אגרת הקודש

THE STEINSALTZ TANYA

Iggeret HaKodesh

VOLUME V

THE MAGERMAN EDITION

THE STEINSALTZ TANYA

IGGERET HAKODESH
18–26

COMMENTARY & TRANSLATION BY

RABBI ADIN EVEN-ISRAEL STEINSALTZ

Steinsaltz Center

Maggid Books

The Steinsaltz Tanya:
Iggeret HaKodesh 18–26, Volume 5
First edition, 2024

Maggid Books
An imprint of Koren Publishers Jerusalem Ltd.

POB 8531, New Milford, CT 06776-8531, USA
& POB 4044, Jerusalem 9104001, Israel
www.maggidbooks.com

This book was published in cooperation with
the Israeli Institute for Talmudic Publications.

We acknowledge with gratitude the generous support of
Terri and Stephen Geifman, *who made possible an earlier edition of this commentary.*

Steinsaltz Center is the parent organization of institutions
established by Rabbi Adin Even-Israel Steinsaltz
POB 45187, Jerusalem 91450 ISRAEL
Telephone: +972 2 646 0900, Fax +972 2 624 9454
www.steinsaltz-center.org

Cover design by Tani Bayer

ISBN 978-1-59264-588-6, hardcover

Printed and bound in the United States

Executive Director, Steinsaltz Center
Rabbi Meni Even-Israel

Editor-in-Chief
Rabbi Jason Rappoport

Translators
Zev Bannet
Sara Fenton
Rabbi Zalman Margolin
Avi Steinhart
Yaacov David Shulman
Oritt Sinclair

Editors
Sara Fenton
Nechama Unterman

Proofreader
Shlomo Liberman

Hebrew Proofreader
Avichai Gamdani

Hebrew Edition Editors
Rabbi Meir Hanegbi, Senior Editor
Rabbi Hillel Mondshein
Rabbi David Brokner

Hebrew Vocalization
Rabbi Hillel Mondshein

Technical Staff
Adena Frazer
Adina Mann
Avi Steinhart

Dedicated to

my wife, **Debra**,

and my children,
Elijah, **Zachary**, **Sydney**, and **Lexie**.

May this new translation of the Tanya,
along with the commentary from Rabbi Steinsaltz (*z"l*),
bring us closer to hasidic teaching and
help us connect with the mystical meaning
behind the Torah.

May all the children of Israel use
the Tanya's knowledge and wisdom
to work together to hasten the coming of Mashiaḥ.

David M. Magerman

ספר התניא מלמד אותנו שהנפש האלוקית מסורה כל כולה לקב״ה והיא מבחינה זו חסרת אנוכיות או תחושת ישות. הנפש הבהמית לעומת זאת מרוכזת בעצמה ומסורה לקיומה הנפרד.

לפיכך לימד אותנו האדמו״ר האמצעי שכאשר שני יהודים לומדים או משוחחים בענייני עבודת ה׳ הרי אלו שתי נשמות אלוקיות כנגד נפש בהמית אחת. הנפש הבהמית לא מצטרפת עם חבירתה משום שכאמור היא מסורה לעצמה אבל הנפשות האלוקיות מצטרפות יחד בלי כל חציצה או הבדל.

(מתוך: ״היום יום״ כ׳ לטבת)

לזכות
משה ליב בן זיסל שיחי׳ לאיוש״ט
שולמית בת זהרה שתחי׳ לאיוש״ט

The *Tanya* teaches us that the divine soul is fully devoted to G-d, and therefore it is selfless. By contrast, the animal soul is selfish, devoted only to maintaining its own existence.

The Mitteler Rebbe, Rabbi Dovber of Lubavitch, taught that when two Jews learn or discuss matters pertaining to service of God, there are two divine souls against one animal soul. The animal soul thinks only of itself and will not attach itself to the animal soul of the other. But the two divine souls are joined together with no division or barrier.

(Cited from *HaYom Yom*, 20 Tevet)

In the merit of
Moshe Leib ben Zisel
Shulamit bat Zohara

A blessing from the Lubavitcher Rebbe, Rabbi Menaḥem Mendel Schneerson, dated 21 Av 5721 (August 3, 1961), viewing with favor Rabbi Steinsaltz's project of writing a short commentary, with longer explanations, on the *Tanya* in a style accessible to the contemporary reader:

(ושאלות ותשובות – כהמצורף למכתבו) בענייניר המובאים בתניא, כן ביאור קצר או גם ארוך, ובסגנונו, ערוכים בלשון בני דורנו...

בברכה לבשו"ט

In December 2012, the final volume of the Hebrew edition of *The Steinsaltz Tanya* was published. That year, at a hasidic gathering, Rabbi Adin Steinsaltz shared why he wrote the book. He explained that Rabbi Shneur Zalman of Liadi, the author of the *Tanya,* had poured his entire soul, his love and awe, his soul-wrenching oneness with God into that concise book, into pages that obscured his immense spirit so well. Through his commentary, Rabbi Steinsaltz strove to reveal to us this spirit, that powerful fire just barely contained by the words of the *Tanya.*

And he certainly succeeded. Yet he failed to mask his own burning spirit, his own love, awe, and closeness to God, as he had attempted to do his entire life.

The publication of this English edition of *The Steinsaltz Tanya* is the fulfillment of Rabbi Steinsaltz's vision to make the teachings of the *Tanya* accessible to every single individual. At the height of the preparations for this edition, our teacher Rabbi Adin Even-Israel passed away.

In this book, one learns how the life of the tzaddik lives on in this world, in those who learn his works. It is through those students who are open to receiving his teachings and are inspired to build upon his words that his light remains with us. We pray that this commentary of Rabbi Steinsaltz will introduce many generations of Jews to the world of the *Tanya* and to the path of authentic devotion to God.

May it serve to elevate his soul.

Contents

IGGERET HAKODESH/THE HOLY EPISTLE

For the Hebrew Tanya Vilna edition, open from the Hebrew side of the book.

אִגֶּרֶת הַקֹּדֶשׁ

Iggeret HaKodesh

The Holy Epistle

Epistle 18

THIS IS NOT AN ORDINARY EPISTLE WRITTEN BY THE Rebbe to his hasidim about a particular matter. Rather, like epistles 15, 19, and 20, it is a kind of discourse explaining a hasidic concept. This epistle expounds on two contrasting types of love of God: love of delights and love of yearning to cleave to God.

Love is probably the most significant and influential force in a person's life, the depth of which in one's inner world, being love of God. Hasidic works address love of God frequently, possibly more than they discuss any other attribute or spiritual capacity. They explore its scope, its various levels, and its modes of expression in the finest of detail. They describe each of its aspects and every dynamic it could possibly be involved in. In order to gain an understanding of an abstract, spiritual matter, we compare and contrast its various manifestations. Therefore, in this epistle, love of God is explained through differentiating between these two types of love.

It is commonly known that *Iggeret HaKodesh* is arranged by topic.[1] Accordingly, we should look for the conceptual connection to the previous epistles especially here. Epistle 17 discusses the reward for a mitzva, the Garden of Eden, and the resurrection of the dead. The beginning of this epistle, too, deals with a type of love that constitutes the

1. It is not arranged chronologically according to when the epistles were written, nor in any other, similar manner; see the comment of the Lubavitcher Rebbe, Rabbi Menaḥem Mendel Schneerson, based on *Sefer HaSiḥot* 5705, p. 110 (published in *Shiurim BeSefer HaTanya*).

reward for divine service rather than divine service itself. Furthermore, the two levels of reward discussed in the previous epistle, the "principal" and the "fruits," may be said to correspond to the two levels of love addressed here: love of delights and concealed love. Love of delights comes from above. It is a gift that follows divine service, much like the "principal." Concealed love, on the other hand, is present in every Jew at all times, felt most when one is engaged in divine service. This corresponds to the "fruits." This epistle adds an emphasis that the reward that is manifest in our world and is therefore the driving force behind all divine service is the faculty of love. We worship God by means of this faculty, and we seek it out within our acts of divine service.

27 Elul
23 Elul (leap year)

כְּתִיב: ״מַה יָּפִית וּמַה נָּעַמְתְּ אַהֲבָה בַּתַּעֲנוּגִים״ (שיר השירים ז,ז).

The verse states, "How fair you are and how pleasant you are, love in its delights!" (Song 7:7).

This verse speaks of a specific kind of love, which is known as love of delights. It may be inferred from here that there is also another kind of love, which is not comprised of delights.

הִנֵּה ב׳ מִינֵי אַהֲבוֹת הֵן הָ־א׳ ׳אַהֲבָה בְּתַעֲנוּגִים׳ דְּהַיְינוּ שֶׁמִּתְעַנֵּג עַל ה׳ עוֹנֶג נִפְלָא בְּשִׂמְחָה רַבָּה וַעֲצוּמָה שִׂמְחַת הַנֶּפֶשׁ וְכִלּוֹתָהּ בְּטַעֲמָהּ כִּי טוֹב ה׳ וְנָעִים נְעִימוּת עֲרֵיבוּת עַד לְהַפְלִיא מֵעֵין עוֹלָם הַבָּא מַמָּשׁ שֶׁנֶּהֱנִין כו׳.

Now, there are two kinds of love. The first is love of delights, meaning one enjoys a wondrous pleasure in God, coupled **with a great and powerful joy, the joy of the soul and its infatuation as it tastes that God is good and delightful, and marvelously sweet.** This experience is **literally like** the experience of **the World to Come, where** "the righteous…**enjoy** the splendor of the Divine Presence" (*Berakhot* 17a).

While there are many types and levels of love, detailed in hasidic works, that are characterized by external factors such as the object of one's love,[2] here the author of the *Tanya* discusses the two essential aspects of love itself. In the first, the emotion relates to the process, to the desire for closeness and to the shortcomings of a reality in which the lovers are not together and do not actualize their love. The second aspect arises when they are actually together. The first kind of love is not actually concerned with the object of love, but rather with its memory and with one's passion and longing for it. While the second kind of love is felt when the object of one's love is present, and this love relates to it directly. ☞

This love is not called first because it is first chronologically, nor does "first" mean the most common. Rather, it is the highest love. It is called love of delights because the love itself is a delight. Unlike a love of desire and longing to fill some lack, which could be a love of anguish, love of delights is entirely a pleasure. It requires nothing and constitutes wondrous bliss. This can be true only of love of God, because a perfect, eternal love that never lacks anything cannot exist in relation to anything else. Anything that pertains to the limited, incomplete realms that are bound by time contains some kind of deficiency, some element that is not currently complete or from which the soul is disconnected. A delight is "wondrous" only when it is "in God." The literal translation of the Hebrew that is loosely rendered as "in God" literally means "over" God. This means that this delight is above all the worlds, and moreover, it is even above the name of God, which refers to

THERE ARE TWO KINDS OF LOVE

☞ Every "complete" love is a relationship between two parties. Consequently, every whole love is actually comprised of two loves: that which is experienced by the first party and that which is experienced by the second. With regard to love of God, there is the love felt by the human being, who is distant and separate and who wants to come closer to be with God. Additionally, there is God's love. Nothing is separate or distinct from God. A person's higher being can experience love of God from God's standpoint, (on the level of *da'at elyon* (higher knowledge) and higher emotion). This is "love of delights."

2. For example, love of one's child, love of one's spouse, and so forth. Although we are discussing love of God here, the many forms of love of God correspond to the different types of love that exist between human beings.

the manifestation of God that forms and gives life to the worlds. Such love is about being together with God Himself, with all the emotion and meaning that this entails. This is a "wondrous" delight. "Wondrous," as explained elsewhere, means separate, for the pleasure taken in God is distinct from all conceivable earthly pleasures. ☞

"Joy" is a revelation, while "pleasure" is internal. The source of "pleasure" may be unconscious and imperceptible, even to the person himself, while "joy" means the revelation of something's essential meaning, both to the individual and to others.[3]

Joy is revelation, both in the sense that when a person is happy, he reveals and is revealed, and in the sense that revelation brings joy. The soul rejoices when it gets a taste of the fact that God is good and delightful.[4] Of course, we cannot grasp with our minds, nor even with our emotions, the manifestation of God's goodness, which is the object of "the love of delights." We are unable to fully comprehend this; we can receive only a taste of it. A "taste" is like a spark of *Ḥokhma,* a flicker of light that the soul can subsequently interpret. The soul can then live based on this memory.[5]

When one receives a "taste" of the fact that God is good and

FAIR AND PLEASANT

☞ Elsewhere (*Torat Ḥayyim*, Gen., from 149c onward, at length), the connection between the beginning of the verse, "How fair you are and how pleasant you are," and its continuation, "love of delights," is elucidated. Specifically, it is explained why the term "delights" is in the plural. "Fair" and "pleasant" always relate to the complementarity between two different elements. Like the attribute of *Tiferet*, Splendor, which includes both *Ḥesed* (Kindness), and *Gevura* (Restraint), "fairness" occurs when there is a harmonious blending of two colors, two musical notes, and so forth. "Pleasant" refers to the spiritual pleasure found within splendor. Based on the verse, it may be said that love of delights, too, comprises two aspects or forms of love. This may refer to *Ḥesed* and *Gevura*, direct light and reflected light, or internal and surrounding light. "Delights" is in the plural because it is the relationship between the two contrasts that brings about that which is fair and pleasant, and arouses the sensation of pleasure in this type of love.

---

3. See *Likkutei Torah, Derushim LeSukkot* 80a.
4. In accordance with Ps. 34:9, 135:3.
5. It is explained in the kabbalistic works that the cantillation notes (*te'amim,*

delightful, he attains a general idea of the matter rather than complete comprehension of it. Essentially, God and everything connected to Him is exceedingly pleasant and sweet, and this is wondrous to the point that it is impossible to grasp. The soul cannot bear what it cannot grasp, and it begins to pine as a result of all the pleasantness and sweetness.[6] As was explained in the commentary to the previous epistle, the soul reaches the level of pining when it attains what it can from the light that "fills all worlds," the light that is first grasped by *Ḥokhma*. When this light fills the soul with consciousness and sensation until it can bear no more, the soul reaches the level of "pining," a state in which the vessel can no longer contain the light.

As was explained in the previous epistle, there is a general distinction between the time for "work" and the time for receiving one's "reward."[7] This world is essentially for divine service, which means observing mitzvot, studying Torah, and praying. The World to Come, on the other hand, is for receiving one's reward. There, it is no longer possible to act, but only to view and take pleasure from all that we accomplished while in this world. Therefore, love itself is "divine service."[8] It is performed by means of contemplation, purification of the soul, transformation of one's desires, and effort to bring it to fruition in this world. This effort is made with one's spiritual faculties as well as through speech and action in the realm of Torah, prayer, and mitzvot. In contrast, the "delight" obtained from love of delights is a "reward," rather than "work." Even if there was an act of service that led to this pleasure, the pleasure

---

or "tastes") on the letters of the Torah relate to the *sefira* of *Ḥokhma*. (There are four levels: cantillation notes, vowels, the decorations above the letters, and the letters themselves. The cantillation notes correspond to *Ḥokhma* in the soul, as well as to the world of *Atzilut*. It is likewise explained that memory pertains to the part of brain that relates to *Ḥokhma*. The *Kadesh* section (Ex. 13:1–10) of the *tefillin*, which relates to the brain of *Ḥokhma*, contains the phrase "It shall be ... a remembrance" (Ex. 13:9).

6. This description corresponds to that of the *Or HaḤayyim* on Lev. 16:1, which is cited in many hasidic works.

7. As the Talmud states, "Today [is the time] to do them, [but only] tomorrow, [the ultimate future, is the time] to receive reward for [doing] them." (*Eiruvin* 22a).

8. In a certain sense, it is the essential act of worship in this world. This is referring to prayer. The *Zohar* states, "There is no worship like worship out of love." See *Likkutei Torah*, Num. 42c.

itself would not be a direct, unequivocal consequence of the service, but rather something additional, a gift. Even if one receives a taste of "love of delights" in this world, it is not a part of this world. Rather, it is "like the actual experience of the World to Come, where the righteous enjoy the splendor of the Divine Presence."

וְעַל זֶה כְּתִיב: "שִׂמְחוּ צַדִּיקִים בַּה'" (תהלים צז,יב). וְלֹא כָּל אָדָם זוֹכֶה לָזֶה וְזוֹ הִיא בְּחִינַת כַּהֲנָא בִּרְעוּתָא דְלִבָּא שֶׁבַּזּוֹהַר הַקָּדוֹשׁ.

Regarding this kind of love **the verse states, "Rejoice in the Lord, you righteous ones"** (Ps. 97:12). **Now, not everyone merits to** attain **this** kind of love; **it is the kind** described **in the holy *Zohar*** (3:177b) by the phrase, **"The *kohen*** serves God **with the innermost desire of the heart."**

The revelation of the delight that is found in love, the joy that is found in God, is the reward of the righteous. ☞

It says in *Likkutei Amarim* that not everyone can be a tzaddik or receive the reward of the tzaddikim, which is love of delights. Anyone can achieve that which comes as a result of divine service. If he invests the time and effort and does the necessary work, then he will succeed. However, not everyone receives an additional gift from above. These endowments are given by the grace of God, and do not depend on the strength of a person's will or service, but rather, on the unique essence of a given soul and the awakening of divine will from above, to which not every person is privy.

LOVE OF DELIGHTS: DELIGHT THAT IS THE VERY ESSENCE OF LOVE

☞ When the pleasure that one derives from love is the result of external things that he receives, whether physical or spiritual, this is not "love of delights." When it comes to love of delights, one is not a recipient. Rather, all a person's emotional reactions relate only to the object of his love: its presence, its greatness, and so forth. It is the sole source of his pleasure. It is explained elsewhere (for example, in *Likkutei Amarim*, chap. 10) that this describes the divine service of the righteous, who are called people of ascension. Their worship and their desires revolve entirely around that which is above them, rather than themselves. They are merely vessels, or channels, for the higher forces and emotions that pass through them.

The priests were singled out from among the Jewish people to worship God in a unique manner than the rest of the Jewish people. An Israelite can never become a priest. Parallel to this clear-cut delineation of roles, with regard to spiritual divine service, the righteous possess unique faculties and their own special modes of worship. Like the priests,[9] they teach, guide, and lead the people in the ways of divine service, and they themselves have a form of worship that is unlike everyone else's.

As explained in the *Zohar*,[10] and in more detail elsewhere,[11] unlike the service of the Levites, the priestly service is "concealed." This essentially internal work that demands intention and thought, happens in the heart, therefore, it differs from person to person. In contrast, the external service of performing mitzvot, is alike for everyone.

The essential, innermost desire of the heart is not a desire that is formed in the mind through contemplation and deep reflection. It does not pertain to objects in the outside world, but to that which the soul itself longs for. It precedes rational understanding of one's external reality. When divine service is performed with the innermost desire of the heart, one's deepest, most essential desire is manifest in the soul. In other words, the soul does not need to attain something that it does not have or that is concealed from it. In contrast, when divine service is performed with the faculties of the soul, the mind tries to attain that which is above it, and the attributes strive to relate to that which is beyond their grasp. The person is thus left only searching and longing, running and returning from one side to the other of the seemingly unbridgeable gap between humankind and the Divine, between the revealed and the concealed. However, in the case of divine service through the innermost desire of the heart, one has already "arrived." Something much greater overpowers the soul and all its faculties; a divine space from above. The *Zohar* explains that the priestly service is

---

9. See, for example, Rashi on the phrase "You shall be for Me a kingdom of priests [*kohanim*]" (Ex. 19:6): "Senior ministers, like in the verse 'And David's sons were *kohanim*' (II Sam. 8:18)."

10. See also *Zohar* 3:39a. The *Zohar* speaks of the concealed nature of the priestly service. It is concerned with one's will, intent, and thought. The Levite service, on the other hand, can be seen and heard.

11. See *Likkutei Torah*, Lev. 9d.

"concealed," while service of the Levites is loud and melodious, because the priestly service requires no additional exertion. It does not need to break down any barriers or cross any divides, because everything is already present. The soul can pass comfortably and effortlessly from realm to realm. This kind of worship and love is called love of delights because the very experience of it is an unparalleled pleasure. One who loves with this kind of love needs nothing else.

וְעַל זֶה נֶאֱמַר: "עֲבֹדַת מַתָּנָה וגו' וְהַזָּר הַקָּרֵב וגו'" (במדבר יח,ז), כִּי אֵין דֶּרֶךְ לְהַשִּׂיגָהּ עַל יְדֵי יְגִיעַת בָּשָׂר כְּמוֹ הַיִּרְאָה שֶׁשּׁוֹאֲלִין עָלֶיהָ: יָגַעְתָּ בְּיִרְאָה? וְאוֹי לַבָּשָׂר שֶׁלֹּא נִתְיַיגֵּעַ בְּיִרְאָה, כְּמוֹ שֶׁכָּתוּב בְּרֵאשִׁית חָכְמָה.

Moreover, **of this** kind of love **the verse states, "As a service that is a gift** I give your priesthood; **the non-priest who approaches…"** (Num. 18:7), **for there is no way to attain it by human effort, like** there is with **fear** of God. **Regarding** fear, **one is asked** in the next world, **"did you toil with fear?" and, "Woe to the person who did not toil to** attain **fear," as stated in *Reshit Ḥokhma*** (*Sha'ar HaYir'ah*, chap. 12).

The author of the *Tanya* quotes a verse that characterizes the way in which the priestly service entails the innermost desire of the heart: "You and your sons with you shall keep your priesthood with regard to any matter of the altar and with regard to that which is within the curtain.... As a service that is a gift I give your priesthood; the non-priest who approaches shall be put to death" (Num. 18:7). In Jewish history, this service of love and the "innermost desire of the heart" was reserved only for the priests, and performed inside the Temple. In the spiritual realm, only the righteous and those individuals who have received it as "a gift" engage in this type of service. This type of worship is not attainable by others.

This reflects God's attribute of kindness, for He gives it "free of charge," not in exchange for a person's worship. However, it also contains an aspect of the attribute of judgment, for the only way to attain it is as a gift, and it is given only to those who are chosen by God. No one else may acquire it, and moreover, they are prohibited from even trying. This is reflected in the end of the verse: "The non-priest who approaches shall be put to death."

There are some spiritual faculties that are received as gifts, and there are others that are received as rewards for a person's efforts. That which a person is capable of attaining, he is obligated to attain. The human being was brought to this world in order to work hard and receive his reward, not to receive gifts.[12] However, the limitation involved in this is that one's reward relates directly to the work he performs, and each person's work relates directly to the faculties that he possesses. Therefore, through hard work, a person is only able to reach levels of love and fear that are within human grasp, levels that already exist in some form in his reality in a more constricted expression for example, in the love and fear he feels for other people. In contrast, one cannot attain the level of "love of delights" through hard work. There is nothing like it in this world, and it may be acquired only as a gift. ☞ ☞

It says in *Reshit Ḥokhma* that after a person's death, he is asked if he made an effort to achieve the attribute of fear while in his body.

HUMAN EFFORT

☞ This refers to continual exertion in order to reach that which we have not yet reached, that which we do not understand, and that which we do not yet feel. Constant effort knocks at the door, and ultimately opens it. The underlying premise of divine service is that God does not give us a task that we are unable to perform. We lack none of the necessary faculties or hard-wiring. Everything we need is available to us, and all we have to do is to make an effort. Effort, therefore, is the "key" that opens the "door" to unearth the treasures behind it. Every person is called to open the door by means of continual effort in Torah study, prayer, and divine service in general. Each individual does this in accordance with his own character and level.

HUMAN EFFORT AND SPIRITUAL EFFORT

☞ In the works of the author of the *Tanya*, the term "human effort" usually appears together with the term "spiritual effort."[13] Human effort refers to overcoming the physical and worldly obstacles that we are subject to and drawn to. In order to connect one's mind and attributes to the Divine, see the Divine in everything, and love and fear God and not the world, one needs to trample and subdue the body so

---

12 It is explained elsewhere that the souls were brought into the world was so that they would not receive "the bread of shame," which is the abundance that is benevolently bestowed upon God's creations in the form of gratuitous gifts. Instead, we earn our bread with honor, through work. See *Likkutei Torah*, Lev. 6d;.

13. *Likkutei Amarim*, chap. 42.

From this question it is clear that this matter depends only on effort. Not only is it possible to acquire fear by means of hard work, but moreover, everyone is obligated to do so, and a person who does not will encounter misfortune.[14]

וּכְתִיב בְּיִרְאָה: "אִם תְּבַקְשֶׁנָּה כַכָּסֶף וגו'" (משלי ב,ד–ה), מְלַמֵּד שֶׁצְּרִיכָה יְגִיעָה רַבָּה וַעֲצוּמָה כִּמְחַפֵּשׂ אַחַר אוֹצָרוֹת.

Also, regarding fear, the verse states, "If you seek it like silver..." (Prov. 2:4), **which indicates that** acquiring fear **requires a great and mighty effort, like** that of **one searching for treasures.**

The verse states, "If you seek it like silver and search for it like for hidden treasures, then you will understand fear of the Lord" (Prov. 2:4–5). The following analogy is brought in *Likkutei Amarim* (chap. 42): Just as a person digs in the ground with tremendous effort when searching for treasure, one must dig with the same amount of effort in order to uncover the treasure concealed within the understanding of the heart. This treasure, concealed fear of God, is present in the soul of every Jew. (It is part of "concealed love," for it is the fear of being separated from

that it is not a substantial reality. The way to accomplish this is through thoughts of repentance in the depths of the heart. In other words, we do not disregard the body, but we "repent" from wherever its faculties have strayed through thought, speech, and actions that do not concern God and His Torah. We repent from the deepest part of our soul's essence. Spiritual effort, on the other hand, refers to effort made through the deep contemplation of God's greatness for extended periods of time. Both types of effort are necessary, for the light that enters this world is limited and concealed. Human effort is chiefly concerned with overcoming the "concealment" of the physical realm so that it does not become a hindrance, while spiritual effort is about contemplating whatever glimmer of light a person sees more and more until the soul becomes greatly illuminated. Although only "human effort" is mentioned here, it seems to be referring to spiritual effort as well. This term may have been employed because it relates to the quote that follows: "Woe to flesh that did not toil with fear." In any case, human effort is evidently the first stage, which connects more to the aspect of fear. As has been explained, contemplation that requires fear is mainly concerned with refraining from contemplating, or being drawn to, other matters. This is included in "human effort."

14. *Reishit Hokhma*, Gate of Fear:12 (Only the sentence, "Woe to the flesh ...") See also *Shabbat* 31a.

God). One must search inside himself in order to uncover it, whether by garnering an actual emotion or by resolving to more carefully, observe the Torah's commandments. Since fear (and love) are certainly present in every soul, the attainment of fear depends only on effort. In the words of the Sages, "If a person says to you ... I have labored and I have found, believe him."[15] ☞

אֲבָל אַהֲבָה רַבָּה זוֹ [אַהֲבָה בְּתַעֲנוּגִים] נוֹפֶלֶת לָאָדָם מֵאֵלֶיהָ, מִלְמַעְלָה, בְּלִי שֶׁיָּכִין וִיכַוֵּין לָהּ, אַךְ וְרַק אַחַר שֶׁנִּתְיַיגַּע בְּ'יִרְאַת הָרוֹמְמוּת' וְהִגִּיעַ לְתַכְלִית מַה שֶּׁיּוּכַל לְהַשִּׂיג מִמֶּנָּה לְפִי בְּחִינַת נִשְׁמָתוֹ - אֲזַי מִמֵּילָא בָּאָה הָאַהֲבָה בְּתַעֲנוּגִים מִלְמַעְלָה לִשְׁכּוֹן וּלְהִתְיַיחֵד עִם הַיִּרְאָה, כִּי דַּרְכּוֹ שֶׁל אִישׁ לַחֲזֹר כוּ' (קידושין ב,ב), כְּמוֹ שֶׁנִּתְבָּאֵר בְּלִקּוּטֵי אֲמָרִים (פרק מג).

By contrast, this great love [**love of delights**] **descends by itself upon a person from Above, without him preparing for or intending it,** and **only after one has exerted himself regarding** the attainment of **fear of the exalted, having reached the full capacity** of fear **his particular soul is capable of. Then, the love of delights comes automatically from Above, residing within and becoming united with the fear, for "it is the way of a man to pursue** a woman" (*Kiddushin* 2b)**, as explained in *Likkutei Amarim*** (chap. 43).

REGARDING FEAR

☞ Why does the author of the *Tanya* begin speaking of fear here when this epistle is chiefly concerned with love? As will be explained below, every expression of divine service that a person embarks upon must begin with fear, not love. This is because that which is essential is safeguarded by means of fear. It is also because love will inevitably follow fear, while the opposite is not always true.: Moreover, when we refer to that which depends on the individual's efforts, we

15. *Megilla* 6b. The Lubavitcher Rebbe, Rabbi Menaḥem Mendel Schneerson, comments on this statement in several places: "Ostensibly, to 'find' something means to discover it without having intended to. If so, how does this connect to 'laboring'? After a person has labored as much as he can, he receives something from above that is beyond the scope of his efforts. It is as though he 'finds' it." See *Torat Menaḥem*, vol. 23, p. 231.

Elsewhere, it is explained that great love and love of delights are two levels of love. ☞

Love of delights is, as mentioned, a type of worship that is a gift rather than the result of effort. It is impossible to receive it by means

are speaking of fear, for, as the Sages say, "Everything is in the hands of Heaven, except for fear of Heaven" (*Berakhot* 33b). Since this depends on the individual, it is also required of him. It is a basic requirement that a person have an active spiritual faculty of fear. On the other hand, love and the acts that arise from it are additional, and are carried out in accordance with one's own free will.: Furthermore, effort in divine service is made through fear rather than love. This is because one's efforts can only affect the lower realm; this is man's duty. Hasidic works explain that to arouse love, it is enough to contemplate God's greatness and kindness within the worlds. However, this is not the case with regard to fear. Since the essence of fear is nullification, it requires a profound understanding of and connection to God's essence, and these arise from effort (See *Torat Menaḥem*, vol. 3, pp. 279ff).

It is important to understand that love and fear are not two separate faculties, but two sides of the same coin. There is no love of God without fear of God, and there is no fear of God without love of God. All divine service is composed of both, and our perception of reality in general, and of the Divine in particular, contains both. Nevertheless, when we speak of what a person can and should do in order to bring about love and fear, we begin with fear. In some situations, the inception of people's divine service is love, but these are unique circumstances, although not rare, where the person is more sensitive and open to love, and God shines His light upon him with kindness as an awakening from above. However, even in such cases, when the person eventually returns to the beginning, to build the foundation of his divine service from within, it necessarily involves the attribute of fear.

GREAT LOVE AND LOVE OF DELIGHTS

☞ In *Likkutei Amarim* (chap. 43) it says that "great love" is love of delights. However, elsewhere it is explained that they are not the same, and that love of delights is on a higher level than great love (see *Torah Or* 48a). Yet another source states that there are two levels of great love, and love of delights is the higher one, which is manifest as pleasure (see *Torah Or* 47c).: Love of delights is the higher aspect, while great love relates also to the lower realm and the soul. These types of love correspond to the two levels of the *sefira* of *Keter*, Crown: *Arikh Anpin* and *Atik Yomin* (Ancient of Days). *Atik Yomin* relates to the higher, spiritual level of essential pleasure, which is detached and distinct from the lower worlds. *Arikh Anpin* is more external, like the level of will, which relates to the worlds. Therefore, while great love is a supernal love, a gift that comes from above, it is also connected to the divine service of the lower realm, for it "pursues" fear (see below). Even though it does not arise from effort and mental exertion, it is bound to and "pursues" higher fear, which is itself tied to effort, as has been mentioned.

of effort, preparation, or intention, and moreover, it comes specifically when one has not prepared for it. By nature, when one prepares for something, he does so according to his perceptions, expectations, and anticipations. However, when something comes from above, from far beyond the individual and the farthest reaches of his expectations, preparation only interferes with its arrival.

There is, nevertheless, a stipulation. This gift is not a totally independent process with no correlation whatsoever to the individual; it is simply not direct, as in the case of wages, which are paid in accordance with the amount of work that has been done. One's actions in the lower realm are indirectly pertinent. Although God freely gives us that which He desires to give us, even if it is not what we deserve, in order to receive it in a significant and impactful way, there must be some level of preparation in the person's soul. The spiritual "vessel" that is able to relate to this kind of love is "fear of the exalted." ☞

LEVELS OF FEAR

☞ As with love, there are many levels and aspects of fear, which boil down to two basic types "lower fear" and "higher fear." Hasidic works refer to these different fabrics of fear using different names lower fear is also called "fear of punishment" and "fear of sin," and higher fear is also referred to as "fear out of shame" and "fear of the exalted." The essential difference between them is that when a person feels lower fear, he is afraid of punishment. This fear pertains to the individual and what will happen to him. Just as one fears an evil person or an injury, he is afraid of what will befall him if he violates the commandments. "Fear of sin," too, is about the individual: One is afraid of stumbling and engaging in sin. In contrast, higher fear is concerned with God alone. The person recognizes that God is infinitely higher than everything else, and as a result of this realization, a great and powerful fear descends upon him. In this kind of fear, there is no room for one's own emotions. The person's entire existence is nullified and inconsequential, and as a result, he feels great shame when he thinks of himself, and more generally, when he thinks anything at all. He recoils at the slightest sensation of any ego. This is exalted fear, which the individual experiences as "fear out of shame" (see *Likkutei Amarim*, chap. 43). As mentioned above, lower and higher fear are the attributes that we toil for. The effort to cultivate fear is carried out primarily with the mind, which forms the awareness that produces the emotion and the response of fear. This awareness is when a person feels the clarity of perceiving the objective reality of the Divine. Recognizing that the Divine is real and present, not an illusion or a projection of the soul, is the basis for understanding the attribute of judgment and the line that delineates where one's self ends and the other begins. This relates both to fear of punishment and fear

The deeper a person contemplates higher fear or "fear of the exalted" on a more abstract level, the more he is able to actualize the full capacity of his fear. How a person comprehends his world depends on his personal "vessels." He cannot acquire more than what his "vessels" are able to contain. Every person acquires such "vessels of awareness" throughout his life: knowledge, study, effort, abstraction, subtly, and so forth. However, at the foundation of all a person's abilities and vessels lies his "particular soul." This refers to the essence and root of his soul, the spiritual world it derives from, and so on. One receives his unique soul from his father, his mother, and God. He has no choice in this matter, nor does he need to perform any work for it. There is, however, work that a person can and should perform in accordance with the soul that he has received. He must use the talents and abilities he was born with in order to realize his full potential.

When a person reaches the full capacity of his comprehension, and attains the sensation of the fear of the exalted that accompanies this, then love of delights descends upon him from above. As mentioned, this love is not the result of divine service performed in the lower realm. Rather, it arises automatically and naturally. It is not commensurate with the level of the human being, but with God. It is God's love: meaning, it is the feeling of actually loving God Himself, of loving His love, not just the comprehensible, limited way in which that love expresses itself in one's life. But rather, a love that cannot be grasped, for no thought can fully perceive God. It is a feeling that is somehow an extension of God's own feeling, not as it humanly perceived. As stated, in order for this supremely transcendent feeling to be registered and resonated with within one's soul, the soul must attain fear of the exalted, higher fear, to the fullest extent that it is capable of. Higher fear, like higher love, belongs to a level that is above comprehension, above the soul, and above the worlds. It is God's, and therefore it is the only way for a person to perceive a glimpse of "love of delights," which comes from above. ☞

of the exalted. Fear of punishment is the fear of something that may harm the individual. This threat arises from within the confines of the world that he understands, yet has no control over. Fear of the exalted is the recognition of God's real, awesome existence. God is just as real as any human being standing before us, yet He is so great and sublime that He is beyond all comprehension.

Once a person has put in the necessary effort and aroused within himself the highest level of fear that he is able to garner, he can also be privy to love of delights. It is explained in *Likkutei Amarim* that love is considered "male" (*zakhar*), as it says, "He recalled [*zakhar*] His kindness" (Ps. 98:3). Fear, on the other hand, is considered "female": The verse states, "a woman who fears the Lord" (Prov. 31:30), which could also be translated, "Woman is fear of the Lord." These abstract concepts are reflected in the observable dynamic between men and women, that generally the man pursues the woman, and not the other way around, as stated in the Talmudic quote here. He does this in order to be with the woman and give to her. ☞

The power of bestowing kindness and love always seeks to flow from above to below, into vessels and defined boundaries. It is like water, which naturally runs from a higher place to a lower place. Consequently,

LOVE OF DELIGHTS COMES AUTOMATICALLY

☞ Why does higher love come automatically while higher fear comes through effort? By definition, both defy comprehension. When a person loves, his comprehension is positive, meaning that he apprehends a perceptible phenomenon, an attribute or an action to which love can attach. With regard to the highest levels, such comprehension is impossible. Fear, on the other hand, does not require a person to understand something specific. One needs only to understand that the divine reality is dissimilar from him and far more exalted. Fear requires the comprehension of the fact that this matter is incomprehensible. This means glimpsing the vast distance and internalizing the fact that God is supernal, exalted, and beyond all else. This is negative knowledge, which one can attain even when it relates to levels that are beyond comprehension. This kind of understanding is what evokes the attribute and sensation of fear.

IT IS THE WAY OF A MAN TO PURSUE

☞ This analogy conveys the idea that love is an active "giver," and fear is a passive "receiver." Similarly, it is explained elsewhere (see the introduction to *Sha'ar HaYiḥud VeHa'emuna*) that love of God is the root of all positive commandments, and fear of God is the root of all negative commandments. The spiritual faculty of love corresponds to the capacity to act, while the faculty of fear relates to the capacity to maintain that which already exists so that it does not become spoiled. Likewise, "male" and "female" signify the giver and the receiver, respectively. Fear forms the "vessel," the ability to receive, and love creates the light and flow. Love pursues fear because love without fear is worth nothing. It is insubstantial. Even if it fills the entire world, if it has nothing to grasp onto and project on, it is like a nonentity. Love pursues fear because it is not manifest or real unless fear is present.

although an awakening from below cannot arouse love of delights or draw it down, if and when it awakens by itself, it descends to the space where higher fear is found. As stated, fear, especially higher fear, characterizes the inestimable higher realm. Likewise, it characterizes that which is in the lower realm and relates to the inestimable, the supernal level of love of delights. Therefore, higher love will find its place to a greater degree wherever exalted fear is stronger and the person feels lowlier and more subsumed.

28 Elul

24 Elul (leap year)

וְהַשֵּׁנִית, הִיא אַהֲבָה וְתַאֲוָה שֶׁהַנֶּפֶשׁ מִתְאַוָּה וְאוֹהֶבֶת וַחֲפֵיצָה לְדָבְקָה בַּה׳, לִצְרוֹר בִּצְרוֹר הַחַיִּים, וְקִרְבַת אֱלֹהִים טוֹב לָהּ מְאֹד וּבוֹ תַּחְפּוֹץ, וְרַע לָהּ מְאֹד לְהִתְרַחֵק מִמֶּנּוּ יִתְבָּרֵךְ חַס וְשָׁלוֹם לִהְיוֹת מְחִיצָה שֶׁל בַּרְזֶל מֵהַחִיצוֹנִים מַפְסֶקֶת, חַס וְשָׁלוֹם.

The second kind of love **is a love characterized by desire.** It is **when the soul desires, loves and aspires to cleave to God, to be bound in the bond of Life; when** it appreciates how **God's closeness is so good for it, and that is what it aspires to.** Conversely, it appreciates **how it is so bad to be distanced from Him, God forbid, to be separated, God forbid, by an iron barrier** caused **by the external forces of impurity.**

The second type of love discussed in this epistle is different in almost every respect from the first. The first is a love that not everyone is able to attain, while the second is found in every Jew. The first is a gift that can never be acquired by means of effort, while regarding the second, not only is it possible, but it is obligatory to toil for it. The first is love of delights, and the second is not.[16] This does not mean that it is the opposite of pleasure; however, its main concern, rather than experiencing delight, is achieving its objective, as will be explained below.

Unlike love of delights, this love includes within it an element of desire. The soul yearns to receive something it lacks.

Before the soul descends into this world, it is literally bound to-

16. That is not to say that this kind of love involves no pleasure or joy. However, the delight that it brings is not the pleasure of love itself. Rather, it causes a kind of gratification at having filled a void and fulfilled a desire.

gether with God,[17] the Source of All Life. Once it is in this world, far away from its source, it longs to be back there, cleaving to God. It lacks God's closeness, which is so good for it, as the verse says, "As for me, nearness to God is good" (Ps. 72:28). When it is in this world, the soul becomes enclothed in the body and the animal soul, which conceal and separate it from that closeness and goodness. Consequently, it desires and aspires to attain that connection once again. ☞

The opposite of this love is fear: the fear of becoming distanced or separated from God.[18] When the object of a person's love is not yet present, and he only desires, loves, and aspires to it, his longing is always accompanied by the fear of failure, that the object will never come. As long as the beloved object is not yet part of the perfect union that the person seeks, he is in a kind of twilight: There is light and warmth on one side, and darkness and desolation on the other. The strength

DESIRES, LOVES, AND ASPIRES TO CLEAVE

☞ This multiplicity of terms reflects the many different levels through which the soul must ascend, beginning in the material world and culminating in the supernal space of closeness to God. When the soul is in the almost-total concealment of this world, it "desires." The body and the physical world recognize desire, because through it, they act to obtain what they lack. Above this level is the spiritual world, the realm of emotion, love, and the desire to come closer and to give. Here, the soul "loves." This level corresponds to the world of *Yetzira*. On the next level, the soul "aspires," with the innermost aspect of will. While the external aspect of will is desire and overt emotion, in this realm the soul aspires with the deepest levels of emotion, at their very root in the mind. This level corresponds to the world of *Beria*. The culmination of all these levels is the state of cleaving to God becoming one with Him, attached to Him, and incorporated within Him like in the world of *Atzilut* It says in *Likkutei Levi Yitzḥak on HaTanya*, "It may be said that 'desires' is in *Asiya*; 'loves' is in *Yetzira*; 'aspires' is in *Beria*; 'to cleave to God' is in *Malkhut*, Kingship (which is enclothed in *Asiya*); 'to be bound in the bond of life' is in the Yesod of *Zeir Anpin* and in *Zeir Anpin* in general (which is enclothed in *Yetzira*); and 'God's closeness' is in *Bina*, (which is enclothed in *Beria*), where God's name *Elokim* is found." See there for more on this idea.

---

17. This is in accordance with I Sam. 25:29. The "bond of life" is the repository of souls, the place where souls are found before they descend into bodies in this world.

18. See *Likkutei Amarim*, chap. 25.

of one's yearning for God demonstrates his fear of being distanced from Him. This kind of love is not love of delights. The feeling that accompanies it does not include pleasure at having fulfilled a desire, and moreover, it involves the unpleasant apprehension that stems from the fear of being distanced. ☞

The concern is that the soul will be separated from God by *kelippot* (husks) that conceal the holiness found within. When the Sages use the term "iron barrier,"[19] they mean the strongest and most impermeable kind of barrier.[20] The fear hiding in the soul of every Jew is that this kind of barrier will separate it from God. The divine soul does not fear anything. It is bound to the Divine and not connected to the world. Likewise, it does not receive anything from the world. As a result, the only thing in the world that can threaten or harm it is the cessation of the connection between it and the Divine. ☞ ☞

When they accumulate, these external forces become an "iron barrier," a closed, complete system that does not allow anything to pass through it. This is like a worldview that leaves no room for any other perspective, or a strong emotion that leaves no space for any other feelings in the soul. Of course, if the barrier were completely

BAD FOR THE LOVE TO BE DISTANCED

☞ Although this love is not love of delights, and although it may involve yearning and even pain and anguish, it by no means feels bad. As long as a person experiences love, there is contact and connection between him and God, whether it is concealed or revealed. Any emotion aroused in one's connection to holiness, anything that comes up through the toil and search, is fundamentally good. It may be difficult and even frustrating, but it is certainly not experienced as a bad feeling of dread or despair. Nevertheless, when a person feels the pain of distance from God, dark, despairing emotions are not far from his emotional radar. The love that he feels is colored by fear that if he would lose all contact, the connection would be lost. This is what the author of the *Tanya* is referring to when he writes that the soul appreciates how "It is so bad to be distanced from Him." When distance turns into detachment, matters become "bad." While there is love, there is nothing but closeness. However, just as darkness emphasizes light by virtue of the contrast between them, this love is emphasized by the potential for "bad."

19. The Sages use this term in *Pesaḥim* 85b and *Sota* 38b.
20. See *Eiruvin* 28b; Jerusalem Talmud 5:5.

impermeable, it would not be so bad for the person, because he would not be aware that there was anything on the other side. However, it is not totally sealed. Just as concealed love is always present, whether hidden or shining, so too the different levels of barriers conceal while occasionally reveal. The human being, who feels love on the one hand and the barrier on the other, finds himself between the longing to be completely connected and the fear of the "iron barrier," of being totally separated.

וְאַהֲבָה זוֹ הִיא מוּסְתֶּרֶת בְּלֵב כְּלַל יִשְׂרָאֵל, אֲפִילוּ בָּרְשָׁעִים, וּמִמֶּנָּה בָּאָה לָהֶם הַחֲרָטָה.

This love is hidden in the heart of every Jew, even in the wicked; that is where their feelings of remorse come from.

IRON BARRIER

☞ This phrase is taken from a statement of the Sages that actually asserts the opposite "Even a barrier of iron does not separate between the Jewish people and their Father in Heaven" (*Pesaḥim* 85b). In truth, the connection between God and all Jewish souls is essential. They are truly one entity, and nothing can divide them. This essential union is expressed in the love that is concealed within the soul. This love never detaches from God, even in a case of true self-sacrifice. This love, along with the Divine that it loves, is concealed, but only from our viewpoint. From the heavenly perspective, the concealment does not exist. This is the "iron barrier." It does not really separate the Jewish people from their Father in Heaven. However, because of our sins, we may perceive it as an obstruction, and the divine soul experiences fear and anguish at this.

EXTERNAL FORCES

☞ This is the accepted term for *kelippa*, the external aspect of reality. It does not express the divine reality that flows within it, but its own reality. Absolutely everything has an internal and an external aspect. For example, when a person does something, whether in the physical or the spiritual realm, the internal aspect is his will with regard to that matter, the purpose for which he acts, speaks, or thinks. The external aspect is the vessel or instrument through which the act is performed and within which it exists. The internal aspect, therefore, reveals the individual: his will and his thoughts about the matter. The external aspect might not reveal these things since it pertains to the vessel. The internal aspect cannot exist without the external aspect. Consequently, the external reality is not fundamentally bad. However, if instead of being subsumed and subordinate to the internal aspect it becomes the end in itself, it becomes an "external force of impurity," signifying evil and *kelippa*.

There are two aspects of this love: It is concealed, and it is present in every Jew. Love of delights, on the other hand, is revealed and reveled in by only certain individuals. ☞

What is "concealed love," a love that is not felt? It is explained in several places in *Likkutei Amarim* that "concealed" pertains to the revelation of emotion. On some levels and in certain circumstances, a person does not feel his love of God. However, regardless of one's situation or level, every person is capable of revealing it in other ways and through other emotions, and certainly through thought, speech, and action.

Clearly, love of God is not obviously manifest in the hearts of the wicked; they lead sinful lives. Nevertheless, this love is revealed in them as well. The Sages say, "The wicked are filled with remorse all their days."[21] A wicked person commits a transgression, but this love, which is embedded in his soul, gives him no rest. Even after the animal soul and its desires have overcome him and he no longer feels or even thinks of holiness, love of God keeps him from being able to enjoy the fruits of his actions. He experiences remorse, which stems from this love.

The author of the *Tanya* does not describe the complexity of the human soul at length here as he does in *Likkutei Amarim*. Rather, he addresses the question that pertains to this love: How is it possible that a person has love of God within him, and a desire to come closer to Him, yet he acts in a way that is diametrically opposed to this, with wickedness, violating God's will and distancing himself from Him?

CONCEALED LOVE

☞ Because it is concealed, people may not know of its existence, so this should be publicized. Indeed, throughout the *Tanya*, the author repeatedly mentions, in different ways and from different angles, that every Jew possesses a love for God (see e.g., *Likkutei Amarim*, chap. 18–19). Likewise, he remarks that we all have a divine soul that lusts after God and loves Him because the soul is itself a part of God (see e.g., *Likkutei Amarim*, chap. 2). He further states that anyone can be a *beinoni* and reveal this love (*Likkutei Amarim* 14).

21. This is cited in *Shevet Mussar*, chap. 25. A similar phrase appears in *Nedarim* 9b, but the exact quote has not been found in either the Talmud or the Midrash.

אַךְ מִפְּנֵי שֶׁהִיא מוּסְתֶּרֶת וְנֶעֱלֶמָה בִּבְחִינַת גָּלוּת בַּגּוּף, הֲרֵי הַקְּלִיפָּה יְכוֹלָה לִשְׁלוֹט עָלֶיהָ, וְזֶהוּ רוּחַ שְׁטוּת הַמַּחֲטִיא לָאָדָם.

However, because it hides in concealment, in a state of exile within the body, the *kelippa* is able to dominate it. This is the "spirit of folly" that causes a person to sin.

Love of God is the love of a person's divine soul. Just as the soul is concealed, as it is in a state of "exile" within the body in its corporeal faculties, so too this love is concealed. It is not revealed in a person's heart, nor in his life. It may manifest occasionally, at extreme moments when he is being tested and receiving revelation,[22] but it is not part of a person's everyday experience. ☞

EXILE WITHIN THE BODY

☞ The soul is in a state of exile within the body. A person is in "exile" when he is somewhere where he does not belong, where he cannot express himself. Instead, he is subservient to the place, its people, its aspirations, and its values. In some cases, the person feels the difficulty and frustration of being in exile. However, when the exile is especially overpowering, the person identifies with it so strongly that he does not realize that he is in exile. He is convinced that the paradigms of that place are his own. The same is true regarding the soul that is in exile within the body. The body has desires, needs, and a particular way in which it views the world and relates to it. The soul inside the body naturally accepts this approach. The physical body is concerned with the physical world. From its perspective, the physical world is what is important and real. The soul exiled to a body sustains the body with all its preoccupations. While the soul brings deeper dimensions, and wisdom to one's life, which stem from its own strength, understanding, and sensitivity, nevertheless, corporeal concerns are at the center, while the soul and all its affairs, are relegated to the secondary spiritual realm.

It is explained elsewhere[23] that exile is not merely a terrible ordeal. It contains deeper meaning, a purpose that becomes revealed and actualized upon coming out of exile. Emerging from exile signifies the refinement and rectification of the exile. The sparks of holiness that were in that place are removed, and the exile itself is transformed into an instrument, a hoist that elevates holiness even higher. This is the case with regard to all types of exile, from the exile of the Jewish people among the nations to the exile of the divine soul within the physical body in this world. Through Torah and mitzvot, the soul that is in a body in this world is able to achieve attachment to the Divine on a higher, deeper level than it can when it is not in a body.

---

22. See *Likkutei Amarim*, chaps. 18, 25.
23. See *Likkutei Amarim*, chap. 37; *Torah Or* 49a, 61a.

Exile is *kelippa*, an impenetrable covering that conceals the holiness that comprises it, and professes instead to be a self-sustaining entity. Since the soul is in exile, *kelippa* is able to dominate the individual to the extent that he forgets his divine soul, with its innermost wisdom, and desires. Instead, he identifies with the *kelippa* and its whims. This is the "spirit of folly," which causes a person to act contrary to his inner will. He disregards his understanding of what is good and what is not, of what is vital to his existence and what leads him to the path of ruin. ☞

וְעַל כֵּן עֲבוֹדַת הָאָדָם לְקוֹנוֹ הִיא לְהִתְחַזֵּק וּלְהִתְגַּבֵּר עַל הַקְּלִיפָּה בְּכׇל מִכׇּל כֹּל, דְּהַיְינוּ מִתְּחִלָּה לְגָרְשָׁהּ מֵהַגּוּף לְגַמְרֵי מִמַּחֲשָׁבָה דִּיבּוּר וּמַעֲשֶׂה שֶׁבַּמּוֹחַ וְלָשׁוֹן וּרְמַ"ח אֵבָרִים.

Therefore, because the *kelippa* opposes this love, **serving one's Creator consists of standing strong to overcome the *kelippa* altogether. This means to first expel it completely from the body, from the thought, speech and action that are in the mind, the tongue and the 248 organs.**

The soul that is in exile in the body, or in any kind of exile, must carry out some work, an act of service. This is an act that involves overcoming difficulties and obstacles. A person's service to his Creator consists of overcoming the "concealment" of the body and the world, as well as

THE SPIRIT OF FOLLY

☞ This phrase comes from the statement of the Sages, "A man commits a transgression only if a spirit of folly enters him" (*Sota* 3a). Although a person's essential desire is to cleave to the Divine, inspired by his concealed love within, a spirit of folly can become enclothed in him, covering up his genuine love and desire. "Spirit" relates to the attributes, and "folly" refers to a time when they are not operating in accordance with reason. The individual begins to believe that he wants and loves other things that distance him from his actual thoughts and desires. For, as previously explained, when a person is in exile within the body, he considers the body's desires as though they are his own. This is the "spirit of folly" that comes as a result of exile within the body.

In *Likkutei Amarim* (chap. 24) it is explained in more depth that concealed love, a person's inner desire to cleave to the Divine, is unalterable. Since it is an expression of the soul itself, no desire, will, or rational argument can stand against it. This does not apply only in extreme cases where people are tested and must sacrifice their lives and possessions in order not to be parted from God. The truth is that a Jew will never consciously do anything that will defeating the spirit of folly, which distances the individual from himself and from his God. The purpose of this service is to come closer to God and to cleave to Him, bringing one's love for Him to fruition. Nevertheless, it cannot begin with love, because the soul is concealed within the body and cannot openly see or desire spiritual light and objective good. Rather, it begins with exerting some force to overcome the *kelippa* and its concealment, and only subsequently reveal the love. ☞

The author of the *Tanya* explains that we must overcome the *ke-*

distance himself from God. Even the sinner does not sin because he wants to pull away from God. He does so because the spirit of folly leads him to think that even if he sins, he will not be parted from Him. The spirit of folly does not engage in a battle against the inner desire to cleave to the Divine. Rather, it diverts the individual and misleads him. It tells him, "If you do this, you will not be cut off from God," "If you do that, you will still be a good Jew," "The most important thing is what is in your heart," and so forth.

SERVICE: TO OVERCOME

☞ In contrast to the light and influence that we receive from above, from God, service is performed below, by the human being himself. This is seen elsewhere as well: The array of "divine service" in the structure of the ten *sefirot* is unlike the arrays of Torah and "acts of kindness." It is the left array, that of *Gevura*, which progresses from below to above. This corresponds to the Temple sacrifices, which ascend upon the altar. It also corresponds to prayer: The essence of prayer is the individual's ascent from the material world and his attachment to supernal holiness. This epistle discusses two types of love "love of delights," which we receive from above, and "concealed love," which is already found within the human being, for he receives it as an inheritance. The question may be asked, What is the part of the individual in all this? What is the service that he is to perform? The service of the human being is to prevail over the *kelippa*. We know that love is present. There is no need to create it or draw it from elsewhere. However, we do need to break down the concealing *kelippa* so that it may be revealed.

Nevertheless, as will be stated later on, this is not a simple matter. There is not merely a layer of *kelippa* that needs to be broken down in order for love to immediately be revealed. The primary "concealment" that occludes one's inner love of God is not physicality; one's psychological and emotional paradigms and loves are much more difficult to overcome. For example, physical hunger can be suppressed relatively easily, but the emotional relationship that a person has with food is almost impossible to overcome. This is true to an even greater extent in other areas: We do not triumph by merely removing and rejecting "concealment," but rather by cultivating new goals and objects of connection and love. Furthermore, the soul that is embedded in the body, and its loves and desires, may lose its capacity to perceive or connect to spiritual matters. It

lippa "*bakol mikol kol*,"[24] which is loosely translated as "altogether." The precise language of this Hebrew phrase however, includes the repetition of the word *kol*, "all," three times. The simple implication of this repetition is that the *kelippa* must be completely vanquished, in all ways and in every aspect. Yet this phrase certainly also alludes to the talmudic statement[25] about the three individuals to whom God gave a taste of the World to Come, and over whom the evil inclination did not rule: Abraham, Isaac, and Jacob. It is written regarding them, "*bakol*," "*mikol*," and "*kol*."[26] God gave the forefathers "everything," *kol*. This was the reward for the mitzvot that they performed, and it was everything that could possibly be received, *hakol*. The forefathers, on their part, performed their service perfectly. As has been explained, they were perfect "chariots" of the divine attributes, and they bore no desire or love for anything else. This "perfection" of the forefathers, expressed by the terms "*bakol*," "*mikol*," and "*kol*," is also found in their descendants. Every Jew has the capacity to overcome the *kelippa* in the same way: "*bakol*," "*mikol*," and "*kol*." It is explained in *Likkutei Amarim* (chap. 18 and onward) that in a certain sense, the forefathers bequeathed to their descendants the "perfection" that they achieved. This is the inheritance of concealed love, which is present in every Jew. This love is that which enables us to observe the mitzvot fully, and become "chariots" of the Divine, through carrying out the mitzvot, just like our forefathers.[27] ☞

The beginning of a person's service is to expel the *kelippa* completely.

may no longer have the words or concepts necessary for this. Therefore, here too, for concealed love to be revealed as an overt feeling of love of God, it is not enough to merely break down the *kelippa*. One must also develop the faculties and skills necessary to relate to higher worlds and realities, for that is where God is more revealed and "real."

---

24. This phrase also appears in *Likkutei Amarim*, chap. 30.

25. *Bava Batra* 17a. The phrase also appears in the fourth blessing of the Grace after Meals.

26. Regarding Abraham, it is written, "And the Lord blessed Abraham, in everything [*bakol*]" (Gen. 24:1). Regarding Isaac, it is written, "I ate from all [*mikol*]" (Gen. 27:33). And regarding Jacob, it is written, "I have everything [*kol*]" (Gen. 33:11).

27. See *Likkutei Amarim*, chap. 37.

Thought, speech, and action are the three garments of the soul.[28] They are the ways in which the body expresses and reveals the soul in this material world. Thoughts are expressed through the mind, speech through the tongue, and actions through the 248 body parts. A person is required to expel the *kelippa* "*bakol mikol kol.*" These three terms signify the three garments of the soul. *Bakol,* which is said regarding Abraham, relates to action, or acts of kindness, on the right array of the sefirot. *Mikol,* which is said with regard to Isaac, refers to thought, or divine service and prayer, on the left array. *Kol,* which is said of Jacob, relates to speech, or Torah, is aligned on the middle array of the sefirot.

In *Likkutei Amarim,* the author of the *Tanya* explains that the divine service of a *beinoni* relates entirely to the garments of the soul, and not to the spiritual faculties themselves. A person can toil and make changes and corrections only regarding these garments; what he does, says, and thinks. He cannot alter his spiritual faculties, or what he feels. A *beinoni* cannot change his emotions except in certain cases, and then only indirectly, through the garments of the soul. A person's service is to refrain from thinking, speaking, and doing certain things, and instead to think, speak, and do other things. The first step of one's service, when he is still in the exile of the body, and still thinking and speaking through the thoughts and loves of the *kelippa,* is to reject these thoughts and loves. He must stop thinking of them, speaking of them, and acting on them. ☞

BAKOL MIKOL KOL

☞ The different terms used with regard to the forefathers show that each one's "perfection" is not exactly the same as the others'. Rather, there are three different types of perfection within service. These are the three arrays, which are embodied by the forefathers' Torah, divine service, and acts of kindness (see *Likkutei Amarim*, chap. 4).

EXPEL IT COMPLETELY FROM THE BODY

☞ The obligation to "completely" reject and expel foreign thoughts and loves requires an explanation. Why can love of God and worldly loves not exist side by side, just as a person can love a particular food and a particular person, and these loves do not interfere with each other? Love and fear of God are unique. There is a fundamental

28. See *Likkutei Amarim,* chap. 4.

וְאַחַר כָּךְ יוּכַל גַּם כֵּן לְהוֹצִיא מִמַּסְגֵּר אָסִיר בְּחוֹזֶק יָד, דְּהַיְינוּ לִהְיוֹת חָזָק וְאַמִּיץ לִבּוֹ בַּגִּבּוֹרִים לִהְיוֹת הָאַהֲבָה הַמְסוּתֶּרֶת נִגְלֵית בְּגִילּוּי רַב בְּכָל כֹּחוֹת חֶלְקֵי הַנֶּפֶשׁ שֶׁבַּגּוּף.

Then, one will be also be able to release the captive love **from** its captivity, and to do this **with a strong hand, that is, to stand strong like a stouthearted warrior so that the hidden love will be revealed, with immense revelation, within all the powers of the** various **components of the soul vested in the body.**

Once a person has banished all thoughts, speech, and actions that pertain to this world, he will be able to extricate the divine soul from all worldly matters. Until then, the divine soul is shackled and confined within these matters.[29]

Even when the outer barriers are removed and there seem to be no more obstacles, concealed love does not reveal itself. It needs to be brought out "with a strong hand." It is written regarding the exodus from Egypt, "For with strength of hand the Lord took us out of Egypt" (Ex. 13:16), and in numerous other places it says that it was done "with a powerful hand" (Ex. 13:9). To bring the children of Israel out of Egypt, it was not enough merely to remove the impediment of "Egypt."[30] When no one was trying to stop them from leaving any more,

contradiction between love of God and love of this world; they cannot coexist. A person whose soul is bound to this world, to earthly desires and fears, can achieve love and fear of God only in his imagination. At most, he will achieve an occasional, temporary sensation, but this will have no real basis or continuation. The reason for this is that God is separate and distinct from everything else. There is truly nothing besides Him. Therefore, a real perception of Him cannot exist on the same scale, in the same dimension, or within the same conceptual framework as anything else. The loves cannot coexist because the vessels are the same vessels: In a certain sense, a person loves God with the same spiritual vessels with which he loves another person. A vessel that relates to a worldly object cannot concurrently relate to God. Every trace of the other love must be cleared out for love of God to be revealed in it. If this is not the case, then that person's love of God is not actual love of God, but rather love of himself or merely a fleeting spark of inspiration, that he thinks is love of God.

29. The wording of the *Tanya* comes from Isa. 42:7; see also Ps. 142:8.

30. A similar idea is mentioned in *Likkutei Amarim*, chap. 31, regarding the phrase "The people had fled" (Ex. 14:5).

the exile still continued in their souls. They felt no need or desire for anything different, anything supernal, spiritual, or holy. They did not know where to go, and they did not understand why this was happening to them. It is the same regarding the soul. The removal of external impediments does not fill the internal void. At this stage, the soul still has no supernal, holy aspirations. Therefore, one needs to bring it out with a strong hand, with will and faith alone, in order to begin moving forward, despite the fact that we do not yet understand why, nor do we desire anything to be different.

This requires courage and restraint.[31] One must bolster his heart against all that he is used to loving, and against his fears of "emptiness" and the unknown. This courage, and this closing off of the heart, stems from restraint, which is the force within the soul that safeguards, curtails, and preserves.

The powers of the soul include the capacity of intellect in the brain, and love, fear, and so forth in the heart. These are enclothed in thought, speech, and action.

דְּהַיְינוּ, הָעִיקָּר בַּשֵּׂכֶל וּבַמַּחֲשָׁבָה שֶׁבַּמּוֹחַ שֶׁהַשֵּׂכֶל יַחֲשׁוֹב וְיִתְבּוֹנֵן תָּמִיד כְּפִי שִׂכְלוֹ וְהַשְׂכָּלָתוֹ בַּבּוֹרֵא יִתְבָּרֵךְ, אֵיךְ שֶׁהוּא חַיֵּי הַחַיִּים בִּכְלָל וְחַיֵּי נִשְׁמָתוֹ בִּפְרָט, וְעַל כֵּן יִכְסוֹף וְיִתְאַוֶּה לִהְיוֹת דָּבוּק בּוֹ וְקָרוֹב אֵלָיו כּוֹסֶף טִבְעִי, כְּבֵן הַכּוֹסֵף לִהְיוֹת תָּמִיד אֵצֶל אָבִיו, וּכְמוֹ אֵשׁ הָעוֹלָה לְמַעְלָה תָּמִיד בְּטִבְעָהּ לִמְקוֹרָהּ.

This means that the love is revealed **primarily in the intellect and thought in the brain, so that** one's **intellect, according to its cognitive ability and** capacity for **understanding, constantly thinks about and contemplates the Creator, blessed be He, how He is the Life** source **of** all **life in general, and the Life** source **of his soul in particular. Thus, he will yearn and desire to be bound to Him and close to Him,** with **a natural longing, like a son who yearns to always be with his father, and like fire, whose nature** it is **to constantly rise above to its source.**

31. The phrasing in the *Tanya* comes from Amos 2:16, "The courageous of heart among the valiant."

Until now, we have primarily discussed the prelude to divine service: what one must eliminate or reject, and what he must be sure not to think or do, so that the concealed love will be revealed. From here on, the author of the *Tanya* describes, in detail, what a person needs to actually do.

Most of this divine service takes place in the brain. There is intellectual thought within the brain, but there are also thoughts within the heart, which pertain to the attributes, love and fear. Here, the author of the *Tanya* mentions the thoughts of the brain first, because at this stage, when love is still concealed and the soul does not yet feel or yearn by itself, most of the divine service is performed by the intellect. ☞

One should not consider these matters on just one random occasion. Rather, he should engage in serious, prolonged contemplation that ingrains the ideas within him. The impression of this contemplation should remain with him always.

Every individual engages in contemplation with his own intellect,[32] which may be deep or broad, detail-oriented or big-picture-oriented. One's mind moves at a unique pace and employs personally developed

IN THE INTELLECT AND THOUGHT IN THE BRAIN

☞ The understanding that divine service is mainly in the intellect is based on two assumptions: The first is that the mind is fundamentally more rectified and perfect than the attributes of the heart. It is well known that the "breaking of the vessels," generally speaking, pertained to the attributes and not the brain. The same is true regarding the relationship between the world of *Atzilut* and the worlds of created beings, and likewise between human beings and animals, for example. The human sheds light on the animal, *Atzilut* sheds light on the other worlds, and so forth. It is explained in *Likkutei Amarim*, chap. 9, that the abode of the divine soul is in the brain, while the abode of the animal soul is in the heart, in the left ventricle. The second is that the mind rules over the heart: The intellect has the power to change and correct the attributes and the soul itself.

A person is able to control his mind much more than he can control his emotions. He can choose which thought to think, and if other thoughts arise in his mind against his will, he can decide not to continue thinking them and think of something else instead. This is not true of feelings.: A person cannot decide to feel a particular way. Therefore, with regard to divine service and what a person in the lower realm is able to do on his own, the main factor is the service of the mind.

32. One must not try to contemplate from someone else's perspective, for this is external to him. He might attempt to understand what another person thinks, and why and how he does so, but this does not relate to him in any way.

imagery and paradigms about that which is pertinent to him and affects any aspect of his being.

"Understanding" refers to what a person knows, that which he has already learned. Contemplation of the Divine is not like contemplation of the material objects that one sees. An ordinary person does not see the manifestation of the Divine in all things. He merely sees the world, and he must learn about the Divine from the teachings of scholars and books, as well as from his own contemplation. This is the main reason for studying the deeper levels of the Torah in general, and hasidic discourses in particular: to acquire material for contemplation. A kind of example of this is brought below, and likewise, this idea is expounded upon in great detail in many hasidic discourses. It is explained[33] that only a vast amount prolonged contemplation can lead to a true awakening of love of God.

The subject of this contemplation is not the essence and being of God Himself, which we cannot possibly grasp with our intellect. Rather, broadly speaking, it is the revelation of God as the Creator and Ruler of the world.

In order to evoke an attitude of love toward God, a person must contemplate God's attitude of love toward us and our world. This attitude is manifest in the most meaningful gift possible, which we receive from Him: life in this world in general, and the life of one's individual soul in particular.

Every individual possesses some level of understanding of this life and of the world, according to his level and the kind of life he leads. Therefore, he may also get some conception of the source of life: on the cosmic scale and of a personal level. This conception that every person seeks is not only intellectual, but is a glimpse of love. To the same extent that a person loves life in general, and his own soul's life in particular, he will open up and discover love when he contemplates the Source of life; the Creator. ☞

THE CREATOR

☞ The author of the *Tanya* uses the term *Boreh* here, as opposed to other terms that also mean Creator, *Yotzer,* He who Forms, or *Oseh,* He who makes. The word *Boreh*

---

33. See *Kuntres HaHitpa'alut,* written by the second Lubavitcher Rebbe, Rabbi Dovber Schneuri, and the introduction to *Kuntres HaAvoda* and *Kuntres HaTefilla,* by the fifth Lubavitcher Rebbe, Rabbi Sholom Dovber Schneersohn.

People love their lives and their souls. In the simplest sense, "life" refers to the food one eats; the work he carries out; his relationships with his family, friends, and acquaintances; his experiences; and so forth. These are the elements that make up life. However, above all this, there is life itself, and occasionally, at moments of great salvation or spirituality, the individual is able to feel it. Therefore, in a certain sense, life is what a person desires, labors for, and longs for all his days. When one contemplates the fact that the Creator is the Source of all life, forming it, bestowing it upon us, and sustaining it, his mind yearns for God and he desires to cleave to Him. ☞

points to the world of *Beria*, which embodies "existence from nothingness." The worlds of *Yetzira* and *Asiya* devolve from other worlds, and are thus "existence from existence." Only the world of *Beria*, which originates from God Himself (or more precisely from the world of *Atzilut*, which is one with God), is "existence from nothingness." Consequently, contemplation of the *Boreh*, the name that refers to God as Creator in the world of *Beria*, amounts to the contemplation of nothingness. This contemplation signifies the total nullification of the worlds and of oneself. Just as the *Boreh* is "nothingness" to the creations, for a created being cannot comprehend a Creator that is distinct from itself, so too all of creation, *beria*, is "nothingness" with regard to the *Boreh*: It is totally subsumed and incorporated in Him, and accordingly, there is nothing besides Him.

YEARNING WITH THE INTELLECT

☞ While the term "yearn" used here is an expression of love,[34] it is a special kind of love, not that which is revealed in the heart, but rather that which is concealed. See *Torah Or* 113c. In *Sefer HaMa'amarim*, 5692–5693, p. 352, it is explained that the term for yearning, *yikhsof*, is connected to the term for silver, *kesef*, because silver is found in nature in combination with other elements, and in order to reveal the silver, one must refine it in fire. The same is true of concealed love. The love a person feels toward his soul is the most elementary form of love, which is revealed at all times. However, regarding the love of the Source of one's soul and the Source of life itself, one understands intellectually that it exists and that this is how he should relate, yet he does not feel it at all times. This love is concealed from the heart and revealed in the intellect. The individual understands that he should love, and he even acts as though he does, yet this love is not always apparent in his heart. When one does not feel or enjoy the love in his heart, then he feels the lack, as well as the yearning to fill it as much as possible.

34. This term used here for "yearning," *yikhsof*, is seen in the verse "because you longed [*nikhsof nikhsafta*] for your father's house" (Gen. 31:30); see *Likkutei Amarim*, chap. 50.

There are also different levels when it comes to love between human beings. The first and most basic level is the love that a person feels for himself and for his own life. This is the love that is called in *Likkutei Amarim,* "My soul, I desired you."[35] The next level is the love that one feels for his father and mother, as it says in the same chapter of *Likkutei Amarim,* "like a son who tends to his father and mother, loving them more than his own body, soul, and spirit." This human love is also natural, though it is not obvious, for it requires some development on the part of the individual, who must have an awareness of something that is not physical or immediately apparent: the hidden source of that which is visible. Nevertheless, as is also explained there, once a person attains this level of awareness, this kind of love can be even stronger than the love of "My soul, I desired you."

The author of the *Tanya* alludes to another level of concealed love, which is also mentioned in *Likkutei Amarim* (chap. 19). This level is compared to fire, whose nature it is to constantly rise. The metaphor for this higher level of love is an inanimate object; that does not depend on any understanding or knowledge and seems to be even more basic than that of the previous levels. The idea, which is explained in *Likkutei Amarim,* is that a flame, which is compared to the light and life force of the soul, naturally strives to ascend, to escape its wick and reunite with its source, even though its own light will be extinguished if it succeeds, becoming subsumed in that source. The first level mentioned was based on love of one's own life, and the next was based on love of the Source of one's life. This, even higher level, is when a person is willing to sacrifice his life and disappear from worldly reality for the sake of love of God.

וְכָל מַה שֶּׁיַּתְמִיד לַחֲשׁוֹב בְּשִׂכְלוֹ כּוֹסֵף זֶה כָּכָה יִתְגַּבֵּר וְיִתְפַּשֵּׁט כּוֹסֵף זֶה גַּם בְּפִיו וּבְכָל אֵבָרָיו לַעֲסוֹק בַּתּוֹרָה וּמִצְוֹת, לְדָבְקָה בָּהֶם בַּה׳ מַמָּשׁ, דְּאוֹרַיְיתָא וְקוּדְשָׁא

The more one's mind constantly contemplates this yearning for closeness to God, **the more this yearning will grow stronger, and it will spread to the mouth and to all the organs as well,** motivating them **to be occupied with Torah** study **and** performance of the **commandments,**

35. See *Likkutei Amarim*, chap. 44, based on Isa. 26:9.

בְּרִיךְ הוּא כּוּלָּא חַד. **by which he will truly bond with God, for the Torah and the Holy One, blessed be He, are entirely one.**

As explained earlier, a person can choose to think about these matters and to continue thinking of them for an extended period of time. He can decide to think about the fact that God is the Source of life and of his soul, and that he should therefore yearn to cleave to Him as much as he is able to do so. As this thought continues to grow over time and permeates all one's other thoughts, the yearning will overflow beyond his thoughts and fill his speech and action.

Every person's revealed yearning and love seek actualization. This love, be it intellectual yearning, or heartfelt longing, is not a "love of delights," but rather a love of longing, which seeks to fill that which is missing. Longing occurs in the soul, while fulfillment takes place in the body. All yearning in this world is actualized through the body. A person desires something, and then he performs some act: He says something, does something, or goes somewhere, and this fulfills his soul's desire in some way, quieting and alleviating the yearning. With regard to love of God, too, the yearning is ultimately satisfied through the mouth and other body parts.

This fulfillment takes place through studying Torah and performing mitzvot, and as a result, becoming attached to God. It is difficult to speak with God like one speaks with another person, and it is certainly impossible to hug or kiss Him. Nevertheless, out of His great love for us, He desired that the soul within the body be given the Torah, which is enclothed in worldly matters. In the Torah, God expressed and enclothed His will and wisdom in the most essential way. This means that we are given God Himself with no filters. The Torah was not given to us by means of an intermediary such as an angel, a messenger, a parable, or a metaphor. The Giver and the gift are one. Therefore, when a person thinks thoughts of Torah with his mind, speaks its words with his mouth, or performs its mitzvot with his 248 body parts, he is thinking God's most essential thoughts, speaking His deepest words, and performing His actions. He is united and attached to God by means of a union that is unparalleled in this world. At that moment, not only are God and the Torah one,[36] but the individual, God, and the Torah are all one.[37]

וְעַל כּוֹסֶף זֶה שֶׁבְּגִילּוּי רַב כְּתִיב "צָמְאָה נַפְשִׁי וגו'" (תהלים מב,ג), כְּאָדָם הַצָּמֵא לְמַיִם וְאֵין לוֹ תַּעֲנוּג עֲדַיִין כְּלָל.

Of this yearning that is so **greatly manifest the verse states, "my soul thirsts** for God…" (Ps. 42:3), **like a person thirsty for water who does not yet feel any pleasure at all,** unlike the love of delights mentioned above.

Usually, a person cannot feel the attachment to God with the same intensity as he feels the yearning. If he does, then this is love of delights. Therefore, one is constantly in a state that is like thirst. Thirst is a yearning-feeling. It is a sense of lack that becomes progressively more tangible. It grows stronger the more one contemplates the fact that God is the Source of life, and that he longs to cleave to Him. Since God is infinite, a person can accomplish this only through the Torah, which is compared, for this reason, to water.

However, because the Torah is enclothed and concealed in this world, when a person studies Torah and fulfills mitzvot, he does not necessarily quench his feeling of thirst. He may feel the same way he does when he engages in worldly affairs: He may not sense the Divine within them. For like the Torah, human beings are similarly enclothed in the body and in this world. A person understands worldly matters easily and thoroughly, and has emotional reactions toward them. In the future, we will be able to feel attachment to the Divine in the Torah and mitzvot that we engage in. This was explained at length in the previous epistle. Right now, however, a person can feel this intimate closeness only if he purifies his body and senses, so that his spiritual senses are no longer numbed by material input. Even if he succeeds at

36. In *Likkutei Amarim*, chaps. 4 and 23, this statement is quoted in the name of the *Zohar*. There, it states there that it is from *Zohar* 1:24a. *Likkutei Torah*, Deut. 46:1, refers to *Zohar, Beshalaḥ* 60a. See also *Tikkunei Zohar* 6 and 22 (the Lubavitcher Rebbe, Rabbi Menaḥem Mendel Schneerson).

37. See *Zohar* 3:73a, which states, "There are three interconnected levels: God, the Torah, and Israel."

attaining such purity, he is able to feel the Divine in holy matters only to a minimal degree.

וְגַם עַל כּוֹסֶף זֶה וְאַהֲבָה זוֹ הַמּוּסְתֶּרֶת בָּנוּ אָנוּ מַעְתִּירִים לַה׳ לִהְיוֹת בְּעֶזְרֵנוּ לְהוֹצִיאָהּ מִמַּסְגֵּר וְשֶׁיִּהְיֶה הַלֵּב מָלֵא מִמֶּנָּה לְבַדָּהּ וְלֹא תִּכָּנֵס צָרָתָהּ בְּבֵיתָהּ, שֶׁהִיא תַּאֲוֹת עוֹלָם הַזֶּה, רַק שֶׁתִּהְיֶה הִיא עֲקֶרֶת הַבַּיִת לִמְשׁוֹל בְּצָרָתָהּ וּלְגָרְשָׁהּ הַחוּצָה מִמַּחֲשָׁבָה דִּיבּוּר וּמַעֲשֶׂה עַל כָּל פָּנִים.

Also, concerning this yearning and this love hidden inside of us, we beg God to come to our aid and **to** help us **release it from** its **captivity.** We pray **for the heart to be filled with this** yearning and love **alone, and that its "rival" – worldly desires – not enter its "house,"** which is the heart. **Rather,** this love **should be the master of the house, dominating its rival and expelling it from thought, speech, and action, at the very least.**

The author of the *Tanya* adds that the contemplation described above is not enough to reveal this love. Rather, one must also pray for it to be revealed.[38] Prayer, which is also called the service of the heart (*Ta'anit* 2a), is concerned with instilling a person's contemplation in his heart. It is work that involves transforming and purifying the heart's innate feelings toward this world and redirecting them so that they connect to the Divine instead, as is explained at length elsewhere. The word *avoda,* which means service or work, is related to the term *ibbud,* which means processing and enhancing of an item, such as an animal hide, which is treated to make it into leather. ☞

PRAYING FOR LOVE

☞ When a person prays to God for love of God, he says, "I have done all that I can. I have contemplated, studied Torah, and fulfilled mitzvot. Now it is Your turn to act. Not because I have done something great, nor because I deserve it, but because in truth, only You can do it." In prayer, the devotee connects the mind with what is

38. The Lubavitcher Rebbe, Rabbi Menaḥem Mendel Schneerson, remarks that the author of the *Tanya* was compelled to add this here in order to affirm what is written in epistle 4, that revelation does not come through contemplation but rather by means of prayer and charity; see there (this is cited in *Likkutei Biurim*).

The "heart" refers to the capacity of love within the soul. This can be focused on worldly matters such as food, money, and people, or it can be directed to the Divine. As has been stated, the *beinoni,* who needs to uncover the concealed love within him, cannot rid his heart entirely of his desires for worldly objects. However, he can render them insignificant and inactive, and disempower them from factoring in the decisions he makes regarding how to behave.

It is explained in *Likkutei Amarim* that the *beinoni* is able to completely expel his worldly desires from the garments of his soul: thought, speech, and action. This means that one does not think or speak, and certainly does not make choices informed by his desire or love for worldly matters, nor by the concerns of his body or animal soul.

הֲגַם שֶׁלֹּא יוּכַל לְשַׁלְּחָהּ לְגַמְרֵי מִלִּבּוֹ, עַל כָּל פָּנִים תִּהְיֶה הִיא מוּסְתֶּרֶת בִּבְחִינַת גָּלוּת וַעַבְדוּת לַעֲקֶרֶת הַבַּיִת גְּבִרְתָּהּ, לְהִשְׁתַּמֵּשׁ בָּהּ לִדְבָרִים הֶכְרֵחִיִּים לָהּ לְבַד כַּאֲכִילָה וּשְׁתִיָּה, כִּדְכְתִיב: "בְּכָל דְּרָכֶיךָ דָעֵהוּ" (משלי ג,ו).

Even if one cannot send the "rival" **away from his heart completely, at the very least it**, the rival, **should be** the one **hidden in a state of exile,** like a rival wife, **subservient to her master, the master of the house, serving her** master's **needs alone, such as eating and drinking, as the verse states, "In all your ways be cognizant of Him"** (Prov. 3:6).

If beforehand, love of God was concealed, now, when it is revealed, the many forms of worldly love will be concealed instead. They cannot

above the mind. He joins his "reality," that which is attainable, with "nothingness," the unlimited and omnipotent. This principle pertains to all of divine service: Everything we do in the lower realm with regard to contemplation and hard work is merely an opening for God, who completes it for us. Only the Creator Himself can truly shift things and free them from the confinement and boundaries of this world. A person can achieve this only through prayer, during which he is void of all that he has done and all that he is, and connects to God like an empty vessel. Then, it is not he who is acting. Rather, God is acting through him; sending him a livelihood, healing, and so forth, and likewise revealing within him the love that God feels for him and that he feels for God.

operate together, as previously explained: When one ascends the other descends; when one is revealed the other is concealed. ☞

Even in worldly matters that are not explicit commandments, a person must worship God, connect with Him, and cleave to Him. As stated, even if he is not able to engage in these matters out of love of God, he can nevertheless do them for reasons other than fulfilling his worldly desires. This is how one is able to serve God by means of worldly matters.

The directive to "In all your ways be cognizant of Him" does not just describe a level of especial piety: It is cited as a *halakha* in the *Shulḥan Arukh*.[39] Here, however, the author of the *Tanya* adds a new dimension to this command. The *Shulḥan Arukh* states that all a person's actions, such as eating and drinking, must be for the sake of Heaven, and certainly not for physical pleasure. Yet in addition to this, the inner strength and desire derived from such bodily pleasures must be used for the sake of divine service. In other words, a person must not engage in these actions like one who is forced to do so, with no vitality. Rather,

THE EXILE OF WORLDLY DESIRES

☞ Here, the author of the *Tanya* uses the same language he used earlier regarding love of God. When love of God is revealed, worldly desires are concealed and are essentially in "exile." Previously, it was described how the divine soul and love of God are exiled in the body and the animal soul. Here, it is the exact opposite.The animal soul and worldly love are exiled in the divine soul's love of God. "Exile," as explained elsewhere, is not only inescapable captivity where the captive cannot act as he chooses. It is also a kind of "slavery." The exiled individual is in servitude to the place of the exile. He must channel his vitality and strength into concerns that are not his own. Then the animal soul, with the passion and power of its worldly desires, is not nullified; rather, it is bound to serve the love of God.

39. See *Shulḥan Arukh, Oraḥ Ḥayyim* 231: "And likewise with anything that is pleasant for him in this world, his intent should not be for his pleasure, but rather for the service of the Creator, may He be blessed; as it is written, 'In all your ways be cognizant of Him.' And the Sages said, 'Let all of your actions be for the sake of Heaven.' As even optional things, such as eating, drinking, walking, sitting, getting up, sexual relations, conversation, and any physical need, all of them should be for the service of your Creator." The Lubavitcher Rebbe, Rabbi Menaḥem Mendel Schneerson, also remarks on this.

he must utilize the power and vitality that he possesses with regard to these matters and make them part of his divine service. Food should not be a despised necessity, but a mitzva, or the means to a mitzva, which one must perform with excitement. This, in turn, awakens the innate vitality and excitement within the action itself. Therefore, when a person perfects and elevates not only a physical action but also the life force and desires of this world, he is carrying out the verse "In all your ways be cognizant of Him" to the fullest extent possible. ☞

This epistle-discourse deals with two kinds of love of God, which are also two ways of serving God. The first is "love of delights," wherein the human soul has ascended to the higher realm, seeing and experiencing reality as it truly is: Every aspect of life is good, clear manifestations of the will of God for the sake of serving God. Through the prism of this love, a person sees only God's will in all his endeavors. God's kindness, His unending love, is showered upon the individual always. This is reflected in the verse "How fair you are and how pleasant you are, love of delights." The second type of love is that which is concealed within a person who is in the lower realm. His love of God is hidden, and his experiences are of this world: the desire for it and the dread of it. This person does not experience the pleasure of finding God in all his endeavors, and he must therefore work hard, mentally and spiritually, to make peace with this lack, and link his endeavors to God nonetheless. A tremendous degree of strength is necessary for this, and the person receives it from the place of concealed love, which is where he feels absence, yearning, and thirst for God. This love is concealed

IN ALL YOUR WAYS BE COGNIZANT OF HIM

☞ This commandment comprises one of the most fundamental tenets of Hasidism. Hasidism does not pertain only to particular actions, times, places, or spiritual faculties. Rather, it is relevant to every path a person takes, whether physical or spiritual, whether the path of a mitzva, a "way of God," or any kind of pursuit, any of "your ways." Hasidism does not distinguish between different kinds of actions or thoughts. Everything a person does, and the way in which he does it, has the potential to be divine service. However, a person should not be foolish. This fact is not supposed to make his life easier or more difficult. Rather, it is intended to permeate his being and his actions, making him cognizant of the fact that everything is connected to God.

but it is not foreign to him: It is his, and is a part of him. Therefore, when it is not manifest as love, it is manifest as the absence of love, as horror at the idea of a reality where divine love is not present, and as a strong desire to fill this void. This not only pushes and mobilizes the person to express that love through thought, speech, and action but it lends additional energy to his holy soul from the concealing forces themselves: the tangible satisfaction of worldly passions get channeled into one's love of God

Epistle 19

This epistle, like the previous one and the following one, resembles a hasidic discourse. Epistles such as these clarify the hasidic approach to a particular theoretical topic or aspect of divine service. One of the most important and difficult questions in Judaism pertains to the connection between the Torah that we possess and the supernal source of the Torah in the Divine. Does the Torah as we know it really constitute the wisdom and inner will of God, despite its seemingly "practical content of everyday *halakhot* and stories about human beings? Also, how exactly does the transition from above to below take place? Understanding these matters greatly enhances a person's reverence for both the Written Torah and the Oral Torah, for he comes to the realization that all realms of reality depend on every single stroke and dot in the Torah for their existence. Moreover, he recognizes that God's very essence is found in the Torah. These topics, which are dealt with in this epistle, relate to prophecy, wisdom, human comprehension, and the path of decent from above to below by way of the external dimension and the inner dimension. These topics are difficult to understand, for they are exceedingly complex and go beyond the rational.

Because of the significance of this epistle, it is mentioned frequently in later hasidic works. It is also called the epistle of "Enveloping with light as if with a cloak," for this is the verse that is cited at the start of it. Additionally, it is known by several other names that are related to its content, such as "*Netzaḥ* (Dominance), *Hod* (Splendor), and *Yesod*

(Foundation) of *Abba*," "The virtue of the internal over the external," and "You will See My back."

29 Elul
25 Elul (leap year)

"עוֹטֶה אוֹר כַּשַּׂלְמָה וגו'" (תהלים קד,ב). הִנֵּה בְּ'לִקּוּטֵי תוֹרָה' שֶׁל הָאֲרִיזַ"ל פָּרָשַׁת 'כִּי תִשָּׂא' וּפָרָשַׁת 'וַיִּקְרָא' כָּתַב כִּי הַשָּׂגַת מֹשֶׁה רַבֵּינוּ עָלָיו הַשָּׁלוֹם לֹא הָיְתָה בִּבְחִינַת פְּנִימִיּוּת דְּחָכְמָה עִילָּאָה הַנִּקְרָא 'אַבָּא דַּאֲצִילוּת' וְכָל שֶׁכֵּן בִּסְפִירַת הַכֶּתֶר שֶׁלְּמַעְלָה מִמֶּנָּה, הַנִּקְרָא 'אֲרִיךְ אַנְפִּין'.

The verse states, "**Enveloping with light as if with a cloak...**" (Ps. 104:2). **Now, the Arizal writes in his *Likkutei Torah,* in *Parashat Ki Tisa* and *Parashat Vayikra,* that the** level of **comprehension** attained **by Moses, our teacher, may he rest in peace, did not** draw **from the inner dimension of supernal *Ḥokhma,* which is called "*Abba* of *Atzilut,*" and all the more so,** it did not draw **from the *sefira* of *Keter,* which is called "*Arikh Anpin,*" which transcends** supernal *Ḥokhma.*

This epistle begins with a quote from Tanakh. The author of the *Tanya* generally begins the epistles in *Iggeret HaKodesh,* as well as many of his hasidic discourses, with a biblical verse. Occasionally he brings a quote from the Sages as well, that relates to the verse, and sometimes he raises questions on the verse. He then explains these matters and answers the questions according to the hasidic approach. In this epistle, the connection between the opening verse and the rest of the epistle is not explained. However, a connection can be inferred by looking at other places where this verse is quoted in the works of the author of the *Tanya.*[1] "Enveloping light as if with a cloak" conveys the subject of this epistle, which is concerned with how divine influence descends from above: The inner light is enclothed in an outer garment. "Light" refers to the highest levels of supernal matter, and "cloak" refers to the garments, the external forms in every world and on every level, in which the light is enclothed so that it can descend, be revealed, and illuminate that particular realm.

The Torah is the great light, the "secret" of God Himself. It is found

---

1. See epistle 23; *Torah Or* 49b; *Likkutei Torah,* Lev. 27a, Num. 31b; and see *Reshimot HaTzemaḥ Tzedek* (*Yahel Or*) on this verse in Psalms, p. 395.

within everything that God has created and conveyed. Little by little, this lofty secret is revealed below, descending from one world to the next and from one time to the next, until the essence of all the worlds reaches the lowest realm, our physical world. This epistle describes the way in which the light descends from world to world and from concealment to concealment. It is not extinguished, nor does it lose any of its radiance or holiness, as alluded to in the verse "enveloping light as if with a cloak."

First, the author of the *Tanya* clarifies concepts related to Moses's comprehension of the Torah. The Torah was given to us through Moses, and an insight into how he understood it enables us to understand the way in which he transmitted it to us.

Likkutei Torah of the Arizal was commonly found among the early hasidim. The author of the *Tanya* quotes it frequently in his writings. It is a collection of sermons arranged according to the *parashiyot* of the Torah, Prophets, and Writings.[2] Appended to it is another work, *Ta'amei HaMitzvot,* which explains the mystical reasons for several of the mitzvot mentioned in each *parasha.*

It has been noted[3] that the ideas presented here are not quoted exactly as they are written in *Likkutei Torah*. Rather, they are derived from the ideas in that work. In *Parashat Ki Tisa* there, it is explained at length that Moses is from the secret of the back side (*aḥor*) of the knowledge of *Zeir Anpin,* and this is why it is said, "You will see My back [*aḥorai*]" (Ex. 33:23). In *Parashat Vayikra* a similar idea is expounded upon regarding the small letter *alef* in the word *vayikra,* which signifies a considerable constriction and is like the back side of the original.

The ideas cited here in the name of the Arizal are stated in the words of the author of the *Tanya,* and we may interpret and relate to them in the same way as we interpret and relate to the rest of this epistle.

Moses's comprehension is not his own private concern. Moses was

---

2. Some of them correspond to homilies in *Sha'ar HaPesukim* and *Sefer HaLikkutim.*

3. A comment of the Lubavitcher Rebbe, Rabbi Menaḥem Mendel Schneerson, which was published in *Shiurim BeSefer HaTanya,* states, "Examine that text well in order to understand how we learn that which is written in *Iggeret HaKodesh* from *Likkutei Torah,* and specifically from the wording in *Parashat Ki Tisa* and *Parashat Vayikra.*"

the greatest prophet and the "father" of the prophets: All the prophets were his students, and all their prophecies are like offshoots of his prophecy. Moreover, the entire Torah that is in our possession, the Written Torah and the Oral Torah, was given to us through Moses's prophecy. Moses's comprehension is therefore the source of our whole comprehension of God, and accordingly, it is important that we understand its essence. ☞

The highest level of revelation is within *Ḥokhma*. The same is true with regard to the soul: The first moment of understanding in the soul takes place through *Ḥokhma*, which is like a flash of light that receives input from the inconceivable "*ayin*" in a single instant. At this initial point, comprehension is at its deepest. It is totally pure and all-encompassing. This is before we understand what it is and certainly before we grasp its meaning.

Supernal *Ḥokhma* is called "the father of *Atzilut*." The terms "father" and "mother" refer to *Ḥokhma* and *Bina*, respectively. Accordingly, this is the *sefira* of *Ḥokhma* of the world of *Atzilut*: the highest *sefira* of the highest world. ☞

Why does the author of the *Tanya* mention the fact that supernal *Ḥokhma* is called "*Abba* of *Atzilut*"? This remark appears to be redundant. One possible explanation is that the term "supernal *Ḥokhma*" refers not only to the world of *Atzilut*, but also to the realms above

MOSES'S COMPREHENSION

☞ The test of comprehension within the lower reality is simple: Does the person understand or not? However, when the comprehension relates to a higher, more abstract, and more spiritual reality, the distinction becomes more complex. This is especially true with regard to comprehension of the Divine. On the one hand, God is totally incomprehensible, yet on the other hand, He gives life to everything, and can thus be revealed at every level. Therefore, the first test of comprehension is: Which level and realm does the comprehension pertain to? And the second test is: Does this comprehension relate to the inner or outer dimension? The difference between inner and outer comprehension, in the most general sense, is the difference between grasping the idea itself and grasping its outcomes. Outer comprehension splits up into numerous levels. The higher levels are expressed through conscious and emotional connection, and the lower levels involve physical action. With regard to Moses's comprehension, the complex answers to these questions are presented here in accordance with the writings of the Arizal.

Atzilut, such as *Ḥokhma* of *Akudim*, or *Adam Kadmon*, and even higher realms.[4] Therefore, he adds that it is called "*Abba* of *Atzilut*," which means *Ḥokhma* of the world *Atzilut*.[5] This emphasizes the fact that Moses's comprehension did not extend to supernal *Ḥokhma*: It did not even extend to *Ḥokhma* of the world of *Atzilut*, which is the lowest level of supernal *Ḥokhma*. ☞

Once again, there is a double definition here: "the *sefira* of *Keter*, which is called *Arikh Anpin* (long face)."[6] *Arikh Anpin* is another *partzuf*, just like "father," "mother," and so on. Since the author of the *Tanya* wrote that Moses's comprehension did not reach the inner dimension of *Ḥokhma* of *Atzilut*, one may have thought that it did reach the

ḤOKHMA AND *ATZILUT*

☞ The *sefira* of *Ḥokhma* and the world of *Atzilut* are unlike other levels and realms. *Atzilut* is not truly a "world," because relative to the worlds of created beings, *Atzilut* is actually totally Divine. All its *sefirot* are divine forces that act on and are revealed within the other worlds. Likewise, *Ḥokhma* is not like the other *sefirot*. It is explained in Kabbala that *Ḥokhma* is not just a particular force or manifestation, but a revelation of God Himself. However, it is only revealed in a tangible way, by becoming enclothed in the other *sefirot*. It follows that comprehension on the level of the supernal *Ḥokhma* of *Atzilut* is not merely an understanding of the life force that God confers on the worlds. It is the comprehension of God Himself in the worlds, to the extent that this is possible on the part of the person receiving it.

ABBA OF *ATZILUT*

☞ The term *Abba*, father, is not exactly the same as the term *Ḥokhma*. *Ḥokhma* is one of the ten *sefirot*, while *Abba* is one of the *partzufim*, "faces," of *Atzilut*: father, mother, *Zeir Anpin*, and *Malkhut* (Kingship). Each *partzuf* is a whole, complex entity, a complete structural analogue of *sefirot*, whose components are organized in a particular order. Since the discussion here concerns the inner and outer dimensions of *Ḥokhma*, it is certainly referring to a complex entity that is comprised of many different aspects, and not to an individual *sefira*, which is like a single, simple source of light. Perhaps that is why this repetition is followed by other, similar repetitions in the *Tanya*: "the *sefira* of *Keter*, which is called '*Arikh Anpin*,'" and "the seven lower *sefirot*, called *Zeir Anpin*." This is explained below.

---

4. See *Likkutei Torah*, Lev. 43c.
5. This is how it is explained in *HaLekaḥ VehaLibuv*.
6. The meaning of *Arikh Anpin* and the difference between it and *Zeir Anpin* will be explained below

external dimension of *Keter*. It was therefore necessary to state that it did not. ☞ ☞

כִּי אִם בִּבְחִינַת אֲחוֹרַיִים דְּחָכְמָה הַמִּתְלַבְּשִׁים בְּבִינָה הַמִּתְלַבֶּשֶׁת בְּ־ז' סְפִירוֹת תַּחְתּוֹנוֹת שֶׁנִּקְרָאוֹת 'זְעֵיר אַנְפִּין' סוֹד הַתּוֹרָה, וּמִתְפַּשֶּׁטֶת עַד סוֹף ד' סְפִירוֹת הַתַּחְתּוֹנוֹת שֶׁהֵן נהי"מ.

Rather, Moses's comprehension extended to **the external dimensions of *Ḥokhma,* which are clothed in *Bina,* which** in turn **is clothed in the seven lower *sefirot,* called *Zeir Anpin.*** The enclothement of *Ḥokhma* in *Zeir Anpin* is **the secret of the Torah.** Within *Zeir Anpin, Ḥokhma* **extends to the bottom of the four lowest *sefirot, Netzaḥ*** (Dominance)*,* ***Hod*** (Splendor)*,* ***Yesod*** (Foundation) **and *Malkhut*** (Kingship).

ARIKH ANPIN

☞ Here, it does not mention the inner or external dimension of the *sefira*, for *Arikh Anpin* is itself the external dimension of *Keter*. *Keter* contains two *partzufim: Arikh Anpin* and *Atik Yomin*. *Arikh Anpin* is the external dimension of *Keter*, while *Atik Yomin* (see *Torah Or* 33b) is the inner dimension.

MOSES'S COMPREHENSION DID NOT EXTEND

☞ The detailed description of what Moses did not comprehend is puzzling because in general we cannot learn about something in detail from a description of what it is not. However, this assertion is not an absolute negation. Rather, it shows that Moses did have some degree of comprehension on that level, though not of its inner essence, as will be discussed later in the epistle. Furthermore, the reason why the author of the *Tanya* mentions the *sefira* of *Keter* here is to teach us that the source of what is understood is even higher than the inner dimension of *Ḥokhma*. There is technical comprehension, which is concerned with the various modes of revelation, but this usually has no significance beyond the level at which it is revealed. However, when it comes to the comprehension of the essence of a matter, even when it is enclothed in the most external of externalities, there is also meaning to the inner dimension and the root of its root, all the way up to the highest realm. Certainly here, regarding Moses's comprehension, and regarding our comprehension of the Torah, it is important to know what is understood, but it is also important to know what is not understood, for that which is not understood is the root of that which is understood and revealed.

From here, the author of the *Tanya* will discuss that which Moses did comprehend in his prophetic vision:

The external dimensions of *Ḥokhma* are not the inner essence of *Ḥokhma*. Rather, they are what is revealed on the outside. *Bina* is the garment that enclothes these dimensions. It is like a vessel for the light of *Ḥokhma*.

Comprehension extends to the light that is enclothed, and this pertains to the external dimension, for the inner dimension is never enclothed. Moses's comprehension extended to the external dimension of *Ḥokhma*. In other words, it did not extend to *Ḥokhma* itself, but to the side of *Ḥokhma* that is perceived in other realities. Every utensil in the material world has a particular purpose: A cup is used to hold liquids, a knife is used for cutting, and so forth. However, in order for the utensil to be used for its intended purpose, it must have an exterior, a side that connects with the external environment. In this sense, the "exterior," or "back," of *Ḥokhma* is that which is enclothed, that which connects to the level that receives from *Ḥokhma*, which is *Bina*. ☞

THE EXTERNAL DIMENSIONS OF *ḤOKHMA*

☞ This does not mean that the inner dimension of *Ḥokhma* cannot be grasped at all, for this too is *Ḥokhma*. However, the attainment of the inner dimension cannot be converted into understanding or feeling, even within the individual himself. The comprehension of *Ḥokhma* is like intuition. The object of this type of comprehension cannot be defined or analyzed. We have no way of relating to it and no instrument that can grasp or even touch it. Quintessential, inner dimension-*Ḥokhma* is like light without a vessel. It constitutes pure inception. The following stages, the consequences and projections of that initial spark of *Ḥokhma* can only be translated into *Bina* and the lower levels of apprehension through the external dimension of *Ḥokhma*.

Comprehension that is enclothed in a vessel is the comprehension of the external dimension. Moreover, the comprehension being discussed here is intended to advance into other realms, into one's emotion, thought, and speech, and from there to other people's perceptions, emotions, and so on. Internal comprehension remains as is. It simply exists within the essence of the matter, so it cannot continue to become more revealed. That which is grasped within *Ḥokhma* stays within *Ḥokhma*. In contrast, the comprehension of the external dimension can move from level to level. A person is able to see a particular sight, but he cannot hear it. Nevertheless, he can hear the external dimension of that sight. He can hear of its impact from those who see it, even if he himself does not. Comprehension that continues to move downward must certainly be ad-

After having discussed the enclothement of the external dimension of *Ḥokhma* within *Bina*, the author of the *Tanya* continues:

After *Ḥokhma* is enclothed in *Bina*, *Bina* is enclothed in the seven emotive *sefirot*: *Ḥesed* (Kindness), *Gevura* (Restraint), *Tiferet* (Beauty), *Netzaḥ* (Dominance), *Hod* (Splendor), *Yesod* (Foundation), and *Malkhut* (Kingship). ☞

The composite of the seven lower *sefirot* is more than just a group of individual *sefirot*. Like in the human soul, the attributes form an all-encompassing entity much like a world or an individual. They act as one unit that possesses a head and feet, a front and a back, and its own par-

vancing by way of the external dimensions: The external dimensions of the high levels are enclothed in the inner dimensions of the levels below them.

ENCLOTHED IN EMOTIVE ATTRIBUTES

☞ In the human soul, being enclothed in *Bina* means being enclothed in the mind, where matters are perceived in terms of inner "letters" that define and form our intellectual consciousness. However, being enclothed in the lower *sefirot*, the emotive attributes, means being enclothed in emotion as well. We cannot connect to *Ḥokhma* because it constitutes an overall awareness that cannot be broken down. Yet *Bina* creates characterizations that can be contrasted to one another to form a perceivable image: what the matter in question is, its nature, and so forth.

When the information reaches one's attributes, he begins to form personal connections: He loves a certain object or is afraid of it; he realizes that this object is good and that one is bad; and so on. This occurs on the level of *Ḥesed*, *Gevura*, and *Tiferet*. When the person reaches conclusions that relate to action: Run toward it, run away; and so forth, it is on the level of *Netzaḥ*, *Hod*, and *Yesod*. Being enclothed in emotive attributes means being enclothed in a level that is lower but also more tangible. Because a person's sense of himself develops through the attributes, he can truly understand a concept only when it is enclothed in the attributes. The mind only tells us that the matter exists, and while this fact may indeed interest us, only when the matter enters the realm of the emotive attributes, does it become the reality in which we live.

It is the same with regard to the *sefirot* and the worlds. When divine essence, or, God's infinite light, is enclothed in the cognitive *sefirot*, it is beyond the world. It is on the level of the divine realm that precedes God's speaking reality into existence, on the level of God who thinks about the world, so to speak. On the other hand, the divine life force that gives actual existence to the worlds is enclothed in the attributes. The verse states, "In six days the Lord made the heavens and the earth" (Ex. 20:11), and hasidic works explain that this refers to the six attributes of *Zeir Anpin*. Accordingly, our comprehension, which is an inherent part of the worlds, cannot relate directly and truly to the Divine unless it is enclothed in the seven lower *sefirot*.

ticular purpose and way. In Kabbala, an entity like this is called a *partzuf*. The *partzuf* of the emotive *sefirot* is called *Zeir Anpin*, which means "small face" in Aramaic. *Partzuf* means "face," and refers to an entire level. This *partzuf* is called "small" because relative to the large "long face," *Arikh Anpin*, it is small. *Arikh Anpin* pertains to the all-encompassing *sefira* of *Keter*, which contains all ten *sefirot* from *Keter* to *Malkhut*. *Zeir Anpin* is like a microcosm of the large entity of *Arikh Anpin*.

The "secret of the Torah,"[7] which is essentially the subject of this epistle, refers to the wondrous way in which the Torah progresses from being God's pure essential *Ḥokhma*, and descends to a level compatible with our world. Here, it is concerned with practical commandments, both positive and negative, and with classifying all things: What is holy and what is impure, what is permitted and what is forbidden, and the way in which every aspect of life can be channeled toward holiness. *Zeir Anpin*, of the world of *Atzilut*, relative to the worlds of created beings, describes God's "face," which is turned toward us, as it were. This is why it is called the "small face," for it relates to the world. On the other hand, *Arikh Anpin*, the large face, signifies the broad view from above, from God's perspective. This "face" that looks at the world, from above, sheds light and shines with the true form and essence of every aspect of reality. This is the Torah: the holy perspective that reveals within this small, lowly world how things truly are, unearths the meaning of everything, and moreover, cultivates the manifestation of God Himself, who relates to us with His *Ḥesed*, *Gevura*, *Tiferet*, and so forth. ☞

SECRET

☞ Whenever something is defined as "secret," the implication is that the matter is not entirely clear or revealed, that it involves a concealed process of heavenly "intervention" that we cannot explain. The "secret of the Torah" is the secret of the connection between the higher realm and the lower realm. The lower realm refers to our reality: the place where we are located, and the realm that we are able to understand. The higher realm refers to that which is concealed, which is beyond the framework of our consciousness and thoughts. Since a connection between the higher realm and the lower realm seems to be impossible, it is termed a "secret."

7. See *Etz Ḥayyim*, *Sha'ar HaKelalim*, chap. 1; *sha'ar* 20, "the Mohin)", chap. 3, *sha'ar* 25, "*derushei hatzalam*," *derush* 8. et cetera

Within *Zeir Anpin*, the *sefirot* are further divided into "internal" and "external." In the most general sense, *Ḥesed, Gevura,* and *Tiferet* are "internal," and *Netzaḥ, Hod, Yesod,* and *Malkhut* are "external." In the soul, the attributes are similarly divided into two types: *Ḥesed, Gevura,* and *Tiferet* are the emotive attributes, and they define the soul's real, intrinsic feelings. *Netzaḥ, Hod, Yesod,* and in a certain sense even *Malkhut,* are the *sefirot* that process one's internal world and connect them to the "outside," defining what they mean, what to do with them, how to do it, and so forth.

וְשָׁם הָיְתָה הַשָּׂגַת נְבוּאָתוֹ בִּבְחִינַת פְּנִימִיּוּת, דְּהַיְינוּ מִבְּחִינַת פְּנִימִיּוּת דְּנהי"מ.

There, the **comprehension of** Moses's **prophecy extended to the inner dimensions, that is, the inner dimension of *Netzaḥ, Hod, Yesod* and *Malkhut*.**

Every level, even if it is entirely "external," consists of both an internal dimension and an external dimension. Therefore, although *Netzaḥ, Hod, Yesod,* and *Malkhut* pertain to the connection and "outside" affect toward other people, they contain an inner dimension as well. This inner dimension, like in the soul, is concerned with the "inner" meaning of the flow. It relates to the enjoyment and meaning that a person derives from the influence that he has on others. ☞

Moses was privy to apprehending the inner dimension of supernal *Netzaḥ, Hod, Yesod,* and *Malkhut*. This means that he did not grasp

THE INNER DIMENSION OF *NETZAḤ, HOD, YESOD,* AND *MALKHUT*

☞ The author of the *Tanya* describes at length in several places in *Iggeret HaKodesh* how the essence of the mitzva of charity is its power on the person who is doing the giving. God did not issue this commandment so that people would receive money: He has many other, simpler ways to accomplish this. Rather, this commandment was enacted primarily so that people would give. When a person gives from that which belongs to him, when he gives of himself, even though he is not compelled to do so and even though the other person did not earn it, then he brings the essence and inner dimension of the mitzva of charity to fruition. This is true with regard to all other types of spiritual give and take as well: The giver becomes infused with spiritual light from the inner dimension of the mitzva, from the good that he dispenses. The external dimension, on the other hand, impacts the receiver.

God's inner being (*Ḥokhma, Bina, Da'at* [Knowledge], *Ḥesed, Gevura, Tiferet*), but only the realm of God's influence within the worlds (*Netzaḥ, Hod, Yesod, Malkhut*). However, he grasped the inner dimension of these: the essential meaning of divine influence from God's own perspective. God's divine vitality creates of all the worlds and gives them life. The inner dimension of this, therefore, is the Torah and the words of the prophets, which express God's side of divine influence: His love, His gratification when we do His will, and the opposite when we do not. This is what comprised Moses's prophetic comprehension.

אֲבָל לְמַעְלָה מִנהי״מ לֹא הָיְתָה לוֹ שׁוּם הַשָּׂגָה בִּפְנִימִיּוּת כִּי אִם בִּבְחִינַת אֲחוֹרַיִים דְּחָכְמָה הַמְלוּבָּשִׁים בְּבִינָה הַמְלוּבֶּשֶׁת וּמִתְפַּשֶּׁטֶת תּוֹךְ פְּנִימִיּוּת דְּנהי״מ בְּסוֹד 'נוֹבְלוֹת חָכְמָה' שֶׁלְּמַעְלָה - תּוֹרָה שֶׁהִיא בִּבְחִינַת 'זְעֵיר אַנְפִּין', וּכְדִכְתִיב: "וְרָאִיתָ אֶת אֲחוֹרָי וּפָנַי לֹא יֵרָאוּ" (שמות לג,כג) עַיֵּין שָׁם, וּבְשַׁעַר הַנְּבוּאָה, פֶּרֶק א'.

But *in the sefirot* **higher than *Netzaḥ, Hod, Yesod* and *Malkhut*, he did not have any comprehension of** their **internal dimensions.** He **only** comprehended **the external dimension of *Ḥokhma*, clothed in *Bina*, which is clothed in and extends into the inner dimensions of *Netzaḥ, Hod, Yesod* and *Malkhut*, by the secret of the "vestige of *Ḥokhma* above,** which is **Torah."** As mentioned above, **this** secret of the Torah **is the level of *Zeir Anpin*, reflected by the verse, "you will see My back, but My face will not be seen"** (Ex. 33:23). **See there** in the Arizal's *Likkutei Torah* **and in *Sha'ar Hanevua*, chap. 1.**

Moses did not comprehend the inner dimension of the cognitive or emotive *sefirot*. He did, however, comprehend the inner dimension of *Netzaḥ, Hod, Yesod,* and *Malkhut*. This is the difference between Moses's prophetic comprehension and the comprehension of the rest of the world: Like its existence, the world receives its comprehension from the external dimension of *Netzaḥ, Hod, Yesod,* and *Malkhut.*

This seems to be a repetition of an idea that was already stated previously.[8] Perhaps to emphasize the power of this concept which shows how the inner dimension that is revealed in the lowest of realms embodies the entire spectrum of spiritual progressive descent, all the way up to the highest level. In other words, when Moses comprehended the inner dimension of *Netzaḥ, Hod, Yesod,* and *Malkhut,* he did not just grasp the inner dimensions of *Netzaḥ, Hod, Yesod,* and *Malkhut,* but also that which is enclothed in them: *Ḥokhma, Bina,* and so forth. This is the overarching rule: comprehending inner essence on any level includes and reflects the inner dimensions of all levels, up to the very highest. The external dimension connects to, and is enclothed in, the lower levels, and therefore its comprehension is separate from that which is above it and in a certain sense also conceals that which is above it. In contrast, the inner dimension is not enclothed in the lower levels, but actually enclothes the higher levels. Consequently, all levels, including the most supernal, are revealed and reflected within the inner dimension. ☞

The term *novlot,* "vestige," refers to fruits that fell from the tree before they were fully ripened. This is a metaphor for the Torah that is in our possession:[9] It constitutes supernal *Ḥokhma,* yet it has "fallen" from its place in the higher realm, and is no longer directly connected to the heavenly source of its life-force and development. *Novlot* are still the same fruits, but because they have fallen and become, to all appearances, detached from the tree, the tree's essential life force is not apparent within them, neither in their taste nor in their appearance.

Zeir Anpin pertains to the emotive *sefirot,* and the emotive *sefirot* establish connections, such as: I love this, I fear that, I do this, I do not do that. In a sense, this is the essence of the Torah that is revealed to us: categorization of objects in the world. The Torah tells us which items are kosher and which are not, for example. The connection between this and supernal *Ḥokhma* is not clear: It lies in the secret of "the vestige of *Ḥokhma* above." The Torah finds its source is supernal *Ḥokhma,* yet descends to the lower realms, and along the way, becomes enclothed in garment after garment. This also occurs within the soul,

8. The Lubavitcher Rebbe, Rabbi Menaḥem Mendel Schneerson, raises this in *He'arot VeTikkunim LaTanya.*

9. See *Bereshit Rabba* 44:17.

where *Ḥokhma* is pulled down toward the external, emotive attributes. These attributes express only the final verdict of the soul regarding a particular matter: One desires an object or does not desire it, an item is kosher or not kosher, and so on.

The author of the *Tanya* cites the words of the Arizal concerning Moses's level of comprehension. This idea is expressed through the verse in *Parashat Ki Tisa*. Moses beseeched God, "Please show me Your glory" (Ex. 33:18), and the response was that he could grasp the external dimension but not the internal.

Likkutei Torah is the work of the Arizal that was cited at the beginning of this epistle. *Sha'ar HaNevua* is likewise a work of the Arizal,[10] in which it is explained at length what prophecy is, what makes Moses's prophecy different from that of the other prophets, and more.

THE EXTERNAL DIMENSION OF *ḤOKHMA*, ENCLOTHED IN *BINA*

☞ As the Lubavitcher Rebbe, Rabbi Menaḥem Mendel Schneerson, points out (*He'arot VeTikkunim LaTanya*), only *Ḥokhma* and *Bina* are mentioned here as being enclothed in the inner dimension of *Netzaḥ*, *Hod*, *Yesod*, and *Malkhut*. The emotive *sefirot* of *Ḥesed*, *Gevura*, and *Tiferet*, which are within *Zeir Anpin*, are not mentioned. In other words, *Bina* is directly enclothed in the inner dimension of *Netzaḥ*, *Hod*, *Yesod*, and *Malkhut*, and not by way of the emotive *sefirot* of *Ḥesed*, *Gevura*, and *Tiferet*.

One could say that broadly speaking, this is the difference between the light that descends through the unfolding succession of worlds, which is what creates and directs these worlds, and the light of revelation within the worlds. In the unfolding succession of worlds, light is enclothed on all levels in the proper order. In the case of revelation, on the other hand, the final stage of enclothement before revelation is always bypassed, and sometimes other stages are omitted as well (a similar idea is discussed in *Likkutei Amarim*, chap. 53). Here, the author of the *Tanya* explains how comprehension and revelation occur by way of enclothement in the inner dimension of *Netzaḥ*, *Hod*, *Yesod*, and *Malkhut*, and not through the emotive *sefirot* of *Ḥesed*, *Gevura*, and *Tiferet*. The life force that forms reality is enclothed in the emotive *sefirot*, while the ideas, reasons, and thoughts behind creation are enclothed in the cognitive *sefirot*. This is the essence of divine revelation in the world: The light and the wisdom within things are revealed to the creations not as they are now, in the realm of physical creation, but rather as they are from the heavenly perspective.

---

10. It is unclear to which book this is referring. Some posit that it refers to "*Sha'ar Ruaḥ HaKodesh*" from *Shemona She'arim*, and others posit that the intention is to the book printed today under the name *Sha'ar HaYiḥudim*."

Up to this point, the author of the *Tanya* has been quoting the words of the Arizal. Moving forward, he goes on to develop these ideas further, offering an explanation that is based on the deepest, most mystical levels of the Torah, which have been handed down to us, by the scholars of truth, in the *Zohar* and in the writings of the Arizal.

וְלִכְאוֹרָה יֵשׁ לְהַפְלִיא, הֲרֵי נֶאֱמַר "וְלֹא קָם נָבִיא עוֹד בְּיִשְׂרָאֵל כְּמֹשֶׁה" (דברים לד,י), וְאֵיךְ הִשִּׂיג הָאֲרִיזַ"ל יוֹתֵר מִמֶּנּוּ וְדָרַשׁ כַּמָּה דְּרוּשִׁים בִּבְחִינַת פְּנִימִיּוּת, אֲפִילוּ בִּסְפִירוֹת וּמַדְרֵגוֹת רַבּוֹת שֶׁלְּמַעְלָה מֵהַחָכְמָה וְכֶתֶר דַּאֲצִילוּת?

But **it seems surprising. After all, the verse states, "There has not risen another prophet in Israel like Moses"** (Deut. 34:10). **How is it then, that the Arizal comprehended more than** Moses, **and taught a number of teachings concerning the internal dimensions, even of many *sefirot* and spiritual levels that transcend *Ḥokhma* and *Keter of Atzilut*?**

Moses was the greatest of the prophets, and no other human being was ever able to comprehend on the same level or to the same degree that he did. It says here that Moses grasped only the lower *sefirot* and the external dimensions of the *sefirot* of the world of *Atzilut*. However, in the writings of the Arizal, there are descriptions of much higher levels, and not only their external dimensions, but also their inner dimensions. Moreover, not only are the *sefirot* of the world of *Atzilut* described, but so are levels that lie beyond it.[11] ☞

HOW DID THE ARIZAL COMPREHEND MORE THAN MOSES?

☞ Ostensibly, this question pertains not only to the Arizal, but also to us: How can we relate to and speak of such high levels? If Moses could not comprehend them, how do we have the words and concepts to say that he could comprehend this but not that? When we speak of levels of understanding, it must be noted that every progressively lower level, is like the external dimension of the level above it. The many various levels can be broadly divided into three. The first two are the level of prophecy and the level of the comprehension of the kabbalists. These levels will

11. These are the levels of *Arikh Anpin, Atik, Adam Kadmon,* and even the constriction and pre-constriction.

1 Tishrei
26 Elul (leap year)

אַךְ הָעִנְיָן הוּא פָּשׁוּט וּמוּבָן לַכֹּל, שֶׁיֵּשׁ הֶפְרֵשׁ גָּדוֹל בֵּין הַשָּׂגַת חַכְמֵי הָאֱמֶת כְּרַשְׁבִּ"י וְהָאֲרִיזַ"ל, שֶׁהִיא הַשָּׂגַת חָכְמָה וָדַעַת, וּבֵין הַשָּׂגַת מֹשֶׁה רַבֵּינוּ עָלָיו הַשָּׁלוֹם וּשְׁאָר הַנְּבִיאִים בִּנְבוּאָה הַמְכוּנָּה בַּכָּתוּב בְּשֵׁם רְאִיָּה מַמָּשׁ, "וְרָאִיתָ אֶת אֲחוֹרָי" (שמות לג,כג), "וָאֶרְאֶה אֶת ה'" (ישעיהו ו,א), "וַיֵּרָא אֵלָיו ה'" (בראשית יח,א).

But the truth is plainly obvious to all that there is a big difference between the comprehension of the kabbalists like Rabbi Shimon bar Yochai and the Arizal – which is a comprehension that they were privy to due to their **wisdom and knowledge – and the comprehension of Moses, our teacher, may he rest in peace, and the other prophets.** Moses and the prophets experienced **prophecy, which the Torah calls actual seeing,** as in the verses **"you will see My back"** (Ex. 33:23); **"I saw the Lord"** (Is. 6:1); **"The Lord appeared to him"** (Gen. 18:1).

be discussed below. The third level is that of any individual who can read the works of Kabbala and talk about the concepts mentioned there. Regarding this level, the Arizal comprehended the "inner dimension." Through his wisdom and prophetic intuition, the Arizal grasped the essence of reality as no human being had ever grasped it before. In contrast, the way in which we discuss this teaching is completely external, because we do not comprehend the actual concepts, but only the fact that they exist and the fact that there are those who comprehend them. *Likkutei Torah* (Lev. 5a and onward) comments on the verse "You shall not withhold the salt" (Lev. 2:13) that our comprehension of the concealed Torah, the Kabbala, is an understanding of that which exists rather than the essence. For people in a particular field, the words and concepts of that field have meaning. They recognize and understand them, and have a conscious and even an emotional connection to them. On the other hand, people who come from the outside can say these words and even use them in the correct way, but do not possess a real sense of them. For example, almost anyone can conceptualize and relate to the number five in a tangible way, but most of us have no real concept of a quantity like five million. With regard to Kabbala, this is the difference between the scholars of truth (the kabbalists) and other people: The kabbalists, who are engaged in the field not only in terms of their knowledge but also in terms of the work of perfecting and purifying their souls, are able to perceive the essence of these matters, to feel their presence and their depth. Such individuals, even if they are not on the level of prophecy, are certainly in a totally different spiritual, mental and emotional space from people who are merely able to say the words.

The level of Rabbi Shimon bar Yoḥai's comprehension is expressed in the *Zohar*. The level of comprehension in the writings of the Arizal and his disciples comprises another layer of mystical teachings in addition to those of the *Zohar*.

The two types of comprehension are completely dissimilar. The comprehension of the kabbalists came through their intellectual faculties; their wisdom, understanding, and knowledge. On the other hand, Moses's comprehension and that of the other prophets is prophetic. There is no way to compare their levels of comprehension. First, we must discern the nature of the comprehension in question and the way in which it is acquired. Then, it is possible to compare different levels of this comprehension.

Comprehension through the intellectual faculties is something that we have a frame of reference to recognize and understand. Prophetic comprehension, on the other hand, is a type of comprehension that most people do not experience, and therefore it requires some explanation.

Prophetic comprehension is referred to in *Tanakh* in terms of sight.[12] The author of the *Tanya* brings examples of this. The first verse that he cites is about Moses, the second is about Isaiah, and the third is about Abraham. All levels of prophetic revelation are referred to as "seeing," not only the prophecy of Moses, which was higher than all other prophecies and was, in a sense, on the level of the giving of the Torah itself. Isaiah did not convey original teachings but rather rebuked the people and called on them to observe the Torah's commandments, yet his prophecy is also described in these terms. Even the prophecy of Abraham, which took place before the Torah was given, is referred to in this way.

וְאַף שֶׁזֶּהוּ דֶּרֶךְ מָשָׁל וְאֵינָהּ רְאִיַּית עַיִן בָּשָׂר גַּשְׁמִי מַמָּשׁ, מִכָּל מָקוֹם הַנִּמְשָׁל צָרִיךְ לִהְיוֹת דּוֹמֶה לַמָּשָׁל, וּכְתַרְגּוּם "וַיֵּרָא אֵלָיו ה'" (בראשית יח,א): "וְאִתְגְּלִיָא לֵיהּ

Although this is merely **a metaphor and doesn't mean vision of the physical eye in the literal sense, nevertheless, the analogue must be similar to the analogy. Thus,** *Onkelos* **translates** the verse, **"The Lord appeared**

12. For example, Samuel says, "I am the seer" (I Sam. 9:19).

וכו'", שֶׁהוּא בְּחִינַת הִתְגַּלּוּת, שֶׁנִּגְלָה אֵלָיו הַנֶּעְלָם בָּרוּךְ הוּא בִּבְחִינַת הִתְגַּלּוּת.

to him" as "God **became revealed to him...,"** **reflecting** a divine **revelation, in which the hidden** God, **Blessed be He, became openly manifest to** Abraham.

The physical eye sees the physical realm, yet prophetic vision is certainly not physical. It is on such a high and pure level that it sees only the Divine. It does not register physicality visually, nor does it see spirituality. It sees God's will, wisdom, thoughts, and speech. They are enclothed in whatever level that the prophet has attained, and yet they are beyond any created level. The concept of physical vision here is only a metaphor.

Prophetic vision must be similar to physical vision, for the verses of *Tanakh* draw a parallel between them. In order to understand their connection, we must consider another, more abstract term for vision.

Onkelos translates prophetic comprehension, which is, as mentioned above, similar to physical vision, a revelation. This term does not signify a physical vision. Nonetheless, spiritual vision is a kind of revelation. ☞

Unlike all the other senses, vision does not refer only to the sensing of an object. Rather, it indicates revelation. This is not a revelation in the sense that we discover one detail and then another and try to construct an image of the object in our minds. Rather, the object itself is revealed at once, as with physical vision, where the entire object is perceived instantaneously just as it is. Only after this stage can the mind analyze what it has seen, learn more details about it, and draw conclusions. However, "vision" itself refers to the overall, unmediated perception of the object as a whole. Revelation means that the very

ABSTRACT LANGUAGE IN ONKELOS

☞ In almost every case where the Torah speaks anthropomorphisms, Onkelos uses an abstract expression, thus moving further away from the physical realm. The abstract term admittedly provides a less accurate metaphor. However, being more abstract, it is able to mediate between the metaphor and the reality, illuminating the metaphor and helping us understand and connect to the physical images used in the Torah.

message is revealed and is present. The person who perceives it is, at that moment, inactive. Similarly, when a person comes to a new place such as a new school, a "world" in and of itself, he is not yet familiar with all the rooms, people, or relationships in the place, yet he is there. This is the stage of revelation: The divine display itself is present and visible even though the person does not yet understand it and certainly cannot yet explain to others what he sees. ☞

That which the prophet "sees" in his prophecy is the reality into which he has been absorbed. During the prophecy, he is not in the ordinary realm, but rather "there," in the place that he sees in the prophecy. According to all his senses, he is there: It becomes his entire reality. There is a second stage of prophecy, in which the prophet conveys to us what occurred "there." He describes what he saw in his own words. This is subject to the individual prophet and his personal level. The ideas of the prophecy are expressed through his unique conceptualizations. Yet the essence of prophecy is the Divine Presence that is revealed to the prophet and into which he is immersed at that moment. This is what is being discussed when we address the level of Moses's comprehension.

The advantage of revelation at this level is its palpable clarity. It is the same experience as when a person sees and senses the physical reality around him. This is real in every sense of the word, even more so than something that the person hears about, although he may understand what it is, how it behaves, and so forth.

מַה שֶּׁאֵין כֵּן בְּהַשָּׂגַת חַכְמֵי הָאֱמֶת שֶׁלֹּא נִגְלָה אֲלֵיהֶם הֲוָיָ"ה, בִּבְחִינַת הִתְגַּלּוּת, רַק שֶׁהֵם מַשִּׂיגִים תַּעֲלוּמוֹת חָכְמָה הַנֶּעְלָם [נוּסָּח אַחֵר: בַּנֶּעְלָם] וּמוּפְלָא מֵהֶם.

By contrast, the comprehension of the kabbalists, to whom *Havaya* was not openly revealed, but who merely **comprehend** intellectually, without vision, **the secret wisdom that is concealed [another version:** the secret wisdom **within the concealed] and beyond them.**

The name of *Havaya* itself is not revealed to the kabbalists. In our world, the name of *Havaya* is enclothed in the name of *Elokim* and the name of *Adnut*, but it itself is not manifest. The prophet sees the essence of the matter just as it is the higher realm, beyond the concealing confines of our world. The kabbalist, however, cannot see this. Rather, he "hears" of it from below. He hears of the reality of the matter from those who can see it.

The kabbalists comprehend that which is within the realm of the concealed. This is in tandem with the second version included here, "within the concealed." The prophet is actually in that realm, so he comprehends it with all his senses and spiritual faculties, just as we comprehend the physical reality in which we are located. The kabbalist, however, comprehends by means of his wisdom. He is not truly in that realm. He receives information about it and images of it. He may encounter people, or angels, who have been there, and he may even experience certain things as though he were there, but he himself is not actually there. This is why it says that the kabbalist comprehends "the secret wisdom." He comprehends matters that are not revealed to him, but remain concealed to him. For the kabbalist, the concealed remains concealed and is never truly revealed. However, his strength lies in his ability to absorb that which is concealed, that which is essentially beyond him, into his spiritual faculties, intellect, and emotions. He understands and relates to such matters, some to a greater degree and some to a lesser. ☞

VISION AS THE FACULTY OF WISDOM

☞ Elsewhere (see *Torah Or* 75a), spiritual vision is equated with the faculty of *Ḥokhma*, while the faculty of *Bina* is compared to the sense of hearing. *Ḥokhma* is not like the other spiritual faculties. The soul is active to some degree in its other faculties, but in *Ḥokhma*, it is subsumed: It nullifies its sense of itself. It is opened up and experiences the all-encompassing truth of reality as is, beyond its categorization into details and its enclothement in the spiritual faculties of understanding, emotion, and so forth. The revelation that the author of the *Tanya* is discussing here is like the essence of wisdom itself, if one could remain within it, unlock it, and experience it.

GRASPING ESSENCE THROUGH PROPHECY AND EXISTENCE THROUGH WISDOM

☞ Elsewhere in the works of Hasidism (see *Likkutei Torah*, Deut. 6c–d, Lev. 5d; *Derekh Mitzvotekha* 173a), it is explained that there are two fundamental levels of comprehension: comprehension of essence and comprehension of existence. Comprehension of essence means truly grasping the essence of an object in a direct, unmediated

וְלָכֵן אָמְרוּ: "חָכָם עָדִיף מִנָּבִיא" (בבא בתרא יב,א), שֶׁיָּכוֹל לְהַשִּׂיג בְּחָכְמָתוֹ לְמַעְלָה מַעְלָה מִמַּדְרֵגוֹת שֶׁיּוּכְלוּ לֵירֵד לְמַטָּה בִּבְחִינַת הִתְגַּלּוּת לַנְּבִיאִים בְּמַרְאֵה נְבוּאָתָם כִּי לֹא יוּכְלוּ לֵירֵד וּלְהִתְגַּלּוֹת אֲלֵיהֶם, רַק מַדְרֵגוֹת הַתַּחְתּוֹנוֹת, שֶׁהֵן נהי"מ.

Therefore, the Sages have **said, "a sage is greater than a prophet"** (*Bava Batra* 12a), **for with his wisdom** a sage **can comprehend** spiritual levels **far higher than the levels that can be revealed below to the prophets with their prophetic vision.** This is **because only the lowest levels, namely,** ***Netzaḥ, Hod, Yesod*** **and** ***Malkhut,*** **are able to descend and be revealed to** the prophets.

fashion, in the same way that we comprehend ourselves, the physical reality we live in, and all the objects that are part of our world. We intuitively know how these things feel and behave. Comprehension of existence, on the other hand, refers to understanding things even if we have not seen them with our own eyes and we do not know precisely what they are. This is the understanding of matters that someone has told us about, or matters that we know exist based on our intellect. These two types of comprehension are comparable to the two levels discussed here: prophetic comprehension and the comprehension of the kabbalists (*Derekh Mitzvotekha* 173a; *Ma'amarei Admor HaZaken* 5563, vol. 1, pp. 278 and elsewhere. This is also frequently discussed in the discourses of the Lubavitcher Rebbe, Rabbi Menaḥem Mendel Schneerson). Prophetic comprehension is the comprehension of essence: The prophet truly sees the object in a real, palpable way; it is his reality. On the other hand, the comprehension of the kabbalist is the comprehension of existence. The kabbalist is able to comprehend, by means of his wisdom and understanding, the fact that certain realms exist. He can learn about their appearance and nature, and even develop feelings toward them. Nevertheless, he has merely acquired an external knowledge of their existence.

The author of the *Tanya* has a discourse (*Likkutei Torah*, Lev. 4b, and elsewhere: "You shall not withhold the salt") in which he discusses the differences between studying the revealed Torah and studying the concealed Torah. To some extent, the ideas correspond to what is being discussed here. The study of the revealed Torah is concerned with this world, with matters that are concerned with oxen, donkeys, woolen *tzitzit*, and so forth. Consequently, although the wisdom enclothed in these matters is the inner dimension of supernal *Ḥokhma*, we are able to comprehend its true essence, because it is enclothed in worldly objects. The concealed Torah, on the other hand, is not enclothed in this world, but in the concepts of higher and more abstract worlds. As a result, we have no comprehension of its essence, but only of its existence. It is understandable, therefore, why the author of the *Tanya* refers here to the kabbalists and the inner dimension of Torah. Regarding the revealed Torah, the prophet is not superior, for the kabbalist, too, can acquire knowledge of

Clearly, this talmudic statement is not saying that a sage is superior to a prophet,[13] but rather that there is an aspect of wisdom that is on a higher level than prophecy. The sage's comprehension does not require direct experience of a matter. External understanding, through messengers or other means, is adequate. As a result, the sage's comprehension can reach higher and farther. By analogy, imagine a traveler who walks on foot through different places, in the wind and rain, encountering the people and animals that reside there. In this way, he discovers those regions. A different person, however, could access an online map and move from one country to another with just one click. The person who physically travels to a place certainly has the more real experience. Nevertheless, he is limited by his humanity. He cannot travel extremely far, nor reach an exceedingly large number of places. In contrast, a person with books and maps can "reach" farther. He can "experience" an incalculable number of places, and he can do so in a short amount of time. This is comparable to the sage's advantage over the prophet.

Prophetic comprehension involves the revelation of the object itself. The prophet ascends and experiences it in its supernal place. For this to occur, there must be a real, essential connection between the "giver" (the source) and the "receiver." They must truly meet, and this is possible only in the realm that the receiver's essence can relate

its true essence. However, regarding the concealed Torah and the comprehension of matters as they are in the higher worlds, there is a big difference between these individuals: The prophet achieves comprehension of essence, while the kabbalist achieves only comprehension of existence. As stated, this means that the matter is not truly revealed to him. Instead, he grasps "the secret wisdom." The kabbalist understands the fact that the matter exists, but its essence is forever concealed from him.

13. For prophets are also "scholars of truth," of the concealed Torah, as the Sages say, "The Holy One, blessed be He, rests His Divine Presence)only upon [one who is] mighty, and wealthy, and wise" (*Nedarim* 38a). See *Or HaTorah, Tanakh*, vol. 2, p. 954, citing the Arizal, *Likkutei HaShas*. The Lubavitcher Rebbe, Rabbi Menaḥem Mendel Schneerson, notes the precise language of the author of the Tanya, that while prophets are unable to comprehend the higher spiritual levels by means of their "prophetic vision," however, with regard to their wisdom, they too are "scholars of truth."

to. A receiver cannot receive from the inner essence of a giver, from his intellect and emotions, exactly as they are. Rather, he can receive only that which derives from the giver's intellect and emotions, or in other words, their external aspect. This refers to the attributes of *Netzaḥ, Hod, Yesod,* and *Malkhut*. In contrast, the kabbalist does not need to comprehend the concept itself. He can hear about it, or see images or an outline of it. He could create a whole system of names and symbols, and through this, relate to vast, high levels even though they have no direct connection to his character or essence.

שֶׁהֵן הֵן הַיּוֹרְדוֹת תָּמִיד וּמִתְגַּלּוֹת מֵהַמַּשְׁפִּיעַ לְהַמְקַבֵּל בִּבְחִינַת מוֹחִין וְחַיּוּת, כַּיָּדוּעַ לְיוֹדְעֵי חֵן שֶׁהַנהי״מ שֶׁל הָעֶלְיוֹן מִתְלַבְּשִׁים בַּתַּחְתּוֹן לְהַחֲיוֹתוֹ, שֶׁהֵן הֵן כְּלֵי הַהַשְׁפָּעָה וְהוֹרָדַת הַחַיּוּת מֵהָעֶלְיוֹן לַתַּחְתּוֹן בְּכָל הָעוֹלָמוֹת וְהַמַּדְרֵגוֹת.

It is those lowest levels **that always descend from the** higher level of **a giving** source **and are revealed to the** lower, **receiving** level **on an intellectual level,** as **a creative** force, **as known to those initiated in the esoteric wisdom of Kabbala that the** ***Netzaḥ, Hod, Yesod*** **and** ***Malkhut*** **of the higher** spiritual level **are clothed in the lower** level **to give it life.** This is **because they are the means by which the life force flows down from the higher** level **to the lower** level. This happens **in** progressive descents between **all the worlds and** spiritual **levels.**

It is explained in the works of Kabbala that every flow from above to below in the unfolding succession of the worlds occurs in the same manner: The lower *sefirot* (*Netzaḥ, Hod, Yesod,* and *Malkhut*) of the upper level are enclothed in the upper (cognitive) *sefirot* of the lower level. Divine vitality from the *moḥin* and life force cannot descend as is, in the exact same state, just as a person cannot transfer his intellect or emotions directly to another person. The transfer from person to person is accomplished through words, speech, and so on, which are converted into "*moḥin*" in the other individual. That individual absorbs, understands, and tries to internalize these matters as best he can, enclothing them in his wisdom, understanding, and knowledge. The emotive and cognitive elements of the higher level are enclothed in speech, which is *Malkhut*, the final *sefira*. However, here too, it is not the higher attributes that are enclothed in speech, but only the lower attributes, the external dimension of the inner attributes (*Hesed, Gevura, Tiferet*). These are *Netzaḥ*, *Hod*, and *Yesod*. ☞

וְלָכֵן גַּם כֵּן הֵן הֵן הַמִּתְגַּלּוֹת לַנְּבִיאִים בִּבְחִינַת הִתְגַּלּוּת מַמָּשׁ.

Therefore, they are also the levels **that are revealed to the prophets in an openly manifest way.**

Prophetic comprehension takes place through the actual revelation of the higher realm. This means that *Netzaḥ*, *Hod*, *Yesod*, and *Malkhut* of the higher realm are revealed within the prophet's spiritual faculties. This is the reality that the prophet sees and feels. ☞

HIGHER LEVEL ENCLOTHED IN THE LOWER LEVEL

☞ This is explained elsewhere (*Likkutei Torah*, Lev. 29c and elsewhere) by means of the following analogy: When a person is greatly excited, whether with love, anger, or some other emotion, he is unable to speak. The depth and force of the emotion that he feels cannot be enclothed in speech. Only after the excitement passes can he sum up what he went through to some extent. At that point, he is able to talk about it. *Netzaḥ*, *Hod*, and *Yesod* comprise the ability to view and interpret matters "from the outside," and consequently, the ability to relate to the outside world. Accordingly, these are the *sefirot* that are enclothed in speech, (which is itself enclothed in the soul of the receiver.)

NETZAḤ, *HOD*, *YESOD*, AND *MALKHUT* ARE REVEALED TO THE PROPHETS

☞ It is explained elsewhere (see *Derekh Mitzvotekha* 172b) that the difference between prophets lies in the particular "*Netzaḥ*, *Hod*, *Yesod*, and *Malkhut*" that are revealed to them. Even though every revelation of prophecy is a revelation of *Atzilut*, Moses's revelation was enclothed in "*Netzaḥ*, *Hod*, *Yesod*, and *Malkhut*" of *Atzilut*, while the revelations of other prophets are enclothed in "*Netzaḥ*, *Hod*, *Yesod*, and *Malkhut*" of the lower worlds. According to *Derekh Mitzvotekha*, the prophecy of Isaiah was enclothed in "*Netzaḥ*, *Hod*, *Yesod*, and *Malkhut*" of the world of *Beria*, and the prophecy of Ezekiel was enclothed in "*Netzaḥ*, *Hod*, *Yesod*, and *Malkhut*" of the world of *Yetzira*.

וּבְתוֹכָן מְלוּבָּשׁ אוֹר הַבִּינָה שֶׁהִיא בְּחִינַת הֲבָנַת הָאֱלֹהוּת מֵאוֹר [נוּסָּח אַחֵר: וְאוֹר] אֵין סוֹף בָּרוּךְ הוּא, וּבְתוֹכָהּ מְלוּבָּשִׁים אֲחוֹרַיִים דְּחָכְמָה, שֶׁהִיא מַדְרֵגָה שֶׁלְּמַעְלָה מֵהַשֵּׂכֶל וְהַהֲבָנָה בֶּאֱלֹהוּת בָּרוּךְ הוּא, כִּי שֵׁם חָכְמָה מוֹרֶה עַל מְקוֹר הַשֵּׂכֶל וְהַהֲבָנָה.

Now, **clothed in them is the light of** ***Bina,*** **which is the understanding of Godliness from the light of** ***Ein Sof,*** [**another version: and the light** of *Ein Sof,*] **blessed be He. Clothed in** *Bina,* in turn, **are the external levels of** ***Ḥokhma.*** Now, *Ḥokhma* **is the level that transcends intellect and the understanding of God's Divine** being, **blessed be He, for the term** ***Ḥokhma*** **reflects the source of intellect and understanding.**

The *sefirot* of *Netzaḥ, Hod, Yesod,* and *Malkhut* are revealed to the prophets, and within these revelations, the higher *sefirot* are also revealed: the emotive (*Ḥesed, Gevura, Tiferet*) and the cognitive (*Ḥokhma, Bina, Da'at*). The cognitive *sefirot* are not only revealed as the source of the emotive *sefirot,* but also in and of themselves. For *Bina* does not mean only an understanding of the worlds, but also an understanding of the Divine, of the way in which God is perceived as an understandable entity, so to speak. Of course, an understandable image is necessarily some kind of reflection of the worlds. However, there is a difference, which lies in the question: What is the subject? Here, the subject being perceived is the light of *Ein Sof,* not the world. The world merely contains the vessels and concepts through which we think of the Divine.

In the unfolding succession of the worlds, the external dimension of the higher level is enclothed in the inner dimension of the lower, receiving level. The same thing occurs between *Ḥokhma* and *Bina*: The external dimension of *Ḥokhma* is enclothed in the inner dimension of supernal *Bina,* which is the understanding of the Divine. *Ḥokhma* itself is beyond the intellect and the understanding of the Divine.

As was explained in *Likkutei Amarim* (chap. 18), *Ḥokhma* is composed of the letters *ko'aḥ ma,* "the power of what." This indicates nullification and that which cannot be grasped. The link between *Ḥokhma* and *Bina* is the same as the link between that which can and cannot be comprehended, between reality and that which precedes it, between "nothingness" and "existence." *Bina* is likened to a river: The waters of the river flow and diverge in plain sight, yet the river itself begins at a concealed source of water. This is *Ḥokhma,* which is compared to a spring. Likewise, prophecy is revealed and illuminated on the lowest and most external levels of the *sefirot,* and ultimately in the physical realm. Yet its source is in supernal *Ḥokhma* or even higher, for *Ḥokhma* is the opening and the vessel for the actual revelation of *Ein Sof.*[14]

Until now, this epistle has dealt with prophetic comprehension in general, and that of Moses in particular: its nature, its quality, and its various levels. However, prophecy does not pertain only to the prophet himself. Rather, it is relevant and even binding on all individuals, including the prophet.[15] The authoritative status of prophecy is the result of the fact that it is a direct revelation. The prophet sees and knows it rather than merely hearing about it. Consequently, no one can negate it.[16] The substance of the prophecy is the crucial element, particularly in the case of Moses's prophecy, which is the vessel through which we received the Torah. Accordingly, this epistle will explore the giving of the Torah: how it descends from on high, from a place no thought can occupy, to each of us, and penetrates our intellect and emotions, as well as our thoughts, speech, and actions.

וְלָכֵן אָמְרוּ בַּזֹּהַר דְּאוֹרַיְיתָא מֵחָכְמָה נָפְקַת, כִּי טַעֲמֵי מִצְוֹת לֹא נִתְגַּלּוּ וְהֵם לְמַעְלָה מֵהַשֵּׂכֶל וְהַהֲבָנָה.

Therefore, it is stated in the *Zohar* (3:28a) **that "the Torah is derived from *Ḥokhma,*" for the reasons behind the mitzvot were not revealed, and they transcend the intellect and understanding.**

14. See the gloss in *Likkutei Amarim,* chap. 35, citing the Maggid of Mezeritch.
15. *Ḥokhma,* too, can be relevant and binding, yet this actually stems from prophecy: *Ḥokhma* clarifies and reinforces the matters revealed in the prophecy. The connection between prophecy and *Ḥokhma* can be seen in the connection between the Written Torah and the Oral Torah, as well as the link between the Oral Torah and the kabbalistic traditions passed down from generation to generation until Moses's prophecy.
16. Rambam, *Sefer HaMadda, Hilkhot Yesodei HaTorah* 8:1 contains a similar idea. Rambam adds that the authority of Moses's prophecy (the Torah) stems from the fact that at Mount Sinai, all the children of Israel experienced prophecy. Consequently, even after their prophecy ceased, they had the same degree of certainty regarding the rest of Moses's prophecy: the Torah.

Like the prophecy that is revealed to the prophet, the Torah that is revealed to us reaches the lower, physical, tangible realm. Its hidden source, on the other hand, is beyond comprehension. It lies in supernal *Ḥokhma* or even higher.[17] ☞

THE TORAH IS DERIVED FROM *ḤOKHMA*

☞ Elsewhere (see *Torah Or* 11c; *Likkutei Torah*, Num. 7a), this statement is understood in a different sense: The revelation of the Torah is derived from *Ḥokhma*, but its root lies even higher; in *Keter*. The Torah is indeed enclothed in the mind, but its source is higher: in the simple divine will, which is above and beyond all comprehension. Here, however, the emphasis appears to be on *Ḥokhma* and the fact that there is a concealed source to the conceivable Torah. Nevertheless, this source is within the mind. Although it is concealed, it is rational and relates to the perception of the intellect. The idea that there is a concealed, intellectual source of the Torah has far-reaching implications. If we were to say that God Himself (*Keter* and so on) gave us the Torah that is revealed to us, enclothed in *Bina* and that which is below it, this would mean that God gives us only practical conclusions, a definitive model of how we should think and what we should do. In a certain sense it would be as though He gave us only the *Kitzur Shulḥan Arukh*. If this were the case, the Torah would be an important, wise, and sensitive work, which could bring people to spiritual elevation. However, it would not be anything beyond that. On the other hand, the idea that God gave us a Torah that is derived from *Ḥokhma* means that He gave us the light of *Ein Sof* enclothed in *Ḥokhma* (see *Likkutei Amarim*, chaps. 18–19; epistle 20). In other words, He gave us Himself. The Talmud (*Shabbat* 105a) states that the word *anokhi*, which begins the Ten Commandments, is an acronym for the phrase "I Myself wrote and gave [*ana nafshi ketivat yehavit*]." The Ba'al Shem Tov teaches that this Aramaic phrase should actually be read as, "I wrote and gave Myself" (see *Ba'al Shem Tov al HaTorah, Yitro* 9ff).

The idea that the Torah is derived from *Ḥokhma* and not *Keter* is exceedingly significant for human beings in the lower realm: The Torah that we possess is not comprised only of external understanding but of the essence of *Ḥokhma*, the deepest point of the Torah. There, the Torah is not merely what God reveals to us, but also God Himself. For *Ḥokhma* is the vessel of nullification. This vessel possesses no reality of its own, and therefore it does not define or complete anything. It serves only as an indicator of something that is itself infinite.

Moreover, from the idea that there is a concealed, intellectual source of Torah, it is implied that there is a rationale not only for the Torah in general, but also for each individual mitzva in the Torah. If we were addressing only the source of the Torah that is in the divine will, we would not be discussing rationales at all. However, since we are speaking of a source that lies in *Ḥokhma*, we are addressing the reasons for the mitzvot, although they are not revealed, for they are found in the concealed, intellectual source.

17. See *Zohar* 3:182a.

Ḥokhma is enclothed in intellect and understanding. However, the rationales for the mitzvot are beyond *Ḥokhma* and they are not enclothed or revealed in intellect or understanding.

Each mitzva in the Torah is a revelation of the essential divine will, on the level of *Keter,* higher than *Ḥokhma* and all the other *sefirot.* Therefore, the rationales for the mitzvot cannot be grasped by any faculty lower than *Ḥokhma.* Every mitzva has an explanation, however, it is relegated to the level of concealed *Ḥokhma,* to the light of *Ein Sof,* which transcends the farthest reaches of human apprehension. Every so often, a glimmer of the actual reason for a mitzva is revealed in certain places within the revealed Torah. This will be discussed below.

וְגַם בְּאֵיזֶהוּ מְקוֹמָן, שֶׁנִּתְגַּלָּה וְנִתְפָּרֵשׁ אֵיזֶה טַעַם הַמּוּבָן לָנוּ לִכְאוֹרָה - אֵין זֶה הַטַּעַם הַמּוּבָן לָנוּ לְבַדּוֹ תַּכְלִית הַטַּעַם וּגְבוּלוֹ, אֶלָּא בְּתוֹכוֹ מְלוּבָּשׁ פְּנִימִיּוּת וְתַעֲלוּמוֹת חָכְמָה שֶׁלְּמַעְלָה מֵהַשֵּׂכֶל וְהַהֲבָנָה.

Even in those places where some ostensibly understandable reason for a mitzva **has been revealed and transmitted** to us, **this understandable reason alone is not the ultimate and full reason** for the mitzva. **Rather, within it is clothed the inner, mysterious dimension of *Ḥokhma* that transcends intellect and understanding.**

There are sections of the Written and Oral Torah that disclose the reasoning behind a mitzva. For example, the king is prohibited from having many horses, so that "He shall not return the people to Egypt" (Deut. 17:16). One is commanded to honor his father and mother "so that your days will be extended" (Ex. 20:12). We are obligated to don *tefillin* because "It shall be a sign for you on your arm and a remembrance between your eyes" (Ex. 13:9). Most of the monetary laws, for instance, can be explained simply in terms of establishing a just society.[18]

The rationales given in the Torah do not explain the entire reason

18. While all mitzvot that are *edot* or *mishpatim* (which include most of the mitzvot) have comprehensible reasoning behind them, the author of the *Tanya* uses the phrase "those places" to point to instances where the verses of the Torah explicitly explain the reason behind the given mitzva. *Eizehu mekoman,* is a literary phrase that is used at the beginning of Mishna *Zevaḥim,* chap. 5, as well as in the prayer book.

for a particular mitzva in such a way that there is nothing else left to be said about the matter. Some of the rationales merely expand on that commandments' parameters and spiritual implications. Others relate to the reasons for the act and its consequences, yet they do not entirely encompass the whole matter to the point where we can unequivocally say that this is the whole reason, and that were it not for this reason, the mitzva itself would not exist.

Within the given rationale lies the essential, true reason for the mitzva, which cannot be defined on the level of the intellect or simple understanding, but only on the deeper, concealed level of *Ḥokhma*. As is explained in Kabbala, "The rationales are within *Ḥokhma*."[19]

We are able to understand different aspects of each object: What it is comprised of, what it does, and so on. However, these matters are within the bounds of *Bina*, the understanding of discrete details. As has already been mentioned, *Bina* is like the sense of hearing: We hear one thing from one person and something else from another, and sometimes we are able to form an image of the object in our minds. However, only through sight are we able to observe the object as a whole. Only in the flash of light that we receive on the level of *Ḥokhma*, which is compared to the sense of sight, can the essential reason for a matter be grasped. ☞

This applies to everything in the world, but with regard to the rationales for the mitzvot, it has an even deeper, more palpable significance.

THE TEST OF TRUTH

☞ How do we know that something is true? All our perceptions merely reinforce one hypothesis or another, but they cannot provide absolute confirmation of the truth. The understanding that a particular matter is true must come through the light of *Ḥokhma*, for "In *Ḥokhma*, things become clear" (see *Etz Ḥayyim* 23:8). This is what the author of the *Tanya* is saying: Enclothed in the explicit reason is the inner, concealed reason. This cannot be grasped with the intellect, for it is the essence of *Ḥokhma* itself.

---

19. According to Kabbala, there are four aspects to the words written in the Torah: the cantillation marks, the vowels, the crowns, and the letters themselves. These correspond to the four *partzufim* of *Atzilut*, as well as the four worlds, the four letters of the name of *Havaya*, and so on. The structure is as follows: The cantillation marks (*te'amim*, which also means "rationales") correspond to *Ḥokhma*, the vowels correspond to *Bina*, the crowns correspond to *Zeir Anpin*, and the letters correspond to *Malkhut* (see *Likkutei Torah*, Num. 57d).

Worldly phenomena are extensions or products of other factors. They are the "external dimensions" of one level or another, as was explained earlier. Accordingly, they do not possess their own essential, inner reason. They can be explained only through their connection to something else, to the complex whole if which they are a part. With regard to the mitzvot, however, apart from the overall reason of doing God's will, each one possesses an essential reason of its own. Each mitzva constitutes the essential will of God, in all time periods and situations. God desires that the mitzva be performed in exactly that way, for that specific reason. Enclothed in each mitzva is a unique rationale from the inner, hidden dimension of *Ḥokhma*, which transcends intellect and understanding.

וְכֵן בְּכָל דִּיבּוּר וְדִיבּוּר שֶׁיָּצָא מִפִּי הַקָּדוֹשׁ בָּרוּךְ הוּא לַנְּבִיאִים הַכְּתוּבִים בַּתַּנַ"ךְ, הֵן דִּבְרֵי תוֹכָחָה וְהֵן סִיפּוּרֵי מַעֲשִׂיּוֹת, מְלוּבָּשׁ בְּתוֹכָם בְּחִינַת חָכְמַת אֱלֹהוּת שֶׁלְּמַעְלָה מֵהַשֵּׂכֶל וְהַהֲבָנָה.

The same applies to every single statement that emerged from God's mouth and was transmitted **to the Prophets, which are written in the *Tanakh*, whether words of rebuke or narratives of events. Within them is clothed divine *Ḥokhma* that transcends the intellect and understanding.**

God's words in the Torah and prophecies[20] likewise constitute His essential, inner speech. Inner speech reveals God Himself. It does not conceal Him like the external speech through which the world was created. Instead, it reveals Him through the terminology of this world and the souls within it: what He wants, "thinks," "feels," and so on. Not only does every mitzva possess a rationale, but every word and letter in the Torah and Prophets also has an essential, spiritual nucleus, a part of divine *Ḥokhma*, which transcends intellect and understanding. ☞

DIVINE *ḤOKHMA* THAT TRANSCENDS INTELLECT AND UNDERSTANDING

☞ "Intellect and understanding" does not refer to a particular level of intellect, but to the overall essence of intellect. Worldly creations, which are formed by divine

20. This refers to the prophecies that were recognized by the Sages and those that were written in *Tanakh*. These are the word of God and were merely placed in the mouths of the prophets.

כַּנִּרְאֶה בְּחוּשׁ מֵעִנְיַן הַקְּרִי וְהַכְּתִיב, כִּי הַקְּרִי הוּא לְפִי הַהֲבָנָה הַנִּגְלֵית לָנוּ, וְהַכְּתִיב הוּא לְמַעְלָה מֵהַשֵּׂכֶל וְהַהֲבָנָה, שֶׁתֵּיבָה זוֹ כִּכְתִיבָתָהּ אֵין לָהּ לְבוּשׁ בִּבְחִינַת הַהֲבָנָה, וּבִקְרִיאָתָהּ בַּפֶּה יֵשׁ לָהּ לְבוּשׁ. וְכֵן הָעִנְיָן בְּאוֹתִיּוֹת גְּדוֹלוֹת שֶׁבַּתַּנַ"ךְ, שֶׁהֵן מֵעָלְמָא עִילָּאָה וּמְאִירוֹת מִשָּׁם בְּגִילּוּי בְּלִי לְבוּשׁ כִּשְׁאָר הָאוֹתִיּוֹת.

This is seen clearly from the concept of the written form and vocalized form of certain words in the *Tanakh*. **The vocalized form accords with** our **understanding** of the word as **revealed to us, while the written form transcends the intellect and understanding.** This means **that this word as it written has no garment** and cannot be clothed **in the realm of understanding, but when it is read by mouth, it has a garment. The same concept applies to the enlarged letters that** appear **in the** ***Tanakh;*** their enlarge format indicates **that they are derived from a supernal world, and shine openly from there, without** any **garment** concealing them, **as is the case with the rest of the letters.**

speech, but not the speech of Torah and prophecy, are created with intellect and understanding. Some creations are created with such an exceedingly high, divine level of intellect and understanding that ordinary human beings cannot plumb their depths, yet still, they are within the scope of human comprehension. The creation functions as a cog in the grand structure of the world and contains intellect and understanding which constitutes the true, inner reason for its existence. Without it, nothing would exist. As stated, everything in this world is the "back side" of something else. It is part of a structure that is built to contain and express spiritual life-force. In contrast, speech of Torah and prophecy is the innermost dimension. It is said that the Ark of the Covenant, which symbolizes the Torah within the Temple, was entirely spiritual (see *Derekh Mitzvotekha, Mitzvat Masa HaAron BaKatef;* Likkutei Torah, Num. 17b, *Derushim LeRosh HaShana* 57c). The content and meaning of this kind of speech is beyond all intellect and understanding. It pervades all worlds as the essential, inner meaning enclothed in all things. This is what the author of the *Tanya* refers to as, "divine *Ḥokhma* that transcends intellect and understanding."

The understanding that we do attain with regard to the stories and words of rebuke in the Torah and Prophets is external. This understanding can itself be beautiful and full of wisdom. However, there is also an inner reason, which we are unable to grasp. Our understanding connects us to the words of the text: We can relate to them, remember them, act on them, and so forth, and as a result, the concealed rea-

Although divine wisdom cannot be seen with the human eye or the human mind, there are nevertheless traces of it that can be perceived with the sense of sight and the intellect.

Like all words, the words of divine speech in the Torah present in two ways: in the form of written letters, and in the form of oral expression. There is usually no perceptible difference between the spoken and the written form: We read what is written and articulate it, and the assumption is that the meaning of what we have read and what we have spoken aloud is the same. However, there are numerous words in the Torah in which there is a noticeable difference. These words are written in one way and according to the oral tradition they are read in a different way.

The works of Kabbala explain that there is deep meaning to these discrepancies. We vocalize words according to our conscious understanding of life. The difference between the spoken and the written form is that the written form is the expression of the object alone. A person can see it, but he has no part in its expression. In contrast, when one reads a word aloud, it is no longer just the object, but rather it is the object as it is expressed by the individual. The person is now involved in the mode of expression. On a deeper level, the written word is not enclothed in the human soul. Although there is concealed meaning that

son also comes to us. When there is content that belongs in one realm, a person might be able to form it into a combination of letters, such as a poem or story, that has meaning in a different realm. When this formulation is brought into to the other realm, the concealed content itself likewise enters that realm, even though it is incomprehensible when it is by itself with no garments around it. An example from a different area is the book *Gulliver's Travels* (1726) by Jonathan Swift. This is a political allegory written in the form of a children's book. To this day, children read it and are oblivious to the messages inserted by the writer. There are holy names of God that mean nothing to most people: They appear to be meaningless combinations of letters. Sometimes, however, people create meaningful acrostics or other compositions from these letters, which others are able to relate to. For example, the *Ana BeKo'aḥ* prayer, a poetic composition that is full of meaning, appears in several places in the prayer book. Together, the initial letters of the words of this prayer form a holy name of forty-two letters. In some prayer books, including the one compiled by the author of the *Tanya*, these forty-two letters are also written beside the prayer so that the person reciting it can regard the letters of this name, which we do not recite aloud.

descends and is enclothed in the letters, it is not enclothed by means of the supernal intellect in such a way that it can also be enclothed in the intellect of the soul. Rather, the written form of the words of the Torah are the essential, supernal content itself, precisely as it is in the higher realm. In contrast, vocalization is enclothed in human garments and human terms, and therefore in the higher realm, too, this type of expression is enclothed in the intellect.[21]

As has been stated, we are unable to see or comprehend the inner meaning, which is in the concealed dimension of *Ḥokhma*. However, when the entire difference between two words, the vocalized form and the written form, is that in one, the inner meaning is enclothed, and in the other it is not enclothed, we can understand clearly that there is a difference between them. This is one way to understand the difference between the spoken and written forms of a word. When we know that the difference stems from the fact that in one of them, supernal *Ḥokhma* is enclothed in understanding and comprehension, and in the other, it is not – we are able to perceive the fact that this word of the Torah contains divine *Ḥokhma*, which is beyond the intellect.

In several places in *Tanakh* there are letters that are larger or smaller than the other letters.[22] The disproportion indicates that these letters convey additional meaning on a higher level. We are generally unable to grasp such meaning. Nonetheless, we are able to see the disparity in size, and it demonstrates to us the fact that there is something else, something deeper, to be found here. ☞

We know that there are written forms of particular words that are not the same as their vocalized forms. Even if we cannot grasp the deeper meaning that they convey, the very fact that such vessels exist in

---

21. Several Chabad discourses it is brought that the written form is in the concealed realm and the vocalized form is in the revealed realm. This is the meaning of "I am not read as I am written" (*Pesaḥim* 50a; *Kiddushin* 71a). In the future, "The Lord will be one and His name one" (Zech. 14:9): This refers to a time when the concealed and the revealed will be combined. See also *Likkutei Torah, Shemini Atzeret* 92c, where it states that the written form is in the higher realm.

22. According to Kabbala, enlarged letters hail from *Bina* and smaller letters exist in *Malkhut*; see *Likkutei Torah*, Lev. 47d; *Peirush HaMilot* 39b; *Peri Etz Ḥayyim, Sha'ar HaSeliḥot*, chap. 8; see also *Hemshekh Ayin Bet*, vol. 2, p. 854.

our world is evidence that this kind of meaning is also present in other commandments, words, and letters where it is not overtly apparent.

2 Tishrei

27 Elul (leap year)

וְהִנֵּה בְּחִינַת חָכְמַת אֱלֹהוּת בָּרוּךְ הוּא, הַמְלוּבֶּשֶׁת בְּתַרְיַ"ג מִצְוֹת הַתּוֹרָה, נִקְרֵאת בְּשֵׁם בְּחִינַת אֲחוֹרַיִים דְּחָכְמָה, כִּי כָּל 'אֲחוֹרַיִים' שֶׁבַּסְּפִירוֹת הֵן מַדְרֵגוֹת הַחִיצוֹנוֹת וְהַתַּחְתּוֹנוֹת בְּמַעֲלָה שֶׁבִּסְפִירָה זוֹ מַה שֶּׁיּוּכְלוּ לֵירֵד וּלְהִתְפַּשֵּׁט לְמַטָּה לְהִתְלַבֵּשׁ בַּבְּרוּאִים לְהַחֲיוֹתָם.

Now, the level of Divine *Ḥokhma* clothed in the 613 mitzvot of the Torah is called the "back of *Ḥokhma*," for the back of any of the *sefirot* refers to the most **external and lowliest levels of that *sefira*, whatever is able to descend and expand below to be clothed in creations to sustain them.**

Divine *Ḥokhma* is, as mentioned above, concealed. It is enclothed in the revealed dimension of the Torah in such a way that we are able to relate to it, whether through the intellect and understanding involved in Torah study, or the active performance of a mitzva.

The *sefirot* are not one-dimensional or simple. Rather, they are complex systems that consist of different parts and levels. They have an upper and a lower dimension, as well as an inner and an external dimension.[23] Within this complex structure, the "back" intrinsically

LARGER AND SMALLER LETTERS

☞ It is explained elsewhere that letters are "vessels," and that the enlarged letters in the Torah signify larger vessels than the small letters, which signify small vessels. Just as a greater amount of light can shine in a large vessel, the light of supernal *Ḥokhma* shines in a more revealed state within the enlarged letters the Torah. It is enclothed in *Bina*, not *Malkhut* like the other letters. In contrast, the smaller letters indicate an immense constriction of the vessels. This occurs when a much greater light is constricted into human vessels.: The enlarged letters are from a higher realm. In other words, they are vessels, but not vessels that belong to our world. They come from a higher reality, and therefore they are able to contain the light of *Ḥokhma*, which is beyond the intellect. This does not mean that there is intelligence and understanding in that reality. Rather, there is a reality that is above ours, and it has the sensitivity to be able to recognize a light that is not within intellect and understanding.

23. Essentially, every *sefira* is composed of all the *sefirot* as well as all the "worlds."

expresses a lower degree of essence and relates to that which is outside the *sefira*. The external dimension is on a lower level and it reveals less of the essential, inner light.

As stated above, the "innermost dimension" refers the essence itself. No one is capable of relating to this because external aspects of an essence are needed to forge some connection with something outside of it. Similarly, the only one who can relate to a person's true essence is the individual himself. And even he himself must tap in to the deepest, innermost aspect of his being to recognize his own quintessence. Other people can relate only to that individual's "external dimensions." The closer one is to him, the more internal this connection can be. It may reach the individual's thoughts or even his emotions. One who is distant from the individual, however, can connect only to that which is most external: his speech, and sometimes only his physical actions. Likewise, it is the external dimensions of the *sefirot* that are able to descend and sustain the creations. ☞

GOD'S BACK

☞ In truth, there is no "other" with respect to God, for there is truly no other besides Him. He brings every iota of reality to life from absolute nothingness. Nevertheless, the holy *sefirot* have a "front" aspect and a "back" aspect, and these *sefirot* are unified with God and give expression to Him, His *Ḥokhma*, His *Ḥesed*, and so on. Consequently, through the "back" aspect of the *sefirot*, God sustains and gives life to an external reality. As has been explained, the creations that receive from the external dimension are created as a result of the fact that the *sefirot* possess an external dimension. God's capacity of providing for "others" results in the actual creation of "others."

It is crucial that we understand that with regard to the *sefirot*, the external dimension and everything that evolves from it are not intrinsically inferior to the inner dimension. A *sefira* is one entity that has an external and an internal dimension, as well as an upper and a lower dimension. There is nothing in reality that lies outside of God, which means, outside of His sefirot: It is just a question of higher or lower, inner or outer, front or back manifestation. Therefore, even those places that reveal divine essence less and more so eclipse God's light, simply manifest a particular facet of a given sefira that expresses divine essence in an entirely different way.

The highest world means the deepest, most inner realm of reality, and the lowest world is synonymous with the external layers of reality. So, for example, *Atzilut* of *Atzilut* is the inner dimension, *Asiya* of *Atzilut* is the external dimension of that world, and so on.

וּבְחִינַת הַפָּנִים הִיא הַסְּפִירָה עַצְמָהּ הַמְיוּחֶדֶת בְּמַאֲצִילָהּ אֵין סוֹף בָּרוּךְ הוּא בְּתַכְלִית הַיִּחוּד, כְּגוֹן דֶּרֶךְ מָשָׁל סְפִירַת חָכְמָה שֶׁהִיא מְיוּחֶדֶת בְּמַאֲצִילָהּ אֵין סוֹף בָּרוּךְ הוּא בְּתַכְלִית הַיִּחוּד.

By contrast, **the "face"** of the *sefira* **is the *sefira* itself, which is united with its Creator, the light of *Ein Sof*, blessed be He, in the ultimate union. For example, by way of analogy, the *sefira* of *Ḥokhma*, which is united with its Emanator, *Ein Sof*, blessed be He, in the ultimate union.**

Similarly, a human being's inner spiritual faculties, that which he thinks or feels inside, do not have any particular purpose. They are simply the way in which he knows, feels, and so on. These faculties are united with him: They express his wisdom, his love, and so forth. ☞

THE *SEFIRA* AND THE CREATOR

☞ This is even more true regarding the higher *sefirot*. They give expression to the Creator Himself and nothing else, but moreover, they have no reality apart from Him. A human being can separate himself from his understanding and emotion. An "understanding" has meaning even when it is detached from the person who understands, since others can relate to it as well. This is not the case with regard to the upper *sefirot*: They have no substance or reality that is separate from the Creator. In this sense, a *sefira* is somewhat like a name. A name, unlike a spiritual faculty, is meaningless in and of itself. All its meaning and substance come only from its connection to the person who bears that name. It is like a gesture, a smile, or facial expression that is unique to a certain individual, and as a result, it is impossible to think of it without thinking of him. This is the kind of union being discussed here: the union of the *sefira* and its Creator.

On the deepest level, it can be said that that which is grasped or perceived by a *sefira* is the *sefira* itself and nothing else. A similar idea is mentioned in *Likkutei Amarim* (chap. 2) and *Sha'ar HaYiḥud VeHa'emuna* (chap. 9). As Rambam states, "He is the Knower, He is the subject of knowledge, and He is the knowledge itself. All is one" (*Sefer HaMadda*, *Hilkhot Yesodei HaTorah* 2:10). It is explained in *Sha'ar HaYiḥud VeHa'emuna*, chapter 8, that this is true with regard to all the *sefirot*. God is truly one, and there is no reality whatsoever apart from Him. Consequently, the concept of His *Ḥokhma*, of His being wise, includes within it the existence of wisdom itself, as well as everything that may be grasped with it. God's *Da'at* incorporates the concept of knowledge as well as everything that may be known, for it is all formed with *Da'at* and is united with it. Likewise, God's *Ḥesed*, through which He gives to others, includes the giving, the gift, and the one who receives. They are all united within *Ḥesed*.

כִּי הַקָּדוֹשׁ בָּרוּךְ הוּא וְחָכְמָתוֹ אֶחָד (כְּמוֹ שֶׁנִּתְבָּאֵר לְעֵיל), וּמַה שֶּׁמֵּאִיר וּמִתְפַּשֵּׁט מֵחָכְמָתוֹ יִתְבָּרֵךְ לְמַטָּה בַּתַּחְתּוֹנִים, שֶׁהֵם בַּעֲלֵי גְבוּל וְתַכְלִית וּמִתְלַבֵּשׁ בָּהֶם, נִקְרָא 'אֲחוֹרַיִים'.

For the Holy One, Blessed be He, and His wisdom are one (as explained above); whatever shines forth and expands from God's wisdom below in the lower worlds, **which are finite and limited beings, and is clothed in them, is called** the **"back."**

God and His wisdom are one.[24] Therefore, *Ḥokhma* itself does not shine and fill the creations. As has been explained, something's essence must be revealed through its external dimension, and cannot manifest through its inner dimension alone. ☞

The lower worlds, the worlds of created beings, are limited. Their purpose is clearly defined. The light of God's *Ḥokhma* that is enclothed in the lower worlds does not merely surround lower beings: providing the backdrop of their existence. If that were the case, it could not change them or influence them in any way. Rather, it is like the inner light that is enclothed within their defined parameters; in particular

ḤOKHMA

☞ While all the *sefirot* in the world of *Atzilut* (and in general) are united with their Creator, it is the *sefira* of *Ḥokhma* that the author of the *Tanya* brings here as an example. *Ḥokhma*, in essence, epitomizes all the *sefirot* of *Atzilut*, and in fact the world of *Atzilut* itself. It is well-known that of all the *sefirot*, *Ḥokhma* corresponds to the world of *Atzilut*, while *Bina* corresponds to *Beria*, *Zeir Anpin* to *Yetzira*, and *Malkhut* to *Asiya*. The world of *Atzilut* is the realm where the *sefirot* are one with their Creator: "He and the light are one" (*Tikkunei Zohar* 3b).

Similarly, a person's *Ḥokhma* is a spiritual faculty that is united with the very essence of his soul. A person's *Ḥokhma* is not separate from him. *Ḥokhma* does not grasp anything but one's very soul. *Ḥokhma* can be explained as a revelation of the very essence of the soul, to the extent that this is possible. Not only does *Ḥokhma* not comprehend that which lies beyond it, but each revelation of *Ḥokhma* causes a total reset, and whatever we knew previously becomes null and void. It is proof of the existence of the soul. The soul is revealed only through *Ḥokhma*, and *Ḥokhma* is entirely connected to the soul. Likewise, in the higher realm, the *sefira* of *Ḥokhma* in *Atzilut* reveals the Infinite One, who is enclothed within it.

24. This idea is explained in *Likkutei Amarim*, chaps. 2, 52; *Sha'ar HaYiḥud VeHa'emuna*, chaps. 7–8.

worlds and souls, in their *Ḥokhma, Bina, Da'at,* and so on. It is even enclothed in a person's speech and his performance of the mitzvot, as mentioned above. ☞

This is not referring to the inner aspect of the light of *Ḥokhma* itself, but to its external aspect.

וְנִקְרָא גַּם כֵּן בְּחִינַת עֲשִׂיָּה שֶׁבַּאֲצִילוּת. פֵּירוּשׁ עַל דֶּרֶךְ מָשָׁל, כְּמוֹ שֶׁבָּאָדָם הַתַּחְתּוֹן, שֶׁיֵּשׁ בְּנִשְׁמָתוֹ ה׳ מַדְרֵגוֹת זוֹ לְמַטָּה מִזּוֹ, שֶׁהֵן בְּחִינוֹת: הַשֵּׂכֶל וְהַמִּדּוֹת וּמַחֲשָׁבָה וְדִבּוּר וּמַעֲשֶׂה,

It is also called ***Asiya*** (Action) **of** the world of ***Atzilut*** (Emanation). To **explain by way of analogy,** it is **like the soul of a physical person, which consists of five levels, one below the other, that is, intellect, emotion, thought, speech and action.**

The part of supernal *Ḥokhma* that shines and is enclothed in the lower worlds is still supernal *Ḥokhma* and Torah. However, it is the external aspect of supernal *Ḥokhma*. This is the Torah that is revealed to us, which is, as stated, "the vestige of *Ḥokhma* above." It is also called *Asiya* of *Atzilut*. Each of the four worlds – *Atzilut, Beria, Yetzira,* and *Asiya* – contains each of the four worlds within it. Therefore, it is possible to speak of a level in the world of *Atzilut* that is called *Asiya* of *Atzilut*. Just as the lower *sefirot* are the external aspect with respect to the higher *sefirot,* the same is true regarding the worlds: *Asiya* of *Atzilut* is the external aspect of *Atzilut*. It is that which descends from *Atzilut* and is enclothed in the lower worlds in order to provide them with vitality.

In order to explain the concept of *Asiya* of *Atzilut* in a more tangible way, the author of the *Tanya* draws an analogy to the human soul:

FINITE WORLDS

☞ Unlike the higher worlds, the lower worlds are finite and limited. The higher worlds are the *sefirot* in *Atzilut*, especially *Ḥokhma* of *Atzilut*, which is, as mentioned, united with its Creator, with the light of *Ein Sof* enclothed in it. Just as God is limitless and infinite, so too His *Ḥokhma* is limitless and infinite. In spiritual matters, the difference between "above" and "below" is like the difference between "giver" and "receiver." The giver is above, and the receiver is below. Although this is not the case regarding the giver, the receiver must be finite and limited, because to receive means to take into account one's own limits and capacity.

This version of the five levels of the soul, found in several places in the *Tanya*,[25] is not the well-known list of *nefesh, ruaḥ, neshama, ḥaya,* and *yeḥida*. It is a list that refers to the revelation of the soul through succession. *Nefesh, ruaḥ, neshama, ḥaya,* and *yeḥida* point to levels of the soul itself, or in essence, to five different "souls." We refer to them much like we do the different worlds and *sefirot*. In other words, they are beings that exist in and of themselves. They interact with each other and receive from each other, but do not evolve from each other. In contrast, the levels of intellect, emotion, thought, speech, and action refer to the light that passes through and is revealed within the levels of the soul, as well as outside of it.

As levels of the light's revelation, rather than measures of the reality in which the light is revealed, these levels evolve from one another and are linked like cause and effect. The light that is manifest on one level is revealed to a greater extent on another. On the one hand, all the vitality and reality of the "effect" derives from the "cause," yet it is close enough to the "cause" to be able to recognize it and its absolute existential dependency on it. All this binds the five levels into one entity. They are not five separate points of revelation but rather a spectrum of revelation ranging from *Ḥokhma* to *Asiya*. ☞

THE SHORTCOMINGS OF MAN AS ANALOGY

☞ These levels relate to the soul only by way of analogy, for regarding divine revelation, the difference between levels is tremendous. Nevertheless, since the only concepts we have are those that come from within us, we employ these terms, from "*Ḥokhma*" to "*Asiya*," with regard to divine revelation as well. We do so even though in the case of the Divine, the meaning behind these terms is unfathomably vast. We say *Ḥokhma*, when in truth this means something infinitely greater and loftier than wisdom, but we have no words or concepts to be able to say or think anything more than this. The verse "In wisdom have You made them all" (Ps. 104: 24) is explained in this way: *Ḥokhma* is the pinnacle of revelation for us, but for God it is like action, the lowest level of expression (see *Sha'ar HaYiḥud VeHa'emuna*, chap. 9). For Him, the entire scope of our consciousness and existence is considered to be only on the level of "action," although of course in divine terms this means much more than just action. One can get a glimpse of this dynamic in his life: When he grows and today comprehends more through his wis-

25. For example, *Iggeret HaTeshuva*, chap. 9; *Sha'ar HaYiḥud VeHa'emuna*, chap. 9.

וְהַמַּעֲשֶׂה הִיא הַתַּחְתּוֹנָה שֶׁבְּכוּלָּם, שֶׁהַחַיּוּת הַמִּתְפַּשֵּׁט מֵהַנְּשָׁמָה וּמְלוּבָּשׁ בְּכֹחַ הַמַּעֲשֶׂה הוּא כְּאַיִן לְגַבֵּי הַחַיּוּת הַמִּתְפַּשֵּׁט מִמֶּנָּה וּמְלוּבָּשׁ בְּכֹחַ הַדִּבּוּר, שֶׁהוּא כְּאַיִן לְגַבֵּי הַחַיּוּת הַמִּתְפַּשֵּׁט מִמֶּנָּה וּמְלוּבָּשׁ בְּמַחֲשָׁבָה וּמִדּוֹת וָשֵׂכֶל.

Action is the lowest of them all, for the life force that expands from the soul to be clothed in the power of action is considered **like nothing compared to the life force that expands from** the soul **to be clothed in the power of speech, which** in turn **is** considered **like nothing compared to the life force that expands from** the soul **to be clothed in** the powers of **thought, emotion and intellect.**

dom than he could yesterday, the peak of his comprehension from the previous day becomes the launchpad of his comprehension today.

Nonetheless, as in all analogies to the human soul, there is also a side to it that is not merely an analogy. The advantage of an analogy to the human soul is not only the fact that this is what we can comprehend: It is also the fact that what we comprehend in the higher realm is, in a certain sense, true. Divine revelation occurs in our consciousness. There is no other place where the Divine is revealed in a way that is meaningful to us. Therefore, there is always a certain correspondence, which varies from person to person, between divine revelation and the revelation within one's mind.

Moreover, the more a person learns, the more it becomes clear that just as we cannot comprehend the divine truth, we likewise cannot comprehend the full depth and purpose of our existence as human beings. The more we comprehend of the Divine, the deeper and higher we are able to reach in our understanding of ourselves, and vice versa. The power of an "analogy" to the human soul is that we comprehend these matters through direct experiences, and when we grasp them, we are able to traverse all realms. Each human being is able to do this to a different degree, in accordance with his personal level. As long as we are holding fast to the truth within us, we do not err in the higher realm. However, if we are deceiving ourselves, then in the higher realm, too, we can no longer be certain.

Nevertheless, as is highlighted elsewhere (*Sha'ar HaYiḥud VeHa'emuna*, chap. 9; *Likkutei Amarim*, chap. 20; see also *Hemshekh Samekh Vav*, pp. 462ff), the author of the *Tanya* is referring to the range of revelation, which means the five levels mentioned here. Our comprehension lies within this range, as does divine revelation. However, the verse states, "I the Lord did not change" (Mal. 3: 6). God Himself does not change or become confined to human comprehension. On every level at which we perceive reality, God seems to be separate. He is the One who gives life to, sustains, and relates to the reality, and therefore He appears to "change," because reality is sometimes physical, sometimes spiritual, and sometimes not there at all. Nonetheless, God Himself is always beyond the five levels. He is unchanging and impossible to grasp.

Action is the lowest level of the revelation of the soul. As has been stated, we are not speaking here of the levels themselves – intellect, emotion, and so on – but rather of the revelation of the life force that flows in them from the soul itself. This life force is first revealed on the level of the intellect, in a person's recognition of the existence and nature of something. The second level is emotion, where one's connection to that thing is established: whether it is good or bad for him, whether or not he desires it, and so on. The difference between these two levels is immense. Emotion does not relate to the entire scope of consciousness, but only to one's personal, emotional conclusions concerning the object. With regard to the revelation of the soul, that which is revealed through emotion is insignificant compared to that which is revealed through the intellect. The third level, thought, is a garment that enclothes the soul. A garment tries to convey to the outside, through signs and symbols, what is happening on the inside. Here too, that which a person can think of and define with thought is like nothing with respect to the soul's actual consciousness and emotion. We feel something deep, vast, and full, and we assign it a symbol. Such external symbols are significant to the individual who receives them, but they are inconsequential in relation to the objects that they represent. The same is true with regard to the connection between speech and thought and between action and speech.

These connections convey the essential dynamic of what hasidic teachings mean when they speak of unfolding succession: The lower level evolves entirely from the level above it, and therefore it does not occupy any place in that higher level. It has nothing more than what it receives from its originating "cause," and as a result it is like "nothing" with respect to it.[26]

---

26. As is explained elsewhere (see epistle 20), "succession" signifies a relationship of "existence from existence," rather than the higher-level connection, such as the one between Creator and creation, of "existence from nothingness." It may be said that we are addressing the matter from a top-down perspective: With regard to the higher level, the lower level is "nothing." However, from a bottom-up perspective, the lower level is able to grasp, in accordance with its capacity, the higher level from which it evolved. The "effect" comprehends its "cause," and accordingly, from its perspective, it constitutes "existence from existence" and not "existence from nothingness."

28 Elul (leap year)

כֵּן עַל דֶּרֶךְ זֶה מַמָּשׁ, הִיא בְּחִינַת חָכְמָתוֹ יִתְבָּרֵךְ, מַה שֶּׁיּוּכַל לְהִתְפַּשֵּׁט מִמֶּנָּה (לְהַשְׁפִּיעַ) [לְהִתְלַבֵּשׁ] בַּתַּחְתּוֹנִים כּוּלָּם, הֵם כְּאַיִן לְגַבֵּי בְּחִינַת פָּנִים, הַמְיוּחָד בְּמַאֲצִיל בָּרוּךְ הוּא, דְּכוּלָּא קַמֵּיהּ כְּלָא חֲשִׁיב.

God's wisdom is exactly the same way. Whatever can expand forth from it (to be clothed) in the lower worlds is considered **like nothing compared to the inner dimension** of divine *Ḥokhma* **which is united with its Emanator, blessed be He, for everything before Him is considered nothingness.**

In accordance with the analogy drawn above, God's *Ḥokhma* is like the human soul. It is united with *Ein Sof*, the Creator Himself. There is a flow that expands from God's *Ḥokhma* into the "unfolding succession of the worlds," which includes all the *sefirot* and each of the physical worlds: *Beria*, *Yetzira*, and *Asiya*. These three worlds correspond to the three garments: thought, speech, and action. The flow enters its receiving vessel and is enclothed in it.[27]

On all levels where the life force expands, it relates only to the external dimension of *Ḥokhma*. The result is an external culminating sign of the life force. However, as stated, this is insignificant relative to the life force itself, and all the more so with regard to the Creator, who is the source of the life force.

וְהַהַשְׁפָּעָה לְכָל הַנִּבְרָאִים כּוּלָּם, שֶׁהֵם בַּעֲלֵי גְבוּל וְתַכְלִית, נֶחְשֶׁבֶת יְרִידָה וְצִמְצוּם כִּבְיָכוֹל לְגַבֵּי הַמַּאֲצִיל אֵין סוֹף בָּרוּךְ הוּא עַל דֶּרֶךְ מָשָׁל, כְּמוֹ שֶׁנֶּחְשֶׁבֶת יְרִידָה וְצִמְצוּם לְשֵׂכֶל הָאָדָם הַמַּשְׂכִּיל, הַמְצוּמְצָם בְּאֵיזֶה עֲשִׂיָּה גַּשְׁמִיּוּת וְחוּמְרִית מַמָּשׁ.

The divine **flow** that gives life **to all creations, which are finite, limited beings, is considered a descent and constriction, as it were, compared to the Emanator, the light of** *Ein Sof*, **blessed be He, by way of analogy, just as it is considered a descent and constriction for the intellect of a thinking person** when it is **constricted in some entirely physical and mundane act.**

27. There is another type of divine influence that is not enclothed within its receptacle, but rather encompasses it. *Torah Or* (92b) and *Likkutei Torah* (Num. 89b–c) discuss the flow that takes place by way of transition and the flow by way of enclothement.

The creations – the physical words, the spiritual worlds, and all that is in them – are immeasurably vast from our perspective, yet in truth they are finite and limited. Their limits are immense and exceedingly lofty, but they are still limits. Consequently, with regard to the Creator, who is infinite, the flow toward the creations, which sustains them and gives them life, is considered a "descent" and a "constriction."

The intellect of a thinking person can engage in extremely abstract concepts that are on the level of the spiritual realm and even higher. Therefore, when a person's intellect engages in physical activities that pertain to his finances, his home, his food, and so forth, this constitutes a significant descent. As was described above, the descent and constriction span five levels, from the revelation of the soul in the intellect to its revelation in the limited spiritual capacity of physical action.

וְלָכֵן מֹשֶׁה רַבֵּינוּ עָלָיו הַשָּׁלוֹם, שֶׁהִשִּׂיג עַד אֲחוֹרַיִים דְּחָכְמָה, זָכָה שֶׁתִּנָּתֵן עַל יָדוֹ הַתּוֹרָה שֶׁהִיא 'נוֹבְלוֹת חָכְמָה' שֶׁלְּמַעְלָה. פֵּירוּשׁ, מַה שֶּׁנּוֹבֵל מִמֶּנָּה וְיוֹרֵד לְמַטָּה וּמִתְלַבֵּשׁ בַּתּוֹרָה גַּשְׁמִיּוּת שֶׁלָּנוּ שֶׁעִיקָּרָהּ וְתַכְלִיתָהּ הוּא קִיּוּם הַמִּצְוֹת לֹא תַעֲשֶׂה וַעֲשֵׂה בְּפוֹעַל וּמַעֲשֶׂה מַמָּשׁ.

Therefore, Moses, our teacher, may he rest in peace, whose comprehension extended to the external dimension of *Ḥokhma*, merited that the Torah be given through him. The Torah **is the "vestige of *Ḥokhma* above," meaning,** it is **what is shed** from *Ḥokhma*, **and descends below and is enclothed in our physical Torah, whose primary** focus **and whose ultimate purpose is performance of the mitzvot, the prohibitory** mitzvot **and the obligatory** mitzvot, **in actual action and deed.**

Now, the author of the *Tanya* connects these ideas to that which was discussed at the beginning of the epistle: Moses's comprehension and the nature of the Torah.

The verse "enveloping with light as if with a cloak" describes the way that light – the light of *Ḥokhma* and Torah[28] – descends into the

28. It is explained elsewhere that these two things are not the same, for Torah is beyond the enclothement of supernal *Ḥokhma*. It states in *Likkutei Torah* (*Parashat Ḥukat*) that there is a kind of divine service that is concerned with bringing the Torah down from above, from higher *Ḥokhma* to lower *Ḥokhma*. However, this is not the topic of discussion here.

worlds. This process originally took place through Moses, who was the greatest of all the prophets. Through his prophecy, he grasped the truth and conveyed it into the lower reality, where he and all the children of Israel resided. As has been explained, in the process of descent, the external dimension of the higher level becomes enclothed in the lower level, and this continues, one level after the next. Because Moses grasped the external aspect of supernal *Ḥokhma,* he was able to bring it into the lower realm, and accordingly, the Torah was given through him. If he had grasped the inner dimension of *Ḥokhma,* he would not have been able to bring it down, for the inner dimension (*penimiyut*) does not move downward. This can be seen in God's words to Moses: "You will not be able to see My face [*panai*], as man shall not see Me and live" (Ex. 33:20). One who sees the inner dimension is no longer "among the living." Instead, he is incorporated into supernal *Ḥokhma,* which is subsumed in *Ein Sof* and no longer relates to human beings or their world. Therefore, by virtue of the fact that Moses grasped the revelation of the external dimension of *Ḥokhma,* as described in the verse "You will see My back," he merited to have the Torah given through him.

The *Ḥokhma* of the Torah, as we know it, is divine *Ḥokhma,* but not in the form that it exists above. Divine *Ḥokhma* descended and was enclothed in all the various levels of all the worlds until it eventually became the Torah that is enclothed in our physical world.[29] ☞

Until now we have discussed the descent of light from *Ḥokhma,*

THE VESTIGE OF *ḤOKHMA* ABOVE

☞ It is important to note that the Torah that is in our possession is described as the vestige of *Ḥokhma* above, and not the vestige of Torah above. As is explained in several places, the Torah itself is higher even than supernal *Ḥokhma.* It is ingrained in God's essence, so to speak, and is beyond any definition or perception. It is beyond the boundaries of our physical world just as it is beyond supernal *Ḥokhma.* Nonetheless, the revelation of the Torah, on all levels, takes place through *Ḥokhma. Ḥokhma* is the source and the essence of revelation, and all the levels that are below it evolved from it. The original, deepest revelation of the Torah takes place through supernal *Ḥokhma,* much like the light that is revealed on the various levels of the soul and in the different worlds. Thenceforth, through the "succession" described above, the Torah is revealed through *Ḥokhma* on each successive level and in each world. On every level, the revelation is like "nothing" compared to the revelation on the

29. The term "vestige of *Ḥokhma* above" comes from *Bereshit Rabba* 44:17.

from the initial revelation of *Ein Sof* until the level of action. Seemingly, there is no elevation involved in this, but only descent and an increasing degree of distance and concealment, until the point where the light can descend no further. Nonetheless, in the final portion of this epistle, there is a change in focus: What is truly important and what is not? What is truly "above" and what is "below"?

In the higher worlds, it is possible to intend, with the mind and emotions, to fulfill the mitzvot on a spiritual level. One does not require a body, nor physical surroundings, for this. However, fulfilling the mitzvot through action is possible only in the material world. The fact that the unfolding succession continues and does not stop in some upper world, but rather descends into this world, is a sign that the essential focus and purpose of the Torah lie in this world, is the observance of the mitzvot through real actions.

כְּמַאֲמַר "הַיּוֹם לַעֲשׂוֹתָם" (דברים ז,יא), וְ"גָדוֹל תַּלְמוּד שֶׁמֵּבִיא לִידֵי מַעֲשֶׂה" (קידושין מ,ב), וְ"הַלּוֹמֵד שֶׁלֹּא לַעֲשׂוֹת נוֹחַ לוֹ שֶׁנֶּהֶפְכָה שִׁלְיָיתוֹ" וכו', וְכָל אָדָם מוּכְרָח לְהִתְגַּלְגֵּל עַד שֶׁיְּקַיֵּים כָּל הַתַּרְיָ"ג מִצְוֹת בְּפוֹעַל מַמָּשׁ, כַּנּוֹדָע מֵהָאֲרִיזַ"ל.

As the verse **states, "Today, to perform them"** (Deut. 7:11), **and** the Talmud states, **"Study is greater, as it leads to action"** (Kiddushin 40b). Similarly, **"One who studies not for the sake of action, it would have been better for him had his placenta turned over…"** (Jerusalem Talmud, *Shabbat* 1:2). **Indeed, every person must be reincarnated** as many times as necessary **until he physically performs all the 613 mitzvot, as known from the Arizal.**

The author of the *Tanya* brings proof of this idea from the words of the Sages. On the verse "today, to perform them," the Talmud states, "Today [is the time] to do them, [in this world,] and tomorrow [is] not [the time] to do them" (*Eiruvin* 22a). "Today" refers to the present day and the current circumstances. From our perspective, this means

level above it. This process continues until the level of physical Ḥokhma in this world. This is the meaning of the phrase "the vestige of Ḥokhma above."

that the soul is in the body, in the physical world. Only through the physical body and the concealment of the Divine can the mitzvot be carried out in practice. "Tomorrow" refers to the World to Come, the spiritual realm, in which the soul and its concept of the self, continue to exist, albeit without the body and without the ability to fulfill the mitzvot through action. ☞

From the verse "today, to perform them," we learn that physical action takes place specifically in this world. However, we do not yet know if this is more important than the spiritual experience. To answer this, the author of the *Tanya* quotes a passage from the Talmud. The Sages disagreed with regard to which is more important: study or action. This is an important question that pertains to all realms, not only our world, which is where physical action occurs. More generally, the question can be expressed in the following terms: In which direction is the whole progression moving? What is the objective? The answer, "Study is greater, as it leads to action," is complex. On the one hand, it states that study is greater, yet on the other hand, the rest of the sentence says almost the opposite: Why is study great? Because it "leads to action." There are many hasidic discourses that discuss this matter, but simply put, it may be said that "Study is greater" describes the reality. This is how the worlds are structured at present. The spiritual is above the physical. General principles are more exalted than specific life instances, influencing them and setting them in motion. However, the phrase "leads to action" indicates that the purpose of everything is, in fact, action. Therefore, with regard to worldly action, the ruling

"TODAY, TO PERFORM THEM"

☞ The physical realm is a product of the almost total concealment of the Divine, and as a result, divine service is not the obvious choice for an individual in this world. Consequently, "today, to perform them" necessarily involves effort and a struggle against obstacles and difficulties. A physical act of holiness is not like a spiritual one. With regard to a spiritual act, like those of the angels, the loftier it is, the less difficult it is to perform, for it is the only and obvious way to comprehend that spiritual realm, feel it and function within it. However, in the lower, physical realm, where holiness is almost imperceptible, divine service is carried out in opposition to, and in spite of, the fact that our senses tell us something different. As will be explained later on, this kind of divine service is an expression of higher spiritual faculties, and it brings down a higher level of light from above.

is that "Study is greater," for through study, we have more success in our actions. Nevertheless, on the larger scale, according to the full, true reckoning, the whole purpose is action, and study is great only because it leads to action.

Accordingly, physical action is more important than its spiritual manifestation. However, we do not yet know the extent of this concept. The next statement that is brought from the Sages[30] says that if a person studies Torah not in order to act, it would have been better if he had not been born. Since the entire purpose of the spiritual reality, and of spiritual endeavors such as Torah study, is physical action, if a spiritual experience does not lead to physical action there is no justification for it. In such a case, all the stages of spiritual cognition and emotion lack value and meaning. Instead, they are viewed as essentially flawed, as something that did not reach the point it was supposed to reach. The entire being of a person who studies not for the sake of action, lacks purpose.

Action is so important that a person's entire existence in this world is for the sake of this alone. If one does not perform acts of holiness, there is no point or meaning to his existence here, to the joining of his body with his soul. However, we have not yet seen whether this is significant only with regard to the union of body and soul, or whether it is also consequential with regard to the holy soul itself. Put another way, we do not yet know if it is significant to the human being (a soul within a body), or to God Himself, as it were, that God sends the soul into this world again and again until it has fulfilled His supernal will. Therefore, the author of the *Tanya* includes the teaching of the Arizal.[31]

Reincarnation refers to the soul's return to this world. It is enclothed in a different body for an additional life cycle in order to finish carrying out all the mitzvot physically. In the spiritual realm, the soul can fulfill all the mitzvot in one life cycle, and it can do so without ever descending into this world. However, physical action is so critical that if the soul does not fulfill this objective the first time it descends into a body, it must descend again and again, for only through action is it

---

30. This quote also appears in *Vayikra Rabba* 35:7.

31. See *Sefer HaGilgulim*, chap. 4; *Sha'ar HaGilgulim*, *Hakdama* 11.

able to find the sole elements that it lacks from *Ein Sof* Himself, which is the only way that it will be able to truly unite with God.

This epistle addresses how the divine light descends from *Ein Sof*, which is above and beyond the *sefirot* and the worlds, and how it is revealed in the worlds, including, ultimately, the physical world of *Asiya*. This descent took place through the comprehension of the prophets, beginning with Moses, who brought the Torah down into our world and revealed it, and ended with the rest of the prophets, who revealed the Divine to each generation in the way that they needed to receive it, appropriate for their context. Generally speaking, the inner light is enclothed in the external dimension of *Ḥokhma*, which is, in turn, enclothed in the inner dimension of the emotive attributes, and so on, until its enclothement in the receiver; creation. Accordingly, the garment of the inner light is all that is ever revealed, while the inner light itself is enclothed within it.

From all this, we learn that the Torah's central purpose lies in its revelation in the lower, physical world of *Asiya*. Accordingly, that which has been described throughout this epistle as a "descent," a shift from the inner dimension to the external dimension, incorporating more and more constriction and concealment, is not simply a descent, for there is a tremendous, mystical secret that is being gradually revealed through it. The great, original light, the inner dimension of supernal *Ḥokhma*, constitutes an immense, unparalleled revelation. However, as great as it is, it also conceals *Ein Sof*, which is not a "light," and which cannot be revealed. Subsequently, one level after the next, there is concealment, or "enveloping with light as if with a cloak." This concealment requires faith and caution, and it takes place through the prophets, the Sages, and each individual Jew, until all the light is concealed except for its final resolution. This final result descended and went through various incarnations until it ultimately arrived here, and is expressed through action alone. Now, without the presence of the light, it reveals that which the great light conceals: *Keter*, which is above *Ḥokhma*, and *Ein Sof*, which cannot be revealed within any kind of boundary. *Likkutei Torah* (Num. 69) describes a place of darkness, where a person has no consciousness or knowledge with regard to how he is supposed to act.

He has neither love nor fear. When this person nonetheless acts as a result of the supernal will within him, which is far beyond his reason and knowledge, he is also bringing something down from above, from supernal *Keter*, which is beyond *Ḥokhma*.

This is significant not only with regard to the Torah's ultimate purpose but also with regard to the way in which it descends. The questions that are asked at the beginning of the epistle are: How does the Torah descend to this low place? Is its holiness preserved the whole way down? How is it sustained despite all the concealments? The answer is that it descends this way precisely because of its purpose, which is to reach the lowest point, the most external of externalities. The essence of holiness is transmitted downward, not only in the general sense, but at each stage of "enveloping with light as if with a cloak," where the external dimension replaces the inner dimension, descends, and is enclothed in the level below. The revelation of holiness is not transmitted, and neither are the great, supernal attributes of love and fear, which become more and more occluded with each descent. Nonetheless, in that final moment of concealment, the very light of holiness itself, which transcends all explanations and emotions, shines forth.

In summary, a person must serve God through action. To do so, he must find within himself the capacity to forgo all that "exists" in this world, including virtues, experiences, comprehension, spiritual attainments, and anything that allures him at all. He must be willing to relinquish all this for the purpose outlined here, which does not pertain to this world. Even if he is not yet on the level at which he is able to do this, he must be prepared for it. This is why the author of the *Tanya* mentions Moses in this epistle. Moses was the greatest prophet and Sage, and the Torah was given through him, yet he was also the humblest of people. In fact, humility was his central attribute and the source of all his other virtues. Moses was truly nullified, as can be seen in his statement, "And what are we?" (Ex. 16:7, 8). See *Torah Or* 57a and *Likkutei Torah*, Lev. 6b, where it is explained that the phrase "What are we?" expresses total nullification and lowliness. The capacity of nullification, which is drawn from Moses into all the levels to which the Torah descends, and into all those who receive it, is the driving force behind the entire process described here. Furthermore, it is what propels each individual to actively learn, teach, observe, and perform what is written in the Torah. It causes a person to stop feeling and seeing himself: He is simply a vessel for the fulfillment of the heavenly objective, which is impossible to understand or experience. As a result, no experience or understanding occurs, and the individual himself is no longer an emotional being with his own separate existence. He is simply attached and subsumed to the one real thing, the Divine, in the only way that makes it possible for the Divine to manifest: through the observance of Torah by means of action. This phenomenon exists in nature as well: The "giver" longs to give to the "receiver," which is on a lower level, even though doing so causes the giver to descend from its original, high level, and moreover, as its "flow" descends, it loses more and more of its radiance. This aspect of nature indicates that the world is in its perfected state, since it is behaving in a way that reflects the heavenly objective within it. When the opposite occurs, when the "giver" does not desire to give or to procreate, this is a sign that the world has become spoiled and corrupted. This is the meaning of the assertion stated at the beginning the epistle, "Moses's comprehension extended to the external dimensions of *Ḥokhma,* which are clothed in *Bina,* which in turn is clothed in the seven lower *sefirot*... in which *Ḥokhma* extends to the bottom of the four lowest *sefirot, Netzaḥ, Hod, Yesod,* and *Malkhut.*"

Addendum to Epistle 19

ALTHOUGH IT IS NOT GIVEN ITS OWN NUMBER, THE following text is not part of epistle 19. It is a short, separate epistle or hasidic exegesis.

The addendum was a later addition to *Iggeret HaKodesh*: It was included only in the 5660 (1899) edition.[1] Ostensibly, it was added here because of its thematic connection to epistle 19. It serves as a kind of supplement or commentary to the content of the epistle. This is particularly apparent at the end of the addendum, which connects almost unequivocally to the epistle.

Epistle 19 discusses the successive descent of the divine light that is in the Torah, from *Ein Sof* to the physical world of *Asiya*. This brief yet comprehensive addendum does not discuss the light or that which descends. Instead, it explains the vessels: the letters through which the light descends. It examines the nature of these letters and the way in which they are revealed and felt on all the levels in the different worlds, as well as in the soul: in thought, speech, and action.

1. For that edition, the text of *Iggeret HaKodesh* was compared to available manuscripts, and two passages were added: this addendum and the one after epistle 22. The two passages were added in these particular places, although they are not part of these epistles, because they belong there according to the manuscripts. However, in the index printed in that edition listing all the discourses in *Iggeret HaKodesh*, they are recorded separately (Rabbi Yehoshua Mondshein, *Sefer HaTanya: Mahadurotav, Targumav, VeBiurav*, 21, 26).

הָאוֹתִיּוֹת הַנִּגְלוֹת לָנוּ הֵן בְּמַעֲשֶׂה דִּבּוּר וּמַחֲשָׁבָה.

The letters revealed to us exist in action, speech, and thought. ☞

THE LETTERS THEMSELVES

☞ Ostensibly, the revelation of the letters themselves is inconsequential: Meaning is not contained within the letters, but in the content that is transmitted through them. The letters seem to be solely a means of communication, of transferring knowledge, directions, and so on, to others. We use commonly recognized combinations of letters for this purpose. However, it is explained in Kabbala that the letters are much more than this. Unlike other methods of communication, the letters consist of an additional dimension that is deep and concealed, even more so than the content that they transmit. This dimension is referred to extensively on the deepest levels of Torah, in particular in Hasidism, both with regard to theoretical concepts and in terms of the way divine service is carried out. The letters are not merely an instrument for the transmission of information. Rather, they create the information. Likewise, they do not merely convey insights and emotions: They create them as well as the reality, both spiritual and material, that they represent. Deeper still, the letters are the building blocks of all of reality.

This understanding of speech and letters stems from the recognition that speech is the vessel of divine expression, and therefore it is the vessel of creation, of the flow of life force and existence into all of reality. This concept pertaining to the letters of divine speech extends to our speech and the letters that comprise it as well. This is reiterated in Hasidism, in the concept that our speech is not separate from God's speech. Of course, it can sometimes be separate. Our speech lacks intrinsic value when it is spoken only with the mouth and directed outward. However, when it comes from a place of inner connection, it is bound to divine speech and to God Himself, who is speaking the very same words. At that moment, the letters are not merely sounds being vocalized or conventional symbols being formed on paper. Rather, they are themselves the creative forces acting upon the world.

Therefore, that which we understand through the letters is not the actual essence that runs through them, but only our particular comprehension of it. The essence itself remains within the letters. We attempt to connect to this essence, which encompasses all possible perceptions and comprehensions of it, by relating to the letters (see *Tzava'at HaRivash* 118; *Likkutei Yekarim* 227). We can therefore understand the endeavors described in many hasidic works to connect, in various ways, not only to the combinations of letters and their meanings, but to the letters themselves: their sound, appearance, quality, and so forth. This likewise explains the desire to "taste" the letters: A person yearns to achieve the most tangible sensation of the letters that he can. This is a vital part of divine service according to Hasidism. It is therefore clear why this discourse is concerned with the revelation of the letters on all levels: thought, speech, and action. As will be explained, it is not concerned only with the human understanding of these terms but also with their higher connotations, which pertain to divine revelation in the *sefirot* and in all the worlds.

3 Tishrei
29 Elul (leap year)

The author of the *Tanya* is discussing the revealed letters here. There are also concealed letters, but they are not addressed in this discourse. The Torah has a revealed dimension and a concealed dimension, as does the human soul and the Divine.[2] Like the Torah, the soul contains revealed letters and concealed letters. ☞

The revealed letters are the letters within the three garments of the soul. These garments constitute the ways in which the soul is revealed: It is revealed to itself through thought, to others through speech, and to the lowly reality of inanimate objects through action. ☞

REVEALED AND CONCEALED LETTERS

☞ Generally, revealed letters refer to the letters of speech, and concealed letters are those that comprise thought. Here, however, we are discussing letters that are revealed through action, speech, and thought. Accordingly, the "concealed letters" mentioned here must comprise something even deeper. Perhaps the revealed letters are the letters of the soul's garments – thought, speech, and action – and the concealed letters are those that are within the soul's faculties (See *Sefer HaMa'amarim* 5708, p. 158. Regarding the soul's garments and the faculties, see *Likkutei Amarim*, chaps. 3–4).

Broadly speaking, letters are a revelation. It is explained in several sources (see *Likkutei Torah*, Song 33c) that the word *otiyot*, letters, is derived from the same term as "The morning comes [*ata*]" (Isa. 21:12), in the sense of conveying and revealing. Accordingly, it is not clear how letters could be "unrevealed." The explanation is that they are concealed in comparison to the letters that are revealed in thought, speech, and action. Nonetheless, they too are conveyed from a more concealed being, which indirectly leads to revelation in thought, speech, and action.

ACTION, SPEECH, AND THOUGHT IN THE DIFFERENT WORLDS

☞ As in most hasidic discourses, we are not discussing only the realm of the soul here, but also the higher worlds, which serve as "garments" of the divine light. These two domains are indivisible: They are interwoven and shed light on each other. That which happens within the soul happens in the worlds, and vice versa. Not only do they affect each other, but more than that: They are exactly the same thing. Thought, speech, and action correspond to the worlds of *Beria*, *Yetzira*, and *Asiya*, respectively, while the world of *Atzilut* corresponds to the soul itself.

Revelation of the letters means, in general, the revelation of the supernal letters

2. The *Zohar* states, "There are three levels that are interconnected: the Holy One, blessed be He, the Torah, and Israel. Each one [comprises] level upon level, the concealed and the revealed" (*Zohar* 3:73a).

דְּמַעֲשֶׂה, הֵן תְּמוּנַת הָאוֹתִיּוֹת שֶׁבִּכְתָב אַשּׁוּרִי שֶׁבְּסֵפֶר תּוֹרָה.

The letters **of action are the** visual **forms of the** Hebrew **letters in the Assyrian script that** appear **in the Torah scroll.**

In the realm of action, the letters are revealed by means of the act of writing. Each letter conveys a unique power and life force that are not evoked from any other letter. This is expressed through the unique physical form of each letter in the Assyrian script in the Torah scroll. One is able to see this form and to feel it with his hands.[3]

Written letters correspond to "action." After the action has been carried out, it becomes a separate entity from the person who performed it. In contrast, the vocalized letters of speech exist only when they are spoken.

Just as action is on a lower level than speech and the world of *Asiya* is on a lower level than the world of *Yetzira*, written letters are on a lower level than spoken letters. With regard to the spiritual worlds, "lower" means that there is less divine revelation there.[4] The written letters are on a lower level than the spoken letters because the person who writes them can be completely hidden. This resembles the world of *Asiya*: God gives it existence and life, yet He is concealed to the extent that the world can perceive itself as totally separate from Him. In the case of spoken letters, however, the speaker is recognizably present. Likewise,

in the world of *Asiya* and in the realm of action, as opposed to the more spiritual realms. The revelation of the letters in speech constitutes the revelation of the letters in the entire world of *Yetzira*, the realm of supernal speech, where objects are created by means of combinations of letters. The revelation of the letters in thought constitutes the revelation of the letters in the world of *Beria*, the realm of supernal thought, which signifies a departure from nothingness: Thoughts emerge from the "nothingness" of the concealed soul, and likewise, creation (*beria*) takes place from the "nothingness" that is united with the Divine in the world of *Atzilut*. The revelation of the letters in thought is unlike the revelation of the letters in speech and action. While this revelation creates thoughts about different objects, on a deeper level it is like the revelation of thought to itself, which does not imprint upon the physical reality, but only upon the spiritual realm that is connected with it.

3. See *Sha'ar HaYiḥud VeHa'emuna*, chap. 12, in the gloss.
4. See *Likkutei Amarim*, chap. 40.

with regard to the world of *Yetzira,* God gives it existence and He is not concealed there, but rather His presence is felt. ☞

וְאוֹתִיּוֹת הַדִּבּוּר נֶחְקָקוֹת בְּהֶבֶל וְקוֹל הַמִּתְחַלֵּק לְכ״ב חֲלָקִים שׁוֹנִים זֶה מִזֶּה בְּצוּרָתָן, שֶׁהִיא הֲבָרַת וּמִבְטָא הַכ״ב אוֹתִיּוֹת בְּכָל לָשׁוֹן.

The letters of speech are engraved in the breath and voice used to speak, **which is divided into twenty-two parts, different from one another in their** spoken **form, namely the enunciation and pronunciation of the twenty-two** different **letters in any language.**

The letters revealed through speech are those that are said and heard by human beings. As in the case of the written letters, there are twenty-two different forms, which are divided among the five organs of speech. These are the pronunciations of the letters. Each letter has its own unique sound, through which it reveals the essence of its power. ☞ ☞

ASSYRIAN SCRIPT

☞ This is based on the idea that the shapes of the letters written in the Torah scroll constitute their true, original forms, which were given to us from on high. Just as Biblical Hebrew is considered God's "language," through which He created the world, gave us the Torah, and reveals Himself to us, these shapes were given to us from above, and they contain the full scope of the letters' potential meaning. Of course, other languages also convey meaning and possess creative power, but they do not possess the perfection of the letters through which the world was created and is sustained. It says in *Torah Or* (10b) that Hebrew letters are called "stones," while the letters of other languages are called "bricks." Both are used to build structures, but stones are created by God, whereas bricks are man-made. Likewise, different handwritten or printed forms of the Hebrew letters serve only as symbols of the original letters. One symbolizes *alef,* another symbolizes *bet,* and so forth, yet they are not truly *alef* and *bet.* The true *alef* is the *alef* written in Assyrian script, which is found in the Torah scroll. It is written in accordance with the *halakhot* given in the Written Torah and elucidated in the Oral Torah with regard to the particulars of each letter's form.

ENGRAVED IN BREATH AND VOICE

☞ While the letters revealed through "action" are written in ink on parchment or some other material, the letters of speech are "engraved in the breath and voice." Elsewhere (*Likkutei Torah,* Lev. 46b, Num. 56a), the author of the *Tanya* explains the difference between "written letters" and "engraved letters." Written letters are those

In the physical realm, "breath" refers to the air in the lungs. Speech is created through this air. In the spiritual realm, "breath" refers to the very beginning of speech before the individual letters are revealed to themselves. This resembles the revelation of the soul itself, the emanation of its "name." This not an actual revelation, nor is it the actual soul. Rather, it is the illumination of the soul's initial expression. The soul is about to reveal itself but does not yet possess a concrete form of any kind (see *Ba'al Shem Tov al HaTorah, Bereshit* 91; *Likkutei Amarim*, chap. 20).

"Voice" is what connects "breath" to speech. Like "breath," it does not actually form the letters. Rather, it creates the extraordinary connection between the intangible, spiritual breath, which is united with the soul, and the physical letters, which are separate from the soul and can therefore be transmitted to others. In the books of the ancients, it is explained that "voice" contains fire and water, which are *Ḥesed* and *Gevura*. In other words, it contains both the act of strengthening the inner essence and the act of emerging and expanding into space. These simultaneous elements combine and intersect, and each one incorporates the other. This is what causes the intangible and the all-encompassing to be transferred into a limited, seemingly distinct entity. Indeed, this "voice," which includes *Ḥesed* and *Gevura*, is the aspect of *Tiferet*, which signifies the forefather Jacob. This is explained in several places (see *Torah Or* 57c–d; *Likkutei Torah*, Deut. 23b; Introduction to *Siddur Sha'ar HaTefilla*, s.v. "*hakol kol ya'akov*") with regard to the verse "The voice is the voice of Jacob" (Gen. 27:22).

"Division" refers to the classification of "voice" into the twenty-two

that are formed with ink on parchment, for example, while engraved letters are carved into a material such as stone, like the letters of the Torah which were engraved on the stone tablets. Here, the author of the *Tanya* indicates that there is a similar distinction between written letters and spoken letters, which are "engraved" on a person's breath and voice. In *Likkutei Torah*, he explains that written letters are a separate entity from the parchment on which they are recorded. Letters engraved on stone, however, are truly part of the stone. They comprise nothing additional or independent: The stone itself forms the shapes of the letters. In the same way, written letters are a separate entity from the person who writes them, while spoken letters are not detached from the breath, the voice, or the speaker himself.

fundamental forms of the letters. "Breath" is not heard, and "voice" is, yet "voice" still has no definition or meaning: It is a channel that conveys expression from "nothingness." Unlike "nothingness," which is a specific point, this channel can be divided up. Its division among the five organs of speech reveals the letters of speech as we hear and recognize them, and adds expansion.

כִּי אֵין הֶפְרֵשׁ בֵּין לְשׁוֹן הַקּוֹדֶשׁ וּבֵין שְׁאָר לְשׁוֹנוֹת בְּמַהוּת הֲבָרַת הָאוֹתִיּוֹת כִּי אִם בְּצֵירוּפָן.

For there is no difference between the Holy Tongue (Hebrew) **and the other languages in the core enunciation of the** sounds made by individual **letters;** the difference is **only when** the letters are **combined** to form words.

In this, spoken letters differ from written letters. The shapes of the written letters are unique to Hebrew. However, the enunciation of the letter *bet* involves a physical movement that is found in every language, and the same is true of the other letters as well. Of course, there is not always a one-to-one correspondence. Some languages may use a combination of letters to express the sound of one Hebrew letter, and vice versa. Nonetheless, in essence, the vowels and consonants are universal. They reveal what the human body's five organs of speech – the tongue, lips, throat, and so on – can do with the voice. With regard to the spoken letters, languages differ only in the combinations of the letters: the words and sentences, which carry meaning.

וְאוֹתִיּוֹת הַמַּחֲשָׁבָה הֵן גַּם כֵּן, בְּכָל לָשׁוֹן שֶׁאָדָם מְחַשֵּׁב תֵּיבוֹת וְאוֹתִיּוֹת הַלָּשׁוֹן, שֶׁהֵן כ"ב לְבַד.

Likewise, the letters of thought – of any language in which a person thinks – are the words and letters of that language; there are only twenty-two core letters.

The revelation of the letters in thought is less tangible and more difficult to grasp. In action and speech, the revelation occurs in a physical way. Even though it has spiritual meaning, it is revealed within a physical vessel, which is clearly evident and distinct in our world. In thought, however, even the letters themselves are spiritual. They are not revealed like the "physical" letters, through a sound or a shape, but rather through intricate, spiritual vessels. As will be stated below, within thought, there are different levels of connection to the letters. On the lower levels, which are closest to speech, a person thinks about the letters and words as they are revealed through speech and writing. Although he does not enunciate them, they are still the same twenty-two letters. The words and letters of speech are no different from the words and letters of thought. Moreover, even in the case of more abstract thought, which does not directly employ words and letters, but rather abstract concepts, the foundation of these concepts is composed entirely of the very same twenty-two letters, from *alef* to *tav*. These letters comprise absolutely everything, in both the physical realm and the spiritual realm. ☞

Just as the spoken letters are considered more closer expressions of one's essence than the letters of the realm of action, the letters of thought are closer expressions of one's essence than the spoken letters. The letters of action can be completely separate from the person who forms them, and in this respect, they are the most external expression of the letters. Spoken letters, on the other hand, cannot be detached from the speaker: He is always present. Likewise, the letters of thought cannot exist without the person who thinks them, but moreover, that person cannot help but think them. A person can decide whether or not to say certain letters aloud, but he cannot help but "think" letters.

THE HEBREW NAME

☞ In *Sha'ar HaYiḥud VeHa'emuna* (chap. 1) it says that the Hebrew name of each object is the combination of letters spoken by God with regard to that object. It is the soul, life force, and being of that object. Just as this is true in the realms of action and speech, it is likewise the case in the realm of thought. Before a thought is even enclothed in spoken letters, the ideas within it contain a soul, a divine life force that gives them life and sustains them. Like the life force within all objects, this life force comprises a unique combination of the twenty-two Hebrew letters, and this is what gives life to that particular thought.

רַק שֶׁבַּמַּחֲשָׁבָה יֵשׁ בָּהּ ג׳ מִינֵי בְּחִינוֹת אוֹתִיּוֹת.

But within the letters of **thought** itself, **there are three different kinds of letters.**

Each level encompasses all the levels below it. Each one is like a whole organism that incorporates all its constituent parts, and like an abstract concept that incorporates all concrete expressions of itself. It follows that the roots of all the types of letters lie within thought: the letters of action, speech, and thought itself. ☞

שֶׁהֲרֵי כְּשֶׁרוֹאֶה בְּסֵפֶר תּוֹרָה תְּמוּנַת הָאוֹתִיּוֹת הֵן מִצְטַיְּירוֹת בְּמַחֲשַׁבְתּוֹ, וְזֶה נִקְרָא בְּחִינַת ׳עֲשִׂיָּה שֶׁבַּמַּחֲשָׁבָה׳.

For when one sees the forms of the letters in a Torah scroll, they are pictured in his thought; this is called the "action of thought;" it corresponds to the level of *Asiya* (Action).

The author of the *Tanya* elaborates, beginning with "action of thought." As mentioned above, we are referring here to the forms of the letters as they are written in the Torah scroll, for this is how they reveal their inner essence in the realm of action. The revelation of the letters in the realm of action can also be manifest in thought. This is known as "action of thought." A person thinks in words, and there is a particular way of thinking in which one sees the images of the words and letters, as they are written, in his mind. Some people are more inclined to thoughts of this kind. They remember and relate to things this way. Others are more inclined to abstract thought, and they are less likely to think in this way, unless they are actually about to form the letters or are thinking about doing so. There is also a broader reference here

THREE ASPECTS OF LETTERS

☞ Other sources discuss a type of parallel to these three kinds of letters within speech and action as well, such as "thought of speech," "speech of speech," and "action of speech" (see, for example, *Imrei Bina, Sha'ar HaKeriat Shema*, chaps. 31–32; *Sefer HaMa'amarim* 5710, pp. 34ff. The Lubavitcher Rebbe, Rabbi Menaḥem Mendel Schneerson, comments on this entire addendum that one should study and understand *Imrei Bina, Sha'ar HaKeriat Shema*, chap. 32, which appears to contain a slightly different explanation of this matter).

to a general connection between thought and a certain level of action. Thought does not relate only to the inner dimension of the letters, which is associated with the thinking soul. Rather, it relates also to the letters' external dimension, which is able to connect to that which is truly inanimate and separate from the soul.

וְכֵן כַּאֲשֶׁר שׁוֹמֵעַ אוֹתִיּוֹת הַדִּבּוּר, הֵן נִרְשָׁמוֹת בְּמַחֲשַׁבְתּוֹ וּמְהַרְהֵר בָּהֶן, וְזֶה נִקְרָא בְּחִינַת 'דִּבּוּר שֶׁבְּמַחֲשָׁבָה' וּבְחִינַת יְצִירָה.

Likewise, when one hears spoken letters, they are etched in his thought, and he thinks about them. This is called the "speech of thought," and it corresponds to **the level of *Yetzira*.**

The next level is "speech of thought." When a person thinks of the words and letters as they are pronounced verbally, this is "speech of thought." Such thoughts are more abstract than thoughts of the written forms of the letters. Here, the meaning of the words is also significant, and furthermore, so is the speaker, as well as his voice, manner of speaking, purpose, and personality, which are revealed in his speech. Here too, some people are more suited to this type of thought. They recall sounds and can hear the deeper meaning within them. Moreover, as above, there is a deeper connotation here, which concerns speech as the creator of connections between worlds and between people. If action relates to the "other" and thought relates to the self, then speech is the link between them.

As has been discussed,[5] the garments of the soul – thought, speech, and action – are connected to, and correspond to, the worlds of *Beria, Yetzira,* and *Asiya* (the world of *Atzilut* corresponds to the soul itself, and the ten faculties of the soul are parallel to the ten *sefirot* of the world of *Atzilut*). Action corresponds to the world of *Asiya.* It signifies the "final outcome," and inanimate objects.[6] No life force can be plainly seen in this realm, and as a result, it is perceived as separate from the source of its life force. Speech corresponds to the world of *Yetzira,* for the letters combine to create words and sentences that contain worlds of

5. In the commentary to this epistle, and at length in epistle 15; see also *Likkutei Amarim,* chaps. 3–4.

6. In the same vein, the world of *Yetzira* is parallel to the category of "vegetable" and the world of *Beria* is parallel to "animal," and sometimes to human beings.

meaning. *Sefer Yetzira* compares the letters to stones that join together to create houses and cities in which people dwell.

וְאוֹתִיּוֹת הַמַּחֲשָׁבָה לְבַדָּהּ בְּלִי הִרְהוּר אוֹתִיּוֹת הַדִּבּוּר, נִקְרָאוֹת 'מַחֲשָׁבָה שֶׁבְּמַחֲשָׁבָה' בְּחִינַת בְּרִיאָה.

Finally, **the letters of pure thought alone,** that is, when one thinks **without being conscious of the letters of speech, is called "thought of thought."** It corresponds to **the level of *Beria*.**

The third level is "thought of thought." This refers to abstract thought, which is not made up of letters or spoken words. The letters of speech and action each have a physical garment: their sound or shape. Therefore, even when one thinks of them, he thinks of them within their physical garments and then gives them meaning. This is what is known as "speech of thought" and "action of thought." In contrast, the letters of thought have no physical garments, so even when one thinks of them there is no vessel or image that one can bring to mind. There is, however, an extremely subtle differentiation in these letters; the meaning and substance of them comprise the vessel, or form, of the letters of a thought. In this sense, the vessel and the light come together. They are not one entity, yet we are unable to separate them. These thoughts come directly from the indefinable "nothingness," from the soul itself. They are comprised of the substance of thought within the vessel of thought: "thought of thought." This signifies the true expression of the idea itself, just as it occurs in the soul. "Speech of thought" and "action of thought" bring an idea outward and make it relatable to the "other." However, its inner essence is expressed through the letters of "thought of thought."

If the world of *Yetzira* signifies the combining of letters, then *Beria* is the revelation of the letters in the sense of "existence from nothingness." ☞

THOUGHT CORRESPONDS TO *BERIA*

☞ *Beria* is the realm of transition from "nothingness" to "existence," from total concealment to the inception of revelation. This kind of revelation is internal, and it is not independent, yet it is still a revelation. It is known as "revelation to the self." Thought, too, is a "revelation to the self," whereas speech constitutes a "revelation to the other." The revelation of a thought is united with the person who thinks it, for

Now, these ideas are linked to epistle 19. The epistle dealt with how supernal *Ḥokhma* is transmitted down until it reaches the world of *Asiya*: The external dimension of the highest level is enclothed in the level below it, and this process continues through each of the levels. This addendum began with a description of the letters on each level and in each world, and now it goes on to explain how light is transmitted from level to level through the letters.

Now, the letters of actual speech are created by and receive their life force from these very letters of thought.

וְהִנֵּה אוֹתִיּוֹת הַדִּבּוּר מַמָּשׁ הֵן מִתְהַוּוֹת וּמְקַבְּלוֹת חַיּוּתָן מֵאוֹתִיּוֹת אֵלּוּ עַצְמָן שֶׁבַּמַּחֲשָׁבָה.

Here, the author of the *Tanya* is discussing the letters of speech itself, not "speech of thought." The letters of actual speech receive their life force from the letters of "speech of thought." The general principle is that speech receives from thought. A person cannot speak if he does not first think about the matter he is speaking about. However, pure thought does not bring about speech. Only thoughts that relate to speech can comprise speech. They must be structured like speech and must carry the intent to be expressed as speech. The letters of thought on this level are called the letters of "speech of thought."

Though a person sometimes says one thing while thinking about something else,

וְאַף שֶׁלִּפְעָמִים מְדַבֵּר אָדָם וּמְהַרְהֵר בְּדָבָר אַחֵר,

According to this, speech seems to be unconnected to thought. Consequently, there may be speech that is not created by means of thought and does not "receive" from thought.

it cannot exist without him. Moreover, the thinker carries that thought forever. A person can choose whether or not to speak, but he is always thinking, and is unable to refrain from doing so. On a deeper level, one's thoughts reveal that which is inside him, and therefore they are never separate from him. On the other hand, once something has been said aloud, it has its own existence and meaning, independent of the speaker. With regard to our relationships with others, too, a person's thoughts are obscured, just like the individual himself. Only our speech is able to touch others.

הֲרֵי אֵינוֹ יָכוֹל לְדַבֵּר כִּי אִם אוֹתָן דִּבּוּרִים וְצֵירוּפִים שֶׁכְּבָר דִּבְּרָם וְהָיוּ בְּמַחֲשַׁבְתּוֹ פְּעָמִים רַבּוֹת מְאֹד, וְנִשְׁאַר בַּדִּיבּוּרִים וְצֵירוּפִים אֵלּוּ הָרְשִׁימוּ מֵהַמַּחֲשָׁבָה שֶׁנִּכְנְסָה בָּהֶם פְּעָמִים רַבּוֹת.

nevertheless, he can only speak those words and combinations that he has already spoken in the past, **and which he has thought about many, many times,** so that **the thought that has entered those words and combinations** so **many times leaves an impression.**

There truly is no speech without thought. There may be speech that is unrelated to the thought currently occupying the individual. However, it will relate instead to a thought that occupied him previously. This is possible when a person's current thought is not "complete": It is not a thought that leads to speech, but rather a "thought."[7] This refers to the stage at which a thought arises, when it is still only "thought of thought." Furthermore, in such a case, the speech must be "external." It must not express the soul's inner dimension, its present emotions and perceptions, but rather conclusions that the speaker has already drawn. It must comprise a thought pattern he has experienced in the past, which exists in his soul even if it does not currently carry his soul's inner light. ☞

וְזֶהוּ בְּחִינַת אֲחוֹרַיִים וְחִיצוֹנִיּוּת נה"י מִפַּרְצוּף הָעֶלְיוֹן שֶׁנִּכְנָס בְּתַחְתּוֹן לִהְיוֹת לוֹ בְּחִינַת מוֹחִין

This is the "back" and the external dimension of *Netzaḥ* (Dominance), ***Hod*** (Splendor), and ***Yesod*** (Foundation) **of the higher *partzuf* which**

SAYING ONE THING WHILE THINKING ABOUT ANOTHER

☞ Speech always receives from thought. However, as has been mentioned, there are several different levels with regard to the letters of thought. Speech may, for example, receive from the letters of "action of thought" (or perhaps the letters of "speech of thought"). Like action, the letters of "action of thought" can be separate from the thinking soul. Consequently, the person is able to think of something else at the same time, with the letters of "thought of thought."

---

7. It says in *Likkutei Amarim*, chap. 37, "Contemplation is not tantamount to actual speech." See also *Kuntres Aḥaron* 1–2, where it states, "Contemplation accomplishes nothing."

וְחַיּוּת כַּנּוֹדָע. **enters the lower** level, **becoming its *moḥin* and life force as is known.**

This final sentence connects the addendum to epistle 19. As is explained there, thought and speech are like a higher realm and a lower realm, or a higher *partzuf* and a lower *partzuf*. The letters of "speech of thought" that are enclothed in the letters of actual speech are, in the words of epistle 19, *Netzaḥ, Hod,* and *Yesod* of the upper *partzuf* that are enclothed in the lower *partzuf*, becoming its intellectual faculty and life force. In other words, the external dimension (*Netzaḥ, Hod,* and *Yesod*) of the letters of thought, which is comprised of "speech of thought" and "action of thought," descends to the realm of speech and becomes the substance and life force of the spoken letters.

What does this addendum include that we did not know previously? What is so important in this section that it is inserted here, in this specific place in *Iggeret HaKodesh,* in the *Tanya*? Its significance lies in its focus on the letters themselves. Epistle 19 is concerned with content: *Ḥokhma,* its descent into the worlds, and that which we are able to understand and feel of it. In contrast, the addendum contains an essentially technical description of the shapes and pronunciations of the letters. This adds another, fundamental layer of meaning to the epistle. Although they are inanimate and seem to lack substance, the letters, too, proceed outward and affect others. "Content" conveys only a certain degree of enlightenment and revelation, in accordance with our capacity to perceive it with our intellect. On the other hand, the letters transmit the essence of the matter itself. Although we may not see it, but only believe in it, as they descend, the letters convey this essence through thought, speech, and action. They realize in the lower realm that which is merely theoretical in the higher realm.

Epistle 20

This letter is truly unique. First, it bears the characteristics not of a letter, but rather of a discourse. Of course, *Iggeret HaKodesh* is comprised not only of letters;[1] it is a compilation of the author's written thought that supplements the teachings published in the rest of the *Tanya*. The uniqueness of this passage lies mainly in its being one of the last written by the author of the *Tanya*. His grandson, Rabbi Menaḥem Mendel Schneersohn, who later became the third Lubavitcher Rebbe (the Tzemaḥ Tzedek), and who was in close proximity with him in his last days, described this discourse as follows: "This is the holy work of the Rebbe that he wrote in the days before his passing, in the village of Pena."[2] However, its uniqueness is based not only on the circumstances of its authorship but on its content and style as well. The previous letters (and in a certain sense the *Tanya* as a whole, as it is described in the introduction) were written with specific people and circumstances in mind, and the author of the *Tanya* refers to them directly. However, in this passage, the style is more personal. It is written in the

1. The author's children corroborate this in their endorsement of the *Tanya*: "It is called *Iggeret HaKodesh* because it consists mainly of missives that were dispatched." See the introduction to Rabbi Yehoshua Mondshine, *Sefer HaTanya: Mahadurotav, Targumav, VeBiurav*.

2. *Derekh Mitzvotekha*, p. 170. In *Kitzurim VeHe'arot LeSefer Likkutei Amarim*, p. 40, it is stated with regard to this epistle: "This is the holy writing of the Rebbe himself, whose words are like gold. He wrote it exactly one week before he fell ill and was taken by God. He was summoned to the heavenly academy at the conclusion of the holy Sabbath, *Parashat Shemot*, in the year 5573."

manner of an individual expressing his private thoughts in his own words.[3] The language in this discourse is harder to understand, and the topics that it addresses are some of the most profound and difficult in Hasidism. Furthermore, not only was it written by the author of the *Tanya* at the conclusion of his physical life, but it constitutes a kind of summary of several of his most significant teachings. It is not truly a summary, for his teachings are elaborate and varied, and they are too deep and multifaceted to be summed up in one short treatise. Nonetheless, it touches upon the deepest and most fundamental themes that permeate the hundreds of discourses written or voiced by him during his lifetime.

The location of this letter within *Iggeret HaKodesh* is related to its content.[4] The preceding letters speak of movement from above to below, from concealed, supernal *Ḥokhma* (Wisdom) to the revealed Torah, which is concerned with this world and with real, physical matters. They discuss the fact that this motion constitutes a descent with regard to the diminishing light and its constricted revelation, but note that it is also an ascent, as it reveals the higher divine intent, which is the root of everything, and which belongs specifically in the lower realm. This letter, too, discusses the supremacy of the lower levels, where God Himself, the Infinite One, is revealed.

In this epistle the author of the *Tanya* delves more deeply. He endeavors to discern the essence of the lower levels. What is it about them that is so sublime? Is the lower realm truly "low," or is it actually a higher realm, or could it be both simultaneously? What is beyond these realms that is perhaps not "existence" but rather *ayin*, "nothingness"? And

---

3. A similar style is found in several other texts, such as in the discourse in *Torah Or* 16c. Regarding that discourse it is stated: "This is written in the Rebbe's own words."

4. The sixth Lubavitcher Rebbe, Rabbi Yosef Yitzḥak Schneerson, remarks elsewhere that the letters in *Iggeret HaKodesh* are arranged according to subject matter, and not in chronological order (see *Sefer HaSiḥot* 5705, p. 110).

whatever it is, does it exist in the world only in a general sense, in that it provides it with its basic existence from above, or is it actually within the world? This crucial fact would attest to God's presence in the world of each individual. This letter addresses all the above questions. When we try to understand these matters, even though they were not directed explicitly at us, then we, as the author's hasidim, are engaging in a process of elevation. We contemplate and comprehend with increasing clarity, each of us according to his potential, and beyond.

אִיהוּ וְחַיּוֹהִי חַד אִיהוּ וְגַרְמוֹהִי חַד בְּהוֹן **He and His life forces are one, and His attributes are one in them.** 4 Tishrei / 1 Tishrei (leap year)

This opening sentence, adapted from the introduction to *Tikkunei Zohar* (3b),[5] is also the motto of the whole discourse, as well as the key that unlocks it. Indeed, in many hasidic works where this text is quoted, it is referred to as "The one that begins, 'He and His life forces are one.'"

The first word, "He," is referring to God Himself. The rest of the sentence thus requires clarification, for the assertion that something is one with God is at first glance incomprehensible.

(פֵּירוּשׁ, עֶשֶׂר סְפִירוֹת דַּאֲצִילוּת **(This is referring to the ten *sefirot* of *Atzilut*.**

The ten *sefirot* of the world of *Atzilut* are what being "one with God" is referring to. We identify the *sefirot* of *Atzilut* with God Himself, for God is enclothed in them when He reveals Himself within the worlds.

5. It states there, "For the King is in the ten *sefirot* of *Atzilut*. He and His attributes are one there; He and His life forces are one there. This is not the case in the ten *sefirot* of *Beria*, for they and their life forces are not one, and they and their attributes are not one." The same quote appears in *Pardes Rimmonim*. However, it is cited differently in *Etz Ḥayyim*: "He and His life and His attributes are one there" (*Sha'ar* 26, chap. 1). The phrasing in the *Tanya*, where "He and His life forces" comes before "He and His attributes," is also cited with *Tikkunei Zohar* as its source in several places in *Emek HaMelekh* (*Sha'ar* 5, chap. 5; *Sha'ar* 16, chap. 37) and in the works of Rabbi Menaḥem Azarya of Fano.

These *sefirot* are not a garment that "is created" and that conceals,[6] but rather one that is a pure expression of the Divine and is not tainted by the presence of any other entity. This garment is solely revelatory; no matter which angle one views it from, he discerns the Divine. The ten *sefirot* of *Atzilut* are the means by which we see and relate to the Divine.

'חַיּוֹהִי' הֵן הָאוֹרוֹת וְ'גַרְמוֹהִי' הֵן הַכֵּלִים **"His life forces" are the lights, and "His attributes" are the vessels,**

Lights and vessels are the two most basic components of reality in all of the worlds. From the lowest realm to the world of *Atzilut*, there is no being that is not composed of these two constituents. "His life forces" corresponds to light, which reveals its source but is not in itself a distinct reality. "His attributes" are the vessels, much like the various body parts, which serve as vessels for the soul's life force: The feet reveal the capacity to walk, the head reveals the capacity to think, and so on.[7] ☞

The lights are unbound, and therefore the fact that they are one

"HIS LIFE FORCES" ARE THE LIGHTS, AND "HIS ATTRIBUTES" ARE THE VESSELS

☞ The author of the *Tanya* draws this comparison (which is elaborated upon in the introduction to *Tikkunei Zohar* [17a], in the section known as *Pataḥ Eliyahu*) to show that the life force that sustains each *sefira* is not like the flow of the soul's life force within the body, which has its own reality. Rather, he depicts it as a simple light that has no reality of its own. Likewise, the vessels are not defined and constrained as are body parts. Instead, their limitations are exceedingly abstract, as will be explained below.

---

6. Like the garments of the soul, and like the worlds of *Beria*, *Yetzira*, and *Asiya*; and see *Likkutei Amarim*, chap. 4.

7. The Lubavitcher Rebbe, Rabbi Menaḥem Mendel Schneerson, comments that there is a different way to interpret "His life forces" and "His attributes" (see *Lessons in Tanya*). It states in *Hemshekh Mayim Rabbim* 5636, 151, and in *Hemshekh Ayin Bet*, chap. 153: "In *Etz Ḥayyim* it states that 'His life forces' are the first three and 'His attributes' are the lower seven." However, the author of the *Tanya* writes that "'His life forces' are the lights, and 'His attributes' are the vessels," which indicates that both terms refer to all ten *sefirot*. Therefore, this sentence is not

with the Divine is more understandable. The distinction between the lights and the vessels serves to emphasize the fact that the vessels are also unbound. Indeed, it is mainly the vessels that are discussed below, and how they are one with the Infinite One.

שֶׁכּוּלָּן אֱלֹקוּת **as they are all divinity,**

The *sefirot* of *Atzilut,* the lights as well as the vessels, are entirely a revelation of the Divine. *Ḥokhma* of *Atzilut* is divine *Ḥokhma,* and *Ḥesed* (Kindness) of *Atzilut* is divine *Ḥesed.* We are unable to comprehend *Ein Sof* beyond the *sefirot,* so this constitutes our comprehension of the Divine. Nonetheless, the phrase "as they are all divinity" here refers to something more: Within the *sefirot* and vessels of *Atzilut,* there is truly a revelation of divine power, of *Ein Sof* Himself, as will be explained below.

מַה שֶּׁאֵין כֵּן בִּבְרִיאָה יְצִירָה עֲשִׂיָּה כו') **which is not the case for *Beria, Yetzira* and *Asiya*...)**

In each world, there are ten *sefirot.* The *sefirot* sustain that world and reveal the Divine within it. However, the *sefirot* of the created worlds are not united with the Divine with the same total unity as are the *sefirot* of the world of *Atzilut.* ☞

WHICH IS NOT THE CASE FOR *BERIA*, *YETZIRA*, AND *ASIYA*

☞ The world cannot exist without the Divine, and God brings everything into existence from absolute nothingness and sustains it. Nonetheless, from the perspective of the creations themselves, they each have a "self" that is not the same as the Divine. A created being can regard itself as subject to God, subsumed to Him, and merely His instrument, yet that same creation still perceives itself as a separate entity. Although this may be a minor distinction, it nonetheless creates obscurity, and the result is that the subsumption is not divine. In our perception of the one, infinite God, there is a type of fastidiousness that prevents anything else from being present. Consequently, the world does not express itself as essentially divine. It is concerned with God and praises Him, but it does not speak in His name in the first person.

The question is not whether there is only the Divine or whether there could

---

concerned with particulars but with the world of *Atzilut* in general, and it defines the *sefirot* of *Atzilut* relative to the other worlds.

וְצָרִיךְ לְהָבִין הֵיטֵב, אֵיךְ הָאֵין סוֹף חַד עִם גַּרְמוֹהִי הֵן הַכֵּלִים? הֲרֵי הַכֵּלִים הֵן בִּבְחִינַת גְּבוּל וְתַכְלִית כְּמוֹ שֶׁכָּתוּב בְּעֵץ חַיִּים

It is necessary to achieve a full understanding – how is *Ein Sof* one with the attributes, which are the vessels? After all, the vessels represent limits and finitude, as written in *Etz Ḥayyim*.

Although we are discussing the *sefirot* of *Atzilut*, it is not clear how a defined, bound entity, as abstract as it may be, can be one with *Ein Sof*. *Ein Sof* is that which is beyond any definition or binding, while the ten *sefirot* are the definitions of *Ḥokhma, Ḥesed, Gevura* (Restraint), and so forth.

This question pertains to the "attributes," the vessels and not the lights.[8] Light itself does not possess a defined reality: It is a radiance that emanates from *Ein Sof*. For the most part, the limitations of the *sefirot* derive from the vessels.[9] ☞ ☞

possibly be something else, for it is exceedingly clear that the Divine is all that exists. Rather, the question is: Can something be itself and simultaneously be one with the Divine? The answer is that this occurs only in the emanated world of *Atzilut*. In the created worlds (*Beria, Yetzira*, and *Asiya*), there are creations or there is the Divine. When we regard the Divine, there is nothing besides Him, yet when regarding the creations, we perceive only the creations, while the Divine is not evident, at least not directly.

---

8. It has been observed that the *Zohar* does not state, "He and His life forces and His attributes are one," that they possess the same "oneness." Rather, it states, "He and His life forces are one… He and His attributes are one." On a particular level and in a specific way, God is one with the lights, and in a different way He is one with the vessels. This distinction is very significant, and it is referred to in several places. For example, in *Torah Or* (71a), it is explained that the soul descends into the body so that it may ascend and be elevated from the level of "He and His attributes are one" to the level of "He and His life forces are one."

9. The fifth Lubavitcher Rebbe, Rabbi Sholom Dovber Schneerson (see *Sefer HaMa'amarim* 5669, p. 32), writes that the reference to *Etz Ḥayyim* here is to the beginning of chap. 2 in *Sha'ar* 42 (*Derushei Atzilut, Beria, Yetzira, Asiya*) of that work. He notes that the author of the *Tanya* expressly states, "As written in *Etz Ḥayyim*," which indicates that he does not maintain, like the *Pardes Rimmonim*, that the vessels of *Atzilut* are a limiting force, but are not limited themselves.

IT IS NECESSARY TO ACHIEVE AN UNDERSTANDING

☞ This phrase and other, similar ones are common in hasidic discourses. They refer to a kind of thinking that is not the same as "a question and its answer." A question signifies more than a lack of understanding. It represents a void, something flawed in one's previous understanding. This is not in itself a bad thing. On the contrary, it is part of a healthy process of thinking and developing one's understanding. Nonetheless, even after the answer is given, the question remains. It provides a glimpse into chaos, disorder, and darkness. In this vein, the *Zohar* states that all difficulties and disputes are from the side of evil and strife (*Zohar* 3: 124b; see also epistle 26). In contrast, "One needs to understand" is not intended to answer a question or resolve a difficulty. Consequently, it does not bear the negative implications of a difficulty or a discrepancy. Generally speaking, it raises no problem with the matter itself. Rather, the issue lies with the individual, who does not understand and who "needs to" understand. On a deeper level, as is explained in epistle 26, this is the difference between the inner dimension of the Torah and its revealed dimension. The revealed Torah is concerned with this world, the realm of matter and *kelippa* (husk), and therefore its purpose is to dispel difficulties, resolve disputes, and so forth. In contrast, the inner dimension of the Torah is concerned mainly with the higher levels of reality. These levels are more "transparent," for the divine light itself is revealed in them. Consequently, the inner dimension of the Torah is direct and is not articulated through concealment and "difficulties." Of course, this is not an absolute rule, for there are many hasidic discourses that begin with difficulties. Nonetheless, such difficulties usually appear at the beginning of the discourse, which is situated in the lower realm. As the discourse progresses into the inner, more spiritual realms, the language and style change to reflect the idea of "One needs to understand."

VESSELS HAVE LIMITS

☞ In a discourse in *Derekh Mitzvotekha* (s.v. "*veshavta*," p. 169a), the third Lubavitcher Rebbe, Rabbi Menaḥem Mendel Schneersohn, cites a different approach. He explains that the statement of the *Zohar* "He and His attributes are one" indicates that the vessels in the world of *Atzilut* are truly infinite, like *Ein Sof*. The "vessel" in *Atzilut* is the Infinite One's capacity to limit, and this capacity must be no less infinite than His capacity to reveal and illuminate. Accordingly, that which is limited is not the vessel itself but rather its action, its limitation of the light. The vessel itself is infinite and is therefore one with *Ein Sof*. In a comment at the end of the discourse, the third Lubavitcher Rebbe states that the approach of the author of the *Tanya* here is different: He maintains that the vessels themselves are limited and quantifiable. The third Lubavitcher Rebbe adds that we should particularly trust the words of the author of the *Tanya* here, since he wrote them in the days immediately preceding his passing, as mentioned in the introduction to this epistle. A similar idea is mentioned in *Lessons in Tanya*, citing *Or HaTorah* (*Vayetze* 182b).

אָמְנָם הַכַּוָּונָה הִיא לוֹמַר שֶׁהֵן אֱלָקוּת לִבְרוֹא יֵשׁ מֵאַיִן כְּמוֹ הָאֵין סוֹף

But the meaning is that they are divinity with respect **to creating existence from nothingness, like *Ein Sof*,**

In truth, the light of *Ein Sof* is not one with the vessels. The *Zohar* is speaking of a different kind of unity: the unity of action. Two objects that are completely disconnected can be united through an action that is unique to them alone. Here, there is an action that only God can perform: creating existence from nothingness. This does not refer to creating something from something else that already exists, but rather something new from absolute nothingness. This kind of creation is also found in the vessels of *Atzilut*, in relation to the created worlds. With respect to the higher realm of *Atzilut*, the creations are truly "existence from nothingness." This explanation is founded on the idea that the dividing line between the Divine and the world, between existence and nothingness, runs between *Atzilut* and *Beria*. *Atzilut* is not essentially a "creation." Consequently, within this line between *Atzilut* and *Beria*, and particularly in the vessels of *Atzilut*, which are what "move" into *Beria*,[10] God's capacity to create "existence from nothingness" is revealed.

Unity of action does not mean that the two perform exactly the same action. Rather, the action that *Ein Sof* alone performs is revealed within the vessels of *Atzilut*. It can be manifest only in these vessels.[11]

To help us understand this matter, the author of the *Tanya* begins by explaining the meaning of "existence from nothingness." Like many abstract concepts, it is impossible to explain this phrase by itself. Instead, it is juxtaposed to a similar yet distinct concept.

וְלֹא בִּבְחִינַת הִשְׁתַּלְשְׁלוּת עִילָּה וְעָלוּל לְבַד

and not simply through the unfolding succession of cause and effect.

---

10. This can be seen in the realm of speech: The "vessels" of speech are the letters, and the letters are what pass from one person to another. It is explained in Kabbala that the vessels of *Malkhut* (Kingship) of *Atzilut* become the soul of the worlds of *Beria*, *Yetzira*, and *Asiya*.

11. See the comment of the Lubavitcher Rebbe, Rabbi Menaḥem Mendel Schneerson, printed in *Lessons in Tanya*.

Everything in reality originated from something that existed before it. There are two main ways in which this occurs: "existence from existence" and "existence from nothingness." "Existence from existence" occurs by way of "unfolding succession": Each object evolves from a different object,[12] and from every reality, another reality is created. The relationship between two objects is that of cause and effect. The causal relationship operates in two directions: top-down and bottom-up. Top-down refers to the fact that the "effect" is created from the "cause," while bottom-up refers to the "effect" recognizing its "cause." In contrast to the relationship between cause and effect, "existence from nothingness" refers to an entirely new creation that is formed from total nothingness. There is no causal connection between creator and that which is created. The creation is not the outcome of any other creation that had a prior existence. The Creator created it, but the creation plays no role in the act of creation. There was no process, causal or otherwise, that preceded it, to which it has a connection. That which is "above" the creation is not physical matter or a "cause": It is "nothingness."[13] Therefore, there is no "bottom-up" perspective through which the creation can comprehend its Creator.

"Existence from existence" resembles how a person creates objects from other objects, such as a vessel that one forms from clay and energy. Similarly, a human being can connect two thoughts. He can relate an outcome to its cause and thus understand the origins that brought about the outcomes that he is able to see. Consequently, it is stated in Kabbala that "unfolding succession" refers to the relationship between the created worlds, *Beria*, *Yetzira*, and *Asiya*, and between the

---

12. As the author of the *Tanya* writes elsewhere, "Unfolding succession (*hishtalshelut*) is like a chain (*shalshelet*) in which each link is attached to the next one, without any break in between them" (*Likkutei Torah*, Song 42b).

13. The relationship of "existence from nothingness" between the world (and humanity) and the Divine plays a role in the general human difficulty with recognizing the existence of the Divine. There are clear-cut ways to attain all other things in this world. These ways may be long and difficult, but they are observable and provable. However, with regard to the Divine, there is a chasm that cannot be crossed. This jump of creation, of "existence from nothingness," cannot be replicated by a person through his understanding and knowledge.

components of each of these worlds, all the way down to the spaces in the physical world of *Asiya*. In contrast, "existence from nothingness" does not refer to the connections between the worlds, but to the connection between the Divine and the worlds. *Ein Sof*, the Divine, can be defined as the Creator of "existence from nothingness." As described above, the same connection exists between *Atzilut* and the worlds of *Beria, Yetzira,* and *Asiya*, for *Atzilut* is not like those worlds. Rather, it is the manifestation of *Ein Sof* as He creates the worlds "from nothingness." ☞

וּמַה שֶּׁכָּתַב הרמ"ק עִנְיַן הִשְׁתַּלְשְׁלוּת, עִילָּה וְעָלוּל, וְכֵן הוּא בַּזּוֹהַר הַקָּדוֹשׁ פָּרָשַׁת בְּרֵאשִׁית הַיְינוּ בְּהִשְׁתַּלְשְׁלוּת הַסְּפִירוֹת בַּסְּפִירוֹת עַצְמָן

As for that which Rabbi Moshe Kordevero wrote, that unfolding succession occurs through cause and effect, and the same is implied **in the holy *Zohar*, *Parashat Bereshit*, that is referring to the unfolding succession of the *sefirot* within the *sefirot* themselves**

"EXISTENCE FROM NOTHINGNESS" AND THE METHOD OF STUDYING THE CONCEALED TORAH

☞ An interesting point arises below that relates to the study of the concealed Torah. After the author of the *Tanya* defines the *sefirot* of *Atzilut* as "nothingness," for they cannot be grasped in the worlds of *Beria, Yetzira*, or *Asiya*, he goes on to refer to them as something that may be spoken about, described, and debated. The same matter is thus addressed from different angles. At one time it is referred to as "nothingness," beyond human thought, and elsewhere it is referred to as "existence," a reality that is spoken and thought of. In truth, on our level, we have no real comprehension of this matter. The words and concepts that we have are mere symbols and markers of the essences that bear the same names. Nonetheless, because there is a connection between the higher realm and the lower realm, true knowledge and sensation are present on our level, and they are capable of moving from level to level, from the physical realm to the spiritual realm, and ultimately from level to level within the spiritual realm. This explanation deals mainly with the relations between the terms. We are able to change our perspective and see the matter on a different level. However, since we cannot see or comprehend its essence, but can only discuss its relative reality, we should be very cautious when engaging with it. This engagement relies mainly on information and principles passed on by the rabbis to their most perceptive students. It lies in the intricacies of thought and sensation that are acquired with time and effort.

Rabbi Moshe Kordevero[14] and the *Zohar* (1:19b and onward) also speak of the connections between the *sefirot* of the world of *Atzilut*. These sources appear to contradict that which is written here, that unfolding succession occurred only in the worlds of *Beria*, *Yetzira*, and *Asiya*. However, they are referring to unfolding successions between the *sefirot* of *Atzilut*, not to the unfolding successions that occur in relation to the other worlds.

Unfolding succession can occur only between components of the same entirety. Consequently, it occurs within the created worlds, but not between the Divine and the creations. Just as it occurs within the boundaries of *Beria*, *Yetzira*, and *Asiya*, it happens within the world of *Atzilut* as well. The "world of *Atzilut*" is not like the other worlds, yet it is still a world in the sense that it is a "whole." It is an entity of divine revelation and of supernal *sefirot*. It is a world with respect to the divine essence, which is at more elevated and loftier levels. Therefore, there can be "unfolding succession"[15] between the *sefirot* of *Atzilut*, even though relative to us, *Atzilut* is the "nothingness" that is beyond unfolding succession, and we are elements of "reality," which are transmuted from one another.

(בִּבְחִינַת הַכֵּלִים) (with regard to the vessels).

One can speak of unfolding succession with regard to the vessels of the *sefirot* of *Atzilut*, but not with regard to the lights within those vessels. The lights within *Atzilut* are absolutely simple. They are the

14. *Pardes Rimmonim*, *Sha'ar* 6 (*Seder Amidatan shel HaSefirot*), chap. 6. Rabbi Moshe Kordevero was one of the greatest kabbalists prior to the Arizal, and it is said that he outlined the central tenets of Kabbala that prevailed before the Arizal's time. Although Lurianic Kabbala has been generally accepted in the Jewish world, hasidim continue to refer to Rabbi Moshe Kordevero's teachings as well, as can be seen here and elsewhere. This is based on the understanding that Hasidism, and the hasidic approach to all things, incorporates both systems of Kabbala. Neither Kabbala negates the other.

15. "Within the *sefirot* themselves" means from *Ḥokhma* to *Bina* (Understanding), from *Bina* to *Zeir Anpin*, and from *Zeir Anpin* to *Malkhut*. However, with regard to that which is above it, *Ḥokhma* itself is "existence from nothingness." Likewise, *Malkhut* is "existence from nothingness" with regard to the worlds that descend from it (see *Sefer HaMa'amarim* 5666, p. 338).

direct illumination and revelation of *Ein Sof* Himself. There is one revelation, and it is not divided into different levels. Therefore, there is no unfolding succession between levels with respect to the lights, but only with respect to the vessels.

This parenthetical statement pertains to *Atzilut* in particular since that is where the lights are first enclothed in the vessels. Lights are not really enclothed in vessels before *Atzilut*. Furthermore, in the worlds below *Atzilut*, light is the outcome of unfolding succession. It descends from a light that has already been enclothed in vessels.

They are called "*beli ma*" ("nothingness"; see Job 26:7) **in *Sefer Yetzira*, for they do not have a substance and a defined essence,**

שֶׁנִּקְרָאוֹת 'בְּלִי מָה' בְּסֵפֶר יְצִירָה שֶׁאֵינָן בִּבְחִינַת יֵשׁ וּמַהוּת מוּשָּׂג

The ten *sefirot* that are one with *Ein Sof* are called *beli ma*,[16] connoting *beli mahut*, "without essence." In any case, they lack a comprehensible essence.

Although we are talking about a defined number of *sefirot*, which have a defined essence, they are called *beli ma*. This is because we, who are "creations," cannot comprehend them. Our comprehension is limited to the realm of "existence," or "substance." "Substance" can be defined and related to, while "nothingness" is totally incomprehensible. The essence of the *sefirot* lies in the realm of "nothingness." We can comprehend this realm's existence, but not its essence.[17]

like *Ein Sof*, whom no thought can comprehend at all, as it is written, "But My face shall not be seen" (Ex. 33:23),

וּכְמוֹ הָאֵין סוֹף, דְּלֵית מַחֲשָׁבָה תְּפִיסָא בֵּיהּ כְּלָל וּכְמוֹ שֶׁכָּתוּב: "וּפָנַי לֹא יֵרָאוּ" (שמות לג,כג)

16. They are referred to this way in *Sefer Yetzira*, chap. 1, *mishnayot* 2–8. For example, "The ten *sefirot* of *beli ma* are analogous to the ten fingers," "The ten *sefirot* of *beli ma*, their measure is ten that have no end," "The ten *sefirot* of *beli ma* appear like a flash of lightning and they have no end."

17. See epistle 19 regarding the difference between the prophets' comprehension and the Sages' comprehension. See also *Likkutei Torah*, Deut. 6a.

With regard to our comprehension, the essence of the *sefirot* is the same as *Ein Sof*, God Himself, who is of course above and beyond the ten *sefirot*.[18]

Moses asks God, "Please show me Your glory" (Ex. 33:18), and God answers him, "You will see My back, but My face will not be seen" (Ex. 33:23). This statement can be understood to relate to all of human understanding: The "face," which is in the spiritual, inner realm, can never be comprehended. It is comparable to a person's inner self, what he thinks and feels, as opposed to what he communicates to others. A human being can never convey his true inner self to someone else, and this is all the more true with regard to God's "face": It cannot be seen or understood. Only God's "back," that which He reveals to the outside, that which relates to the creations and to the particular individual, can be comprehended by that individual.

Generally speaking, the *sefirot* of *Atzilut*, which are united with God, are part of the "inner realm." On the other hand, God's revelation in the worlds is the expression of His "external dimension." His revelation in the worlds is analogous to the way an individual speaks to others or performs an action in this world. In contrast, His revelation in *Atzilut* corresponds to that which the person understands and feels within his soul. Concerning the revelation of a person's spiritual faculties such as knowledge or love, it is impossible to distinguish between the soul and the faculties through which the revelation takes place, for the person, his soul, and its faculties are one. So too with regard to the Divine, the understanding within the level of *Atzilut* is divine understanding, which is understood by God. Likewise, *Ḥesed* of *Atzilut* is divine *Ḥesed*, and so forth. This is the unity between God and the *sefirot* of *Atzilut*. In any case, that which He understands, we do not understand.

If even Moses himself could not comprehend the essence of the *sefirot* of *Atzilut*, which constitute God's "face," where did his comprehension of these levels come from, and furthermore, where does our (external) comprehension of these levels come from?

---

18. It is stated in the introduction to *Tikkunei Zohar* (17a), "*Pataḥ Eliyahu*," that no thought can grasp *Ein Sof*.

וּנְבוּאַת מֹשֶׁה רַבֵּינוּ עָלָיו הַשָּׁלוֹם וְהַשָּׂגָתוֹ הָיְתָה מִפֶּרֶק עֶלְיוֹן דְּנֶצַח דז"א.

while the prophecy of Moses our teacher, may he rest in peace, and his comprehension, was from the upper portion of *Netzaḥ* of *Zeir Anpin*.

As explained in epistle 19, Moses' (inner) comprehension did not extend to the inner realm of *Atzilut*, but only to its external dimension. Human beings cannot comprehend the divine intellect and understanding that is manifest in the *sefirot* of *Ḥokhma*, *Bina* (Understanding), and *Da'at* (Knowledge). They can, however, comprehend the effects and expression of the divine intellect within the *sefirot* of *Atzilut*, which are referred to in Kabbala as the *partzuf* of *Zeir Anpin*, or "Small Face." In fact, the effects and expression of the divine intellect can be comprehended only in the lower *sefirot* of *Zeir Anpin*: *Netzaḥ*, *Hod* (Splendor), *Yesod* (Foundation), and *Malkhut* (Kingship). These *sefirot* relate to the outside: to the created beings and their perceptions. The author of the *Tanya* is explaining that Moses' comprehension came from below and reached the highest point of *Netzaḥ*. ☞

COMPREHENSION FROM THE UPPER PORTION OF *NETZAḤ* OF *ZEIR ANPIN*

☞ It is believed that within the *sefirot* there is also a division between the inner dimension and external dimension, and that there are *sefirot* whose very purpose is to "translate" the inner dimension and convey it to the outer realm. By definition, these *sefirot* contain some kind of instrument enabling the comprehension of the other.

The *sefirot* are divided into three groups. The first is made up of *Ḥokhma*, *Bina*, and *Da'at*; the second of *Ḥesed*, *Gevura*, and *Tiferet* (Beauty); and the third of *Netzaḥ*, *Hod*, and *Yesod*. Elsewhere, the *sefirot* are divided "vertically," into right, left, and middle "arrays": *Ḥokhma*, *Ḥesed*, and *Netzaḥ* make up one array; *Bina*, *Gevura*, and *Hod* make up another; and *Da'at*, *Tiferet*, and *Yesod* comprise the third. However, the groups mentioned here constitute a "horizontal" division of the *sefirot*. These groups correspond to the "top," "middle," and "bottom," just as the human body can be divided into head, body, and legs, and the soul can be divided into intellect, emotion, and recognition (this refers to the recognition of higher levels. On this level, emotion and consciousness are attained only in the form of an instinct to act in a certain way). These three fundamental levels proceed from the highest to the lowest and from the innermost to the outermost: The cognitive sefirot, *Ḥokhma*, *Bina*, and *Da'at*, form the innermost level. They are the essence that precedes manifestation, like the intuitive, or external under-

The author of the *Tanya* now returns to his main point. In order to explain his earlier statement that the *sefirot* are divine with respect to creating existence from nothingness, but not with respect to transmutation, he expounds on the concept of transmutation.

וּבְהִשְׁתַּלְשְׁלוּת, הֶעָלוּל הוּא מוּקָּף מֵהָעִילָּה וּבָטֵל בִּמְצִיאוּת אֶצְלוֹ **In an unfolding succession, the effect is encompassed by the cause, and is subsumed in its reality,**

As stated above, unfolding succession refers to the connection between cause and effect. This is a close and essential connection: The effect is not separate from the cause, but is encompassed within it. The author of the *Tanya* states that the effect does not have its own essence. Unlike when something is created "from nothingness," nothing about it is obviously new. Rather, it develops and detaches from the existing entity.

כְּזִיו הַשֶּׁמֶשׁ בַּשֶּׁמֶשׁ **like the radiance of the sun in the sun,**

This idea can be better understood through a physical example, which is cited several times in the *Tanya*.[19] Light cannot be separated from its

standing that comes before the manifestation of the object within the soul. *Ḥesed*, *Gevura*, and *Tiferet* are the "body," the expression of the object within the soul itself. Finally, *Netzaḥ*, *Hod*, and *Yesod* are the relationship between that expression and other beings. They relate to the external beings and address the question of whether and how to flow toward them.

This division into three parts is likewise found within each *sefira*. Each *sefira* consists of three "portions." The "upper portion of *Netzaḥ* of *Zeir Anpin*" is thus the highest section of the highest *sefira* of the "external" *sefirot*. In other words, it is the highest level with respect to all that is comprehensible. This was the level of Moses' comprehension. Nonetheless, "My face," the inner dimension of the *sefirot* of *Atzilut*, is incomprehensible. These *sefirot* are "*beli ma*," like *Ein Sof* Himself. No one can enter their realm, the realm of "nothingness," which does not exist within the vessels or concepts of the creations.

However, as is explained at length in epistle 19, this is referring to the inner comprehension of an object's essence, as, for example, prophetic comprehension. It cannot reach any higher than the upper portion of *Netzaḥ* of *Zeir Anpin*. In contrast, the external comprehension of an object's reality and essence can reach higher. This is seen, for example, in the comprehension of the kabbalists.

---

19. *Likkutei Amarim*, chap. 33; *Sha'ar HaYiḥud VeHa'emuna*, chaps. 3, 10.

source. It has no reality in and of itself. If it is separated from its source, then it does not exist.

As is explained in the *Tanya*, it sometimes seems as if the light is a separate entity. For example, the sunlight that shines on the earth appears to exist independently of the sun. However, this is only because we cannot see the sun itself when we see this light. Likewise, divine light (and speech) appears to exist independently because we do not see the divine Speaker at the same time. God, however, is present everywhere, and thus the most appropriate analogy is to sunlight that is within the sun itself. There, it is clear that the sunlight is not a separate entity, but is encompassed within the sun.

The effect is encompassed and subsumed in the cause: another example. Elsewhere in the works of Chabad,[20] an additional example is brought, which pertains to the human, spiritual experience: the example of a teacher and student. The teacher has his own intellect and way of understanding, and the student has his. Before the teacher begins teaching, the student's intellect is encompassed within that of the teacher. The teacher's intellect incorporates every aspect of what he knows and has known in the past. Even after the teacher has finished teaching and the student's intellect exists within the student, ostensibly separate from the teacher's intellect, it is still encompassed within the teacher's intellect. The entirety of the student's learning is like a light that emanates from the teacher's intellect. It is completely subsumed in the teacher's intellect and has no essence of its own.

כְּמוֹ שֶׁכָּתוּב בְּפַרְדֵּס מֵהָרְמַ״ק (שער ו פרק ו). **as written in *Pardes* Rimmonim, by Rabbi Moshe Kordevero** (6:6).

Pardes Rimmonim discusses the unfolding succession that occurs between the *sefirot*: In unfolding succession, the effect is subsumed and encompassed within the cause; thus there can be no reality of "existence from nothingness," whether between the *sefirot* or between the different spiritual levels in the higher worlds.

---

20. See *Likkutei Torah, Derushim LeRosh HaShana* 56a. See also *Or HaTorah*, Deut., vol. 5, p. 2106, which refers to this letter; this is mentioned in *Tanya im Likkutei Peirushim.*

וְאַף גַּם צִמְצוּמִים רַבִּים מְאֹד לֹא יוֹעִילוּ לִהְיוֹת גֶּשֶׁם עָב כֶּעָפָר מֵהִשְׁתַּלְשְׁלוּת הָרוּחָנִיּוֹת מִשְּׂכָלִים נִבְדָּלִים **And even a very great many constrictions will not be effective to form physical matter as dense as dust, from the unfolding succession of spiritual from transcendent intellects,**

"Transcendent intellects" are entirely spiritual and are wholly distinct from our material conceptions. Consequently, physical matter cannot be transmuted from them. There are a certain number of stages of constriction and unfolding succession that must take place for a small "existence" to evolve from a greater one. However, when there is no connection between two entities, when they are not on the same conceptual plane, no number of constrictions or transitions can link them. Thus the transition from spiritual to physical is an example of "existence from nothingness." ☞

אֲפִילוּ שֶׁל הַמַּלְאָכִים **even of the angels,**

THE TRANSITION FROM SPIRITUAL TO PHYSICAL

☞ It may be said that the path from *Ein Sof* to the worlds consists of successive unfolding successions, and that in between these unfolding successions, there are also transitional stages of "existence from nothingness." These stages reveal the infinite gap between above and below, which cannot be bridged by any number of steps. Although this is an extremely complex subject, and these stages are in fact present relatively or in actuality in everything, it is possible to generally identify three of them: The first is between *Ein Sof* and the world of *Atzilut*, the second is between the world of *Atzilut* and the created worlds, and the third is between spiritual reality and physical reality. Although the distance between these three stages is great, they belong to the same distinctive class, and they parallel one another. Therefore, although this letter mainly discusses the transition between *Atzilut* and the created worlds, it relates to the other stages as well, both above *Atzilut* and below it, all the way down to the lowest point of all, where physical matter is created.

Unlike transitions that take place on higher levels, we are able to sense, in our world, the transition between the spiritual and the physical. We can observe unfolding successions within physical forms: Matter becomes matter; matter becomes energy; inanimate matter becomes organic matter; simple matter is transformed into a complex structure, and so forth. Likewise, we can observe spiritual unfolding successions. This refers to different spiritual, mental, and social concepts that are connected to each other and that give rise to one another. However, the transition between the spiritual realm and the physical realm remains concealed from us. We know that it exists, but we cannot observe it directly, nor determine the ex-

Unlike the divine intellect, which is all-encompassing, angels are distinct spiritual beings. They are appointed to connect the Divine, which is separate and infinite, to the creations within the worlds. Even the greatest angel relates only to one part of the world. For example, each animal on the divine chariot, such the face of the lion, the face of the ox, and so on (see Ezek. 1:10), relates to one aspect of creation. Although these beings possess immense spirituality, they are each concerned with only one aspect of creation, and thus cannot bring about the creation of physical reality, no matter how many stages are involved.[21]

אֶלָּא לִהְיוֹת רוּחַ הַבְּהֵמָה מִפְּנֵי שׁוֹר **except in there being an animal spirit from "the face of the ox,"**

The angel that is "the face of the ox" on the divine chariot cannot create a physical ox. However, it can create the "spirit" of the ox.

Every physical reality in the world has a spiritual force that gives it life. The "animal spirit" is the unique abstract form of a specific animal. The "face of the ox," on the other hand, is the general spiritual force pertaining to the concept of "the animal." It is the source of all animals, and of all the "animalism" found in human beings and in the world. There is a vast distance between the "face of the ox" and the "animal spirit." In one sense, they signify the full scope of what the mind is able to perceive, from the smallest detail to the general rule that applies to a

act point at which the spiritual becomes physical or vice versa. The reason is that this transition is not merely a constriction (or an expansion) of light and of life force. Rather, it is a transition to an entirely different realm, which the forces and beings of the first realm cannot penetrate. The term "transcendent intellects" signifies concepts that are separate from the material world and are not revealed within it. No thought process can comprehend these concepts, and no number of steps or constrictions can connect them to physical matter. No matter how many constrictions take place, they will all remain in the realm of "transcendent intellects" and will never enter the physical realm.

21. The Lubavitcher Rebbe, Rabbi Menaḥem Mendel Schneerson, elucidates the phrasing of the *Tanya* with the following insertion: "even [the 'transcendent intellects'] of the angels" (*Lessons in Tanya*).

matter in its entirety. Nonetheless, even this extends only as far as the animal spirit, and not to the physical animal itself. The final stage, the transition from individual spirituality to physical reality, is not merely an additional step in the process. It is a transition of a different kind. It does not constitute "existence from existence," but rather "existence from nothingness."

כְּמוֹ שֶׁנִּתְבָּאֵר בְּמָקוֹם אַחֵר וְעַיֵּין שָׁם. **as explained elsewhere; see there.**

These other works written by the author of the *Tanya*[22] are not mentioned to provide a source for the matter under discussion, but rather to expand on it. The emphasis here is on the great descent of "existence" from "nothingness." In *Torah Or*, however, the emphasis is on the ascent within "existence." Existence is on a very low level, but due to this very fact, we can understand that its origins are exceedingly high. The vast disparity attests not only to the lowliness of the lower realm, but to the loftiness of its supernal source, which is so high that it cannot be comprehended below. When a source is in the realm of comprehension (and unfolding succession), the lower realm is subsumed in it and is not "existence from nothingness." However, when the source is so high that it cannot be comprehended, that which is created from it can sense itself to be "existence from nothingness," meaning it was created from the high source but does not perceive any relationship between them.

5 Tishrei
2 Tishrei (leap year)

וְיֵשׁ מֵאַיִן נִקְרָא 'בְּרִיאָה' בִּלְשׁוֹן הַקּוֹדֶשׁ **And** something coming into being as **existence from nothingness is called "*beria*"** (creation) **in the sacred tongue** (Hebrew).

The term "*beria*" describes the transition, the leap, from "nothingness" to "existence." Regardless of the number of stages of evolution, of cause and effect, that may be traversed, none can lead from "Creator" to "creation." Likewise, there is no sequence of thought and comprehension

22. This appears to be referring to what was later published in *Torah Or* 90b, s.v. "*yaviu levush malkhut*," according to the comment of the Lubavitcher Rebbe, Rabbi Menaḥem Mendel Schneerson, printed in *Lessons in Tanya*.

through which a creation is able to comprehend its Creator. As stated, something akin to this leap is found also in the created worlds, between the spiritual realm and the physical realm. Regardless of the number of steps that may be taken, the spiritual cannot become physical, and likewise, the physical can never comprehend the spiritual with the means at its disposal. ☞ ☞

וְהָגַם שֶׁהַיֵּשׁ הַנִּבְרָא הוּא גַּם כֵּן כְּלָא חָשִׁיב קַמֵּיהּ דְּהַיְינוּ שֶׁבָּטֵל בִּמְצִיאוּת

Granted that the entity [*yesh*] **that was created is also considered nothingness before Him; that is, it is subsumed in His** divine **reality,**

When we say that a particular creation is "existence from nothingness," this means that it is not subsumed in the Creator. Rather, it perceives itself to be an "existing" being. The author of the *Tanya* explains that this does not mean that the creation truly is an "existence." Instead, it

THE "NOTHINGNESS" THAT IS NOT "EXISTENCE"

☞ The "nothingness" discussed here is not referring to naught, to that which does not exist, but rather to that which cannot be conceived of by the creations. Rambam speaks of this in a different way in his explanation of negative theology (see *Guide of the Perplexed* 1. 58). It is impossible to describe the Creator by means of positive attributes: We cannot say that He "is" any particular attribute. We cannot even say that He exists, because this associates Him with our reality's definition of "existence." The only way we can define God is through negation; for example, by saying that He is not nonexistent. This is similar to what is stated here: The Creator is "nothingness" in the sense that He cannot be included within any definition of "existence."

THE SACRED TONGUE

☞ Through the Hebrew language, we are able to understand the true, definitive meaning of a word, and not merely what a particular individual intended when he uttered it. This is because this language did not originate through agreement among human beings about the definitions of specific words. Rather, the sacred tongue is composed of the true name for every object. As explained in *Sha'ar HaYiḥud VeHa'emuna*, the letters and words of the sacred tongue are what create, sustain, and give life to the objects that they name. Whether an object is physical or spiritual, its Hebrew name is its essence and life force. Although there are several words that appear to be synonymous with *beria*, such as *yetzira*, *asiya*, and even *ha'atzala*, the exact meaning contained within the word *beria* is "existence from nothingness" (See Ramban, Gen. 1: 1, s.v. "*ve'ata shema*").

appears to be an "existence," because from its perspective, the Creator is "nothingness." This is because the creation is not situated "before" the Creator, but rather is found behind barriers and concealments that obscure His presence, and as a result it seems as though He is not there. The creation is "existence" in the shadow of the Creator. It is like a small light that shines in a shaded area. However, when the creation is "before Him," when the shadow is removed and the great light is revealed, and the Creator can be seen together with the creation, then the creation is like nothing. It is subsumed in the divine reality.

לְגַבֵּי הַכֹּחַ וְהָאוֹר הַשּׁוֹפֵעַ בּוֹ מֵהַכֵּלִים דְּעֶשֶׂר סְפִירוֹת דאבי״ע

in relation to the force and light which courses through it from the vessels of the ten *sefirot* of *Atzilut, Beria, Yetzira,* and *Asiya,*

The creation is not subsumed only to the essence and being of God, who is beyond the bounds of the world and of creation.[23] Rather, it is nullified also in relation to the *sefirot* in which God is revealed, and through which He creates and gives life to the worlds. The creations are thus nullified not only in the divine light within the *sefirot,* but also in relation to the vessels of the *sefirot.* Furthermore, they are nullified not only with regard to the *sefirot* of *Atzilut,* but also in relation to the *sefirot* of the other three worlds.

The world of *Atzilut* consists of ten *sefirot.* These are the universal *sefirot,* which pertain to all the worlds. In addition, each world has its own ten *sefirot*: the *sefirot* of *Beria,* the *sefirot* of *Yetzira,* and the *sefirot* of *Asiya.* In each world, the ten *sefirot* are the embodiment of the Divine: divine *Ḥokhma,* divine *Ḥesed,* and so forth. In other words, the Divine is revealed in each world through the *sefirot* of that world. For example, in the world of *Beria* there is *Ḥokhma* of *Beria, Ḥesed* of *Beria,* and so forth; and in the world of *Yetzira* there is *Ḥokhma* of *Yetzira,* and so forth. Thus with regard to each world, the divine revelation in the *sefirot* is akin to the "Creator" in relation to a creation. Likewise, it corresponds to the soul in relation to the body, light in relation to its vessel, and the spiritual dimension in relation to the physical dimension.

---

23. This is a comment of the Lubavitcher Rebbe, Rabbi Menaḥem Mendel Schneerson, printed in *Lessons in Tanya.*

שֶׁהַקַּו אוֹר אֵין סוֹף בָּרוּךְ הוּא מֵאִיר בָּהֶם **in which the line of the light of *Ein Sof*, blessed be He, illuminates,**

As explained at the beginning of *Etz Ḥayyim*, this line refers to the light that illuminates the space that remains after a constriction. It is called a "line" because it is an "inner" light that enters the vessels. In contrast, light that is a "circle" encompasses the vessels but does not enter them. The source of the "circle" is the light of *Ein Sof* in its pre-constriction state. The "line" is therefore the divine light that illuminates the worlds through the vessels of the ten *sefirot*. The divine light illuminates divine *Ḥesed* within the vessel of *Ḥesed*, divine *Ḥokhma* within the vessel of *Ḥokhma*, and so on. The vessels, which are the *sefirot* in the different worlds, adapt the light to each particular world. For example, the *sefira* of *Ḥesed* of the world of *Beria* reveals a light of *Ḥesed* that pertains to *Beria*. In any case, the divine light, which is the light of the primordial line, radiates part of the light of *Ein Sof* in all of the *sefirot* within all of the worlds. Consequently, even though the light of *Ein Sof* passes through the *sefirot*, all creations are nullified before it, just as they are subsumed to the Creator Himself.

וּכְזִיו הַשֶּׁמֶשׁ בַּשֶּׁמֶשׁ, כְּמוֹ שֶׁנִּתְבָּאֵר בְּלִקּוּטֵי אֲמָרִים חֵלֶק ב. **like the radiance of the sun in the sun, as explained in *Likkutei Amarim*, part 2.**

It is explained in *Sha'ar HaYiḥud VeHa'emuna* (chap. 3) that the nullification of the creations in relation to the Creator is analogous to the nullification of sunlight within the sun. Sunlight has no reality in and of itself, separate from its source. Likewise, the light of the "line" and all the creations that exist within it are completely subsumed to the Divine, the source of this light.

This analogy, which was already mentioned in this letter, is cited here once again in order to emphasize the asymmetry that it contains. On earth, sunlight is perceived as a real, self-contained "entity," because we do not see it alongside the sun itself. However, on the surface of the sun, this light is nothing.

הַיְינוּ קַמֵּיהּ דַּוְקָא, שֶׁהִיא יְדִיעָתוֹ יִתְבָּרֵךְ מִלְמַעְלָה לְמַטָּה אֲבָל בִּידִיעָה שֶׁמִּמַּטָּה לְמַעְלָה הַיֵּשׁ הַנִּבְרָא הוּא דָּבָר נִפְרָד לְגַמְרֵי, בִּידִיעָה וְהַשָּׂגָה זוֹ שֶׁמִּמַּטָּה, כִּי הַכֹּחַ הַשּׁוֹפֵעַ בּוֹ אֵינוֹ מוּשָּׂג כְּלָל וּכְלָל

Yet this applies specifically "before Him," which is His knowledge, from above to below. However, with regard to knowledge that is from below to above, the created entity is a completely separate thing, in this knowledge and comprehension from below, as the force that courses through it is not comprehensible in the slightest.

With regard to the sun, there can be light that is "before" the sun, within the sun itself, and light that is far from the sun and concealed from it. However, the meaning of "before Him," with regard to God, is unclear, for God is everywhere, and nothing is "external" to Him or distant from Him. The author of the *Tanya* defines this term: "Before Him" pertains to God's knowledge of the creations, from above to below. The creations' reality is entirely nullified in this knowledge. In contrast, the creations' knowledge, from below to above, is a limited knowledge that cannot comprehend *Ein Sof*. Accordingly, within this knowledge a creation is a real entity, and the incomprehensible Divine is "nothingness." ☞

THE "NOTHINGNESS" OF THE DIVINE AND THE "NOTHINGNESS" OF THE CREATIONS

☞ This is a matter of perspective. A person who looks toward the heavens sees the divine "nothingness," for he is incapable of "seeing." Likewise, from above, the person's "nothingness," and the "nothingness" of all of creation, are evident, for the creations are truly subsumed in the Divine. As has already been stated, creation that is "existence from nothingness" signifies an absence of connection, a gap that cannot be bridged. Therefore, just as the Creator is "nothingness" from the creation's perspective, the creation is "nothingness" from the Creator's perspective. However, there is a significant difference: The Creator is "nothingness" from the creation's perspective because the Creator is totally incomprehensible to the creation, which experiences itself as "existence." On the other hand, from the Creator's perspective, "nothingness" means that the creation has no existence of its own, separate from the Creator's reality. The Creator's "existence,"

וְגַם אֵין עֲרוֹךְ זֶה לָזֶה כְּלָל וּכְלָל **Also, there is no comparison between them whatsoever,**

In addition to the fact that created "existence" cannot possibly comprehend the force that forms and sustains it, and accordingly, it constitutes an "existence" that is not nullified, there is an ontological disparity between them, not merely an epistemological one.

This is a crucial point, because an ontological gap means that the "existence" is not merely an illusion. Rather, it is a reality that is desired by God. It has a purpose, and it exists as a result of His inner will. The idea that it is "existence from nothingness" because it cannot comprehend its source through *da'at taḥton* is an important element of its divine service. It can nonetheless be subsumed in God's knowledge, for its entire being is dependent on God's knowledge. ☞

however, is unending. It is one "existence," which precludes all other "existence."

This is analogous to a one-way mirror. One side of the mirror is transparent, while on the other side, the individual sees only himself. Likewise, from God's perspective, reality is transparent: It has no existence in and of itself, but is an unbroken continuation of the divine light, the light of the "line." On the other hand, from the lower realm, the individual sees only his own existence, while the Divine is imperceptible: It is "nothingness."

Elsewhere (*Siddur im Divrei Elokim Ḥayyim* 44b; *Torah Or* 15a, 19d; *Likkutei Torah*, Deut. 24a), the author of the *Tanya* refers to these two viewpoints in terms of the verse "The Lord is the God of knowledge" (I Sam. 2:3). One is *da'at taḥton*, lower knowledge, that of the creations, which proceeds from below to above. The other is *da'at elyon*, the Creator's knowledge, from above to below. The verse indicates that God possesses both of these types of knowledge. From above, He sees the worlds and their nullification, yet He also sees the individual's heart in the lower realm. On the larger scale, God "knows" with *da'at taḥton* as well as *da'at elyon*. This means that He perceives the "existence" of the lower realm, and through this knowledge, He "exists" and is significant. Accordingly, the knowledge with which we know ourselves and the world is not completely false or an illusion. There are certainly falsehoods and distortion, but there is also true knowledge regarding this world and every being within it. Furthermore, there is true purpose to our life and to our endeavors in Torah and mitzvot within this "existence."

THERE IS NO COMPARISON

☞ This means that the "nothingness" of the Divine and the "nothingness" of the creations have no common factors or concepts that would allow us to say that one contains "more" of a certain thing and the other contains "less." Consequently, there is no way to compare them directly. They cannot be found in the same place, nor in the same conceptual space. If one is present, the other cannot be there.

לָא מִינֵּיהּ וְלָא מִקְצָתֵיהּ מֵהָעֵרֶךְ שֶׁמֵּהֶעָלוּל אֶל הָעִילָּה, שֶׁהֶעָלוּל יוֹדֵעַ וּמַשִּׂיג אֵיזֶה הַשָּׂגָה בְּעִילָּתוֹ וּבָטֵל אֶצְלוֹ עַל יְדֵי יְדִיעָה וְהַשָּׂגָה זוֹ

not from the whole nor from part of it, from the value of the effect to the cause. For the effect knows and attains a certain comprehension of its cause and is nullified in relation to it by means of this knowledge and comprehension.

While "existence from nothingness" signifies a relationship in which no comparison can be made, a "cause and effect" relationship incorporates comparison. The cause is in the same conceptual realm as the effect. This pertains to the effect's highest level, the summit of its comprehension. On this level, the effect is able to comprehend the reality and essence of the cause, the fact that the cause is the source of its existence. Consequently, the effect perceives itself as nullified in relation to the cause.

וְגַם בְּמַהוּתָם וְעַצְמוּתָם אֵין הֶפְרֵשׁ גָּדוֹל כָּל כָּךְ, רַק שֶׁזֶּה עִילָּה וְזֶה עָלוּל

Likewise, with regard to their existence and essence there is no great difference, only that this is a cause and this an effect,

In terms of their essence, cause and effect belong to the same realm and their essence is aligned in the same manner. The difference between them pertains to their respective levels: One is higher and the other is lower. Nonetheless, they are successive levels. ☞

וְלָא מִינֵּיהּ וְלָא מִקְצָתֵיהּ, מֵהַהֶפְרֵשׁ שֶׁבֵּין מַהוּת הַיֵּשׁ הַנִּבְרָא לְמַהוּת הַכֹּחַ וְהָאוֹר הַשּׁוֹפֵעַ בּוֹ לְהַוּוֹתוֹ

but there is not the slightest measure **of the difference between the essence of a created entity and the**

CAUSE AND EFFECT IN THE INTELLECT AND EMOTIONS

☞ Cause and effect are not two separate entities. They are two sides of the same coin. They are made up of the same elements, and as a result, they are able to relate to one another. Only the scope differs, and the relationship between the entities that define them. Intellect and emotion are an example of cause and effect. Emotion incorporates intellect, and intellect incorporates emotion. In other words, both contain both. The difference between them is that the emotions within the intellect are cognitive, while the intellect within the emotions is emotive.

מֵאַיִן לְיֵשׁ וְלָכֵן נִקְרָא ׳יֵשׁ מֵאַיִן׳ דַּוְקָא.

essence of the force and light that courses through it and brings it to existence from nothingness. Therefore, it is called specifically "existence from nothingness."

The difference between cause and effect is not the same as the difference between a created being and the force that causes it to exist. Like this force, the cause influences the effect and brings it into existence. However, the force is essentially distinct from the creation. It is neither of the same type, nor of the same order of magnitude. Consequently, the creation is called "existence" in comparison to this force, which is called "nothingness." That which forms the creation is of a completely different essence. It is incomprehensible and is not found on the same plane of reality, and as a result, we refer to it as "nothingness." ☞

In order to clarify what he wrote at the beginning of this letter, that

TRUE "EXISTENCE" AND "NOTHINGNESS"

☞ The Lubavitcher Rebbe, Rabbi Menaḥem Mendel Schneerson, remarks that it is also truly "existence from nothingness" (*Lessons in Tanya*).

This may be inferred from the repeated statement that "existence" comes from "nothingness" not only in the sense it cannot comprehend the "nothingness" that forms it, but also in the sense that there is an essential difference between them. Thus "existence" is not a reality only from its own perspective, due to the fact that it is unable to perceive that which forms it. Rather, it is a genuine reality. It does not arise only from "below to above," but also from "above to below."

The objective definition of "nothingness" is one of nullification. It refers to a higher reality in which the light of *Ein Sof* is not concealed, but enters from all sides. As a result, this reality is truly part of the essence of *Ein Sof*. There are no limits demarcating it as a separate entity. Thus, it is not "nothingness" only from the perspective of "existence" in the lower realm. Rather, it is true "nothingness," as seen from the perspective of *Ein Sof*.

Likewise, the great wonder of creation, the immeasurable distance between the Creator and the creation, which does not even partially correlate to the difference between cause and effect, is expressed through the idea that "existence" is formed from "nothingness." Consequently, "existence" does not refer only to a creation's inability to comprehend the Creator. Rather, it has its own unique purpose and significance.

Elsewhere, it is explained that creation is called "true existence from nothingness" because its source is like nothingness: It is insignificant relative to God Himself. For example, God's kingship, and the name by which we call Him, are mere glimmers of His true essence (*Likkutei Torah*, Deut. 19d, 1b; Num. 86a at length).

the *sefirot* are like the Divine with respect to the creation of "existence from nothingness," the author of the *Tanya* has explained the concept of "existence from nothingness." He explained that the term *beria*, creation, pertains to this concept. "Existence," the creation, stands on one side of an infinite and incomprehensible chasm, and on the other side there is "nothingness," the Creator. Now, the author of the *Tanya* goes on to explain that the border between "existence" and "nothingness" is not only the border between this world and the essence of *Ein Sof*. It relates also to the more subtle and complex definitions of "existence" and "nothingness." This allows space for the concept of the *sefirot* as the Divine with respect to the creation of "existence from nothingness."

6 Tishrei

וְהִנֵּה רֵאשִׁית הַיֵּשׁ הַנִּבְרָא וּתְחִילָּתוֹ הֵן הַכֵּלִים דְּעֶשֶׂר סְפִירוֹת דבי"ע

Now, the beginning of the created entity and its initial state are the vessels of the ten *sefirot* of *Atzilut, Beria, Yetzira,* and ***Asiya,***

The phrase "the beginning of the created entity and its initial state" indicates that the created entity does not comprise one fixed point but rather a wide range of levels and definitions. The line separating the Creator from the creation is not a fixed one. Instead, there are various fine lines that wind between the worlds, between the lights and the vessels, and between the definitions of "existence" and "nothingness," as will be explained below. ☞

THE CREATED ENTITY AND THE ENTITY OF *ATZILUT*

☞ The term "created entity" indicates that there are also "entities" of "existence" that are not created. In the world of *Atzilut*, too, there is "existence." It is known as "emanated existence," as will be explained below. This is comparable to the concept of *Ḥokhma* as "existence from nothingness" with regard to that which is above it, and of *Bina* as "existence from nothingness" with regard to *Ḥokhma*, as well as other concepts, which will be discussed below. The broad term "existence" refers to anything that becomes revealed, that advances from a place that is not an "entity" to a place that is an "entity." The "entity" in the world of *Atzilut* is not a real entity of "existence," one that perceives itself as a separate being. Rather, it is a particular expression of the Divine. While it is subsumed to the Divine, it forms a reality that is also distinct, in its own unique way, from the divine unity. In contrast, the "created entity" is true "existence." Its vessel conceals the Divine to some extent, causing it to perceive itself as separate from God.

"The beginning of the created entity" refers to the vessels of the ten *sefirot* of the worlds of *Beria, Yetzira,* and *Asiya*. It was explained above that each world has ten *sefirot*. They are the revelation of the Divine in that world, which forms the world and sustains it through *Ḥokhma, Ḥesed, Gevura,* and so forth. Thus, the term "created entity" chiefly refers to the created worlds themselves, as well as all that they contain. The divine light that shines in a particular world is the light of the ten *sefirot* of that world, and "the beginning of the created entity" is a reference to the vessels of these *sefirot*.

The *sefirot* occupy a unique position between *Ein Sof* and the creations. From the perspective of the creations, the *sefirot* are an expression of the Divine and there is no separation between them and the Divine. However, from the perspective of *Ein Sof*, the *sefirot* are distinct essences, light within vessels, which relate to the "created entity." In this sense, the line between "existence" and "nothingness" passes through the *sefirot* as well, and the precise location of its passage is yet to be determined. The first distinction is between the "lights" and the "vessels." This is why the author of the *Tanya* states here that the beginning of the created entity relates to the vessels.

וְגַם הָאוֹרוֹת נֶפֶשׁ רוּחַ וְנִבְרְאוּ מִבְּחִינַת הַנְּשָׁמָה דְּעֶשֶׂר סְפִירוֹת דִּבְרִיאָה יְצִירָה עֲשִׂיָּה שֶׁהוּא אֱלֹקוּת

and also the lights – *nefesh* and *ruaḥ* – were created from the level of the *neshama* of the ten *sefirot* of *Beria, Yetzira,* and *Asiya,* which is divinity,

Moreover, within the category of the "lights," there is another, more subtle distinction that concerns "the beginning of the created entity."

With regard to the light within the *sefirot*, there are different levels, just as there are in the soul that inhabits the body. These levels are *nefesh, ruaḥ,* and *neshama*. *Neshama,* the highest level, is the expression of the Divine, the Creator, both in relation to the vessels of the ten *sefirot* and in relation to the light on the levels of *nefesh* and *ruaḥ*. The levels of *nefesh* and *ruaḥ* pertain to the "created entity." ☞

וְהֵן הַלָּמֶ"ד כֵּלִים דְּמַלְכוּת דַּאֲצִילוּת.

and they are the thirty vessels of *Malkhut* of *Atzilut*.

The *neshama* animates, with divine vitality, the *sefirot* in the created worlds. This level of "*neshama*" in each world – *Beria, Yetzira,* and *Asiya* – derives from the thirty vessels of *Malkhut* of *Atzilut.*[24]

As explained previously, the world of *Atzilut* is the expression of the Divine in relation to the created worlds. The divine light flows from there. It becomes enclothed in each of the other worlds and gives them life. The *sefira* of the world of *Atzilut* that descends and is enclothed in the other worlds is *Malkhut.*

The formation of any "created entity" that is separate and distinct occurs in the *sefira* of *Malkhut.* Just as human speech is a spiritual force that connects to others, divine speech, *Malkhut* of *Atzilut,* is the attribute that relates to the "created entity." As stated elsewhere, the essence of *Malkhut* is the concept of "There is no king without a nation."[25] Kingship has no reality unless the king rules over other people who are separate from him and far inferior to him. *Malkhut* and sovereignty signify rulership over some other being. This being can be ruled over only if it perceives itself as separate. The attribute of

NEFESH, RUAḤ, AND *NESHAMA* IN THE DIVINE LIGHT OF THE TEN *SEFIROT*

☞ In the human soul, the *nefesh* is that which animates the body and the person's physical being, much like the soul of an animal. The *ruaḥ* gives life to the person's emotional vitality. Although this chiefly relates to the spiritual realm, it is concerned with the spiritual aspect of the physical experience the person's innate feelings and emotions. These are centered around the existential and experiential aspects of the individual's life: He desires something, or he does not desire it; he loves someone or fears them, and so forth. In contrast to these two levels, the level of the *neshama* is "divine." It alone relates to the divine soul and to that which is beyond the self and the world. The same three levels are present also in the light of the *sefirot* in every world: *Nefesh* and *ruaḥ* are levels of light that pertain to the worlds and the "created entities," while *neshama* is the expression of the incomprehensible "nothingness," the Divine, the Creator of "existence from nothingness."

24. Regarding the descent of the thirty vessels of *Atzilut* to the worlds of *Beria, Yetzira,* and *Asiya,* see *Siddur im Divrei Elokim Ḥayyim,* at the start of *Sha'ar HaKeriat Shema.*

25. See *Sha'ar HaYiḥud VeHa'emuna,* chap. 7. This phrase is very ancient. It is found in *Rabbeinu Baḥya al HaTorah,* Gen. 38:4, and *Kad HaKemaḥ, Rosh HaShana* 2. It is also quoted in *Emek HaMelekh; Megaleh Amukot;* and *Shela.*

Malkhut is thus the key to the existence of the separate "created entity." Any such reality, on any level, derives in one way or another from the *sefira* of *Malkhut*.

Malkhut is concerned with the "vessels." The lights embody that which is within, and the vessels signify the external dimension, that which relates to the other. In human communication, it is not the speaker's intentions and thoughts that are transmitted to the hearer. Instead, it is the letters of the alphabet, the "vessels" of speech rather than its "lights."

Why are there thirty vessels? Each set of ten *sefirot* is the expression of the Divine in relation to the specific world in question. Consequently, these frameworks are not mere unfolding successions that descend from the world that preceded them. Rather, the light within each set of *sefirot* is connected to the Divine within *Atzilut*, and to *Malkhut* of *Atzilut*. However, the *Malkhut* of *Atzilut* that gives life to the ten *sefirot* of *Beria* bears no resemblance to that which gives life to the *sefirot* of *Yetzira*, nor that which gives life to the *sefirot* of *Asiya*. The difference lies in the fact that there are three levels of vessels within *Malkhut*: internal, middle, and external. Thus, there are three levels, each of which comprises all of the ten *sefirot*, and these are the thirty vessels of *Malkhut*. The inner ten become the soul of the *sefirot* of *Beria*, and likewise, the middle ten are drawn into *Yetzira* and the external ten are drawn into *Asiya*.

וְכֵן בַּאֲצִילוּת מֵחִיצוֹנִיּוּת הַכֵּלִים דְּעֶשֶׂר סְפִירוֹת דַּאֲצִילוּת שֶׁהֵן אֱלֹקוּת 'נִבְרְאוּ' הַהֵיכָלוֹת דַּאֲצִילוּת

The same is the case for *Atzilut*: From the externality of the vessels of ten *sefirot* of *Atzilut*, which are divinity, the palaces of *Atzilut* were "created,"

Even within the world of *Atzilut*, there is a comparable transition from that which is divine to that which is worldly, from "nothingness" to "existence." There is "existence" in the world of *Atzilut*, although it is more subtle than the "existence" in other worlds. It is not a true "created entity," but rather what is referred to elsewhere[26] as "emanated

---

26. See *Hemshekh Ayin Bet*, vol. 1, p. 212, 394; vol. 2, p. 815. See also the note on this concept above.

existence." Nonetheless, in terms of the inner dimension of *Atzilut*, this too is "existence from nothingness."

The ten *sefirot* of *Atzilut*, the lights and the vessels of that world, reveal the Divine, not only in relation to the worlds of *Beria*, *Yetzira*, and *Asiya*, but also in relation to the reality that they create in *Atzilut* itself. This is the transition that is referred to here. The reality that is formed is known as "the palaces of *Atzilut*," and it constitutes "existence" with respect to the *sefirot* of *Atzilut*. ☞

PALACES OF *ATZILUT*

☞ Unlike the *sefira* of *Malkhut*, the higher *sefirot* of *Atzilut* do not relate to "existence," which is truly separate from them. Likewise, human speech relates to other people, while one's spiritual faculties, his intellect and emotions, are not revealed to others. A person's feelings and insights are private and concealed, occurring within his soul.

Nevertheless, here we are discussing the external dimension of the vessels. A vessel's inner dimension is concerned with the vessel's relationship to itself and to the light within it: how it receives the light and unites with it. The vessel's external dimension, on the other hand, connects to that which is outside of it. A vessel's inner dimension is analogous to human emotion, while its external dimension is like the individual's connection to that emotion. In *Derekh Mitzvotekha* (156b), the third Lubavitcher Rebbe, Rabbi Menaḥem Mendel Schneersohn, brings another example to explain the difference between a vessel's inner and outer dimensions. The external dimension is likened to a knife or an axe. These bring the body's actions into the outer realm, enabling a person to perform the act of chopping. The verse states, "In wisdom [*Ḥokhma*] have You made them all" (Ps. 104: 24). This refers to the external dimension of the vessels of *Ḥokhma*. A vessel's inner dimension is like a receptacle, which does not act, but only receives and encompasses something else. The light of *Ein Sof* rests in the inner dimension of the vessels of *Ḥokhma*. For example, the inner dimension of love is the emotion of love, the love for another that is within me. The external dimension of love, on the other hand, is the sense of self that I gain from that love.

Such an entity (an "emanated entity") can also be compared to a thought that has not yet become a thought in the conventional and defined sense of the term. It is no longer part of the soul and its faculties. However, it receives from them, but it has not yet become something "well defined."

This is like an intersection of two infinite lines. Their very meeting defines, in some sense, that which is boundless from two opposite directions.

In any case, this external flow does not actually emerge outward (like the *sefira* of *Malkhut* that creates real worlds). However, it does "create" a kind of reality in relation to the world of *Atzilut*. It is not a created entity, but an emanated existence. Nonetheless, with regard to the divine light, it is regarded as "existence."

The author of the *Tanya* refers to this "existence" as "the palaces of *Atzilut*." As

שֶׁמִּתְלַבֵּשׁ בָּהֶן בְּחִינַת הָעִיגּוּלִים דְּעֶשֶׂר סְפִירוֹת

in which the aspect of the "circles" of the ten *sefirot* is enclothed,

As mentioned, palaces are a scope, rather than specific objects. Thus, the light that is enclothed in the palaces, which gives them life and sustains them, is that of the "circles." It is not an Inner Light, but an encompassing one, which creates an encompassing reality, that of the palace.

The aspect of the "circles" of the ten *sefirot* is enclothed in the palaces. As explained earlier, the light of the "line," is the Inner Light that moves from level to level and creates a connection of unfolding succession between cause and effect. This is an unbroken connection in which the effect comprehends its cause. Accordingly, the effect can never be a separate entity from the cause. The line is the light's path. It comprises one line that extends from above to below. In contrast, with regard to the Encompassing Light of the circle, the "receiver" is unable to comprehend it, and as a result, this light forms the reality of "existence." Although generally speaking, Encompassing Light is on a higher level than Inner Light, it facilitates the creation of the more distant reality, which is seemingly separate from its supernal source. As explained, this is the reality of the palaces, which resembles a world, and likewise, in a certain sense, a "vessel" and the human body. The light is not constricted in order to enter a particular boundary or vessel. Consequently, it encompasses a "whole." This encompassing "perimeter" is like a foundation upon which each object grows and develops

stated, in every world, there is the world itself, and there are its ten *sefirot*. The *sefirot* are the expression of the Divine in that realm, for God forms and rules each world through its *sefirot*. In the world of *Atzilut*, too, there are ten *sefirot*. In addition to creating the worlds of *Beria*, *Yetzira*, and *Asiya*, these *sefirot* also "emanate" a certain level of flow within the world of *Atzilut* itself. This is called "the palaces of *Atzilut*."

A palace is, in a certain sense, like a world. It is a space that accommodates a certain type of object, and where certain kinds of events take place. Similarly, in our world, there are different types of buildings: homes, banks, synagogues, and so forth. Each type of building is constructed in a particular way. These buildings contain certain types of objects, and specific individuals enter them in order to engage in the functions for which they were built. Likewise, each of the palaces has specific boundaries: the sanctum of love, the sanctum of repentance, the sanctum of the Messiah, and so on.

in its unique way. Thus, the palaces of *Atzilut* are the place within the world of *Atzilut* that contains the entities of "emanated existence."

וְגַם גּוּפוֹת הַמַּלְאָכִים דַּאֲצִילוּת, שֶׁהֵן בְּחִינַת 'יֵשׁ' **as well as the bodies of the angels of *Atzilut*, which are considered as "substance,"**

The bodies of the angels of *Atzilut* were likewise created from the external dimension of the vessels of the *sefirot* of *Atzilut*. The palaces of *Atzilut* are a "place," and every place has a "soul." This refers to beings that exist in that place and reveal its Inner Light. The angels of *Atzilut* are such beings. ☞

וּכְמוֹ שֶׁכָּתוּב: "וּבְמַלְאָכָיו יָשִׂים תָּהֳלָה" (איוב ד,יח) **as it is written: "And to His angels He attributes misconduct"** (Job 4:18) –

The simple interpretation of this verse is concerned with the deficiency of the angels.[27] "His angels" are the angels near Him, the angels in

ANGELS OF *ATZILUT*

☞ Notwithstanding the fact that they are on an extremely high level, the angels of *Atzilut* have an element of substance in relation to the *sefirot* and the light of *Ein Sof* that shines within the *sefirot*. This substance is the "body" of the angel. Angels, too, have a soul and a body (see *Siddur im Divrei Elokim Ḥayyim, Sha'ar HaḤanukka* 275d), spiritual and physical substance, which are comparable to the lights and vessels of the *sefirot*. The angel's light, its spiritual substance, is its nullification with regard to the Divine, and its "body" signifies the bounds of its reality.

The term *malakh*, angel, means emissary, for this is the role of the angel. Additionally, the angel has its own reality, through which it performs its task. It states in *Kuntres Aḥaron* (159a) that when an angel is engaged in carrying out its mission, it is referred to by God's name. However, it also possesses another name, which is used whenever it is not engaged in its mission. This name relates to the angel's role. In other words, when the angel is functioning as an emissary, its soul is the part of it that is active. Accordingly, it is an expression, or an extension, of the Divine, like the hand of God, and it is referred to by God's name. When the angel is not functioning as an emissary, its body is acting. This is its framing border, its unique character, and the way in which it is able to perform its task. The angel's "body" is the "existence" of the world of *Atzilut*.

---

27. Many commentators explain that the word *tahala* signifies light, as in the verse "When His lamp would shine [*behilo*] over my head" (Job 29:3). These

Atzilut. Just like God's servants in the lower worlds, the angels of *Atzilut* are deficient in some sense, despite the fact that they are His own angels and are close to Him.

שֶׁאֵינָן בִּבְחִינַת בִּיטּוּל לְגַמְרֵי כְּעָלוּל לְגַבֵּי עִילָּתוֹ.

for they are not entirely subsumed, like an effect in relation to its cause.

The word *tahala* in the verse comes from the term for light. The light of the angels is not perfect, for they are not entirely subsumed in holiness. The angels possess a body, which assigns to them their own reality and thus conceals the infinite divine light to some degree. As stated at the outset, an "effect" is completely subsumed in its "cause." Because the effect is able to comprehend its cause and the fact that it is the sole source of its entire existence, any feelings experienced by the effect necessarily derive from and exist within the cause. "Existence," on the other hand, whether large or small, occurs in the space that is not subsumed, in the fog that obscures its ability to perceive its source.

After explaining the meaning of "existence" in the world of *Atzilut* – the palaces and the bodies of the angels – the author of the *Tanya* goes on to discuss "nothingness," the beings in the world of *Atzilut* that are an expression of the Divine.

7 Tishrei
3 Tishrei (leap year)

אַךְ נִשְׁמוֹת הַמַּלְאָכִים שֶׁיָּצְאוּ מִזִּיוּוּג הַנְּשִׁיקִין

However, the souls of the angels that emerged through the act of **coupling of kissing,**

Unlike the bodies of the angels, their souls do not constitute "existence." Rather, an angel's soul is something more spiritual. It is like a flow of the light of the *sefirot* into the angel's reality. This spiritual flow is called "coupling of kissing." It is like the kiss of a human being, which constitutes a more spiritual connection relative to physical coupling. ☞ ☞

---

commentators also maintain that the term *lo*, "does not," applies to both the first and second parts of verse 4:18. Accordingly, they interpret this phrase as "And toward His angels He does not shine a light" (Ralbag; *Metzudot*). Others state that *tahala* relates to the term *holelot*, debauchery (Rashi; Ibn Ezra).

וְכֵן נִשְׁמוֹת הָאָדָם שֶׁיָּצְאוּ מִזִּיווּג דזו"נ דַאֲצִילוּת **and likewise the souls of man that emerged through the** act of **coupling of *Zeir Anpin* and *Nukva* of *Atzilut*,**

The human soul in *Atzilut* is on an even deeper level than the souls of the angels in *Atzilut*. For this reason, and because it is ultimately enclothed in a physical body, the human soul emerges through the coupling of *Zeir Anpin* and *Nukva*, whereas the souls of the angels emerge, as explained above, through the coupling of kissing. ☞

SPIRITUAL COUPLING

☞ What is "spiritual coupling"? When a person constructs physical objects, such as a house or a tool, the act is external to the individual. He does not put his inner essence into it, but only some degree of external will or intelligence. However, there is also a more spiritual form of creation, in which the person contributes of his true essence. For example, in addition to conveying information to his student, a teacher might also impart his own personal perspective. The same thing can occur, on various different levels, in the realm of nonmaterial creation: writing, artistic expression, and so on. This type of spiritual giving can occur only through "coupling," a deep connection that extends from a person's essence to a different space. While external creation does not require inner connection, here the bonding of one being with the other is essential.

COUPLING OF KISSING

☞ This is a kabbalistic concept that conveys spiritual coupling, in contrast to physical coupling. It is analogous to a kiss between two people, which does not constitute actual coupling, yet it comprises a convergence and a spiritual union. It expresses the intention and emotion that are felt regarding the union, sometimes even more than the act of sexual intercourse itself does. Since "coupling of kissing" is essentially a spiritual union of emotions, desires, and so forth, it engenders spirituality. This is referring to the souls of angels. The angel is a spiritual being, like an emotion or an idea. Even in the realm of *Asiya*, angels are not physical beings and do not inhabit physical bodies. Rather, they are concerned with the ideas and perceptions of action. The angels of *Atzilut* are on such a high spiritual level and are so firmly attached to the Divine that we possess virtually no connection to them. They do not belong to the worlds, but are God's own angels. Even if their "bodies," their external dimensions, contain some connection to worldly reality, and in this sense they constitute "existence," in their souls they are entirely one with God Himself. Accordingly, with regard to "existence," even that of *Atzilut*, these angels are "nothingness," the expression of the Divine.

SOULS AND ANGELS IN *ATZILUT*

☞ In every world and in all realms, the soul is on a deeper level than the angels (*Torah Or* 3b; and see *Likkutei Amarim*, chap. 39). The soul derives from the vessels' inner dimension, and the angel derives from the vessels' external dimension (see

The difference between these two types of "coupling" is like the difference between spiritual coupling and physical coupling.[28] The coupling of *Zeir Anpin* and *Nukva* is analogous to physical human coupling. This does not result only in the creation of a spiritual reality. Instead, it can produce an actual physical reality, another human being, who is not merely a spiritual illumination that derives from the father or mother, but rather is a real, complete reproduction of the father and mother. Likewise, in the higher realm of *Atzilut*, *Zeir Anpin* and *Nukva* embody the "male" and "female" in relation to the worlds. *Zeir Anpin* is the "small face" of *Atzilut*. It comprises the attributes that reflect the inner dimension of *Atzilut* in a way that relates to the worlds. *Nukva* is *Malkhut*, the source of all the worlds as they are manifest in *Atzilut*. This refers to the Divine Presence, which permeates everything and gives life to all things, even the very lowest, by means of divine life force. The coupling of *Zeir Anpin* and *Nukva* is thus the most comprehensive definition of the union of giver and receiver, of God and the worlds. While "coupling of kissing" is on a deep level, a kind of preparation for union within the divine being, the coupling of *Zeir Anpin* and *Nukva* constitutes a true union with *Malkhut*, with reality, and with the "other." From this type of union, the souls that are enclothed in a body in our world emerge, becoming separate beings. Each one is like a copy, or a "child," of God Himself.

קוֹדֶם שֶׁיָּרְדוּ לבי"ע אֵינָן בִּכְלָל 'יֵשׁ' וְדָבָר נִפְרָד בִּפְנֵי עַצְמוֹ, אֶלָּא הֵן מֵעֵין בְּחִינַת אֱלֹקוּת

before they descended to *Beria*, *Yetzira*, and *Asiya*, they are not in the category of "existence" and a separate thing in and of themselves. Rather, they are a kind of divinity

Likkutei Torah, Deut. 26c, and *Derushim LeYom HaKippurim* 70c). The angel is a kind of illumination that constitutes an outward revelation. The soul, on the other hand, is like a copy of the entire divine essence, a reflection of the whole structure of *Atzilut* as it is manifest in each world.

28. See *Torah Or* 4d.

The souls are destined to descend to the worlds of *Beria, Yetzira,* and *Asiya,* and to be enclothed in the physical body. However, before they descend, they are rooted in a higher realm, the world of *Atzilut.*

The souls are like something "divine" in the sense that they are not separate beings. They are a part of the divine and contain nothing that is not divine. However, they do not possess Godliness in all its infinite scope. A specific angel or soul has already been designated, and it will become a creation once it has descended into the created worlds and become enclothed in the vessels of *Beria, Yetzira,* and *Asiya.* However, while it is still in *Atzilut,* it is comparable to an internal desire or thought that relates only to the self, as though painting a picture on the inside that will correspond to the external actuality. In the supernal realm of *Atzilut,* this desire is united with the Divine, the One who desires and envisages it. However, there is still no connection to the worlds and their boundaries at this point. There is no consideration of precisely how and to what extent the soul will be manifest within these boundaries.

בְּצִמְצוּם עָצוּם **in an immense constriction.**

The souls are a kind of divinity, but immensely constricted. ☞

וּכְעֵין הַכֵּלִים דְּעֶשֶׂר סְפִירוֹת דַּאֲצִילוּת שֶׁהֵן בִּבְחִינַת גְּבוּל, עַל יְדֵי צִמְצוּם אוֹר הָאֵין סוֹף הוּא הַקַּו

And they are like the vessels of the ten *sefirot* of *Atzilut,* which are considered limits, by means of the constriction of the light of *Ein Sof,* which is the line

CONSTRICTION

☞ The author of the *Tanya* uses this kabbalistic term because the transition from *Ein Sof* to the souls within *Atzilut* resembles the fundamental transition to the world of *Atzilut* itself, even more than it resembles the transition of "existence from nothingness" from *Atzilut* to *Beria.* It parallels the earliest constriction, which is described in the works of the Arizal. Like that constriction, all constrictions relate in some way to the first stage of transition, the shift from the infinite to the finite, at which *Ein Sof* seems to stop being infinite. Accordingly, constriction is the source and essence of all limitations.

The souls in the world of *Atzilut* are like the vessels of the *sefirot* of *Atzilut*. As stated at the beginning of this letter, these vessels are united with the Divine. They are part of the divine "nothingness" rather than the "existence" in that realm.

The following passage applies to both the souls and the *sefirot* of *Atzilut*, although below, in the parenthetical statement and afterward, it seems to refer only to the souls.

The vessels of the *sefirot* and the souls in *Atzilut* are limited as a result of the constriction of the light of *Ein Sof*.

The dimensions of the constricted light of *Ein Sof* are severely limited. When this light enters the empty space formed by the constriction of *Ein Sof* and becomes enclothed in all the vessels and worlds, it is referred to in Kabbala as the "line." ☞

הַמְלוּבָּשׁ בְּנֶפֶשׁ רוּחַ נְשָׁמָה שֶׁלָּהֶם וּכְמוֹ צִמְצוּם הָרִאשׁוֹן לִהְיוֹת חָלָל וכו׳

that is enclothed in their *nefesh, ruaḥ,* and *neshama,* and like the first constriction, for there to be a void...

The "line" is the constricted light of *Ein Sof*, that is enclothed in the vessels. In *Atzilut*, the vessels are the ten *sefirot* of *Atzilut*, and in the soul, they are the levels of *nefesh, ruaḥ,* and *neshama*. It is well known

THE RAY

☞ This is a kabbalistic term that describes the light that shines in the space that remains after constriction. After the aforementioned constriction, when the void, the open, empty space, remained... there issued from the light of *Ein Sof* a single straight line from its circle light, from above to below" (*Etz Ḥayyim, Heikhal Adam Kadmon* 1: 2).

Thus, constriction affects the light of *Ein Sof*. It is important to note that it is a fundamental point in hasidic thought that *Ein Sof* Himself is not constricted in any way. Rather, as mentioned, His infinite will is constricted: the thought, light, and revelation of *Ein Sof*. This, however, is not the literal interpretation of the concept of constriction (see *Sha'ar HaYiḥud VeHa'emuna*, chap. 7; *Torah Or* 14b; *Hemshekh Samekh Vav*, p. 465). It forms a "void" in it, where the light of *Ein Sof* is constricted and not revealed. The "line" shines in this space. This refers to the light that is no longer infinite, as it was prior to constriction. It is not a line of *Ḥesed, Ḥokhma, Gevura*, or any of the other individual *sefirot*. Rather, it a general line that encompasses everything. It is the primordial "line," the light of *Ein Sof* after constriction. It is referred to as a "line" because it is like a straight line, in contrast that of the five levels of the soul – *nefesh, ruaḥ, neshama, ḥaya,* and *yeḥida* – the lower three souls' light is enclothed in these three levels as an inner light. In contrast, the soul's light shines within *ḥaya* and *yeḥida* as a surrounding light.[29]

The constriction of the line that is enclothed in the *sefirot* and souls of *Atzilut* is like a continuation of the very first constriction.

The significance of this statement, that the constricted light in the vessels of the *sefirot* and in the soul is like the first constriction, lies in the fact that the transition point from *Ein Sof* to the limited realm and the creations is not far beyond us, at the inception of the unfolding succession. Rather, it penetrates the *sefirot,* the worlds, and the soul. It may be said that this transition point, as well as the Infinite One Himself, is with us in all places, and is not found only in the realms far above us. ☞

to a circle. No point on the circumference of a circle is different from any other. The circle has no beginning or end. The points on the circumference cannot be compared and contrasted with regard to their dimensions and attributes, because they are all identical. Accordingly, the circle is analogous to *Ein Sof.* In contrast, a line has a beginning and an end. The line begins where it emerges from the circle of *Ein Sof.* It ends on the other side, where it extends into the created worlds, the worlds of "existence," until ultimately their essence becomes so substantial that it seems to obscure the light altogether. While the circle is the source of all the encompassing lights, the line is the source of all the inner lights, which enter and fill the worlds and vessels. The line thus signifies the entry of the infinite divine light into the limited realm.

THE FIRST CONSTRICTION

☞ This is a fundamental concept in Kabbala, which describes the first and most significant stage in the unfolding succession (see *Etz Ḥayyim, Heikhal Adam Kadmon* 1: 2; see also the beginning of *Otzrot Ḥayyim,* the beginning of *Mevo She'arim,* and *Likkutei Torah,* Lev. 51c). In the beginning of everything, there was God alone.

---

29. This does not pertain only to the soul: In Kabbala, these concepts are used also with regard to the worlds and the higher *sefirot,* which are compared to the levels of the soul. The light of the all-encompassing ray, which is the source of the Inner Light that descends into the worlds, is enclothed in the *sefirot* and vessels of *Atzilut,* which absorb and reveal the Inner Light. This occurs on three levels, which correspond to the three levels of the soul: The *partzufim* of father and mother correspond to *neshama, Zeir Anpin* corresponds to *ruaḥ,* and *Malkhut* corresponds to *nefesh.*

The following parenthetical statement relates to what was said above. The description of the order of unfolding succession, from the *sefirot* of *Atzilut* to the created worlds, addressed the unique status of the palaces, angels, and souls in the world of *Atzilut*. The palaces and the bodies of the angels are distinguished from the souls of the angels and the souls of human beings. The palaces and the bodies of the angels constitute "existence" in relation to the *sefirot*. The souls, on the other hand, are not

There was nothing apart from Him, and there was no "space" for anything.

It is important to note here that we are incapable of truly grasping the concept of *Ein Sof*. We lack the tools to relate to it. At most, we can think of it in terms of various analogies, each person in accordance with his capabilities and nature. Any understanding we reach relating to these matters is achieved this way.

In order to form a "space" for objects to exist, constriction occurred. Constriction does not involve the formation of any objects. It is only a withdrawal, so to speak, of the presence of *Ein Sof*. This leaves a "void," which is ostensibly free of *Ein Sof*. *Ein Sof* cannot be changed, diminished, divided, or limited, because from the moment it is touched, it is no longer *Ein Sof*. Thus we understand the first constriction in terms of a withdrawal of light. The light is not diminished or limited, but is entirely removed, forming a space that is totally empty. This is the essence of the first constriction.

It is important to understand that just as the light of *Ein Sof* is a divine force, its constriction, too, is a divine force. Consequently, the empty space is not truly free of the divine essence, but only of divine light and revelation. Accordingly, the light of the line that shines in the space reveals both elements: the light of *Ein Sof* and its constriction. It reveals and gives expression to the light of *Ein Sof*, for there is nothing else to reveal. Nonetheless, it also reveals that light's constriction, for the line is itself the light of *Ein Sof* that has been limited by constriction.

The term "the first constriction" indicates that there are other constrictions. Indeed, other constrictions in the unfolding succession are discussed in several sources. However, these are not absolute constrictions like the first constriction. Rather, they are constrictions in a simpler sense. They involve the concealment and reduction of light. Only the first constriction, which pertains to the "Absolute Infinite" that preceded everything, by necessity involves a complete withdrawal and the formation of an empty space, as explained. Nonetheless, the first constriction produced "aftershocks," reverberations that spread to other places in the unfolding succession. These expressions of constriction are found wherever there is an encounter of some kind between the infinite and the finite, even if it does not involve the light of *Ein Sof* as it was before the constriction, but is merely a manifestation of this light within the light of the line. As mentioned above, the manifestation of the light of *Ein Sof* within the line extends into the *sefirot* of *Atzilut*. Consequently, the limited vessels of the *sefirot* can come into being only through a constriction that is like the first constriction, where a void is formed and there is a complete withdrawal of *Ein Sof*.

"existence." They are not separate entities, but are a kind of expression of the Divine and the *sefirot*. However, this description of the souls pertains to when they are still in the world of *Atzilut*. The parenthetical statement addresses the possibility that certain souls could descend into the worlds in the same state that they are in in the world of *Atzilut*. Would these souls then be "existence" or "nothingness"?

(וְאַף גַּם לְאַחַר שֶׁיָּרְדוּ הַנֶּפֶשׁ רוּחַ נְשָׁמָה דַּאֲצִילוּת לְעוֹלָם הַזֶּה לַצַּדִּיקִים הָרִאשׁוֹנִים

(And even so, after the *nefesh*, *ruaḥ*, and *neshama* of *Atzilut* descended to this world, to the first tzaddikim,

Souls that descend to the worlds just as they are in *Atzilut* are conferred upon the great tzaddikim, those who possess what is called "a soul of *Atzilut*." Even while they are in the physical body, such souls think and feel as though they were in the world of *Atzilut*. ☞

SOULS OF *ATZILUT*

☞ All souls originate in *Atzilut*. All are enclothed in a physical body in the world of *Asiya*, and all act within this body. Nonetheless, there are different kinds of souls. The nature of their existence differs, as does their revelation on various levels. There are souls of *Asiya*, of *Yetzira*, and of *Beria*, and additionally, there are a very small number of souls of *Atzilut*. Each soul of *Asiya*, with its unique character, faculties, and experiences, is formed in the world of *Asiya*. Each one possesses roots and sparks in higher worlds, yet it exists in this particular form only in the world of *Asiya*. The same is true of the souls of *Yetzira* and *Beria*, which are enclothed in the body in the world of *Asiya*, but, with regard to their essential concerns and experiences, belong to higher worlds. Souls of *Atzilut*, however, are different. They are not formed or enclothed in other places or objects. Rather, wherever they are found, they manifest just as they are at their source, in *Atzilut*. They have the same unity with the divine light itself, not in the form in which it had been influenced and shined upon in the palaces and worlds. Like the souls in the world of *Atzilut*, they are "nothingness," as opposed to "existence," even in the world of *Atzilut*.

Elsewhere, the souls are referred to in terms of two different levels: the souls of *Atzilut*, and the souls of *Beria*, *Yetzira*, and *Asiya*. In *Torah Or* (74c and onward), these two levels are called the souls that are "the seed of people" and the souls that are "the seed of animals" (see Jer. 31: 26). Most of the souls throughout the ages have been souls of *Beria*, *Yetzira*, and *Asiya*, while souls of *Atzilut* were bestowed upon the few tzaddikim in each generation, such as the patriarchs and Rabbi Shimon bar Yoḥai (see *Likkutei Torah*, Song 19c). This is why the author of the *Tanya* refers to them here as "the first tzaddikim." It is also explained in *Torah Or* that what sets these early tzaddikim apart is their knowledge of God (see also *Torat Ḥayyim*, Ex., vol. 2,

אֶפְשָׁר שֶׁלֹּא נִשְׁתַּנָּה מַהוּתָן לִהְיוֹת דָּבָר נִפְרָד מֵאֱלֹקוּת, וְלָכֵן הָיוּ מִסְתַּלְּקוֹת כְּשֶׁרָצוּ לַחֲטוֹא בְּטֶרֶם יֶחֶטְאוּ.

it is possible that their essence did not change to become a separate thing from divinity, and therefore they would depart when they wanted to sin, before they would sin.

Even when they descend into this world, these souls are still in *Atzilut*. In all their manifestations, they comprise one essence and revelation, and it is united with God just like it is in the world of *Atzilut*.[30]

These souls do not become part of the physical world, but rather they are borne on it for as long as this remains possible. Since the Divine is completely concealed here, this world is capable of sin. Our

277a). They simply and truly know the Divine, just as we know the physical world. God's existence is like something they can see with their own eyes: It is plainly true. On the other hand, for the souls of the other tzaddikim and the *beinonim*, which are the souls of *Beria*, *Yetzira*, and *Asiya*, the divine reality is like something they have heard about from others: Even if they understand it and are convinced of its existence, they do not possess the same certainty as one who sees it for himself. At the root of this distinction is the fact that all souls descend to this world, but the descent of the souls of *Beria*, *Yetzira*, and *Asiya* occurs by means of enclothement in *Beria*, *Yetzira*, and *Asiya*, while the descent of the souls of *Atzilut* occurs simply by their passage through those worlds (*Haggahot LeDibbur HaMatḥil Pataḥ Eliyahu* [1898], p. 20). In other words, it is as though the souls of *Beria*, *Yetzira*, and *Asiya* are reborn and created anew in this world, as a new reality that does not recall or have any sense of its earlier reality in the world of *Atzilut*. These souls are found in the physical world and are enclothed in the garments of this world, which conceal the divine light from the soul. On the other hand, the souls of *Atzilut* only pass through the worlds, but are not enclothed in them. The physical world exists for them, but not as a reality in which they are confined. They are not compelled to think and feel only through this reality. Rather, it is like a world that belongs to someone else, a screen that obscures someone else's view. For the souls of *Atzilut*, everything is an expression and a revelation of the Divine as He is seen from above.

30. The Lubavitcher Rebbe, Rabbi Menaḥem Mendel Schneerson, comments (printed in *Lessons in Tanya*), "It is possible to connect this concept to the verse 'Moses Moses' (Ex. 3:4). There are no cantillation marks interrupting the two mentions of Moses in this verse. In contrast, in the phrase 'Abraham, Abraham' (Gen. 22:11), there is a break (*Torah Or, Parashat Mishpatim*; *Torat Ḥayyim, Parashat Mishpatim*)."

world can take on the form of *kelippa,* and this does not contradict its reality. The world's "reality" refers to the order of things, which can be seen as flowing from and receiving from the Divine, yet can also be seen as standing on their own. Thus, in its essence, the physical world can take on the form of sin and *kelippa.* This is not true in the higher worlds, and it is certainly impossible in the world of *Atzilut,* whose entire essence is a direct, unmediated expression of the Divine. Consequently, a soul of *Atzilut* can be in the physical world as long as there is no sin there, and all is arranged in a way that does not contradict the divine revelation. The world might not reveal the Divine, but in any event, it must not express the opposite. However, from the moment that the matter of "sin" arises as a possibility, the souls of *Atzilut* can no longer remain in the world, and they depart.[31]

The line between "existence" and "nothingness" in the world of *Atzilut* runs between the palaces and the bodies of the angels, which constitute "emanated existence," and the human souls and the souls of the angels, which constitute "nothingness." The author of the *Tanya* comments that there are other worlds beyond this, which, like the souls, constitute "nothingness," and not "existence."

וְקָרוֹב לוֹמַר שֶׁגַּם הָאֲלָפִים וּרְבָבוֹת עָלְמִין דְּיָתְבִין בְּגוּלְגַּלְתָּא דְּאָרִיךְ אַנְפִּין וּזְעֵיר אַנְפִּין, אֵינָן עָלְמִין מַמָּשׁ, כְּעֵין הַהֵיכָלוֹת דַּאֲצִילוּת וּבְחִינַת 'יֵשׁ', אֶלָּא כְּעֵין נִשְׁמוֹת הַמַּלְאָכִים שֶׁיָּצְאוּ מִזִּיווּג הַנְּשִׁיקִין

It is reasonable to say that even the thousands and myriads of worlds that are seated in the skull [*gulgalta*] **of *Arikh Anpin* and *Zeir Anpin* are not actual worlds, like the palaces of *Atzilut,* and considered a substance, but rather are like the souls of angels that emerged through the** act of **coupling of kissing**

31. In the same vein as the comment of the Lubavitcher Rebbe, Rabbi Menaḥem Mendel Schneerson, brought in the previous footnote, it is possible to link this concept to Hanokh. According to several hasidic sources, Hanokh was, like Moses, a soul from the first *shemitta,* the world that God created before ours. Hanokh was taken from this world before he had committed any sins (see Rashi, Gen. 5:24).

The "skull"[32] refers to *Keter* (Crown), which is higher than *Atzilut*. It corresponds to the human skull, which is superior to the brain and also encompasses it. Like the human souls and the souls of the angels, which were discussed in connection with the palaces of *Atzilut*, the worlds in the skull do not constitute "existence." They are not a separate entity, but rather are a kind of expression of the Divine. These spiritual manifestations arise from the spiritual "coupling of kissing." They are analogous to the emotions that result from a kiss between two people, in contrast to the actual, living child that results from physical coupling.

וְנִקְרָאוּ עָלְמִין לְגַבֵּי בְּחִינַת הַגּוּלְגַּלְתָּא וְדִיקְנָא) **and are called worlds in relation to the skull and beard.)**

These higher worlds, which are located in the skull, are referred to as "worlds," *olamot*. This word derives from the term *he'elem*, concealed. The Divine is concealed in these worlds. As a result, they perceive themselves as separate entities, as "existence," but only in relation to the skull and the beard. These worlds do not obscure the divine light in *Atzilut* at all. Nonetheless, they are called "worlds," because they conceal the Divine on a level that is higher than *Atzilut*: the level of the skull and the beard. ☞

WORLDS THAT ARE SEATED IN THE SKULL

☞ Like the definitions of many other kabbalistic concepts, this definition is relative. The more abstract a concept is, the harder it is to define without relating it to other concepts. A word or concept may carry different levels of meaning, depending on the frame of reference. Consequently, that which is not considered "existence" or a separate entity with regard to the world of *Atzilut* may be called a "world" and "existence" with regard to the skull and the beard.

Broadly speaking, the skulls of *Arikh Anpin* and *Zeir Anpin* are the "*Keter*" of these *partzufim*. They are analogous to the human skull, the bone that covers the brain. In the spiritual realm, they are the all-encompassing *Keter*, which is above the faculties of the intellect. The skull of *Arikh Anpin* is the *Keter* of the large "Long Face." This is the giant encompassing entity of all of reality, including the world of *Atzilut*. The skull of *Zeir Anpin* is the *Keter* of the "Small Face" of the world of *Atzilut*, which

32. Discussed in *Zohar* 3:128b.

Now, the author of the *Tanya* returns to that which he was discussing before the parentheses: The souls, which, like the *sefirot* of *Atzilut*, are a kind of expression of the Divine.

אַךְ אֵינָן אֱלֹקוּת מַמָּשׁ לִבְרוֹא יֵשׁ מֵאַיִן **Yet they are not actual divinity, to create existence from nothingness,**

These souls are like the *sefirot* of *Atzilut*. However, they are not exactly the same. As explained earlier, the *sefirot* of *Atzilut* are actually divine.

flows (on the necessarily small, constricted scale) directly to the forces that give life to the worlds of *Beria*, *Yetzira*, and *Asiya*, and the physical world. Thus, the worlds in the skulls of *Arikh Anpin* and *Zeir Anpin* are the worlds of the skull and *Keter* of *Atzilut*. Consequently, they are "worlds" and "existence" with regard to the skulls (just like the palaces of *Atzilut* constitute "worlds" and "existence" with respect to the world of *Atzilut*). However, the worlds of the skull are "nothingness," like the skull itself, with regard to the world of *Atzilut*.: With regard to the "beard" mentioned together with the skull, it is taught that the hairs of the beard are part of the flow from that which "encompasses" to that which is "within," from the skull and the *Keter* to the inner faculties: the intellect and the attributes. Accordingly, in relation to *Atzilut* and the other worlds, the beard is akin to the skull, which conveys supernal *Keter* to the worlds and gives it expression within them.

It is explained elsewhere that the worlds in the skull are in the state that precedes their becoming created worlds (see *Or HaTorah*, Ex., p. 199, which is cited by the Lubavitcher Rebbe, Rabbi Menaḥem Mendel Schneerson, in his comments; and see *Torat Shmuel* 5638, s.v. "*ve'amdu raglav*," section 12). This is analogous to a thought that precedes speech, or perhaps even to the stage that precedes thought. God created all the worlds by means of speech and letters. The created worlds – *Beria*, *Yetzira*, and *Asiya* – were created with the letters of speech. In contrast, the concealed, spiritual worlds are comparable to the letters of thought. Just as one's thoughts exist inside him and are not revealed on the outside, the worlds of "letters of thought" are likewise concealed. Thought is closer to a person's true, inner self than speech is. Through thought, a person expresses himself to himself. In contrast, speech relates to other people, in the external realm. With regard to the letters of thought, there are different levels. They become progressively smaller and more spiritual, until they are subsumed in and united with the person, on an even deeper level than his spiritual faculties, consciousness, and emotions. There is no separation whatsoever between the soul itself, its inner will, and these tiny letters, through which the individual expresses himself to himself. Nonetheless, they are still letters, and regardless of their size, they are a type of instrument that defines and creates content and conveys it from one place to another. Thus, these letters and worlds have been defined through some element of *Ein Sof*. Accordingly, they are referred to as "worlds" with regard to *Ein Sof*.

The shared aspect between God Himself and the *sefirot* is defined as the ability to create existence from nothingness. ☞

מֵאַחַר שֶׁכְּבָר יָצְאוּ וְנִפְרְדוּ מֵהַכֵּלִים דְּעֶשֶׂר סְפִירוֹת, שֶׁבָּהֶן מְלוּבָּשׁ הַקַּו מֵאוֹר אֵין סוֹף שֶׁהָאוֹר הוּא כְּעֵין הַמָּאוֹר

since they already emerged and were separated from the vessels of the ten *sefirot*, in which the line is enclothed, from the light of *Ein Sof*. For the light is like the luminary itself,

The souls came from the inner dimension of the vessels of *Atzilut*. They were not a separate entity, and were subsumed to the vessels. Nonetheless, once they emerged from the vessels, they were no longer the same thing. The line that comes from the light of *Ein Sof*, which carries the power of *Ein Sof* to form existence from nothingness, is no longer manifest in the souls: It does not act through them to create existence from nothingness.

Light is merely a glimmer of the luminary. Nonetheless, since

THE SOULS' SOURCE AND SITE OF REVELATION

☞ Elsewhere, it is taught that the souls' source is even higher than this. It is higher than everything else, a part of the supreme Divine (*Likkutei Amarim*, chap. 2). It states in several places that the souls of Israel are on a higher level than the Torah. For example, in *Bereshit Rabba* (1: 4), it states that the thought of Israel preceded everything, even the Torah. Furthermore, it is said that the level of the souls of Israel preceded even the constriction (*Sha'arei Ora* 77a; *Hemshekh Ayin Bet*, vol. 1, p. 169; see also *Torat Menaḥem*, vol. 18, p. 91, 108).

Nonetheless, here, the author of the *Tanya* is not discussing the general source of the souls of Israel, but rather the revelation and "birth" of specific souls in *Atzilut*. The souls of *Beria*, *Yetzira*, and *Asiya* are likewise revealed and "born" in those worlds, after which they descend and become enclothed in the body. Thus, the soul's reality, even in the world of *Atzilut*, is of a being that has already emerged and been born. The soul is a reality in its own world. In contrast, the *sefirot* are the divine revelation that creates and gives life to that world. However, it is explained elsewhere that through its descent into the worlds, its enclothement in the body, and its labor of overcoming and transforming evil, the soul ascends from its "created" reality. It becomes incorporated, like the *sefirot*, in a union of "He and His life forces are one." Consequently, the line that comes from the light of *Ein Sof* is enclothed in the soul just as it is enclothed in the *sefirot* (see *Sefer HaMa'amarim* 5656, p. 256; 5650, p. 288).

there is nothing in the light aside from the luminary, it transmits and expresses part of the luminary's essence that is "like the luminary" because what the light emits is a pure expression of the luminary's essence. ☞

הוּא מַהוּתוֹ וְעַצְמוּתוֹ שֶׁל הַמַּאֲצִיל בָּרוּךְ הוּא, שֶׁמְּצִיאוּתוֹ הוּא מֵעַצְמוּתוֹ, וְאֵינוֹ עָלוּל מֵאֵיזֶה עִילָּה שֶׁקְּדָמָה לוֹ חַס וְשָׁלוֹם.

which is the essence and being of the Emanator, blessed be He, and is not the effect of some preceding cause, God forbid.

The luminary's essence is that of emanator and creator. Nothing else emanated it. It emanates other entities, and it alone is the original source.

This kind of reality does not exist in our world, where every reality was preceded by a different one. Consequently, it is incomprehensible to the human mind. This is exactly what the author of the *Tanya* is teaching here: Beyond that which is familiar to us, there is something that is not created or emanated. Instead, it is the Creator and the Emanator, who is above all that is created and emanated. This is God Himself.

THE LIGHT IS LIKE THE LUMINARY

☞ God and the life force that flows from Him are compared to a luminary and its light (see *Or HaTorah, Inyanim*, pp. 110ff; *HaMa'amarim Melukat*, vol. 2, pp. 293ff; vol. 3, p. 106, 275). This ancient metaphor applies in several different ways. One of these is the idea of "the light is like the luminary." Light has no existence independent of the luminary. This does not pertain only to the moment when the light was formed, but to the entire duration of its existence. If the luminary is not emitting it, it does not exist. It has no other essence, no other features, and no other name. In its entirety, it is a particular revelation of the luminary. In reality, the light does not appear by itself. Rather, it is enclothed in vessels. As it moves further away from the luminary, it is enclothed in more and more vessels. These vessels are all different, and they increasingly conceal the light's source. Likewise, the "ray," in its entirety, is from the light of *Ein Sof*, whose source is in *Ein Sof* Himself. In the worlds of *Beria*, *Yetzira*, and *Asiya*, where the vessels are "existence" and are separate from the Divine, the light does not reveal *Ein Sof* or His might. Only in the world of *Atzilut*, where "He and His life forces are one; He and His attributes are one," is it revealed through the vessels, too, that the light is like the luminary.

וְלָכֵן הוּא לְבַדּוֹ בְּכֹחוֹ וִיכָלְתּוֹ לִבְרוֹא יֵשׁ מֵאַיִן וְאֶפֶס הַמּוּחְלָט מַמָּשׁ בְּלִי שׁוּם עִילָּה וְסִיבָּה אַחֶרֶת קוֹדֶמֶת לַיֵּשׁ הַזֶּה.

Therefore, He alone has the power and ability to create existence from nothingness and actual absolute nullity, without any other cause or reason that preceded this existence.

Since God was not created by something that preceded Him, He alone is able to create existence from nothingness. None of the creations or emanations can do so. Before God, there was no "existence," but only absolute and total nothingness.

The idea of God as "one" coheres with the idea of God as the Creator of existence from nothingness. God's unity makes it impossible for any other reality to coexist with Him. He alone, set apart from all the worlds, is able to start from absolute zero and create existence from nothingness.

וּכְדֵי שֶׁיִּהְיֶה הַ'יֵּשׁ' הַזֶּה, הַנִּבְרָא בְּכֹחַ הָאֵין סוֹף, בַּעַל גְּבוּל וּמִדָּה נִתְלַבֵּשׁ אוֹר אֵין סוֹף בְּכֵלִים דְּעֶשֶׂר סְפִירוֹת דַּאֲצִילוּת וּמִתְיַיחֵד בְּתוֹכָן בְּתַכְלִית הַיִּחוּד עַד 'דְּאִיהוּ וְגַרְמוֹהִי חַד' לִבְרוֹא בָּהֶן וְעַל יָדָן, בְּרוּאִים בַּעֲלֵי גְּבוּל וְתַכְלִית

In order for this "substance," which is created through the power of *Ein Sof*, to have a limit and measure, the light of *Ein Sof* becomes enclothed in the vessels of the ten *sefirot* of *Atzilut* and is united within them in the ultimate union, until "He and His attributes are one," creating with them and through them creatures of limits and finitude,

Just as the luminary, or Emanator, is infinite, the light that it emits is also infinite, for the light is like the luminary. However, "created entities" are by nature limited. By definition, a "substance," or "existence," must have a "border" that separates it from *Ein Sof*. In the phrase "He and His attributes are one," "He" refers to the luminary, as well as the light that is like the luminary, while "attributes" refers to the vessels of the ten *sefirot*, which are finite. Only through the complete union of these can finite creations be formed. The creations are brought into being by means of the finite *sefirot*, and the light that is enclothed in these *sefirot*. The phrase "limits and finitude" indicates that a creation's limits are its very end and purpose. The purpose of creation is realized through these limits. ☞

EXISTENCE FROM NOTHINGNESS

☞ This phrase does not pertain only to two separate stages: "nothingness" followed by "existence." The great secret of this matter relates to their union. "Existence from nothingness" refers to the "existence" that comes from "nothingness," that receives from it and knows that it is derived from it. "Nothingness" by itself is a concept in almost every human culture: There is a God, an Infinite One, somewhere out there in the heavens. Hasidism uses the talmudic term for this concept: "the God of Gods." He is not ours, and is not connected to us in any way. Rather, He is far beyond us (see *Likkutei Amarim*, chaps. 22, 24). "Existence" is likewise a concept that maintains numerous realms, worlds where the creations believe, whether wholly or partially, that they alone are responsible for producing what they have. The concept of "existence from nothingness," however, is tremendously deep and all-encompassing. It conveys the depth of the Jewish worldview that "existence" draws with all its strength and being from "nothingness." Existence is subsumed into nothingness, yet it exists by the will of nothingness. It has already been mentioned that the transition of "existence" from "nothingness," and the connection between them, is the central theme of this letter, which tracks the course of the transition and attempts to identify and define its paths in all realms. The union of "He and His attributes are one" is essential to this matter, because it is the spiritual union that lies at the source of "existence from nothingness."

It is stated in several places that this phenomenon has a parallel in divine service. "Existence from nothingness" is a movement of God, an act of the Creator that gives life to all worlds. In contrast, there are also movements from below: human acts, which are also known as "an awakening from below," and "the elevation of the feminine waters." These acts of worship are referred to in a number of places as "opposite" movements: "nothingness from existence" instead of "existence from nothingness." A person understands himself and what he perceives to be his needs through his "being": his intellect, desires, and emotions. When he nullifies his being to the unfathomable divine will and wisdom, he is nullifying the "existence" that is familiar and tangible to him, to "nothingness." The two movements are, of course, extremely different. Nonetheless, the human movement, which everyone experiences occasionally, illuminates, to some degree, the creation of "existence from nothingness," in accordance with the verse "From my flesh I will view God" (Job 19:26).

Although the transition from below, from "existence" to "nothingness," appears to be the opposite of the movement from above, it is actually the same thing. Since ancient times, the question has been asked: What are true "existence" and true "nothingness"? The "existence from nothingness" within creation is usually defined in accordance with our understanding: "Existence" is what we feel

וּבִפְרָט עַל יְדֵי הִתְלַבְּשׁוּתָן בבי״ע.

especially by means of their enclothing in *Beria, Yetzira,* and *Asiya*.

The created worlds, *Beria, Yetzira* and *Asiya,* and in particular this world, the physical world of action, constitute the main limits that are the purpose of the creations, and the final outcome of unfolding succession.

8 Tishrei
4 Tishrei (leap year)

אָמְנָם מוּדַעַת זֹאת שֶׁעִיקַּר הִתְהַוּוּת הַיֵּשׁ וְדָבָר נִפְרָד לְגַמְרֵי

However, it is known that the main coming into existence of a substance and an entirely separate entity

"Existence from nothingness" is not comprised of only one level. As mentioned, there is a subtle degree of "existence" in the world of *Atzilut,* and more discernible levels in the created worlds. Three additional levels are discussed here: "entirely," "separate," and "entity." Each one relates to one of the three created worlds: *Beria, Yetzira,* and *Asiya.* The lower down a world is in the unfolding succession, the darker and more closed off it is. The "existence" within it is more separate and pronounced, until ultimately it perceives itself to be completely independent, as though there is no higher force that forms it and gives it life. ☞

and perceive as "existence," and "nothingness" is whatever is beyond that. However, in truth it is the opposite: True "existence" is the eternal God, who brings everything into being, while "nothingness" is the mirage that appears to us to be "existence." Our task of transforming "existence" into "nothingness" actually means transforming false "existence," which is in fact "nothingness," into real "existence," which only appears to be "nothingness." In other words, the purpose of all our labor in this world is to create "existence from nothingness" just as God does. We must reveal the real, divine "existence" and "nothingness" within the false "existence from nothingness" found in creation.

THE LEVELS OF "EXISTENCE" IN HUMAN PERCEPTION

☞ Something akin to this occurs within a person's perceptions as well. The first stage is that of "I exist." This does not contradict the existence of anything else, namely God. It is not even distinct from God. Rather, it is the perception of one's own reality. Sub-

הוא מִמַּלְכוּת דַּאֲצִילוּת is from the *Malkhut* of *Atzilut*,

In order to connect to the finite creations, the light of *Ein Sof* is enclothed in all ten *sefirot* of *Atzilut*. However, the formation of the separate "existence" takes place primarily through *Malkhut* of *Atzilut*. This *sefira* gathers the light from all the *sefirot* and conveys it to the domain of the other worlds. Similarly, in the soul, *Malkhut* is speech, which combines the faculties of the soul – the intellect and emotions – and releases them in the appropriate form and garments so that others are able to receive them.

Apart from the fact that *Malkhut* is the last of the ten *sefirot* of *Atzilut*, and accordingly, it is the outcome of all their activities, there are also deeper reasons why *Malkhut* is the source of the other worlds' existence. The author of the *Tanya* goes on to outline these reasons.

שֶׁנַּעֲשָׂה עַתִּיק דִּבְרִיאָה which becomes the *Atik* Yomin (Ancient of Days) of *Beria*,

Malkhut of *Atzilut* is the *Keter* of the world of *Beria*. The inner dimension of *Keter* is called *Atik*. This signifies "ancient," or "beyond," or "detached," as in the verse "He who moves [*hama'etik*] mountains" (Job 9:5). The full name of this level is *Atik Yomin*: that which is beyond worldly time and dimensions. A physical crown that a person wears is not part of his body like his head or heart is. It is above him and separate from him, yet it belongs to him. Likewise, *Keter* belongs to the ten *sefirot*, yet it is distinct from them and connects to that which is beyond them. Essentially, *Keter* is the mediator between the ten *sefirot* and that which is above them. *Keter* of *Atzilut* is the mediator between the Emanator and the emanated, *Keter* of *Beria* is the mediator between *Beria* and

sequently, on less refined levels, the individual becomes more removed from the divine unity. He feels his own existence as an independent being that is separate from the reality above him. Only his intellect reminds him that there is "nothingness," a Creator, and tells him of the Creator's absolute oneness. On the lowest levels, in the reality of *kelippa*, the "existence" of the individual and the world can perceive itself as completely separate. One is able to conclude that even if God exists, He has no connection to, nor influence over, the details of worldly events. An entity may even become trapped in this realm of *kelippa*, where the Divine has no meaning and therefore no reality, and there seems to be nothing besides "existence."

Atzilut, and so forth. As with any mediator, *Keter* contains something from both of the levels that it connects. The external dimension of *Keter* relates to and encompasses the world and *sefirot* that are below it. This dimension is called *Arikh Anpin*: the long, large, all-encompassing face. On the other hand, the inner dimension of *Keter* is *Atik Yomin*. It is distinct from the world and *sefirot* that are below *Keter*. Instead, it relates to the reality that is above and beyond the ten *sefirot*. Thus, *Malkhut* of *Atzilut*, which becomes the *Atik* of *Beria*, is the source and sustainer of the world of *Beria*, yet at the same time, it is detached from it. This combination of impact and distance creates the reality of a separate "existence" below. It receives the flow of the life force and sustenance, yet it does not perceive *Malkhut* of *Atzilut*, which is "*Atik*," separate from it. Instead, it sees itself as a separate entity.

כִּי 'אֵין מֶלֶךְ בְּלֹא עָם' וכו' as "there is no king without a people..."

This concept is now explained in another way. The phrase "There is no king without a nation"[33] is mentioned in the ancient works in relation to the *sefira* of *Malkhut*. It indicates that this *sefira* exists and has meaning only when there is an "*am*." In its most basic sense, this is referring to an actual nation: the people over whom the king rules. The king cannot be called a king if he has no people to rule over. However, on a deeper level, the word *am* can be explained differently.[34] It derives from the term *imum*, dimming, as in the phrase "dying [*omemot*] coals." This refers to any object whose source of vitality and existence does not shine within it in a way that is clear and revealed. Rather, it is blurred and concealed. As a result, it is not subsumed to its inner source, but appears to be a distinct, independent entity. "There is no king without a nation" means that one is not "king" over himself or his children, for children are subsumed to their parents and are essentially united with them. He is "king" only over others.[35] Other attributes do not have this

33. This phrase appears in *Rabbeinu Baḥya al HaTorah*, Gen. 38:30; *Kad HaKemaḥ*; and elsewhere. See also *Sha'ar HaYiḥud VeHa'emuna*, beginning of chap. 7.

34. *Sha'ar HaYiḥud VeHa'emuna*, beginning of chap. 7.

35. *Sha'ar HaYiḥud VeHa'emuna*, beginning of chap. 7. Elsewhere, it states that he is also not "king" over the officials who enforce his commands, but only over the citizens who carry them out and who accept him as their sovereign. Furthermore,

requirement, even when they relate to others. For example, a person may possess the attribute of kindness. If there are other people around him, he can express this attribute through giving. However, even if he does not reveal his kindness, he is still a kind person: The qualities of kindness are found in his essence. With regard to the attribute of kingship (*Malkhut*), however, if the one who is ruled over is removed, nothing remains of the essence of kingship.

Malkhut refers to power and authority, and power is something that is held over others. There is no power involved if an act would have been carried out in any case. When a person's hand performs his will, for example, it has no choice in the matter and no desire to do anything else. There is power and *Malkhut* only when there is a conflicting desire that must be changed, whether by means of coercion or persuasion. As explained with regard to the phrase in the prayer book, "And His kingdom they willingly accepted upon themselves," *Malkhut* exists only when it is willingly accepted by another.[36] ☞

וְגַם רִיבּוּי הַנִּבְרָאִים וְהִתְחַלְּקוּתָן, שֶׁנִּבְרְאוּ בְּכֹחַ הָאֵין סוֹף יָחִיד וּמְיוּחָד בְּתַכְלִית הוּא עַל יְדֵי רִיבּוּי הָאוֹתִיּוֹת

In addition, the multitude of created beings and their divisions, which were created through the

THERE IS NO KING WITHOUT A NATION AND THERE IS NO NATION WITHOUT A KING

☞ Just as the nation makes the king, it is also true that the king makes the nation. Regarding God, this pertains to our very existence. In the beginning, there was nothing besides God. Everything else came into being as "existence from nothingness." If God were not the King, the nation would not be called a nation, and there would be no relationship between the King and the nation. But more than that, there would simply be no nation. There would be nothing whatsoever. The author of the *Tanya* explains here that the reality of "existence from nothingness," the very fact that things – the world, the sky, human beings, and so forth – exist hinges on *Malkhut*.

---

he is not "king" over trees and rocks, but only over people, who are "like him." A king's subjects can willingly accept his reign upon themselves only when these two conditions are met: They are distinct from him, yet are also similar to him (see *Likkutei Torah*, Deut. 44d, Num. 6a).

36. See *Likkutei Torah*, Deut. 51b.

הַיּוֹצְאִין מִמַּלְכוּת, פִּי ה׳

power of *Ein Sof*, who is absolutely, completely one, is achieved **by means of the multiplicity of the letters that emerge from *Malkhut*, the mouth of God,**

Thus, *Malkhut* creates "existence from nothingness." Now, the author of the *Tanya* describes an additional aspect of *Malkhut*: God is absolutely and entirely "one," whereas creation is comprised of a multitude of creatures that are distinct from one another. Accordingly, in addition to its state of "existence from nothingness," creation's state as a "plurality" derived from "unity" is likewise unique to the *sefira* of *Malkhut*.

Malkhut is the speaking mouth, the five organs of articulation from which the letters that "speak" and create the worlds emerge. While the other *sefirot* do not contain letters, but one indivisible, internal concept, *Malkhut* is a multitude of letters. *Ḥokhma*, for example, perceives one overall picture. In the emotive *sefirot*, too, the internal emotion is one, just as the soul is one. Speech, on the other hand, breaks down knowledge and emotions into many different letters and words. Of course, letters and words combine to form particular meanings. Nonetheless, only the letters themselves are transmitted. They are the essence of speech. ☞

"וּבְרוּחַ פִּיו כָּל צְבָאָם" (תהלים לג,ו) וה׳ מוֹצְאוֹת הַפֶּה הֵן מה׳ גְּבוּרוֹת דְּנוּקְבָא.

"by the breath of His mouth, all their hosts" (Ps. 33:6). **The five organs of articulation are from the five aspects of *Gevura*,** restraining forces, **of *Nukva*.**

THE SECRET OF THE LETTERS

☞ No matter where the letters are conveyed, they can never completely recreate the upper *sefirot* that affected them, nor the wisdom or emotions expressed by those *sefirot*. This is because the world is "separate," just as the person who hears one's speech is separate from him. Nonetheless, the letters also contain a secret, and this secret is their power. It is passed from world to world within the letters themselves, without the various connotations that those letters bear. For the unadulterated letters are the only things that move from world to world and from person to person. When letters receive meaning, they always reveal something to someone, but beyond that, the secret of the letters themselves is transmitted. This secret does not have a "meaning." "Nothingness," which is inherent to it, is able to reveal and create more and more by means of the letters that transmitted it.

"The heavens" refers to the spiritual reality, the source and vitality of our physical reality. "All their host" are the multitudes of angels who convey the spiritual abundance into the worlds and divide it among them. There are many angels are because they are "by the breath of His mouth": They are created and sustained by means of the letters of divine speech, of which there are a vast number when one considers all their combinations.

The pronunciations of the twenty-two letters result from the voice being employed in twenty-two different ways. First, however, the voice is divided into five parts. As in human speech, these are the five organs of articulation: the throat, palate, tongue, teeth, and lips. They form the twenty-two letters, which join together in countless different combinations, and these combinations create the worlds.

Divine light, like the human voice, is divided up by the aspects of *Gevura*. *Gevura* is the force that separates and limits, while *Ḥesed* is the connecting and unifying force. Thus, the five aspects of *Gevura* are what break down the simple voice at the outset, dividing it up into the five organs of articulation. ☞

וְלָזֹאת נִקְרֵאת עָלְמָא דְּאִתְגַּלְיָא **For this reaon, *Malkut* is called the revealed world,**

As mentioned above, *Malkhut* is divine speech. It corresponds to human speech, which is revealed to other people, while the other faculties of the soul are concealed from them. ☞

FIVE ASPECTS OF *GEVURA*

☞ This is a kabbalistic concept that is juxtaposed with the five aspects of *Ḥesed*. It embodies all the types of *Gevura* that are conveyed to the worlds from above. It pertains to the lights that flow from the five *sefirot* – *Ḥesed, Gevura, Tiferet, Netzaḥ*, and *Hod* – into *Yesod*, and from there, into *Malkhut*. In this regard, there are two types of lights: aspects of *Ḥesed* and aspects of *Gevura*. The aspects of *Ḥesed* accumulate that which flows from the different forms of *Ḥesed*, and the aspects of *Gevura* incorporate all that derives from the different forms of *Gevura*. The elementary illumination of the five aspects of *Gevura* and *Ḥesed* is what creates the multitudes of letters and letter combinations.

THE REVEALED WORLD

☞ This term is usually interpreted as "the world that is revealed to us," the world we live in. In contrast, "the concealed world" is not revealed to us. Accordingly, "the re-

כִּי בָהּ נִגְלֶה כֹּחַ אוֹר אֵין סוֹף לִבְרוֹא יֵשׁ מֵאַיִן, שֶׁלֹּא עַל יְדֵי עִילָּה וְעָלוּל.

since in it the strength of the light of *Ein Sof* is revealed, to create existence from nothingness, not through cause and effect.

"Existence from nothingness" is a type of creation that does not occur through cause and effect.

Here, a deeper reason is given for why *Malkhut* is called "the revealed world." The capacity of *Malkhut* to reveal the divine light in the lowest realms, so that it is perceived as "existence from nothingness," derives from a supernal power that is manifest in *Malkhut*. This power is essentially higher than all the other *sefirot*. It was explained in epistle 5 that with regard to human speech, the information conveyed may be on a lower level than that which is found within the intellect and emotions, the faculties of the soul. Nonetheless, the capacity of speech to flow outward, toward others, reveals a higher force, which the other spiritual faculties do not possess. This force comes from beyond the human being, from *Keter*, which is what enables the person to convey part of himself to the outside, to other people. Thus the term "the revealed world" is not used to diminish *Malkhut* of *Atzilut* in relation to the other *sefirot* because of the fact that it is revealed, whereas they are concealed due to their loftiness. Rather, it expresses the superiority of *Malkhut* of *Atzilut*, which reveals the power of the light of *Ein Sof* Himself, while the other *sefirot* reveal only what is within them. It said at the beginning of this epistle that only God Himself can create "existence from nothingness." Consequently, any creation of "existence from nothingness" is from Him, and it is possible to say that He is revealed in that place. The power of *Ein Sof* is revealed specifically through *Malkhut* of *Atzilut*, because "existence," that which is separate from the higher "nothingness," is formed through this *sefira*. ☞

vealed world" includes the worlds of *Beria*, *Yetzira*, and *Asiya*, for there is "existence" in these realms. They contain beings that we are able to relate to, and through these beings, we can relate to the divine light as well. Since the divine light is enclothed in these structures, it can be revealed to us through them. As explained, *Malkhut* of *Atzilut* is the source of these worlds in the Divine. The term "the revealed world" is thus interpreted in a deeper way here.

אֲבָל ט׳ סְפִירוֹת הָרִאשׁוֹנוֹת, נֶאֶצְלוּ בְּהִשְׁתַּלְשְׁלוּת עִילָּה וְעָלוּל וְאוֹר הָאֵין סוֹף הוּא מְלוּבָּשׁ בְּחָכְמָה לְבַדָּהּ.

The first nine *sefirot*, by contrast, emanated through unfolding successions of cause and effect, and the light of *Ein Sof* is enclothed in *Ḥokhma* alone.

The nine *sefirot* of *Atzilut* that are above *Malkhut* did not emanate through the process of "existence from nothingness," in which the power of *Ein Sof* is manifest. Instead, they emanated from one another through unfolding successions of cause and effect: In each level, the level directly above it is revealed, but nothing higher than that.

As mentioned above, the light of *Ein Sof* Himself is manifest only in the transition of "existence from nothingness," which constitutes a transformation to a completely different essence and world. This light is not revealed in the *sefirot* that evolve from one another by way of cause and effect, with the exception of *Ḥokhma*. *Ḥokhma* is the first *sefira* and it receives from the "nothingness" beyond the limits of the *sefirot*. Consequently, the verse states, "Wisdom, where [*me'ayin*] will it be found?" (Job 28:12). This can be interpreted to mean that *Ḥokhma* comes from the light of *Ein Sof*, which is "*ayin*," "nothingness." Thus *Ḥokhma* alone is an emanation of *Ein Sof*, a kind of "existence from

THE STRENGTH OF THE LIGHT OF *EIN SOF* IS REVEALED IN IT

☞ The Talmud states: : Moses came and said in his prayer: "The great, the valorous, and the awesome God" (Deut. 10: 17). Jeremiah the prophet came and said: Gentiles, that is, the minions of Nebuchadnezzar, are carousing in His sanctuary; where is His awesomeness? Therefore, he did not say awesome in his prayer etc. Until the members of the Great Assembly came and returned the crown of the Holy One, Blessed be He, to its former glory. They said: On the contrary, this is the might of His might, meaning the fullest expression of it, that He conquers His inclination etc. (*Yoma* 69b).

Put another way, every revelation in this world is in fact a manifestation of its opposite. When a person "sees" the Divine, he is really seeing an extremely limited revelation, which certainly does not convey God's innate essence. On the other hand, when one sees only a world that functions as though there were no God, this is a profound revelation of untold greatness and power. The ultimate creative force is manifest when a being or world is created whose entire existence derives from and is sustained by the Divine, yet it is able to feel and behave as though there were no God. This is the creation of "existence from nothingness," which only God has the power to bring about.

nothingness." However, after *Ḥokhma* itself, there is no creation of "existence from nothingness" in the nine *sefirot* above *Malkhut*. There is only cause and effect, which is akin to "existence from existence."

וְזֶה שֶׁנֶּאֱמַר: 'נָעוּץ תְּחִלָּתָן בְּסוֹפָן' (ספר יצירה פרק א משנה ז).

This is the meaning of the statement: "Their beginning is affixed to their end" (*Sefer Yetzira* 1:7).

This statement describes the connection, that exists within every system/structure between beginnings and endings. The initial thought that constitutes the very beginning of a process is revealed in its conclusion, which is where the original intention is fully realized. Here, as in *Sefer Yetzira*, this is mentioned in relation to the *sefirot*. There is a special connection between the "beginning" and "end" of the *sefirot*, between *Keter*, which is above the *sefirot*, and *Malkhut*, which influences the worlds below the *sefirot*. In the soul, too, there is a connection between a person's initial, internal desire, and the act that is ultimately carried out in accordance with that desire. The desire is brought to fruition only through the act, and it is formed only through the act. The act is the only thing that can be said to embody the desire itself. ☞

כִּי כֶּתֶר הוּא מְמוּצָּע בֵּין הַמַּאֲצִיל לַנֶּאֱצָלִים

For *Keter* is a mediator between the Emanator and the emanated,

The mystical works contain various interpretations of the status of *Keter*.[37] Some include it among the *sefirot*, while others state that it is part of *Ein Sof*. It is concluded that *Keter* of *Atzilut* is a mediator

"THEIR BEGINNING IS AFFIXED" REFERS TO *KETER*

☞ Although the first *sefira* is *Ḥokhma*, which is why it is called "*reshit* (the beginning) *Ḥokhma*," the phrase "Their beginning is affixed to their end" pertains to *Keter*. It has been pointed out that this phrase employs the term *teḥilatan*, rather than *roshan*, to mean "their beginning." *Hatḥala* is both prior to and higher than *rosh*. It signifies *Keter*, which is above *Ḥokhma*. Furthermore, the term *na'utz*, "affixed," expresses more than just a connection. It indicates that *Keter* itself descends and becomes embedded in *Malkhut*. In other words, *Keter* acts upon *Malkhut*.

37. See *Hemshekh Samekh Vav*, p. 165; *Likkutei Torah*, Lev. 46c.

between the Emanator and the emanated.[38] In all other realms, too, *Keter* is a mediator between successive worlds. A mediator is one who stands in the middle, between two levels. It does not entirely belong to either one of them, for it contains something from both.

וְיֵשׁ בּוֹ בְּחִינָה הָאַחֲרוֹנָה שֶׁל הָאֵין סוֹף. **and it contains the final aspect of *Ein Sof*.**

Every mediator contains something from each of the two levels that it stands between. Thus in *Keter* of *Atzilut*, there is something from *Atzilut* and something from the Emanator, *Ein Sof*. When *Keter* is affixed to *Malkhut* it conveys that essence of *Ein Sof*, of God Himself, to *Malkhut*. As explained above, this is the power of *Ein Sof* that is found in *Malkhut*, the power to create "existence from nothingness."

Nonetheless, the "final aspect of *Ein Sof*" is not derived from the inner dimension of *Ein Sof*, but the external dimension. To some degree, it may be regarded as the "conclusion" of *Ein Sof*. This is analogous to two people who are very different from one another, such as one who is spiritually great and the other spiritually deficient. They cannot meet on the spiritual plane, through their wisdom or emotions. However, they are able to meet in the practical results of their internal processes.

וְלָכֵן נִקְרָא 'כֶּתֶר מַלְכוּת' כִּי אֵין כֶּתֶר אֶלָּא לַמֶּלֶךְ. **This is why it is called *Keter* of *Malkhut*** (Crown of Sovereignty), **for no one but a king has a crown,**

The *sefira* of *Keter* is called *Keter* of *Malkhut*.[39] Since "Their beginning is affixed to their end," *Keter* is designated for *Malkhut*. It is bound to *Malkhut*, and they are essentially one.

Kings have crowns, whereas sages, warriors, and so forth, do not. Likewise, with regard to the *sefirot*, *Keter* relates to *Malkhut* more closely than any of the other *sefirot*. As explained above, the power of

38. This is the opinion of the Arizal, cited in *Etz Ḥayyim* 41:3.

39. "Supernal *Keter* is *Keter* of *Malkhut*" (Introduction to *Tikkunei Zohar*, 17a, "*Pataḥ Eliyahu*").

Ein Sof within *Keter*, the ability to create "existence from nothingness," is revealed only through *Malkhut*.

This phrase emphasizes the unity of the concepts of *Keter* and *Malkhut*: There is no such thing as a crown without a king, and likewise, there is no such thing as a king without a crown. They are two sides of the same coin. *Keter* connotes surrounding and encompassing. It signifies that which is beyond the scope and confines of reality. It refers specifically to the crown of a king, for the king is raised above his kingdom, and is separate from his nation. Consequently, *Malkhut* signifies power, for this is the only way that a king is able to relate to his "nation," to those beings that are separate from him. Because of the very fact that he is elevated and distinct, the king allows, and sustains, the existence of this distant, separate reality. This is akin to the creation of "existence from nothingness."

וְגַם כִּי בְּחִינָה אַחֲרוֹנָה דְּאֵין סוֹף הִיא מַלְכוּת דְּאֵין סוֹף.

and also because the final aspect of *Ein Sof* is the *Malkhut* of *Ein Sof*.

The essential connection between *Keter* and *Malkhut* is clear from all sides. Previously, it was described how we see *Keter* from below, conveying its light and flow to *Malkhut*. However, the connection between them is also apparent from above. In essence, *Keter* is *Malkhut*, for at its source, it is the *Malkhut* of *Ein Sof*. In relation to the worlds, *Ein Sof* is the "*Keter*," which is separate from, and elevated above, everything else. Accordingly, *Malkhut* of *Ein Sof* has the essence of *Keter*. ☞ ☞

KETER OF *MALKHUT* ON EVERY LEVEL

☞ There is a general principle in Kabbala that the general structures are also found within individual entities, and likewise, individual structures recur and become ever larger in scope. This is true with regard to the basic structure of the ten *sefirot* as well. While in general, we refer to the ten *sefirot* of the world of *Atzilut*, the same structure is present on a smaller scale too, such as in the created worlds. Moreover, this structure also exists on a larger scale, where *Atzilut* and all the worlds below it correspond to the world of *Asiya*. This is called *Asiya DiKhlalut* or *Adam DeAsiya* (See *Likkutei Torah*, Lev. 8d). Accordingly, the matters being discussed here have broader significance. Our *Keter* is the "*Malkhut*" of that which is above this realm. Likewise, in the lower realms, which are the created worlds, the *Malkhut* of each world is the *Keter* of the world below it.

וְלָכֵן גַּם הַמַּלְכוּת דַּאֲצִילוּת נִקְרָא כֶּתֶר מִמַּטָּה לְמַעְלָה **Therefore, the *Malkhut* of *Atzilut* is also called *Keter*, below and above,**

Thus, when viewed from above, *Keter* is *Malkhut*, and when viewed from below, *Malkhut* is *Keter*. Consequently, from all angles, *Malkhut* is *Keter*.

What is the meaning of *mimata lemala*, "below and above"? Ostensibly, *mimata*, literally "from below," indicates the world of *Beria*: Just as *Malkhut* of *Ein Sof* is the *Keter* of *Atzilut*, *Malkhut* of *Atzilut* is the *Keter* of the created worlds. While this is indeed true, based on what is written below, *mimata lemala* refers primarily to the world of *Atzilut* itself, rather than to the transition between worlds.[40] In other words, the power of *Ein Sof* in *Malkhut* of *Atzilut* does not relate only to the worlds of *Beria*, *Yetzira*, and *Asiya*, which are like "existence from nothingness" with respect to this *sefira*. Rather, from all possible angles, this is the reality. Regardless of which level we look at, and from which perspective, *Malkhut* is *Keter*, in relation to both that which is below it and that which is above it. This is because the power of the light of *Ein Sof*, which is beyond any definition, is revealed within *Malkhut*. Accordingly, just as *Keter* emits the light of *Ein Sof* from above, *Malkhut* emits it from below, in a different way.

MALKHUT OF *EIN SOF*

☞ This does not refer simply to the level above the world of *Atzilut*. As explained elsewhere, it is the highest level that we are able to relate to. It pertains to the essence of *Ein Sof* before constriction, before any divine intent or desire have even been established. *Malkhut* of *Ein Sof* is the only part of *Ein Sof* that we are able to comprehend. It belongs to *Ein Sof*, just as *Malkhut* of *Atzilut* belongs to the ten *sefirot* of *Atzilut*, yet at the same time, it defines the connection to the "nation," in the broadest sense. This includes the first constriction and the unfolding succession of the worlds. The significance of our connection to *Malkhut* of *Ein Sof* lies in the fact that we understand that the flow of divine power conveys the true power of *Ein Sof* from *Malkhut* of *Ein Sof*, which, as mentioned, is part of *Ein Sof* prior to constriction. This is the power to create "existence from nothingness," which enters *Malkhut* of *Atzilut* as well as *Malkhut* of the lower worlds.

40. This is also based on other sources; see *Derekh Mitzvotekha, Shoresh Mitzvat HaTefilla*, chap. 26. It is also interpreted this way in *Lessons in Tanya*.

Elsewhere, two types of light are discussed: direct light and returning light.[41] Direct light is the light of the ray, which illuminates from above to below. It is analogous to visible light that emanates from its source and increasingly diminishes as it moves further away from it, eventually reaching a point where it ceases to flow. Returning light corresponds to light that is reflected from below, from that faraway place where the light no longer penetrates. Direct light is referred to as "direct" because it shines directly from the luminary onto whichever object it reaches. Returning light is the light that is sent back from the threshold where the direct light vanishes.

Direct light refers to the unfolding succession in its current state, as we see it. From its abstract, spiritual source above, it descends, unfolding and becoming more and more material as it moves further down. Similarly, within the human being, every action begins on the higher plane of the soul, within one's consciousness. From there, it descends to the realm of emotion and relationship, and from there, to thought, speech, and action. In contrast, returning light refers to the uncertain, inner unfolding of the same. One's actual deeds constitute the end of the process, and accordingly, it can be said that action precedes and causes all the other stages, even the most spiritual and abstract. Direct light is obvious and apparent: It is the world that was formed by the Creator, and this the world that we perceive at first sight. On the other hand, returning light is never clear. The place that returns it possesses no light of its own, and it is uncertain that it will be light, that it will shine, as it were, even on the Creator Himself, for this depends on how the human being reacts down below, in the physical world. The returning light is a mystery that God has concealed since the beginning of Creation. It may be said that direct light is revealed because it comprises God's "speech" to the worlds and the souls. This is the speech that forms us and is directed toward us. In contrast, returning light is concealed, because it is not intended for us or our world, but for God Himself. From His concealed place on high, God Himself asked the question "Which is the direct light?" and He alone receives the answer "The returning light." This "answer" is what *Malkhut* sends back from the lowest realm. As a result, it is higher than all direct light,

41. *Derekh Mitzvotekha, Shoresh Mitzvat HaTefilla*, chap. 26; see also *Torat Ḥayyim, Vayigash*; *Torah Or* 5a, 33a.

because it is the "speech" that addresses God Himself, who is above all worlds and limits.

Thus *Malkhut* is the tenth and final *sefira* with respect to the path of the direct light that comes from above. However, it is the first *sefira* with respect to the returning light that comes from below. This is the meaning of what is written here, that *Malkhut* is *Keter* "*mimata lemala*," "below and above."

וּמַה גַּם כִּי בְּרִיאַת הַנְּשָׁמוֹת מִמֶּנָּה לִהְיוֹת יֵשׁ וְדָבָר נִפְרָד בִּפְנֵי עַצְמוֹ בְּעוֹלַם הַבְּרִיאָה

and especially as the creation of souls occurs through it, to become a substance and a separate entity in and of itself in the world of *Beria*.

This is another aspect of the revelation of the power of *Ein Sof* in *Malkhut* of *Atzilut*. It was explained above that the creation of "existence from nothingness" occurs through the power of *Ein Sof* (*Keter*) alone. In addition, there is also a true revelation of *Ein Sof* in the creation of souls. When a soul descends and is enclothed in the lower world, it perceives itself as "existence," as a separate entity, much like the lower world itself. Nonetheless, the soul is truly a part of the Divine, and the creation of the soul, whereby it is drawn down into the created worlds, is a revelation of the power of *Ein Sof* through *Malkhut*. This revelation is revealed by the Inner Light into the worlds, into the "existence" where the Divine is not manifest. When an internal revelation like this develops and ascends properly, it will be deeper and more essential than the revelation of the encompassing light of *Ein Sof* in *Keter*.[42] ☞

KETER OF MALKHUT

☞ The descriptions given here form a multifaceted view of "*Keter* of *Malkhut*." This concept is fundamental to our understanding of the relationship between God, the world, and the human being. It is not fully realized in the human experience, and consequently, there is no way for us to comprehend or recognize it perfectly. We do not even possess a word for it, but only this combination of two terms, which comprise an attempt to express its true essence. Therefore, in this passage,

42. The Lubavitcher Rebbe, Rabbi Menaḥem Mendel Schneerson, comments here, "From this, it is clearly understood that there is no contradiction with regard to what is written about the souls' creation." It appears that the Rebbe is referring

וְנִקְרָא בְּשֵׁם לֵידָה This is called birth,

In Kabbala, the creation of the souls into the lower worlds through *Malkhut* of *Atzilut* is called "birth."

Above, the author of the *Tanya* discussed the "souls of *Atzilut*." These souls exist in the world of *Atzilut*, and the most exceptional ones descend, in their "*Atzilut*" state, into the created worlds.[43] However, in truth, all souls originate in *Atzilut*. The souls that are referred to as souls of *Beria*, *Yetzira*, or *Asiya* are called this by virtue of their revelation in those worlds: They are enclothed in the vessels and forms of a particular world. They are found in *Atzilut* within the general source of all souls: Their component parts derive from it, and those components are part of the essence of the congregation of Israel, of all Jewish souls. However, as individual souls, they are not in *Atzilut*. Accordingly, their descent into the created worlds is seen as a "birth." When a fetus is in the womb, it is part of its mother. It becomes a distinct individual only upon being born. This does not pertain only to the body, but also to the soul, which is no longer subsumed in the supernal source of all souls, but is enclothed in

the author of the *Tanya* examines this concept from several angles and on several different planes. First, he describes the view from above. Supernal *Keter* is the highest point, or "heaven," with regard to all of reality. When observed from above, it is the *Malkhut* of *Ein Sof*. Thus from this perspective, *Keter* is *Malkhut*. Next, he describes the view from below: *Malkhut* is the lowest and final point of the divine lights (the world of *Atzilut* and all that is above it), yet when viewed from below, it is the *Keter* of our lower worlds. In other words, *Malkhut* is *Keter*. The third and final dimension is that of the creation of the souls. It embodies the essential meaning of "*Keter* is *Malkhut*." Regarding the first two levels, the author of the *Tanya* defined the scope of "*Keter* is *Malkhut*," but in the last one, he defines "*Keter* is *Malkhut*" itself. The final stage can occur only after the first two, because a king can reveal himself as the king only in the context reality of "king and nation" ("There is no king without a nation"). Only when the divine soul descends into the world and perceives itself as "existence from nothingness" like the world itself, is it able to nullify this "existence" when it accepts God's kingship. This, too, constitutes "*Keter* is *Malkhut*." However, in this instance, instead of concealing Himself, God reveals *Keter* within *Malkhut*.

---

to the discrepancy in the matter of the souls' source. In one place, it states that it is in *Malkhut* of *Atzilut*, yet elsewhere, it states that it is in the highest realm, in *Ein Sof* Himself, who is above everything.

43. See *Likkutei Torah*, Lev. 18a and onward, where it states that these souls are like "the fish of the sea."

the physical body and world. The moment of birth is the moment of the formation of a person's unique self. From that point on, he begins to feel things like hunger and fear. However, unlike other creations, the soul is a part of God even after birth. No matter where it is, it is an expression of the Divine. It is the divine element within the human being and the world, and it reveals and illuminates God to the extent that it is able to do so. Thus the soul, which was formed through *Malkhut* of *Atzilut* (also referred to as "the congregation of Israel," the gatherer of all Jewish souls), is not only a product of the power of *Ein Sof*, like the worlds themselves are. It also manifests the light of *Ein Sof* wherever it is found.

כִּקְרִיעַת יַם סוּף, דִּ'בְעַתִּיקָא תַּלְיָא'. **like the splitting of the Red Sea, which "depends on** the level of ***Atik***."

It is stated in Kabbala that the splitting of the Red Sea is analogous to the birth of all souls. The kabbalistic works explain the calendar year in terms of the life cycle of the soul: its birth, development, and coupling, followed by birth once again.[44] The seventh day of Passover, when the Red Sea was parted, is identified as the day when the souls were born.[45]

The *Zohar* states that the splitting of the Red Sea "depends on the level of *Atik*" (*Zohar* 2:48a). It was explained above that *Atik* is the inner dimension of *Keter*, or in other words, the power of *Ein Sof* within *Keter*. Thus, the splitting of the Red Sea, like the birth of the souls, depends on *Atik*, the power of *Ein Sof*, since *Ein Sof* is the only One with the capacity to create "existence from nothingness." From this perspective, the splitting of the Red Sea is not merely "existence" that originates from "nothingness," but rather "existence" that reveals the "nothingness" within all the "existence" in this world. ☞

LIKE THE SPLITTING OF THE RED SEA

☞ Hasidic discourses explain that at the splitting of the Red Sea, God "turned the sea into dry land" (Ps. 66:6). "The sea" refers to the concealed world, the one divine reality of the world of *Atzilut*, which is not revealed in our world. "Dry land," on the other hand, is the revealed world, the world of *Beria*. The removal of that which

44. Birth occurs on the seventh day of Passover, growth and weaning on Shavuot, and coupling on *Shemini Atzeret*.

45. *Peri Etz Ḥayyim, Sha'ar HaLulav* 8; see also *Likkutei Torah*, Lev. 16b and onward.

וְגַם כָּל גִּידּוּל הַנְּשָׁמוֹת כָּל ז׳ חֳדָשִׁים, מִזִּיווּג שֶׁל שְׁמִינִי עֲצֶרֶת עַד שְׁבִיעִי שֶׁל פֶּסַח

Likewise, the entire growth of the souls all seven months,[46] from the coupling of *Shemini Atzeret* until the seventh day of Passover,

Here, the author of the *Tanya* goes into further detail about the souls' birth. *Shemini Atzeret* is the culmination and conclusion of the festivals that fall in the month of Tishrei. It couples with *Malkhut* (the Divine Presence), for on *Shemini Atzeret*, *Malkhut* receives a new flow from God. This flow issues from the essence of *Ein Sof* and is absorbed into *Malkhut*. This is why we start saying *morid hageshem*, "He makes the rain fall," in our prayers on *Shemini Atzeret*. Accordingly, the winter months, until the seventh day of Passover, are the months of "gestation."[47]

הוּא כְּמוֹ גִּידּוּל זו"נ בְּבֶטֶן אִימָּא עִילָּאָה שֶׁהוּא עַל יְדֵי אוֹרוֹת עֶלְיוֹנִים מֵאִימָּא עִילָּאָה, וּמִלְמַעְלָה לְמַעְלָה

is like the growth of *Zeir Anpin* and *Nukva* in the belly of the "Higher Mother," which occurs by

is concealed and unified with the Divine to the revealed reality constitutes a "birth." However, the transformation of sea into dry land at the splitting of the Red Sea was an extraordinary miracle. It does not pertain to the creation of the world of *Beria* through the world of *Atzilut* by means of "existence from nothingness," as described above. Rather, it signifies the visible entry of *Atzilut* itself into *Beria*. As explained, this is akin to the birth of a soul.

Birth is itself the transition of a fetus from existing in "water" to existing on land. Elsewhere, it is explained that before birth, the soul is a "fish of the sea." Moreover, there are extremely high souls, the souls of *Atzilut*, which the *Zohar* refers to as "fish of the sea that walk on land." These are the few tzaddikim, like Moses and Rabbi Shimon bar Yoḥai, who do not really belong in this world but are put here for a particular purpose (*Likkutei Torah, Parashat Shemini*).

46. See *Likkutei Hagahot LaTanya*, p. 76, which contains an explanation of how this time amounts to seven months, since there are actually six months (less one day) from *Shemini Atzeret* until the seventh day of Passover.

47. See *Peri Etz Ḥayyim, Sha'ar Ḥag HaMatzot* 8, *Sha'ar HaLulav* 8; *Mishnat Ḥasidim, Sukka* 12:8. This idea is also mentioned in *Likkutei Torah*, Lev. 16b. See also *Likkutei Hagahot LaTanya*, p. 76, which contains an explanation of how this time amounts to seven months, since there are actually six months (less one day) from *Shemini Atzeret* until the seventh day of Passover.

עַד אֵין סוֹף הַמִּתְלַבֵּשׁ בָּהּ כָּל ט׳ אוֹ ז׳ יַרְחֵי לֵידָה.

means of the supernal lights from the "Higher Mother," and even higher, until *Ein Sof*, which enclothes itself in it throughout the nine or seven months of birth.

The development of the soul before its birth is akin to the growth of *Zeir Anpin* and *Nukva* in the belly of the "Higher Mother," which is *Bina*. *Zeir Anpin* and *Nukva* are compared to children, and *Bina* is their "mother." Before *Zeir Anpin* and *Nukva* are revealed, before they begin to influence the worlds, they are encompassed within *Bina* like a fetus in the womb. Like the fetus, they receive nourishment from that which their "mother" ingests, namely, the supernal lights of *Bina* itself, which *Bina* receives from *Ḥokhma*, and *Ḥokhma* receives from *Ein Sof*.

Thus during these months, there is no revelation or birth of "existence from nothingness." Nonetheless, the spiritual preparation for this takes place. All those higher forces, the forces of *Ein Sof*, are gathered together.

Coupling, gestation, and birth in the soul. For an emotion to be "born" in the human soul, and even more so, for speech or action to be "born," the stages of "coupling" and "gestation" must first take place. "Coupling" refers to the union of *Ḥokhma* and *Bina*, the father and mother of everything that happens within the human being. There is a flash of consciousness, or *Ḥokhma*, and this is absorbed by *Bina*. In the stage of "gestation," the person contemplates and integrates the matter, and the insight grows and takes on a particular form. Finally, at "birth," the emotion itself is born. It is no longer incorporated within the intellect, in *Bina*, but can perceive itself as totally separate, and behave accordingly. For example, if someone bumps into a person, and the person who he collided with does not think about it further, then nothing happens. However, the flash of a thought may enter his mind that perhaps the other person was attempting to hurt him. He might continue to contemplate this, ruminating over the idea that the person planned the act, considering what he may have been thinking, and so forth. The more he thinks about it and paints a picture of it in his mind, the more this picture grows and evolves, and ultimately, a feeling of fierce anger is generated. This feeling can then become independent of one's understanding, and of what actually took place. The same thing can occur with regard to love for another person, and likewise, as is explained at length in other hasidic works, with regard to the "holy" emotions: love of God and fear of God. One's contemplation must be continuous, one step after another, and it must take place over the course of time. The process and time are essential to the "birth" of a real, viable, concrete emotion such as love or fear. ☞

וְכָכָה הוּא בִּבְרִיאַת נְשָׁמוֹת וּמַלְאָכִים לְעוֹלַם הַבְּרִיאָה

So too, with regard to the creation of souls and angels for the world of *Beria*.

Above, it was explained that the souls of humans and angels that descend into the worlds are formed through *Malkhut* of *Atzilut*. Their creation is comparable to the development of *Zeir Anpin* and *Nukva* in *Atzilut*. *Malkhut* of *Atzilut* is like the "(lower) mother" of the souls born in the world of *Beria*. ☞

וְגַם כָּל עִיקַּר וְשֹׁרֶשׁ הַטִּיפָּה שֶׁמְּקַבֶּלֶת וּמִתְעַבֶּרֶת מז"א הוּא מְמוֹחִין דְּאַבָּא וְאִמָּא

In addition, the whole essence and root of the drop that it receives and with which it **is impregnated by *Zeir Anpin* is from the mind of father and mother,**

NINE OR SEVEN MONTHS OF BIRTH

☞ There are either nine or seven months of "gestation," and some sources also mention twelve months. Here, the author of the *Tanya* does not relate to the discrepancy, but only to the fact that these two alternatives exist. Elsewhere (see *Torat Menaḥem*, vol. 2, p. 73) it is explained that the gestation period is necessary for the transformation from a single, all-encompassing "drop," to a "fetus" with recognizable body parts: head, legs, and so on. As more time passes, the distinction between the different organs becomes clearer and more defined. When this is important, the gestation period is longer, and when the opposite is required, the gestation period is shorter. Regardless, there must be a period of time during which the soul grows and develops and draws light from the light of *Ein Sof*.

THE CREATION OF THE SOULS IN THE WORLD OF *BERIA*

☞ As stated, with regard to the created world as a whole, the power of *Ein Sof* is revealed only in the fact of its existence, but not in its life force or capacity

Zeir Anpin is the male "counterpart" of *Malkhut*. Through it, *Malkhut* conceives and gives birth to the souls. This is akin to physical intercourse, where the woman receives a "drop" that contains the essential male forces necessary for a child to grow, and the essential forces that will exist within the child. *Malkhut* receives the drop from *Zeir Anpin* (the emotive *sefirot*). However, the source of the drop is not in *Zeir Anpin*, but in the "mind of father and mother," which are *Ḥokhma* and *Bina*. In ancient texts, it is common to represent the source of a man's semen as being in his brain.

Just like in the physical world, every birth, the formation of every new being, is the result of coupling. On all levels, the union of male and female is the only thing that can create a new entity that is not merely an extension of that which existed previously. This is true with regard to the spiritual dimension of the soul, and likewise with regard to the divine being in the world of *Atzilut*. The "drop" that *Zeir Anpin* places within *Malkhut* derives from the union of the higher levels, *Ḥokhma* and *Bina*.

וּבְכָל זִיווּג נִמְשֶׁכֶת לְאַבָּא וְאִמָּא מֵאֲרִיךְ אַנְפִּין וְעַתִּיק יוֹמִין וּמִלְמַעְלָה לְמַעְלָה עַד אֵין סוֹף.

and in each coupling it is drawn to father and mother, from *Arikh Anpin* and *Atik Yomin*, and even higher, until *Ein Sof*.

Furthermore, each coupling of "father and mother" is drawn from a coupling on an even higher level.

"Coupling" refers to the joining of male and female, two opposites. A connection between opposites is possible only by virtue of a flow from above, because that which connects them cannot be a

for comprehension. On the contrary, *Ein Sof* is concealed in this realm. In contrast, the soul is, in essence, a revelation of *Ein Sof*. Wherever it is found, including during its development and birth, it perpetually reveals the power of *Ein Sof* in *Malkhut*, to the point where it may almost be said that the soul and *Malkhut* are one continuous progression. Indeed, the soul is a member of the "congregation of Israel." This is *Malkhut*, the Divine Presence, from which a spark descends into the worlds. This spark is what constantly, in all places, illuminates and reveals the Divine Presence, *Malkhut*, and the power of *Ein Sof* enclothed within it.

part of either one of them. Rather, it must come from a higher place that incorporates both of them. Both must recognize and accept its superiority and authority. Moreover, coupling does not evoke a flow only from the level above it. Essentially, it evokes the entire unfolding succession, because each flow from above stems from an even higher level. Here, the lower coupling in *Atzilut*, the union of *Zeir Anpin* and *Malkhut*, which leads to the birth of the souls, starts with a flow that is higher than both of these dimensions: a flow from the brain. This flow into the lower realm derives from the higher coupling in *Atzilut*, the union of "father" and "mother," or *Ḥokhma* and *Bina*. The coupling of "father" and "mother" is drawn from *Keter*: from *Arikh Anpin*, the external dimension of *Keter*, which relates to the worlds, and beyond that, from *Atik Yomin*, the inner dimension of *Keter*, the Emanator in relation to Himself up to *Ein Sof*.

The process is similar within the soul, and likewise, in the human body. Prior to the creation of the "drop," both in the male and the female, a hidden biological and psychological process takes place. This process leads to the formation of the "drop": for example, the structure and essence of the sperm cell. The process is a personal, internal one. Even the individual himself is usually not aware of it. Thus in the soul, *Ḥokhma* and *Bina*, which are the "father" and "mother," come together and form a particular insight. However, one may ask why this specific flash of *Ḥokhma* is created, and furthermore, why it is formed in this particular manner. Moreover, what causes a person to understand it the way that he does? When we consider these questions, it becomes clear that there are entire systems of preconsciousness in the innermost dimensions of the soul, and these give rise to each specific insight.

רַק שֶׁהַכֹּל בְּהֶעְלֵם בַּמּוֹחִין **Only, everything is concealed in the mind**

The internal processes through which the light of *Ein Sof* passes into *Malkhut* are concealed, just as a person's consciousness and thoughts are invisible from the outside. They are concealed in the "mind," for this is the term used to represent the Inner Light that comes from above. In contrast, the "attributes" embody the connection between this light and the lower realm.

עַד לֵידַת הַנּוּקְבָא, הַנְּשָׁמוֹת וְהַמַּלְאָכִים וְהַהֵיכָלוֹת לְעוֹלַם הַבְּרִיאָה

until the *Nukva* gives birth to the souls, angels, and the palaces for the world of *Beria*.

Nukva is *Malkhut*, and this "birth" is "existence from nothingness." The power of *Ein Sof* is found throughout the unfolding succession, in every one of its stages. However, it is not revealed within all of these stages. It is analogous to a fetus that is concealed in its mother's womb: It cannot be seen, and its development is hidden. It is revealed only at its birth. When it becomes revealed within a particular form of "existence," it expresses, whether directly or indirectly, all that is above it: the fact that it has a "father" and "mother," and so forth.

נִמְצָא שֶׁזֶּהוּ גִּילּוּי אוֹר אֵין סוֹף מַמָּשׁ עַל יְדֵי הָעִיבּוּר וְהַלֵּידָה.

It follows that this is an actual manifestation of the light of *Ein Sof*, by means of the gestation and birth.

The stages of gestation and birth conclude a process that begins, as mentioned previously, before the onset of the unfolding succession. Accordingly, the force of creation and birth that is revealed in *Malkhut* is not merely a manifestation of *Malkhut*. Moreover, it is not just a manifestation of *Atzilut* either. Rather, through this "birth," the creation of "existence from nothingness," *Ein Sof* Himself is revealed.

וּבָזֶה יוּבַן הֱיוֹת הַמִּצְוֹת בְּמַלְכוּת ה׳ שֶׁל שֵׁם הֲוָיָ״ה, וְהַתּוֹרָה בִּזְעֵיר אַנְפִּין, וָא״ו שֶׁל שֵׁם הֲוָיָ״ה

Now we can understand the fact that the mitzvot are in *Malkhut*, the final letter ***heh*** of **the name of *Havaya*, whereas the Torah is in *Zeir Anpin*, the *vav* of the name of *Havaya*,**

9 Tishrei

5 Tishrei (leap year)

Having explained the concept of "Their beginning is affixed to their end" on a general, theoretical level, the author of the *Tanya* goes on to discuss its meaning and application with regard to an individual's life and divine service.

The final letter *heh* of the name of *Havaya* symbolizes *Malkhut*, while the *vav* symbolizes *Zeir Anpin*.

The connection between the Torah and mitzvot as we know them is akin to the connection between *Zeir Anpin* and *Malkhut*. *Malkhut* is the present reality, the final outcome of all higher levels, forces, and processes. *Zeir Anpin*, on the other hand, is the inner dimension of all the higher spiritual forces with respect to *Malkhut*. It gives expression, in the lower realm, to everything in the higher realm.[48] Thus Torah corresponds to *Zeir Anpin*. It comprises all teachings, insights, and communications from above, presenting the ideal image of how reality should be. The mitzvot, on the other hand, correspond to *Malkhut*, for they constitute the physical implementation of these teachings. ☞ ☞

NOW WE CAN UNDERSTAND

☞ The shift seen here from a general, abstract description to a practical, concrete application is typical of hasidic discourses, for a number of reasons. One reason is that hasidic discourses are not written merely in order to provide theoretical explanations of the mystical teachings. They always contain implications for what hasidim refer to as *avoda*, "work." The individual must ask himself: What does this mean for me? How can I worship God in this regard, both spiritually and physically? Sometimes the answer is obvious, and other times, the author trusts the readers to reach it on their own. However, in certain cases, such as this one, the author explains exactly how the subject relates to the realm of spiritual and physical service.

The practical applications of a concept are important, for "Action is the most important thing." This phrase appears frequently in hasidic texts, beginning with the works of the author of the *Tanya* (*Likkutei Torah*, Lev. 34b). It is derived from the statement of the Sages, "Study is not the most important thing, but actions" (Mishna *Avot* 1:17). It expresses the idea that one should endeavor to translate every abstract, theoretical concept, at least partially, into physical action.

Furthermore, practical applications are important also because Hasidism is particularly concerned about "giving life" to words so that they do not remain mere concepts and phrases. One can use a term proficiently without knowing what it truly means. In the hasidic view, however, the important thing is to connect to the words: We should inhabit them, and likewise, they should inhabit us. A human being is like a small world. Everything that exists in the larger world exists within the individual as well. In order to give life to the world and to himself, one must find and carry out within himself the idea that he is articulating. One way to begin is to transfer the concept into a familiar realm: that of the soul and its faculties, or that of physical action. Subsequently, when a person carries out or contemplates these words, or experiences feelings in relation to them, he

48. See *Torah Or*, *Teruma* 79c and onward.

הֲגַם שֶׁלְּמַעְלָה בַּאֲרִיךְ אַנְפִּין **and also that above, in *Arikh Anpin*,**

Arikh Anpin, the large or "long" face, is the larger domain beyond the world of *Atzilut,* which includes the world of *Atzilut* within it. In this space, the relationship between the Torah and the mitzvot is different.

The *partzuf* of *Arikh Anpin* is associated with *Keter* of *Atzilut.* This level is above *Atzilut,* yet it is connected to that which is below it. It contains the source of everything in the world of *Atzilut,* including the

is also able to achieve knowledge of them. We understand the highest concepts by means of the things that are most tangible to us, and as a result, we are able to effect the necessary unification and correction in ourselves and all of reality.

ZEIR ANPIN AND *MALKHUT* IN *ATZILUT* AND IN DIVINE SERVICE

☞ The ten *sefirot* of the world of *Atzilut* are divided into four "*partzufim.*" They are father, mother, *Zeir Anpin,* and *Malkhut.* Each one corresponds to one of the four letters of the name of *Havaya,* which is the general term for the world of *Atzilut.* This is what the author of the *Tanya* is referring to when he writes that *Malkhut* is the final *heh* of the name of *Havaya,* and *Zeir Anpin* is the *vav. Zeir Anpin* also corresponds to the number six, which is the *gematriya* of *vav,* for there are six *sefirot,* or emotive attributes, in this *partzuf.*

A *partzuf* is either one *sefira* or a number of *sefirot* that together make up an entire, self-contained "layer." The *partzuf* includes all the same elements as the general structure of the ten *sefirot,* and it acts as a whole, separate entity. Thus *Zeir Anpin* and *Malkhut* are the *partzufim* of "male" and "female," or the "giver" and the "receiver." Together, they constitute the reality of our world: *Malkhut* is the reality, and *Zeir Anpin* comprises the flow and life force that are received by reality. The same is true with regard to the Torah and the mitzvot. These were given to the world, and they are themselves the essence of giving, the revelation of the Divine: God reveals His essential will and wisdom in worldly garments. Accordingly, just as our worldly reality is *Zeir Anpin* and *Malkhut,* Torah and mitzvot are likewise *Zeir Anpin* and *Malkhut.*

"Torah" and "mitzvot" first and foremost refer to the Torah that we study and the mitzvot that we perform, and these truly are *Zeir Anpin* and *Malkhut* within us. When we engage in Torah study, we are *Zeir Anpin,* and when we do mitzvot, we are *Malkhut.* Torah and mitzvot are not merely objects in our world that we choose to interact with. Rather, they are part of us, and of our divine souls in particular. This is who we are, and this is how we live our lives and reveal our essence, which is one with the Divine. When we fulfill the King's commandments and accept His kingship, we embody divine *Malkhut.* Likewise, when we engage in Torah study, in God's will and wisdom, and we desire what He desires and understand it (each person in accordance with his level of understanding of the Torah), in this regard, we are *Zeir Anpin.*

Torah and mitzvot of that world. However, in *Arikh Anpin,* the Torah and mitzvot are in a different form, for it contains the abstract source of the mitzvot. In the world of *Atzilut,* only the effect, or "impression," of this form is present. The difference is not merely that one form is more abstract than the other. As will be explained below, it is like the difference between a seal and the impression that it makes. That which protrudes in the seal is depressed in the impression, and vice versa.

the mitzvot are in the skull, in the whiteness, which is the path of the splitting of hairs, which split into the 613 paths of the Torah that is in *Zeir Anpin.*

הַמִּצְוֹת הֵן בְּגוּלְגַלְתָּא, בְּלַבְנוּנִית, הִיא הָאוֹרְחָא דִּבְפַלְגוּתָא דְשַׂעֲרֵי דְּמִתְפַּלְגָא לְתַרְיָ"ג אוֹרְחִין דְּאוֹרַיְיתָא שֶׁבִּזְעֵיר אַנְפִּין.

In *Arikh Anpin,* the mitzvot are in the "skull." The human skull is the bone that encloses the brain from above, and similarly, with regard to the *sefirot,* the "skull" is *Keter,* which surrounds the cognitive forces from above. In the higher realm of *Arikh Anpin,* the "skull" is "*Keter* of *Keter.*" The skin that can be seen between the hairs on the human head is referred to as the "whiteness." Elsewhere, this is compared to the white of a piece of parchment that can be seen between the written letters. The whiteness is also described as "the path between the hairs." The hairs represent the Inner Light that is drawn from the Encompassing Light through immense constriction. The path between the hairs, on the other hand, symbolizes the path of the Encompassing Light itself from world to world. This is like a physical path that people walk on from place to place, which is free of weeds (which represent the hairs). This path splits into 613 separate paths, which signify the 613 mitzvot, for the mitzvot are called "the paths of God."[49] These paths connect God Himself, in the most supernal realm, to the world of *Asiya,* where the mitzvot are performed. At the source in *Arikh Anpin,* there is one path, but in *Zeir Anpin* of *Atzilut,* which illuminates the other worlds, it separates into the 613 mitzvot. These can also be described as the 613 "body parts" of the King.[50]

---

49. *Zohar* 3:136a, based on Ps. 25:10.

50. All of these concepts are derived from the conceptual framework of the *Idra Rabba* section of the *Zohar,* which is elucidated in the writings of the Arizal.

The presence of the mitzvot in the "skull" indicates that their source is in the simple divine will that is beyond the intellect. Furthermore, this source is in the "whiteness," the path between the "hairs" that grow from the skull. The hairs symbolize the constriction and the emergence of *Ḥokhma* from the skull. They signify the Inner Light that is derived from the Encompassing Light. In contrast, the whiteness represents a higher level within the Encompassing Light itself: the ancient divine will, which is not constricted and drawn out as Inner Light. Even when it descends to the world of action, this level is an encompassing garment. Even in the lower realm, it resembles the simple divine will itself. It is above the intellect and beyond any definition.

Having explained that the source of the mitzvot in *Arikh Anpin* is in *Keter* of *Arikh Anpin,* or "*Keter* of *Keter,*" the author of the *Tanya* goes on to indicate where the source of the Torah is in *Arikh Anpin.*

The source of the Torah, which emerges from the supernal wisdom, is in the sealed mind of *Arikh Anpin,*

וְשֹׁרֶשׁ הַתּוֹרָה, דְּנָפְקָא מֵחָכְמָה עִילָּאָה הוּא בְּמוֹחָא סְתִימָאָה דַּאֲרִיךְ אַנְפִּין

The Torah emerges from supernal wisdom,[51] which is *Ḥokhma* of *Atzilut.* The Torah's source is in the "sealed mind of *Arikh Anpin,*" which is the level of concealed *Ḥokhma,* also referred to as *Ḥokhma* of *Keter.* ☞

EMERGING FROM *ḤOKHMA*

☞ This means that the Torah's departure from divine concealment, and its entry into the world, take place through the essence and vessels of *Ḥokhma.* We can clearly see that the Torah is enclothed in the intellect: We study Torah, understand it, and so forth. The Torah is worldly wisdom and reason. Through it, we perceive the meaning behind every worldly object. In the higher realm, too, the light of *Ein Sof* is enclothed in *Ḥokhma,* for *Ḥokhma* is the perfect, repaired "vessel," the trace of *Atzilut* in every reality. Furthermore, this "vessel" does not yet contain the definitions and limitations of a being. Consequently, it is within *Ḥokhma,* the essence on the borders of the worlds, that *Ein Sof* is enclothed. In other words, the Torah, and in a certain sense God Himself, enters the world through *Ḥokhma.* Since the Torah as we

51. This is stated in the *Zohar* (2:121a) and is explained in many hasidic sources.

וְהַיְינוּ הַחָכְמָה דְּטַעֲמֵי הַמִּצְוֹת **and this is the wisdom of the reasons for the mitzvot,**

The concealed *Ḥokhma* of *Keter,* which is higher than the *Ḥokhma* of the revealed Torah, is the wisdom of the divine meaning within the mitzvot. One aspect of *Ḥokhma* is concerned with the definitions of the mitzvot and how they should be performed. This aspect connects to the lower worlds. It relates to the way in which the Torah meets the world of action, and how the supernal will within the mitzvot moves from world to world until the mitzvot are physically carried out. However, at its source, in *Keter, Ḥokhma* does not relate to the act of the mitzva, but rather to its inner meaning, the meaning of the supernal will itself. The mitzva is performed in the lower realm, but its reason is revealed only above, in the concealed reality of *Keter,* which is beyond *Ḥokhma.* That is where the divine meaning behind the practical mitzvot is revealed.

Thus in *Atzilut,* the Torah is in *Zeir Anpin* and the mitzvot are in *Malkhut*: In other words, Torah is above and the mitzvot are below. However, in *Arikh Anpin,* which precedes *Atzilut,* this relationship is reversed: Torah is in *Ḥokhma* of *Keter,* while the mitzvot are higher up, in *Keter* of *Keter.* Below, the author of the *Tanya* explains this in accordance with the aforementioned principle of "Their beginning is affixed to their end," which refers to *Keter* and *Malkhut.*

אֶלָּא שֶׁהוּא כְּחוֹתָם הַמִּתְהַפֵּךְ **except that it is like a reversed seal.**

A wax seal, for example, leaves an impression that is the exact opposite of itself: Whatever is on the right on the seal is on the left in the impression, whatever protrudes is depressed, and so forth. This "inversion" represents the relationship between that which is in *Atzilut* and that which is in *Keter* (*Arikh Anpin*), which is above *Atzilut.* The higher levels are able to descend further, and consequently, when a

know it derives from *Ḥokhma,* its source in *Arikh Anpin* is found in *Ḥokhma* of *Arikh Anpin,* which is also known as *Ḥokhma* of *Keter.* In Kabbala, this level is referred to as the "sealed brain." Generally speaking, *Ḥokhma* is revelation. In the soul, for example, *Ḥokhma* is the onset of revelation: It is the means by which we begin to recognize and feel all things. However, in *Arikh Anpin,* in the *sefira* of *Keter,* which comprises all that is beyond and concealed from the intellect, *Ḥokhma* too is concealed.

level descends to an extremely low point, this indicates that its source is very high. The source of the mitzvot is exceedingly high, and as a result, when they move into the worlds, they reach the lower levels. Conversely, the Torah's source is lower, and accordingly, the Torah is higher in *Atzilut* and in relation to the other worlds. ☞

וְנָעוּץ תְּחִלָּתָן בְּסוֹפָן הוּא כֹּחַ הָאֵין סוֹף בָּרוּךְ הוּא, לִבְרוֹא יֵשׁ מֵאַיִן, וְלֹא עַל יְדֵי עִילָּה וְעָלוּל, שֶׁיִּהְיֶה הֶעָלוּל מוּקָּף מֵעִילָּתוֹ וּבָטֵל בִּמְצִיאוּת

And "Their beginning is affixed to their end" is the strength of *Ein Sof*, blessed be He, to create existence from nothingness, not by means of cause and effect, with the effect encompassed by its cause and negated in existence,

The concept of the "inverted seal" is akin to that of "Their beginning is affixed to their end." As explained above, "their beginning" refers to *Keter*, which is higher even than *Ḥokhma*, the first level of *Atzilut*. "Their end," on the other hand, pertains to the physical creations that are below *Atzilut*, in the created worlds.

The strength of *Ein Sof* is beyond all the worlds, but it is revealed in *Malkhut*, in the force that creates "existence from nothingness." This is a reference to the lower worlds, which are created through *Malkhut*.

A SEAL IS REVERSED ONLY WHEN ITS INNER DIMENSION IS IMPRINTED BELOW

☞ An impression is formed when the seal's design is pressed into the wax below it. Likewise, the "inversion" described here occurs only when there is a transition, when the "substance" is imprinted on a lower reality. Only with regard to the illumination of light above, there is no inversion: That which exists above is present below as well. The reversal takes place only when this light is absorbed into a different realm. This may be compared to the case of a teacher who wants to convey a certain idea to his student. The teacher realizes that it is not enough that he himself understands the concept. He must find a way to convey it to his student that is higher, at its source, than his own understanding, such as through a sense of the matter, or through a story or a fine analogy, for example. The teacher cannot conjure these things up on his own: They come to him only when he is in the midst of teaching. This unattainable goal that he is facing evokes within him higher powers than those he can attain by himself. In turn, these powers are capable of reaching the level of the student.

The *sefirot* in the world of *Atzilut* are connected to one another by means of "cause and effect" relationships. In a "cause and effect" relationship, the effect recognizes the cause. It perceives the fact that the cause is the source of its entire existence, and that it has no reality without this cause. Consequently, the effect is entirely subsumed in the cause.

רַק יִהְיֶה הַיֵּשׁ דָּבָר נִפְרָד מֵאֱלֹקוּת בִּכְדֵי שֶׁיִּהְיֶה הַמַּאֲצִיל בָּרוּךְ הוּא מֶלֶךְ עַל כָּל הַנִּפְרָדִים עַל יְדֵי שֶׁיְּקַיְּימוּ מִצְוֹתָיו שֶׁיְּצַוֶּה עֲלֵיהֶם

but with the substance as a separate thing from divinity, so that the Emanator, blessed be He, will be King over all separate entities, by means of their fulfilling His mitzvot that He commands them.

A creation that is formed as "existence from nothingness" is separate from its source. It cannot comprehend the source's essence, and moreover, it might not even be aware of its existence. Thus, by definition, the created entity views itself as separate from the Creator, or in other words, from the Divine.

As explained, *Malkhut* which is kingship, is applicable only if there are entities that are separate from the ruler. God desired to be King, and consequently, beings were created that bear a separate/distinct "existence". Nonetheless, their existence by itself does not give rise to *Malkhut*. For *Malkhut* to be established, these created beings must express their relationship to it. If a king declares his sovereignty by issuing a command to the people, the people must express their recognition of his rule by fulfilling the command of their own free will. As the prayer states, "His kingdom they willingly accepted upon themselves." In other words, the king's desire for sovereignty is not sufficient to establish a kingdom. The desire and will of the nation are also necessary. The people's desire is separate and distinct from the king's. It is the desire to accept the king's rule and fulfill his commands.

וְ׳סוֹף מַעֲשֶׂה בְּמַחֲשָׁבָה תְּחִלָּה׳.

And "the final stage of action is first in thought."

This phrase, from the *piyyut Lekha Dodi*, describes the other side of the phrase "Their beginning is affixed to their end." It expresses how the final stage of action, God's Kingship over the separate beings in the world of action, was present at the inception of "thought," which preceded speech and action. It was in the internal desire for *Malkhut*, which is referred to as *Keter* of *Malkhut*.

Thus, the source of the holy deeds, the practical mitzvot, are the highest source of holiness. Henceforth, the author of the *Tanya* discusses the virtues of the practical mitzvot.

In the same vein, it is stated in the Jerusalem Talmud: "But doesn't Rabbi Shimon maintain that one pauses from his Torah study **for the** mitzva of ***lulav*?"**

וְלָכֵן אָמְרוּ בִּירוּשַׁלְמִי: וְלֵית לֵיהּ לְרַבִּי שִׁמְעוֹן שֶׁמַּפְסִיק לַלּוּלָב? וכו'

The rabbis of the Jerusalem Talmud discuss various situations where a person is required to halt what he is doing in order to recite *Shema* or *Amida*.[52] Rabbi Shimon bar Yoḥai takes an extreme approach with regard to the importance of Torah study. He posits that a person should not interrupt his Torah study, even for the purpose of reciting *Shema*. Nonetheless, it becomes clear that even Rabbi Shimon acknowledges that one must suspend his Torah study in order to perform a practical mitzva that has a fixed time and cannot be carried out later, such as the taking of the *lulav*.

---

52. "Rabbi Yoḥanan said in the name of Rabbi Shimon ben Yoḥai, 'For example we, who are engaged in the study of Torah, do not interrupt even for the recitation of the *Shema*'.... Rabbi Ḥananya ben Akiva said, 'Just as they interrupt for *Shema*, so they interrupt for prayer, *tefillin*, and all other commandments of the Torah.' Would not Rabbi Shimon ben Yoḥai agree that one interrupts to make a *sukka* or a *lulav*? Does not Rabbi Shimon ben Yoḥai make the distinction between one who studies to do and one who studies in order not to do? Because he who studies in order not to do would have been better off had he not been born. And did not Rabbi Yoḥanan say, 'He who studies without the intent to put into practice would have been better off if the placenta he was in was twisted around and he never would have entered the world'?" (Jerusalem Talmud, *Shabbat* 1:2). There is a similar discussion in Tractate *Berakhot* (1:2) of the Jerusalem Talmud. However, the Lubavitcher Rebbe, Rabbi Menaḥem Mendel Schneerson, remarks that the author of the *Tanya* is apparently referring to Tractate *Shabbat*.

וְכָל הַלּוֹמֵד שֶׁלֹּא לַעֲשׂוֹת נוֹחַ לוֹ שֶׁנֶּתְהַפְּכָה שִׁלְיָיתוֹ עַל פָּנָיו וכו׳

And: "Whoever studies without the intent to put into practice would have been better off if the placenta he was in was twisted around..."

This statement is made by Rabbi Yoḥanan in the abovementioned discussion in the Jerusalem Talmud. He is emphasizing the importance of the practical mitzvot. With regard to Torah study, study that relates to action is superior. This means study that is undertaken in order to act. The imagery here indicates that the entire reason a person is brought into the world is to perform mitzvot. For spiritual endeavors alone, there is no need for a physical body. Consequently, regarding a person who studies Torah without the intent to put it into practice, it would have been better if he had not been born.

כִּי הַשִּׁלְיָא נוֹצְרָה תְּחִלָּה מֵהַטִּיפָּה וְהִיא לְבַדָּהּ הָיְתָה עִיקַּר הַוָּלָד עַד מ׳ יוֹם, שֶׁהִתְחִילָה צוּרַת הַוָּלָד

For the placenta was initially formed from the drop, and it alone was the essence of the child until forty days after conception, **when the child began to take shape.**

Here, the author of the *Tanya* explains the abovementioned image. The placenta is the vessel through which the fetus is formed during gestation. Before the fetus has any form or definition, the placenta is the major entity. According to the Sages, this stage lasts until forty days after conception. At that point, the fetus's essential structure has been formed, and its basic characteristics, such as its gender, have been defined. Before the fortieth day, there is only the reality that preexists the fetus: the reality of the placenta. This early reality continues to develop, and it is fully realized only after the person's birth and growth, when he performs a physical act with his body. If a person does not perform this act, he negates the whole course of human development by way of the placenta. In a certain sense, he reverts back to that earlier, placental stage.

The author of the *Tanya* emphasizes the fact that this does not mean a return to the state that existed prior to conception, but rather the state that existed at the very beginning of conception, before the fetus came into being. In a certain sense, this refers to the period before the soul truly descends into the body. The groundwork and intention for this event are present, but there is not yet any connection between body and soul. There is bodily matter, namely the placenta, and there is a soul that is destined to enter into it. However, there is no real connection whereby the physical matter takes shape in accordance with the soul and its worldly role, and whereby the soul assumes the constraints of the physical body. Thus the author of the *Tanya* is describing neither the body nor the soul, but rather the soul that is within the body. When the soul within the body carries out God's commandments in the physical world of *Asiya*, it is realizing this connection by uniting the different parts of the whole. However, if the soul within the body does not carry out the mitzvot, all of this has no meaning for man himself and his descent to the world. It is as though he does not exist at all, and the only thing that remains is what existed previously: the placenta alone.

וְכָכָה הַמִּצְוֹת הֵן עִיקַּר הַתּוֹרָה וְשָׁרְשָׁהּ הֲגַם שֶׁהַמִּצְוָה הִיא גּוּפָנִית וְהַתּוֹרָה הִיא חָכְמָה, רַק שֶׁזֶּה בְּחִיצוֹנִיּוּת וְזֶה בִּפְנִימִיּוּת

So too, the mitzvot are the essence and root of the Torah, especially as a mitzva is corporeal and the Torah is wisdom, only that this one is in the externality and that one is in the internality,

The source of the mitzvot is higher, yet they occur only in the lower, external layer of this world. On the other hand, the source of the Torah is lower, but it is manifest in the inner dimension of our world, in the spiritual reality of the intellect.

Because the source of the mitzvot is so high, it has no expression in the inner dimension of our lowly world. Its manifestation is entirely external. We are incapable of comprehending the magnitude of the mitzvot: All we can do is perform them. This is the meaning of the idea that the mitzvot are in the external dimension. ☞

THE MITZVOT ARE THE ESSENCE AND ROOT

☞ Thus the mitzvot take precedence within the supernal source of everything, which is far beyond our comprehension. Furthermore, this precedence has implications for our lives and our divine service in this world. It is explained in many different

וּכִדְלְקַמָּן. **as will be explained below.**

Later on in this letter, the author of the *Tanya* explains these elements of our divine service, Torah study, and mitzva observance. However, he does not return to this topic specifically, aside from a brief remark at the end of the letter. It is possible that he wrote more, and that the text he is referring to is no longer in our possession. This accords with the publishers' note at the end of the letter, "Until here we have found of his holy writing." However, it is also possible that the author of the *Tanya* is referring to the ideas that emerge based on the words that he writes below, despite the fact that they are not stated explicitly.

Now, the author of the *Tanya* returns to the central theme of the letter: the creation and unfolding succession of the worlds from "nothingness" wherever *Ein Sof* reaches and creates "existence from nothingness."

10 Tishrei
6 Tishrei (leap year)

וְהִנֵּה, כְּמוֹ כֵן, מִזִּיווּג זו"ן דבי"ע נִבְרְאוּ מֵאַיִן לְיֵשׁ כָּל הַנִּבְרָאִים וְהַנּוֹצָרִים וְהַנַּעֲשִׂים **Now, in the same manner, all the created, formed, and fashioned entities were created from "nothingness" to "existence," from the coupling of *Zeir Anpin* and *Nukva* of *Beria, Yetzira,* and *Asiya,***

As discussed earlier, the souls of the world of *Atzilut* were "born" out of the union of *Zeir Anpin* and *Nukva* of *Atzilut*. Through this union, they emerged from "nothingness" in the form of "existence." Likewise,

sources that when a person carries out the positive and negative commandments, his soul becomes purer, and his mind is more capable of comprehending Torah (*Torah Or* 1b; *Likkutei Torah LeGimmel Parshiyot, Bereshit* 1c). This is said with regard to actual deeds, as well as Torah study that is carried out in order to act. These matters constitute a concealed process of preparation in the inner dimension of the soul, which ultimately enables the soul to receive the Torah's wisdom. In general, these stages are not clearly evident. One might conclude that they are not, in fact, real, and that the Torah truly begins with *Ḥokhma* and has no connection to the mitzvot or their spiritual effects. Consequently, it is important to mention this fact. One should contemplate it and remember that "at first [the world] was dark and then light [followed]" (*Shabbat* 77b). Prior to the light of the Torah, which is revealed through *Ḥokhma* and *Bina*, there is a hidden foundation of all-encompassing divine will. We receive this in an external manner, and subsequently, we are able to receive the Torah's wisdom in an internal way.

the creations in the world of *Beria* were formed through the union of *Zeir Anpin* and *Nukva* of the world of *Beria*; the creations in the world of *Yetzira* were formed through the union of *Zeir Anpin* and *Nukva* of the world of *Yetzira*; and the creations in the world of *Asiya* were formed through the union of *Zeir Anpin* and *Nukva* of the world of *Asiya*. With regard to each world, the joining of the *sefirot* of *Zeir Anpin* and *Nukva* is what forms the world itself, as well as the souls and angels within it.

עַל יְדֵי אוֹר הַנְּשָׁמָה שֶׁבְּתוֹכָן שֶׁהִיא אֱלֹקוּת **by means of the light of the soul within them, which is divinity,**

As mentioned at the beginning of the epistle, what creates "existence from nothingness" is *Ein Sof* Himself, and His revelation in the form of the divine light within all things. The *sefirot* are "the Divine" with respect to the worlds. Within the *sefirot*, the light is "the Divine" with respect to the vessels. And within the light itself, the light on the level of *neshama* is "the Divine" with respect to the lights that are on the levels of *nefesh* and *ruaḥ*.

As explained, the line between "existence" and "nothingness," between the Divine and the world, does not have one fixed path. Rather, it enters all places. In a certain sense, the same pattern is replicated on each subsequent level. Each time, there is a shift from the more general context to the more specific. This is how we must relate to the definitions given here, as well as the flexible use of kabbalistic terms.

מֵהַכֵּלִים דְּעֶשֶׂר סְפִירוֹת דְּמַלְכוּת דַּאֲצִילוּת. **from the vessels of the ten *sefirot* of *Malkhut* of *Atzilut*.**

The light of the soul is the manifestation of the Divine within the ten *sefirot* of each of the created worlds. It is drawn into those *sefirot* from *Malkhut* of *Atzilut*. *Malkhut* of *Atzilut* is a *sefira* of the world of *Atzilut*, and the world of *Atzilut* itself is the manifestation of the Divine in relation to all of the worlds.

Specifically, as mentioned at the beginning of the letter, *Malkhut* of *Atzilut* contains thirty vessels. This is because each of the ten *sefirot* has an internal, a middle, and an external vessel. The ten internal vessels become the "soul" of the world of *Beria*; the ten middle vessels become the "soul" of the world of *Yetzira*; and the ten external vessels become the "soul" of the world of *Asiya*.

Thus we understand, and this point is further strengthened later on in the letter, that the line of divine Inner Light, the light of *Ein Sof* Himself, runs from above to below throughout the unfolding succession of the worlds. The unfolding succession begins above the world of *Atzilut* and extends all the way to the world of *Asiya*. It occurs by means of the vessels' descent and division among the different worlds. The light described here, the light of the soul, reaches all the way to *Zeir Anpin* and *Nukva* of *Asiya*, and comes directly from *Malkhut* of *Atzilut*. It carries the divine essence wherever it goes, and this essence is what creates "existence from nothingness."

וְגַם בְּתוֹכָהּ, הֶאָרַת הַקַּו דְּאוֹר אֵין סוֹף, הַמְלוּבָּשׁ בַּאֲצִילוּת

Within it, as well, is **the illumination of the line of the light of *Ein Sof*, which is enclothed in *Atzilut*,**

The light of the line flows into *Malkhut* of *Atzilut*. In Kabbala, the "line" is the light drawn into the space formed by constriction, from the light of *Ein Sof* that precedes constriction. Unlike the light of *Ein Sof* before constriction, the line's light has a "top," a "bottom," and directionality. The "top" is the line's starting point in the light of *Ein Sof*, and the "bottom" is the path it travels and illuminates. The line itself becomes smaller and smaller at each level as it moves further away from the top. These attributes of the line are what enable it to emit the light of *Ein Sof* even into the vessels. For the *Ein Sof* is not purely an infinite, encompassing reality. Rather, it is able to relate, to a certain extent, to the creations. It is in the world of *Atzilut* that the light of the ray begins to shine within the vessels, for while *Atzilut* is a reality of lights within vessels, it is a divine reality. This means that it is completely nullified and transparent with regard to the Infinite One, and its vessels, even those of *Malkhut* of *Atzilut*, are able to enclothe and reveal the light of *Ein Sof* that is in the line.

עַד הַפַּרְסָא.

until the *perasa* (the partition).

The direct, revealed light of *Ein Sof* reaches the partition between the world of *Atzilut* and the world of *Beria*. This *perasa* is the essential divider between the divine reality and the created reality. Below it, the light of *Ein Sof* is no longer fully revealed. As will be explained, the light of *Ein Sof* does enter the realm below the *perasa*, but it is not as visible there as it is in *Atzilut*. Below the *perasa*, there is only an "illumination of the illumination" of *Ein Sof*, which portrays His presence and nature. ☞

וְהֶאָרַת הַקַּו שֶׁהָיָה מֵאִיר בִּכְלֵים דְּעֶשֶׂר סְפִירוֹת דְּמַלְכוּת, בָּקַע הַפַּרְסָא עִמָּהֶם, וּמֵאִיר בָּהֶם בבי"ע

The illumination of the line, which cast its light in the vessels of the ten *sefirot* of *Malkhut*, split the *perasa* with them, and casts its light upon them in *Beria, Yetzira,* and ***Asiya*,**

As explained, *Malkhut* of *Atzilut* is what creates the worlds of *Beria, Yetzira,* and *Asiya* by means of the power of *Ein Sof* that is manifest within it. In other words, the vessels of *Malkhut* of *Atzilut*, together with the light of *Ein Sof* that radiates within them, descend, and thereupon, they form and give life to the worlds of *Beria, Yetzira,* and *Asiya*. The power of *Ein Sof* within *Malkhut* that creates "existence from nothingness" is thus drawn into the created reality. It continuously forms this reality and gives it life, even though it is not revealed in it, and even though the limited and separate reality of the creations seems to contradict the reality of *Ein Sof*. Nonetheless, the light of *Ein Sof* is found in each of the worlds. It is the aspect of the soul within each one: It gives life to that world, yet it also exists within it as the light of *Ein Sof*. ☞

PERASA

☞ The *perasa* is not a third entity that separates *Atzilut* from *Beria*. Rather, the *perasa* is the "existence" of the created world itself, and its perception of itself as "separate." Vessels that are capable of revealing *Ein Sof* are those that are essentially subsumed in *Ein Sof*. When *Ein Sof* reaches the created vessels, which are not totally subsumed, and which perceive their own existence as well, it is no longer revealed as *Ein Sof*. Instead, it is revealed as light, as a revelation that is limited to the vessels of a particular world, yet portrays the unlimited light of *Ein Sof*. It cannot be seen, yet it can be understood from that which is seen.

SPLITTING THE *PERASA*

☞ As this letter repeatedly explains, the line between "existence" and "nothingness" (and in a certain sense, the presence of *Ein Sof*) does not end in the higher realm, at the partition between *Atzilut* and *Beria*. Rather, the light of *Ein Sof* pen-

כְּמוֹ בַּאֲצִילוּת מַמָּשׁ. **exactly as in *Atzilut*.**

The light of *Ein Sof* in the worlds of *Beria, Yetzira,* and *Asiya* is exactly the same as it is in *Atzilut*. This fact is emphasized here because it is not self-evident. *Ein Sof* is not as clearly revealed in the created worlds as He is in the world of *Atzilut*. Nonetheless, He is present, not relatively or nearly, but truly. The difference arises from the created worlds, which willfully conceal themselves. However, the line of the light of *Ein Sof* flows from above to below in these worlds exactly as it does in *Atzilut*. ☞

etrates this *perasa* in a concealed manner and passes through it to the other side, to the created worlds. The *perasa* is a principle that is constantly perpetuating, and it conceals and reveals the "*Ein Sof*" that pertains to each level.

THE *PERASA* IN THE HUMAN EXPERIENCE

☞ The *perasa* is explained elsewhere in relation to the human experience (see *Torah Or, Parashat Vayera,* s.v. "*pataḥ Eliyahu,*" 13c and onward): It performs the same function as an analogy. There are two ways to convey an understanding of a certain point from one person to another. One way is to make it as abstract as possible so that it can pass from vessel to vessel, from person to person. This is possible only when the giver and the receiver possess a shared foundation, so that they both understand the meanings of the words and concepts in more or less the same way. The receiver's vessel must be capable of receiving. In the words of the Sages, he must "understand on his own" (see Mishna *Ḥagiga* 2: 1). Subsequently, all that remains is to form a connection and transfer the light and substance from one "vessel" to the other. The second way to convey understanding is by means of an analogy. When the receiver's vessels are not of the same order as the giver's, the giver can "dress up" his understanding in something else, such as within a story or an image of a reality that relates to the receiver's experience. This story or image creates a form, or vessel, which contains the knowledge and understanding that the giver wishes to convey. However, in this case, he does not need to convey the knowledge itself, but only the story, which may be transmitted to the receiver without obstruction. This mode of transmission is what is called the *perasa*, and it is how light is conveyed from the world of *Atzilut* into the worlds of *Beria, Yetzira,* and *Asiya*. What is special about this mode of transmission is that it does not involve the transfer of only light or meaning. Rather, light is transferred together with a vessel. The receiver does not receive abstract content that he must place in his own vessels. Instead, he receives the content together with the vessel that holds it. In the case being discussed here, the light of *Atzilut* is received enclothed in the vessels of the ten *sefirot* of *Malkhut* of *Atzilut*. Just like the knowledge conveyed through an analogy, once this light is transmitted, it is not visible, and one must contemplate the analogy in order to reveal it. Nonetheless, it can still be revealed, because it was transmitted through

Below, the author of the *Tanya* explains that the light emitted by the line can indeed be found in the lower realm, but first and foremost, the line itself is to be found there. The light emitted by the line is enclothed in the vessels of *Atzilut,* and it descends within them, through the *perasa,* to the worlds of *Beria, Yetzira,* and *Asiya,* just as the external dimension of the higher realm descends to the inner dimension of the lower realm. The line itself is present in the lower realm just as it is in the higher realm. It is the essential Inner Light, and it is akin to the initial, essential desire that achieves its ultimate objective. It is the "end" that is affixed to the "beginning." Similarly, when a person explains a particular matter, the explanation descends by means of the vessels of the giver to the vessels of the receiver, and it continues in this way, moving downward, from giver to receiver. However, throughout this process there is an additional element: the desire to give, and the pleasure derived from giving. This is all-encompassing and unchanging from start to finish.

וְכֵן גַּם הַקַּו בְּעַצְמוֹ, הַמְלוּבָּשׁ בְּסִיּוּם וְסוֹף נה״י דְּאָדָם קַדְמוֹן

The same is true of the line itself, which is enclothed in the conclusion and end of *Netzaḥ, Hod,* and ***Yesod* of *Adam Kadmon,***

As explained above, the light emitted by the line is enclothed in the vessels of *Atzilut,* and furthermore, it splits the *perasa.* The line itself, however, is not enclothed in *Atzilut,* nor in any single part of it. It is enclothed only in the fundamental structure that encompasses the entire line. This structure is called *Adam Kadmon.* ☞

an analogy. Moreover, when this light is revealed, it is even more complete, in a certain sense, than it is when conveyed in an abstract form. When an idea is abstract, its meaning is never transmitted precisely or fully. There is always a difference between the receiver's vessel and the giver's vessel. By necessity, the content is conveyed in separate parts, and these parts are reassembled in a different way when they reach the receiver. However, when an analogy is used, the content proceeds in its entirety, in exactly the same form as in the higher realm.

NETZAḤ, HOD, YESOD OF ADAM KADMON

☞ The plane of *Adam Kadmon*'s ancient and abstract, and it is far removed from all that we know. Nonetheless, since it includes the term "adam," "human being," we connect it to our understanding of the ten *sefirot,* which are thought to be

Adam Kadmon is the first and broadest *partzuf*. It encompasses the entire line, from when it emerges from the light of *Ein Sof* until it stops flowing. This is indicated in its name. *Adam* is the structure, the *partzuf*. It is analogous to the human body and soul in the physical world, and to the ten *sefirot*, which are also referred to as *adam*. This particular *adam* is *kadmon*: It comes before (*kodem*) every other *partzuf* and structure. This does not simply mean that it is the first one. Rather, it precedes everything: the beginning, the middle, and the end. It is the structure that enclothes the line itself, before its light shines on any level.[53]

In our human understanding, it is possible to compare *Adam Kadmon* to God's "original thought," or "original desire," concerning everything that will eventually exist. "I will reign"[54] was God's earliest thought, which arose before He emanated, created, or said anything. It embodies His desire to be King. Earlier, it was explained that the existence of the "King" necessarily entails the existence of all the worlds, because the worlds comprise the reality of the "nation" that accepts God's Kingship. The original thought is not merely the beginning of a process that goes on to unfold. It is the thought of God, who is all-knowing and all-powerful. Consequently, before the existence of time, it includes everything that has happened, that will happen, and that could happen before the thought is fully realized. Moreover, just as *Adam Kadmon* ends in *Asiya*, this thought, too, reaches the lowest level of the world of *Asiya*.

Thus "original desire" contains everything that will ever have existence, although these objects are not yet situated within the vessels

arranged in the shape of a human being, and are identified with the ten faculties of the soul and body. The lower segment of the ten *sefirot*, which is made up of *Netzaḥ*· *Hod*, and *Yesod*, relates to the lower, external reality. These sefirot correspond to the "feet" of both the soul and the body. The author of the *Tanya* specifies, "the conclusion and end of *Netzaḥ*· *Hod*, and *Yesod*," because the enclothement of the line ends at the outer edge of these *sefirot*. The line is not enclothed in *Malkhut*, for in *Malkhut* of *Adam Kadmon* (which becomes the *Atik* of *Atzilut*), it is the light of the line that shines, rather than the line itself (see *Or HaTorah*, Gen., vol. 2, 428a).

53. See *Kuntres Torat HaḤasidut*.

54. See *Torah Or* 78b.

or boundaries that will contain them in reality. Accordingly, the line encompasses the potential for everything that exists in actuality, down to the lowest level of *Asiya*. This is what the author of the *Tanya* goes on to explain.

שֶׁהוּא סוֹף רַגְלֵי הַיּוֹשֶׁר שֶׁלּוֹ, הַמִּסְתַּיְּימִים בְּמַלְכוּת דַּעֲשִׂיָּה.

which is the end of *Adam Kadmon's* **"feet of straight lines"** [*raglei hayosher*], **which conclude in the** ***Malkhut*** **of** ***Asiya.***

Adam Kadmon is all-encompassing in the same way as "original desire." It spans from "main" *Keter*[55] to the lowest point of *Netzaḥ, Hod,* and *Yesod* of *Adam Kadmon*. These three *sefirot* of *Adam Kadmon* are the "feet" of *Malkhut* of *Asiya,* the lowest point in the entire unfolding succession.[56] ☞

FEET OF STRAIGHT (*YOSHER*) LINE

☞ This term, which will be expanded upon below, is related to the distinction in the mystical works between two aspects of the unfolding succession: the aspect of the circles and the aspect of the lines (*yosher*). Every level in the unfolding succession possesses both of these aspects. The circles surround one another: Each level encircles the level below it. In contrast, with regard to the aspect of the line, each level evolves and connects to the next one as though along a straight line that extends from above to below. The "circles" aspect of *Adam Kadmon* is a circle that encompasses all the levels below it. Both the highest and lowest point of *Adam Kadmon* are part of this circle, and both *Atzilut* and *Asiya* are encircled. In contrast, the "line" aspect of *Adam Kadmon* extends from the beginning of everything to the end of *Asiya,* such that each level connects to a level in the unfolding succession. Thus, when the author of the *Tanya* states here that *Netzaḥ, Hod,* and *Yesod* of *Adam Kadmon* end in *Malkhut* of *Asiya,* this means that the line within these three *sefirot* of *Adam Kadmon* shines in *Malkhut* of *Asiya.*

Similarly, the "circles" aspect of original thought comprises the groundwork and atmosphere that enable the thought to materialize. It encompasses all the events that could possibly take place within the scope of the thought, but it does not include the particulars. On the other hand, the "line" aspect of thought is enclothed in specific circumstances and in the way each one leads to the next. A thought that is enclothed in the realm of action is a more practical thought, while a thought that is enclothed in speech is more abstract, and even deeper than this is a thought that is not enclothed in anything.

---

55. See *Likkutei Torah,* Lev. 20d, Num. 95a; *Hemshekh Ayin Bet,* vol. 1, p. 19.
56. See *Etz Ḥayyim, Sha'ar* 43, Introduction (cited in *Likkutei Siḥot,* vol. 15, p. 472).

הִנֵּה הֶאָרַת הַקַּו מְאִירָה מִשָּׁם, וּמִתְלַבֶּשֶׁת בְּאוֹר הַנְּשָׁמָה דְּעֶשֶׂר סְפִירוֹת דבי"ע שֶׁהוּא אֱלֹקוּת.

Now, the illumination of the line shines from there, and is enclothed in the light of the soul of the ten *sefirot* of *Beria, Yetzira,* and *Asiya,* which is divinity.

As explained, the ten *sefirot* of each world contain lights and vessels. The light within a vessel corresponds to the soul within a body. Accordingly, this light has various levels, which are analogous to the levels of *nefesh, ruaḥ,* and *neshama* in the soul. The border between the realm of the Creator and the realm of the creations, between the world and the Divine, runs between the vessels and lights of the *sefirot,* and within the lights, between the levels of *nefesh* and *ruaḥ,* which are "the worlds," and *neshama,* which is the expression of the Divine. Thus, the light of the divine line itself, whose essence is not revealed even in the world of *Atzilut,* illuminates the lower realm. There, the line's initial purpose is fulfilled, for it gives expression to its essence. This light is enclothed in all the levels of the unfolding succession, in the "light of the *neshama*" within each separate world and level, and this too reveals the line's essence.

Two different types of illumination have been discussed here. Above, the author of the *Tanya* described the revelation that descends in the vessels of *Atzilut,* traverses the *perasa,* and enters the *sefirot* of the worlds, moving from *Beria* to *Yetzira* and then to *Asiya.* The further this light descends, the more it is concealed and separated from its source. In contrast, here, the author of the *Tanya* describes an illumination that is not a revelation in the usual sense. It does not occur in the intellectual and emotional vessels of a particular world or soul. Rather, it is akin to a bestowal of essence, which is received by the final stage of action. At that level, the initial desire is fulfilled. It illuminates all the previous levels, and within them, reveals the starting point, reawakening the potential that arises from desire, and the pleasure that is felt when it is realized.

וְהֶאָרָה דְּהֶאָרָה מִתְלַבֶּשֶׁת בְּנֶפֶשׁ רוּחַ דְּעֶשֶׂר סְפִירוֹת דִּבְרִיאָה יְצִירָה עֲשִׂיָּה וְאַף גַּם בְּכָל הַכֵּלִים שֶׁלָּהֶם

An illumination of the illumination is enclothed in *nefesh* and *ruaḥ* of the ten *sefirot* of *Beria, Yetzira,* and *Asiya,* as well as in all their vessels,

The illumination of the line is enclothed in the level of *neshama* within the ten *sefirot* in the worlds of *Beria, Yetzira,* and *Asiya,* while an illumination of this illumination, which is an effect even further from the source, is enclothed in the levels of *nefesh* and *ruaḥ*. As mentioned earlier, the vessels of the *sefirot* and the lights of *nefesh* and *ruaḥ* make up the outer dimension of the *sefirot*. The inner dimension, the aspect of the Divine within the *sefirot,* is the illumination of the line itself that is present in all things. On the other hand, the outer dimension and the vessels are the illumination of the inner dimension, also called the illumination of the illumination. ☞

וְהֶאָרָה דְּהֶאָרָה דְּהֶאָרָה, הוּא בְּכָל הַנִּבְרָאִים וְנוֹצָרִים וְנַעֲשִׂים כְּמוֹ שֶׁכָּתוּב: "הַיַּמִּים וְכָל אֲשֶׁר בָּהֶם וְאַתָּה מְחַיֶּה אֶת כּוּלָּם" (נחמיה ט,ו).

and an illumination of the illumination of the illumination is found in **all created, formed, and fashioned entities, as it is written: "The seas and everything that is in them, and You sustain them all"** (Neh. 9:6).

The "illumination of the illumination of the illumination" is likewise fundamentally different from the "illumination of the illumination." If "illumination" is a revelation of the Divine and "the illumination of the illumination" corresponds to divine action, then "the illumination of the illumination of the illumination" is akin to the outcome of the action.

The "illumination of the illumination of the illumination" is that which is formed by means of the divine force within the *sefirot*. This

ILLUMINATION OF ILLUMINATION

☞ The difference between "illumination" and "illumination of illumination" is an essential one. The illumination of an object is, of course, not the object itself, yet it illuminates it, and accordingly, it reveals it. The illumination of the illumination, on the other hand, is separate from the object. It does not reveal the object itself, but only traces of it: one of its actions, one of its functions, an indication of its presence, and so forth. Thus the illumination of the line is enclothed in the level of *neshama*, which is "the Divine": It still bears the name and unity of its divine source. Although it is just an illumination, it is a revelation of *Ein Sof*, and it performs the operations of *Ein Sof*. The illumination of the illumination, however, is akin to the action itself, which can be totally separate from the one performing it. Consequently, the illumination of the illumination is not "the Divine."

term pertains to all the beings on every level, or in other words, all the creations in the worlds of *Beria, Yetzira,* and *Asiya.*

God Himself gives life to all of the creations, and sustains them on every level. This is referring to God's initial intention, the "original thought" of *Adam Kadmon,* which is one with God's essence. The creations of *Beria, Yetzira,* and *Asiya* bring this thought to fruition through their existence and life force. ☞

וְכָל זֹאת בִּבְחִינַת הִתְפַּשְּׁטוּת הַחַיּוּת לְהַחֲיוֹתָם. **All this is by the expansion of the life force, in order to sustain them.**

The different levels of illumination, such as "illumination," "illumination of illumination," and so on, are stages in the illumination and expansion of the life force from the light of *Ein Sof.* However, they pertain only to the "illumination" of *Ein Sof.* Consequently, unlike the actual light of *Ein Sof,* the illumination is enclothed in a "garment" and animates all objects in accordance with their scope, boundaries, and vessels. This divine illumination is referred to as "the light that fills all worlds."

7 Tishrei (leap year)

אָמְנָם מְצִיאוּתוֹ וּמַהוּתוֹ שֶׁל אוֹר הָאֵין סוֹף אֵינוֹ בְּגֶדֶר מָקוֹם כְּלָל **However, the existence and essence of the light of *Ein Sof* is not in the category of a place at all,**

With regard to the light that fills all worlds, there is always a place that is filled and given life by the light. In contrast, the light of *Ein Sof* Himself is not identified with any particular space. In fact, the light of *Ein Sof* does not relate to the concept of space at all. With regard to this light, reality is not divided into separate places or periods of

YOU SUSTAIN THEM ALL

☞ As explained in *Sha'ar HaYiḥud VeHa'emuna* (chap. 2), the word *atta,* "You," is made up of the letters of divine speech: *Alef* and *tav* signify the entire Hebrew alphabet, for they are its first and last letters, respectively, while *heh,* which is the fifth letter, symbolizes the five organs of articulation. Speech is the *sefira* of *Malkhut.* Through *Malkhut,* the capacity of *Ein Sof* to create "existence from nothingness" is revealed in each world.

time, and it does not distinguish between the creations of *Atzilut*, the creations of *Beria*, and so on. The light of *Ein Sof* is beyond all such definitions, and consequently, they do not limit or affect it in any way.

וְסוֹבֵב כָּל עָלְמִין בְּשָׁוֶה, וְ"אֶת הַשָּׁמַיִם וְאֶת הָאָרֶץ אֲנִי מָלֵא" (ירמיה כג,כד), בְּהַשְׁוָואָה אַחַת וְלֵית אֲתָר פָּנוּי מִינֵּיהּ' אַף בָּאָרֶץ הַלֵּזוּ הַגַּשְׁמִית

but rather **it encompasses all worlds equally, and** this is expressed in the verse **"Do I not fill the heavens and the earth – the utterance of the Lord?"** (Jer. 23:24), **in a single equalization, and "there is no space devoid of Him," even on this corporeal earth,**

The light of *Ein Sof* is akin to a circle: Everything that the circle encompasses is equally "surrounded" by it. The statement that this light is not defined by space does not mean that it is not present in every aspect of reality.[57] Rather, it indicates that it is indeed present in all things, and moreover, it is equally present in everything. It is present in the lowest realm to the same degree that it is present in the highest realm, because "high" and "low" have no meaning with respect to the light of *Ein Sof*. This divine illumination is called "the light that encompasses all worlds."

Hasidism teaches that the verse "Do I not fill the heavens and the earth" refers to the light that encompasses all worlds. "Heaven" and "earth" are the broadest concepts of space: The heavens constitute the entire upper realm, and the earth constitutes the entire lower realm. It is not clear how it is possible to fill both of these realms equally, without them being on the same level. Rather, the light that "fills all worlds" encompasses the heavens and the earth separately. It fills each one in a different way and with a different light. Together, the heavens and the earth can be filled only by God, or in other words, by the light of *Ein Sof* Himself, which encompasses all worlds. As mentioned, this light fills everything, and it is present everywhere, in both the higher realm and the lower realm, in equal measure.

One might have thought that this lofty aspect of the Divine would

57. See *Likkutei Amarim*, chap. 48.

occur only in the vast, infinite, upper realm. Therefore, the author of the *Tanya* clarifies that it pertains to the physical world as well.[58] ☞

רַק שֶׁהוּא בִּבְחִינַת מַקִּיף וְסוֹבֵב, וּכְמוֹ שֶׁנִּתְבָּאֵר הַפֵּירוּשׁ בְּלִקּוּטֵי אֲמָרִים (פרק מח).

only that He is considered to encompass and surround it, **as the meaning was explained in *Likkutei Amarim*** (chap. 48).

Chapter 48 of *Likkutei Amarim* emphasizes what was stated above: One should not think that the light that "encompasses all worlds" is present only in the higher realm, surrounding the worlds. In fact, it is present also in the lower realm, within all things. However, it is not enclothed in any "garments." Instead, it envelops each object. It does not animate the object from within. Rather, it constitutes the space that allows the object to exist in its current form. It provides the object with its place, its essential nature, and its processes.

וְלֹא הִתְפַּשְּׁטוּת וְהִתְלַבְּשׁוּת הַחַיּוּת לְהַחֲיוֹתָם וּלְהַוּוֹתָם מֵאַיִן לְיֵשׁ כִּי אִם עַל יְדֵי הֶאָרָה דְּהֶאָרָה דְּהֶאָרָה וכו׳ מֵהַקַּו כַּנִּזְכָּר לְעֵיל.

It is not the expansion and enclothing of the life force, to sustain them and to bring them into being from nothingness to existence; rather, it is by means of the illumination of the illumination of the illumination…, from the line, as stated above.

"DO I NOT FILL THE HEAVENS AND THE EARTH"; "THERE IS NO SPACE DEVOID OF HIM"

☞ These two statements describe the encompassing light, and both of them are necessary. "Do I not fill the heavens and the earth" refers to the light: What fills the heavens and the earth is the light that is present in everything in equal measure. All boundaries and definitions are nullified in relation to this light. All vessels and realms are meaningless, and there is no difference between heaven and earth. On the other hand, the statement "There is no space devoid of Him" relates to the realms and vessels. It teaches that they are not devoid of the encompassing light. This statement does not negate the vessels. In fact, it attaches great importance to every part

58. The phrase "There is no space devoid of Him" appears in *Tikkunei Zohar* 91a, among other places.

The life force is enclothed in the creations, and this animates and sustains them in the form of revealed, visible entitles. This process does not occur by means of the encompassing light, for this light is concealed in relation to the creations. Instead, it occurs by means of the light that fills all worlds. The light that fills all worlds descends from level to level, becoming more constricted each time it does so. It is the "illumination" of the line's light, then the "illumination of the illumination," and so on.

וְגַם מֵאוֹר אֵין סוֹף הַסּוֹבֵב וּמַקִּיף לְאַרְבַּע עוֹלָמוֹת אבי"ע בְּשָׁוֶה, מֵאִיר אֶל הַקַּו הַפְּנִימִי דֶּרֶךְ הַכֵּלִים דְּעֶשֶׂר סְפִירוֹת דבי"ע.

Furthermore, the light of *Ein Sof*, which surrounds and encompasses equally the four worlds of *Atzilut*, *Beria*, *Yetzira*, and ***Asiya*****, shines onto the inner line, by way of the vessels of the ten *sefirot* of *Beria*, *Yetzira*,** and ***Asiya*****.**[59]

Thus, the light that "encompasses all worlds" surrounds all the worlds in equal measure, and furthermore, it is beyond them all and serves as the foundation for their very existence. However, it also extends its infinite illumination into the worlds. This means that the power of *Ein Sof* enters into the framework of *Beria*, *Yetzira*, and *Asiya*, and manifests itself in specific places and forms. Ostensibly, this is impossible: If

of them, for there is no single part that is devoid of this light and all that it signifies. Thus, the light that encompasses all worlds contains both of the aspects discussed here. It is beyond all limits, and is separate and distinct from everything else. However, it is also found within every boundary. It allows the boundaries to exist and is the foundation of every object: For an object to exist, it must do so within the framework of the encompassing light.

59. Here, the author of the *Tanya* refers to the light that encompasses all four worlds. However, he concludes the passage by mentioning the *sefirot* of only three of these worlds: *Beria*, *Yetzira*, and *Asiya*. The Surrounding Light does indeed encompass all four worlds. Furthermore, its illumination of the inner line through the vessels is what gives the vessels the ability to create "existence from nothingness." Earlier in this letter, the author of the *Tanya* stated that the "created entity" originates in the vessels of the *sefirot* of *Beria*, *Yetzira*, and *Asiya*.

the light is infinite, it is "Surrounding Light." On the other hand, if it is "Inner Light," it is not infinite, but limited. Therefore, the author of the *Tanya* explains here that *Ein Sof* enters the worlds by means of the vessels of the ten *sefirot*, and not by means of the lights. Generally, we regard a vessel as something that restricts the light within it. However, in a certain sense, it "encompasses" the light. Therefore, on every level, the vessel signifies the limitation of the light, and that which is beyond the light. Yet it also signifies that which is beyond the limitation of the light, namely, all the light that is not revealed in the vessel, since it is "infinite" and beyond revelation.[60] Consequently, the light of *Ein Sof* is able to enter the worlds through the vessels.

וּבְהֶאָרָתוֹ תּוֹךְ הַכֵּלִים נוֹתֵן בָּהֶם כֹּחַ וָעוֹז לִבְרוֹא יֵשׁ מֵאַיִן.

By means of its illumination within the vessels, it grants them the strength and might to create existence from nothingness.

One might ask how the light of *Ein Sof*, the light that encompasses all worlds, is revealed in the worlds, in view of the fact that it cannot be manifest within worldly limits. The answer is that it is revealed through the power to create "existence from nothingness," which it conveys to the vessels of each world. As explained at the beginning of this letter, the ability to create "existence from nothingness" comes solely from *Ein Sof*.

Here, the author of the *Tanya* refers specifically to the ability to create "existence from nothingness," and not to the act of creation itself, since it is impossible to have a true revelation of *Ein Sof*, of God Himself, in the worlds of *Beria*, *Yetzira*, and *Asiya*. The ability to

60. It is taught that the source of the vessels is found in the *reshimu*, or "trace." After the light of *Ein Sof* constricted itself the first time, an impression remained at the place of the constriction: a trace of the infinite light of *Ein Sof* that was manifest there prior to the constriction. Accordingly, in the space produced by the constriction, there is light of the ray, which was emitted by *Ein Sof*, and additionally, there is the trace of the light that was there prior to the constriction. It may be said, very generally, that the ray's light is the source of the "lights," and the trace is the source of the "vessels."

create "existence from nothingness" is an expression of the power of *Ein Sof*. However, the creation, and the creations themselves, are not *Ein Sof*. Rather, they are the "illumination of the illumination of the illumination" of the light that fills all worlds.

וּמֵאַחַר שֶׁהַבְּרִיאָה הִיא עַל יְדֵי הַכֵּלִים לָזֹאת הֵם הַנִּבְרָאִים בִּבְחִינַת רִיבּוּי וְהִתְחַלְּקוּת וּגְבוּל וְתַכְלִית וּבִפְרָט עַל יְדֵי הָאוֹתִיּוֹת כַּנִּזְכָּר לְעֵיל.

Since the creation is through the vessels, they are therefore created in the form of multiplicity, division, limit, and finitude, especially by means of the letters, as stated above.

As mentioned, the vessels "encompass" the Inner Light, and accordingly, they are able to give expression to the encompassing light. In contrast, the Inner Light found in the vessels comprises only that which is revealed within it. Consequently, it evolves from one illumination to the next by way of "cause and effect," but it does not have the ability to generate anything not contained within it, or in other words, to create "existence from nothingness."

The vessels are external and limited relative to the light, and in contrast to the light's oneness, they generate a multitude of creations. Similarly, the light within the soul is one entity, but when it is bound by the vessels of the soul's faculties, which include all the different kinds of emotion and comprehension, it is split into many diverse, clearly defined sections.

The letters are the vessels of the *sefira* of *Malkhut*, the vessels of "speech." Through these vessels, the flow moves outward to the creations, from one entity to another. This is analogous to human speech. The vessels of the soul define the properties of a person's soul as they are manifest in his thoughts and feelings. However, speech and the letters that comprise it go even further. In speech, concepts are not represented in a subjective manner, but in a way that enables them to be conveyed to others. When letters are "liberated" from their speaker, they become a separate entity, and what results are countless additional interpretations and combinations of these letters that are in no way connected to the person who uttered them. The thoughts and emotions of a specific individual are limited by what he understands, feels, and knows. However, once he expresses them outwardly through speech, any other individual can hear and interpret them in accordance with his own perceptions and feelings, and there is no end to the possible interpretations.

11 Tishrei
8 Tishrei (leap year)

וְעוֹד זֹאת יָתֵר עַל כֵּן, עַל כָּל הַנִּזְכָּר לְעֵיל, הֶאָרָה דְּהֶאָרָה דְּהֶאָרָה וְכָל הַנִּזְכָּר לְעֵיל הִיא מַרְאָה כֹּחָהּ וִיכָלְתָּהּ בִּיסוֹד הֶעָפָר הַגַּשְׁמִי, בְּגִילּוּי עָצוּם בְּיֶתֶר עָז מִיסוֹדוֹת הָעֶלְיוֹנִים מִמֶּנּוּ

What is more, in addition to everything stated above, the illumination of the illumination of the illumination, and all that was mentioned earlier, displays its power and ability in the element of the corporeal earth, in an immense manifestation and great power, from the elements that are higher than it,

Although the surrounding lights shine in all places, their manifestation is strongest in the lower realms.

The first part of this sentence is difficult to follow.[61] However, it appears to reflect a transition: It summarizes that which was stated above so that it can base the latter material on it.

The element of earth is the lowest of all the levels in the lowest of all the worlds. The physical realm is found below all the spiritual worlds, and furthermore, earth is the lowest of the four elements of the physical world, which are wind, fire, water, and earth. As explained elsewhere, these four elements correspond to other, higher levels, such as the four worlds, and the *partzufim* of the *sefirot*.[62] The element of earth can therefore be equated with *Malkhut* of *Malkhut*, for in a certain sense it is the realization of the attribute of *Malkhut*. Accordingly, the divine power of *Ein Sof* is more fully revealed within this element than it is on any higher level.

61. The Lubavitcher Rebbe, Rabbi Menaḥem Mendel Schneerson, comments in *He'arot VeTikkunim LaTanya* that the wording of this phrase requires further study, as does its intended meaning.

62. See *Likkutei Torah*, Num. 75d, 205d, Deut. 34c.

וְגַם מִצְּבָא הַשָּׁמַיִם שֶׁאֵין בְּכֹחָם וִיכָלְתָּם לְהוֹצִיא יֵשׁ מֵאַיִן תָּמִיד, כִּיסוֹד הֶעָפָר הַמַּצְמִיחַ תָּמִיד יֵשׁ מֵאַיִן.

even from the hosts of heaven, which do not have the power and ability to bring forth existence from nothingness consistently, like the element of earth, which is always sprouting existence from nothingness,

This manifestation is greater than the manifestation in the other earthly elements, but moreover, it is greater than the manifestation in the heavenly elements. The hosts of heaven are God's servants in the spiritual realm. They have constant love and fear of Him, and they praise Him and do His will with utter devotion, without a trace of their own essence. Nonetheless, the divine manifestation in the physical element of earth is greater than the divine manifestation in these beings.

As explained above, the ability to bring forth "existence from nothingness" is essentially different: It is beyond all other powers of creation and influence. Consequently, the upper elements, the angels and the hosts of heaven, do not possess this ability. Even if they were to concentrate all their efforts on this objective, they would not be able to achieve it even once. This power is not acquired by accumulating other powers. It has an entirely different essence, and it is not found in the upper realms, but only in the element of earth. Accordingly, the earth is continually growing "something" from "nothing," for this is its essential nature. ☞

TO BRING FORTH EXISTENCE FROM NOTHINGNESS CONSISTENTLY

☞ When a force or attribute is always present in a particular place, this indicates that it is innate and essential to that place. It might be revealed elsewhere when necessary, but it remains there only temporarily. In other sources, the author of the *Tanya* discusses the concept of "truth" (see *Likkutei Amarim*, chap. 13; *Likkutei Torah*, Lev. 40a, Num. 93b): The sign of the truth is that it is constant and unchanging. If it is applicable only some of the time, then it is not "the truth." Accordingly, when the ability to bring forth "existence from nothingness" is constant, this indicates that it is "true," that it is the essential power of this particular level.

In the relationship between cause and effect, the cause and the effect are linked. The difference between them is that one is concealed and the other is revealed. Consequently, in the "cause and effect" relationship, the power of creation is limit-

הֵם עֲשָׂבִים וְאִילָנוֹת namely herbs and trees

Where there was previously nothing but earth, plants continually emerge and grow. There is a spiritual force in the earth, known as "the power of growth." Through this force, the earth produces vegetation, thus creating "existence from nothingness." Of course, a seed must be planted in the earth before this happens, but the seed simply indicates to the "power of growth" how it will ultimately be manifest: as grain or an apple tree, for example. The seed is not a tiny "entity" that grows into a plant. In fact, it is consumed into "nothingness" when the new entity sprouts. Thus new growth from the earth is "existence from nothingness," rather than a preexisting entity in a new form. ☞

ed. It comes to fruition by revealing that which was previously concealed, and subsequently, it ceases to act. In contrast, with regard to "existence from nothingness," there is no correlation whatsoever between nothingness and existence. Accordingly, there is no limit to the power of creation: It perpetually forms existence from nothingness (see *Hemshekh Ayin Bet*, vol. 2, pp. 647 and onward).

THE POWER OF GROWTH

☞ Today, science attempts to provide explanations for such phenomena that can be understood according to the laws of nature. We are not used to viewing phenomena such as plant growth as "supernatural," as the creation of "existence from nothingness." However, it is possible to look at things differently. Since we always find what we look for, we must change what we look for. The wording of our question defines the methods of our research as well as its findings. When we formulate a problem in numerical terms, we approach it mathematically and obtain a numerical solution. We could study the connections that our research uncovers, observing how one factor explains or causes another, while failing to see beyond the particular wording of our question. Yet it is also possible to seek out that which is beyond: the wonder, the Divine, the infinite in all things. The power of growth that is found in the earth is, after all, a metaphor. When one hears a metaphor, he might consider only its literal meaning, and not what it represents. Indeed, there are many factors that make it easier for a person to do this. However, one could also seek the reality beyond the metaphor, the hidden thread of meaning that rearranges the content, transferring it onto an entirely different plane.

In truth, this is not merely a metaphor proposed by the author of the *Tanya* or the rabbis who preceded him. Rather, fundamentally, this metaphor comes from God Himself. After all, the entire lower world is merely the "ramification," the physical realization of the upper realm. Elsewhere, it is stated that the upper worlds are in fact the "ramification" of all that happens in our world. In this vein, the Maggid of Mezeritch interprets the phrase "Know what there is above you" (Mishna *Avot* 2:1) as "Know

(וְהַמַּזָּל הַמַּכֶּה וְאוֹמֵר 'גְּדַל', הַיְינוּ לְאַחַר שֶׁכְּבָר צָמַח הָעֵשֶׂב, וְאֵינוֹ אוֹמֵר לוֹ לִצְמוֹחַ מֵאַיִן לְיֵשׁ אֶלָּא מִקּוֹטֶן לְגוֹדֶל וְלָשֵׂאת פְּרִי כָּל מִין וּמִין בִּפְרָטֵי פְּרָטִיּוּת. אֲבָל בְּטֶרֶם יִצְמַח לְמִי יֹאמַר כָּל מַזָּל וּמַזָּל לְכָל עֵשֶׂב וְעֵשֶׂב בִּפְרָטֵי פְּרָטִיּוּת?)

(and as for **the constellation which strikes and declares "grow,"** that occurs **after the herb has already sprouted. It does not tell it to sprout** in a manner of **existence from nothingness, but from a small to a large size and to bear fruit, each and every species in all of its particular details. Before it sprouts, however, to whom would each and every constellation, of each and every herb, instruct with all the particular details?**)

Here, the author of the *Tanya* further explains the metaphor of the "power of growth."

He refers to the Sages' pronouncement that "You find no blade of grass below that does not have a constellation of stars in the heavens that protects it and strikes it, telling it, 'Grow.'"[63] Ostensibly, this contradicts what was stated above, that plants grow from the earth in the manner of "existence from nothingness." The "constellation"[64] of a blade of grass is its concealed source before it has a physical form,

that what is above is from you" (see *HaYom Yom*, 13 Iyar; *Maggid Devarav LeYaakov* 198). There is nothing in this world that is not a direct or indirect expression of the higher reality, which may be revealed plainly, allegorically, or esoterically. Thus a person should certainly endeavor to correctly interpret explicit metaphors like this one. He must not be diverted by the metaphor's superficial, transitory meaning, but must seek out its deeper significance. He must perceive the allusion, and certainly the more direct references, to the higher reality, to the meaning that is unending and divine.

63. *Bereshit Rabba* 10:6.

64. The Sages identify the term *mazal*, "constellation," with the fixed constellations in the spheres. The author of the *Tanya* explains that it is one part of the unfolding succession: The *mazal* receives from the seventy ministering angels, the ministering angels from the guarding *ofanim*, the *ofanim* from the holy *ḥayyot* in the divine chariot, and so forth (*Torah Or* 9a; *Likkutei Torah*, Num. 77c).

yet after it has received a name and has been designated as a separate entity in relation to all other worldly beings. Thus, each blade of grass grows from its own dedicated spiritual source. This seems like "cause and effect" and "existence from existence," rather than "existence from nothingness."

The relationship between the blade of grass and the constellation, in which the constellation says, "Grow," and the grass grows, arises only after the grass has been formed from nothingness. This is comparable to the flow of life force in the unfolding succession of "cause and effect." The life force determines the scope and nature of the outcome, but not its size and form. The outcome's existence comes from the power of *Ein Sof* alone. Likewise, the flow and nature of the life force in the grass are determined by the constellation. However, the grass's creation from nothingness takes place by means of the "power of growth" in the earth, which is the power of *Ein Sof* to create "existence from nothingness."[65] ☞

מֵהַכֹּחַ הַצּוֹמֵחַ שֶׁבּוֹ, שֶׁהוּא אֵין וְרוּחָנִי וְהֵם גַּשְׁמִיִּים.

from its power of growth, which is insubstantial and spiritual, whereas they are corporeal.

The "power of growth" in the earth is a spiritual force, whereas plants are physical entities. As stated, the transition from spiritual to physical is a transition from "nothingness" to "existence." An increase in spiritual power does not bring about physical creation. When a physical entity appears, its arrival cannot be explained in terms of the spiritual forces

THE POWER TO GROW EXISTENCE FROM NOTHINGNESS

☞ Elsewhere, the author of the *Tanya* draws an analogy to a person who builds something with his hands. Even though his hands carry out each stage of the construction, we do not say that the hands made the object, but rather that he, the person, made it, and that he did so with his hands. Likewise, the grass grows by means of the constellation. However, both the constellation and the grass were created by the power of *Ein Sof*, which is revealed through the "power of growth" found in the earth (*Likkutei Peirushim* [manuscript], 5572).

65. See also *Or HaTorah*, Num., vol. 1, p. 196.

that preceded it. There is no spiritual level that clearly leads to physical creation. Consequently, when a physical entity emerges from the spiritual realm, it is always a surprise, because it is "something from nothing." As explained, when "existence" is formed from "nothingness," the power of *Ein Sof* is manifest. This power is beyond both the physical and the spiritual, and when it enters the inner system, it brings with it something entirely new.

Now, the author of the *Tanya* addresses the question of why this power is revealed in the element of earth, the lowest point of the unfolding succession.

וְאֵין זֹאת אֶלָּא מִשּׁוּם דְּרַגְלֵי אָדָם קַדְמוֹן מִסְתַּיְּימִים בְּתַחְתִּית עֲשִׂיָּה

This is the case only because the feet of *Adam Kadmon* culminate at the bottom of *Asiya*,

As stated, *Adam Kadmon* is the *partzuf*, the very first form, that enclothes the line that emanates following constriction. Consequently, it encompasses the entire length of the line, from the point where it emerges from the light of *Ein Sof* before constriction, until the lowest level of the world of *Asiya*. The kabbalistic works contain a schematic representation of a circle with a line extending into it from one point on the circumference.[66] The line reaches close to the other side of the circle, but does not actually touch it.

וְתַחַת רַגְלָיו מֵאִיר אוֹר אֵין סוֹף בָּרוּךְ הוּא הַסּוֹבֵב כָּל עָלְמִין בְּלִי הֶפְסֵק רַב בֵּינֵיהֶם רַק עִיגּוּלֵי אָדָם קַדְמוֹן לְבַדּוֹ.

and under his feet the light of *Ein Sof*, blessed be He, illuminates, He who surrounds all the worlds without any great break between them, with the sole exception of the encircling lights of *Adam Kadmon*.

Thus the line that emerged from the circle approaches the circle once again, coming as near as it possibly can, at its endpoint, which is under the feet of *Adam Kadmon*.

---

66. The *Etz Ḥayyim* (*Heikhal Adam Kadmon, Derush Iggulim VeYosher, Anaf* 2) includes this diagram: ⦶

Only the surrounding light of *Adam Kadmon* separates the feet of *Adam Kadmon,* which enclothe the line all the way to its lowest point, from the larger circle on its other side. It was explained above that there are two aspects to the unfolding succession: circles and straight lines. The straight lines represent the light of the line, which is enclothed and revealed in the worlds, at every level, in accordance with each level's nature. The circles are the lights that surround each level and world. Along the length of the line, the *partzufim* and worlds evolve from one another. The higher structures incorporate the lower, more segmented structures, and the circles that surround the higher structures encompass the circles of the lower structures. Since the first and highest structure, or *partzuf,* is *Adam Kadmon,* it encompasses all the others: Its head is beyond all boundaries, and its feet reach the bottom of *Asiya*. Likewise, the surrounding light of *Adam Kadmon* is the circle that surrounds all the worlds and domains along the line. Above *Adam Kadmon* is the light of *Ein Sof,* which encompasses everything, and all levels are subsumed in it. In the spiritual realm, distances are measured in "levels." The closest thing to the all-encompassing light of *Ein Sof* is only one level away from it, and this is the level of the circles of *Adam Kadmon*.

The lowest level of *Asiya* is exceptional because it is the closest point to the light of *Ein Sof* prior to constriction. However, its proximity to the light of *Ein Sof* has no obvious effect on it, since there is no direct connection between them, no light that shines directly from one to the other. Instead, the light is concealed from this level. It is like a reality that exists just beyond its border, a reality that affects it profoundly. In a certain sense, this reality creates a different atmosphere. It produces a strong will to go beyond the limits, and additionally, it generates the capacity to achieve this. This is precisely what the author of the *Tanya* is referring to here: the power to create "existence from nothingness," or in other words, the actual ability to grow grass and trees from the earth.

וְגַם הַקַּו מֵאוֹר אֵין סוֹף הַמִּסְתַּיֵּים בְּסִיּוּם רַגְלֵי אָדָם קַדְמוֹן מֵאִיר מִמַּטָּה לְמַעְלָה בִּבְחִינַת אוֹר חוֹזֵר

In addition, the line from the light of *Ein Sof* that culminates at the conclusion of the feet of *Adam Kadmon* illuminates from below to above, in the form of returning light,

There is another way in which the light of *Ein Sof* is manifest in the lowest level of *Asiya*, which is the lowest world:

The surrounding light is not the only light that shines with tremendous strength in the lowest level of *Asiya*, the "feet of *Adam Kadmon*." The direct light has almost no energy when it reaches the bottommost point, yet it returns with a new vigor that stems from below.

When the light that descends from the top of the line reaches the point where it cannot descend any further, it is reflected back up. The returning light returns along the same path on which the direct light descended. Since it simply returns to all the places where the direct light has already been, it does not appear to reveal anything new. However, the returning light is fundamentally new and different because of the fact that it comes from below: Ostensibly, it emanates from the world, from human beings, rather than from God. Therefore, as explained elsewhere, although it does not appear to reveal anything that the direct light did not reveal already, on a deeper level it is referred to as a "new light." It has never before entered the world, and consequently, it carries the power of *Ein Sof*, which is beyond the revelations of the direct light.

כְּמוֹ שֶׁהַמְלוּבָּשׁ בא"א ואו"א וזו"נ דַּאֲצִילוּת מֵאִיר בְּאוֹר חוֹזֵר מִמַּלְכוּת דַּאֲצִילוּת.

just as the light **that is enclothed in** ***Arikh Anpin*****, father and mother, and** ***Zeir*** **and** ***Nukva*****, of** ***Atzilut*****, illuminates via a returning light from** ***Malkhut*** **of** ***Atzilut*****.**

These are the *partzufim* of the world of *Atzilut*, in descending order: *Arikh Anpin* is part of the *sefira* of *Keter*; father and mother are *Ḥokhma* and *Bina*, the cognitive *sefirot*; and *Zeir* and *Nukva* are the emotive *sefirot* and *Malkhut*. The direct and returning light in the world of *Atzilut* were discussed earlier in this letter. In *Atzilut*, the vessels are completely permeable to the light within them, and the light within them is completely permeable to the light of *Ein Sof*. At the lowest level of *Atzilut*, in *Malkhut*, the permeability ceases, and the light is reflected back up.

וּמַלְכוּת דַּאֲצִילוּת הִיא בְּחִינַת כֶּתֶר מִמַּטָּה לְמַעְלָה וְ'נָעוּץ תְּחִלָּתָן בְּסוֹפָן' וְכָכָה הוּא בְּסִיּוּם הַקַּו דְּאוֹר

And that ***Malkhut*** **of** ***Atzilut*** **is a form of** ***Keter*****, from below to above, and "their beginning is**

אֵין סוֹף, הַמִּסְתַּיֵּים בְּסִיּוּם הַיּוֹשֶׁר דְּרַגְלֵי אָדָם קַדְמוֹן.

affixed to their end." This is also the situation at the culmination of the line of the light of *Ein Sof*, which culminates at the conclusion of the straight feet of *Adam Kadmon*.

Thus in a sense, *Malkhut* is the source of the returning light, which flows from below, just as *Keter* is the source of the direct light, which flows from above.

The highest *sefira*, *Keter*, is affixed to the lowest *sefira*, *Malkhut*, since each of these *sefirot* embodies both the element of *Keter* and the element of *Malkhut*. Both contain the source of a "new light," which was not received from any higher level, and which illuminates the entire world of *Atzilut*.

The symmetry of the direct and returning light in the world of *Atzilut* is present also on a wider scale: that of the entire line. This is the scale of *Adam Kadmon*, which begins above *Atzilut* and ends at the lowest point of *Asiya*.

מֵאִיר מִמַּטָּה לְמַעְלָה, לִבְחִינַת אוֹר הַנְּשָׁמָה דְּמַלְכוּת דְּמַלְכוּת דַּעֲשִׂיָּה, שֶׁהוּא אֱלֹקוּת מַמָּשׁ מֵחִיצוֹנִיּוּת הַכֵּלִים דְּמַלְכוּת דַּאֲצִילוּת.

It illuminates from below to above, in the form of the light of the soul of the *Malkhut* of *Malkhut* of *Asiya*, which is actual divinity, from the externality of the vessels of *Malkhut* of *Atzilut*.

As mentioned, the light of the *neshama* within each world is "the Divine" in relation to the light of the *nefesh*, the light of the *ruaḥ*, and the vessels of that world. It forms the border between the Divine and the world. This border runs through all worlds in the exact same place. Thus at the lowest point of *Asiya*, also called *Malkhut* of *Malkhut* of *Asiya*, the returning light shines first into the lowest vessel that is able to receive it: "the Divine" within the lowest level of *Asiya*.

Like the "Divine" on all levels of *Beria*, *Yetzira*, and *Asiya*, the light of the *neshama* of *Malkhut* of *Malkhut* of *Asiya* receives from the external dimension of the vessels of *Malkhut* of *Atzilut*. *Atzilut* is essentially divine, and *Malkhut* of *Atzilut* is the element of *Atzilut*, of the Divine, that descends into the worlds. That which descends within *Malkhut* of

Atzilut is the external dimension of the vessels. Similarly, speech, which corresponds to *Malkhut*, is conveyed from one person to another. First and foremost, speech transmits letters and words: not their meanings, but their external forms and pronunciations.

There is a back-and-forth motion of "running and returning" between the direct light and the returning light. The returning light comes from below. It conveys powers that are beyond any that existed previously: powers of creation. However, the returning light does not actually create anything. It transmits the power to reveal the divine light of *Ein Sof*, yet it does not reveal it in practice. Only the direct light, which comes from above, from the divine aspect of each world and level, reveals the Divine and creates "existence from nothingness." The author of the *Tanya* describes the returning light that comes from the lowest point of *Asiya* and illuminates the divine element within *Asiya*. Although it is in *Asiya*, the divine light is truly divine. It is part of the line, the light of *Ein Sof* that proceeds through the worlds of *Beria*, *Yetzira*, and *Asiya* from the vessels of *Atzilut*.

וּלְפִי מַה שֶּׁכָּתוּב בְּסֵפֶר הַגִּלְגּוּלִים, פֶּרֶק כ׳, הוּבָא בְּלִקּוּטֵי אֲמָרִים מִתְלַבֶּשֶׁת תְּחִלָּה הֶאָרָה זוֹ שֶׁל הַקַּו דְּאוֹר אֵין סוֹף בְּאוֹר הָאֲצִילוּת שֶׁבָּעֲשִׂיָּה וּמִמֶּנָּה לִבְרִיאָה וִיצִירָה שֶׁבָּעֲשִׂיָּה, וּמֵהֶן לִבְחִינַת אוֹר הַנְּשָׁמָה דְּמַלְכוּת דְּמַלְכוּת דַּעֲשִׂיָּה.

9 Tishrei (leap year)

According to what is written in *Sefer HaGilgulim*, chapter 20, as cited in *Likkutei Amarim*, this illumination of the line of the light of *Ein Sof* is first enclothed in the light of the *Atzilut* that is in *Asiya*, from where it proceeds **to *Beria* and *Yetzira* that is in *Asiya*, and from them to the form of the light of the soul of the *Malkhut* of *Malkhut* of *Asiya*.**

Now, the author of the *Tanya* again describes the divine light's descent into the worlds.

Sefer HaGilgulim is a work by the Arizal. The works cited here[67]

67. The Lubavitcher Rebbe, Rabbi Menaḥem Mendel Schneerson, comments, "See *Likkutei Amarim*, gloss to chapter 6, chapter 18; see also the end of chapter 51 and the end of chapter 52." The gloss to chapter 6 refers to *Sefer Gilgulim* and to *Etz Ḥayyim* 47:2. See also *Likkutei Torah*, Num. 2b.

outline the descent of the light of *Ein Sof* to the lowest levels of the worlds, as well as the lowest levels of the soul. They explain that the world of *Asiya* enclothes ten *sefirot* of *Asiya*, and these in turn enclothe ten *sefirot* of *Yetzira*. Within the ten *sefirot* of *Yetzira*, there are ten *sefirot* of *Beria*; within the ten *sefirot* of *Beria*, there are ten *sefirot* of *Atzilut*; and within the ten *sefirot* of *Atzilut* is the light of *Ein Sof*. The aforementioned sources address the descent through the four worlds. The principles are the same here, although the author of the *Tanya* focuses either on the specifics of the world of *Asiya*, or on the wider scale: the entire line of the light of *Ein Sof*.

There is a kabbalistic principle that the same structures are repeated in all things. Thus within the world of *Asiya*, there are four levels. These levels correspond to the four worlds, and they too are called *Atzilut*, *Beria*, *Yetzira*, and *Asiya*. The light of *Ein Sof* is enclothed in the world of *Asiya* in the same way as it is enclothed in the four worlds: First, it is enclothed in *Atzilut* of *Asiya*, and from there, it proceeds to *Beria* of *Asiya*, *Yetzira* of *Asiya*, and *Asiya* of *Asiya*. The final level of its enclothement, which the author of the *Tanya* refers to here, may also be described as "*Atzilut* of *Asiya* of *Asiya* of *Asiya*." As mentioned, this is the lowest level that enclothes "the Divine."

וְעַל יְדֵי זֶה יֵשׁ כֹּחַ וָעוֹז בְּסִיּוּם הַכְּלִי דְּמַלְכוּת דְּמַלְכוּת דַּעֲשִׂיָּה שֶׁבִּיסוֹד הֶעָפָר, וְהוּא מַאֲמַר "תַּדְשֵׁא הָאָרֶץ וכו'" (בראשית א,יא) לִהְיוֹת פּוֹעֵל בְּקֶרֶב הָאָרֶץ תָּמִיד לְעוֹלָם וָעֶד

In this manner, the conclusion of the vessel of the *Malkhut* of *Malkhut* of *Asiya*, which is in the element of earth, has power and might. This is the meaning of **the utterance "Let the earth sprout grasses…"** (Gen. 1:11), **to be constantly active in the midst of the land forever and ever**

Thus there are three types of light that illuminate this level, the *Malkhut* of *Malkhut* of *Asiya*:

1. the illumination from the line of the light of *Ein Sof*, which emanates from above, from *Atzilut*;
2. the returning light, which emanates from below;
3. the light of *Ein Sof*, which "encompasses all worlds," and which is adjacent to this level.

As a result of all this illumination, this level has a unique power that derives from *Ein Sof*: the power to perpetually create "existence from nothingness." This capacity is revealed through the power of growth within the earth.

The "power of growth," which generates "existence from nothingness," and in a certain sense forms all life on earth, is the embodiment of the verse "Let the earth sprout grasses." This is one of the ten utterances through which the world was created.

Because this utterance is embodied in the physical earth, it contains a power that is derived from *Ein Sof* alone: It is able to continue creating "existence from nothingness" unceasingly, without any limitations. ☞

Only one of the ten utterances, "Let the earth sprout," has been mentioned so far in this letter. This utterance contains the creative power of *Ein Sof*: the capacity to form "existence from nothingness." Here, in parentheses, the author of the *Tanya* comments on the difference between this utterance and the others.

(בְּחִינַת אֵין סוֹף, וְלֹא בִּלְבַד בְּשֵׁשֶׁת יְמֵי בְרֵאשִׁית; כְּמַאֲמַר "יִשְׁרְצוּ הַמַּיִם" וּמַאֲמַר "תּוֹצֵא הָאָרֶץ נֶפֶשׁ חַיָּה", מֵחָכְמָה דְּמַלְכוּת דְּמַלְכוּת דַּעֲשִׂיָּה

(in the form of *Ein Sof*, and not in the six days of Creation alone, as in the utterance "Let the waters swarm" and the utterance "Let the earth bring forth living creatures," from the *Ḥokhma* of *Malkhut* of *Malkhut* of *Asiya*,

The power to create "existence from nothingness" contained within the utterance "Let the earth sprout" endures forever. However, this

THE TEN UTTERANCES THAT CREATE THE WORLD

☞ The author of the *Tanya* discusses the ten utterances in *Sha'ar HaYiḥud VeHa'emuna*. There, he explains that as long as the world continues to exist, all ten utterances are continuously being stated. They create and sustain all of reality at every moment in time, just as they did during the six days of Creation. In this regard, there is no difference between the six days of Creation and any other day in the history of the world. We refer to all the days when we recite in the *Yotzer Or* blessing, "In His goodness He renews the work of Creation each day." Human speech exists while it is being spoken, and it ceases to exist once the speaker stops speaking. Likewise, the worlds are "the word of God," and thus they exist, and are continually recreated, while God "speaks" them.

is not the case with regard to the other utterances. For example, the species of the animal kingdom were created through the utterances made on the fifth and sixth days. As mentioned, these utterances, too, continue to be stated in perpetuity. They continue to create and sustain each being that is formed from nothingness. However, they do not continue to create new beings that did not exist previously. Instead, they "renew the old."[68] In contrast, the utterance "Let the earth sprout" is enclothed in the physical earth, and consequently, it becomes the power of growth within the earth. This power continues to create new beings unceasingly, even after the six days of Creation. Everything that the earth generates, at all times, comes from total "nothingness." The seed that is planted in the earth returns to "nothingness": It does not function as a small entity that evolves into a larger one, or as a single unit that multiplies.

A person may find it difficult to accept this distinction between animal and plant life. However, his difficulty is with the analogy, and it should not hinder his ability to understand the underlying concept. The physical earth symbolizes the lowest level of the lowest realm. At this level, the power of creation is constantly being nourished by the returning light that comes from below, as well as the surrounding light, which "encompasses all worlds" and is adjacent to this level. This does not occur in the case of an utterance that receives its life force only from above.

The light of *Ein Sof* that emanates from above comes from *Ḥokhma*. It is enclothed in *Ḥokhma*, both in the world of *Atzilut* and in the worlds below *Atzilut*.[69] "*Ḥokhma* of *Malkhut* of *Malkhut* of *Asiya*" is the level

---

68. Several hasidic works distinguish between the creation of a new essence and light that never existed previously, and the formation of new beings "so that the worlds can continue to exist." Although the latter also involves the creation of a new entity of "existence from nothingness," it derives from an essence that already exists. In Hasidism, this is referred to as "the renewal of the old"; see *Bati LeGani*, vol. 1, p. 160.

69. In *Likkutei Amarim* (gloss to chap. 35), it states that the light of *Ein Sof* is enclothed only in *Ḥokhma*. The reason given for this is that the letters of *Ḥokhma* can be rearranged to spell *ko'aḥ ma*, which signifies nullification. *Ḥokhma* does not limit or block *Ein Sof*, but serves as the conduit for the flow of *Ein Sof* into the worlds.

of *Ḥokhma* that pertains to the lowest level of *Malkhut,* which is the divine speech that forms the reality of physical action. ☞

שבז׳ יְמֵי בְּרֵאשִׁית הֵאִיר בָּעוֹלָם הַזֶּה הֶאָרָה מֵאוֹר אֵין סוֹף בְּחֶסֶד חִנָּם בְּלִי הַעֲלָאַת מַיִין נוּקְבִין כְּלָל)

for in the seven days of creation there shone in this world an illumination from the light of *Ein Sof,* through gratuitous kindness, without any elevation of the feminine waters).

This light of *Ein Sof,* through *Ḥokhma* of the divine speech of the utterances, the "new" aspect of that speech which did not previously exist, was there only during the six days of Creation. After the six days of Creation, however, the speech was no longer completely new and unprecedented. Instead, it was like an extension of the first utterances, which had not ended. The first time each utterance was spoken, it was expressed through gratuitous kindness. Gratuitous kindness is performed without being requested, without anything being given in return. In the six days of Creation, the world did not ask for anything or give anything, because it did not yet exist. However, once the world existed, it no longer received by means of gratuitous kindness. Now, it receives only if it "asks" first. It receives only in such a manner that it perpetuates its previous existence,

ḤOKHMA OF *MALKHUT*

☞ Just like in the soul, within the Divine as well, there is a special connection between speech and wisdom, or "*Ḥokhma.*" It is explained in numerous sources (see epistle 5) that speech has an external and an internal dimension. The external dimension pertains to the physical forms, or sounds, of the letters at the final stage of the unfolding succession, and the internal dimension is the light of *Ḥokhma* that shines directly into the letters. Obviously, speech is not just the enunciation of the letters. A very small child is able to make the sounds of the letters, yet he cannot speak. In order for there to be speech, *Ḥokhma* must illuminate the letters. This illumination transmits a life force into the letters. The life force does not reach the letters through the unfolding succession, but directly from the highest realm, from *Ein Sof.* This is evident when the speaker himself perceives new meaning in his words that he had not comprehended before expressing them aloud. The illumination of *Ḥokhma* that is revealed in speech is what gives speech the power of *Ein Sof* that creates "existence from nothingness."

only if its existence yesterday justifies and gives rise to its continued existence today. The hasidic works, citing the *Zohar,* explain that "an awakening from above is contingent upon an awakening from below."[70] Similarly, the Arizal writes that the flow of masculine waters from above comes only after the elevation of the feminine waters from below. Accordingly, gratuitous kindness is akin to "existence from nothingness," because it does not emerge from any other existence, but rather from "nothingness." It has no apparent cause. Thus, the power of *Ein Sof* that creates "existence from nothingness" flowed into the ten utterances only during the six days of Creation. Subsequently, this flow was determined by the actions of the world, specifically of human beings, who have free will. This kind of flow is comparable to "existence from existence." Although we recite, "In His goodness He renews the work of Creation each day," this refers to that which existed the previous day, and to the renewal, once again, of the old. It is not describing something genuinely new, which is not derived from some other creation. In contrast, the utterance "Let the earth sprout" is, as mentioned, the power of growth within the earth. Every day, it generates totally new entities in the earth that did not exist previously, just as it did in the six days of Creation.

The utterances of the other days of Creation are analogous to a speech delivered from a podium. The speaker articulates a particular idea that he has thought of, and the listeners hear it. Subsequently, each time one of the listeners asks a question or requests an explanation, the speaker reveals additional aspects of the topic. These additions depend on the listeners: If they do not ask anything, no new aspects are revealed, and the speech above remains as it was. On the other hand, the utterance "Let the earth sprout" takes the form of the power of growth in the earth, which comes from below. It is comparable to the force that propels people to ask questions and to request more. This force leads the individual to believe in the *Ein Sof* above, even though he cannot see Him. Likewise, as a result of this force, the individual comes to understand that it is both possible and vital to ask for more and more year after year.

---

70. See *Zohar* 1:86b.

לְהַצְמִיחַ עֲשָׂבִים וְאִילָנוֹת וּפֵירוֹת, מֵאַיִן לְיֵשׁ תָּמִיד, מִדֵּי שָׁנָה בְּשָׁנָה, שֶׁהוּא מֵעֵין בְּחִינַת אֵין סוֹף, שֶׁאִם יִתְקַיֵּים עוֹלָם הַזֶּה רִיבּוּי רִבְבוֹת שָׁנִים יַצְמִיחוּ מִדֵּי שָׁנָה בְּשָׁנָה.

This served **to sprout herbs, trees, and fruit, consistently from nothingness to existence, year in year out, which is a kind of *Ein Sof*, for if this world will last for many multitudes of years, they will sprout from year to year.**

Now, the author of the *Tanya* returns to discuss the power of growth, which is constantly producing truly new entities within the earth.

Herbs, trees, and fruit signify three ways that *Ein Sof* is expressed in our world: Herbs demonstrate continuous reproduction; trees exhibit incalculable growth in relation to their seeds; and fruit possesses an essentially different quality from its seeds, which makes it akin to "existence from nothingness."

The power of growth in the earth is infinite: There is no limit to what is able to grow. However, there is a certain quantity that may be produced each year. Plant growth is cyclical, and the previous year's growth impacts the current year's. If there were truly no limits, then this growth would not constitute creation. *Ein Sof* enters the realm of the creations and is revealed within its limits. Nonetheless, when plant growth continues to occur every year for many years, the power of *Ein Sof* is revealed within it. ☞

The utterance "Let the earth sprout" is unique in that it is not revealed through the creation of the heavens, the earth, or the earth's contents. Rather, it is revealed through the creative power itself: the raw, all-encompassing power of creation that enters the earth. As mentioned, the earth is *Malkhut*, which is the last of all the levels. Accordingly,

YEAR IN, YEAR OUT

☞ The Lubavitcher Rebbe, Rabbi Menaḥem Mendel Schneerson, comments that this term seems to contradict the term "consistently [*tamid*]," which immediately precedes it. In contrast, above, *tamid* was joined to and equated with the term "forever," which was followed by "in the form of *Ein Sof*." Here, however, the word *tamid* must be interpreted as it is in epistle 14: There, the author of the *Tanya* cites a verse that contains this word (Deut. 11: 12), and explains that it means "every year" (cited in *Lessons in Tanya*).

the divine light that is concealed in this level contains the power of *Ein Sof*: the power to continue creating "existence from nothingness" indefinitely, like *Ein Sof* Himself. ☞

אֶלָּא שֶׁיֵּשׁ מֵהֶן, עַל יְדֵי הַעֲלָאַת מַיִין נוּקְבִין, וְהֵם הַזְּרוּעִים וְהַנְּטוּעִים, וְאַף עַל פִּי כֵן הֵם כְּמוֹ יֵשׁ מֵאַיִן, שֶׁהַגַּרְעִין הַנָּטוּעַ אֵין לוֹ עֵרֶךְ כְּלָל לְגַבֵּי הַפְּרִי וְגַם נֶגֶד כָּל הָאִילָן עִם הָעֲנָפִים וְהֶעָלִין, וְכֵן בְּמִינֵי זֵרְעוֹנִים וִירָקוֹת, וְגַם בְּמִינֵי תְּבוּאָה לְהִתְהַוּוֹת מֵאוֹת גַּרְעִינִין מִגַּרְעִין אֶחָד הוּא כְּמוֹ יֵשׁ מֵאַיִן, וּמִכָּל שֶׁכֵּן הַקַּשִּׁין וְהַשִּׁבֳּלִים.

However, there are some of them that come into being **by means of the elevation of the feminine waters, and they are those that are sown and planted. Even so, they are like** things that are created in the manner of **existence from nothingness, as the planted kernel has no value at all relative to the fruit, nor in relation to the whole tree, with the branches and leaves. The same applies to types of seeds and vegetables, and also types of produce – the formation of hundreds of seeds from a single seed is like** creation in the manner of **existence from nothingness, all the more so straw and stalks.**

Although it was stated above that the power of growth within the earth is "existence from nothingness," and there is no visible cause

"LET THE EARTH SPROUT" WAS STATED ON THE THIRD DAY

☞ It may be said that the first two days of Creation comprised the entirety of Creation. On those days, God created and gave us heaven and earth, light and darkness, *Ḥesed* and *Gevura*, and the universe and its limits. Only on the third day did creation begin in relation to the returning light. This does not mean that the returning light itself was formed, for this requires an awakening from below, as can be seen in the verse "No vegetation of the field had yet sprouted; because the Lord God had not caused it to rain upon the earth, and there was no man to till the ground" (Gen. 2:5). However, the potential for it was created. As stated, this refers to the power of *Ein Sof*, within the earth, to reflect the light and to create real "existence from nothingness."

that induces it, we see sprouting after seeds are sown, and growth after small seedlings are planted, and these processes resemble "existence from existence." However, the seed is not of the same order as the plant. The fact that it has no value in relation to the plant shows that this is not a case of "existence from existence." The formation of "existence from existence" occurs when a small being becomes larger. The original entity is still evident in the new entity. Although it may have changed, it is of the same order as the new entity. Here, the seed is not evident in the fruit's appearance or sweetness, the tree's size, or the ear of grain's abundance and the quality of these seeds in the ear of grain.

Some plants grow even though human beings did not plant them. This means that the essential ability to generate plant life does not depend solely on "the elevation of the feminine waters," on human actions and prayers. Rather, this ability is an infinite, divine, creative power: the power to create "existence from nothingness." Below, the author of the *Tanya* discusses the difference between vegetation that grows naturally and vegetation that is planted. In kabbalistic terms, this is the difference between a flow that derives from the elevation of the feminine waters, and one that does not.

וְהִנֵּה הַפֵּירוֹת שֶׁעַל יְדֵי הַעֲלָאַת מַיִין נוּקְבִין, הִיא הַזְּרִיעָה וְהַנְּטִיעָה, הֵם מְשׁוּבָּחִים מְאֹד מְאֹד מֵהָעוֹלִים מֵאֲלֵיהֶן מִכֹּחַ הַצּוֹמֵחַ לְבַדּוֹ שֶׁבָּאָרֶץ.

Now, these fruits, that are formed **by means of the elevation of the feminine waters, which is sowing and planting, are of exceedingly better quality than those that rise of their own accord, merely through the strength of that which sprouts in the earth.**

Fruits that are sown and planted are larger, more abundant, and better tasting. However, their superiority[71] mainly in the fact that they provide

71. The Lubavitcher Rebbe, Rabbi Menaḥem Mendel Schneerson, comments here that the term "exceedingly [*me'od me'od*]" relates to the virtue of the practical mitzvot, which is discussed in this letter. Specifically, when the flow comes from above by virtue of a person's mitzva or prayer, it is of "exceedingly greater quality." This idea is elucidated further in *Likkutei Torah* (*Parashat Shelaḥ*, s.v. "*vayomeru el kol adat Yisrael*," mainly 38c), in the interpretation of the verse "The land is

for human needs. Plants that grow naturally do not take human needs into account. They include thistles and weeds, as well as trees that do not produce fruit. They are not necessarily essential or beneficial to humans or animals. On a deeper level, the power of growth within the earth does not sustain only plant life, but also the higher levels: the animal kingdom and humankind. Thus, plants have an additional purpose that is not connected solely to themselves, which is to nourish and sustain animals and humans. In this regard, planted vegetation is superior, not only from the human perspective, but also from the perspective of the plants themselves, since it fulfills the aforementioned purpose.[72]

וּמִזֶּה נַשְׂכִּיל הַמְשָׁכוֹת אוֹרוֹת עֶלְיוֹנִים באבי״ע (שֶׁהוּא תַּכְלִית בְּרִיאַת הָאָדָם) כְּמוֹ שֶׁנִּתְבָּאֵר בְּמָקוֹם אַחֵר.

From this we can learn about **the drawing of the supernal lights in *Atzilut, Beria, Yetzira,*** and ***Asiya*** **(which is the purpose of the creation of man), as explained elsewhere.**

Based on what we know about the power of growth in the physical earth, and the fact that the plants are superior when they are produced by means of human labor, we are able to learn about the flow of light in general, even in the spiritual realm. A flow, or a light, that emanates from above by means of an awakening from below, "the elevation of the feminine waters," is superior to a flow that does not emanate by means of an awakening from below.

The flow of the light of *Ein Sof* into the world by means of human effort, and the superiority of this flow over the flow that emanates by itself, is described in detail elsewhere.[73] This superiority is the purpose

---

exceedingly [*me'od me'od*] good" (Num. 14:7), which was Joshua and Caleb's statement denying the spies' claim.

72. In *Torah Or* 44c, plants that grow by themselves are compared to the innate, concealed love of God, while those that were planted are compared to world-centered love, which a person awakens within himself by means of contemplation. However, that source is concerned mainly with the virtue of natural vegetation, which signifies the essence of divine service, as well as its higher source.

73. See *Likkutei Torah*, Deut. 50a, s.v. "*ki ha'aretz totzi.*"

of the creation of the world in general, and the creation of humankind in particular.

Our efforts in this world constitute the elevation of the feminine waters. The world is comprised of a mixture of good and evil, and the individual's task is to choose the good: to identify it and to separate it from the evil. When a person does this, the good ascends and the evil descends, and this, in essence, is the elevation of the feminine waters. The elevation of the feminine waters is "superior" because it is followed by the flow of the masculine waters from above. As explained, the quantity and quality of the lights contained in this flow would have been impossible without the elevation of the feminine waters. A flow that descends continuously, not as a result of the elevation of the feminine waters, is entirely superficial. It is a general flow that sustains the external structures but does not relate to their content and significance. It spreads out, reaching both those who need it and those who do not, both the good and the evil. All in all, it sustains the worlds superficially without giving expression to their inner purpose, which is the revelation of the Divine. In order to focus the flow so that it reveals holiness in the world and in our souls, there must be an elevation of the feminine waters: Good must be chosen and separated from evil, and the concealment, the lower reality, must be nullified. Subsequently, the flow from above will be for good and not evil. It will reveal the Divine rather than conceal Him, and it will be endlessly spacious rather than through scarcity and sorrow. ☞

The flow of the masculine waters above the feminine waters. Elsewhere, it is explained that this is what occurs today, when people are

THE POWER OF THE FEMININE WATERS

☞ Every elevation of feminine waters is an act of giving, and every act of giving is a kind of self-sacrifice. This is analogous to a seed that is planted in the soil and subsequently disappears. However, this dissipation can actually open the door to a flow from above that is beyond anything that existed previously. Only by nullifying the limits of the previous reality can one procure a completely new reality that is infinitely different from what existed before, as the plant is infinitely different from the seed. This does not mean that something, however large it may be, is simply added to the previous reality. Rather, the act of self-nullification brings with it the concept of the infinite, and it draws God into the world: not into the previous reality, but into the reality that "chose" Him and prepared a space in which He could dwell.

required to labor and rectify (see *Or HaTorah*, Gen. 4a). However, in the future, once the rectification is complete, there will be another, even higher reality. In fact, this reality already exists in a certain sense, since the highest realms incorporate the future. Today, the flow of the masculine waters, which occurs by means of the elevation of the feminine waters, is determined according to the scope of the feminine waters. This is analogous to a response given to a question, a response that relates directly to what was asked, to the concepts used by the questioner, but does not extend beyond this. On a higher level, however, it is possible to have an awakening from above that is not caused by an awakening from below, a flow that is not determined by the receiver's petition, or the limits of his vessels, but rather by the Giver. In other words, this is a flow of *Ein Sof* that will be found in the external realm as well as the inner realm, so that even physical matter will constitute a divine revelation. This future reality is described in the verses "For the earth will be filled with knowledge" (Isa. 11:9), and "All flesh will see" (40:5).

12 Tishrei / 10 Tishrei (leap year)

וּמִזֶּה יוּבַן הֵיטֵב בְּעִנְיַן סֵדֶר מַדְרֵגוֹת דּוֹמֵם צוֹמֵחַ חַי מְדַבֵּר, שֶׁהֵן בְּחִינַת עָפָר מַיִם אֵשׁ רוּחַ.

And through this, one can fully understand the matter of the order of classifications: mineral, vegetable, animal, and **articulate, which correspond to** the four categories of **earth, water, fire,** and **wind.**

From the fact that the power of *Ein Sof* is manifest in the physical earth to a greater degree than it is manifest in the higher levels, we are able to understand the order, from highest to lowest, of the four classes of matter: mineral, vegetable, animal, and human. These classes correspond to the four elements: Earth corresponds to mineral, water to vegetable, fire to animal, and wind to human.[74] With regard to the four elements, there is a clear progression from highest to lowest.[75]

---

74. In Kabbala, more parallels are added: the four letters of the name of *Havaya*, the four worlds (*Atzilut*, *Beria*, *Yetzira*, and *Asiya*), the *partzufim* of *Atzilut*, the levels and faculties of the soul, and others. See also *Likkutei Torah*, Num. 5b (citing *Etz Ḥayyim*), 7a, Deut. 34c.

75. See Rambam, *Sefer HaMadda*, *Hilkhot Yesodei HaTorah*, chap. 4.

Although at first glance the classes of matter appear to be ordered in the same way as the four elements, with human at the top and mineral at the bottom, it is possible to discern a different order.

שֶׁאַף שֶׁהַחַי הוּא לְמַעְלָה מֵהַצּוֹמֵחַ וְהַמְדַבֵּר לְמַעְלָה מֵהַחַי, אַף עַל פִּי כֵן הַחַי נִיזּוֹן וְחַי מֵהַצּוֹמֵחַ וְהַמְדַבֵּר מְקַבֵּל חַיּוּתוֹ מִשְּׁנֵיהֶם.

For although the animal is above the vegetable, and the articulate is above the animal, even so the animal is sustained and lives from the vegetable, and the articulate receives his vitality from them both.

This question arises in many hasidic discourses: Since humans are on a higher level than animals, and animals are on a higher level than plants, why does the flow from above to below not adhere to this order? After all, a higher level is by nature closer to the source, and life force flows from this level to the levels below it. The elements of the human soul, for example, follow this order: from wisdom to understanding, from the intellect to the emotions, and so forth. Nonetheless, in reality, the order is reversed: Animals receive their life force from the plants that they eat, and humans receive their life force from both plants and animals. The explanation given here[76] is that, as mentioned, the power of *Ein Sof*, which is the force of creation and life, is revealed in the lowest level, the element of earth at the bottom of *Asiya*. This is where the power of growth, which perpetually produces vegetation from the

---

76. In many hasidic sources, this question is explained in terms of the connection between "chaos" and "rectification." The human being, who signifies rectification, rectifies the chaos, which is found in the animals and plants. In this regard, he is above them. However, since chaos is, at its source, higher than rectification, and the person who rectifies the chaos reveals its higher source, he is able to receive his life force from it (see *Torah Or* 65d and onward, 74d; *Likkutei Torah*, Lev. 13b, Deut. 14a). In truth, this explanation connects to the one given here, since the power of *Ein Sof* can ascend only through rectification. This could be, for example, a mitzva or an intention for the sake of Heaven. If there is no rectification, the power of *Ein Sof* remains where it is. This rectification is in fact the same thing as "the rectification of the chaos," for it is the only way for the power of *Ein Sof* to be released from the chaos so that it may ascend. This can be seen below, where the author of the *Tanya* describes, in connection with this matter, how animals that are sacrificed on the altar ascend to the angels in the divine chariot.

earth, is manifest. Subsequently, animals and humans, living beings, receive this life force from the plants, which are below them. It was also explained that this flow is called "returning light": It returns from the bottom of *Asiya*, giving life to the levels above it as it ascends. This light carries the power of *Ein Sof*, the aspect of *Keter* that illuminates in it, both from the top of the line and the circles of *Adam Kadmon*, which are adjacent to it.

וְגַם חָכְמָה וָדַעַת, שֶׁאֵין הַתִּינוֹק יוֹדֵעַ לִקְרוֹת אַבָּא וְאִימָּא עַד שֶׁיִּטְעוֹם טַעַם דָּגָן כו' (בבא קמא עב,א): וַעֲדַיִין לָא אֲכִילְנָא בִּישְׂרָא דְּתוֹרָא כו'.

This is the case **even for wisdom and knowledge, as a child does not know how to call "father" and "mother" until he has tasted the taste of grain…; and "because I had not yet eaten ox meat…"** (see *Bava Kamma* 72a).

This matter is also revealed in the human soul. Wisdom and knowledge are the highest levels of the soul, yet they are contingent on physical sustenance. When a child is able to tell the difference between his parents and others, and to perceive their existence to some extent, even if not their essence, this is a very significant stage in his development. According to the Sages, he cannot reach this stage while he is still exclusively breastfeeding, but only once he has begun to eat plant products and to receive vitality from them.[77]

Similarly, in the Talmud, Rabbi Naḥman explains that he made an incorrect statement the previous day because he had not yet eaten meat when he uttered it. In other words, a lack of physical sustenance impacted on his intellectual and spiritual abilities.

כִּי הוּא בְּחִינַת אוֹר חוֹזֵר מִמַּטָּה לְמַעְלָה, מִתַּחְתִּית הָעֲשִׂיָּה, שֶׁמִּתְגַּלֵּית שָׁם בְּיֶתֶר עַז הֶאָרָה דְּהֶאָרָה כו'

For it has the form of returning light, from below to above, from the bottom of *Asiya*, where the illumination of the illumination manifests with great power…,

77. *Berakhot* 40a. It is explained at length in hasidic literature, in relation to unleavened bread as well as food in general, how physical sustenance produces a tremendous elevation of the soul's faculties.

The flow that a person receives from eating animals and plants, which are inferior to him, is "returning light." This is the light that ascends from the lowest point reached by the direct light. As mentioned, the direct light becomes more and more constricted as it descends, taking the form of "an illumination of an illumination," and so on. The point from which the light returns is not simply the next stage of the direct light's path. Rather, it is a turning point, a new beginning. The direct light is exceedingly strong where it begins in the higher realm, for it has just emerged from the luminary. Likewise, the point of reflection is akin to a new luminary, which shines the light all the way back to the highest realm, even more strongly than the direct light when it first emerged.

מֵאוֹר אֵין סוֹף הַסּוֹבֵב כָּל עָלְמִין, וּמֵהַקַּו אוֹר אֵין סוֹף שֶׁבְּסִיּוּם רַגְלֵי הַיּוֹשֶׁר דְּאָדָם קַדְמוֹן בִּבְחִינַת אוֹר חוֹזֵר כַּנִּזְכָּר לְעֵיל.

from the light of *Ein Sof*, who surrounds all the worlds, and from the light of *Ein Sof* at the conclusion of the straight feet of *Adam Kadmon*, in the form of returning light, as stated above.

This illumination in the lower realm is from the light of *Ein Sof* Himself, which encompasses all worlds. This refers to the great circle that surrounds all space, but shines more strongly at the bottom of *Asiya*, which is closest to it, as explained.

It was stated that the returning light is greater than the direct light. One might have thought that the opposite was true. In the physical world, for example, the light that is reflected from the moon is weaker than the direct light that strikes it, and the same is true of the light that is reflected from a mirror. The advantage of the returning light is not readily apparent, and moreover, it is indeed weak and lacking in relation to the parameters of the direct light. Nonetheless, it is possible to look at this matter in a different way. The returning light is stronger than the direct light, even at the point where the direct light first emerges. The direct light embodies revelation, proceeding from God's essence, to His will and wisdom, to His relationships and actions. Consequently, this light is revealed, since it "speaks" to us and our vessels. The returning light, on the other hand, does not involve any kind of revelation, because it is not directed at the world, but rather at God Himself. This is the hidden advantage of the returning light: It does not illuminate the external dimension of creation, but the inner dimension of the supernal intent to create. The direct light may be compared to that which a person desires, thinks, understands, and does, while the returning light corresponds to the hidden, underlying factors that lead him to desire, think, and do these things. The author of the *Tanya* explains that the returning light comes from the light that encompasses all worlds, and moreover, the light that encompasses all worlds is the concealed foundation of the worlds' entire existence and the illumination of the direct light. When the returning light comes back to the light that encompasses all worlds, it first draws its power from that encompassing light.

Put another way, the returning light is greater than the direct light in the same way that light is greater than darkness, and the penitent is greater than the tzaddik. The Talmud states, "In the place where penitents stand, even the full-fledged righteous do not stand" (*Berakhot* 34b). This is explained at length in numerous places.

וְיוּבַן הֵיטֵב בָּזֶה, טוּב טַעַם וָדַעַת, מַה שֶׁמַּלְאָכִים עֶלְיוֹנִים שֶׁבַּמֶּרְכָּבָה, פְּנֵי שׁוֹר וּפְנֵי נֶשֶׁר, נֶהֱנִים מְאֹד וְנִיזּוֹנִים וּמִסְתַּפְּקִים מֵרוּחַ הַבְּהֵמָה וְהָעוֹף הָעוֹלֶה אֲלֵיהֶם מֵהַקָּרְבָּנוֹת שֶׁעַל גַּבֵּי הַמִּזְבֵּחַ

In this context, one can fully understand, with intellectual **discernment and awareness, the fact that the higher angels in the** divine **chariot, the face of an ox and the face of an eagle, receive great enjoyment and are sustained and satisfied from the spirit of the animals and fowl that ascends to them from the sacrifices that are upon the altar,**

The higher angels mentioned in the vision of the divine chariot (Ezek. 1:10) are called "the face of an ox" and "the face of an eagle," because they are the source of all the animals and birds on earth. Obviously, the divine chariot does not contain a physical ox or a physical eagle. Rather, these terms refer to the highest forms of these creatures, such as a love and fear of God that have the strength of a beast and the swiftness of a bird, metaphorically speaking. Generally, we perceive these angels as conferring vitality on all animals and birds, in both the spiritual and physical realm: The "animal life force," in addition to the creatures that graze in the field. Indeed, the direct light proceeds in this way, from above to below. However, there is also movement in the opposite direction, whereby the higher angels receive their vitality from the physical animals in the lower realm. The returning light proceeds in this way, from below to above. An animal that is sacrificed on the altar, which ascends and is consumed by the altar's fire, is a manifestation of the returning light. It ascends from the beast's physical body, elevating all the animals in the entire world along with it. This includes each and every corporeal creature, as well as the animal elements in the soul and the spiritual worlds. This ascent is one aspect of the returning light. It conveys vitality and power to the entire animal kingdom, all the way to its highest levels, namely, the face of an ox, the face of an eagle, and so on. The advantage of this flow is the fact that it is not simply the illumination of the direct light that comes from above in the ordinary manner. Instead, this illumination derives from the power of *Ein Sof*, and it is released by means of the rectification and elevation of the lower realm through the act of bringing sacrifices.

וּכְדִקְדּוּק לְשׁוֹן הַזּוֹהַר הַקָּדוֹשׁ (חלק ג רמא,א): וְאִתְהַנְיָין מִיסוֹדָא וְעִיקָּרָא דִּילְהוֹן.

as in the precise formulation of the holy *Zohar* (3:241a): "And they receive enjoyment from their element and essence."

The *Zohar* describes the relationship between the higher angels in the divine chariot and the sacrifices that are brought on the altar. The higher angels, the face of an ox and the face of an eagle, derive enjoyment from the sacrifices. This is because the root of the animals' descent from the higher angels is revealed in the physical creatures that ascend upon the altar.

וְאַחֲרֵי הַדְּבָרִים וְהָאֱמֶת הָאֵלֶּה, דַּעַת לְנָבוֹן נָקֵל לְהָבִין עַל יְדֵי כָּל הנ"ל גּוֹדֶל מַעֲלַת הַמִּצְוֹת מַעֲשִׂיּוֹת, אֲשֶׁר הֵן תַּכְלִית יְרִידַת הַנְּשָׁמוֹת לָעוֹלָם הַזֶּה הַגַּשְׁמִי כְּמוֹ שֶׁכָּתוּב: "הַיּוֹם לַעֲשׂוֹתָם" (דברים

After these words and truth, "knowledge comes easy to the discerning man," to understand by means of all the above arguments **the great virtue of the practical mitzvot. For they are the purpose of the descent**

ז,יא), **וְיָפָה שָׁעָה אַחַת בִּתְשׁוּבָה וּמַעֲשִׂים טוֹבִים בָּעוֹלָם הַזֶּה מִכָּל חַיֵּי עוֹלָם הַבָּא.**

of souls to this corporeal world, as it is written: "Today, to perform them" (Deut. 7:11), **and a single hour** spent **in repentance and good deeds in this world is better than the entire life of the World to Come.**

To conclude this letter, the author of the *Tanya* returns to the significance of the practical mitzvot, which was discussed above.

From this letter, whose scope is deeper and higher than that of all the others, we understand[78] that the power of *Ein Sof*, which is above all worlds, is revealed at the lowest level of *Asiya*. This is expressed in the tremendous importance of the practical mitzvot, which are performed with the body. Not only are they preferred over more spiritual forms of divine service according to *halakha*, but they have immense inherent value as well. The purpose of the world's creation, and of the soul's descent into the body, are fulfilled only through the performance of the practical commandments. Through these mitzvot, the returning light ascends and gives life to all the worlds by means of a new, elevated light.

Regarding the verse cited here, the Sages state, "Today [is the time] to do them, [in this world,] and tomorrow [is] not [the time] to do them" (*Eiruvin* 22a). "Today" refers to this world, where the soul is enclothed in the physical body. This is the time for performing the practical mitzvot.

The term "good deeds" refers to the practical mitzvot, for these are deeds that are entirely "good." God, who is "good," commanded that they be carried out, and He Himself performs them in His own way. Furthermore, when we perform them, the light of "goodness" shines in all the worlds. Repentance, too, takes place in the lower realm. Repentance constitutes a return to God, and on the largest scale, it embodies that which was explained above with respect to the light that returns from the physical world.

These closing words serve as a summation of the epistle's conclusion.

---

78. The author of the *Tanya* uses biblical phrases here: "After these true matters" (II Chron. 32:1) and "Knowledge is easy for the discerning" (Prov. 14:6).

After the exceedingly deep, spiritual topics addressed in the letter, they act as a sort of "seal" that is applied to the "outside" of the document.

עַד כָּאן מָצָאנוּ מִכְתַּב יָדוֹ הַקְּדוֹשָׁה. **Until here we have found of his holy writing.**

The sons of the author of the *Tanya* were the publishers of *Iggeret HaKodesh*, and they added this remark.

In *Kitzurim VeHe'arot LeSefer Likkutei Amarim* (p. 40), it is stated with regard to this letter, "This is the holy writing of the Rebbe himself, whose words are like gold. He wrote it exactly one week before he fell ill and was taken by God. He was summoned to the heavenly academy at the conclusion of the holy Sabbath, *Parashat Shemot*, in the year 5573."

This addition is unusual. Nothing similar to it was added by the publishers anywhere else in this work. It is possible that they added it here because of the tremendous holiness of this particular text, in order to distinguish it from other epistles. Other letters were edited to make them suitable for the general population. However, the editors did not touch this text: It was published exactly as written, from beginning to end.

Moreover, for those hasidim who read the text and are unable to comprehend it fully, it is impossible to sum it up except to say, "Until here we have found of his holy writing."

It is difficult to summarize this "epistle." The author of the *Tanya* himself sums it up as a discourse that reveals the value of the practical mitzvot. Nonetheless, this summary seems far removed from the letter itself. This does not mean that there is no connection between them, or that the value of the practical mitzvot does not in fact emerge from the text. Rather, it means that the "flow from within to without" does not encapsulate all that is "within."

Without going into detail, it is possible to describe this chapter as a journey along the line between "existence" and "nothingness." This is where God Himself is found, since He is the only One who can create "existence from nothingness." "Existence" is not found in only one place. Rather, it is everywhere, since the line between "existence" and "nothingness" passes through every place. However, it is always found at the "lowest point." In every system, including the systems of emotion and thought, the lowest point is the bottom of *Asiya,* the place where God is not evident. This is where "existence" is found, and where the power of *Ein Sof* is revealed.

One interpretative discourse, which accords with the summary given by the author of the *Tanya,* is concerned with the enhancement of "existence" and of the physical realm. Humans and the world reach fulfillment through labor, namely through rectifying and elevating the physical. However, the text also reveals a different interpretative discourse. As we move further along the line between "existence" and "nothingness," the "existence" begins to lose its substance. The power of *Ein Sof,* which forms and sustains everything from "nothingness," is found within physical "existence." More than any contemplation of the spiritual reality, this substantiates the idea that "existence" is not really "existence" at all, but rather, everything is part of the Divine.

In the harsh winter of the year 5573, in a dilapidated hut in a remote village, the author of the *Tanya* lay on his deathbed. Just before he departed this world, he pointed to the hut's ceiling and asked his grandson, who would later become the third Lubavitcher Rebbe, "Can you see the wooden beam?" When his grandson inquired as to why he had asked this, he responded, "All I see now is the divine, life-giving 'nothingness'" (This story appears in *Sefer Shivḥei HaRav,* and a different version of it appears in *Sefer Beit Rabbi,* vol. 1, chap. 22. See the discourse of 24 Tevet 5712 in *Torat Menaḥem,* vol. 4, p. 258, and *Sefer HaSiḥot* 5703, p. 155. It is mentioned in many of the talks and discourses of the Lubavitcher Rebbe, Rabbi Menaḥem Mendel Schneerson. See also Rabbi Yehoshua Mondshine, *HaMasa HaAḥaron,* p. 174, for the full account).

Epistle 21

This epistle revisits a topic that is addressed in many of the epistles in *Iggeret HaKodesh*: the importance of giving charity, and in particular, charity in support of the hasidic communities in the Land of Israel.[1] This epistle was probably written in the year 5553.[2] Around that time, the author of the *Tanya* wrote several epistles on this topic that were not included in *Iggeret HaKodesh*. In them, he urges his hasidim not to give charity only once a year, when rabbinic emissaries arrive to collect funds. Instead, they should set aside money for this purpose each week, or at the very least each month. This epistle, too, addresses this matter as well as its spiritual implications.

The donation itself is not discussed: neither the requirement to donate, nor the amount that one should give. Rather, this epistle is concerned with the manner in which the charity is given. Since the mitzva of charity is carried out in the physical realm, through the act of providing materially for the needy, one might assume that the method and intention are unimportant as long as the money is received by those who need it. However, this epistle explains why these elements are indeed significant. It reveals why the physical outcome is not sufficient, and why one must also be mindful of the way in which the act is carried out and the spiritual intention behind it.

---

1. This is explained in the preface to *Iggeret HaKodesh*, and is expounded on at length in the preface to *Iggerot HaKodesh Admor HaZaken* (5772), edited by Rabbi Shalom Dovber Levin.

2. In *Iggerot HaKodesh Admor HaZaken*, this epistle is epistle 36.

13 Tishrei
11 Tishrei (leap year)

אַחַר דְּרִישַׁת שְׁלוֹמָם, כַּמִּשְׁפָּט לְאוֹהֲבֵי שְׁמוֹ,

After inquiring into their welfare, as befits those who love His name,

This opening, or something similar to it, is found at the start of several epistles written by the author of the *Tanya*.[3] ☞

אֶל הַמִּתְנַדְּבִים בָּעָם לַעֲשׂוֹת צִדְקַת ה׳ עִם אַרְצוֹ הַקְּדוֹשָׁה לָתֵת מִדֵּי שָׁנָה בְשָׁנָה חוֹק הַקָּצוּב מָעוֹת אֶרֶץ הַקּוֹדֶשׁ תִּבָּנֶה וְתִכּוֹנֵן בִּמְהֵרָה בְיָמֵינוּ -

to the people who volunteer to perform the righteousness of God with His holy land, to give each and every year a fixed sum of money for **the holy land – may it be rebuilt and established speedily in our days –**

THOSE WHO LOVE HIS NAME

☞ This is how the addressees of this epistle are referred to. Love is mentioned because the commandment to give charity garners the forces of kindness and love in the soul. The Lubavitcher Rebbe, Rabbi Menaḥem Mendel Schneerson, references a parallel concept brought in epistle 5, that charity is given through the attribute of kindness, whose inner dimension is love. The author of the *Tanya* explains there that the reference to God's name can be explained the *Zohar* that says: "Who makes the holy name every day? One who gives charity to a pauper."

It is explained that when a person gives to those "who do not have" in this world, it prompts God to do the same. God gives to those who "do not have" by extending Himself, so to speak, into reality. He reveals Himself as a Being who relates and gives to the worlds, and in particular the lower worlds, which are complete nothingness in relation to God. The divine reality that relates to the world corresponds to God's "name," just as a person's name is the term used by others to refer to him.

3. The opening of this epistle, like those of many of the epistles written by the author of the *Tanya*, is a tapestry of biblical verses and allusions: "After inquiring into their welfare, as befits those who love His name" is a reference to Ps. 119:132; "to the volunteers on behalf of the people" recalls Judg. 5:9; "to perform the righteousness of the Lord" evokes Deut. 33:21; "with His holy land, to give each and every year" alludes to I Sam. 7:16; "may my word drop" appears in Job 29:22; "and my speech distil as the dew" echoes Deut. 32:2; and "to urge those who are quick and to strengthen weak hands" recalls Isa. 35:3.

The Land of Israel is God's land. It is sanctified to Him, and the lives and deeds of those who live there are sanctified to Him as well. This is why charity given to the inhabitants of the Land of Israel is referred to as "the righteousness of the Lord."

This epistle does not introduce an idea that was previously unknown. Rather, it reinforces a practice that had already been in place for years among the hasidim. At that time, there was an established system for the collection of funds for the Land of Israel. Every household was assessed in order to determine how much it could afford to donate. Each year, this amount was to be given to the designated rabbinic emissaries, who would collect the funds and bring them to the Land of Israel.

אֲלֵיהֶם תִּטּוֹף מִלָּתִי וְתִזַּל כַּטַּל אִמְרָתִי לְזָרֵז לִזְרִיזִים

may my word drop to them, and my speech distil as the dew, to urge those who are swift

In this epistle, the author of the *Tanya* addresses people who are accustomed to giving charity every year, but who nevertheless require encouragement regarding future contributions and the manner in which they contribute, as explained below.[4]

The fact that the author of the *Tanya* uses the expressions "May my word drop" and "may my speech distil as the dew," which are borrowed from the prophetical Writings and the Torah, demonstrates his conviction that this directive is akin to a passage from the Torah itself. The hasidim are not just fulfilling a temporary, socio-economic

---

4. Like most of the epistles in *Iggeret HaKodesh*, this epistle was not printed in its entirety. In the supplements to this epistle, the following passage appears at this point: "I bless the One who is good and who does good, on account of good news, which fortifies the bones, brightens the eyes, and gladdens the heart. For many letters have shone in my direction from many places, amid sounds of proclamation, informing and announcing to me that all members of the community have determined and accepted, with great love and exceptional affection, to set aside funds for the holy land every week or every month. I commend the doers of good. May God do good for those who are good, [giving them] all the types of goodness, spiritual and physical. Just as God's word is precious in their eyes, so their souls will be precious in the eyes of God, who will save them from any misfortune. Amen, may this be His will. However, regarding those who have not yet determined and accepted this, may my word drop to them..."

need, but one of the divine commandments, each of which provides the ultimate opportunity for connecting and cleaving to God's will.

The author of the *Tanya* addresses those individuals who are capable of, and suited to, this tremendous undertaking.[5] This does not necessarily refer to their financial ability, since the amount that each person was asked to give was determined according to what he could afford. Rather, it refers primarily to their spiritual capacities. ☞

וּלְחַזֵּק יָדַיִם רָפוֹת בְּמַתַּן דָּמִים, **and to strengthen weak hands in the giving of money,**

The problem is that our "hands are weak." People want to act, yet their actions are feeble. When the critical moment of action arrives, the difficulty is too great and our inner strength breaks down. This does not occur simply because the act is objectively too hard, or because our will is too weak. Mainly, it occurs because the connection between the act and our will is weak. This is comparable to being in a dream. The dreamer is not fully conscious, or he is in a weakened state of consciousness, and therefore he lacks agency, and his desires and abilities do not correspond to his actions. Therefore, the author of the *Tanya* attempts to "strengthen weak hands." In other words, he endeavors to bolster every level of our awareness, to strengthen the connection between our inner world and outer behavior, with regard to this act.

TO URGE THOSE WHO ARE QUICK

☞ The Lubavitcher Rebbe, Rabbi Menaḥem Mendel Schneerson, was once asked why everyone always complied with his instructions, even when they involved great personal sacrifice. The Rebbe replied that he never instructed anyone to do anything unless he knew they would do it. Here too, the author of the *Tanya* addresses "those who are swift." These individuals have already shown that they are quick to donate, and therefore, have shown that they are capable of increasing their speed. As will be explained below, alacrity is essential to the mitzva of giving charity, as the verse states, "You shall love the Lord with all your...might," which literally translates as, "with all your surplus," and is understood by the rabbis as, "with all of your money." Meaning, a person's ability to give something extra even after he has already given everything demands a certain degree of alacrity.

5. It states in *Sifrei* (*Bemidbar* 1, at the beginning), "One implores only those who are [already] implored." A similar expression appears in *Makkot* 23a.

While the word "*damim*" is a common term for money, it literally means "blood." Indeed, the phrase *matan damim,* which means "the giving of money," is elsewhere used to describe the sprinkling of blood on the altar during the sacrificial worship. Spiritually, the act of bringing an offering signifies the sacrifice of oneself, of one's animal soul, which is his very life force.[6] On an even deeper level, this act represents the elevation of life force from the world below to bring it close to the lofty Divine.

מְעוֹת אֶרֶץ יִשְׂרָאֵל מִדֵּי שַׁבָּת בְּשַׁבַּתּוֹ, וּלְפָחוֹת מִדֵּי חֹדֶשׁ בְּחָדְשׁוֹ,

the money of the Land of Israel, on a weekly basis, or at least on a monthly basis,

When a hasid gives money to the communities of the Land of Israel, he gives of his very life force, and on a deeper level, his act facilitates bringing the soul closer to the Divine and raising the Divine Presence from the dust, as will be explained below.

The charity collectors established the last day of each week and the first day of each month[7] as the times for giving charity.[8] To this day, there is a beautiful custom of placing coins in the charity box of Rabbi Meir Ba'al HaNes each week, immediately before the Sabbath candles are lit.

This regularity resembles that of the additional offerings brought in the Temple, which are alluded to in the phrases used here. The additional offerings of the Sabbath and Rosh Ḥodesh, the first day

---

6. See *Likkutei Torah,* Num. 75a and onward; *Iggeret HaTeshuva,* chap. 2.

7. The phrases "on a weekly basis [*midey shabbat beshabbato*]" and "on a monthly basis [*midey ḥodesh beḥodesho*]" originate from *Tanakh.* Regarding the additional offering of the Sabbath, the verse states, "This is the burnt offering of each Sabbath on its Sabbath [*shabbat beshabbato*]" (Num. 28:10), and regarding the additional offering of Rosh Ḥodesh, the first day of the Hebrew month, the verse states, "This is the burnt offering of the New Moon for each New Moon [*ḥodesh beḥodesho*]" (Num. 28:14). The most similar source, however, is Isa. 66:23: "It shall be that on each and every New Moon [*midey ḥodesh beḥodesho*] and on each and every Sabbath [*umidey shabbat beshabbato*] all flesh will come to prostrate themselves before Me."

8. Based on a comment of the Lubavitcher Rebbe, Rabbi Menaḥem Mendel Schneerson.

of the Hebrew month, were so called because they were brought in addition to the regular daily offerings. As mentioned, here the author of the *Tanya* is likewise discussing the "additional."

Furthermore, on those days, the Temple gates were opened, and as the book of Isaiah describes, at those times, "All flesh will come to prostrate themselves" (66:23).[9] The Temple gates are analogous to the gates between this world and the upper worlds, between humanity and the manifest divine light. When the divine light is revealed, the human being is subsumed to it and prostrates himself to it. The hasidic view is that the Torah is eternal:[10] Every part of the Torah applies always, to every individual, both on the large and small scale. The biblical phrases used here indicate that the same closeness to God and "opening of the gates" that took place in the Temple occur when a person gives charity to the Land of Israel on a weekly or monthly basis.

מֵעֶרְכּוֹ הַקָּצוּב לְעֵרֶךְ שָׁנָה, וְכָל כֶּסֶף הַקֳּדָשִׁים אֲשֶׁר עָלָה עַל לֵב אִישׁ לְהִתְנַדֵּב בְּלִי נֶדֶר,

of the specified amount, for the sum of a year, and all the consecrated money that any person undertook to donate, without a vow,

As mentioned, the charity collectors would assess how much each person was able to give, and one was required to contribute the amount that had been determined for him. Although it was a yearly total, this epistle encourages and obliges a person to give a portion of it each week, or at the very least each month. This was for the sake of the poor, whose needs could not always wait an entire year. However, there were also other reasons, which will be discussed below.

"All the consecrated money" is another image (based on II Kings 12:5) that refers to the Temple service. In the sacrificial worship, there were voluntary gift offerings in addition to the obligatory offerings.

---

9. In *Likkutei Levi Yitzḥak LaTanya* it states, "For on the Sabbath and on Rosh Ḥodesh, the gate of the inner courtyard that faces eastward is opened, and on the Sabbath and Rosh Ḥodesh, 'All flesh will come to prostrate themselves before Me.' See *Likkutei Torah*, Deut. 96d, s.v. '*vehaya midey ḥodesh beḥodesho*.'"

10. See *Likkutei Amarim*, chap. 17. This idea is found in many hasidic sources, for example, *Meor Einayim, Parashat Noaḥ*; *Degel Maḥaneh Efrayim, Parashat Bereshit, Parashat Lekh Lekha*.

Regarding charity, too, people would sometimes undertake to give more than their allocated amount, without necessarily informing the charity collectors of their intention. The words of the author of the *Tanya* apply to these additional sums as well.

Although people used to vow to bring gift offerings in the Temple, here the author of the *Tanya* states that the resolution to give additional charity is made "without a vow." He explains elsewhere, "Now that our hearts have become weaker, we must say, 'without a vow [*beli neder*]'" (*Likkutei Torah*, Num. 82b). ☞

לְפַרְנָסַת אַחֵינוּ יוֹשְׁבֵי אֶרֶץ הַקּוֹדֶשׁ מִדֵּי שָׁנָה בְּשָׁנָה. **for the livelihood of our brothers living in the Holy Land, on a yearly basis.**

One should resolve to give his additional donations, too, in the manner described above, on a regular basis: weekly or monthly, and without a vow. This is referring to the money that he has undertaken to donate in addition to the amount that he is obligated to give.

WITHOUT A VOW

☞ In *Likkutei Torah*, the author of the *Tanya* explains that a vow is an utterance about an object that actually causes the object to become sacred (Num. 81a, s.v. "*vayedaber Moshe*"; 82b). The words of the vow have the power to impact a particular reality and elevate it to holiness, and this gives rise to certain practical obligations. For example, non-sacred objects may become impure, but sacred objects may not; an Israelite is permitted to become impure, but a priest is not; one who approaches sacred objects while impure is liable to receive the death penalty, and so forth. In addition to the practical, halakhic implications, a vow has spiritual implications as well: When the words are uttered, they create a reality of binding, even dangerous, holiness. Therefore, a person who is not capable of being exceedingly careful about his level of holiness, or is not a complete tzaddik, but rather, a *beinoni*, (a person who, with all of his desire to be in a state of holiness, cannot separate himself entirely from the physical realm and his personal desires) such a person must add "without a vow" to his utterance. (See also *Ba'al Shem Tov al HaTorah, Noaḥ*; *Amud HaTefilla* 129–130; *Tzava'at HaRivash*; *Keter Shem Tov*). Here and elsewhere it evident that with regard to all aspects of divine service, the author of the *Tanya* maintains that one should conduct himself as a *beinoni* rather than a tzaddik. For example, he states at the beginning of *Likkutei Amarim*, "Even [if] the entire world says to you, 'You are righteous,' consider yourself like a wicked person" (chap. 1). It is explained in chapter 14 that "like a wicked person" is referring to a *beinoni*.

כִּי הִנֵּה, מִלְּבַד הַיָּדוּעַ לַכֹּל גּוֹדֶל מַעֲלַת הַזְּרִיזוּת בְּכָל הַמִּצְוֹת הַנֶּאֱמַר וְנִשְׁנָה בְּדִבְרֵי רַבּוֹתֵינוּ ז״ל, ״לְעוֹלָם יַקְדִּים אָדָם לִדְבַר מִצְוָה כו׳״,

For behold, apart from what everyone knows about **the virtue of alacrity with regard to all the mitzvot, as stated and repeated by our Rabbis: "A person should always be first** to perform **a matter of a mitzva…,"**

This epistle places special emphasis on the number of donations given. At first glance, the number and frequency of a person's donations appear inconsequential, since the most important element of this mitzva is that the money is received by those who need it. Nonetheless, the author of the *Tanya* explains here why these factors are indeed significant.

To understand this concept, one must first recognize an important rule of divine service: that the mitzvot, and all aspects of divine service, must be done with alacrity. This does not mean that they should be performed quickly, but rather that they should be done as soon as possible. A person must never delay doing them or choose to do other things first.

There are numerous quotes from the Sages that reflect the greatness of the virtue of alacrity.[11]

וּזְרִיזוּתֵיהּ דְּאַבְרָהָם אָבִינוּ עָלָיו הַשָּׁלוֹם הִיא הָעוֹמֶדֶת לָעַד לָנוּ וּלְבָנֵינוּ עַד עוֹלָם.

and the alacrity of our forefather Abraham, of blessed memory, stands forever, for us and our descendants everlasting.

The Sages learn from the verse "Abraham awoke early in the morning" (Gen. 22:3) that despite the hardship involved in fulfilling the commandment of "Take now your son, your only one" (22:2), Abraham did so as early as he could.[12] Moreover, he did not delegate any part of the task to others, but "saddled his donkey" (22:3) by himself.[13] Even more than his ability to pass this difficult personal test, the emphasis

11. The quote cited by the author of the *Tanya* here appears in *Nazir* 23b; *Bava Kamma* 38b; *Horayot* 11a.

12. See Rashi ad loc; *Yoma* 28b. Additionally, in *Pesaḥim* 4a the phrase "Abraham awoke early in the morning" is used to characterize Abraham's fulfillment of the mitzva of circumcision.

13. *Sanhedrin* 105b.

here is on the alacrity with which Abraham did as he was commanded, as will be explained below.

The binding of Isaac, the tenth and most difficult trial faced by Abraham, is considered his greatest source of merit, as well as that of all his descendants. In times of trouble, when we cry out for God's salvation, even when it is not truly deserved, we mention the binding of Isaac. Abraham's act at the binding of Isaac was beyond reckoning. He gave up everything he knew and understood, including his own self and all that was rightfully his, in order to maintain his covenant and connection with God. We ask that God act in the same way toward us: We pray that He will go beyond the letter of the law and beyond the calculation of what we deserve, so that our relationship and covenant with Him will be preserved.

כִּי הָעֲקֵדָה עַצְמָהּ אֵינָהּ נֶחְשֶׁבֶת כׇּל כָּךְ לְנִסָּיוֹן גָּדוֹל לְעֵרֶךְ מַעֲלַת אַבְרָהָם אָבִינוּ עָלָיו הַשָּׁלוֹם,

For the binding of Isaac itself is not considered such a great test in relation to the level of our forefather Abraham, of blessed memory,

What is so remarkable about the binding of Isaac?

All tests are measured relative to the person being tested. A test may be tremendously challenging and nearly impossible for one person, while for someone else it may be minor or not a test at all. A test is only a test if it pushes the individual to the limit of his capabilities, and this limit differs from person to person. Abraham was "the greatest man among the giants,"[14] and therefore, that which is a difficult test for anyone else is not a test with respect to Abraham, since there is no question that Abraham will do what the test asks of him. Bringing one's only son as an offering is unimaginably difficult, even impossible, from our perspective. However, from Abraham's perspective, it is not such a great test, since it is not beyond the scope of his capabilities.

בְּשֶׁגַּם כִּי ה׳ דִּיבֵּר בּוֹ, "קַח נָא אֶת בִּנְךָ כו'" (בראשית כב,ב).

especially as God spoke directly **to him: "Take now your son…"** (Gen. 22:2).

14. Based on Josh. 14:15; and see Rashi ad loc.

Part of the difficulty of any test is the uncertainty that it entails. A person is placed in a situation in which he must decide whether to do one act or another, but sometimes it is not clear which one is preferable. This is especially true regarding matters of self-sacrifice and the sanctification of God's name. In such cases, the decision is exceedingly difficult. The correct choice is derived from an extremely deep force within that cannot be articulated or explained, and is therefore regarded as the greatest test of all. However, God explicitly told Abraham, who was a prophet, "Take now your son." Consequently, Abraham had absolute clarity regarding this matter. He knew that it was God's will and that it was what he was supposed to do. ☞

וַהֲרֵי כַּמָּה וְכַמָּה קְדוֹשִׁים שֶׁמָּסְרוּ נַפְשָׁם עַל קְדוּשַּׁת ה׳, גַּם כִּי לֹא דִּיבֵּר ה׳ בָּם.

And there are a considerable number of holy individuals who gave up their lives in sanctification of God, even though God did not speak to them.

Furthermore, throughout Jewish history, there have been Jews who have given their lives to sanctify God's name. These individuals were not only sages and prophets, but even simple Jews. It could be argued that historically it was the simple Jews who sacrificed their lives for God

GOD SPOKE TO HIM

☞ Even prophets do not have perfect clarity regarding the meaning of their prophecies, and this is particularly true when the revelation pertains to the prophet himself. Only regarding the prophecy of Moses is it said, "A vision that is not in riddles" (Num. 12: 8). For everyone else, including other prophets, divine revelation is enclothed in parables and riddles, which vary in accordance with each person's character and situation. The way in which the words are interpreted is a reflection of the individual's level. A person may have worked hard to refine his soul so that it is no longer bound so tightly to worldly affairs. Someone like this, who is accustomed to "being" in higher realms and relating to the divine reality as the actual reality, perceives the subtle, supernal meaning more swiftly and with greater clarity. However, the more a person is embroiled in his physical life, the more the supernal messages become ambiguous and subject to worldly interpretation. Nonetheless, regarding the binding of Isaac, the directive is explicit, leaving no room for any other interpretations: "Take now your son, your only one...Isaac" (see also Rashi ad loc.). This only reinforces the question: What was the great test that Abraham faced?

the most. Some of them were completely disconnected from holiness throughout the course of their lives, so their acts of self-sacrifice were therefore utterly astonishing. All of these Jews acted without the absolute certainty that God was commanding them to do so. They received no indication of what He wanted from them in that moment. Instead, they acted by virtue of the simple understanding that the alternative was unthinkable. Ostensibly, an act of self-sacrifice like this is comparable to Abraham's sacrifice of his son. In fact, considering who performed these acts, it may be even greater. ☞

Nonetheless, Abraham's sacrifice is regarded as the pinnacle: It is the Jewish people's greatest source of merit, sustaining every generation. We must endeavor to understand why this is so.

רַק שֶׁאַבְרָהָם אָבִינוּ עָלָיו הַשָּׁלוֹם עָשָׂה זֹאת בִּזְרִיזוּת נִפְלָאָה,

However, it is that our forefather Abraham, of blessed memory, did it with wonderous alacrity,

The greatness of the binding of Isaac lies in the alacrity with which it was performed. The degree of alacrity may not seem particularly remarkable, especially in contrast to the self-sacrifice that was involved. Nevertheless, alacrity reflects a person's spiritual state, which is the source of his actions. It reveals the inner intent, the "soul" of the action, as well as that of the person performing it. The alacrity with which Abraham carried out the binding of Isaac indicates the essence and sincerity of his self-sacrifice. His was an even greater act of self-sacrifice than martyrdom. Every act is the outcome of a spiritual process. Abraham's alacrity reveals his spiritual state, the place from which he acted, and accordingly, it reflects the true value of his act.

HANNAH AND HER SEVEN SONS

☞ The rabbis of every generation have emphasized the connection between the binding of Isaac and Jewish martyrdom in sanctification of God's name, which has occurred throughout our history. The Talmud (*Gittin* 57b) relates the tragic story of a woman who had seven sons. According to other sources, her name was Hannah. The woman watches as one by one, each of her sons willingly gives his life to sanctify God's name. Before her last son is taken away, she kisses him on the head and says, "My sons, go and say to your father Abraham, 'You bound one altar, but I bound seven altars.'"

לְהַרְאוֹת שִׂמְחָתוֹ וְחֶפְצוֹ לְמַלְּאוֹת רְצוֹן קוֹנוֹ וְלַעֲשׂוֹת נַחַת רוּחַ לְיוֹצְרוֹ.

displaying his joy and desire to fulfill the wishes of his Maker and to provide satisfaction to his Creator.

Alacrity in the external realm of action reflects the individual's inner reality. In performing God's will with alacrity, Abraham acted as though he were doing something he truly wanted to do, something he enjoyed. He acted immediately, doing everything that he could at the earliest possible moment, even though it goes against basic human nature to want to sacrifice one's child. Nonetheless, Abraham acted not for his own gratification, but God's. Abraham was completely subsumed to the Divine, and as a result, he had no identity of his own, no personal desires or sources of pleasure. He felt only God's desires, and the satisfaction that God would receive as a result of this act. He felt this so completely that it drove him to act quickly, avoiding even a moment's delay.

Consequently, the alacrity with which Abraham performed the binding of Isaac constitutes our greatest merit, which protects us in every generation. This does not mean that Abraham's alacrity is weighed against his self-sacrifice. Rather, these two elements are bound together. An act that serves as a merit for other people and future generations is an act whose value is not related to the particular individual or situation, but is eternal. When a person gives his life to sanctify God's name in a particular time and place, it is a tremendous act, and he is certainly remembered as a martyr. However, this deed does not necessarily have implications for other people. On the other hand, Abraham's alacrity shows that his act was not just an expression of personal self-sacrifice. Abraham transcended himself entirely and did the greatest thing a human being can possibly do. His act was a pure reflection of God's will, unconnected to his personal devastation, struggle, and ability to transcend. The value of such an act is eternal, and accordingly, it safeguards us and all our future descendants.

וּמִמֶּנּוּ לָמְדוּ רַבּוֹתֵינוּ ז״ל לְקִיּוּם כָּל הַמִּצְוֹת בִּכְלָל, וּבִפְרָט מַעֲשֵׂה הַצְּדָקָה הָעוֹלָה עַל כּוּלָּנָה,

The Sages learned from him with regard to the fulfillment of all the mitzvot in general, especially the mitzva of charity, which is greater than all of them,

From Abraham's alacrity,[15] the Sages learned[16] that all mitzvot should be performed in this manner: with joy and at the earliest possible moment. This is how a person fulfills his own desires, and one's own desires should be completely subsumed to God's desires.

The mitzva of charity surpasses the other mitzvot[17] in several different ways. In *Likkutei Amarim* (chap. 37), it is explained that more than any other mitzva, charity acts on this world and elevates the sparks of holiness within it. Elsewhere,[18] charity is described as quintessential "awakening from below." This is the expression of the lower world that has meaning in the higher world, and it evokes the "awakening from above," whereby supernal forces flow into the lower realm.

whose fruit protect and save the doer **in this world from all types of calamities that might erupt, as it is written: "charity will rescue from death"** (Prov. 10:2; 11:4), **and all the more so from other types of suffering that are less** severe **than death.**

הַמְגִינָּה וּמַצָּלָה בְּפֵירוֹתֶיהָ בָּעוֹלָם הַזֶּה מִכָּל מִינֵי פּוּרְעָנִיּוֹת הַמִּתְרַגְּשׁוֹת, כִּדְכְתִיב: "וּצְדָקָה תַּצִּיל מִמָּוֶת" (משלי י,ב; יא,ד), וְכָל שֶׁכֵּן מִשְּׁאָר מִינֵי יִסּוּרִים הַקַּלִּים מִמָּוֶת.

It is explained in the Talmud (*Sota* 21a)[19] that every mitzva "protects and saves" the person who performs it from all types of calamities, both physical and spiritual.[20] This is certainly true with regard to the giving of charity, which is equivalent to all the other mitzvot.

The main reward for the performance of a mitzva, which is referred

---

15. According to a comment of the Lubavitcher Rebbe, Rabbi Menaḥem Mendel Schneerson (*Likkutei Siḥot*, vol. 6, p. 348), this does not simply mean that we learn how to act based on our observations of Abraham's actions. Rather, Abraham and his act of self-sacrifice gives us the capacity to act in this manner. In the same way, we receive his love of God as an inheritance (see *Likkutei Amarim*, chap. 18).

16. *Pesaḥim* 4a.

17. The author of the *Tanya* alludes here to Prov. 31:29. This verse is part of the *Eshet Ḥayil* poem, which pertains to the *sefira* of *Malkhut*, Kingship. The reference is fitting since it is explained here that charity embodies the ascent of *Malkhut*.

18. See epistle 12.

19. See also epistle 3.

20. As Rashi elucidates there, "'Protects' from suffering, and 'saves' from the evil inclination, so that it does not lead him to sin."

to as the "principal," is not received in this world. Indeed, it is stated in a number of sources that the value of a mitzva is so great that the world cannot contain its reward. However, as the Mishna states, "A person enjoys their fruits in this world while the principal remains for him in the World to Come" (*Pe'a* 1:1). In addition to a "principal," which is reserved for the World to Come, certain mitzvot also have "fruit," which are enjoyed in this world. The giving of charity is one such mitzva.

Charity and its fruits do not protect a person only from the calamity of death. They ensure that everything that happens to him in this world happens in a pleasant way, with no suffering.

כָּל שֶׁכֵּן שֶׁטּוֹב לָנוּ גַּם בָּעוֹלָם הַזֶּה, לְהַקְדִּימָהּ כָּל מַה דְּאֶפְשָׁר, שֶׁהֲרֵי אָדָם נִידּוֹן בְּכָל יוֹם.

All the more so it is good for us, in this world as well, to give it priority as much as possible, since man is judged every day.

We do not always recognize the urgency of matters relating to the spiritual realm and the World to Come. Our lives are steeped in physicality, and accordingly, we are fully aware of the exigencies and realities of life in the physical world. Furthermore, this is not just a subjective feeling: Physical actions cannot be postponed or circumvented. Every act occurs at one specific point in time and space, and every moment of inaction signifies a potential act that will never be performed. On the other hand, in the spiritual realm, there is always a space in which one is able to pause and make adjustments. Therefore, the author of the *Tanya* states that one should perform the mitzva of charity, which protects us in the physical world, at the earliest possible moment.

According to *Rosh HaShana* 16a, a person is not judged only at the end of the world or at the end of his life, once he has left the physical world. Likewise, he is not judged only at the end of each year. Rather, he is judged every day. The heavenly judgment determines the spiritual and religious implications of one's thoughts and actions. The spiritual ramifications of one's actions do not remain in the higher world, but permeate the temporal realm and impact the events of his daily life, influencing what happens and how it happens. ☞

JUDGED EVERY DAY

☞ Although this may not be the case in theory, in practice many people treat religion as separate from life in the physical world. Therefore, a person may be conscious of the Divine and compassionate toward others while he is praying and studying Torah, yet when he is walking down the street or doing business, the "religious" factors fade into the background. Such people regard this world as a separate domain where "business is business" and the only concern is taking care of one's own interests. However, according to the view that a person is judged every day, there is no distinction between the higher world and the lower world, between the future and the present, or between the streets and the synagogue. A person is judged by Heaven, according to heavenly values, at all times, no matter where he is. God determines what and how much the individual will receive and how he will receive it. Likewise, God decides who will live, who will die, who will be rich, and who will be poor. Therefore, one must give charity, which protects us in this world, every day, at every possible moment, so that this mitzva will serve as his defense in the judgment being passed on him.

On a deeper level, the heavenly judgment does not refer to the immediate, inevitable outcome that results from every one of a person's actions, utterances, thoughts, and feelings. Rather, the judgment is an accounting, which is rendered after a person dies and at significant times throughout his life, for example, yearly on Rosh HaShana, monthly on Rosh Ḥodesh, and even daily. The judgment is an evaluation of the overall picture: the person's intentions and actions, and all that ensued from them. There is no one prescribed outcome of such an accounting. There are many different possibilities, and the judgment determines what the outcome will be at each stage of the individual's life.

The hasidic approach, which is discussed at length elsewhere and is based on the words of the prophets and Sages, is that the individual determines his own judgment. The heavenly court is a metaphor for what transpires within us. As mentioned, every one of a person's actions and thoughts has an outcome. However, in our complex reality, this outcome has meaning only in the broader context. To determine where a person is headed based on a given choice, there needs to be a birdseye understanding of where it is coming from and where it will ultimately lead.

The outcome of an action is comparable to a letter of the alphabet. By itself, a letter has little meaning. Yet the more the letters are combined to make words and sentences the more they formulate meaningful messages and determine one's reality. Accordingly, our judgment corresponds to speech, which is *Malkhut*, Kingship. These two attributes are juxtaposed in the phrase "The law of the kingdom is the law [*dina demalkhuta dina*]." In the light of this concept, this phrase reads, "the summation of a person's speech is his judgement." His judgment is the way in which he combines the "letters" of his life: the meaning, weight, and direction that he gives to each matter.

The fact that a person is judged every day means that each day, we form different combinations of letters: in the words we say and think, and more generally, in the way we live and the way we view ourselves, others, and the world. When a person performs an act of charity, of helping and giving to others, his act traverses all the worlds, from the highest to our lowly

14 Tishrei
12 Tishrei (leap year)

אַךְ גַּם זֹאת מָצָאנוּ רָאִינוּ בַּעֲבוֹדַת הַצְּדָקָה.

Moreover, we have found and observed, with regard to the work of charity the following:

Until now, the author of the *Tanya* has discussed the importance of alacrity in the performance of all mitzvot, especially the giving of charity. Now, he explains an additional implication of alacrity in the mitzva of charity, and the deeper connotations behind it.

The author of the *Tanya* refers to the "work" of charity, because the emphasis here is on the efforts of the giver rather than the outcome, the distribution of funds to the needy. A person must exert himself spiritually to give of himself when he has almost nothing to give. ☞

מַעֲלָה פְּרָטִיּוּת גְּדוֹלָה וְנִפְלָאָה, אֵין עֲרוֹךְ אֵלֶיהָ,

That charity is an **especially great and wonderous virtue, to which nothing compares,**

This description indicates that the author of the *Tanya* is not referring to a virtue that is embodied in all mitzvot. Rather, this virtue pertains specifically to the spiritual efforts of one who gives charity. ☞

לִהְיוֹת מַעֲשֵׂה הַצְּדָקָה נַעֲשֵׂית בִּפְעָמִים רַבּוֹת, וְכָל הַמַּרְבֶּה הֲרֵי זֶה מְשׁוּבָּח, וְלֹא בְּפַעַם אַחַת וּבְבַת אַחַת, גַּם כִּי הַסַּךְ הַכּוֹלֵל אֶחָד הוּא,

for the act of charity is performed many times over, and whoever does more is praiseworthy, not by doing it **on one occasion or all at once, even though the total sum amounts to the same.**

world. This mitzva arranges the "letters," the outcomes of all his thoughts, utterances, and actions during that period, into an expression of kindness, a flow of vitality toward all those in need. Alacrity is essential in this matter because of the fact that we are judged every day: The letters are constantly being drawn into new combinations, and the ideal combination is one of kindness and charity.

THE WORK OF CHARITY

☞ It was explained above (epistle 12; *Likkutei Amarim*, chap. 15) that "work," and particularly the work of charity, refers to a situation where an individual does more than he is required to do and has been accustomed to doing. It does not pertain to the act itself, namely what the person did or how much money he donated, but to

The additional virtue of the mitzva of charity lies in the act of giving itself, and accordingly, this act should be performed as frequently as possible. This is not simply an aspect of the attribute of "alacrity" discussed above. Its rationale is not that the poor are in need of immediate relief, and therefore one should give without delay even if he is unable to give the full amount. Here, the author of the *Tanya* is discussing funds for the Land of Israel, which were delivered annually. Accordingly, the "alacrity" described here is different, and moreover, it is infinitely greater and more wonderful. It pertains to the giver himself: the manner in which he gives and how this impacts his life and soul.

כְּמוֹ שֶׁכָּתַב הָרַמְבַּ"ם ז"ל בְּפֵירוּשׁ הַמִּשְׁנָה (אבות פרק ג משנה טו) **שֶׁשָּׁנוּ חֲכָמִים ז"ל: "וְהַכֹּל לְפִי רוֹב הַמַּעֲשֶׂה".**

As the Rambam, of blessed memory, wrote in the commentary on the Mishna (*Avot* 3:15), **that the Sages taught: "Everything is in accordance with the abundance of actions."**

Rambam interprets "the abundance of actions" to mean the number of times an action is repeated. He states, by way of example, that there is no comparison between a person who donates a thousand dinars to charity in one payment and a person who gives the same amount

his spiritual efforts. When one does what he has always done, there is no change to his soul, no spiritual elevation, but only a continuation of the status quo. This may not be easy to accomplish, yet it is not termed "work." Change occurs only when the individual stretches himself. When this happens, he is no longer the same person, but a more developed, improved version of himself.

WONDEROUS AND INCOMPARABLE

☞ These terms are usually used to describe the *sefira* of *Keter*, Crown, as well as the encompassing light. *Keter* is separate and distinct from the other *sefirot*, and likewise, the encompassing light signifies that which is "beyond." While the inner light is enclothed in vessels, the encompassing light is not on the same scale as the rest of reality, and does not have any kind of causal relationship with it. Similarly, the virtue of giving charity at the earliest possible moment, and frequently, is on a completely different level, which is not found in any of the other mitzvot or virtues in this world.

one coin at a time. This is because each time one hands out a coin, he is performing an additional act of generosity.

וְהִנֵּה מִלְּבַד כִּי הָרַמְבַּ"ם ז"ל בֵּיאֵר הֵיטֵב טַעֲמוֹ וְנִימּוּקוֹ כְּדֵי לְזַכֵּךְ הַנֶּפֶשׁ עַל יְדֵי רִבּוּי הַמַּעֲשֶׂה,

Now, apart from the fact **that the Rambam, of blessed memory, explained his reasoning and rationale comprehensively – in order to purify the soul by means of the abundance of actions,**

It is a principle of life that what a person does and how he behaves affects his soul.[21] A person cannot separate himself from his actions, for better or for worse. A person's bad deeds damage his soul, even if they were unintentional. The inverse is also true: even if they are initially done mechanically and without the proper intent, one's good deeds refine his soul. The soul is enclothed in the body, and it is therefore compelled to take part in whatever actions the body performs. When an act is repeated many times, the soul becomes accustomed to it, and eventually, the act becomes part of the soul. The person feels and thinks differently, and in the case of giving charity, becomes essentially kind and giving. The action is a vessel for the soul's light, and likewise, the soul takes shape according to the vessel. Rambam interprets this matter in accordance with the revealed Torah. Today, his explanation may be seen as a psychological one: The value of the action is not measured by the external reality but rather in the soul of the doer. More precisely, the experience of the soul ultimately brings about change in the soul itself. Below, the author of the *Tanya* provides an additional, "incomparably wondrous" explanation from the concealed Torah. ☞

RAMBAM VERSUS THE KABBALA

☞ Rambam's explanation regarding the connection between a person's actions and soul derives from the revealed Torah. There is also a deeper, hasidic interpretation, which can in fact also be construed in the words of Rambam. The human soul is not truly separate from the worlds. One is not simply a metaphor for the other. Rather, they are bound together and impact one another. Essentially, they are one entity. However, the approach of the author of the *Tanya* is to identify the interpreta-

21. As it states in *Sefer HaḤinukh*, "Our hearts follow our actions" (mitzva 16).

הִנֵּה מִקְרָא מָלֵא דִּיבֵּר הַכָּתוּב 'פְּעוּלַּת צְדָקָה לְחַיִּים', דְּהַיְינוּ שֶׁפְּעוּלָּתָהּ וּסְגוּלָּתָהּ לְהַמְשִׁיךְ חַיִּים עֶלְיוֹנִים,

Scripture categorically states "the act of charity is life," that is, its impact and power is to draw down supernal life,

Simply put, charity bestows life.[22] Everything that can be considered charity, such as money, food, love, wisdom, and even a smile, affects the perpetuation of life. Furthermore, just as a human being's act of charity in the lower world creates a flow of life toward one who is in need, divine charity entails the unlimited flow of life from the highest realm. ☞

tions that stem from the revealed as well as the concealed Torah. There are several reasons for this, but they are beyond the scope of this note. The author of the *Tanya* never disqualifies a "revealed" teaching, even if it is more limited in scope than the concealed one. First, he thoroughly analyzes the explanations that stem from the revealed Torah, and only afterward, if necessary, he provides the concealed interpretation, citing Kabbala or hasidic teachings. Rambam's explanation here does not embody the "great and wonderful, incomparable virtue" described above. Consequently, the author of the *Tanya* provides an additional explanation, on an altogether different scale. The effect on the human soul is only one element of this interpretation, which derives from the incomparable "wonders" of the Torah: its deepest, most concealed dimensions.

THE ACT OF CHARITY IS LIFE

☞ Essentially, when an individual gives physical charity in this world, it creates a "wave of giving" that spreads throughout all the worlds, encompassing not only those who are deserving, but anyone in need, and anywhere there is a lack. This idea is expressed in different ways in every epistle that is concerned with charity. It is based in the words of the Sages and in Kabbala. The Midrash states (see *Shemot Rabba* 31:15) that all of God's creations borrow from one another: Day borrows from night and night borrows from day; the moon borrows from the stars and the stars borrow from the moon; *Ḥokhma*, Wisdom, borrows from *Bina*, Understanding; and the

22. The Lubavitcher Rebbe, Rabbi Menaḥem Mendel Schneerson, notes that the quote in the text, "The act of charity is life," appears to be a combination of two verses: "The act of the righteous is for life" (Prov. 10:16), and "Charity is the base of a life" (Prov. 11:19). This is problematic since the author of the *Tanya* writes that this phrase is "categorically" stated in *Tanakh*.

מֵחַיֵּי הַחַיִּים, אֵין סוֹף בָּרוּךְ הוּא לְאֶרֶץ הַחַיִּים, הִיא שְׁכִינַת עוּזֵּינוּ,

from the source of life, *Ein Sof*, blessed be He, to the land of life, which is the Divine Presence, our strength,

The term "source of life," which literally translates as the "life of life," is a title for God. The author of the *Tanya* discloses that the vitality that is unleashed from an act of charity stems from the aspect of God that is the infinite source of all life. In contrast to life in the lower realm, supernal life is boundless, indefinable, and entirely beyond the grasp of our rational mind. It is the flow of the divine life force itself, which does not possess any particular form. In our world, and in a certain sense, in all of the worlds, life itself is "enclothed" either in a physical form or a spiritual form that relates to the physical realm of which it is a part. All the different ways in which we see life, feel life, and think life are in fact only fragments of life that have been delineated and "enclothed" in specific forms, such as food, the body, love, light, and so forth. They are necessary to our wellbeing, so we carve them out from within boundless supernal life. Supernal life itself, however, is infinite and undefinable, flowing from God's *Ein Sof*.

The "land of life" is the vessel that receives supernal life. Just as the succession of life culminates in the lowest rung; physical earth, the upper earth, which is called the Divine Presence, or *Malkhut*, is the ultimate receiver of the flow of supernal life. The Divine Presence, therefore, parallels the element of earth, of "receiving," within the Divine. It receives supernal life, the infinite divine flow itself, before it is broken down into different "physical" forms in each world. The "land of life" is the Divine Presence [*Shekhina*] because it receives life, and accordingly, it is where the infinite Divine dwells [*shokhen*].

The implications of this are far-reaching. When we speak about individual creations, such as ourselves, different parts of ourselves, or

Torah borrows from the mitzvot, yet none of them charges interest from any other. In other words, there is a system of giving and kindness at the very foundation of our world, and a human being who charges "interest," who demands payment for his actions, creates a blockage in this system. However, a person who performs acts of charity, who gives gratuitously, opens up the channels through which supernal life flows into all the worlds.

other creations that relate to us in some way, we are speaking only of particular aspects of life, but not of the essence of life, nor of the infinite Divine. Essential life flows from *Ein Sof*, or the "source of life," and we can refer to it only in terms of the Divine Presence. God and the Divine Presence are bound to one another: Only the Divine Presence receives God's flow. In other words, God manifests His essence and infinitude only in the Divine Presence.

Accordingly, the Divine Presence is akin to essential life, and to *Ein Sof*, who emanates life. It is not a specific, defined entity, but rather the nullification of all definitions and boundaries between objects. Since it receives the unconstrained essence of life, it may be said that it embodies the essence of "receiving." This does not pertain to the receiving of any particular object, but rather to the act of receiving itself. ☞

שֶׁעָלֶיהָ נֶאֱמַר: "וְאַתָּה מְחַיֶּה אֶת כּוּלָּם" (נחמיה ט,ו).

regarding which it is stated: "You give life to them all" (Neh. 9:6).

As explained regarding this verse in *Sha'ar HaYiḥud VeHa'emuna* (chap. 2), the word "You," *atta*, spelled *alef-tav-heh*, can be said to encompass all the letters of the alphabet, from *alef* to *tav*, as well as the five organs of articulation, embodied by the letter *heh* whose numerical equivalent is five. Consequently, this word signifies the letters of divine speech, which "speak" all of reality into existence. Creation is made up entirely of divine utterances: God forms and gives life to everything through

PRAYING FOR THE DIVINE PRESENCE

☞ In Hasidism, it is often said the greatest kind of prayer is prayer for the sake of the Divine Presence. In this kind of prayer, the individual does not pray for the sake of his own connection to God. Moreover, he does not pray so that his needs will be fulfilled and his troubles eased, nor even to give thanks for what he has received. Prayer for one's own sake actually separates a person from *Ein Sof*, and from the flow of vitality that He emits, because it diverts some element away from the Divine Presence and toward the self. This does not mean that there is no place for such prayers. However, the most desirable kind of prayer, the prayer that embodies the unification of all of creation within the Divine, is said solely for the sake of the Divine Presence. A person who cries out for the plight of the Divine Presence and gives thanks for its blessings becomes the "mouth" of the Divine Presence. He articulates the letters that form all the remedies and positive influence that the world needs.

speech. According to this view, the Divine Presence is the speech itself. ☞

וְהִיא סוּכַּת דָּוִד הַנּוֹפֶלֶת עַד עָפָר, This is the booth of David, which has fallen to the dust,

In the present day, while we are in exile, the Divine Presence is referred to as "the booth of David, which has fallen" (see Amos 9:11).[23] The "booth of David" is a reference to David's kingdom (*Targum* ad loc., and see the other commentaries on this verse). Its "fall" represents the exile, and its reestablishment the redemption. The kingdom of David, both past and future, exemplifies what God's kingship over our world is supposed to look like: The Jewish people living in their land, fulfilling all of God's commandments, and establishing His kingdom in the world. When this does not describe the current situation, it is said that the booth of David is fallen.

Dust epitomizes the "inanimate object," the lowest class of earthly matter. In ascending order, the higher classes of matter are vegetable, animal, and human being. Today, we are living in the time of "the footsteps of the Messiah," and as we approach the end of the exile, the Divine Presence falls to the "dust": It is concealed within the obscure,

YOU GIVE LIFE TO THEM ALL

☞ Human speech receives vitality from the soul. As a vessel, it does not receive exclusively from one particular spiritual faculty, but from all of them. It is explained in several places (see epistle 5, and in epistle 20, presented differently) that it is actually even greater than them, since speech is the essence of the soul, which is not defined by any particular spiritual faculty. Speech is the vessel that receives the soul's very essence, and the same is true with regard to the Divine Presence. Speech is made up of "*alef-tav-heh*": the letters from *alef* to *tav*, expressed through the five organs of articulation. By themselves, the letters are not yet "defined" as anything in particular, and they do not convey meaning. However, they contain the power of *Ein Sof*: the potential to speak and to create. Once letters combine to make one of the countless possible letter-combinations, they signify a specific form: life force enclothed in matter and limits. In this light, the verse then reads: The letters of speech and the organs of articulation give life to the multitude of particular details that comprise the reality of every world that ever was, is, or will be.

23. See epistles 9, 30; *Likkutei Torah*, Num. 8d.

lowly, physical reality. Consequently, that is also where the rectification and elevation of the Divine Presence begins: with the work of refining the "dust," and elevating the divine sparks scattered in the physical world. ☞

וְכִמַאֲמַר רַבּוֹתֵינוּ ז״ל: גָּלוּ לֶאֱדוֹם שְׁכִינָה עִמָּהֶם כו׳.

in accordance with our Rabbis' statement: When they were exiled to Edom, the Divine Presence was with them…

As explained in *Likkutei Amarim* (chap. 17), this interpretation unlocks the mystery of the exile of the Divine Presence.[24] The Divine Presence is not an independent entity that can elect to be with us at certain times and to be apart from us at other times. Rather, it is the divine life force within us, which sustains us continuously. However, the manner in which it sustains us is determined by our actions. When we do God's will, think divine thoughts, and so on, the Divine Presence is revealed. On the other hand, when we follow the ways of Edom and identify with our fallen state, it is concealed and exiled, and furthermore, it sustains the "Edomite" deeds that we perform. Just as the Divine Presence is exiled because of us, is it also redeemed through us.

FALLEN TO THE DUST

☞ The way to serve God during the exile is to lay the groundwork for the redemption (see *Likkutei Amarim*, chap. 37). This may also be described as building the grand structure of the Messiah. In earlier generations, divine service was primarily concerned with the head, namely the cognitive faculties of wisdom, understanding, and knowledge. The *tanna'im* and *amora'im*, for example, served God first and foremost through Torah study. In contrast, the period of "the footsteps of the Messiah" relates to the heels, the lowest of all the body parts. Accordingly, today, the greater part of divine service is performed in the "dust," the realm of physical action, particularly through giving charity (see epistle 9. This idea is explained in detail in numerous sources, for example, *Sefer HaMa'amarim Melukat*, vol. 1, p. 193).

24. The rabbinic statement quoted here comes from *Megilla* 29a as cited in *Ein Ya'akov*; *Bemidbar Rabba* 7:10.

כִּי בְּאִתְעֲרוּתָא דִּלְתַתָּא לְהַחֲיוֹת רוּחַ שְׁפָלִים דְּלֵית לֵיהּ מִגַּרְמֵיהּ כְּלוּם, אִתְעֲרוּתָא דִּלְעֵילָּא,

For by an awakening from below, to revive the spirit of the humble, who have nothing of their own, there is **an awakening from above,**

When a person in the lower realm gives his own money and material resources to those who have even less than he has, this generates an awakening from above, from the supernal "source of life," which correlates to *Zeir Anpin* of the world of *Atzilut*. This awakening revitalizes the Divine Presence, which is *Malkhut*, the *sefira* that "has nothing of its own." Therefore, a human being's act of charity in the lower world, which gives life to the needy, is what awakens the source of life in the upper realm and causes it to give life to the worlds.

וּבִפְרָט בְּהִתְנַדֵּב עָם, לְהַחֲיוֹת יוֹשְׁבֵי אֶרֶץ הַחַיִּים מַמָּשׁ, וְדַי לַמֵּבִין.

especially when the people volunteer to revive those living in the actual land of life, and this is **sufficient explanation for one who understands.**

When hasidim come together as a community, they reveal the Divine Presence to a much greater extent than any act performed by one individual. As mentioned, the "land of life" is the Divine Presence, *Malkhut*, and the higher element of earth. However, it is also the title given to the lower, physical Land of Israel. As explained in several places,[25] the lower Land of Israel is parallel to the heavenly Land of Israel. When charity and life are given to those who live in the physical Land of Israel, the result is the most direct and ultimate awakening from below. This comprises a flow of life force straight to the essential "land of life," in its most transcendent form: divine *Malkhut*, also known as the Divine Presence, which receives the essence of the divine life force.

וְכָל מַשְׂכִּיל עַל דָּבָר גָּדוֹל וְנִפְלָא כָּזֶה יִמְצָא טוּב טַעַם וָדַעַת, כַּמָּה גְּדוֹלִים דִּבְרֵי חֲכָמִים ז״ל שֶׁאָמְרוּ ״הַכֹּל לְפִי רוֹב הַמַּעֲשֶׂה״, דְּהַיְינוּ מַעֲשֶׂה

Whoever comprehends such a great and wonderful idea as this will discover pleasing rationale and awareness, how great are the

25. See *Likkutei Torah*, Num. 36d–37a.

הַצְּדָקָה, הַנַּעֲשָׂה בִּפְעָמִים רַבּוֹת, לְהַמְשִׁיךְ חַיִּים עֶלְיוֹנִים, לְיַחֵד יִחוּד עֶלְיוֹן פְּעָמִים רַבּוֹת.

words of the Sages, when they said "everything is in accordance with the abundance of actions," that is, the action of charity, which is performed many times over, serving **to draw down supernal life, to unite the supernal unification many times over.**

This epistle expounds on the greatness of the mitzva of charity beyond the magnitude of the physical act performed by the individual. This mitzva has repercussions in every world, and its effects are beyond all measure and comprehension.

The act of giving charity is the principal act of divine worship. The Sages emphasize the importance of an "abundance" of actions because each time this act is performed, it draws down supernal life. Every time a person performs the act of a mitzva, a union is created: He unites opposite "ends" to form one entity. On the most basic level, when a person does any act with intention, he brings together each of the different elements involved in the act's accomplishment: thought, action, and the soul. But more than that, when one performs a mitzva, the union that is created is "supernal." It ascends to the highest heights and is all-encompassing: It joins the upper realm to the lower realm, the Giver to the receiver, and oneness to plurality. This is the union between God and the Divine Presence.

The supernal union formed through the act of giving charity is both broader and deeper than the supernal unions that result from the other mitzvot. This is because, as explained, charity influences the world of action more broadly and deeply than any of the other mitzvot. Additionally, the magnitude of this supernal union is a consequence of the "abundance of actions" that the mitzva of charity involves. While the other practical mitzvot, such as *lulav* and *tzitzit*, can be performed only at a specific time or with a certain object, this mitzva has no such external constraints.Charity may be given anytime and anywhere, and moreover, it may consist of anything. Accordingly, there is no limit to the number of times this mitzva can be performed. When one gives to a pure "receiver," who does not give him anything in return, he thereby forms a union between "giver" and "receiver" that impacts all worlds. The significance of this union goes far beyond the physical outcome of the act, how much money the person gave, and so on. Consequently, although in practical terms there is no difference between donating a sum of money once and donating the same amount by contributing smaller sums on many separate occasions, in spiritual terms the difference is enormous. Every time a person gives charity, his soul experiences "giving" once again, and recreates the union between supernal life and the Divine Presence, which is in the lower realm. Each time this happens, the unification that is formed expands the all-encompassing universal union even further. ☞

וְהַיְינוּ נַמִּי כְּעֵין מַה שֶּׁכָּתַב הָרַמְבַּ"ם לְזַכֵּךְ הַנֶּפֶשׁ,

This is also similar to what the Rambam wrote, that it is **to purify the soul,**

"ABUNDANCE OF ACTIONS" IN EACH PERIOD OF TIME

☞ In *Likkutei Amarim* (chap. 41) it is explained that if a person is unable to maintain the proper intention for the entire duration of a mitzva, particularly Torah study, which is a sustained activity that engages the mind, it is enough that he has the proper intention when he begins to perform it. The author of the *Tanya* cites, by way of example, the *halakhot* of writing a Torah scroll or a bill of divorce. These acts require intention: When writing a Torah scroll, one must write with this purpose in mind, and likewise, when writing a bill of divorce, he must write it for the specific woman who is to receive it. In both of these cases, it is sufficient if when he begins to write, the scribe has the necessary intention with respect to everything that he is about to write. Nonetheless, as explained there, there is a limit to this rule: A person's intention from the previous day, and even from the previous hour, ceases to apply once that period has ended. He must reaffirm his intention when a new period begins. Each period has its own unique essence, and consequently, an intention that pertains to one point in time, one set of circumstances, does not pertain to another. In each new period, the divine life force that flows through the worlds regenerates and becomes an entirely new, different entity (see epistle 14). With regard to the drawing down of supernal life and the union of the upper realm with the lower realm, a person's spiritual intention on a certain day certainly does not correspond to the unique life force of the following day. In order for a union to be formed, the upper and lower realms, as well as the upper and lower intentions, must correspond to one another. This occurs only when we act with intention in the here and now.

In light of this, we are able to understand the instruction given at the beginning of this epistle. Although we are required to pay a set annual amount, this sum should not be given all at once, at the beginning or end of the year. Instead, it should be divided up into separate contributions that are given weekly, or if one finds this too difficult, at least monthly.

Now, at the conclusion of the epistle, the author of the *Tanya* returns to the words of the Rambam, which he previously explained in accordance with their literal meaning.[26] Here, he expounds on them in accordance with the Torah's deeper levels of interpretation. ☞

כַּנּוֹדָע מִזּוֹהַר הַקָּדוֹשׁ דִּשְׁכִינָה נִקְרֵאת 'נֶפֶשׁ' כִּי הִיא חַיֵּינוּ וְנַפְשֵׁנוּ,

as is known from the holy *Zohar*, that the Divine Presence is called *nefesh* (soul), **because it is our life and soul,**

In Kabbala, the five levels of the soul (*nefesh, ruaḥ, neshama, ḥaya,* and *yeḥida*) correspond to the various worlds and heavenly *sefirot*. *Nefesh* signifies the world of *Asiya* and the *sefira* of *Malkhut*, which is the level of the Divine Presence.[27]

The author of the *Tanya* explains the reason for this. As mentioned, the Divine Presence is the divine life force within all things. Nonetheless, the idea that every individual is able to clearly understand and relate to is that the Divine Presence is the divine life force within himself, and more broadly, the entirety of the life force within himself. In order for a person to comprehend the existence of the Divine Presence as an independent entity, he must first nullify, to some extent, his perception of himself as an independent being. Subsequently, he will be able to connect his sense of the reality of his own soul to the Divine Presence,

A KABBALISTIC INTERPRETATION OF RAMBAM

☞ The author of the *Tanya* held Rambam in the highest regard and was deeply connected to him. He quotes Rambam's works frequently. However, in his writings, the author of the *Tanya* usually distinguishes Rambam's teachings from the hasidic teachings, especially those that are based on Lurianic Kabbala. In fact, in several places he carefully explains the differences between them (for example, the gloss to *Likkutei Amarim*, chap. 2). Nevertheless, here, in what is perhaps the exception that proves the rule, the author of the *Tanya* departs from this approach and interprets Rambam's statement in a broader, non-literal sense. He seems to be implying that Rambam actually meant for his words to be interpreted in this way.

26. Above, the author of the *Tanya* cited Rambam's praise of the repeated act of giving of charity because of the fact that this refines the soul.

27. *Tikkunei Zohar* 87b; see also *Zohar Ḥadash*, Ruth 84a. In many hasidic and kabbalistic sources it is an established fact that the level of *nefesh* is *Malkhut* and the Divine Presence.

at least to some degree. Very little is required in order to achieve this: When a person opens himself up to the idea that his life and soul are not completely disconnected from other people's lives and souls, he is able to comprehend the idea that the Divine Presence, which is "the life within all things" and "the soul of the world," is also his own life and soul.

As mentioned, Rambam states that an "abundance of actions" is praiseworthy because it refines the soul. Above, the author of the *Tanya* interpreted this in relation to the individual's soul: The repeated actions cause the person to see reality in a different way. Here, however, the author of the *Tanya* gives a deeper interpretation of Rambam's words: The "abundance of actions" refines the Divine Presence as well. In other words, it causes changes in the reality itself. ☞

וּכְתִיב: "כִּי שָׁחָה לֶעָפָר נַפְשֵׁנוּ" (תהלים מד,כו).

and it is written: "Our soul is stooped over into the dust" (Ps. 44:26).

When the *nefesh*, the Divine Presence, is in exile, it is unclean and coated with "dust." This refers to the physical world, which conceals the Divine. A person's repeated acts of giving with gratuitous kindness, and without recompense, resemble divine giving. These human acts merge with divine giving and draw it into the world, where it refines the individual's soul as well as the Divine Presence, which is also called *nefesh*.

וְלָכֵן אָמְרוּ רַבּוֹתֵינוּ ז"ל: "גְּדוֹלָה צְדָקָה שֶׁמְּקָרֶבֶת אֶת הַגְּאוּלָּה"

And therefore, our Rabbis said: Great is charity, as it advances the

OUR LIFE AND SOUL

☞ The two interpretations that the author of the *Tanya* finds in the words of Rambam actually reflect the two layers of meaning found in this entire epistle. On the one hand, the human soul undergoes purification and becomes subsumed to God, the "Giver." On the other hand, the soul is the Divine Presence. It too is found within the human being, and it is subsumed to the "soul of the world," which is the global Divine Presence, which is also called *nefesh*. All this occurs on the level of the individual human being as well as on the level of the whole world. Yet, the power to unify the two lies in every person's hands and happens through the mitzva act that they do. A single, physical act may seem insignificant in relation to the vast worlds, a tiny speck in the darkness and concealment of the exile. However, when there is an "abundance of actions," each act forms an additional union, and this causes the union to expand further and further, ultimately becoming the all-encompassing union of God and the Divine Presence.

(בבא בתרא י,א), לַהֲקִימָה מֵעָפָר מְעַט מְעַט, **redemption** (*Bava Batra* 10a), **raising it little-by-little from the dust,**

As explained in this epistle, acts of charity have a cumulative effect. The fact that we are instructed to perform them frequently indicates that these acts are not treated separately. Rather, they combine to produce an outcome that is greater than the sum of its parts. When an act of charity is performed in the "dust," which is the lowest world, where the spiritual and holy cannot be seen or felt, light and holiness accumulate and continue to gain strength while remaining concealed. Charity is referred to as "great" because this constitutes its entire purpose. It is "planted" in the "dirt," where it appears to vanish altogether, yet it concentrates there for one single purpose: to raise the Divine Presence from the dust.[28]

This process is intrinsically gradual and concealed. Its concealment is not intentional but simply a consequence of its slow pace. Everyone notices when something changes dramatically, but we do not always perceive small, gradual shifts. The great transformation develops slowly and steadily over time until one day it is revealed to us that we are in a completely different world. This is the redemption.

"עַד כִּי יָבֹא שִׁילֹה" (בראשית מט,י). **"until Shilo arrives"** (Gen. 49:10).

This refers to the Messiah[29] at the time of the complete redemption, when the Divine Presence will arise, whole and perfect, from the dust.[30]

---

28. See also *Likkutei Amarim*, chap. 37.

29. See Rashi ad loc.; see also *Likkutei Torah* of the Arizal ad loc.; *Likkutei Torah*, Song; *Siḥat Aḥaron shel Pesaḥ* 5699. This is also mentioned many times in the discourses of the Lubavitcher Rebbe, Rabbi Menaḥem Mendel Schneerson. "Until Shilo arrives" is an unusual way to describe the redemption. It is possible that this phrase alludes to the aspects of the redemption that are dealt with in this epistle. The Lubavitcher Rebbe cites the *Zohar* (1:237b) in relation to this matter:

> However, in the verse "until Shilo arrives," the word Shilo is written with the letter *heh*, (while in the other verses it is written with a *vav*.) This verse reveals the secret of the holy name *Yah* (*yod-heh*). In some places, Shilo is spelled *shin-yod-lamed-vav*, without a *heh*, and in other places it is spelled *shin-lamed-heh*, without a *yod*. Here, however, it is spelled *shin-yod-lamed-heh*, with both a *yod* and a *heh*. This is the secret of the holy, heavenly name, for the Divine Presence will rise up by means of the name *Yah*, and this is the secret of *yod*.

30. The closing of this epistle was not printed in the *Tanya*, but it appears in

This short epistle deals with one critical point: the need to give charity frequently. Since in monetary terms, the total amount given is the same whether a person donates it all at once or in many separate contributions, the significance of giving repeatedly must be with respect to the spiritual realm and the divine service of the soul. It was explained that just as physical charity bestows life upon a person who does not have enough to live on, the spiritual act sends vitality into *Malkhut*, which has nothing of its own. *Malkhut* is the Divine Presence, which is on such a low level during the exile that it is in the "dust." Nonetheless, while the physical flow is limited by the constraints of both the giver and the receiver, the spiritual flow has no limits. It is the life force itself, prior to being enclothed in a physical form in one specific place, time, and person. The way to open this gate, and keep it open, is through the "work" of giving charity. When a person opens up his heart and his wallet to another, he breaks the boundary between them that defines what is his and what is the other person's. In doing so, he opens the gate and forms a supernal union, which draws the essence of the life force from the highest realm to the lowest. He must expand this union as much as he can, applying it in each period of time and filling every moment, world, and soul with the flow of supernal life.

Regarding this level of giving, the Sages said, "Great is charity, as it advances the redemption." The author of the *Tanya* strongly emphasizes this point here. As a result, his hasidim would give charity as frequently as they were able to, and would strive to give even more.

Iggerot Kodesh Admor HaZaken (epistle 36):

> In light of these words of truth, my beloved ones, my brothers, and my friends, you must spur each other on. Each person must support his neighbor and say to his brother, "Let us be strong for our people and for God's cities in the holy land. Let us seek their prosperity and well-being with all our hearts and souls." I implore you again and again not to cast aside my words, God forbid. May the entreaty of this supplicant, who loves [his people] and seeks their well-being with a yearning heart and soul, find favor.

Epistle 22

THIS LETTER WAS COMPOSED (PROBABLY IN 1793) IN the context of the "Liozna Regulations [*Takanot Liozna*],"[1] which were designed, perhaps for the first time in the history of Hasidism, to define and institutionalize the relationship between the Rebbe and his hasidim. The need for these regulations arose both due to the large number of hasidim who were following Rabbi Shneur Zalman at the time, as well as the fact the hasidic Rebbe is an extremely commanding figure. These considerations led to the enactment of the Liozna Regulations, to which we owe this unique letter in which the author of the *Tanya*, highly uncharacteristically, refers to himself as a party in this relationship. On account of the tension between his love for his followers like his own self and his inability in practice to fulfill all of their wishes, he goes out of his way to express his personal distress in unusually frank terms for his style of writing, which is typically clear and restrained, while avoiding any disclosure of his private turmoil (which surely existed). This letter, especially in the section that was not printed in *Iggeret HaKodesh*, but which is cited in the commentary below, provides a window through which one can glimpse the personality behind the tzaddik and his writings. A fascinating personal story is revealed here in its splendor: Courage and heroism; sensitivity and love for individuals and people in general; and the occasional frustrations and pains, both on account

1. On these regulations, see the Introduction to *Iggerot Kodesh Admor HaZaken*, chap. 6, and the notes to Letter 31 there.

of the behavior of others – as well as himself – and due to the difficulty, which every person experiences, in accepting with peace of mind all that God metes out as for the best.

The printed epistle 22 can be divided into three main sections: In the first part (until the passage that begins "like a merciful, wise and righteous father") the author of the *Tanya* asks his hasidim, in almost pleading terms, not to approach him with questions that involve material matters and the affairs of this world, and he proceeds to give his reasons for this request. The second section (until the passage beginning "My beloved ones, my brethren and friends") partly serves to counterbalance the first section, as he nevertheless offers the hasidim advice – not on how to change and solve the problems of this world, but how to look at them differently. The third part is basically a separate letter, which was added by the publishers to the 1900 edition, and it will be elucidated on its own below.

THE LIOZNA REGULATIONS

Liozna was the town where the author of the *Tanya* first held an official post. At that time, after a group of hasidim led by Rabbi Menaḥem Mendel of Vitebsk and his colleagues departed for the Land of Israel, the hasidim of Rabbi Shneur Zalman, who was left as the only hasidic Rebbe in these regions, greatly increased in number. There were far more hasidim than usual for hasidic courts at that time, indeed more than there had been in earlier periods, even for the Maggid of Mezeritch and the Ba'al Shem Tov.[2] This had

2. These great men differed not only in the number of their followers but also in their style of leadership. In the cases of the Ba'al Shem Tov and the Maggid of Mezeritch, a small circle of hasidim would gather around the Rebbe, and his Torah was directed to them. All the other hasidim were in a more distant circle, and the relationship between them and the Rebbe operated mainly on a personal basis, in that they would come to receive advice and blessings from the Rebbe on various occasions. Rabbi Shneur Zalman, by contrast, not only enjoyed a large number of disciples, but all the hasidim were recipients of his Torah, meaning that they were more than passive receivers – they were hasidim in the full sense

a substantial impact on Rabbi Shneur Zalman's teachings, on the type of divine service he instructed his disciples to engage in, and on the personal relationships between him and the hasidim. Appropriate and viable options for a small group of elite followers were now impossible, both for the Rebbe and the hasidim. It became necessary to regulate the conduct of the hasidim in the Rebbe's "court": When does one approach the Rebbe; who may enter his presence, and in what manner; how should one prepare for this encounter; and so on and so forth. The whole set of regulations, which were formalized in several stages between the years 1793-1800, are called the "Liozna Regulations" in the Chabad hasidic tradition. The regulations were recorded mainly by the hasidic elders and approved by the Rebbe himself. The original written regulations have been preserved to this day in the manuscript treasury of the Chabad - Lubavitch Library. In another, less orderly form, they also appear in several of Rabbi Shneur Zalman's letters to his hasidim.[3] While this letter does not provide an actual list of regulations and instructions, it also belongs to that category of letters, as it shares the same background as them.

By way of an introduction, the beginning of this letter, which was not included in the printed editions of *Iggeret HaKodesh*, is presented here as it appears in *Iggerot Kodesh Admor HaZaken*, Letter 35. It provides important background information for the rest of the letter:

After greetings of peace and everlasting life, my soul pours out in my petition, and my request is spread and laid out before all my beloved ones and friends, all of the members of our fold in general, and especially those engaged

---

of the word, partners in his Torah and service of God, or at least this is how the author of the *Tanya* felt towards them. This factor helps explain Rabbi Shneur Zalman's attitude in several regards, and it also sheds light on the unique nature of his teachings in relation to his predecessors.

3. These have been published in *Iggerot Kodesh Admor HaZaken*, Letters 31, 35, 43, 47, 50, 67.

in holy matters – the charity collectors of the Land of Israel, may it be rebuilt and established speedily in our days. My request to them is doubled with all my heart and soul, that they should watch with an open eye and oversee an actual life-threatening situation, taking authority over the people of the Lord who are journeying to our camp, warning them severely that they should not be a source of bitterness to me, or a cause of aggravation by travelling at an inappropriate time, as explained below. Whether they are residents of their city, or from the nearby settlements, or from another place and are passing through their city, and whether they are new or old members of our community, they should be asked and warned, with a repeated and harsh warning, that in their journey they should not violate one of these terms that have been set up in truth and justice, and they should be shown a copy of this letter.

First of all, none of those travelling on the four established occasions[4] should so much as consider requesting a private audience with me, even for something highly urgent involving the service of God, and all the more so for a worldly matter, even if it is a very great concern. For it is absolutely impossible that all those who have gathered here on those four specific occasions could enter to speak with me. Now, they are all longing to enter, and I cannot differentiate between them, for "jealousy is cruel as the grave" (Song 8:6) with respect to those who force their way in. With my nature and softness of heart, I cannot bear to see the disappointment of those who are barred from entry, and return home in a state of anguish and jealousy, which they consider honorable rivalry among scholars.

Apart from that, as a God-fearing man I am greatly upset, even to death (Jon. 4:9), and it makes me very bitter that we have to push away anyone who wishes to draw near the service of God, from the new members of our community,

---

4. Simḥat Torah; the Shabbat of Hanukkah; Purim; and Shabbat Shuva (the Shabbat between Rosh HaShana and Yom Kippur).

with whom it is highly necessary to speak in private, and this cannot be done in any other manner.

However, what can I do, as there is simply not nearly enough time to speak privately with each and every one of the new members who gather on these four dates, nor can I differentiate between them, by rejecting one person and not the other. Therefore, those new members should not travel at all on the four occasions for a private audience. They have plenty of opportunities to travel in any of the months of the year of their choice, on one of the first three Shabbatot, only they should stay for two or three days after the Shabbat.

As for the fourth Shabbat, which is the Shabbat on which we bless the approaching New Moon, the new members should never travel for that one either, since that Shabbat is set aside for the older members of our community, who are granted an audience specifically once a year, as has been well established. There is not enough time after Shabbat to speak privately with the new members, but only with the older ones, on very important matters regarding which they cannot receive advice from the local members of the community, as they are unable to help them. Also, the other indispensable condition is that the individual in question has two options available to him and he does not know which one to choose. If, however, there is only one avenue open to him, but it is a contemptible one that is causing him great distress, God forbid, and he feels the need to inform me of his sorrow, may God have mercy, then he can apprise me in a letter or through a well-known trustee of mine. He can rest assured that I will hear all of his words in full, without any omissions at all. If I have a response, I will answer through the same means, but he should not try to force his way in to see me in person.

I am tired of conveying in writing the magnitude of the grief that embitters my very life, caused by those who enter to lay out their misery in person, at length, in order that their sorrows and troubles should enter the depths of my heart, may God have mercy. Furthermore, when they ask for advice on issues that involve no sorrow and bitterness at all, I am weary of the confusion this causes me, and the time it takes away from other tasks, when I have to think about and analyze the case in depth, in order to provide a proper answer. This detracts from the numerous and weighty issues facing all the members of our community in general, may God increase you one thousand times over, and bless you (see Deut. 1:11) with the blessing of peace, that they will dwell in their homes in peace; "with repose and pleasantness you will be saved" (Isa. 30:15) forever.

Now, it goes without saying, regarding all my beloved ones and friends, to whom my soul is as dear to them as their own, that had they known from the outset what they are doing to me by asking for their needs and for counsel from afar, they would certainly have found in themselves a way to ease their situation by casting their burden upon the Lord, that He should do what is best in His eyes, instead of bothering me and confusing me with their affairs. However, it seems that some members of our community are suffering from an illusion and false idea, which is truly as far from me as east from west, as they say about me things that apply to great and famous individuals – O Lord, by these things they live (see Isa. 38:16) – who are not surprised by the many varied events that unfold over the course of time, and who can speak about them unequivocally. But what advantage has the charmer (see Ecc. 10:11) in boasting, and the heart knows the bitterness of my lowly soul (see Prov. 14:10) in its absolute true root. I know my own worth, and my heart is aware, for I can feel with my own senses the great and frequent confusion in my brain and heart. On several occasions I have actually despaired of my life at this level, and I have often arrived at the decision that I should uproot my pegs[5] from this country. However, I await the salvation of the Lord, that He will open the eyes of the passers-by,[6] and place in the heart of all those who hear these statements

5. That is, the pegs of my tent; see *Pesaḥim* 80a.
6. *Ha'ovrim*; a pun on "to open blind [*ivrot*] eyes," Isa. 42:7.

of mine the desire to accept them with love and willingness. Let the words of my mouth be acceptable (see Ps. 19:15).

It should be noted that even according to their erroneous assumption, their mixing of the straw with the wheat (see Jer. 23:28), with those great, famous leaders, may they live, their comparison is still inaccurate. For in virtually all of their cases – may God lengthen their days and years in prosperity – their honorable place of residence was in a single country, where the towns were in close proximity, clustered together such that there was not much distance between them. Thus, they could ease the burden from upon the people and bear it with them (see Ex. 12:22).

Who was greater than Moses, our teacher, may he rest in peace, and yet he said: "How can I bear alone [your troubles, and your burdens, and your quarrels," Deut. 1:12]. Now, he only had to deal with communal matters that relate to the people as a whole, not to individuals, and only to judge between them with regard to Torah laws. As our Sages have stated, "judgment" means Torah,[7] and it is one of the pillars of the world, and yet they said: Can it enter your mind that Moses, our teacher, may he rest in peace, would sit and judge all day long? When was his Torah accomplished?[8] This is referring to Moses not having time alone to reflect on the Torah he had heard directly from the Almighty – he never had to dispense advice to each individual person on matters that do not concern the Torah and fear of Heaven.

This concludes the unprinted section; the printed letter follows below:

15 Tishrei 13 Tishrei (leap year)	**My beloved ones, my brethren and friends, with hidden love and an open rebuke:**	אֲהוּבַי אַחַי וְרֵעַי, מֵאַהֲבָה מְסוּתֶּרֶת תּוֹכַחַת מְגוּלָּה:

Since he wishes to speak to the hasidim – whom he loves like brothers and friends[9] – in a manner that sounds like rebuke, he makes an effort

7. See *Berakhot* 6a.
8. Shabbat 10a.
9. The expression "my beloved ones, my brethren and friends" is derived from

to soften the apparently harsh impression of his words. He makes a play on words on the verse: "Better open rebuke than hidden love" (Prov. 27:5) – instead of the contrast of the verse itself, he connects its two clauses, implying that one stems from the other. In other words, the rebuke he is about to deliver is motivated by love, only the love is hidden while the rebuke is out in the open.

לְכוּ נָא וְנִוָּכְחָה, זִכְרוּ יְמוֹת עוֹלָם בִּינוּ שְׁנוֹת דּוֹר וָדוֹר,

Come now, and let us debate together; remember the days of old, consider the years of many generations,

These biblical paraphrases are not merely a stylistic flourish. The author of the *Tanya* often employs biblical expressions always in order to convey a specific message. Here too, he seeks to emphasize that this is not a singular case of a personal shortcoming of leadership; rather, this characterizes the leadership in Israel since time immemorial, even when there was the highest level of direct divine intervention ever, through the prophets Moses.

הֶהָיְתָה כָּזֹאת מִימוֹת עוֹלָם, וְאַיֵּה אֵיפוֹא מְצָאתֶם מִנְהָג זֶה בְּאֶחָד מִכָּל סִפְרֵי חַכְמֵי יִשְׂרָאֵל הָרִאשׁוֹנִים וְהָאַחֲרוֹנִים לִהְיוֹת מִנְהָג וְתִיקּוּן, לִשְׁאוֹל בְּעֵצָה גַשְׁמִיּוּת כְּדָת מַה לַּעֲשׂוֹת בְּעִנְיְנֵי הָעוֹלָם הַגַּשְׁמִי -

has this ever occurred: Where, where indeed, have you found this custom in any one of all the books of the early or later Sages of Israel, that this is a custom and a remedy, to seek counsel from the tzaddik **on the material plane, regarding the proper thing to do involving matters of this physical world –**

This "remedy" means a rectification for the world. The purpose of life on this world is to improve the world. Accordingly, even if a certain

---

Psalms 122:8 (for more on this phrase, see the next letter below); "with hidden love and an open rebuke" is from Proverbs 27:5, as noted in the commentary; "Come now, and let us debate together" is a quote from Isaiah 1:18; "remember the days of old, consider the years of many generations" is a close paraphrase of Deuteronomy 32:7; "has this ever occurred" (below) is based on Joel 1:2; "where, where indeed" is taken from Judges 9:38; and "regarding the proper thing to do" appears in Esther 4:15.

mode of conduct is convenient for a person, if it does nothing to amend the world, he should not follow that path.[10]

People live in the natural, physical world, and thus they inevitably encounter problems. The natural state of the world does not seem fair: Uncertainties abound with regard to all aspects of life – one's livelihood, health, marriage and more. Questions constantly arise; what should one do; how should he react, which path he should follow... Moreover, by its very nature this world hides the future; a person cannot grasp with his limited intellect the direction in which the tide is turning because the world is too complex and unpredictable. These questions are not theoretical: They strike at the heart of life, causing each person suffering, anxiety, and stress at his very core. It is therefore reasonable for people to ask and seek counsel on these matters. They will turn to experts, parents and friends, and they especially expect to receive advice from their teacher and rabbi, to whom they attribute a deep and comprehensive understanding and vision, which goes beyond the insight of an ordinary person.

Even so, we do not find that people would ask the rabbi, the Rebbe, or the tzaddik, about such issues. This does not include inquiring from a friend, a wise person, or an expert, as every person surely consults such individuals on occasion, but rather approaching someone who represents the Torah and matters involving the service of God. Such an individual is expected, consciously or otherwise, to provide a more profound insight, even a supernatural vision, that penetrates the barrier of materiality. Moreover, like little children, they expect their "father" to take upon himself the responsibility for their lives and destiny.

אַף לִגְדוֹלֵי חַכְמֵי יִשְׂרָאֵל הָרִאשׁוֹנִים כְּתַנָּאִים וְאָמוֹרָאִים אֲשֶׁר כָּל רָז לָא אָנֵס לְהוּ וּנְהִירִין לְהוֹן שְׁבִילִין דִּרְקִיעַ,

not even from the early Sages of Israel, like the *tanna'im* and *amora'im*, from whom no secret was hidden,[11] and to whom the paths of heaven were clear,

10. As explained elsewhere, the converse is actually the case: The main rectification in fact occurs when actions are taken on earth, in the form of an "awakening from below," through struggles and difficulties, rather than in fulfillment of an explicit instruction from above.

11. This expression, which is derived from Daniel 4:6, appears in various formulations in many places in the rabbinical literature.

The phrase "to whom the paths of heaven were clear" is from a statement of the *amora* Shmuel (*Berakhot* 58b), who was one of the greatest of the Sages and was considered knowledgeable in secular studies as well. He claimed that paths of heaven, that is, the orbits of the stars and the various constellations, were as clear to him as the paths of his hometown of Neharde'a. According to hasidic interpretation of this saying, the "paths of heaven" includes the spiritual worlds, and thus the meaning of the statement here is that not even those Sages who were experts in the secrets of the Torah, and the paths of the upper worlds that influence this world, would be approached for advice regarding affairs of this material world.

כִּי אִם לַנְּבִיאִים מַמָּשׁ אֲשֶׁר הָיוּ לְפָנִים בְּיִשְׂרָאֵל, כִּשְׁמוּאֵל הָרוֹאֶה אֲשֶׁר הָלַךְ אֵלָיו שָׁאוּל לִדְרוֹשׁ ה׳ עַל דְּבַר הָאֲתוֹנוֹת שֶׁנֶּאֶבְדוּ לְאָבִיו.

but only from actual prophets, who were in earlier times in Israel, such as Samuel the Seer, as Saul went to him to seek God over the matter of his father's lost donkeys.

A prophet is called a "Seer" (I Samuel 9:9) because he sees what is hidden from others. The plain meaning of this verses is that Saul did not go to the prophet Samuel for spiritual guidance but to ask him see what he, Saul, was unable to perceive within the physical world. There is a type of vision that goes beyond space and time. The great individuals of Israel always possessed this vision, tapping into varying levels of the holy spirit. The prophet was unique in his ability to bring down this vision, which is above time and place, and relate it to a specific hour and locale.[12] He can therefore see simply and actually – as we see the physical reality that is before our eyes –what exists now, and what will happen in the future, all over the globe.[13]

---

12. See *Keter Shem Tov*, Additions, 340.

13. This is why the test of whether someone is a true prophet does not concern his vision of the upper worlds, but rather his ability to see what will happen here, in the material world, in the future. See Rambam, *Sefer HaMadda, Hilkhot Yesodei HaTorah* 11:1.

כִּי בֶּאֱמֶת כָּל עִנְיְנֵי אָדָם, לְבַד מִדִּבְרֵי תוֹרָה וְיִרְאַת שָׁמַיִם, אֵינָם מוּשָּׂגִים רַק בִּנְבוּאָה,

For in truth, all of a person's affairs, apart from matters of Torah and fear of Heaven, can be grasped only through prophecy,

By "a person's affairs," the author of the *Tanya* does not mean an ordinary understanding of matters of this world, which every person attains to a greater or lesser degree; rather, he is referring to a grasp of worldly matters like that of prophecy, that is, of absolute certainty: The prophet sees in his mind's eye what will happen in the future in this world and what needs to be done, and so on, with the same clarity and certainty that a person knows what he is seeing with his own eyes.

He adds "apart from matters of Torah and fear of Heaven," as these can indeed be attained by Sages with that measure of certainty, which they can then use to guide the people. In this regard it must be noted, as it will be stated below, that the Torah has already been brought down into time and space. The Sage who studies the Torah does not have to be a prophet himself; his very status as one of the Sages of the Oral Torah means that he is reflecting and transmitting the words of the Torah to this time with the same certainty and reality as the words of an actual prophecy. This is not the case for the rest of a person's affairs in this world – here the Sage has no such advantage and is like all other men.[14] ☞

"APART FROM MATTERS OF TORAH AND FEAR OF HEAVEN"

☞ When it comes to questions of *halakha* and how one should behave in matters of Torah, mitzvot and the fear of God in this world, the Sages can also attain a state of certainty. The problem is that the boundary between the affairs of the material world and words of Torah and the fear of Heaven, which are clothed in the physical world, is not clear and unequivocal. Physical life is a unified network, and it is difficult (if at all possible) to separate its various components. This problem remains unresolved, and as we will see below, it is part and parcel of the unsettled nature of this letter, with all of its contradictions and questions that are left open even at its conclusion.

14. The converse of this point, that the Sage actually does have ability to see in the practical world, more than other people, will be discussed below.

וְ״לֹא לַחֲכָמִים לֶחֶם״ (קהלת ט,יא) כְּמַאֲמַר רַבּוֹתֵינוּ ז״ל: ״הַכֹּל בִּידֵי שָׁמַיִם חוּץ מִיִּרְאַת שָׁמַיִם״ (ברכות לג,ב),

"also not to the wise is bread" (Ecc. 9:11), **in accordance with our Rabbis' statement: "All is in the hands of Heaven apart from the fear of Heaven"** (*Berakhot* 32b),

The verse from Ecclesiastes is understood to imply that in matters involving bread, which signifies one's sustenance in the world, the Sages do not have a greater grasp than that granted by the relative and limited human intelligence. Of course, they can achieve in this field as much as other people, but they have no inherent advantage and no access to another, esoteric form of knowledge, on account of their wisdom in the Torah.

The basic message of the saying from *Berakhot* is that one has free choice in matters involving the service of God and the fear of Heaven; no decree from heaven forcefully decides for man regarding spiritual matters. However, everything else, all the affairs of the material world, are indeed in the hands of Heaven, and man and his counselors cannot do anything to change them. This statement adds to the previous one – not only do we lack the knowledge; we cannot affect the outcome either. Of course, this does not mean that one should sit and do nothing; on the contrary, it is his duty to do as much as he can to earn a living, to heal himself, etc. However, he should conduct himself by following the ways of this world, with its rules and limitations to which he too is subject. What he is not required to do – and in fact cannot do – is bypass these rules by turning to a higher power, to heaven. Concerning this, it is stated here that "all is in the hands of Heaven," and we and the Sages do not have any way (now that prophecy has ceased) to bring down from heaven the knowledge or guidance on how we should best proceed at the current moment. ☞

וְשִׁבְעָה דְבָרִים מְכוּסִּים כו׳, אֵין אָדָם יוֹדֵעַ בַּמֶּה מִשְׂתַּכֵּר כו׳, וּמַלְכוּת בֵּית דָּוִד מָתַי תַּחֲזוֹר כו׳ (פסחים נד,ב). הִנֵּה הוּשְׁווּ זֶה לָזֶה.

and "seven things are concealed…, a person does not know how he will earn a living…, or when the monarchy of the house of David will be restored…" (*Pesaḥim* 54b). **They are thus equated to one another.**

These seven items include the day of death and the day of comfort. The saying thus equates a person's livelihood to events such as the time of the redemption, which are obviously concealed from us, and which not even the greatest of Sages can know. It follows that secrets involving earning a living and other worldly affairs remain hidden and inaccessible to the Sages.

וּמַה שֶּׁכָּתוּב בִּישַׁעְיָה (ג,ג): "יוֹעֵץ וַחֲכַם חֲרָשִׁים", וְכֵן מַה שֶּׁאָמְרוּ רַבּוֹתֵינוּ ז"ל (אבות פרק ו משנה א): "וְנֶהֱנִין מִמֶּנּוּ עֵצָה וְתוּשִׁיָּה", הַיְינוּ, בְּדִבְרֵי תוֹרָה הַנִּקְרָא 'תוּשִׁיָּה',

And with regard to that which is written in the book of **Isaiah** (3:3), **"the counselor, subtle scholar," and similarly the Rabbis' statement** (*Avot* 6:1), **"enjoy counsel and sound wisdom from it," that is referring to the words of Torah, which is called "sound wisdom,"**

These sources appear to indicate that someone who is wise, specifically in matters of Torah, can also dispense advice in affairs of the world, and that others will benefit from his counsel with regard to mundane matters. The answer is that this counsel is referring to the Torah, which the Sages call "sound wisdom."[15] Thus, all the advice focuses solely on matters of Torah, not the dealings of the material world.

"ALL IS IN THE HANDS OF HEAVEN" – ANOTHER INTERPRETATION

☞ An almost diametrically opposed explanation of this rabbinic saying is attributed to the Rebbe Maharash (Rabbi Shmuel Schneerson): When a person prays and asks God for something, "all is in the hands of Heaven" as to whether or not he will receive it, "apart from the fear of Heaven," as here Heaven does not have a choice, as it were – if a person asks for it, God has to give it to him. This explanation suits our context as well: All is in the hands of Heaven as to whether or not to grant something to someone, and the Sages cannot know what will be granted from Heaven, and they certainly cannot change it. The exception is one's fear of Heaven – since this is not in the hands of Heaven, and God is compelled to give it, so to speak, the Sages only have to teach and inform the people of the proper path they must follow in the fear of Heaven, which is the path of the Torah, and God will grant it.

---

15. *Sanhedrin* 26b. The Gemara there offers several explanations for why the Torah is called "sound wisdom [*tushiyya*]," e.g., because it weakens [*matteshet*] a person's strength, or because it was given in secret [*shenittena be-ḥashai*].

כְּמַאֲמַר רַבּוֹתֵינוּ ז"ל: 'יוֹעֵץ' זֶה שֶׁיּוֹדֵעַ לְעַבֵּר שָׁנִים וְלִקְבּוֹעַ חֳדָשִׁים כוּ' (חגיגה יד,א), שֶׁסּוֹד הָעִיבּוּר קָרוּי עֵצָה וְסוֹד בִּלְשׁוֹן תּוֹרָה, כִּדְאִיתָא בְּסַנְהֶדְרִין דַּף פ"ז (עמוד א), עַיֵּין שָׁם בְּפֵירוּשׁ רַשִׁ"י.

in accordance with our Rabbis' statement: "The counselor" – this is referring to **one who knows how to intercalate years and determine months…** (*Ḥagiga* 14a), **as the secret of intercalation is called a counsel and a secret in the language of the Torah, as stated in** *Sanhedrin* 87a; **see Rashi's commentary there.**

Here the author of the *Tanya* provides evidence that matters of Torah are also called "counsel." Rashi's commentary on *Sanhedrin* 87a, to which he directs the reader's attention, reads: "In the intercalation of the year, which is called a secret and a counsel etc." ☞

16 Tishrei
14 Tishrei (leap year)

אַךְ הָאֱמֶת אַגִּיד לַשּׁוֹמְעִים לִי, כִּי אַהֲבָה מְקַלְקֶלֶת הַשּׁוּרָה,

However, I will inform those who will listen to me of the truth, that love upsets the regular order.

Here the author of the *Tanya* addther, more profound reason as to why one should not ask the Rebbe about the affairs of this world: It is not only because of the Rebbe's limitations – as he is not a prophet and it is not in his power – but also because in truth this is not the proper way to serve God. In the well-known saying "love upsets the regular order" (see e.g., *Bereshit Rabba* 55:8), the "order" refers to the accepted customs and arrangements of affairs in every culture by which people think and perform actions. It is more than simply manners – it is the basic operation of the system. When feelings are

THE SECRET OF THE INTERCALATION

☞ The Rambam writes in *Sefer Zemanim, Hilkhot Kiddush HaḤodesh* (11:4): "For these methods [of calculating when the new moon can be seen at the beginning of each month] are abstract and profound methods. This is 'the secret of the intercalation,' which was known to the great Sages, and they would not hand them down to all people, but only to ordained and perceptive individuals…." These matters were and remain a secret that is not revealed to everyone, which a person cannot learn by himself, but for which he requires the advice and guidance of another.

running strong, such as passionate love or the opposite, they upset that regular habit, and it is no longer possible to maintain the order. Regular order can be preserved in formal, restrained associations, whereas love by its very nature breaks down boundaries. In one's desire to reach the beloved, a person disregards the orderly mode of conduct, and "upsets the regular order." Love is fashioned, as it were, out of a different fabric, and its wearer refuses to be obstructed by all the normal orders of operations and structures, but treats them as though they did not exist. ☞

וְהִנֵּה הִיא כְּסוּת עֵינַיִם שֶׁלֹּא לִרְאוֹת הָאֱמֶת, מֵרוֹב אַהֲבָתָם לְחַיֵּי הַגּוּף לְשֵׁם שָׁמַיִם, לַעֲבוֹד בּוֹ אֶת ה׳ בְּרִשְׁפֵּי אֵשׁ וְשַׁלְהֶבֶת גְּדוֹלָה מֵאַהֲבַת נַפְשָׁם אֶת ה׳.

This is a covering of the eyes, to avoid seeing the truth, due to their great love of material life for the sake of Heaven, to serve God with it, with flashes of fire and a great flame, out of their soul's love of God.

The hasidim, in their love for God and their passion to serve Him, fail to see this truth in the "regular order." Their love becomes like a "covering of the eyes," a phrase from Genesis 9:15. The love and desire to worship God, to feel close to Him and cleave to Him through prayer, Torah and mitzvot, can be replaced by an impatience, an inability to tolerate the series of delays between the stages. The author of the *Tanya* is not "accusing" his hasidim of approaching him simply for the sake of their material lives. They indeed come to seek the Lord,

ABRAHAM'S LOVE

☞ The Sages use this very expression, that "love upsets the regular order," to describe both the actions of our forefather Abraham – who saddled his donkey himself in his great love and desire to fulfill God's command – and the Giving of the Torah, where God, in his love for the Jewish people, upset the regular order of creation, by revealing Himself, in order to give them the Torah (see *Torah Or* 60d; *Likkutei Torah*, Num. 52c and onward. According to the regular order, it should have proceeded step-by-step for fifty thousand jubilees, and yet the Holy One, blessed be He, gave the whole Torah to us in an instant). However, despite the beauty of the *Akeida* and the Giving of the Torah, God did not bring us into the world to upset the order. God designed us to function from within the incremental order of development so that we should seek Him and serve Him from inside this arrangement, from within the world and its order.

but their difficulties and troubles – which were truly unbearable – do not allow them to serve God, study and pray in accordance with their desire and love. ☞

וְעַל כֵּן הֵיטֵב חָרָה לָהֶם בְּצַעַר הַגּוּף, חַס וְשָׁלוֹם ה׳ יְרַחֵם,

They are therefore greatly upset by the suffering of the body, God forbid, may the Lord have mercy,

The hasidim are thus "greatly upset" (phrase from Jonah 4:9) by all the material issues, the life and struggles of this world, which appear to prevent them from cleaving to the Divine. The author of the *Tanya* admits that suffering is hard. He understands that these are not the

"LOVE OF LIFE FOR THE SAKE OF HEAVEN"

☞ While there is a love of materiality for its own sake, the author of the *Tanya* is not referring to that at all, for there is also a love of material success that is for the sake of Heaven. When a person feels that the body and the love of materiality are a means and a way to love God, that the body which hides God from view is only fueling the fire of one's love for Him, and that the reality and power of the body is merely indicative of the power and potential of one's love for God – this is the love of material life for the sake of Heaven.

In other words, while the body does indeed hide the Divine, as its entire being and activity are material and earthly, the opposite of heavenly, this is merely the external aspect, while hidden inside the body and matter, lie enormous powers that can be channeled into service of God. One can clearly see that the desire and instinct of the body is stronger and more real than any spiritual sense of holiness. As explained elsewhere at length, the powers attributed to the body belong to a primal layer (the world of chaos, *tohu*) that is far more powerful than the layer on which we normally operate in our lives of holiness (the world of rectification, *tikkun*). All that is required is to extract these powers from their material context, and the like, and attribute them to holiness. This is not simple and is far from easy, in fact it is the most difficult of tasks, but this is the entire service of man in his body and in this world: To use this world and its primal powers for the purpose of sanctity.

The love of the body for the sake of Heaven stems from the recognition that the soul descended into the body precisely for this purpose: To serve God through the body, so that one's closeness to God will thereby be even more intense, with flashes of fire and flames, etc. (see Song of Songs 8:6). However, when the soul lies in the darkness of the body and the confusion of this world, surrounded by thick darkness, his ever-accumulating difficulties and troubles do not allow one to see the light, then it is not enough to love the body for the sake of Heaven. This love by itself cannot withstand the continuous pressure, and ultimately patience runs out and one "upsets the regular order," and unleashes his love to break the structure which is its own very foundation.

grievances of spoiled people, but rather cries from broken hearts, which stem from difficult lives full of distress that one does not know how to bear. He adds these words as his own personal expression, beyond what he as the Rebbe knows is the truth of life, and acknowledges that what his hasidim endure is indeed difficult and terrible – "God forbid, may the Lord have mercy."

וְאֵין יְכוֹלִין לְקַבֵּל כְּלָל עַד שֶׁמַּעֲבִירִם עַל דַּעְתָּם, לְכַתֵּת רַגְלֵיהֶם מֵעִיר לְעִיר לִשְׁאוֹל עֵצוֹת מֵרָחוֹק,

and they cannot accept it at all, until they lose their minds, pounding their feet from city to city, to seek counsel from afar,

They are unable to accept the tribulations of the world and the state of divine concealment, and "lose their minds," meaning, since they actually know the truth, they therefore bypass their minds to embark on arduous journeys to seek counsel from afar. Although they have the truth right "here," and "afar" is not relevant to them, they still wander from place to place. The problem is not only that the solution is distant and hard to achieve, but that it is not one's own, it is not true for him. For what is true for him is right here; there is no need to search for it, but simply to accept it.

וְלֹא שָׁעוּ אֶל ה׳ לָשׁוּב אֵלָיו בְּרוּחַ נְמוּכָה

and they did not turn to God, to return to Him with a lowly spirit

The whole problem is in the form of address, turning one's face to God, which means accepting things as they are. The author of the *Tanya* explains that a person can achieve this state if he resolves "to return to Him with a lowly spirit." This "lowly spirit" is a necessary condition. When a person has a haughty spirit, that is, he considers himself an important individual, a "somebody," and is unable to turn to God. Since his own being is occupying that space, how can God be there too? In simple terms, turning to God, like addressing another person, involves turning one's will and mind away from himself and his needs, and focusing entirely on God. Someone with a haughty spirit is incapable of this.

וְהַכְנָעַת הַגּוּף לְקַבֵּל תּוֹכַחְתּוֹ בְּאַהֲבָה, "כִּי אֶת אֲשֶׁר יֶאֱהַב ה' וכו'" (משלי ג,יב).

and bodily submission, to accept His reproof with love, "for he whom the Lord loves He reproves…" (Prov. 3:12).

One's body is the center and foundation of his sense of being, both physical and mental, and therefore repentance also involves the subjugation of the body. This does not necessarily entail mortifications and fasts, but rather a mental attitude that one does not consider the body and its desires and lusts important, and that they will not serve as factors in his judgment, but merely as instruments and garments for his divine soul.

When one turns to God with a lowly spirit and bodily submission, he can receive even reproof from Him with love. It is easy to accept light and kindness with love, but to receive reproof lovingly, when it is expressed through hardships and suffering – that is difficult. It is possible, however, when one approaches the task "with a lowly spirit and bodily submission," without high expectations, without the sensitivity of someone who has something to lose, and without a conceited self-importance that makes a person quick to take offense.

The full verse from Proverbs reads: "For he whom the Lord loves, He reproves, and he reconciles like a father with a son." God's reproof is an expression of His love. One who is aware of this fact can accept the rebuke with love, even though it is hard and unpleasant, because he can relate to its inner meaning, which is love and goodness. In general, a person can accept with love almost any difficulty and suffering if he knows that it is for the best, that it is not a chance occurrence or an expression of indifference or cruelty, but rather that it stems from caring and affection.

15 Tishrei (leap year)

וּכְמוֹ אָב רַחֲמָן חָכָם וְצַדִּיק הַמַּכֶּה בְּנוֹ,

This is **like a merciful, wise and righteous father who strikes his son.**

In this comparison, the father expresses his love for his son through the very act of striking him.[16] Indeed, a merciful father who strikes

16. Rabbi Yosef Yitzchak Schneerson, of blessed memory, notes that the title of "pious," which appears below, is omitted here. This is because a father who hits

his son thereby demonstrates more than his love. In the language of Kabbala, this is described as "*Gevura* in *Ḥesed*." As explained in many places, each attribute incorporates in its constituent parts all of the attributes, which allows for combinations of attributes and enables them to relate to each other and to the complexity of real life. It is further explained that this is an even more profound revelation of *Ḥesed* than "*Ḥesed* in *Ḥesed*." The reason is that it is natural for a loving person to bestow love; he is simply doing what he is inclined to do by his benevolent nature, and therefore this is no more than the illumination and extension of his love. By contrast, when a loving person follows the path of judgment, as when a father strikes his son, this is not only an extension and expression of love, but a change in his nature, which reveals the essence and depth of his love. Only the essence of love itself can be displayed as the opposite of love, because true love is expressed in accordance with the needs of the loved one, not the needs of the one who loves, as that is characteristic of a superficial love.[17] ☞

"A MERCIFUL, WISE AND RIGHTEOUS FATHER"

☞ The father in the example has to be merciful, wise and righteous. Not all fathers in our world are like that: This is not the case for a father who beats his son for no good reason, simply because he is cruel or stupid. It applies only when the father is merciful and hits his son solely out of necessity; when he is wise and not making a mistake, but is doing what is really for his son's benefit. He is righteous and pious because his conduct is right and he is performing nothing other than kindness for his son. Only then is the example appropriate.

---

his son, even though he is acting of love, cannot be described as pious at that moment (*Sefer Ha-Siḥot* 5704, p. 15).

17. See *Torah Or*, Ex. I, p. 125. See also *Ba'al Shem Tov al HaTorah, Parashat No'aḥ, Amud HaTefilla* 134: "A wise person should consider that when he is rejected by the left hand of the Holy One, blessed be He, God Himself is present there, in all of His glory. For we ourselves can attest that for someone to reject another person he has to be there next to him. He should therefore accept this rebuff with love, kiss the rejection, and tremble with a great trembling, understanding that the purpose of this rejection is for him to draw ever closer to God..."

שֶׁאֵין לְבֵן חָכָם לַהֲפוֹךְ עוֹרֶף לָנוּס, לִמְצוֹא לוֹ עֶזְרָה אוֹ אֲפִילוּ מֵלִיץ יוֹשֶׁר לִפְנֵי אָבִיו, הָרַחֲמָן וְהַצַּדִּיק וְחָסִיד,

A wise son should not turn his back to flee, to seek aid or even someone to plead his case before his father, the merciful, righteous and pious,

"Someone to plead his case before his father" is the equivalent, in the case at hand, of the tzaddik who turns to God, "his father," in prayer, requesting assistance and for Him to change a decree. One might flee and try to extricate himself from what he thinks is bad for him, but when he realizes that everything that happens is from his good Father, and is appropriate for him, he will not turn away in an effort to avoid accepting it from Him. Rather, the son must be wise, since although what he feels and sees at the moment is rebuke, hardships, and the like, a wise man sees the outcome; he understands where the reproof is coming from and its purpose, and therefore he can sense the good in what is happening to him.

רַק לִהְיוֹת "יָשָׁר יֶחֱזוּ פָנֵימוֹ" (תהלים יא,ז),

but rather one should strive **to be "upright who beholds His countenance"** (Ps. 11:7),

In other words, one should look directly at his situation and not seek out explanations, excuses and rationales, because the truth lies in the situation itself, as it is. When a person trusts in his father, that he is merciful, righteous and pious, it is clear to him that he has no other intention in mind. He realizes that he is not a pawn or a means to some other end, but rather he is his father's main focus, he is the purpose of all other seemingly "secondary actions that his father does." He is aware that everything he experiences is tailor-made for him by his father.

עִם אָבִיו פָּנִים בְּפָנִים,

with his father, face-to-face,

"Face-to-face" means that he shares the same "face," with his father with the same thoughts and intention. Just as the father's inner intent is that everything should be for his son's benefit, the son should likewise see things in the same manner, with the same inner intention as his father. Moreover, when the bestower and the recipient are face-to-face, the connection between them does not go through superficial and backhanded aspects of their relationship at all; rather, it goes straight from one face to the other, much like a thought or a feeling which can transfer from one person to the other without the need to speak. Therefore, if they are positioned face-to-face on a high level, it is even possible that the son will not feel the external blows at all, but only the love that is contained within them.

לִסְבּוֹל הַכָּאוֹתָיו בְּאַהֲבָה לְטוֹב לוֹ כָּל הַיָּמִים.

to bear his beatings with love, for his own good always.

One should not focus on the unpleasant externality of the beating, but on his father's inner will, which is for his benefit, out of love. "To bear" does not mean that he must suffer, but rather that he must endure the beatings. Indeed, carrying burdens involves difficulty and even pain that must be overcome. This demands work and effort. (As opposed to kindness and love, which are in a sense, weightless, and carry themselves.) However, when a person accepts difficulty with love, knowing that it is for his good, he can bear the burden "for his own good always,"[18] that is, in all the vicissitudes of time, even on those occasions when he cannot clearly feel his father's love.

וְהִנֵּה לְמַעְלָה בְּחִינַת 'פָּנִים' הוּא הָרָצוֹן וְהַחֵשֶׁק אֲשֶׁר אָבִינוּ שֶׁבַּשָּׁמַיִם מַשְׁפִּיעַ לְבָנָיו

Now, on the higher plane, the aspect of "face" is the will and desire with **which our Father in Heaven bestows upon His children**

Here, the author of the *Tanya* offers a deeper understanding of the phrase "face-to-face." Opposed to the face, there is a "backside" of influence from above, through which God bestows divine influence upon those to whom He does not desire to give, as it were. We can glimpse this dynamic through our own experiences as well: We have objects and people that we want and desire, and others that we do not want and do not desire. Nevertheless, they have to be present so that what we really want can exist, so that the world which we want to live in, will be sustained. We invest our time and energy in all of those secondary pursuits, not out of passion and desire, but as a kind of ne-

18. A paraphrase of Deuteronomy 6:24.

cessity, a required routine. This is how the world is built and how one's life is structured – there is always a backside, an aspect of life that can be compared to a chair whose whole purpose is to support the person sitting upon it, the primary purpose. A man's relationship with his son, who is the innermost and essential continuation of the father, is also his most profound relationship. On a higher plane, God's "countenance," His front, so to speak, is how He relates and gives to His children Israel, in general and in particular, in contrast to the "backside," which is His mode of conduct with all the worlds and everything in them. ☞

כָּל טוּב עוֹלָמִים וחַיֵּי נֶפֶשׁ וְגוּף בְּאַהֲבָה וְרָצוֹן חֲשִׁיקָה וַחֲפִיצָה,

all the good of the worlds, and the life of the soul and body, with love and willingness, desire and longing,

God bestows upon us "all the good of the worlds" and does not hold anything back from us, as all of this goodness is designated for His children. The term "worlds" in the plural, alludes to the two worlds, this world and the World to Come.[19] The difference between this world and the next is, to a certain extent, the most overarching division of reality and parallels above and below; materiality and spirituality; present and future; the world of service and the world the reward, and so on.

On the individual scale, the inner goodness which God bestows

FRONT AND BACKSIDE

☞ The face, or front, contains life, everything that is living and breathing and currently active, while the backside contains, in a sense, what has already happened, the framework and background to what is currently unfolding. This follows the temporal meaning of "front" and "back" – "front" refers to what is before me, what is happening at the moment, while "back" denotes what has already occurred. In this light, everything written in the Torah, and everything that unfolds as an expression of Torah, constitutes life and its inner meaning, whereas material existence, as the world sees it, is only the "backside," providing framework and background to the Torah.

19. This is derived from the verse "for God [*Yah*; the letters *yod* and *heh*] the Lord is the Rock of the worlds" (Isa. 26:4). This is explained by the sages as (*Menaḥot* 29b): The World to Come was created with the letter *yod*, and this world was created with the letter *heh*. This concept frequently cited in hasidic works.

upon Israel is directed toward both our spiritual state, "the life of the soul," and toward our material situation, "the life of the body." "Love and willingness, desire and longing" are expressions of the innermost levels of the Divine from which both of these influences, spiritual and material, flow to Israel.

עַל יְדֵי תּוֹרַת חַיִּים שֶׁהִיא רְצוֹנוֹ יִתְבָּרֵךְ, אֲשֶׁר נָתַן לָנוּ, כְּמוֹ שֶׁאוֹמְרִים: "כִּי בְאוֹר פָּנֶיךָ נָתַתָּ לָנוּ תּוֹרַת חַיִּים כו'",

by means of the Torah of life, which is His will that He gave us, as we say: "For with the light of Your face You gave us the Torah of life…,"

The citation here is from the *Amida* prayer.

The vessel for this deep divine influence is the Torah, which is "His will," as it reveals God's internal desire. Quintessential inner essence, by its very definition, has no vessel other than Torah, which is itself internality. And yet the Torah did not remain up above, in the form of the concealed supreme will of the Creator, but was given to us, Israel, down here below.

לַעֲשׂוֹת בָּהּ רְצוֹנוֹ, וְעַל זֶה נֶאֱמַר: "בְּאוֹר פְּנֵי מֶלֶךְ חַיִּים וּרְצוֹנוֹ כו'" (משלי טז,טו).

with which to perform His will, and it is stated regarding this: "Life is in the light of the king's countenance, and his favor is like a cloud of the late rain…" (Prov. 16:15).

This is referring to all of the mitzvot we perform in this world, when the soul is in the body. The Torah is thus the inner light that comes from high above, from the innermost levels of the Divine – the inner desire and delight – down to the personal, physical reality of each member of Israel. Therefore, the same person who fulfills the highest will in the Torah below is the one who receives all the inner abundance, "all the good of the worlds," which is bestowed through the Torah. Not only was the Torah given in the light of God's countenance, as the verse states, but it is the very light of His countenance itself. If you wish to know the focus of God's attention, what He is looking at and to where He is turning His face, so to speak, you have to look in the

Torah. The Jewish people, who received the Torah, are destined for it and they uphold it; they are the ones who receive all of this abundant innermost divine connection.

מַה שֶּׁאֵין כֵּן לְעוֹבְדֵי גִילּוּלִים, מַשְׁפִּיעַ חַיֵּי גוּפָם

This is not the case with regard to idol worshippers, upon whom **He bestows the life of their bodies**

Unlike Israel, God bestows upon the gentiles the life of the body alone, which is an external influence. "The life of their bodies" is the life of this world, the physical abundance that is amply granted to gentiles, especially during the period of our exile. While this influence is also spiritual, it is a spirituality that relates to the life of the body, meaning, it is always channeled into the ego of physical existence.[20]

שֶׁלֹּא בִּרְצוֹן וַחֲשִׁיקָה וַחֲפִיצָה.

without willingness, desire and longing.

When God gives to the gentiles, to those who worship idols rather than God, to those who turn their backs to the Lord, He does do so without willingness and desire, unlike when He bestows the internal influence. For in practice, this act of giving serves to amplify the physical being, which is the opposite of holiness and the subsummation of one's internality to the Divine.

לְכָךְ נִקְרָאִים 'אֱלֹהִים אֲחֵרִים', שֶׁיּוֹנְקִים מִבְּחִינַת אֲחוֹרַיִים.

This is why they are called "*elohim aḥerim*" (foreign gods), **as they suckle from the aspect of the "backside"** [*aḥorayim*] of God's will.

Those who receive this influence and live through it are thus called "foreign gods." Someone who is giving willingly and with desire turns his face to his recipient, because he wants to see him and enjoy his reaction, whereas a person who is giving unwillingly and without desire turns his back on the beneficiary, as he takes no pleasure in the act and sometimes even "suffers" from it. Meanwhile, all of his attention and

20. See *Likkutei Amarim*, end of chap. 1.

interest are focused elsewhere. The same applies above, with regard to the divine influence granted to the world.

The difference between "front" and "back," as explained here and elsewhere,[21] is the difference between God's bestowal upon Israel, which is internal, and His giving to the nations, which is external and in a "backside" manner. It follows that all the influence that a Jewish person receives, even if it seems bad and comes in the form of suffering, is really good and true kindness. The converse is also true: All the physical influence that reaches the gentiles, even if it appears in the form of giving and kindness, is not internal; it is always external, and therefore in the larger picture it is a manifestation of divine judgment; it is merely the tool and the framework, which carry the inner essence.

וְכָךְ הוּא בְּאָדָם, הָרָצוֹן וְהַחֵשֶׁק הוּא בְּחִינַת פָּנִים, **The same applies to man; the will and desire is the aspect of countenance,**

The same applies to a Jewish person with respect to how he receives the influence from above. While "the will and desire are the aspect of countenance," the face, the contrary is also the case: When you get something that you don't want, from someone you don't want to receive it from, this is "backside." Accordingly, when a Jew receives from God, from the outset the giving from above is "the aspect of countenance," which means that it depends solely on us – if we receive it in the aspect of countenance, the face, it will be "face-to-face."

"Face-to-face" means that the countenance below should be turned towards the countenance above, to unite with a commensurate intention of inner presence. To use a mundane comparison, when people love each other, the truer and deeper their love becomes, the more blurred the difference between the needs of one and the needs of the other become. The line that differentiates between the pleasure they each receive evaporates, since each of them takes delight in the pleasure of the other. Therefore, one does not need anything from the other, except for his very presence, since the enjoyment of the one, is itself the pleasure and fulfillment of the other's love.

21. See e.g., the commentary to *Likkutei Amarim*, chap. 2, p. 77-78; chap. 4, p. 134.

וְאִם אֵינוֹ מְקַבֵּל בְּאַהֲבָה וְרָצוֹן, כְּאִלּוּ הוֹפֵךְ עוֹרֶף וְאָחוֹר חַס וְשָׁלוֹם.

and if one does not accept it **with love and willingness,** it is **as though he is turning away his neck and back, God forbid.**

God gives with love and desire, with "the aspect of countenance." However, it does not always seem this way from the other side. The person on the receiving end may not accept what God is sending him with love and willingness, face-to-face, instead, he may turn his back away from the giver. ☞

17 Tishrei

וְעֵצָה הַיְּעוּצָה לְקַבֵּל בְּאַהֲבָה, הִיא עֲצַת ה׳ בְּפִי חֲכָמֵינוּ ז״ל, לְפַשְׁפֵּשׁ בְּמַעֲשָׂיו וְיִמְצָא לוֹ עֲוֹנוֹת הַצְּרִיכִין מֵירוּק יִסּוּרִים

The recommended counsel, to accept with love, is the counsel of God, as expressed by our Sages, to examine one's deeds and find transgressions of his that require the cleansing of suffering

"AS THOUGH HE IS TURNING AWAY HIS NECK"

☞ Turning one's neck away is a serious act. Although, externally, it is not as bad as actually violating the King's will, like performing a sin, internally, it is even more serious. A sinner might still feel close to God in his heart; perhaps there was a reason why he transgressed; a lust that he did not anticipate, a temporary mishap. By contrast, one who turns his face is like a rebel; it is as though he is declaring that his attention is elsewhere, that his will and inner focus are not with God. There is also an aspect to turning one's back that is even graver than an act of rebellion, since one who revolts against God still relates to Him, whereas someone who turns his face away maintains no relationship with Him at all. He is neither for nor against, he completely ignores His existence, so to speak, and there is nothing more insolent than that. Therefore, it seems that the comparison here is not total; someone who does not receive suffering with love is considered only "as though" he is turning his back, not actually, God forbid. This is similar to the teaching that "whoever grows angry, it is as though he engaged in idol worship" (see *Shabbat* 105b; see also *Iggeret HaTeshuva*, chap. 7, and Letter 25, below).

When described in this manner, it seems unlikely – how is it possible for someone to turn his back on God, when He is giving him with inner desire and will?! Because that individual is situated down here, and he first of all sees and senses this world as the true reality that he cannot ignore, he perceives and feels only trouble and distress, with respect to his children, health, and sustenance, and thus it is no longer self-evident that he will accept it with love and willingness.

The author of the *Tanya* understands this. He realizes that people are really suffering, and that he has to make some allowance for such hasidim.

This is not a complete solution to the problems of this world, an instruction from above on what will happen and how to act, but only advice on how "to accept with love," how to change one's attitude towards those problems. The teachings of our Sages[22] are called "the counsel of God" because the words of the Sages in the Talmud and midrashim are not their own statements but the Oral Law, the word of God clothed in human terms.

The Talmud (*Berakhot* 5a) states that if a person sees that suffering is befalling him, he should examine his deeds. In other words, he should search amongst his previous actions, "and find transgressions of his that require the cleansing of suffering." The sufferings and troubles of this world can be viewed in different ways. When one sees suffering as caused by malicious intent, such as evil events that are the result of someone else's calculations, then they are indeed unbearable. However, when one has the attitude that they are specifically directed at oneself and with good intentions, as the foundation for something good that will occur later, similar to a medical treatment that will save his life and the like, this makes it easier to bear the suffering, to the point where one can even accept them with love.

Adjusting one's perspective in this manner is not easy. It involves a change in worldview, in one's entire approach from its very foundation. In order to make such a transformation, one has to find a fulcrum within reality, something real that exists no matter how one looks at life, upon which the new outlook can be constructed. The author of the *Tanya's* advice is to find transgressions in one's past, even slight sins, each person in accordance with his level, which caused a defect and a deficiency in his soul that has not yet been corrected. This transgression, whose rectification is achieved through suffering, as explained in the sources,[23] can be the axis by means of which one's attitude towards the suffering can change. Misery, and all the difficulties of this world in general, now have a purpose. They are not wholly destructive, as they help a person build on another plane – one that is more fundamental and internal – a better, purer and more stable life.

---

22. It should be noted that the author of the *Tanya* typically uses the term "our Rabbis," and only rarely "our Sages." Certainly, when he states "our Sages," here and elsewhere, there is a reason for it.

23. See the beginning of *Iggeret HaTeshuva*.

וְיִרְאֶה לָעַיִן גּוֹדֶל אַהֲבָתוֹ אֵלָיו הַמְקַלְקֶלֶת הַשּׁוּרָה.

and then he will clearly see His great love for him, which upsets the regular order.

From now on, not only is he no longer resentful of the suffering which leads him to turn his back on God, as it were, but he actually views it as an expression of God's great love for him. The author of the *Tanya* reiterates here an expression he used earlier in the letter, "upsets the natural order," which refers to a love that is so great that it changes the normal operation of the worlds. However, unlike the previous mention, the phrase has a positive meaning in this context.[24] Earlier, it referred to upsetting the unique way that God manages the affairs of a man, who, out of love, does not have the strength and patience for what he interprets as concealment and distancing, and instead of accepting things with love, seeks to change them. Here, by contrast, the phrase indicates an even higher recognition, that the way God is treating him is not merely following the correct order, but it involves upsetting the order, a change in his favor from God's regular manner of operating the worlds. ☞

"HIS GREAT LOVE FOR HIM, WHICH UPSETS THE REGULAR ORDER"

☞ This "regular order" is referring to God's external operation and influence, and the way that He gives to the worlds by building life's systems step-by-step, following the order of progression and other spiritual and physical laws that he dictates. God's love, which "upsets the regular order," is His conduct and bestowal upon His children, the Jewish people, which is an inner influence: With a shining countenance, with love, readiness, and desire.

Great love and "upsetting the regular order" thus exist both above and below. The difference is that in God's case it is manifested in practice, through a different mode of conduct, and even in a manner that does not follow an order of operation at all, which is reserved for those who love Him. By contrast, in the case of man, the upsetting of the regular order is when his inner consciousness, empowered by his exceedingly great love, succeeds in

24. It is true that even regarding the earlier mention, it cannot be claimed that the meaning was negative, as the love that upsets the regular order is the love of God, and the author of the *Tanya* uses this expression in praise of such individuals. Nevertheless, they lack knowledge, which leads to impatience etc., and this is exactly what he wants to further rectify in this letter.

כְּמָשָׁל מֶלֶךְ גָּדוֹל וְנוֹרָא הָרוֹחֵץ בִּכְבוֹדוֹ וּבְעַצְמוֹ צוֹאַת בְּנוֹ יְחִידוֹ מֵרוֹב אַהֲבָתוֹ. כְּמוֹ שֶׁכָּתוּב: "אִם רָחַץ ה' צוֹאַת בְּנוֹת צִיּוֹן כוּ' בְּרוּחַ מִשְׁפָּט כוּ'" (ישעיה ד,ד).

This is **like the parable of a great and awesome king who washes off with his own hands the excrement of his only son, out of his great love, as it is written, "When the Lord will have washed the excrement of the daughters of Zion…, with the spirit of judgment…"** (Isa. 4:4).

A king has many attendants, who themselves have servants, and these can and should do anything for him. And yet there are things even a king wants to do by himself. What is important to him, what he loves very much, he will want to do personally, even those tasks that in any other situation would be considered difficult and demeaning. Accordingly, all at once a person can view what he is going through in a different light: He is like the only son of the Almighty King; and the sufferings, difficulties, and troubles that he is undergoing serve to absolve him, as he is being cleaned by his Father.[25] As the author of the

ignoring everything he sees – an immeasurably long order and procession of reasons, causes and factors that supposedly create his reality – and treats all of these as the very hand of God Himself, watching over and guiding him personally for his own good, in every moment and situation. At that moment, such a person "upsets the regular order," breaks through and penetrates the entire order of progression, and transforms it into a channel of light and revelation. All of this contrasts with the type of "upsetting of the regular order" that the author of the *Tanya* initially opposed, which is when a person tries to execute that which he does not have permission to do, to change the order of his world in an external fashion (not as someone working within the natural order of things, as in that respect he must make every effort to succeed). That which God can do, because the world is in His palm, a person cannot do. It is neither in his power, nor is it part of his duty. He is the recipient, and as such his role is to receive and give back. If he is not prepared to receive a certain circumstance, he is breaking the rules of the game, and effectively removing himself, as it were, from this relationship (unless he is considered a prophet, as discussed earlier, in which case he comes with his power of prophecy from up above, so to speak, as a "representative" of God.)

25. As the Lubavitcher Rebbe notes, although the Hebrew here reads "*tzo'at*," in the verse itself it appears as "*et tzo'at*."

Tanya explains elsewhere, the Hebrew term for absolution also means "rinsing and scouring."[26]

As previously stated, sometimes it is the "*Gevura* in *Ḥesed*," the expression of the judgment in love, which reveals the essence of the love itself even more than a display of love and the giving it entails. In terms of the parable brought here, the king can give gifts to others who are not his only son, but he will only wash off the excrement of his son whom he loves. Therefore, although not always apparent, it is precisely when God treats us in this manner, through judgment, trouble, and suffering, that He is demonstrating how much He loves us.

וְכַמַּיִם הַפָּנִים אֶל פָּנִים, **And as water reflects a face to the face,**

This is a paraphrase of a verse in Proverbs, which continues: "So does the heart of a person to a person" (27:19). Water reflects the image of the face of the person who is looking at it. The human heart is compared to water in this regard – it gives back what is shown. The face and emotion that one person shows to another engenders the same feeling in the other person's heart as well. The same applies to the relationship between man and the "higher Man."

תִּתְעוֹרֵר הָאַהֲבָה בְּלֵב כָּל מַשְׂכִּיל וּמֵבִין יְקַר מַהוּת אַהֲבַת ה׳ אֶל הַתַּחְתּוֹנִים, אֲשֶׁר הִיא יְקָרָה וְטוֹבָה מִכָּל חַיֵּי הָעוֹלָמִים כּוּלָּם, **the love will be aroused in the heart of every intelligent person who understands the precious essence of God's love for the lower creations, which is more precious and better than all** forms of **life in all the worlds,**

The "lower creations" are those souls that are situated below, in bodies, enmeshed in the lowly affairs of this world. As explained, God's love for lowly man is considered internal in contrast to His bestowal of all the life of the worlds, both the upper and the lower worlds, which is external. For this reason, it is more "precious," not only in quantity, but also in qualitative, internal terms, than "all the forms of life in all the worlds."

---

26. As stated in *Iggeret HaTeshuva*, chap. 1.

כְּמוֹ שֶׁכָּתוּב: "מַה יָּקָר חַסְדְּךָ וכו'" (תהלים לו,ח) "כִּי טוֹב חַסְדְּךָ מֵחַיִּים כו'" (שם סג,ד).

as it is written, "How precious is Your kindness, God, men take refuge in the shadow of Your garment" (Ps. 36:8) and **"For Your kindness is better than life…"** (Ps. 63:4).

The most precious thing is God's kindness which He bestows upon man, the benevolence He personally gives, which is clearly His singular, unique kindness.

Likewise, "Your kindness is better than life," than the life of all the worlds. "Life" refers to the illumination as it manifests in practice, which is limited by the parameters of what it gives vitality to, as opposed to "Your kindness," which is the source that illuminates the life of all worlds. *Ḥesed* expresses the inner essence of life, the life as it pulses in the will and internal pleasure of the One who bestows it. The same dynamic applies to people as well; their *Ḥesed* is always an expression of an inner feeling of love, as opposed to giving materially, which can also be external and compulsory, as stated above.

כִּי הַחֶסֶד שֶׁהוּא בְּחִינַת אַהֲבָה הוּא חַיֵּי הַחַיִּים שֶׁבְּכָל הָעוֹלָמוֹת,

For *Ḥesed*, which is the aspect of love, is the infinite **source of life in all of the worlds,**

Life is the spiritual force and being that animates everything in the worlds. However, even life has its own life, a higher and more abstract inner influence that vitalizes it. This life of life is divine kindness, which is an expression of God's internal love for us.[27]

כְּמוֹ שֶׁאוֹמְרִים "מְכַלְכֵּל חַיִּים בְּחֶסֶד".

as we say, "who sustains the living with kindness."

This phrase, which is from the *Amida* prayer, means that He provides the needs of living creatures with *Ḥesed*. In other words, kindness and love are the inner sustenance, the hidden life-force within visible life. Even if life does not appear outwardly kind, even if it seems to be an

27. As explain in Letter 15, above, the internality of *Ḥesed* is love.

expression of judgment, the life of life within is always true, divine kindness and love. ☞

וְאָז, ״גַּם ה׳ יִתֵּן הַטּוֹב״ וְיָאֵר פָּנָיו אֵלָיו בִּבְחִינַת אַהֲבָה מְגוּלָּה אֲשֶׁר הָיְתָה תְּחִלָּה מְלוּבֶּשֶׁת וּמְסוּתֶּרֶת בְּתוֹכֵחָה מְגוּלָּה וְיִתְמַתְּקוּ הַגְּבוּרוֹת בְּשָׁרְשָׁן,

Then "indeed, the Lord will bestow the good," and He will shine His countenance toward him in a manner of an open love that was initially enclothed and hidden in an open rebuke, and the *gevurot* will be sweetened at their root,

When an individual accepts the inner kindness and love from his side, when he transforms the externality that appears as judgment and suffering into inner essential kindness and love, then "indeed, the Lord will bestow the good,"[28] and "He will shine His countenance toward him in a manner of an open love."[29] He will show us the love within the difficulties and sufferings we felt, the love "that was initially enclothed and hidden in an open rebuke."

"As water reflects a face to the face" is an unfolding process, which moves from side to side and back and forth, penetrating deeper each time. This is how interpersonal relationships develop: A countenance on one side evokes a countenance on the other side, which in turn induces even more inner connection and even more trust and closeness. Here too, at the initial stage the inner light shining from above transforms the

"WHO SUSTAINS THE LIVING WITH KINDNESS"

☞ Elsewhere (*Torah Or* 36b), Rabbi Shneur Zalman explains that "sustains [*mekhalkel*]" is "a vessel within a vessel [*keli betokh keli*]." That is, in order to draw life into the worlds, which is the "life of life," a great constriction of the vitality is required, for it to enter into a vessel within a vessel. This indicates that the life of life, the kindness and love that constitute life, can also manifest in the form of a constriction and limitation, and it is in that very state that they clearly express God's true kindness and love. When we recite the phrase "who sustains the living with kindness," we are thanking God that even the judgment and constriction "sustains" us "with kindness," as a demonstration of His kindness and love.

---

28. Ps. 85:13.
29. Based on Num. 6:25 and Ps. 67:2.

exteriority of below into a "countenance" of loving acceptance of the open reproach, and subsequently the inner loving acceptance below also transforms the exteriority of above – the rebuke and suffering – until it resembles the inner, revealed kindness and love.

What might appear to be *gevurot* and judgment is actually love and kindness at its root. Sometimes there is a need to set a boundary, to reprimand, to enact some kind of cleansing, precisely out of love and caring. When the root of that strictness, which is love, is revealed, this is the mitigation of the *gevurot* at their root. ☞

וְיִתְבַּטְּלוּ הַדִּינִין, נֶצַח סֶלָה וָעֶד.

and the harsh **judgments will be nullified, eternally, Selah, forever.**

This is an even more significant stage than the sweetening; it is an absolute negation, that there will be no judgments at all. In other words, the cancellation will not be merely temporary, or to a certain extent, but rather the judgment will be nullified at its root, and there will be only kindness and love both within and without.

Continuing with the metaphor of "sweetening the *gevurot,*" a bitter or spicy food can be sweetened by mixing sugar into it. However, even though one can even add so much sugar that the bitter taste is no longer noticeable, that would not lead to a change in its essence: The bitter will remain bitter, and likewise the judgment will remain judgment; it has simply been mixed with other substances. In contrast, sweetening at the root constitutes a change in the very properties of the substance.[30] At that time, the judgments are entirely abolished, and the judgment ceases to be a judgment at all.

"SWEETENED"

☞ "Sweetening," or mitigating, is a common term in the esoteric sources for the transformation of judgment into mercy. The sweet taste, representing kindness, is contrasted with the bitter (or spicy) taste that represents *Gevura* (see *Likkutei Amarim*, chap. 27, and in several other places. See also the whole discussion in *Torah Or*, Num. Section 6, p. 1388). As one can sense, sometimes a spicy taste is even more delicious and satisfying for the palate than the sweet.

30. See *Torah Or*, 12a; *Ma'amarei Admor HaZaken* 5566, Section 1, p. 97, which provides the example of lupines that are boiled over and again, in order to sweeten them.

The terms "eternally; Selah; forever,"[31] which serve to indicate the conclusion of the discussion, signify the reinforcement of the previous claims: "So it should it be truly, forever, without a pause." This is the mark of the truth: It does not change with the vagaries of place or time. The same will apply to the abolition of judgments – truly and forever – when the *gevurot* are sweetened at the root.[32]

---

31. See *Eiruvin* 54a: A Sage of the school of Rabbi Eliezer ben Ya'akov taught: Wherever it states *netzaḥ* ["eternally"], Selah, or *va'ed* ["forever"], [the implication is that the subject to which the word is attached] will never cease. *Netzaḥ,* as it is written, "For I will not contend forever; neither will I be eternally [*lanetzaḥ*] angry" (Isa. 57:16). Selah, as it is written, "As we have heard, so have we seen in the city of the Lord of Hosts, in the city of our God; may God establish it forever, Selah" (Ps. 48:9). *Va'ed,* as it is written, "The Lord shall reign forever and ever [*va'ed*]" (Ex. 15:18).

32. The following are concluding words and a summary that were appended to the original letter. While they do not appear here, they were printed in the complete version that appears in *Iggerot Kodesh Admor HaZaken*:

"I will further demand and seek, and make known what is surely the case (see Hos. 5:9), that all those who yearn to enter so that I will speak with them in private, specifically from the older members of our community, are deluding themselves by thinking that I know more than them. We can ourselves see that "in the multitude of people is the king's glory" (Prov. 14:28) and that God is with us (Num. 14:9), and I cannot relay in private even a whisper (see Job 4:12) of what needs to be said and spoken about us each month, on the Shabbat when we bless the New Moon. Nevertheless, one who occasionally has something urgent involving the service of God, [which requires him] to ask me specifically in private, must wait for about two weeks; perhaps then there will be a suitable and available hour to speak with him as he wishes.

Now, whoever violates one of these terms, apart from his judgment at the hands of Heaven – to which I do not deliver him, God forbid, and therefore I do not have the power to forgive – I will also impose upon him some kind of fine for the Holy Land, may it be rebuilt and reestablished speedily in our days, [to be given] to his local charity collectors, as they see fit and in accordance with his means, as a safeguard, to serve as a remembrance and a sign. The main thing is that I have requested many times over from the charity collectors, may they live, to oversee all of this carefully, so that not a single detail of it should go unfulfilled, Heaven forfend.

Even if they see others violating all of these terms and forcing their way in, they should not say that the vow must have been nullified, as we do not learn from an incident that occurred. Perhaps there was a special reason here – they should not infer from it to depart from all of those conditions, not even in the slightest. Please, please, I beg of you, with great compassion, not to banish me from our country at an inopportune, unfit time of ill favor before the Lord.

The meaning of the mitigation of the *gevurot* and the nullification of the judgments, as expressed by the terms "eternally; Selah; forever," is that this will be the eternal state of affairs not only with regard to the future, but in a certain sense with respect to the past as well. When an object breaks, it can be fixed in such a manner that it is no longer smashed. However, such a repair job, which rectifies only the future, is not a true and complete amendment at the root of the object, since the past remains broken. It is not accounted for, so to speak, and there is no justification for why the item was in its previous state. By contrast, the repair referred to here (which is how the act of rectification works in general, according to Hasidic teachings) sweetens the past as well. It clarifies why everything occurred, as it shows that in fact, all the bitterness was nothing but goodness and kindness from the very outset, only it was hidden, similar to a "chair,"[33] the means to achieve perfection and a greater level of the visible good and sweetness.

The sweetening of the *gevurot* in this manner is, in fact, the topic of this letter. It began with the *gevurot,* the difficult situation, the troubles and tribulations that Jews have endured in their daily lives, until they could bear them no longer and came to the Rebbe to seek help. The Rebbe's answer can be divided into two parts: The initial reply appears at first glance to be the Rebbe's personal reaction – an expression of his own pain for the plight of the hasidim, a virtual apology for his inability to provide an adequate response to them and something almost approaching anger that they are turning to him with such requests. However, when everything he says is taken into account, there is not even a hint of helplessness here. His answer is, fundamentally, the reply of a "Rebbe" – not a personal, human response but an illumination of the truth in relation to the questioner. His statements should be

---

I await and look forward to your response in writing, [to hear] in which places these statements were accepted and where they were not, God forbid. I will then devise plans (see Ps. 13:3), how and what to correct, and may God place within us good counsel to do what is good and right in His eyes (see Deut. 12:28).

I also wish to announce that in the month of Nissan, and Iyar, until the Shabbat before the start of the month of Sivan, and likewise after Simḥat Torah until the Shabbat of Hanukkah, nobody should travel at all, neither new members nor old ones."

33. On the meaning of this term, see *Ba'al Shem Tov al HaTorah, Parashat Bereshit,* 41-43.

understood as follows: It is correct that in these circumstances the truth seems difficult, demanding for the hasid and hard and painful for the Rebbe who has to deliver this truth to the hasid whom he loves. This explains the shakiness of the tone at the beginning of the letter. Nevertheless, one can discern from the very start how the Rebbe, with public and personal heroism – for he surely accepts his personal responsibility for it all, as he feels what the hasid is feeling – directs the problem towards the only solution he sees. The issue become even clearer in the second part of the letter (from the words "like a merciful, wise and righteous father etc."), where he explains both the theoretical basis for this path and its practical fulfillment.

This is not the solution that every Rebbe would offer, but it is characteristic of the author of the *Tanya*. After all, it is also possible to sweeten the *gevurot* in a temporary, external manner, such as when the Rebbe intervenes and halts the oppression, by taking the issue upon himself and changing that reality or the hasid himself. However, if the Rebbe were to do this, the hasid will be left with something unfinished, unsweetened *gevurot* that he merely does not feel at the moment. For the author of the *Tanya*, however, there are no shortcuts or compromises. A person can and must work with the actual reality of his life, and he must travel the whole path himself. The Rebbe will accompany him, he will be alongside him in all his difficulties, to offer explanations, encouragement, and support – but he cannot go in his place. The sweetening is not external but internal, performed by the man himself, by thinking and attending to the whole and to each and every detail. The author of the *Tanya* portrays this path through his maxim from the start of the *Tanya*: "A long and short path." It is "long" because there are no shortcuts or skipping of stages, but it is also "short" because this sweetening is at the root, and one will not have to repeat anything that has been sweetened in this manner in another cycle of life. ☞

ASKING THE REBBE FOR MATERIAL ADVICE

☞ After all that has been stated and explained in this letter, that one should not ask the Rebbe for material advice involving the affairs of this world, the question still remains: As one can see, hasidim come to their Rebbes with such problems all the time, and they even approached the author of the *Tanya* himself, and continued to do so. Surely, they did not come in vain!: The simplest explanation is that even though he is not a prophet, the "Rebbe," in the hasidic sense, still has an advantage over ordinary people. Therefore, he can advise people even in matters of this world not only as a friend or an expert, but through an inner vision, by which he perceives reasons and solutions that another person cannot see. The Rebbe is a true leader of Israel, who is connected to the hasidim – and to all members of Israel – and he loves them deeply, even more than a man loves his own soul. Accordingly, he first of all listens – he is the great listener who attends to other people with unlimited patience – and therefore he can absorb details and subtleties that someone else might miss, while keeping the larger picture in mind. Furthermore, because it concerns him as well, since he sees those personal problems in all areas of life with the same degree of closeness, pain and joy as the person telling him, he can find solutions with the strength of someone who is truly affected by the issue. As is known, when a matter affects someone on the inside, he discovers hidden, inner forces within his soul, and is able to act beyond his normal capabilities.[34] This is especially true of the Rebbe, who in addition to his involvement and closeness to the petitioner also retains the detachment and breadth of mind of a Rebbe, one who sees the entire picture; a true head of the body of the community.

In addition, a hasidic rabbi, and certainly the author of the *Tanya*, has a kind of *ruaḥ hakodesh*, prophetic intuition, and even actual prophecy when he answers questions on these issues. See *Keter Shem Tov*, Additions, 340: "When Samuel said to Saul 'I am the Seer'...as a prophet sees the matter with his very own eyes. The Omnipresent does not conceal it from him, and thus he saw the donkeys etc. This is achieved through the disclosure within time and space of something that is above time and place etc. The Ba'al Shem Tov, of blessed memory, was on this level." Paradoxically, it is precisely the author of the *Tanya's* reply here, that the answers in these matters belongs to "actual prophets," which proves that he could provide a response to such problems because he himself was like an "actual prophet" (see *Torat Menaḥem*, vol. 2, p. 107; ibid vol. 16, p. 48, and in several other places. See also *Torat Shalom*, *Sefer HaSiḥot*, p. 169).

But in that case, after all the explanations, we are left puzzled by the comments of the author of the *Tanya* in this letter, as he seems to completely reject this claim: "Has this ever occurred, etc.!" One possibility is that Rabbi Shneur Zalman is referring specifically to "counsel on the material plane, regarding what to do involving matters of this physical world," that is, when the sought advice concerns material matters alone. Here, he maintains, one has to be on the level of a prophet, someone who does not exist today. Therefore, when the hasidim come to him, as described, with all the weight of this world and its troubles on their shoulders, his initial response is that "these are the affairs of this world; they are hidden from my eyes and I cannot deal with them." The various levels of *ruaḥ hakodesh* and prophecy are not like powers

---

34. See *Hayom Yom*, 9 Elul, on Torah study, which states that when one is "involved" in a topic he understands it better. Proof is cited from several occasions where the Talmud suggests that ignorant people might make various claims. It asks how those individuals can come up with such arguments, and explains that

and abilities that a person can acquire for himself and act upon them as he wishes. Apart from the requisite work of personal preparation, these skills are always associated with a state of mind and an environment that one does not choose, and they are granted only through a supernal act of kindness from Above.

The author of the *Tanya*, like every true tzaddik, does not know ahead of time whether he will see with *ruaḥ hakodesh*. He listens, receives an impression and relates to the matter at hand, and only then does he try and see. But beforehand he declares, in humility and truth, that he does not know, and he cannot say what he does not see. This is what he states in this letter. Nevertheless, with that background in mind, this reply is also the response of a "Rebbe." It should be understood not as a personal reaction with respect to himself – as there is no such thing for a Rebbe – but as an expression of the illumination of truth directed towards the hasidim. For in actual fact, nowadays that is not the way to deal with material problems as such. Not because he is unable to do so due to not having reached the necessary level of prophecy, but because this is not the correct path for his hasidim. The author of the *Tanya* is discussing this basic conception throughout this letter, and outlining the path that should be avoided with regard to such issues, and the path that should be taken.

Admittedly, when the hasidim approach him at other times, and he delves into these problems in a different manner, it becomes clear that for the hasidim in particular, and for Jews in general, this separation between the affairs of this world and the service of God does not exist in practice, as the two are always intertwined. This opens the way to deal with all issues in the context of the Torah and the service of God. In this manner, through Torah[35] and divine service, it turns out that there is a place for these questions as well, and that there are degrees of *ruaḥ hakodesh*, and even of actual prophecy, that are revealed even in our times.

---

when something affects one personally, even weak-minded people can come up with complex logical arguments.

35. See, for example, the Sages' comments with regard to the light of the first day of creation, that through it one could see from one end of the world to the other, and the midrash states that it was hidden away by God for the righteous. The Ba'al Shem Tov explains that God concealed it within the Torah, and not for the righteous in the future, but for the righteous at all times, since the Torah itself enables one to peer from one end of the world to the other (*Ba'al Shem Tov al HaTorah, Parashat Bereshit*, 27 and onward). See also *Likkutei Torah*, Lev. 22d, s.v. "*ka miflegei*," section 2 and onwards.

Addendum to Epistle 22

THIS SECTION OF THE PRINTED EPISTLE 22 IS ACTUALLY a separate letter that was included here only in later additions.[1] It is possible that the letter was not given its own number and title because it was added to an existing typeface, and the printers did not want to change the numbering of the letters. It was likely placed alongside epistle 22 because that is where it appeared in the manuscripts from which it was taken.[2] Furthermore, in its content and style it also resembles epistle 22 and the other letters and documents that pertain to the Liozna Regulations.[3] The similarity can already be seen in its opening, which, like epistle 22, expresses the difficulties of the Rebbe who, due to the multitude of hasidim and their problems, can no longer lead them in the old, direct ways, which entails the regulations and restrictions in the Rebbe's relationship with the hasidim. However, unlike the previous letter, which dealt with the worldly problems of the hasidim, this letter focuses on the service of God – prayer, and specifically public prayer. The letter can be divided into two parts: The first concerns the strengthening of the hasidim in the service of prayer, while

1. *Iggeret HaKodesh* was published as part of the *Tanya* for the first time in the Shklov 5574 (1814) edition. This addition was included only in the edition of 5660 (1900).

2. See the introduction to Rabbi Yehoshua Mondshein (of blessed memory), *The Book of the Tanya – its Editions, Translations, and Commentaries*" (Heb.). See also *Iggerot Kodesh Admor HaZaken*, in the note on the introduction to Letter 14.

3. Indeed, the manuscript of this letter was found amongst the manuscripts of essays from the year 5553 (1793), the period of the Liozna Regulations.

the other involves an apparently separate issue – the bonding of the hasidic group and the love of Israel.

18 Tishrei

16 Tishrei (leap year)

אֲהוּבַיי אַחַיי וְרֵעַיי, **My beloved ones, my brethren and friends,**

This term of address to the hasidim also appears in the previous letter and in several other places in the letters of Rabbi Shneur Zalman.[4] Its threefold expression of affection is reserved for the closest hasidim, those who are not only beloved but also "brethren and friends," meaning that the Rebbe can treat them as equal brothers, who are helping him lead the hasidic movement and ideas forward. The Rebbe speaks to the hasidim in this manner when he is demanding from them the same service as he expects from himself: That they should join him, as his brothers and friends, in the service of God. He is not addressing them like a father to his sons, or as a teacher to students who are listening to him, but as a Rebbe calling upon his hasidim to accompany him, ascend with him, and accept responsibility alongside him. Indeed, on almost every occasion when this expression appears, it is followed by a demand for a high level of divine service, whether in reference to the affairs of this world or the direct service of God, especially prayer.[5]

מִגּוֹדֶל טִרְדָּתִי אֲשֶׁר הִקִּיפוּ עָלַי יַחַד וְסַבּוּנִי כַּמַּיִם כָּל הַיּוֹם וְכָל הַלַּיְלָה תָּמִיד לֹא יֶחֱשׁוּ, **on account of my great preoccupation, which have together encompassed me and surrounded me like water all day and night, forever not holding their peace,**

The letter begins with a description of the "preoccupations"[6] of an individual who, in addition to his status as a great rabbi, indeed one of the leading halachic authorities of his time, and a Rebbe of hasidim

4. See e.g. *Iggerot HaKodesh* 9, 22, 24, and 27. Likewise, this phraseology appears often in the letters of his rabbi and colleague, Rabbi Menaḥem Mendel of Vitebsk.
5. It should be noted that this term of address is also used in *Kuntres HaHitpa'alut* ["Tract on Ecstasy"] of the Mitteler Rebbe, Rabbi Dovber of Lubavitch.
6. The Lubavitcher Rebbe notes that although the Hebrew word here is *tirdati,* "my preoccupation," it should probably read *tirdotai,* "my preoccupations," in the plural, as below.

who is innovating a new way of serving God – the Chabad tradition –is also a leader and head of Israel in his milieu, who feels and bears responsibility for the material needs of every Jew. As depicted here, those preoccupations "surrounded me like water all day," the waters of the struggles for the world's sustenance and against its ills,[7] which envelop him not only during the day but also throughout the night, "without holding their peace."[8] These preoccupations disturb him like a constant background noise, until he is unable to find a moment of silence from it all to shift his focus elsewhere, to other and higher layers of reality, which is the main work of a Rebbe – Torah, prayer, and souls.

I am unable to deliver the burden, to put into writing all that is in my heart. לֹא אוּכַל מַלֵּט מַשָּׂא לֶאֱמֹר עִם הַסֵּפֶר כָּל אֲשֶׁר בִּלְבָבִי.

In other words, "I cannot shake off these preoccupations and write down all that is in my heart in the form of a book or a letter." He apologizes to his "beloved ones, brethren and friends" for his inability to sit and compose for them words of guidance on these matters of an appropriate length and deliberation; "all that is in his heart" – all that he thinks, feels, and understands on these issues. It is not because they are unimportant or that the hasidim are unworthy, but because the preoccupations of this world and its affairs are always more "pressing," as they always inundate the immediate, nearest space. However, in actual fact it is those hasidim who are his "beloved ones, brethren and friends," and the deeper subjects that he discusses with them, which are in his heart, who are most precious to him and touch him deeply.

A Rebbe of hasidim, a tzaddik, is not only a leader in the conventional, political, social and economic senses. Although he also engages in all these areas, his true focus is on the inner, spiritual level of events. It is there, below the surface, that what is really important unfolds: Torah, prayer, and Jewish life, through which the Rebbe can essentially

---

7. See e.g., *Torah Or* 8c, s.v., "*mayim rabbim.*"

8. The phrase "which have together encompassed me and surrounded me like water all day and night" is derived from Psalms 88:18; "all day and night, without holding their peace" is from Isaiah 62:6; "I am unable to deliver the burden" is a rewording of Isaiah 46:2; "to put into writing" is based on Esther 9:25; and "all that is in my heart" is a close paraphrase of II Kings 10:30.

have an effect on external matters as well. When he addresses "my brethren and friends," he expects them to join him in this task. As he will emphasize below, when they are united, by virtue of their status as a community, they will assist him and bear the burden of a Rebbe with him. Only in this manner, through the power of the labor of the hasidim, can the Rebbe also succeed in his task, both from within and without: To establish and maintain the people who are with him, while at the same time building a clear path towards the service of God for future generations as well.

אַךְ בִּקְצָרָה בָּאתִי, כְּמַזְכִּיר וּמַחֲזִיר עַל הָרִאשׁוֹנוֹת בִּכְלָל, וּבִפְרָט אֶל הַמִּתְנַדְּבִים בָּעָם,

However, I will express myself in brief, like one reminding you **and reviewing earlier matters in general form, especially to the volunteers on behalf of the people,**

He states that the brief contents of this letter have already been discussed in the past, both in writing and face-to-face. Therefore, he will not begin by presenting these matters, as he would have done if he were addressing new people and had the leisure to start from the very beginning. This letter – at least the part of it that was printed – is very short, and everything it states should be read as a summary and abbreviated version of many ideas that it does not lay out. It does not provide a methodically presented design or approach to the service of God; rather, as stated here, he is "like one reminding and reviewing" – he mentions certain points and thereby reminds the reader, with the necessary emphases, of what he should already know.

These matters were stated in "general form" and established for all the hasidim, "especially to the volunteers on behalf of the people." This expression, which is from Judges (5:9,) refers to the addressees of this letter, who are unique among the people in that they have taken upon themselves more than their obligatory share of the burden. ☞

לַעֲמוֹד עַל הָעֲבוֹדָה זוֹ תְּפִלָּה,

to stand over the service, which is prayer,

The teaching that "service is prayer" is from *Ta'anit* 2a. This is the essence of his request from his close hasidim, the "volunteers" – to stand and strengthen themselves in the service of the heart, which is the work of prayer. ☞ ☞

"THE VOLUNTEERS ON BEHALF OF THE PEOPLE"

☞ Since prayer, including the service of prayer that the author of the *Tanya* will discuss below, is mandatory rather than an act of piety, why does he address "the volunteers"? Prayer, deemed by the Sages as "service of the heart," is essentially compulsory; praying every day according to the order of the prayer book is an obligation. Yet, by addressing "the volunteers," the author of the *Tanya* implies that the true essence of the service of prayer entails specifically what one adds to that order. As the Mishna states (*Berakhot* 4:4): "One whose prayer is fixed, his prayer is not a supplication." Beyond reciting the words, the real service is in one's thoughts and emotions: What one thinks; what he feels; what he has in mind before he says the words. In this regard, not only is there no fixed measure, but it is crucial to add something each time that goes above and beyond one's previous effort. The ability to feel every time, to self-abnegate and enter the word wholeheartedly so that it will have its effect, requires one to go beyond the standard order in every prayer. This can be only voluntarily, not in fulfillment of a duty.

STANDING

☞ The word and concept of "standing," *amida*, is so inextricably connected to prayer that it has become a virtual synonym for prayer, especially the central prayer of the Eighteen Blessings, known as the *Amida* (*Berakhot* 26b, 28b; *Bereshit Rabba* 68:9; see *Torah Or* 46a). The two are connected in several ways and on different levels. On a simple level, when a person prays, he roots himself in his mental space, by gathering himself and focusing on his source above, away from the environment. When he prays, he also stands firm upon his opinion and intention, resisting all those obstacles and hindrances – nature, habits, this world – that constantly pull him outward and downward. There is also the literal meaning of standing up, when one goes from a position of lying down or sitting to standing. This implies that when a person is situated in this world, it is as if he is crouched over, embroiled in mundane activities through his actions, thoughts and feelings. When he comes to pray, he "stands up," he is lifting his head and spirit from the earth to the sky. Indeed, it is explained in the esoteric texts of the Torah (*Sefer HaMa'amarim Melukat*, vol. 4, p. 297, and in many other places) that standing expresses self-negation, and thus prayer in general and the *Amida* prayer in particular is the process through which one nullifies the self and connects to God.

"THE SERVICE"

☞ The term "service," especially in our times, when we do not have the sacrificial service of the Temple, refers mainly to "the service of the heart," which is prayer. As the Sages taught: "Which is the service that is in the heart? You must say that this is prayer" (*Ta'anit* 2a; cited by the Rambam *Sefer HaAhava, Hilkhot Tefilla* 1:1). Likewise,

בְּקוֹל רָם, in a loud voice,

That is, by pronouncing the letters out loud and actually saying them, not merely leaving them in one's thoughts. Even in the *Amida* prayer, when one should not be heard by others,[9] he must still articulate and enunciate all of the words. ☞

it is well-known that the prayers were established in correspondence with the sacrificial service (*Berakhot* 26b). The word *avoda*, service, work, labor, denotes an action that one performs in opposition to his natural inclinations, against the nature of the world. When he acts in accordance with his nature and habits, with the aid of nature, this is not called "*avoda*." The nature of an object consists of the place and manner in which it is positioned, the form which is ingrained on it within reality, similar to how the shape of a coin is pressed onto it. As long as a person continues to act within nature, even if he achieves great results, his deeds are not considered "*avoda*." *Avoda* always involves a change in nature, when a person ingrains another mode into himself. In this sense, prayer entails more work than any other level of religious life. For unlike the Torah and mitzvot that a person engages in wherever he is, the whole point of prayer is to change one's place, to ascend upwards and make oneself better and purer. When a person articulates Torah ideas, he must understand what he is saying; whereas when he recites words of prayer, he has to be authentically present.

Why specifically prayer? It seems that the author of the *Tanya* viewed prayer as the innovative and unique feature of the hasidic movement. Not in opposition to the study of the Torah or in its stead, but together with it, such that by virtue of prayer, the Torah, mitzvot, and all human life in general would ascend upwards. For this reason, standing for prayer in the hasidic manner – seriously, with devotion, until one reaches the ultimate pining of his soul until he nears expiration – comprises the cultivation of the soul of Hasidism; the inner core through which everything will work out, in one way or another. It is related about Rabbi Shneur Zalman that when he was young, he was deliberating whether to go to the Gaon of Vilna or the Maggid in Mezeritch, and he arrived at a decision through the following reasoning: "I know a little about how to study Torah but nothing about how to pray, and therefore I will go to Mezeritch."

Furthermore, as stated in epistle 22, the author of the *Tanya*'s approach was for the Hasidim to see to the task themselves. They should not wait for God, or the tzaddik, to drag them from their place, but rather they should ascend from their current position through their own efforts. This is the service of prayer.

PRAYER THROUGH SPEECH

☞ The idea that prayer should be recited in a loud voice, by verbally pronouncing the letters, is foundational to Judaism in general and Hasidism in particular. Prayer,

9. *Shulḥan Arukh HaRav* 101:2.

לְהִתְחַזֵּק מְאֹד to be greatly strengthened

which in essence is a connection[10] between man and God and between the Divine Presence and God, should inherently include these two extremes: On the one hand, thought and intention (spirituality), and on the other hand the letters that are spoken "in a loud voice" (inanimate; materiality). Intention alone, without speaking, is like clapping with one hand; it does not forge any connection, and therefore is not in fact prayer at all and does not have the effect of prayer.

There are other facets of the rule that prayer should be spoken out loud: One feature of prayer is that it involves a request for the person's needs. The general hasidic viewpoint is that the very act of articulating a prayer creates the reality of the requested item, or at least the vessel in which to receive it. If one wants the request to be fulfilled in this world and not only in the upper worlds, he must give it expression specifically through the physical voice.

Another feature of prayer, of cleaving to God and self-abnegation in the halakhic sources, is that "the voice awakens the intention." This applies on various levels (for more on raising one's voice in prayer, see *Likkutei Siḥot*, vol. 35, p. 193. The sources there direct the reader, with regard to how the voice awakens one's intention, to *Beit Yosef, Oraḥ Ḥayyim* 101; *Taz,* ibid 101: 1; *Shulḥan Arukh HaRav* ibid 101: 3. See also *Tur* and *Shulḥan Arukh, Oraḥ Ḥayyim* 61:4 (and *Shulḥan Arukh HaRav* ibid 61: 5); *Reshit Ḥokhma, Sha'ar HaKedusha,* end of chap. 15 (cited by the *Shelah, Sha'ar HaOtiyot* 100: 175). See also *Ohr HaTorah*, Ex. Vol. 1, p. 176 and onwards; *Sefer HaMa'amarim* 5659 (of Rabbi Sholom Dovber Schneerson, p. 6.). Simply put, speaking out loud takes a person away from his self-absorption and the meaningless ruminations of his mind and heart, leading him to consider what he is saying. This kind of speech skips over, as it were, a whole psycho-spiritual process that should happen in one's mind, through thought and intention and yet did not happen. When a person talks in this manner, it effectively drags his intention along automatically. What is more, speech has the power to lead the soul[11] farther than any inner mental power, more than the mind can achieve and feel on its own (*dibbur*, "speech," can also mean "leading"; see e.g., *Sanhedrin* 8a: "One leader [*dabbar*] for the generation"). What the word itself contains, through its vocal pronunciation and the articulation of its letters, is the very divine word, which we too recite. Therefore, by simply uniting and adhering to the speech of prayer one transcends every mental intention. It is likewise explained elsewhere that the source of speech lies above the powers of one's soul, intellect, and attributes, as it is from the level called the *kadmut hasekhel*, "primordial reason," which precedes the intellect, from the *Keter* that is above *Ḥokhma*. With regard to the concept that speech is rooted up high in *Ḥokhma*, see Letter 6,

10. As explained in several places, *tefilla*, prayer, is derived from: "I engaged in a great struggle [*naftulei*] with my sister" (Gen. 30:8), or in the language of the Mishna: "One who lines [*hatofel*] a sound vessel" (*Kelim* 3:5; see also e.g., *Torah Or* 79d).

11. *Dibbur*, "speech," can also mean "leading"; see e.g., *Sanhedrin* 8a: "One leader [*dabbar*] for the generation."

In order to stand up in prayer, to shake off the shackles of corporeal and worldly life, each time afresh, one has to greatly strengthen himself. As already explained, this elevation of man runs against nature; the nature both of his body and of the material and spiritual world in which he exists, and anything that goes against nature requires constant reinforcement. It is not enough to do it once and from then on it will stand on its own, because that will not happen if one does not work on it constantly.[12] Therefore, this strengthening must be performed "greatly," consistently and without limit.[13]

בְּכָל עוֹז וְתַעֲצוּמוֹת **with the entirety of** one's **strength and power**

This expression[14] is possibly an allusion to the Torah[15] and the forces that strengthen the soul, as it is only through this power that one can find the strength to oppose the immense, primordial forces of the nature of the world, of the *tohu*, chaos.

נֶגֶד כָּל מוֹנֵעַ מִבַּיִת וּמִחוּץ **against all internal or external obstacles**

"Obstacles" is a general name for anything that hinders and prevents a person from serving God. These obstacles are generally divided into

above. See also *Sefer HaMa'amarim* 5659, p. 6, and the pages before and after. For a different perspective, see at length *Torah Ḥayyim, Parashat Noaḥ,* p. 51a and onwards, regarding employing a loud voice during *Pesukei DeZimra* and the whole of the prayer before the *Amida,* in contrast to the *Amida* prayer itself, which is recited quietly. The idea is that speaking in a loud voice embodies the act of refinement from the *tohu*, chaos, whereas prayer through quiet speech and self-abnegation is the stage of rectification. The ascent of the forces from the *tohu* for the rectification etc. is revealed specifically through the use of a loud voice.

12. For a similar idea, see *Sha'ar HaYiḥud VeHa'emuna,* chap. 2.

13. As is known, "greatly [*me'od*]" always means without limit. See *Likkutei Torah,* Num. 43c, et al.

14. Which is derived from Psalms 68:36.

15. The Torah is called "strength," *oz*. See *Sifrei,* Deut. 343; *Shemot Rabba* 27:4; *Vayikra Rabba* 31:5. See also *Torah Or, Yitro,* s.v. "*baḥodesh hashelishi.*"

two types: "internal" and "external." The "external" obstacles come from outside a person: Other people, the problems of this world and its temptations, and in a sense even one's own body. All of these constantly pull him downward and outwards, countermanding his attempts to venture inwards and connect with the essence of his divine soul and its powers to actualize his desire to ascend and cleave to the Divine. By contrast, "internal" obstacles come from within the individual himself, from those forces of his soul that fail to achieve his goals. The source of these internal obstacles are conflicting forces inside him that impede each other, not because others are interfering with him, but because he sabotages himself. ☞

"INTERNAL" OBSTRUCTERS

☞ Every person has their braking mechanisms, which are certainly necessary at times, but sometimes prevent him from acting as he should; they can occasionally even become mechanisms of self-destruction. It can happen that after much effort, perhaps years of struggle and expectation, one reaches a state where all the external factors that were blocking his path, disturbing him, and distracting him disappear, and yet as time passes, it becomes clear to him that he is still falling short of his goal. All the problems from the outside were nothing more than a cover for deeper, internal issues, which are much harder to overcome. One wants to sit and study but he doesn't have time, he has to take care of his household, his health, his children and his parents, etc. Lo and behold, at some point things settle down, when he no longer needs to run off and deal with this or that, and yet he continues to feel restless. Even if there is nothing left that is preventing him from doing as he wishes, he is unable to find within himself the strength and energy to do what he desires.

For example, in order to study Torah for its own sake, or to pray with proper intention, some level of preparation and purity of the soul is required, a level at which the soul can receive energy from holiness itself, because if not, it will revert back the superficial externality from which it drew its life-force until now. An even more subtle internal obstacle, as described in epistle 15 above, is that even when all of one's attributes are steeped in holiness, there is a mechanism of restraint or balance between the forces, which, although essential, can sometimes cause a person, or indeed, an entire society, to become dysfunctional, to the extent they are unable to perform significant work of any kind. As stated in epistle 15 (see there): "*Netzaḥ* expresses [the ability] to triumph [*le-natze'aḥ*] and stand firm against anything that prevents [that] pouring forth and [that prevents the] learning [from reaching] his son, [whether these impediments are] internal or external. 'Internal' means [that] the father strengthens himself against the attribute of *Gevura* and constriction within him, which arouses contentions in his will against his son, saying that [his son] is not yet ready [to receive] this [learning]."

בְּ'יָד חֲזָקָה' כְּמַשְׁמָעוֹ. **with a "mighty hand," with** all its **implications.**

That is, not with a soft hand, not by means of persuasion, with logic and knowledge, but through a more internal force, which arises from the perception of one's very soul that this is how things should be, and it does not matter what feeling and understanding he has, if any. Therefore, this is a "mighty hand," since it does not take into account one's conscious mental powers, it does not wait for him to comprehend and yearn, but acts upon him through a mighty hand so that he behaves in this manner.

שֶׁהוּא רְצוֹן יְרֵאָיו, אֲשֶׁר לְמַעְלָה מִן הַחָכְמָה וְהַתְּבוּנָה, **This is the will of those who fear Him, which is above wisdom and understanding,**

The "mighty hand" is "the will of those who fear Him," the inner will that comes from the power of one's quintessential fear of God within his soul, "which transcends wisdom and understanding." This is the fear in the supreme will that is within the essence of the soul, which is situated above the levels of the intellect in the soul, at the highest root of the attribute of fear and the manifest *Gevura* in the soul. ☞ ☞

THREE "HANDS"

☞ Elsewhere (see e.g., *Likkutei Torah*, Num. 21b and onwards), the author of the *Tanya* talks at length about three "hands" that are mentioned in the Bible: A "great hand" (e.g., Exodus 14:31); a "mighty hand" (e.g., Exodus 3:19); and a "high hand" (e.g., Exodus 14:8). He explains that these "hands" represent the three attributes of *Ḥesed*, *Gevura*, and *Tiferet* in *Keter*, which are above the intellect, and which penetrate and enclothe themselves in the attributes that are below the intellect (in *Atzilut*). With respect to the soul, these are the hidden attributes in the essence of the soul, which penetrate the life of the soul as an expression of simple will.

"ABOVE *ḤOKHMA* AND UNDERSTANDING"

☞ *Ḥokhma* is the highest level of the inner powers of the soul. It is the source of all their vitality and influence, meaning that a person grasps a concept, and in accordance with his wisdom and understanding he develops feelings and attitudes that are realized through his soul and body. "The will of those who fear Him" is the will that is above *Ḥokhma*; it is not just another level above wisdom, but rather it is of another,

אֲשֶׁר נָתַן ה׳ בָּהֵמָּה לָדַעַת לַעֲשׂוֹת אֶת כָּל אֲשֶׁר צִוָּה ה׳ בְּהַשְׂכֵּל וָדַעַת.

which God placed within them, to know to perform all that God has commanded, with intelligence and knowledge.

Wisdom and understanding are the inner forces of the soul, the powers of recognition that God has placed within each person in accordance with his level and status; how he sees his world and himself, and how he feels and proceeds to act in his life. The phrase "which God placed within them" is derived from Exodus 31:6.

In general, there are two types of service of God: In accordance with the intellect and above the intellect. The service that is in accordance with the intellect, which is the focus of the author of the *Tanya* here, is the service whose origin, strength, and beginning are from the intellect and knowledge – when one attains a certain understanding and awareness, and feels, conducts himself, and behaves accordingly. ☞

infinitely higher essence, and no limb of the body or faculty of the soul relates to it in particular. This is an all-encompassing power whose action goes beyond the individual limbs and powers of the soul, such that when it is revealed it does not take them into consideration and it does not need to persuade them, since it is beneath its dignity to argue with them at all. Everyone feels like this on occasion: A certain will arises within him and it is obvious to him that this is how things should be, and it is also evident to him that it does not matter what he understands, because his

"WHICH GOD PLACED WITHIN THEM"

☞ Although serving God with one's intellect seems to entail a process that man himself creates, through contemplation, and developing and improving his attributes, it is precisely with regard to this service that the author of the *Tanya* states "which God placed within them." In other words, God gave these powers to man, as opposed to "the will of those who fear Him," which the person himself strengthens with a "mighty hand." It seems from this that the powers of the mind are a kind of "work tool" that God grants a person, to a greater or lesser extent. However, the one who activates the tools and uses them is the person himself, and therefore this work appears to be performed by him. By contrast, the faculty of the soul that truly expresses the individual himself, is the will. Through the will one adds to the service that which depends on his own choice, exercising the choice to change life-direction or change the intensity with which he is working on himself. The service of the "mind that controls the heart," which is discussed in many places, is actually a service of the will rather than the intellect, as the author of the *Tanya* himself notes (*Likkutei Amarim*, chap. 12): "Every person can, through the will of his mind, restrain

רַק רָצוֹן פָּשׁוּט וְרוּחַ נְדִיבָה There should be **merely a simple will and a generous spirit**

The service that is above the intellect is the service powered by the simple will, which is above the intellect. "Merely a simple will," stripped of the trappings of reason, "and a generous spirit" of volunteering that is not compelled by anything: Not by fear or desire for any object in the world, but by the power of the simple, primary desire for God.

בְּכָל אִישׁ אֲשֶׁר יִדְּבֶנּוּ לִבּוֹ לַעֲבוֹד עֲבוֹדָה תַּמָּה, לַעֲשׂוֹת נַחַת רוּחַ לְיוֹצְרוֹ. **within every man whose heart renders him willing to perform a perfect service, in order to provide his Creator with gratification.**

This will is present within every Jew, and it finds expression when his "heart renders him willing" (based on Ex. 25:2), when his heart is opened "to perform" such work of his own accord, even if the mind does not instruct him to do so. It is on those very occasions when he is not tied down or directed towards any particular action that the simple will, the essence of his divine soul can be revealed within him, which is to serve God.

A "perfect service" means one that is not compromised by any personal interests or other intent, but rather its whole purpose is "to provide his Creator with gratification," solely for the sake of Heaven.

"For the sake of Heaven" does not necessarily mean for a spiritual purpose, or even solely for sacred ends, as even spiritual matters can be contaminated by one's ego. An intention for the sake of Heaven should completely exclude the ego from its considerations and awareness, and this is the what "to provide his Creator with gratification" means. This intention does not even mean that the ego will unite with Him and abnegate itself to Him, but only that God should receive gratification.

himself and control the spirit of lust in his heart..." It is precisely by means of this faculty, which goes beyond, which is undefined and unlimited by the faculties of the soul, which expresses the soul itself more than anything else, that man can make the choice to serve God, and change his attributes and ways. soul and very life depend on this matter.

וְעַל זֶה נֶאֱמַר: "כִּי עַם קְשֵׁה עוֹרֶף הוּא וְסָלַחְתָּ" (שמות לד,ט).

And it is stated regarding this, "For it is a stiff-necked people; may You forgive" (Ex. 34:9).

This verse is applied to the simple will that exists within every Jew, to provide his Creator with gratification. At first glance, Moses' argument appears strange: He is asking God to forgive the people, and the reason he gives for this request is "for it is a stiff-necked people." "A stiff-necked people" is not usually an expression of praise, as we can see from other places where God refers to the people of Israel in this manner.[16] How, then, can this serve as a reason for forgiveness? It has been explained that being "stiff-necked" is an essential feature of the people of Israel which can be an advantage or a disadvantage. It is a disadvantage when the context is not good, as then it expresses the stubbornness of Israel and their refusal to listen to God's voice. Although they are going against the words of the prophets and what every reasonable person can see and understand, they stiffen their necks in order not to hear. However, in a positive context, when Israel is performing the will of God, it is an expression of great praise: They hold fast to the Torah and God's mitzvot with a tenacity that goes beyond all explanation, even against what all the nations are telling them, against reason, against all odds, even when they are threatened with death. In this sense, the expression does indeed provide a justification for forgiveness.

כִּי הַסְּלִיחָה הִיא גַּם כֵּן לְמַעְלָה מִן הַחָכְמָה, כִּי "שָׁאֲלוּ לַחָכְמָה כּו'".

As forgiveness is also above wisdom, as "they asked *Ḥokhma*..."

Forgiveness, like the inner will, also transcends wisdom. The full account of this quotation appears in the Jerusalem Talmud, *Makkot* 2:6:[17] "They asked *Ḥokhma*: What is the punishment for a sinner? It replied: 'Evil pursues sinners' (Prov. 13:21). They asked Prophecy: What is the punishment for a sinner? It replied: 'The soul that sins, it will die' (Ez. 18:4). They asked the Holy One, blessed be He: What is the punishment for a sinner? He replied: 'Let it repent and receive

16. See e.g., Ex. 32:9, 33:3, Deut. 9:13.
17. See also *Pesikta deRav Kahana* 25:7.

forgiveness.'" According to *Ḥokhma*, the intellect, one who sins must bear the consequences. This accords with the entire intellectual perception of reality, which maintains that there is an order to the world, that causality exists, that everything which happens has repercussions that cannot be changed. In contrast, forgiveness and the ability to repent mean that there is no necessary causality, that there is nothing that cannot be changed, that beyond all the connections and rules that *Ḥokhma* perceives there is another reality where these do not apply. *Ḥokhma* is the vessel with which God created the worlds; it is like the superstructure of the world, the thought and intelligence by which the world is run. Therefore, when it is asked about the punishment of a sinner, it replies: "Evil pursues sinners." This is how the world is built and this is how it operates. *Ḥokhma* cannot change this, as that goes against its nature. However, above the world, higher than even *Ḥokhma*, is God Himself, for whom there can be a superstructure that is ultimately transcendent, and that is forgiveness.

וּמֹשֶׁה רַבֵּינוּ עָלָיו הַשָּׁלוֹם בִּיקֵּשׁ מִדָּה כְּנֶגֶד מִדָּה, וְדַי לַמֵּבִין.

And Moses, our teacher, may he rest in peace, requested measure for measure. This is **sufficient** explanation **for one who understands.**

The "measure for measure" is forgiveness corresponding to the stiff-necked people. When a person acts towards God in a stiff-necked manner that goes beyond wisdom, when he persists in cleaving to Him even when there is no rational reason to do so, this leads God to treat him in a similar manner and forgive him.

From here until the end of the letter, the author of *Tanya* makes another, apparently very different, request from the hasidim, that unity and peace should reign amongst them, that they should not think or speak against one another in any manner. And yet, this request is undoubtedly related to the first part of the letter, which focused on prayer. For the first condition towards the service of prayer, and in particular the deeply internal service of prayer of the hasidic group, is unity and love for one another. As cited in the name of the Arizal,[18] and codified

18. See e.g., *Pri Etz Ḥayyim, Sha'ar Olam HaAsiya*, chap. 1; *Sha'ar HaKavanot Derushei Birkot HaShaḥar*.

by the author of the *Tanya* in his Siddur, that one should recite before starting to pray the morning prayer: "I hereby accept upon myself the positive mitzva of 'you shall love your neighbor as yourself.'"

וְעוֹד זֹאת אֶדְרוֹשׁ מִמַּעֲלַתְכֶם **There is an additional matter that I seek of** my **esteemed ones:** 19 Tishrei

Here he "seeks" in the form of a demand, not merely by reminding the "volunteers," as he did earlier. Beforehand he was speaking about prayer, the service of the heart, which no one can really measure, which nobody can fully demand either from himself or from others. Here, however, he is referring to simple interpersonal conduct, observable deeds that every man can and should demand from himself and to which he ought to commit himself. Moreover, such behavior is necessary, as without it there is no room for anything else, no matter how lofty or spiritual.

שֶׁלֹּא לְהַשְׁלִיךְ דְּבָרַי אַחֲרֵיכֶם. **Not to cast my words behind you.**

Although what he will proceed to say is very simple and basic, most people do not like to hear it. The requests require much work and submission, and are not especially exciting or uplifting. That is why people tend to "cast them behind," brushing them off with comments such as "later," "this applies to someone else," "I'll think about it" etc. This is the opposite of dealing with the issues head on: "I myself," "seriously," "really," and "right now."

אֲשֶׁר עָרַכְתִּי שִׂיחַ **For I have arranged** my **discourse**

The letter is addressed to the established hasidim with whom the Rebbe has already held talks, perhaps with each of them on a personal level, and now he is merely writing down the conclusions, in the form of a demand that is binding in practice.

לִהְיוֹת כׇּל אִישׁ יָשָׁר וְהוֹלֵךְ בְּתוּמּוֹ כַּאֲשֶׁר "עָשָׂה הָאֱלֹקִים אֶת הָאָדָם יָשָׁר" (קהלת ז,כט), **so that each man can be upright and walk in his innocence, as "God made man upright"** (Ecc. 7:29),

The clause "so that each man can be upright and walk in his innocence," which is derived from Proverbs 28:6, basically expresses a simple rule:

One must be honest and not cheat people, especially himself. For God created man upright; He treats him with integrity and He demands integrity in return. "Upright" means to see truthfully and simply that God created him as he should be, and that He treats him as he deserves to be treated, in exactly that fashion. There are no complicated calculations here, one cannot say that "the reason is because of such-and-such," or that it occurred "in order for this outcome to happen," and so on and so forth. When one truly accepts this, he will think in an upright manner and walk innocently, with an attitude of inner peace towards everything that unfolds.

It is explained elsewhere[19] that the verse "the Lord made man upright" refers to his divine soul, which is directly connected and rooted high above, a literal "portion of God above." This means that within this entire soul, through all the stages of its descent into the physical body, there are no intermediaries between it and God Himself. The vitality that comes from its essence and strength gives it life from above to below; as it exists above, so it is below, in every degree and every detail. This serves to emphasize all the more so that the life of every Jew, in its every aspect, is directly connected to the ultimate source of all beings.

וְלֹא לְבַקֵּשׁ חֶשְׁבּוֹנוֹת רַבִּים **and not to seek out many calculations**

This phrase comes from that same verse in Ecclesiastes. The problem is that every person has an image – usually distorted – of himself and of the world. Everyone reflects on and tries to understand what is happening and what will occur, but his thoughts are skewed by his attributes, loves and fears, his memories and hopes, and above all by his sense of being. The more materialistic a person is and the more he is immersed in this world, the stronger and more influential is his sense of being. Consequently, when something happens to him that doesn't fit the image he has of his life, the way he thinks it should be, he tries to sort it out through "many calculations."

19. See *Likkutei Torah*, Deut. 37d, Num. 40c.

מֵעֲלִילוֹת מִצְעֲדֵי גֶבֶר וּמַחְשְׁבוֹת אָדָם וְתַחְבּוּלוֹתָיו.

from the paths that a man chooses, a person's thoughts and plans.

One should not take this approach, because "a man's steps are from the Lord" (Ps. 33:23; Prov. 20:24), meaning, one does not understand the path one's life will take and everything that will happen to him, as the verse says, "and a person, what does he understand of his way?" (Prov. 20:24) The same applies to "a person's thoughts;" what he thinks and tries to comprehend and thereby categorize, since "the Lord knows the thoughts of man, that they are vain" (Ps. 94:11).[20] One's calculations and thoughts, by which he attempts to explain and makes sense of reality, are not directed towards man's own benefit or the truth.

כִּי זוּ מְלֶאכֶת שָׁמַיִם הִיא וְלֹא מְלֶאכֶת בָּשָׂר וָדָם.

For that is the work of Heaven, not the work of humans.

One's thoughts cannot grasp "the paths that a man chooses," where one will go, not only in his life in general, but with each step. Real life, even on the most basic level, is the work of Heaven. The calculations, contexts, reasons, and meaning – how, why, and where – are on a scale that goes beyond human comprehension.

This does not mean that a person should avoid thinking about what is happening and not try to understand, learn, amend and plan. However, he should not do so as the creator and master of the events, but as someone who is interpreting what is going on, the people and the incidents, with humility and simplicity, accepting them in an upright manner, as they are, listening in faith without imposing his desires and thoughts upon them. It is only on this basis that a person can and should contemplate, understand and grasp what he should do, accept responsibility, and choose the good path which he can follow, and so on.

וּלְהַאֲמִין בֶּאֱמוּנָה שְׁלֵימָה בְּמִצְוַת חֲכָמֵינוּ ז"ל: "וֶהֱוֵי שְׁפַל רוּחַ בִּפְנֵי כָּל אָדָם" (אבות פרק ד משנה י) בִּכְלָל.

One must believe with a perfect faith in the instruction of our Sages: "Be of lowly spirit before all people" (*Avot* 4:10), **in general.**

20. These verses are allusions to the Rosh Hashana prayer service.

This command, to "be of lowly spirit," requires a "perfect faith." Not the belief that one must do so, but the belief that this is how things truly are. For this instruction involves not action, but thought and feeling, a worldview, and therefore belief here is essential for truly fulfilling this maxim on every level of one's soul.

The adage conveys both a personal and a general outlook. On a personal level, one must be of lowly spirit towards every person that he connects with. This aspect mainly entails one's work with himself; he must refine his moral attributes and behavior. In this particular context, however, the author of the *Tanya* is dealing with one's general attitude, the individual person in relation to a certain generality, to a group and community of Jews, as part of the collective. That is why this teaching refers not to a private person but to the whole: "Be of lowly spirit before all people" – in general.[21]

כִּי יַצִּיבָא מִלְּתָא וְתַקִּין פִּתְגָמָא שֶׁכָּל אֶחָד מְתוּקָּן מֵחֲבֵירוֹ,

For the matter is true, and the saying correct, that each one is perfected through the other,

Although this saying[22] might seem to be merely an educational device, that it is merely good to think in this manner, it is in fact the truth. For every person, there is indeed some quality that he lacks, in which someone else is better off than him. Moreover, the author of the *Tanya* is referring here not only to one's values, but also to his practical aims, each and every person can be improved by his friends. It is only from within the collective, through the experience of being part of a group of hasidim, that one can achieve self-rectification and perfect one's service of God. This is not referring to the perfection of one's private, personal divine service, but the service itself: The prayer that ascends through the community; the light, the spiritual force of goodness that rises from the service of the collective group.

---

21. See the comment of the Lubavitcher Rebbe (published in *Shi'urim BeSefer HaTanya*) on this saying of the Sages, cited in *Likkutei Amarim*, chap. 30.

22. "The matter is true" is from Daniel 6:13; "and the saying correct" follows the translation of Onkelos to Gen. 41:32, as well as the slightly different expression in Ex. 18:17 and Deut. 1:14.

וּכְתִיב: "כָּל [אִישׁ] יִשְׂרָאֵל כְּאִישׁ אֶחָד חֲבֵרִים" (שופטים כ,יא) - כְּמוֹ שֶׁאִישׁ אֶחָד מְחוּבָּר מֵאֵבָרִים רַבִּים, וּבְהִפָּרְדָם נוֹגֵעַ בַּלֵּב כִּי מִמֶּנּוּ תּוֹצְאוֹת חַיִּים.

as it is written, "All the men of Israel… as one man, comrades" (Judg. 20:11); **just as one man is comprised of many limbs, and when they are separated the heart is affected, "for out of it are the issues of life."**

The author of the *Tanya* follows the plain meaning of this citation, that all of Israel is like a single man. There is a difference between a group of people and a group of limbs from one body. People can separate from each other, but the limbs of the body depend on one another. They cannot separate, and if they do, they will cease to live. The author of the *Tanya* is saying that all the souls of Israel are not like a mere group of people but comparable to the limbs of a single body, such that if they become separated, they will have no life, God forbid.

The heart is the center of the life of all the limbs of man, from which life spreads to all the other limbs and to which it returns. All this movement of life, which is life itself, depends on the fact that the organs are all connected to each other, as they receive from one another and give to each other. They are not like separate parts between whom there are calculations and deliberations, but like the limbs of the body, which do not feel that they are in opposition to the others. There is no barrier between one and the other, but rather the person whose limbs they are feels them all as one single unity. If one becomes separated, this concerns more than the limb that was removed, it also affects the heart and impairs the entire network of life-force that spreads throughout all the limbs.

אִם כֵּן אֲנַחְנוּ, הֱיוֹת כּוּלָּנוּ כְּאִישׁ אֶחָד מַמָּשׁ, תִּיכּוֹן הָעֲבוֹדָה בַּלֵּב, וּמִכְּלַל הֵן כו'.

If so, with regard to **us, since we are all literally like one person, the service will be secured in the heart; and from the affirmative…**

"From the affirmative, you can derive the negative," that is, if they are not like one actual person, then the service will not be secured in the heart.

The expressions "affects the heart," and especially "the service will be secured in the heart," have a double meaning. The heart, as in the metaphor, is the organ at the center of life, and its flow of life depends on the unity between the limbs,[23] and correspondingly on the unity between the individuals in the collective. However, the author of the *Tanya* is also undoubtedly referencing the meaning of the expression "the service of the heart" as the service of prayer. Prayer is the heart of Hasidism, the source and result of hasidic life. The vitality of the hasidim depends on prayer, and ultimate hasidic prayer in turn is contingent on the unity amongst the hasidim, like one man.

וְעַל כֵּן נֶאֱמַר: "וּלְעָבְדוֹ שְׁכֶם אֶחָד" דַּוְקָא.

And it is therefore stated: "And to serve Him with one consent" – specifically.

The word *shekhem*, here translated as "consent," also means "shoulder." Elsewhere,[24] the author of the *Tanya* explains that this word for shoulder implies behind the shoulder, which in spiritual terms is another word for the "backside." Everything on the inside has an essential unity, in contrast to the backside, which is the place of multiplicity and separation. The expression "one *shekhem*" thus means that the separate backside unites with the internality, and even nullifies itself in the light of the inner essence. Accordingly, the verse is saying that service, the rectification of man and the world, is to "to serve Him with one *shekhem*,"[25] to unite the *shekhem*, the backside and the other, with the interiority and unity. ☞ ☞

וְעַל כֵּן אֲהוּבַיי יְדִידַיי, נָא וְנָא לִטְרוֹחַ בְּכָל לֵב וְנֶפֶשׁ לְתְקוֹעַ אַהֲבַת רֵעֵהוּ בְּלִבּוֹ,

Therefore, my beloved ones, my friends, I implore you greatly, that you should toil with all your heart **and all** your **soul to secure in your heart, love of one's fellow man;**

23. See also Letter 31, below.

24. See *Torah Or* 102b and elsewhere.

25. The quotation is from Zephaniah 3:9. See also Genesis 48:22: "And I have given to you one section [*shekem*] beyond your brothers."

Here the author of the *Tanya* articulates his practical conclusion, what must actually be done. This is why he does not say that there has to be love, that is too abstract, but that one should work hard and not give up, until the love arises. How should one do this and how much energy should he invest? "You should make every effort (lit. with all the heart and soul)." In other words, a half-hearted attempt, for a half an hour a day, or if there is time, is not enough. Rather, one must toil until nothing is left, not a moment and not a single fiber of the soul that is not committed to this undertaking.

The phrase "to impress into the heart the love of one's fellow man" means to pin one's thoughts on the necessity and truth of this advice, until he feels towards the other as he feels towards himself. He must then etch this feeling firmly "into the heart," and not let the heart stop feeling, but engrave it deeper and deeper.

The author of the *Tanya* here employs a similar expression to the one the Torah used in relation to the love of God, "with all your heart and with all your soul,"[26] but in reference to the love between a person

EXTERNAL UNITY LEADS TO INTERNAL UNITY

☞ On the basic level, the author of the *Tanya* is referring here to the unity between the hasidim, not the unity of souls on high. However, the lofty unity and cleaving (through prayer) can be achieved only by means of unity below, "you shall love your neighbor as yourself." Essential unity cannot be divided; it is impossible for there to be unity above while there is no unity below. Therefore, as long as in one's thoughts, he does not feel unity and love below, towards his immediate, real surroundings, towards the people who are with him, he will be unable to attain unity and love above.

LIKE ONE PERSON, THE SERVICE WILL BE SECURED IN THE HEART

☞ The ascent into the spiritual worlds that a person experiences in prayer, involves an internal transformation – if he does not change, he has evidently not really ascended, but it only seems to him that he has risen upwards. One of the changes is an increasing blurring of the boundaries between the "I" and the "other." The differences in interests, personalities, and at the root of everything the chasm between "me" and everyone else, gradually disappear, becoming less and less significant. If that does not occur, then the individual does not ascend.

---

26. This expression appears in several places in Deuteronomy, the most famous of which is the chapters of the *Shema*. It is not surprising that the author of the

and his fellow man. This is because, as stated here, one love cannot exist without the other, as they are all basically one single dynamic of love.

"וְאִישׁ אֶת רָעַת רֵעֵהוּ אַל תַּחְשְׁבוּ בִּלְבַבְכֶם" כְּתִיב (זכריה ח,יז).

it is written, "Do not think evil in your hearts, each against his neighbor" (Zech. 8:17).

After speaking about the positive side, the love of one's fellow man, he turns to the negative formulation. Generally, one might refer to the injunction against hating one's neighbor in his heart (Lev. 19:17), but here he cites the verse "let none of you devise evil in your hearts against his neighbor." The reason is that, as explained above, this is the way to achieve the desired end; not simply through a general directive on how things should be, but a specific instruction that can be implemented right now. Furthermore, here we are talking about the love of one's neighbor as the foundation for the inner service of prayer. Thinking badly of one's friend obstructs a person, preventing him from even beginning to pray. We have already learned that in Hasidism that a person is located where his thoughts are;[27] negative thoughts of one's friend attest to his own place.[28] It is he who is enmeshed in that evil, he is trapped in that thought and cannot ascend even a step, since it does not allow him to unite either with his friend below or with his Friend above.

וְלֹא תַּעֲלֶה עַל לֵב לְעוֹלָם, וְאִם תַּעֲלֶה, יְהַדְּפֶנָּה מִלִּבּוֹ כְּהִנְדּוֹף עָשָׁן

Such a thought **should never arise in the heart, and if it does, one should drive it from his heart like smoke is driven away,**

Tanya does not mention here the third clause of the *Shema* – "and with all your might" (Deut. 6:5) – as that is a singular expression, which is also unique in terms of its content. Since it applies specifically to the relationship between a single individual and the One God, it is thus certainly inappropriate in this context.

27. In accordance with the saying of the Ba'al Shem Tov that a person is situated in the place of his will and thoughts. See *Keter Shem Tov*, 48.

28. It is stated in the name of the Ba'al Shem Tov, on the verse: "Your own evildoing shall chastise you" (Jer. 2:19), that the evildoing one sees in the other is actually his own. See *Keter Shem Tov*, Additions, 175-176; *Ba'al Shem Tov al HaTorah, Parashat Bereshit*, from 123 and onwards; see also *Torat Menaḥem*, vol. 11, p. 114.

It is possible that one might momentarily entertain a thought of this kind, as the average person does not have full control over the feelings and thoughts that enter his mind. But if so, "one should drive it from his heart" immediately, so that no trace of it remains, "like smoke" (based on Ps. 68:3). Smoke, after it has evaporated, leaves nothing behind – not even a stain or an impression. It is as though it never existed at all.

וּכְמוֹ מַחֲשֶׁבֶת עֲבוֹדָה זָרָה מַמָּשׁ. **and like actual idolatrous thoughts.**

Such a thought, when a person thinks badly of another, is absolute evil, like the thought of worshipping idols. This extreme comparison is designed to counter the following distorted idea that one might consider: "Since I can perceive evil in my friend, perhaps I should focus on that in order to separate myself from the evil." The author of the *Tanya* therefore states that such a way of thinking is like actual thoughts of idolatry, which by definition, are never okay. There is no justification for such contemplations, and there is no way that anything good could come from them, as the very thought is already idolatrous.[29] Furthermore, just as one who thinks of idolatry thereby separates himself from God, so too one who thinks evil of another separates him from that person, and that, as has been explained, is like separating oneself from God Himself.

כִּי גְדוֹלָה לָשׁוֹן הָרַע כְּנֶגֶד עֲבוֹדָה זָרָה וְגִילּוּי עֲרָיוֹת וּשְׁפִיכוּת דָּמִים, וְאִם בְּדִבּוּר כָּךְ כו'.

For great is the transgression of **malicious speech; it corresponds to idolatry, forbidden sexual relations, and murder** combined. **And if this is the case for** mere **speech...,**

The Talmud in *Arakhin* 15b compares malicious speech to these three cardinal sins, regarding which it is stated that one should allow himself to be killed rather than transgress them; they are not even overridden in a life-threatening situation. They are never permitted at all. If malicious speech is like idolatry etc., this applies even more so to one who entertains evil thoughts about another. For with regard to prayer and

29. See Rambam, *Sefer HaMadda, Hilkhot Avodat Kochavim* 2:3.

the inner service of the heart, one's thoughts have more influence and can be an even greater hindrance than speech and action.

וּכְבָר נוֹדַע לְכָל חֲכַם לֵב יִתְרוֹן הֶכְשֵׁר הַמַּחֲשָׁבָה עַל הַדִּבּוּר

as **it is already known to all who are wise at heart the advantage of the preparation of thought over speech**

The "wise at heart," in this explanatory comment, is one who perceives the inner dimension, who feels the internal dimension and its power.[30] From this perspective, thought is surely more influential than speech. Speech is external to the human soul; a person can choose whether to talk or not, he can talk about one thing and think about another. This is not the case with regard to thought; a person cannot refrain from thinking, and he cannot think one thing and feel another. Thought is united with the soul to such an extent that the person himself is unable to separate the two. Thought takes the soul with it, whether it wants to come or not. ☞

THE PREPARATION OF THOUGHT

☞ This concept, *hekhsher maḥshava*, comes from the laws of ritual purity and impurity. For example, food has been "prepared for impurity," meaning, it has the capacity to become ritually impure, once liquids have fallen on it with the owner's consent. If water fell on it without the owner's consent, the food has not been rendered fit to contract impurity. This consent is one's thought, and thus thought alone, even without speech and action, prepares the foods for the possibility of impurity. However, merely being prepared for impurity is not yet impurity itself; it is only the internal readiness, the removal of the option from a state of irrelevance to becoming an important factor – that the food can now become impure. Here too, it is indeed speech that is the active and creative force, but speaking without thought is worthless. It is the thought that prepares the person, or the situation, for the speech to be meaningful. When a person thinks evil of his neighbor in his heart, he prepares the

30. As it is written, "In the hearts of all the wise hearted I have put wisdom" (Ex. 31:6). Only the wise-hearted can detect the wisdom within the external forms that everyone can see. Elsewhere, the author of the *Tanya* defines this label as applying to "one who is wise and has the heart to understand of his own accord" (*Likkutei Torah*, Lev. 43c). In the context there, he is saying that when one writes a clever dictum, only the wise at heart can discern the inner content from the written letters.

הֵן לְטוֹב וְהֵן לְמוּטָב.

both for the good and for that which lacks the good.

The preparation of thought, and its influence upon the soul, can be highly beneficial. The capacity of good thoughts to make a person feel good and act well is among the most well-known of these effects. This includes one's good thoughts not only about himself, but also concerning others. Whoever is in an environment and atmosphere where good thoughts are entertained will reap their great benefits. This applies even to those who lack the good,[31] as stated above.

וַה' הַטּוֹב, הַמְבָרֵךְ אֶת עַמּוֹ בַּשָּׁלוֹם, יָשִׂים עֲלֵיכֶם שָׁלוֹם וְחַיִּים עַד הָעוֹלָם, כְּנֶפֶשׁ אוֹהֵב נַפְשָׁם מִלֵּב וָנֶפֶשׁ.

May the good Lord, who blesses His people with peace, grant you peace and life forever, as in the soul of he who loves their soul with heart and soul.

The author of the *Tanya* concludes this letter with words of blessing and peace. This blessing suits the content of the letter, which dealt with peace among the hasidim as the key for the continuation of hasidic life and vitality. The final note of the conclusion is that peace and love should reign amongst them as in the soul of the Rebbe himself, "who loves their soul with heart and soul." The Rebbe is the head, the brain and soul, of the hasidim as a whole. In this sense, the Rebbe's personal soul incorporates Hasidism and all of the individual hasidim. It is like

situation to receive impurity, and from that moment his speech, and his every movement and hint, will already set off impurity and destruction. By contrast, a good thought will prepare the speech to function well and with holiness. This does not mean that a thought is more important and harmful than speech, but rather that it prepares the ground for speech, qualifying it to have a significant impact, "for the good and for that which lacks the good," as he proceeds to state.

31. This euphemistic use of the phrase, which literally means "for both the good and for the beneficiary," is a relatively late one. In the rabbinic sources the word *lamutav*, "for the beneficiary," is generally deployed in the context of "returning to the right way" (see e.g., *Megilla* 14a), and thus one can take the expression to mean "both for the good and for he who must return to the good path."

the soul itself with respect to the limbs of the soul and body, which contains all of the vitality that spreads through and is expressed in the limbs, in its essence and pure state, which is how it should be. This is his blessing to them, that all of this should apply to them in their material, external forms as it is within his own soul.

This short letter, which relates to the time and concerns of the Liozna Regulations, dealt with another aspect of the construction and formation of the hasidic society, not only the establishments of protocols, but also – and mainly – the spiritual, inner side of Hasidism, which is expressed in the service of prayer. After prayer had been relegated for generations to an uncertain place between the Torah and the mitzvot, which were the main focus of Judaism, Hasidism restored prayer to the center of religious life – less as the request for one's needs and more as a way to connect and cleave to God, and to enable the transcendence of man and the faculties of his soul through his self-abnegation to the Divine. Prayer, in this sense, includes not only the prayer of an individual but also communal prayer in the most comprehensive sense, meaning all of Israel, the Assembly of Israel, and the Divine Presence that is within Israel, for which the *minyan*, quorum, and the group of hasidim serve only as the opening. Even an individual who prays, who ascends and cleaves to the Divine, is no longer a separate entity; he is nullified from that existence and becomes a unique form of expression for reality as a whole. Here the two parts of the letter come together, since a person who prays in this manner cannot afford any separation, especially not from his hasidic brethren. With brotherly love and unity, with the good that each person thinks of his friend, with the reinforcement that he thereby receives – only in this fashion can the individual hasid maintain this stance, and only in this way can they all maintain this service of prayer and their connection to the Rebbe. For in the service of prayer, the hasidim join the Rebbe in his inner task like limbs joining the will of the soul. When the hasidim pray in this manner they are united with the Rebbe, not only as recipients but alongside him in his work. Together they influence and rectify other hasidim, Jews in general, the world, and everything that comes their way. This recalls the story of when the Ba'al Shem Tov prayed at such great length that his entourage had enough time to leave him, go about their affairs, and come back and still had to wait for him to finish. He proceeded to rebuke them for causing a great schism and thereby losing out on very lofty attainment. Cited in *Ba'al Shem Tov al HaTorah, Parashat No'aḥ, Mekor Mayim Ḥayyim* 23.

Epistle 23

This epistle that predates the previous letters, was apparently written during the author of the *Tanya's* early years in Liozna, around the year 5545.[1] Its content is similar to the previous epistle[2] that addressed the topic of prayer and emphasized praying with a quorum of Hasidim. In the same vein, this epistle addresses the power of collective prayer, yet takes it one step further to explain the nature of the collective and the reason why a quorum of Jews that gather not only for prayer, but also for Torah study, and even without any particular activity,[3] draws down a degree of holiness higher than the holiness found in any world, due to their very being together.

The epistle is divided into two parts, the first is theoretical and deep, the second – practical. The first section explores the nature of these phenomena; what is the fabric of that boundless holiness, ungraspable by man and angel alike, that resides particularly on ten Jews? This epistle does not exhaust the topic. However, it sufficiently gives the Hasidim an awe-inspiring, humble recognition of the residing

1. According to the *Iggerot Hakodesh* of the author of the *Tanya* (there it is epistle 5.)

2. As previously mentioned, the letters were arranged for print, not according to chronological order, but according to content.

3. As mentioned in this epistle, and at greater length in other places, that even when those Jews are not engaging in Torah or any other matter of holiness, their very being together, brings about the residing of the Divine Presence. This letter, however, focuses on learning Torah in a group, which draws down the residing of the Divine Presence to another deeper and more powerful degree, than when they are not doing anything.

of the Divine Presence in a quorum of Jews. The second section brings these concepts to their practical application. It arouses the Hasidim to strengthen themselves in the laws and customs of the synagogue, which is the place where the quorum assembles and the Divine Presence dwells.

20 Tishrei

17 Tishrei (leap year)

"בִּגְזֵירַת עִירִין פִּתְגָמָא וּמֵאמַר קַדִּישִׁין" **"By the decree of the angels and the verdict by the word of the holy ones,"**

While this verse addresses angels,[4] the sages related it to Torah scholars who are like the ministering angels (*Pesaḥim* 33a.)[5]

חַכְמֵי הַמִּשְׁנָה עֲלֵיהֶם הַשָּׁלוֹם **the Sages of the Mishna, may they rest in peace,**

The concepts elucidated in this epistle about the holiness of the quorum are not rationally comprehensible, therefore, the author of the *Tanya* connects them to the Sages of the Mishna, whose teachings constitute the oral Torah; like a heavenly decree uttered by angels.

שֶׁשָּׁנוּ בְּמִשְׁנָתָם: "עֲשָׂרָה שֶׁיּוֹשְׁבִין וְעוֹסְקִין בַּתּוֹרָה שְׁכִינָה שְׁרוּיָה בֵּינֵיהֶם" (אבות פרק ג משנה ו). **who taught in their Mishna, "Ten who are sitting and are engaging with the Torah, the Divine Presence rests amongst them"** (*Avot* 3:6).

In a similar saying of the Sages[6] that is brought in *Likkutei Amarim* at the end of chapter eleven and later on in this epistle, it says, "Wherever there are ten Jews, the Divine Presence dwells." The difference is that here it says, the Divine Presence dwells amongst them," meaning within them, in their depths, whereas the former intention of the residing of the Divine Presence is only as a surrounding light.[7] It follows that ten

4. Daniel 4:14

5. Rashi there on *Pesaḥim* (note from the Lubavitcher Rebbe, Rabbi Menaḥem Mendel Schneerson.)

6. *Sanhedrin* 39a.

7. *Likkutei Amarim*, chap. 11 speaks of even totally wicked people, that the holiness

Jews who sit and engage in Torah study, enjoy a double benefit, that of the ten Jews who are gathered together who are privy to the residing of the Divine Presence as a surrounding light, and the effect of their Torah study which brings about the shining of an internal light that can be felt in a tangible way. The combination of both of these, of a surrounding light that penetrates inside, is the topic of the epistle.

כִּי זֶה כָּל הָאָדָם, וְאַף גַּם זֹאת הָיְתָה כָּל יְרִידָתוֹ בָּעוֹלָם הַזֶּה לְצוֹרֶךְ עֲלִיָּה זוֹ, אֲשֶׁר אֵין עֲלִיָּה לְמַעְלָה הֵימֶנָּה.

For this is the whole of man, and moreover, his entire descent to this world was for the sake of this ascent, over which there is no higher ascent.

This is a reference to Ecclesiastes and means, "this is the purpose of man's creation,"[8] to draw down the indwelling presence of the Divine into himself and into the world.

The root of man's soul is incredibly high, literally a piece of God above. Its manifestation in a body in this lowest of worlds entails a gaping descent to the ultimate degree that spans the entire spectrum of reality.[9] A known principle in the service of God is that the purpose of every descent is the ascent that follows it. The bigger the descent, the greater the ascent that follows. If the descent reached the absolute lowest place, then the following ascent will scale the absolute highest place. It follows, that if this is the whole purpose of man's existence, then there cannot be anything higher than it, since it is not a stage that leads to something else, but rather, "this is the whole of man." ☞

DESCENT FOR THE SAKE OF ASCENT

☞ It is explained elsewhere (see *Likkutei Biurim*), that the ascent referred to here is not like every other ascent that follows a "descent that was for the purpose of the ascent." Meaning, with a descent that is followed by an ascent, the two are separate.

---

exists only in a surrounding way upon them and does not shine into the depths of their spiritual faculties.

8. Similarly, the Sages comment on this phrase from Ecclesiastes "For this is the whole of man," Rabbi Elazar said, "God said, the whole world was only created for this purpose."

9. See *Likkutei Amarim*, chap. 36 and also 31 and 45.

כִּי שְׁכִינַת עוּזּוֹ אֲשֶׁר בְּגָבְהֵי מְרוֹמִים, וְהַשָּׁמַיִם וּשְׁמֵי הַשָּׁמַיִם לֹא יְכַלְכְּלוּ אֵימָתָהּ - תִּשְׁכּוֹן וְתִתְגַּדֵּל בְּתוֹךְ בְּנֵי יִשְׂרָאֵל,

As His power's presence, which is in the highest of heights, and whose dread the heavens and the heaven of heavens cannot contain, shall reside and be magnified amongst the children of Israel,

This quote is from King Solomon's prayer for the dedication of the Temple (I Kings, 8:27). King Solomon's sentiment perfectly encapsulates what the author of the *Tanya* is explaining. Beyond all God's manifestations of Self, beyond everything He does, beyond the entire created universe, God Himself exists, "His power's presence, which is in the highest of heights." He surrounds all worlds and transcends all, "whose dread the heavens and the heaven of heavens cannot contain." Neither the heavens above the earth, which are totally refined, spiritual and abstract compared to the earth, nor the "heavens of the heavens," which are absolutely spiritual and abstract compared to the heavens, can contain the dread of the presence of the Divine. When a person contemplates this utterly separate and lofty level, then he feels an immense, overwhelming awe which is called "awe of God's exaltedness." Yet, this unfathomably huge, overwhelmingly infinite Divine Presence can reside, manifest and even grow greater amongst the Jewish people in a quorum of Jews who are learning Torah and praying together. ☞

The ascent is relative to the descent that preceded it, and receives its power and meaning from it, like an answer to a question or payment for work; connected, yet separate. In contrast, here, there is no ascent that follows the descent. This descent turns out to be an unimaginably huge elevation in and of itself.

HIS POWER'S PRESENCE...SHOULD RESIDE AND BE MAGNIFIED

☞ King Solomon presents this very paradox, which is expressed in the version of *kedusha* from the morning prayers of Shabbat and festivals, in his prayer for the dedication of the Temple: "How is it possible that the infinite Divine Presence of God, that even the highest heavens cannot contain, will reside in this house?" By quoting King Solomon's prayer, the author of the *Tanya* hints that the same paradox is at play when ten men engage in Torah and mitzvot together. The Divine Presence not only "resides" with them, but "is magnified amongst the Jewish people," as will be explained later. When the Divine Presence resides with the Jewish people, it gets elevated higher than its original level, the elevation within the descent, as implied by the opening words of this epistle.

כְּמוֹ שֶׁכָּתוּב: "כִּי אֲנִי ה' שׁוֹכֵן בְּתוֹךְ בְּנֵי יִשְׂרָאֵל" (במדבר לה, לד),

as it is written, "For I am the Lord, who rests in the midst of the children of Israel" (Num. 35:34),

This verse speaks of the indwelling Divine Presence particularly amongst the Jewish people, which is why it employs the term "children of Israel" in the collective. This residing of the Divine Presence is the type that arises in the presence of a coalesced group and not for individuals alone. An individual person expresses one instance, one expression of the Jewish essence as refracted through his particular set of life-circumstances. While, when the entirety of the Jewish people, as expressed by a quorum of men, gathers together, the quintessential Jewish essence shines, and the infinite Divine becomes manifest.[10] (This also happens to a certain degree in the deepest depths of every Jew, as will be explained later.)

עַל יְדֵי עֵסֶק הַתּוֹרָה וְהַמִּצְוֹת, בַּעֲשָׂרָה דַּוְקָא,

through engagement in Torah and mitzvot, specifically in a group of **ten,**

However, there is a seeming contradiction in this verse. The verse uses the word *betokh* which, in addition to meaning "among," also means "within." This implies that the light shines as an inner light into each and every person, not only as a surrounding light. Therefore, the author of the *Tanya* adds this piece about Torah learning and mitzva performance to explain that when they are engaged in them, they are privy to both: the surrounding light that comes as a result of the ten simply gathering together and the inner light that is shined into each one personally as a result of the divine service that they do when they are together.

Every Jew, in his essential divine soul, is one with the entire Jewish people; it is the garments of his soul that separates him from the rest of the nation as an individual. When he engages in Torah study and mitzvot, however, his inner divine soul is revealed and made manifest, therefore, the Divine Presence becomes revealed within him individually as well.

---

10. This is the unique power that an assembly of Jews has, like a group that gathers to pray, their prayer is always heard. See *Rosh HaShana* 18a and Rambam, *Sefer HaMadda, Hilkhot Teshuva* 2:6. Conversely, there is a deep rift caused when a group is not humbled in unity, and is rather ridden with hatred and controversy.

כְּמוֹ שֶׁאָמְרוּ רַבּוֹתֵינוּ ז"ל: אָתְיָא "תּוֹךְ" "תּוֹךְ" כו' (ברכות כא,ב).

as our Rabbis stated: It is inferred by a verbal analogy between the words **"among," "among,"** ... (*Berakhot* 21a).

Now the author of the *Tanya* explains the reason for the number ten. The Talmud states that an individual person praying does not recite the *kedusha;* only in the congregation, like the verse says, "I (God) am sanctified amongst (*betokh*) the children of Israel." The term "children of Israel" refers to a group of Jews. This is learned from a Talmudic inference (*gezeira shava*) when the same word appears in two different verses. The word "*tokh,*" amongst, also appears in the verse "Separate yourselves from the midst (*tokh*) of this congregation" (Num. 16:21.) The word for congregation in this verse is "*eida,*" which always means at least ten. That the term "*eida*" always refers to at least ten is learned from another Talmudic inference, in which the group of spies is referred to as an "*eida,*" "How long will it be with this evil congregation (*eida*)?" (ibid 14:27.) There were twelve spies, two of which were not included in this statement; Calev and Joshua did not sin and thus were not considered "evil." Ten are left over.[11]

וְעַל זֶה נֶאֱמַר: "בְּקִרְבְּךָ קָדוֹשׁ" (הושע יא,ט),

Regarding this, the verse states, "I am **sacred in your midst**" (Hos. 11:9),

The surrounding light of God that transcends the awareness of the members of the quorum, will dwell and be manifest through Torah study and mitzva-performance "in your midst," within the realm of your conscious awareness.

---

11. See *Megilla* 23b. The Rebbe Rayatz [Rabbi Yosef Yitzḥak Schneerson] asks, in a conversation quoted also in *Likkutei Biurim* here, "Why do the sages learn that an "*eida*" and "*tzibur*" is specifically ten men from the verse "separate yourselves from the midst of this congregation," that refers to the congregation of Koraḥ? Because in this verse, Moses refers to the surrounding power of evil that plagues the congregation that erred. He could have fixed the inner essence, and would not have had to warn "separate yourselves." Conversely, in holiness, ten draw down a surrounding light of holiness."

וְאֵין דָּבָר שֶׁבִּקְדוּשָּׁה בִּפָּחוֹת מֵעֲשָׂרָה (ברכות שם).

and there is no act of sanctity in a group **fewer than ten** (*Berakhot* 21a).

Since the "holiness" does not dwell upon an individual person but rather upon the group, comprised of a minimum of ten people, therefore, "an expression of holiness" is only recited in the presence of ten people.

"An expression of holiness," refers to the recitation of *kedusha, barkhu,* Torah reading and more, and the order of congregational prayer in general. All of these are ways of drawing down not just a distant revelation of God like an echo of a ripple-effect of His influence, but rather, God Himself, as it were, the great Holy One, that is utterly transcendent of all. As previously explained in relation to the residing of the Divine Presence, this level of revelation cannot manifest in a limited, incomplete vessel, as is every individual person when they are alone. Only a congregation, at least ten Jewish men, who together create a new entity that surpasses all the individual entities that comprise it, can be a vessel for "an expression of holiness."

וּמִשּׁוּם הָכִי נַמִּי אִצְטְרִיךְ לְהוּ לְרַבּוֹתֵינוּ ז״ל לְמֵילַף מִקְּרָא, ״מִנַּיִן שֶׁאֲפִילוּ אֶחָד שֶׁיּוֹשֵׁב וְעוֹסֵק בַּתּוֹרָה כו׳״.

And for this reason, too, our Rabbis had to derive from a verse, "From where is it learned **that** God allots reward **even** for **one who sits and engages in the Torah...?"**

After this whole discussion, one may conclude that Torah study with less than ten people is not worthwhile at all. Therefore, the author of the *Tanya* comments here that the Sages[12] needed to anchor the truth

12. *Avot* 3:2. It is unclear which *Mishna* the author of the *Tanya* was referencing. There is room to say that he intended *Mishna* 6, as brought as the probable source in *Likkutei Biurim*): "From where do we know that even one [who studies alone is privy to the Divine Presence]? As it says, "In every place that I will mention my name, I will come to you and bless you." The beginning of that *Mishna* is the *Mishna* that was brought at the beginning of the epistle: Ten sit and engage in Torah study, the Divine Presence dwells amongst them." Yet, since later on, the author of the *Tanya* speaks about the allocation of reward, it makes sense to say that he was referencing *Mishna* 2 that talks about reward. In several places, *Or HaTorah* of the Tzemaḥ Tzedek, and Lessons in *Tanya*. In *Likkutei Biurim,* he says that *Mishna* 6 is learned from *Mishna* 2, that also there the intention is of an

of the immeasurable value of even one person who sits and learns Torah alone in a verse: "Let him sit alone and be silent, because he took it upon himself" (Lam. 3:28). The fact that a person learning alone is necessary in addition to learning with ten shows that they are not the same thing. There is an essential difference between Torah study in the presence of ten, and with less, as will be detailed below.

וְאַף גַּם זֹאת לֹא מָצְאוּ לוֹ סֶמֶךְ מִן הַמִּקְרָא אֶלָּא לִקְבִיעַת שָׂכָר בִּלְבַד **And even so, they only found support for this from Scripture with regard to the allocation of a reward**

As the *Mishna* says, God allocates reward." Meaning, the illumination that is drawn down to an individual that studies Torah is as reward, not the actual illumination of the Torah that he learned. Receiving reward, as discussed elsewhere (Avot 1:3), is also called "*pras.*" The word "*pras*" also means a piece, a portion. Reward is only a superficial illumination of the thing, a mere part of it, not the thing itself. For example, it is the hired employee who receives payment for working, not the owner of the company. The employee works, and is thus deserving of pay, however, the crux of the work that he does is not actually his.

לְיָחִיד לְפִי עֶרְכּוֹ, **to the individual, in accordance with his worth,**

The reward is a limited illumination that enters the vessel of the receiver, and therefore is received according to the level and vessel of each and every person: according to his intellectual and emotional capacities, his IQ at the present moment, his skill level and effort that he invests. Even more so, it could be that the reward is not the actual thing, but rather makes itself compatible to the recipient. For example, that which we register through our senses is never the actual entity that we are experiencing, but rather, its appearance, its sound, etc. Even of its overall appearance, sound... we only register that which falls within

---

individual (and any number less than ten) it is only talking about allocation of reward (on various levels, because there is a difference between one, two, three...) Yet, only with ten, will there be a residing of the actual Divine Presence.

our audio and visual range. However, when the recipient enters into the domain of the thing itself, the thing does not take into account the observer and his limitations at all.

לְפִי [נוּסָח אַחֵר: וּלְפִי] עֵרֶךְ הַמְרוּבִּים. **in accordance with (an alternative version: and in accordance with) the worth of the many.**

The *Mishna* speaks not only of the individual, but about two people, three, five... who are sitting together learning. Every additional person brings extra value to the learning. Therefore, the illumination of reward that each person receives is not only commensurate to his own personal spiritual level, but is rather a product of the overall level of all the participants combined. Therefore, though they are not privy to the residing of the light of *Ein Sof* itself, they are not only receiving the limited illumination that they would if they were learning alone.

The difference between the two versions is the "*vav* of conjunction," which means "and." The meaning of "according to the worth of the many," without the *vav,* is that when there is more than one person studying Torah together (but less than ten), every individual receives reward according to the overall value of the group. This reward increases as the number of people increase. The version that has a *vav*-of conjunction and reads "*and* in accordance with the many" implies that a person learning with a group reaps the reward of his own spiritual level and effort in addition to the reward of the group as a whole.

Either way, the illumination of the reward is limited, in that it is allocated according to the spiritual level of the individual or the group.

אֲבָל לְעִנְיַן הַשְׁרָאַת קְדוּשַּׁת הַקָּדוֹשׁ בָּרוּךְ הוּא, אֵין לוֹ עֵרֶךְ אֲלֵיהֶם כְּלָל. **However, with regard to the manifestation of the sanctity of the Holy One, blessed be He,** the individual **has no worth in relation to** the congregation **at all.**

The revelation of God's all-encompassing essence that manifests particularly when ten people engage in Torah study together, is not commensurate with the spiritual or intellectual capacity of the individual or group of learners. The residing of the holiness of God is a revelation of the actual light of *Ein Sof* as explained above.[13]

21 Tishrei

18 Tishrei (leap year)

וְהַהֶפְרֵשׁ שֶׁבֵּין 'הַשְׁרָאָה' לִ'קְבִיעוּת שָׂכָר' מוּבָן לִמְבִינֵי מַדָּע, כִּי קְבִיעַת שָׂכָר הוּא שֶׁמֵּאִיר ה' לְנֶפֶשׁ תִּדְרְשֶׁנּוּ בְּאוֹר תּוֹרָתוֹ,

The difference between "manifestation" and "allocation of a reward" is comprehended by those who understand knowledge. For the allocation of a reward is that God illuminates upon the soul that seeks Him, with the light of His Torah,

"Comprehended by those who understand knowledge" refers to anyone who engages in the deeper dimension of the Torah and is familiar with the basic distinction between concepts such as essence versus illumination and surrounding light versus inner light.

The allocation of reward is the allotment of particular illumination from the light of the Torah that a person learned, that he can relate to. This allocation depends on the capacity of one's soul and faculties that the individual cultivated for himself, through his actions, degree of energy-investment, true desires and capacity for receiving. ☞

THE SOUL THAT SEEKS HIM

☞ The reward, the divine light, that reaches a particular soul in a way that it can register and experience, is not an automatic result of one's spiritual aptitude or of performing a particular devotional act. No person can ever reach or acquire the infinite by his own efforts, no matter what. God shining His light unto a person, an experience incalculably beyond human reach, is always a result of God's simple desire to emerge from His infinite realm and connect with a finite being. The vessel, or in the language of Hasidism, the "arousal from below," to draw down this supernal will, is when man leaves his own constricted human realm to relate to the Divine.

---

13. The Lubavitcher Rebbe, Rabbi Menaḥem Mendel Schneerson, comments on a seeming contradiction: It says in *Avot* 3:2, that when two sit together and speak words of Torah, the Divine Presence resides amongst them. He suggests a reconciliation according to *Or HaTorah Ekev* 70, 5542. And see this idea explained at length in the edition of the *Tanya* with *Likkutei Peirushim* adapted by Rabbi Chitrik.

שֶׁהוּא מַעֲטֶה לְבוּשׁוֹ מַמָּשׁ. **which is the actual covering of His garment.**

All light is a revelation, and every revelation is a type of garment of the one who is revealing Himself. The world is filled with lights that reveal every element of the universe, however, the light that reveals God is the light of the Torah.

The Torah is the light which comprises the garment of God Himself. The world is filled with lights that express aspects of the Divine and crystalize to become every aspect of existence, yet the light that reveals God Himself is the light of the Torah. ☞

וְלָכֵן נִקְרֵאת הַתּוֹרָה 'אוֹר' שֶׁנֶּאֱמַר: "עֹטֶה אוֹר כַּשַּׂלְמָה" (תהלים קד,ב). **Accordingly, the Torah is called "light," as it is stated, "Enveloping with light as though with a cloak"** (Ps. 104:2).

This is the light of divine essence. "The truth of the Lord is forever (Ps. 117:2)," besides for God, no other truth or reality exists. This is the One revealed through the Torah.

The Torah is called light, because it is totally and utterly a revelation. Every other revelation is also a concealment. It reveals relative to the

This is the "the soul that seeks Him" (see Lam. 3:25) only the seeking, yearning soul, who is ready to step out of its own box by learning Torah with pure intentions, by praying with every ounce of his being, by cleaving to the Divine, will merit this reward. "According to the pain, that is his reward" (Avot 5: 23). The degree to which the soul sacrifices leaving its comfort zone in the constrictions of this world, does it merit reward, the light of the *Ein Sof* constricting itself by leaving its infinite realm, to fill the dimension of a human being.

THE LIGHT OF THE TORAH; THE COVERING OF HIS GARMENT

☞ The light reveals just like a garment presents the wearer and lends insight into him. The garment mediates between what is being revealed, and the revealer, making them compatible. For example, people do not leave their houses, that is, reveal themselves outwardly, unless they are wearing appropriate garb. Thought only reveals itself when it is clothed in speech that is appropriate and compatible with the receiver; the right language, relevant concepts etc. In this sense, God's garb is the light of the Torah that reveals, not the ripple effect of His action, nor the leftover imprint of something that someone, person, or angel, experienced, but rather God Himself clothed within it.

source, therefore, when one thing is revealed, another is concealed. This does not apply to the Torah, because it reveals the source of all sources, the truth that holds and encompasses everything, the revelation out of whose purview nothing lies; therefore, it is called "Light."

Just like a garment conceals that which it covers, it also reveals an aspect of it.[14] Similarly, the light of the Torah reveals to every person the infinite, limitless, God, in a revelation that is compatible with his level of awareness.[15]

וְהַנֶּפֶשׁ הִיא בַּעֲלַת גְּבוּל וְתַכְלִית בְּכָל כֹּחוֹתֶיהָ, **The soul has defined limits to all of its strengths;**

One's intellectual faculties are limited in their cognitive and analytic capabilities; there is a limit to the number of concepts that a person can internalize in his lifetime. One's emotional faculties are also limited. Some highly intelligent people who are capable of grasping very abstract concepts lack the emotional intelligence to feel those concepts on an emotional level.

לָכֵן גַּם אוֹר ה׳ הַמֵּאִיר בָּהּ הוּא גְּבוּלִי מְצוּמְצָם וּמִתְלַבֵּשׁ בְּתוֹכָהּ. **therefore, the light of God that shines into it is also limited, constricted, and is enclothed within it.**

It is important to emphasize here that the light of the Torah, despite its being constricted more and more with each level that it descends, always remains the garment of light that enclothes God Himself. This is the power of the Torah, wherever and however it may express itself, it always reveals God's inner will (*Ratzon*), true divine wisdom (*Hokhma*).

14. See *Yahel Or* (a commentary on Psalms by the Tzemaḥ Tzedek): The Torah is the light [referred to] in the verse "Enveloping with light as with a cloak."

15. As the Lubavitcher Rebbe, Rabbi Menaḥem Mendel Schneerson, comments, that the verse "a mitzva is a flame and the Torah is the light" seems to be a fitting one for the author of the *Tanya* to bring here. He uses another verse because his intention is to bring a proof that God shines through the light of His Torah, like how a cloak reveals several aspects of its wearer (*Lessons in Tanya.*)

וְעַל כֵּן יִתְפַּעֵל לֵב מְבַקְשֵׁי ה׳ Consequently, the hearts of those who seek the Lord are enthused

When the light of God shines into the "soul that seeks Him" in the form of reward, within the capacity of the recipient, one's heart does not remain apathetic; it is aroused with love and fear for that which is being revealed to it. This is the meaning of this verse, that those who truly seek God are ultimately privy to the enthused heart.

בִּשְׁעַת הַתְּפִלָּה וְכַיּוֹצֵא בָּהּ. at the time of prayer and the like.

The time of prayer is generally the opportunity for a person to seek out God. "The time of prayer" does not just mean the hours of the prayer service, but rather, the entire picture: a settled mind at the opportune time, during the fitting order and version of prayer, articulating words that hold inspiring content. The heart that becomes enthused as it glimpses the light of God is not just a result of doing the right thing at the right time, even with the best of intentions, but rather, it is a gift from above, bestowed to him while being present in those circumstances. Someone who has cleared his head of extraneous thoughts, prepares himself to utter the words of the siddur with intention and deeply settles into prayer, will usually be blessed with an inspired his heart.

The established prayer times are not the only times that one's heart can become enthused. True, the time of prayer is auspicious, this is why the sages established these times and infused the potential for powerful connection into the spiritual fabric of them. The power of the Jewish people lies in these set times, yet still, this concept of the enthused heart is essentially private and personal. Even the same person will experience this heartfelt feeling of inspiration differently depending on his life situation; where he happens to be and the state of his inner world at a given moment. It could be that today it was before the prayer service that a person felt moved when saying a certain psalm, or at any other time that he turned to truly face God. Naturally, it is a beautiful thing for one's heart to be stirred at any time, not necessarily during prayer, which is what these two words, "and the like" connote.

כִּי בוֹ יִשְׂמַח לִבָּם וְיָגִיל אַף גִּילַת וְרַנֵּן, For their hearts rejoice in it, and will be happy, even with joy and exaltation,

This wording that includes several words for joy, appears in many places in the teachings of the author of the *Tanya,* and expresses various degrees of joy in the revelation of the light of God: "*simḥa, gila,* and *rina.*" "*Simḥa*" is the joy of the revelation, because joy and revelation always go hand in hand; when there is joy there is revelation, when there is revelation there is joy. "*Gila*" is a deeper, concealed happiness that relates to the hidden layers of life that have not yet been revealed.[16] And "*rina*" is the exaltation of yearning with perfect trust for the revelation of that which is totally hidden in darkness and concealment.[17]

וְתִתְעַנֵּג נַפְשָׁם בְּנוֹעַם ה׳ and their souls will delight in the pleasantness of the Lord

Elsewhere, in *Iggerot Hakodesh,*[18] the author of the *Tanya* explains that "the pleasantness of the Lord" is the hidden light that God hid for the righteous in the world to come. It has this name because the experience of this revelation of divine light is a bliss that surpasses all the delights of this world. The sages say that in this light one can see from one end of the world to the other (*Ḥagiga 12a*), meaning that the world and all of its noise do not conceal this light. To the contrary, in this light, every detail of life brightly shines with the revelation of its purpose. Anyone privy to reveling in the light of this divine perfection feels inexpressible euphoria. ☞

[נוּסָח אַחֵר: עַל ה׳] (an alternative version: on the Lord)

---

16. As it says, "He engulfed His secret place in darkness," (Ps. 18:12.) And see *Torah Or,* parashat *Miketz, Rani Visimkhi,* and in the *Biur* (36:4).

17. See *Likkutei Torah,* Deuteronomy 1:3, there and 48:2.

18. Epistle 29: "Now this light, which is hidden for the righteous in the messianic future, is called "the pleasantness of Hashem" and "the *tzaḥtzaḥot* to delight in Hashem," And it is called "the 400 worlds of yearning [*kissufin*]" in which the righteous delight. As the verse states: "Four hundred silver [*kesef*] shekels" (Gen. 23:16). This light has a very great many qualities and levels, rising ever higher. But the minute illumination that descends level after level to create this garment belongs to the lowest level of this light. Metaphorically speaking, it is called the external level and that which is rearmost [*aḥorayim*]."

This alternate version emphasizes even more saliently the lesson that the author of the *Tanya* is imparting. The divine name used here, the name of *Havaya*, is the name of God that lends existence to everything. The phrase then reads "higher than the name of *Havaya*." This entails ascending to a realm next to God Himself, as it were, not as creator, which is a role that albeit all-powerful, still works within the parameters and therefore limitations of this world, but rather by the totally transcendent aspect of God, as explained above.

וְאוֹרוֹ, בְּהִגָּלוֹתוֹ מִמַּעֲטֵה לְבוּשׁוֹ שֶׁהִיא הַתּוֹרָה, "וְיָצָא כַבָּרָק חִצּוֹ" (זכריה ט,יד).

and His light, when it is revealed from the covering of His garment, which is the Torah; "and His arrow will emerge like the lightning" (Zech. 9:14).

The garment of the Torah, like any garment, both reveals and conceals. Reveals, since it is only through the garment, its shapes and letters, that any glimmer of the light can be gleaned. Yet, it is the garment that appears outwardly, not the content. To the contrary, the content becomes more and more hidden the more garments are layered on top of it. The Torah, therefore, reveals most supernal content: God's desire and wisdom, His love and fear, yet in the garb of extremely worldly things such as an ox, a donkey, *tzitzit* and lulav.

A person can therefore engage in Torah expressed in an ox, a donkey and a lulav, yet not feel the light and supreme love of God that is hidden there. Only a person for whom God "allocates reward" merits

AND THEIR SOULS WILL DELIGHT IN THE PLEASANTNESS OF THE LORD

☞ The Ba'al Shem Tov teaches that God hid this special light not for any future time period, but for the righteous in the Torah (see *Ba'al Shem Tov al HaTorah, Parashat Bereshit* 27 and onward). The Torah calls every Jew a tzaddik, which implies that when any Jewish person learns Torah, he can be privy to this sublime hidden light as his allocation of reward. His prize is the illumination of light perfectly tailored to him and the content of his study, as brought in this epistle. This provides an answer to the question of, how is it possible that a soul in the body can benefit from this light that even the entire world cannot contain. The answer, in the words of the Ba'al Shem Tov, is that it is hidden in the Torah, which is a vessel wider than the entire world, and can contain this light" (see his comments there, 32).

to see how these worldly phenomena are actually "the covering of His garment," revelation of divine light: Torah.

When the divine light from within the garment of Torah bursts through to its learner, it is like to a bolt of lightning. ☞

וְזוֹ הִיא קְבִיעַת שְׂכַר הַתּוֹרָה הַקְּבוּעָה תָּמִיד בְּנֶפֶשׁ עֲמֵלָה בָּהּ.

This is the allocation of the reward of the Torah, which is always established within the soul that **labors in it.**

This particular illumination through the Torah-garment is the reward that is allocated to the learner that is totally dependent on him; he receives this reward, not only in the time to come, when there will be no more body and temporal world to limit that reward, but at any time, according to his degree of investment in Torah study. This is one of the essential emphases of the author of the *Tanya* and Hasidism in general: the reward of divine light is not just hidden for the future, and resigned to be the portion of only the greatest of tzaddikim, but rather is granted to any "soul that labors in it."

19 Tishrei (leap year)

אֲבָל הַהַשְׁרָאָה הִיא הֶאָרָה עֲצוּמָה מֵאוֹר ה' הַמֵּאִיר בָּהּ בְּלִי גְּבוּל וְתַכְלִית,

However, the manifestation is an immense illumination from that light of God that shines in it without definition or limit,

WILL EMERGE LIKE THE LIGHTNING

☞ "An arrow like lightning" is reminiscent of "the flash of lightning" of *Ḥokhma*, Wisdom (see the end of epistle 15, above, and in many other places in fasidic teachings) The faculties of the soul, the intellect and the attributes, are garments for the light of a person's soul, or in the context of God, garments for the light of the Divine. *Ḥokhma,* the first of all, goes out and into the vessels of the soul like a flash of lightning; it has no meaning in and of itself; it is a visionary flash and nothing more. However, like a flash of lightning, it illuminates the entire world for a split second. *Bina* takes it from that moment to the next, and *Da'at,* brings it into one's inner world, into the love and fear etc. This is how the pleasantness and light of God that is hidden in the garment of the Torah emerge every so often, especially during auspicious times like prayer, yet they are not grasped by anything, because, as mentioned above, no vessel can grasp them. Yet still, God's light illuminates all of reality for an instant through the letters of the Torah.

The residing of the Divine Presence, mentioned in the beginning, upon "ten [who] sit and engage in Torah study, applies particularly to ten people gathered together.

In contrast to the allocation of reward, which is a limited illumination allotted according to the particular person's capacity so that he will feel, experience and be transformed through it, ten people together are privy to an indwelling of the Divine Presence that is absolutely boundless, and surpasses the soul's capacity to intellectually or emotionally grasp. ☞

וְאֵינוֹ יָכוֹל לְהִתְלַבֵּשׁ בְּנֶפֶשׁ גְּבוּלִית, **and which cannot be enclothed in a limited soul,**

The residing of the Divine Presence cannot manifest in one's soul, because the soul has its limits. And the finite is incapable of containing the infinite. ☞

IMMENSE ILLUMINATION...WITHOUT DEFINITION OR LIMIT

☞ This residing of the Divine Presence is not an illumination directed at a particular person for a specific reason, but rather, the illumination of the Divine Presence in and of itself. A distant analogy to this is when an individual is purposely speaking to another in a way that he will be able to understand. That which is spoken has a purpose and therefore is tailored to fit within the particular parameters of the situation. Its purpose is to manifest in the soul of the listener to affect him. In contrast, a person can utter a sentence, or think a thought simply to express himself, without having any other motive. This expression has no defined goal and therefore is not limited in any way. The content of this type of thought, which is one's very soul, is an immense, boundless illumination, without any limitation that restricts it to the content of speech that is directed toward a particular person and must be tailored to that listener's mind.

CANNOT BE CONTAINED

☞ Our physical and spiritual senses are inherently limited, and therefore register only sensations that are intrinsically limited. Furthermore, that which our sensations register is the limit, not the sensation itself. For the sake of illustration, it is known, and even clinically proven, that that which the nerves sense is actually the contrast between sensations. Take for example the famous study of the hot frog. When researchers heated the surface that a frog was sitting on ever so gradually, it did not as much as move and was simply roasted on the spot, because it did not feel any contrast. This is how our physical and even spiritual senses work, to a certain degree.

כִּי אִם מַקִּיף עָלֶיהָ מִלְמַעְלָה, **but rather encompasses over it,** the soul, **from above,**

This illumination relates to us; if it does not penetrate, it surrounds. If it does not become enclothed, it enclothes. ☞

מֵרֹאשָׁהּ וְעַד רַגְלָהּ, **from its head to its foot,**

The encompassing light does not relate to the details of the encompassed. From its perspective, there is no difference between head and

We feel love and fear especially at their outer limit. When one paradigm finishes and another begins, that is when we consciously feel. Only when our love is questioned or threatened do we really become aware of it and learn from it what we need to do. It follows that when a boundless illumination becomes unleashed, our spiritual faculties cannot relate to it. In the author of the *Tanya's* words: "it cannot be enclothed in a limited soul."

THE ULTIMATE ENCOMPASSMENT

☞ All the illuminations that a soul receives can be divided into two types: inner and encompassing. An inner illumination is one that is picked up by the intellect, emotions or any other spiritual faculty. An encompassing illumination lies beyond the reaches of every processing center. (That which lies beyond the encompassing illumination is not relevant to our reality.) The encompassing illumination is in a certain sense, the expression of the objective reality that we are living in; not the way in which it is affecting us. This is why it is called encompassing, because, it certainly exists around us, however, it is always much larger than that which we feel and understand.

Even if we do not comprehend or feel the encompassing dimension in the simplest sense, we are still in it, and sometimes, if it is not too far, we can even feel something of it. No matter the physical or spiritual space that a person is in, there is always some environment around him, affecting him, whether consciously or not. For example, people who are walking around a museum will generally not run, or speak loudly or obnoxiously, not because they were warned by the guard, but because they just sense that it is not appropriate there. When a person is very involved with music, then he will think in musical terms even when there is no music playing; he will be more open to rhythmic and melodic sensations. In a deeper sense, we are always in encompassing "spaces," which is basic reality with all of its layers. Not that which we are consciously aware of, but rather, that which undoubtedly determines how we think and act in a deeper and more foundational sense than anything that we can articulate or sense.

The Divine Presence that dwells in a particular place, amongst a particular group of people, becomes the "space" for the soul to be. It is not that the Divine Presence dwells in the location of the synagogue or quorum, but rather, the Divine Presence becomes the space and context of that location.

foot; it affects everything equally. "Encompassing" does not mean that it exists externally and not internally, but rather, its essence transcends the division of levels that an "inner" illumination relates to, as explained at length in *Likkutei Amarim*, chap. 48. The "inner" illumination spans from the head to the foot, which represent the outer edges of it, from beginning to end, everything in between. There are wise people and people of low intelligence, there are rich people and poor people. However, when no distinction is made between levels of intelligence nor degrees of wealth, then, all are equally important, or equally unimportant. In this sense, the encompassing light exists totally equally in every part of the soul, yet is not grasped by any. This is the meaning of "encompasses over it from above, from its head to its foot."

כְּמוֹ שֶׁאָמְרוּ חֲכָמֵינוּ ז"ל: "אַכָּל בֵּי עֲשָׂרָה שְׁכִינְתָּא שַׁרְיָא", כְּלוֹמַר עֲלֵיהֶם מִלְמַעְלָה,

as our Rabbis said, "The Divine Presence dwells on any place where there are ten," that is, over them, from above,

The author of the *Tanya* shows how the wording of the Talmud, "over,"[19] implies that the revelation of the Divine Presence is from above, not within, meaning that it is not comprehended or enclothed in any spiritual faculty of any person, because it transcends everyone's perception to an equal degree; the different levels of the people gathered do not make a difference. Therefore, the relation of the illumination to those ten is that it dwells from above.

כְּמוֹ שֶׁכָּתוּב: "וִיהִי נוֹעַם ה' עָלֵינוּ וּמַעֲשֵׂה יָדֵינוּ כּוֹנְנָה עָלֵינוּ" (תהלים צ,יז). כְּלוֹמַר, כִּי נוֹעַם ה', אֲשֶׁר הוֹפִיעַ בְּמַעֲשֵׂה יָדֵינוּ בְּעֵסֶק הַתּוֹרָה וְהַמִּצְוֹת -

as it is written, "May the graciousness of the Lord our God be upon us, establishing the work of our hands for us" (Ps. 90:17). **In other words, that the graciousness of the Lord, which appeared through the work of our hands, through engagement in Torah and mitzvot –**

19. *Sanhedrin* 39a. There is also a handwritten version "Upon ten," which fits well with what the author of the *Tanya* says here, "meaning, above them from above."

The graciousness of God is the supernal, quintessential, delight in which God Himself delights in Himself, a manifestation of the Divine that God hid because the world cannot yet endure it.

Although this supernal pleasantness totally transcends the world, it also has a way of manifesting in the world: when the world serves as a tool for the performance of Torah and mitzvot. The Hebrew word for "world," *olam,* shares the same root letters as the Hebrew word for "hides," *ma'alim.* When the world is just a world it conceals the light of *Ein Sof,* and the pleasantness of God does not appear in it. However, when a Jew uses the world as a theatre for the performance of Torah and mitzvot, and turns the world into a vessel for the Divine, then it is no longer an obstinate obstacle standing in the way of spiritual connection, but rather reveals the pleasantness of God, that cannot manifest in any other way.

דְּאוֹרַיְיתָא וְקוּדְשָׁא בְּרִיךְ הוּא כּוּלָּא חַד -

as the Torah and the Holy One, blessed be He, are entirely one –

The Torah is unified with God in perfect, absolute unity.[20] The Torah is not like an external garment, that while externally clothing its wearer, remains an independent item, but rather, like a garment that is not separate, and is one with the wearer.[21]

יִתְכּוֹנֵן וְיִשְׁרֶה עָלֵינוּ מִלְמַעְלָה, לִהְיוֹתוֹ בְּלִי גְּבוּל וְתַכְלִית וְאֵינוֹ מִתְלַבֵּשׁ בְּנַפְשֵׁנוּ וְשִׂכְלֵנוּ. וְעַל כֵּן אֵין אָנוּ מַשִּׂיגִים בְּשִׂכְלֵנוּ הַנְּעִימוּת וְהָעֲרֵיבוּת מִנּוֹעַם ה' וְזִיו הַשְּׁכִינָה,

shall be established and reside over us from above, to be without defined limit, and not enclothed in our souls and our intellect. Therefore, we do not attain with our intellect the grace and pleasantness of

20. Cited in *Likkutei Amarim,* chap. 4 in the name of the *Zohar.* However, until now we have not found this wording. And see the Zohar 3:73a, and there, part 1, 24a, and part 2, 60a, *Tikkunei Zohar* 21b and elsewhere.

21. As brought in several places about the garment that is "like a locust whose garment is part of its body." See *Sha'ar HaYihud VeHa'emuna* 7 and *Likkutei Amarim,* chap. 21. And like letters engraved letters whose instrument of implementation is essentially one with the content itself, see *Likkutei Torah, Vayikra* 53:2 and on, ibid. *Bemidbar* 59:3 and more.

בְּלִי גְבוּל וְתַכְלִית, אֲשֶׁר מִתְכּוֹנֵן וְשׁוֹרֶה עָלֵינוּ	**the graciousness of the Lord and the radiance of the Divine Presence, without defined limit, which is established and resides over us**
בְּמַעֲשֵׂה יָדֵינוּ בַּתּוֹרָה וּמִצְוֹת בְּרַבִּים דַּוְקָא.	**through the work of our hands,** engaging **in Torah and mitzvot particularly in a group.**

These are the three conditions that spark the wonderous connection between the actual, infinite, divine light of the pleasantness of God and us. The first is "through the work of our hands," through action. Action is the lowest rung of the worlds, and therefore has the power to reveal the highest encompassing light that transcends the intellect. Since action lies under the intellect's radar, so to speak, it is not limited by it. A person might not understand intellectually or emotionally why he did a certain mitzva. He does it only because he is obligated to, because he is simply fulfilling the will of God. The second is through Torah and mitzvot as explained above. And the third, through devotion in a group.

For the encompassing light to relate to us, we must have something in common with it. So, while no physical or spiritual power can be more than it is alone, when people gather together for a common purpose, they manifest something that transcends the limitations of each individual. While this is not infinite, it still surpasses the finitude of each person. Every person who joins the group adds another dimension of the infinite, until it reaches the ultimate ten. Ten is the number of wholeness since it encompasses a full circle of the inner dimension. This is true in the "small world" of man, and the ten faculties of his being and how much more so in the world at large, when the ultimate wholeness manifests as ten people with their ten inner faculties joined together. ☞

ON THE POWER OF THE QUORUM

☞ It is true that ten people gathered together do not always embody the ultimate perfection of faculties, complementing each other in the ideal way. The opposite can sometimes be the case. Here the author of the *Tanya* is not talking about the

וְעַל זֶה אָמְרוּ רַבּוֹתֵינוּ ז"ל (קידושין לט,ב): "שְׂכַר מִצְוָה בְּהַאי עָלְמָא לֵיכָּא",

Regarding this, our Rabbis said (*Kiddushin* 39b), "There is no reward for a mitzva in this world,"

In this world, the meaning and infinite divine delight in the performance of a mitzva, cannot be grasped. The reward and significance of a mitzva, "the pleasantness of the Lord," hidden within, are not circumscribed by the dimensions of this world, nor can they be comprehended

quorum as the ultimate perfection of a person's realized faculties, but rather, a connection that surpasses the individual and the group: the encompassing. He gives a definition through negation, when each of the ten says, "there is something beyond me." When a person admits that to himself, it is not so meaningful. Of course, that is the case. However, when a person hears this from another person, then a window is opened into another "beyond," different than his "beyond" and therefore gives meaning to his own "beyond." His infinite is intersected by another person's infinite, and another, and another, until he begins to see a much bigger picture.

We see from here that the joining of different people in one shared context heralds a revelation of the all-encompassing light that can reach every individual to some degree.

That which happens particularly with ten people and not nine, is ungraspable by the mind or heart, since it is a collection of encompassing lights, each of which is inherently incomprehensible. The faculties of the soul can only grasp that which they can register a piece of: the eye sees color only from a particular spectrum of wavelengths, the ear hears the frequencies that it can, the intellect grasps that which it can understand, etc. The senses are incapable of grasping the entirety of the sensations that the world offers and tune in only to particular spectrums of them. However, we can grasp, in a certain sense, the thing itself before it becomes revealed and divided into separate elements.

This revelation, of quintessential essence, happens when every person shows up to the quorum with the absolute fullness of his being to his ultimate capacity. When ten fully manifested people gather with their revealed aspects of selves and their hidden essences, then a perfected wholeness always happens. A person can add anything, and will necessarily add exactly what is missing. One person completes the second, and the third fills in perfectly, etc. until the tenth (and any person can be the tenth) enters and immediately perfects everyone.

It is this perfection of ten that draws down the residing of the Divine Presence, the infinite power of the Divine palpably present, ready for anything, ready to move in any direction. Since these ten people will engage in an act of holiness, Torah or mitzvot, everything begins to move, not even like a river, but more like an ocean, moving everything with it. Therefore, the individual person is not even aware of this all-encompassing, infinite tide that sweeps him up with the entire world, because it lies beyond the reaches of his sensory radar.

or expressed by any definition or measure of our world. This is summed up by the author of the *Tanya's* reading of this Talmudic statement: the reward of a mitzva is not in this world.

כִּי אִי אֶפְשָׁר לְעוֹלָם לְהַשִּׂיגוֹ כִּי אִם בְּהִתְפַּשְּׁטוּת הַנֶּפֶשׁ מֵהַגּוּף,

for it is never possible to achieve it other than through the disrobing of the soul from the body,

In this world the soul is clothed in a body, in which it thinks and feels. Consequently, as long as the soul is within the body and the physical world, sensing through them and thinking with their devices and concepts, it cannot attain the reward of the mitzva. It can achieve this only through the "disrobing" of the soul from the body, when it is freed from the restrictions of this world. ☞

"THE DISROBING OF THE SOUL FROM THE BODY"

☞ On a basic level, the soul's disrobing from the body occurs following a person's death. After the soul separates from the body and frees itself from the memories and habits of its attachment to the physical, it reaches the Garden of Eden, where it can enjoy, to a certain degree, the reward of the mitzvot it has performed. However, by using the phrase "the disrobing of the soul from the body," rather than "after a person's death," the author of the *Tanya* suggests a much broader meaning – that there is a way for the soul to be disrobed from the body even during one's lifetime. This expression also implies that even after a person's death, the main change is the disrobing of the soul from the body. It is possible that even after death the soul will not immediately separate from the body, meaning, when a person was heavily immersed in his body and in this world, when he did not think about the existence of the soul in of itself and it did not affect him at all. In such a case, even after death, although the soul has separated from the body, it cannot divest from the memories and experiences of the body and it does not have the ability to experience anything else. Obviously, a person cannot literally divest himself of the body in this world entirely, because then he will no longer be living in it, but one can change his attitude towards the body and its interests. The question is where is one's "self." As long as the "I" is in the body, and his true feelings and life are immersed in the affairs of the body, he cannot approach the reward of a mitzva at all. However, if someone can – even if only from time to time, at an hour of enlightenment and favor – discover the self in the soul alone, and treat it as the prime self, while the body serves, at most, as the "flesh" he is wearing, he will also be able to experience, to a certain extent, "the pleasantness of the Lord" in the reward of the mitzvot he has performed. This possibility depends on the extent of the disrobing. If it occurs only sometimes, in a contingent manner and through the power of enlightenment from above, then the expe-

וְאַף גַּם זֹאת עַל דֶּרֶךְ הַחֶסֶד, כְּמוֹ שֶׁכָּתוּב: "וּלְךָ ה׳ חָסֶד כִּי אַתָּה תְשַׁלֵּם לְאִישׁ כְּמַעֲשֵׂהוּ" (תהלים סב,יג),

and even then, only **by way of kindness, as it is written, "Kindness is Yours, my Lord, for You render to every man according to his deeds"** (Ps. 62:13),

The reward that God grants for the mitzvot is an act of kindness. Although a reward is generally not considered a kindness, since one is entitled to remuneration for his work, by right and not as kindness or a gift, nevertheless, the divine reward for the mitzvot is always bestowed by way of kindness as well. ☞

וּכְמוֹ שֶׁאָמְרוּ רַבּוֹתֵינוּ ז"ל (סנהדרין ק,ב), שֶׁהַקָּדוֹשׁ בָּרוּךְ הוּא נוֹתֵן כֹּחַ בַּצַּדִּיקִים כוּ׳.

as our Rabbis said, that the Holy One, blessed be He, provides strength to the righteous to receive their reward" (*Sanhedrin* 100b).

It is in fact in order to receive his reward that man requires God's kindness. The practical performance of the mitzva can be performed by a person even if he does not understand or sense what he is doing, which means that in effect one can do something that has no obvious

rience of the reward will also be external, as a mere sense that such a reward does exist. However, when the disrobing is permanent, through the work the person below performs upon himself, the experience can also be internal and touch upon the essence of the reward, which will be real and enduring in his soul.

"KINDNESS IS YOURS"

☞ In a similar manner, albeit from another perspective, of the act of the mitzva itself, it has been explained in the name of the Ba'al Shem Tov (see *Ba'al Shem Tov al HaTorah, Parashat Noaḥ* 34, and *Mekor Mayim Ḥayyim* there), that the relationship between a person and God is not the same as the relationship between one person and another. For the entire existence of a person, everything that he does, is all from the power God. When a person thinks, God thinks through him; when he acts, God gives him the strength, intelligence and ability to do so. Accordingly, even when one performs a mitzva for the sake of Heaven, for God, he does it by means of God's power. Thus, the reward for what he has done is granted by the kindness of God, in that God considers it as that person's "own deed."

value to him. To the contrary, it is sometimes precisely one's lack of comprehension and connection to what he is doing, that enables him to carry it out. The same cannot be said with regard to receiving the reward, which is comprised of one's understanding and sense of the purpose of the mitzva he has done. Here, there must be some sort of correspondence between a person's ability to understand, and what he receives. Since the purpose of the mitzva is God's will and pleasure, which are infinite, whereas the human soul, even when it is divested from the body, still exists within certain boundaries, it is not enough to receive the reward to which one is entitled; rather, God's kindness is required. In other words, one is in need of a kindness that will open up the capacities of the soul, not merely in accordance with the value of its actions, but corresponding to the infinite value of the meaning of the mitzva and its purpose. ☞

In general, whenever a relationship is attained between the infinite and the finite, between the unlimited existence of the Divine and mortal beings, this is necessarily achieved through the kindness of God. After all, no creatures can bridge this gap, and jump from the finite to the infinite. This can be done only through God's kindness. Only He gave us the Torah and the mitzvot and He alone provides us with the strength to receive its reward.[22]

מַה שֶּׁאֵין כֵּן בַּמַּלְאָכִים, **This is not the case with regard to the angels,**

"THE KINDNESS OF GOD"

☞ The shortcoming of all human kindness is that one cannot truly consider all of the factors that will affect how it will be received: Who is receiving it; how it is received; whether it is ultimately for his benefit, etc. Indeed, the bestowal of kindness can even harm the recipient. This is not the case regarding the kindness of God, which is a flawless kindness and a perfect bestowal that incorporates not only the act of giving itself but also the ability to receive it; not only the light but also the vessel that holds it. In this sense, the reward for a mitzva is always granted through the kindness of God, as it includes both the ability and the suitable vessel in which to receive it.

22. See *Torah Or*, 66c and onward.

The angels have not been granted any ability beyond their capacities.[23] The reason is that the angels do not deal directly with the infinite, but always the rank above them in the progression of levels. Unlike the soul, an angel cannot breach the progression of levels, because he himself is part of that progression. The soul, whose root lies above the progression of levels – despite the fact that its current position on the progression might be *lower* than that of an angel – can therefore relate to the existence of the infinite that is above everything, and occasionally even experience it. This is not true for an angel, as his whole essence belongs to that progression – he is the expression of a level, and an agent, an entity that transmits from one level to another.

כְּמוֹ שֶׁשָּׁמַעְתִּי מֵרַבּוֹתַי, כִּי אִילּוּ נִמְצָא מַלְאָךְ אֶחָד עוֹמֵד בְּמַעֲמַד עֲשָׂרָה מִיִּשְׂרָאֵל בְּיַחַד, אַף שֶׁאֵינָם מְדַבְּרִים בְּדִבְרֵי תוֹרָה, תִּפּוֹל עָלָיו אֵימָתָה וָפַחַד בְּלִי גְּבוּל וְתַכְלִית, מִשְּׁכִינְתָּא דִשְׁרְיָא עֲלַיְיהוּ,

as I heard from my rabbis, that, were a single angel standing present in a gathering of ten Jews together, even if they were not conversing in Torah matters, he would be gripped by endless, limitless dread and fear of the Divine Presence that resides over them,

"My rabbis" refers to the Ba'al Shem Tov and the Maggid of Mezeritch.[24] As explained, the Divine Presence that resides over those ten members of Israel is an illumination and revelation from the all-encompassing Divine Presence that is beyond them, which transcends the entire progression of levels. An angel, whose entire essence lies within his place in that progression of levels, cannot bear such a revelation.

Although an angel may not see beyond himself, he clearly perceives the place where he is located, and feels all the love or awe that belongs to that revelation. An angel cannot help but see and feel, because this

---

23. This follows a note of the Lubavitcher Rebbe.

24. The sixth Lubavitcher Rebbe, Rabbi Yosef Yitzḥak Schneerson, relates that when his father, the fifth Lubavitcher Rebbe, Rabbi Sholom Dovber Schneerson, taught him the *Iggeret HaKodesh*, he informed him that the phrase "I heard from my teacher" (e.g., in *Likkutei Amarim*, chap. 35, in the note) refers to the Maggid of Mezeritch, whereas "I heard from my rabbis" means both the Ba'al Shem Tov and the Maggid of Mezeritch.

is the essence of an angel – the emotional expression, etc., of the place where he is situated. In this sense, the resting of the Divine Presence upon ten Jews would be "unnatural" for an angel, as it is the entry of the infinite into his defined and revealed world. Therefore, "he would be gripped by dread and fear of undefined limit," on account of that which cannot be seen and felt, that which would tear him and his whole world apart. ☞

עַד שֶׁהָיָה מִתְבַּטֵּל מִמְּצִיאוּתוֹ לְגַמְרֵי. **until his existence would be entirely subsumed.**

The entire existence of an angel is a precisely demarcated boundary and limit of love and awe, etc. Dread and the fear of undefined limit would nullify his reality entirely.

Having provided a hasidic interpretation of the Mishna: "Ten who are sitting and engaged with the Torah, the Divine Presence rests amongst them," the author of the *Tanya* can now turn to the practical ramifications of his conclusions.

וְעַל כֵּן רַע בְּעֵינַי הַמַּעֲשֶׂה אֲשֶׁר נַעֲשָׂה תַּחַת הַשָּׁמֶשׁ, **Accordingly, the act that is performed under the sun is evil in my eyes,**

22 Tishrei

20 Tishrei (leap year)

This is a paraphrase of Ecclesiastes 2:17. The expression "under the sun" is mentioned here in connection to the statement of the Sages[25] that all the affairs of this world are "under the sun," meaning that there is

MAN VERSUS ANGEL

☞ The essence of an angel is part of the progression of levels, and spiritual make-up of the worlds. Consequently, while it is privy to perceiving and experiencing its spiritual reality and level, it cannot see beyond that. The human soul, on the one hand, does not have experiential awareness of its spiritual level, since it is clothed in a body. On the other hand, since its root lies above the progression of levels, higher than reality and the limitations of all the worlds, it can relate to divine existence (the Divine Presence) itself, which is beyond its own boundaries in the world. Man can activate the Divine Presence in the world, and in a certain manner can also relate to and receive from the essence of this indwelling Divine Presence without being thereby detached from his own inner being, because, in fact, it is his inner essence.

25. See e.g., *Shabbat* 30b; *Zohar* 1:223b.

no gain to be had from them or meaning in their toil, whereas words of Torah are "above the sun." If so, he is saying that what those members of the ten Jews in the synagogue are doing is "evil in my eyes," since instead of engaging in Torah they are occupied with matters of this world, which are "under the sun."

בִּכְלָל, וּבִפְרָט בֵּין אַחַיי וְרֵעַיי, **in general, and especially amongst my brethren and friends,**

The phrase "in general" means "for any Jew who acts in this manner," while "my brethren and friends" are the hasidim, especially those who are close to him, who are like his brethren with respect to the service of God, and who should therefore be attentive to these matters. These "brethren and friends" should be so close to him in heart and mind that even when they are not explicitly told what to do and how, they should still come to this realization of their own accord. Here too, as we will see below, the issue is not prayer itself, but the less clearly-defined margins of the service. In general, the informal service of God, in those places and times where there is no clear-cut obligation to perform a mitzva, pray, or study, is something that Hasidism has always emphasized and reinforced. Therefore, such behavior is especially bad in his eyes when it comes from the hasidim who are "my brethren and friends."

הַנִּגָּשִׁים אֶל ה' - הַגָּשָׁה זוֹ תְּפִלָּה - **who approach the Lord – "approaching" means prayer –**

For them, prayer is truly an act of approaching[26] the Lord.[27] In other words, they performed the service of the soul through prayer, as the author of the *Tanya* demanded from his hasidim, and as explained elsewhere.

וְאַחַר הַתְּפִלָּה אוֹ לְפָנֶיהָ and yet **after the prayer, or before it,**

---

26. See Rashi on the verse: "Abraham approached" (Gen. 18:23).

27. Based on Exodus 19:22: "The priests who approach the Lord etc." Rashi explains that this means "to offer sacrifices," and the prayers are a replacement for the sacrifices (note of the Lubavitcher Rebbe, Rabbi Menaḥem Mendel Schneerson).

The problem is what happens after prayer. True, at the time of prayer they indeed prayed, and even focused on the work of prayer. But what happens following prayer, or before it? Everyone knows and talks about prayer. During prayers one must pray. However, the main issue lies in the margins of prayer – before and after it, when there are no compulsory, defined boundaries – and it is this that he wishes to discuss. ☞

נַעֲשָׂה מוֹשַׁב לֵצִים רַחֲמָנָא לִיצְּלַן, כְּמוֹ שֶׁאָמְרוּ רַבּוֹתֵינוּ ז״ל: ״שְׁנַיִם שֶׁיּוֹשְׁבִין וְאֵין בֵּינֵיהֶם דִּבְרֵי תוֹרָה כו׳״.

a company of scoffers is formed, God save us, as our Rabbis said, "If two are sitting and there are no words of Torah between them this is a company of scoffers" (*Avot* 3:2).

AFTER PRAYER

☞ "After prayer" is a concept involving time and state of mind, which the author of the *Tanya* analyzes at length in the *Tanya* – he is less interested in what occurs during prayer itself, and more on what unfolds after the prayer has concluded. The *Tanya*, including the section of *Iggeret HaKodesh*, is the "Book of *Beinonim*." When it comes to prayer itself, the *beinoni*, if he prays with contemplation and devotion, is in a certain sense like the tzaddik: He serves God with love and awe, ascending upwards and drawing down divine abundance into this world below. However, after prayer the *beinoni* returns to the mundane existence of his daily struggle against concealment, the blurring of boundaries and the spirit of folly. Accordingly, the "Book of *Beinonim*" focuses mainly on what happens after prayer. It is important to state "after prayer," rather than simply "at the time when one falls," since the *beinoni* must experience prayer, and the question of what happens next. "The righteous falls seven times and rises" (Proverbs 24: 16; see *Sha'ar HaYiḥud VeHa'emuna*, "*Ḥinukh Katan*") refers precisely to this: How does one maintain the strengths that were manifested during prayer, and keep them going in the time that follows prayer?: Furthermore, it is important to note that "after prayer" is not a marginal issue, but an essential aspect of one's work in the service of God. According to the *Tanya*, is it is precisely this work that is the purpose of this world and man's descent into it. It is not about one's attainment and devotion, his love and awe, but rather, the challenging path that the *beinoni* must take through his body and this world, which opposes anything holy. As stated, the work of the *beinoni* is more evident before and after prayer, when there is nothing definite in the air – not the uplifting spirit of prayer, not the focus of the soul on the act of a mitzva, but simply the activities of this world at their peak. The question of what to do then, at that time and in this world, will determine the entire world more than anything else.

"Scoffing" refers to those who mock and laugh at everything. Nothing can withstand such an attitude. ☞ ☞

The real problem of scoffing is the removal of the yolk of Heaven. There is nothing wrong with people being happy; on the contrary, joy is a great virtue in the service of God and in all realms of life. The issue is when the joy comes with the removal of the burden of the fear of God. It is then an "open" joy, without limits, because the removal of the burden itself consists of the breaking of all boundaries. In this sense, when Jews meet in a holy place, on a solemn occasion, and yet they do not actively accept the yoke of the kingdom of Heaven upon them, by this neglect alone they have removed the burden of the fear of God from upon themselves.

AN OPEN *KELIPPA*

☞ It is explained elsewhere (see *Torah Or* 61c and onward, based on *Avoda Zara* 19a) and *Torat Ḥayyim Parashat Beshallaḥ*, 137: 1) that scoffing is "the *kelippa* of the Philistines." The word Philistines, *pelishtim*, is connected to the word "open" as in the term "an open alleyway [*mefulash*, this term, which appears in many places in the rabbinical sources, means an alleyway, or a street, that is open on both sides]." It is an open force of negativity that goes from one end of the world to the other, with nothing stopping it. In one's inner world as well, the pleasure of scoffing, like that of debauchery, is experienced in one's very soul, as can be attested by the people for whom this delight is more valuable than all physical lusts. Therefore, its opposite, in the realm of holiness, is the distinctive delight that is wide open towards the essence of the Holy One, blessed be He, which transcends any configuration, depiction, and image.

A COMPANY OF SCOFFERS

☞ This expression refers to a gathering of ridicule, an environment of mockery. Not merely a statement or an act of clowning but a whole atmosphere of scoffing, which has its effect even when no one is saying anything. Therefore, "if two are sitting...this is a company of scoffers." They don't have to engage in any particular, pie-in-the face pranks, or tell a joke at someone's expense. The very fact that they are sitting together – two Jews, two divine souls – with no words of Torah between them, renders it "a company of scoffers." The same can be said of a soldier armed in battle clothes and war colors who is sitting in a concert hall or standing on a city street – he will be an object of bafflement and mockery, like anything that is not in its place or performing its proper function. The same applies to a divine soul that came down to this world but is not engaged in Torah and mitzvot. One Jew can keep to himself, but when there are two Jews together, the issue of whether they are or are not saying words of Torah will affect the space around them, which thereby turns into "a company of scoffers."

וְאִם נַעֲשָׂה מוֹשַׁב לֵצִים בַּעֲשָׂרָה דִשְׁכִינְתָּא שַׁרְיָא עֲלַייְהוּ,

And if a company of scoffers is formed in the presence of **ten, upon whom the Divine Presence resides,**

Two people can already be considered "a company of scoffers," since an interpersonal connection is formed between them, which goes beyond the boundaries of a single person. However, when ten are together, there is a greater degree of the realm of the beyond; there is the presence of the One who is beyond, the real presence of "the Divine Presence that resides over them." The severity of this company of scoffers, and the damage it causes, is accordingly far more significant, as the author of the *Tanya* proceeds to explain:

אֵין לְךָ עֶלְבּוֹנָא וְקָלְנָא דִשְׁכִינְתָּא גָּדוֹל מִזֶּה, רַחֲמָנָא לִיצְלַן.

you have no greater insult and shaming of the Divine Presence than that, God save us.

Ten Jews who are sitting together, and who form a company of scoffers, even if they do not violate a single one of the 613 mitzvot, are thereby ignoring the Divine Presence that resides over them. In interpersonal relations, there is no greater insult than ignoring someone's presence; even if he is beaten, insulted and mocked, they are at least acknowledging his existence, but if he is completely ignored, there is no greater affront than that.

וְאִם אָמְרוּ רַבּוֹתֵינוּ ז״ל (קידושין לא,א) עַל הָעוֹבֵר עֲבֵירָה בַּסֵּתֶר שֶׁדּוֹחֵק רַגְלֵי הַשְּׁכִינָה חַס וְשָׁלוֹם,

If our Rabbis said (*Kiddushin* 31a) **regarding one who commits a transgression in private, that he pushes away the feet of the Divine Presence, God forbid,**

The assumption of one who commits a transgression in private is that there, at least, God does not see him. Accordingly, he is considered to be "pushing away the feet of the Divine Presence" from that place; he is performing an action that, apart from its immediate effect, rids that corner of the presence of God.

Although the plain meaning of "in private" is away from people, nevertheless, the fact that he would not have committed the transgression if people could have seen him shows that the yoke of Heaven is still upon him, that he still fears God to a certain extent. It is important to him that people do not think of him as wicked, or at least, someone who would perform that sin. This means that in his heart he thinks that being evil is repulsive, and that it is praiseworthy to be righteous. Therefore, he is described as "pushing away the feet of the Divine Presence," with "feet" referring to the level of action alone, in contrast to the "body," which represents the emotions of the soul, and the "head," which is the level of the intellect. Thus, one who transgresses in private – a little, temporarily, but not on a regular basis – his heart and head are not in the act, and he is certainly not rebelling against God or removing the yolk of Heaven.

הָעוֹבֵר עֲבֵירָה בָּרַבִּים - דּוֹחֵק כָּל שִׁיעוּר קוֹמָה שֶׁל יוֹצֵר בְּרֵאשִׁית כִּבְיָכוֹל.

yet **one who commits a transgression in public pushes away the whole stature of the Fashioner of creation, as it were.**

This is not the case for one who commits a transgression in public. When someone does something, not only on the level of action – with his "feet" – but with his entire stature, he thereby pushes away the whole stature of the "Fashioner of creation."[28]

"The stature of the Fashioner of creation" is a concept that appears in the early hasidic texts and works of kabbalists.[29] It refers to the entire world, or, to put it another way, all the divine forces (the ten *sefirot*) that constitute and sustain the world. The term "stature" is metaphorically related to the stature of man: His head, body, legs, etc., for man is a "microcosm," who was formed "in the image of God." Like the stature of man, "the stature of the "Fashioner of creation" also includes a head, body, feet, and so forth. This stature is a concept that humans can grasp, and whose totality they can appreciate even with regard to God – "the entire stature" – and thus they can also comprehend the depth of the evil of "pushing away the whole stature."

28. "See *Etz Ḥayyim, Sha'ar HaShemot*, chap. 7; *Yahel Or*, p. 573 and onwards" (note of the Lubavitcher Rebbe, Rabbi Me).

29. "The stature of the Creator of Genesis is 236 thousand myriad parasangs" (*Pirkei Heikhalot*).

From a different perspective, one who sins in public is considered to be pushing away the whole stature of the Creator, so to speak, because the public represents the totality of Israel, the Divine Presence, and thus in essence "the whole stature of the Fashioner of creation." As stated elsewhere, some souls are considered the "head" while others are the legs, and so on, such that the totality of the souls of Israel (in each generation) constitute a whole stature. This entire stature, although it basically refers to the people of Israel, on a deeper level, is "the whole stature of the Fashioner of creation." Accordingly, one who commits a transgression in public, who does not care about those Jews who are "the feet" or those who are the "heads" of Israel, is considered as though he is pushing God away from the full extent of His presence in the world.

כְּמוֹ שֶׁאָמְרוּ רַבּוֹתֵינוּ ז״ל: ״אֵין אֲנִי וְהוּא וכו׳״

As our rabbis said, "Any person who has arrogance within him, the Holy One, Blessed be He, says, '**He and I cannot** dwell together in the world. (*Sota* 5a).'"

God is the infinite One, in every aspect and every place, in general and in particular. He fills all spaces, absolutely; nothing else can serve as a partner to Him, not even in terms of existing in the same place. When a person has arrogance within him, and thinks he is somebody important, it is as though he is removing God from that place, as it were.[30] ☞

"ARROGANCE WITHIN"

☞ Such an individual is not only one who has a sense of his self, as virtually no-one can entirely shake themselves of this feeling, but rather he is one who is not ashamed of it. As long as one senses that something is wrong with feeling like that, this means that he is aware of the presence of God. But when he says "I" and "for me," without feeling that something is wrong, then God cannot be with him in the same world.

30. Compare to *Arakhin* 15b: "Anyone who speaks malicious speech, the Holy One, Blessed be He says about him: He and I cannot dwell together in the world."

אֶלָּא שֶׁ"מֶּלֶךְ אָסוּר בָּרְהָטִים" (שיר השירים ז,ו) כו'. **only that "the king is bound in the chambers"** (Song. 7:6)**...**

These "chambers," as explained in the *Zohar*[31] and mentioned elsewhere in the *Tanya*,[32] are "the rushing thoughts of the mind's chambers."

The verse "the king is bound in the chambers" expresses the absurdity of the Divine Presence in exile. The exile of the Divine Presence means that it is present even where people "push away the feet of the Divine Presence," even in that very place where "He and I cannot dwell together in the world." Nevertheless, it does not depart from that place, as otherwise it could not exist. According to hasidic teachings, the reason for this state of affairs is that "the King is bound in the chambers." In other words, it is as though the King, which is *Malkhut*, the Divine Presence, has bound and tied Himself to the thoughts of man, with the commitment that wherever the thoughts of man go, the Divine Presence will follow and be there. God created man with free choice, in a world that is an "entity" of its own, separate from God, as it were. This is all based on that pledge, by which He binds himself to the thoughts of man, meaning that whatever he thinks and whatever he does – God will be there to fulfill it. This is true to such an extent that a person can push Him out, deny His existence, at the very moment that God is within him, giving him life, and his imaginary world from absolute nothingness. ☞ ☞

"BOUND IN THE CHAMBERS"

☞ This is the essence of the King. When God took it upon Himself to be king, so to speak, this means that there will be a nation, there will be people who live in a reality that is supposedly separate from His infinite being, as in the saying "there is no king without a people," cited in *Sha'ar HaYiḥud Ve-Ha'emuna*, chap. 7, and elsewhere. For the sake of example, the same is true for people as well. If one seeks to educate a child towards independence, to give him an opportunity to build his character, he must accept upon himself – within limits – not to interfere with him, even when he makes mistakes.

---

31. *Tikkunei Zohar, Tikkun* 6 (21b). See also Rashi on this verse.

32. The Lubavitcher Rebbe, Rabbi Menaḥem Mendel Schneerson, likewise comments: "Reference *Iggeret HaTeshuva*, beginning of chap. 7."

אֲבָל וַוי לְמַאן דְּדָחֲקִין לִשְׁכִינְתָּא כַּד יוֹקִים לָהּ קוּדְשָׁא בְּרִיךְ הוּא וְיֵימָא לָהּ: "הִתְנַעֲרִי מֵעָפָר קוּמִי וגו'" (ישעיה נב,ב).

But woe to one who pushes away the Divine Presence, when the Holy One, blessed be He, will raise it up and say to it, "shake off the dust, arise...," (Is. 52:2).

During the exile, it is as though "the King who is bound in the chambers" has undertaken not to react even when people rebel against Him, even when He is disrespected. However, when the exile ends and God will raise the Divine Presence from the dust, woe to those who brought down and pushed away the Divine Presence. It is not a vengeance that God will wreak, but rather,[33] when the Divine Presence shakes off the dust of God's concealment, the person who pushed the Divine Presence down, will be gripped with fear, when he will see the

"THE RUSHING STREAM OF THE MIND'S THOUGHTS"

☞ What is the meaning of this expression? One's thoughts not only reflect his image of the world, they literally conduct the world and the Divine Presence upwards or downwards, just as thought directs speech. There are good thoughts, holy thoughts, which raise the Divine Presence and the world up towards the purpose of creation, whereas other thoughts can *lower* it. When a person contemplates the affairs of this world as separate from the Divine, as though they were a reality to themselves, which he desires or fears, he lowers the Divine Presence into exile and a state of concealment in the physical world. By contrast, when a person reflects upon God as One in heaven and earth, and other thoughts of unity and faith, he thereby raises the Divine Presence from exile. The metaphor of a "rushing stream of the mind's thoughts" depicts the rapid descent and depth of the exile. When thoughts are rushed, they become focused on the material realm, and separated from the holy. The whole ability of this world, of the animal soul and the evil inclination, to "protect themselves" from holiness, to preserve their existence and avoid nullification, is achieved through the rushing of thoughts – faster, faster, from one issue to the next, urgently and with a sense of importance, one thought leading to the next, each idea bound to another. If each person could only stop his train of thought, and for one moment not focus on what he feels he must think about, the King would no longer be "bound in the chambers," and some other thought that is not bound captive to his preconceptions and ingrained patterns of thought, might come to mind.

33. In general, God's punishments are an act not of revenge but rectification, that is, in order for a person to return to the same situations but in a different way; when he experiences them from another perspective, such as from their aspect of corruption, or better, in a manner that helps him act and feel differently.

extent of the damage he caused. Woe to him for that shame, woe to him for that fear.

וְעַל תְּלַת מִילִּין מִתְעַכְּבֵי יִשְׂרָאֵל בְּגָלוּתָא: עַל דְּדָחֲקִין לִשְׁכִינְתָּא וְעַל דְּעָבְדִין קְלָנָא בִּשְׁכִינְתָּא וכו׳, כְּמוֹ שֶׁכָּתוּב בַּזּוֹהַר הַקָּדוֹשׁ.

It is due to three things that Israel are detained in exile: For pushing away the Divine Presence; for shaming the Divine Presence…, as written in the holy *Zohar*.

These are not the exact words of the *Zohar*, but a similar idea does appear there.[34] These three things, on account of which the Divine Presence remains in exile, are not sins that are enumerated in the *Shulḥan Arukh*, but general categories of attitudes – ignorance, contempt and affronts – that can come with or without an actual sin. As described here, when ten Jews are sitting alongside each other, by virtue of their very gathering together, the Divine Presence resides over them, not in theory, but literally, such that anyone who saw it would tremble to his core. But if those Jews not only do not receive the inspiration of the Divine Presence by engaging in matters of holiness such as studying as a group of ten, but they even focus on other, mundane matters, there is no greater insult to the Divine Presence. The Divine Presence, *Malkhut*, has descended through innumerable levels from its place of glory and is now standing over them, declaring "I have come," and yet they pay no attention. ☞

עַל כֵּן אֲהוּבַיי אַחַיי וְרֵעַיי,

Therefore, my beloved ones, my brethren and friends,

"DETAINED IN EXILE"

☞ It is true that when a person violates an explicit negative commandment, he thereby plunges the Divine Presence into a deeper exile, adding another layer of complication to this exile. However, he is not necessarily delayed in exile on account of

34. It seems that the reference is to the *Zohar* 3:75b: "It was taught, due to three things Israel are detained in exile: For shaming the Divine Presence in exile; and that they turn their faces away from the Divine Presence; and for defiling themselves before the Divine Presence."

As stated, this matter is especially serious when it involves "my brethren and friends." For those who are not sensitive and are unaware that the Divine Presence is here, it is not such an affront. However, when it comes to the hasidim who have been trained in this regard, "my brethren and friends," such conduct is insulting both to the Rebbe and to the Divine Presence. Here is where the danger lies, and these are the ones whom he proceeds to warn:

אַל נָא תָּרֵעוּ הָרָעָה הַגְּדוֹלָה הַזֹּאת, וּתְנוּ כָבוֹד לַה' אֱלֹהֵיכֶם, בְּטֶרֶם יַחְשִׁךְ, דְּהַיְינוּ בֵּין מִנְחָה לְמַעֲרִיב כָּל יְמוֹת הַחוֹל לִלְמוֹד בַּעֲשָׂרָה פְּנִימִיּוּת הַתּוֹרָה,

please do not perform this great evil, but give honor to the Lord your God before it grows dark; that is, between the afternoon prayer and the evening prayer on all weekdays, to study in a gathering of **ten the esoteric meaning of the Torah,**

"My brethren and friends please do not perform this great evil,"[35] of engaging in idle chatter before and after prayer, as mentioned, "but give honor to the Lord your God," by focusing on Torah,[36] the service of God, and matters of Heaven. This is the opposite of a company of scoffers, which lacks honor and brings disgrace.

The period between the afternoon prayer and the evening prayer, "before it grows dark,"[37] is specified because it is a convenient time for such affairs. People have prayed the afternoon prayer in a gathering of

this; on the contrary, sometimes the explicit expression of sin can speed up one's ascent and repentance. By contrast, when a person disengages from and ignores the Divine Presence that came to him, there is no greater offence or detachment than this. As a consequence, the Divine Presence lingers in exile and does not reveal itself to him again. The Divine Presence wished to enter, and yet he refused to open the door, but rather, left it in exile while he turned to his affairs that were preoccupying him at that time.

35. "My brethren and friends please do not perform" is derived from Genesis 19:7; while "this great evil" is from, e.g., Genesis 39:9.

36. As "there is no honor other than Torah" (*Avot* 6:2).

37. Based on Jeremiah 13:16: "Give honor to the Lord your God before it grows dark." See Radak there.

ten and are waiting for it to get dark, without dispersing, in order to pray the evening prayer. This is the time when a holy *minyan* can turn into a company of scoffers.[38]

The Divine Presence that resides upon ten Jews, as stated, demands its expression and revelation, as otherwise the Divine Presence is dishonored. The manifestation and revelation of this holiness is now expressed through the study of the Torah by those ten individuals.

What should they study? "The esoteric meaning of the Torah," rather than its revealed teachings. The revealed part of the Torah is when it enclothes itself in the *lower* world, in the material world of *Asiya* that is revealed to us. For we, as soul within bodies, live in the world of physical activity, we feel and think in it. When the Torah is enclothed in these matters, in the practical halakhot, this is the revealed aspect of the Torah. By contrast, the esoteric meaning of the Torah consists of that layer of the Torah which is enclothed mainly in the lofty spiritual worlds,[39] whose meaning concerns the inner parts of the soul. It is not enclothed in our lives in this world but in the separate life of the soul, which touches the Divine itself – those aspects that penetrate our consciousness, our lives, to each individual in accordance with his capacity to receive it, his sensitivity, his knowledge and his deeds. These are the revelations of the inner essence of the soul and the Divine that surrounds our lives. We can thus understand why the author of the *Tanya* instructs the ten to study the esoteric meaning of the Torah, as it draws down the all- encompassing revelation, the resting of the Divine Presence from above, upon those ten, which penetrates the world and all souls. ☞

---

38. The Lubavitcher Rebbe, Rabbi Menaḥem Mendel Schneerson, notes: "He does not begin by referring to the first prayer, the morning prayer, since there is an explicit law in the *Shulḥan Arukh* (89:4) regarding that time, that it is prohibited to engage in one's affairs before the prayer, and similarly that there must be public Torah study after it, [so that one goes straight] from the synagogue to the house of study (155:1)."

39. This is as explained in several places (see e.g., *Likkutei Amarim*, chap. 40, in the note; chap. 26, below; see also *Kuntres Etz Ḥayyim*) that the *Tanakh* belongs to the world of *Asiya*, the *Mishna* to *Yetzira*, the Talmud to *Beria*, and Kabbala to *Atzilut*.

שֶׁהִיא אַגָּדָה שֶׁבְּסֵפֶר עֵין יַעֲקֹב. **which is the *aggada* of the book *Ein Yaakov*.**

Ein Yaakov is a collection of all the aggadic portions of the Talmud.[40] At the time, the book was popular in most Jewish communities and it was studied even by simple Jews, ordinary folk who were not versed in the study of the Talmud. They would read it during the times and occasions discussed here, "between the weekday afternoon prayer and the evening prayer," in a gathering of ten Jews who were anyway in the synagogue waiting for the evening prayer. The author of the *Tanya* is thus not trying to start a new custom, but reinforcing an already existing one, while offering another layer of meaning to it. ☞

ESOTERIC VERSUS REVEALED

☞ "Esoteric" is a general translation for kabbalistic and hasidic teachings called *pnimiyut*, while the literal translation is "inner." Yet, when we refer to the opposite of the "esoteric, or inner meaning" of the Torah, we speak of its "revealed meaning." We do not call it "the external meaning of the Torah," as that term generally has a negative connotation. Furthermore, by definition the Torah has no "externality" – it is all "internal." See e.g., *Kuntres Aḥaron, David zemirot kirit lehu; Derekh Mitzvotekha, Mitzvat Nesi'at HaAron Ba-katef* ["The mitzva of carrying the Ark on the shoulders"]; *Likkutei Torah*, Num. 18a.

THE ESOTERIC MEANING OF THE TORAH AND KABBALA

☞ When one hears the phrase "the esoteric meaning of the Torah," one's thoughts naturally turn to Kabbala, the book of the *Zohar*, and the teaching of the Arizal (it was not possible to study Hasidism at the time). However, the truth is that the esoteric meaning of the Torah is found in all matters, it just depends how a person studies. Hasidim would study the esoteric meaning of everything – each verse, every statement of the Sages, and even halakhic rulings. This is similar to how the teachings of the Sages, in midrashim and the Talmudic *aggadot*, reveal to us, even if sometimes in an obscure manner, the esoteric meaning of the Talmud and revealed Torah.

---

40. The *Ein Yaakov* was written by Rabbi Jacob ibn Habib and his son, Rabbi Levi (the Ralbaḥ) in the early sixteenth century. It was printed alongside Rashi's commentary on the Talmud, the Maharsha's *Ḥiddushei Aggadot*, a compilation of commentaries called *HaKotev*, and other commentaries on the *aggadot* of the Talmud.

שֶׁרוֹב סוֹדוֹת הַתּוֹרָה גְּנוּזִין בָּהּ, **For most of the secrets of the Torah are hidden within it,**

The revealed part of the Talmud discloses the divine will and wisdom that is enclothed in this material world, how exactly one should perform the mitzvot, whereas the *aggadot* of the Talmud reveal and allude to the esoteric meaning of the Torah. This profound, inner meaning, which is more revealed in the upper worlds, is hidden in this world within the teachings of the *aggadot, mussar,* and the wondrous stories. These do not offer practical guidance, but they touch upon the soul, from the most accessible statements to those that are virtually incomprehensible. This is where the "secrets of the Torah" are preserved.[41] A real secret is not something that one hides away, so that it will never be told, but rather something that intrinsically cannot be revealed in this specific place, due to its essential significance. The same applies to the "secrets of the Torah" – they cannot be disclosed in this world of practicality, but as the soul ascends from one level to another they are gradually revealed, thereby transforming from a secret into a lived reality.

The "*aggada* of the book *Ein Yaakov*" is accessible to all people, both because these volumes were available and studied in synagogues, and, mainly, because they are expressed in a language and context which everyone can understand to a certain extent. Works of Kabbala, which deal openly with the esoteric teachings of the Torah, are not suitable for everyone. Their secrets are made explicit; they are not enclothed in matters of this world, and therefore it is evident that there is a secret here, and yet, as the initiated are aware, this secret can be understood only by those who are wise and understand of their own accord, who are engaged in and live in these levels. This is not the case for the rabbinic midrashim of *Ein Yaakov*, where the secrets are mostly concealed within an apparently clear meaning that relates to this world. Even if the meaning, or part of it, is not entirely grasped, nevertheless its revealed aspects still affect the soul.

---

41. See *Shulḥan Arukh HaRav, Yoreh De'a, Hilkhot Talmud Torah*, 2.

וּמְכַפֶּרֶת עֲוֹנוֹתָיו שֶׁל אָדָם, כַּמְבוֹאָר בְּכִתְבֵי הָאֲרִיזַ"ל. **and it atones for a person's transgressions, as explained in the writings of the Arizal.**

The esoteric meaning of the Torah concerns the inner aspect of *halakhot* (the reasons behind the mitzvot). On this level, which precedes the mitzva's crystallization into physical terms in the world of action, one can still change oneself. Thus, if one has committed sins, but still has a handle on the esoteric meaning of the Torah, the inner aspect of what he has failed to implement in practice, he retains the ability, if he engages in them intellectually and spiritually, to achieve some sort of atonement for his transgressions. Whoever grasps the esoteric meaning of the Torah thereby adds depth and breadth to the act of a mitzva, which can both repair defects within the realm of action and also cause new deeds to burgeon forth.

It is unclear where this is explained in the writings of the Arizal. For a related idea, see *Mishnat Ḥasidim, Masekhet HaShekiva,* 1:3: "It is proper to study something that atones for a person's sins, and in which most of the secrets of the Torah are hidden, and that is *aggada,* etc." See the *Tanya im Likkut Peirushim* ["The *Tanya* with a collection of commentaries"], which cites other sources, although those are not from the writings of the Arizal.

וְהַנִּגְלוֹת שֶׁבָּהּ הֵן דַּרְכֵי ה' שֶׁיֵּלֵךְ בָּהֶם הָאָדָם, **Its revealed teachings are the paths of God which a person should follow,**

This is referring particularly to the *aggadot* of the Talmud. They have a revealed layer of meaning, which include words of advice and *mussar,* some of which are stated explicitly while others can be inferred from the stories of the forefathers of the nation or the Sages in general.

They are called "revealed" because they have a direct impact on actual human behavior. They teach "the paths of God" that go beyond the list of mitzvot, including the gaps between the mitzvot, all those aspects of life where no express mitzva is performed, in which one only prepares for a mitzva. For it is only through this complimentary divine service, that a person can truly walk in the path of God, fully and all the time. If all a person has are the halakhot, where will he get the strength to maintain them? What will he do with himself when he is not actively engaged in a mitzva? And while he is dealing with a mitzva, what will he do with his soul?

וְיָשִׁית עֵצוֹת בְּנַפְשׁוֹ בְּמִילֵּי דִשְׁמַיָּא וּבְמִילֵּי דְעָלְמָא, וְכַיָּדוּעַ לְכָל חַכְמֵי לֵב.

and he should devise counsels within his soul, in both **matters of heaven and worldly matters, as is known to all the wise of heart.**

The material that a person studies from aggadic sources will help him both in matters of heaven – Torah and prayer – and worldly matters, in his relations with his friends, his work, his body, and so forth. To an even greater extent than words of halakha, the *aggadot* of the Talmud and all their commentaries are not enough by themselves for one to grasp and understand their message. The only counsel for this is the wisdom of the heart. This applies both to rabbis and people of influence everywhere, when it comes to influencing others and giving advice; wisdom of the heart is needed so that one can truthfully internalize the ideas.

וְגַם לִלְמוֹד מְעַט בְּ'שׁוּלְחָן עָרוּךְ' 'אוֹרַח חַיִּים' הֲלָכוֹת הַצְּרִיכוֹת לְכָל אָדָם,

They **should also learn a little *Shulḥan Arukh, Oraḥ Ḥayyim,* those *halakhot* that are essential for all people.**

The *Shulḥan Arukh,* with its commentaries, is a book of halakhic rulings, a practical summary of the entire progression of the Halakha, formulated as instructions on what a contemporary person is required to do. The *Oraḥ Ḥayyim* section of the *Shulḥan Arukh* deals with *halakhot* that are within the sphere of all people, in contrast to the other sections, which focus on less common matters and which are mainly the concern of halakhic authorities and the courts.

וְעַל זֶה אָמְרוּ רַבּוֹתֵינוּ ז"ל: "כָּל הַשּׁוֹנֶה הֲלָכוֹת בְּכָל יוֹם כו'",

Regarding this, our Rabbis said, "Whoever studies *halakhot* every day he is guaranteed that he is destined for the World to Come" (*Megilla* 28b).

It is considered so worthwhile to review *halakhot* every day that in the merit of this practice one is guaranteed a share in the World to Come.[42] In other words, this act alone gives such value to one's life that it is considered significant and valuable in the next world as well – an eternal value, unlimited in time and in any world.

שֶׁהֵן הֲלָכוֹת בְּרוּרוֹת וּפְסוּקוֹת הֲלָכָה לְמַעֲשֶׂה, כַּמְבוֹאָר בְּפֵירוּשׁ רַשִׁ"י ז"ל שָׁם (בנידה עג,א).

For those *halakhot* referred to there **are the clear, decided *halakhot*** for **practical implementation, as explained in Rashi's commentary there** (*Nidda* 73a).

That is, they offer a summary and ruling of the *halakha* in practice, without the reason for the *halakhot* and without the debate between the various opinions amongst the Sages and the ruling authorities. The ruling of the *halakha* is the revelation of the divine will itself, which is above everything. All the stages of the halachic discussion are part of the enclothing of the will in the level of *Ḥokhma* – the reason behind them, how they are formulated, and so on and so forth, but the supreme will itself, which is above all the worlds, is found solely in the ruling of the *halakha*. It is specifically in this manner that the *halakha* expresses the separateness and eternity of the divine will, and in a certain sense of the Holy One, blessed be He, Himself, within the worlds.

It should be noted that he is not referring here to *halakhot* in general, but to the review of those *halakhot* that all people require, which are those that appear mainly in *Shulḥan Arukh, Oraḥ Ḥayyim*. On a basic level, this is because such *halakhot* provide the additional advantage of study that leads to action, the practical knowledge of what one is required to do. On a deeper level, this constitutes a further extension of the drawing down of the supreme will into our space and time, into the very act that one must perform right now.

---

42. Also found in *Nidda* 73a. This saying also appears in the daily prayer book, followed by several *halakhot*, in order to fulfill its teaching.

22 Tishrei (leap year)

וּבְשַׁבַּת קֹדֶשׁ בַּעֲלוֹת הַמִּנְחָה יַעַסְקוּ בְּהִלְכוֹת שַׁבָּת, כִּי 'הִלְכְתָא רַבְּתָא לְשַׁבַּתָּא' וּבְקַל יָכוֹל הָאָדָם לִיכָּשֵׁל בָּהּ חַס וְשָׁלוֹם,

And on the holy Shabbat, at the time of the afternoon prayer, they should engage in the *halakhot* of Shabbat, as "Shabbat has great *halakhot*," over which a person can easily stumble, God forbid,

This refers to the period before or after the afternoon prayer of Shabbat. The expression "Shabbat has great *halakhot*"[43] means that the laws of *Shabbat* are numerous and complex, such that people are unaware of all the problems and prohibitions they might encounter over the course of every Shabbat. On *Shabbat* we adjust almost every aspect of our behavior from the weekdays; it is the *halakhot* of *Shabbat* that dictate these changes. One who does not know the *halakhot*, and continues to act on *Shabbat* as on the weekdays, is liable to violate serious *Shabbat* prohibitions.

אֲפִילּוּ בְּאִיסּוּר כָּרֵת וּסְקִילָה, מֵחֶסְרוֹן יְדִיעָה,

even over a prohibition that entails excision or stoning, due to lack of knowledge,

Even if one is not literally liable to stoning, as that entails a willful act in the presence of witnesses and after a warning has been issued, but rather he transgresses "due to lack of knowledge," the prohibition against desecrating *Shabbat* is nevertheless one of the most severe prohibitions of the Torah, for which one can – under certain conditions – be held liable for excision or stoning. While in other areas of life, Jews are typically aware of such serious prohibitions and keep far away from them, since the prohibitions of *Shabbat* involve the same actions that one performs every day in a permitted manner, if one does not learn the *halakhot*, he will not have sufficient knowledge to avoid stumbling in severe transgressions.

43. From *Shabbat* 32a, and the comments of the *Rishonim*. This was also the name Rabbi Shneur Zalman gave to a small pamphlet on the laws of *Shabbat* that was printed in prayer books.

וְשִׁגְגַת תַּלְמוּד עוֹלָה זָדוֹן, חַס וְשָׁלוֹם.

and an error in Talmud is considered intentional, God forbid.

In general, a lack of knowledge of a *halakha* renders one exempt from punishment – one who does not know that something is forbidden is considered an unwitting sinner, who is not as liable to punishment as a willful transgressor. Nevertheless, since the knowledge itself is mandatory, meaning, one is obligated to learn the *halakha,* it follows that if one lacks knowledge because he could have learned and yet failed to do so, he is considered a willful sinner from a certain perspective.[44] For even if he did not perform the act itself deliberately, his neglect of study was intentional, and this colors the act as well.[45]

וְאֵין צָרִיךְ לוֹמַר בְּאִיסּוּרֵי דִּבְרֵי סוֹפְרִים שֶׁרַבּוּ כְּמוֹ רַבּוּ לְמַעְלָה,

There is no need to say that the same can be said **of rabbinic prohibitions, of which there are very many more,**

If one can err with regard to severe Torah prohibitions, which are the main part of the *halakhot* of Shabbat, he is all the more liable to make a mistake when it comes to the prohibitions of the Sages, which are decrees and safeguards that were added to the basic *halakhot.* These are extremely numerous in the case of Shabbat, and many are not even aware of their existence.

וּבִפְרָט בְּאִיסּוּרֵי מוּקְצֶה, דִּשְׁכִיחֵי טוּבָא, וַחֲמוּרִים דִּבְרֵי סוֹפְרִים יוֹתֵר מִדִּבְרֵי תוֹרָה,

and especially with regard to the prohibitions of *muktze,* which are highly common; and rabbinic prohibitions are more severe than Torah matters,

44. *Avot* 4:13. See *Bava Metzia* 33b, and Rashi there, who explains that this statement applies specifically to one who issues a ruling of halakha, not ordinary people.

45. In one of his sermons (see *Torat Menaḥem* [*Hitva'aduyot*] 5744 [1984], vol. 3, p. 1751), the Lubavitcher Rebbe infers from the wording "is considered [*ola*] intentional" that although legally speaking this is of course not literally an intentional act, when we ascend [*olim*] to the interiority of a person's soul, an error in Talmud can be regarded as intentional. See also the Lubavitcher Rebbe's comments in *Shi'urim be-sefer HaTanya* ["Lessons on the Book of the *Tanya*"], chap. 32.

Every person encounters prohibitions of *muktze*, which are of rabbinic origin, every Shabbat. One of the reasons for these prohibitions is that they keep a person far from his regular weekday preoccupations, thereby creating the internal sense and atmosphere of Shabbat. Thus, by definition the prohibitions of *muktze* typically involve one's immediate surroundings, and if one is unaware of them, he is liable to violate them. One should not take rabbinic prohibitions lightly, merely because they are not from the Torah, as they are even more precious to God than the words of Torah,[46] and therefore, we too must treat them no less stringently.

כְּמוֹ שֶׁאָמְרוּ רַבּוֹתֵינוּ ז״ל, שֶׁכָּל הָעוֹבֵר עַל דִּבְרֵי חֲכָמִים, אֲפִילּוּ בְּאִיסּוּר קַל שֶׁל דִּבְרֵיהֶם, כְּמוֹ הָאוֹכֵל קוֹדֶם תְּפִלַּת עַרְבִית, וּכְהַאי גַּוְנָא, חַיָּיב מִיתָה כְּעוֹבֵר עַל חֲמוּרוֹת שֶׁבַּתּוֹרָה.

as our Rabbis said, that whoever violates the words of the Sages, even with regard to a light prohibition of theirs, such as one who eats before the evening prayer and the like, is liable to death like one who transgressions the most severe prohibitions **of the Torah.**

The Sages[47] decreed that one should not eat before the evening prayer, in case he falls asleep for the night and fails to pray. Although the transgression of a rabbinic prohibition such as this is considered lighter than violating a Torah command – as it is merely a safeguard and an adjunct to an actual Torah prohibition – nevertheless, the principle that one may not violate the words of the Sages is considered very severe, and is itself a prohibition from the Torah, for which one can, under certain circumstances, be rendered liable for death. ☞

וְכָל יָחִיד אַל יִפְרוֹשׁ עַצְמוֹ מִן הַצִּיבּוּר, אֲפִילּוּ לִלְמוֹד עִנְיָן אַחֵר, כִּי אִם בְּדָבָר שֶׁהַצִּיבּוּר עֲסוּקִין בּוֹ.

No individual may separate himself from the community, even to study a different matter, other than that in which the community is engaged.

46. This is derived from, e.g., Jerusalem Talmud, *Berakhot* 1:4, and *Avoda Zara* 2:7, which reads: "Rabbinic prohibitions are more precious than Torah matters." See also *Eiruvin* 21b.

47. *Berakhot* 4b, *Avot DeRabbi Natan*, chap. 2.

This is referring to the group of ten Jews who are studying between the afternoon prayer and the evening prayer. It includes not only one who separates himself from Torah study completely, in order to focus on other matters, but "even to study a different matter." It is true that each session of Torah study, on every topic and by all people, in private or public, has value, but this letter is dealing with the special status of communal Torah study. In the particular situation described here, when a person is part of a community that is studying together, the virtue of public study is pivotal. The power of the community is always far greater than that of an individual who is part of the community. Whoever the individual may be, the public of which he forms a part

"THE WORDS OF THE SAGES"

☞ In all generations, it was common for unlearned individuals (*amei ha'aretz*) to belittle the words of the Sages, because they failed to understand fully that the requirement to listen to them is an explicit mitzva from the Torah: "You shall do according to the statement that they will tell you...and you shall take care to perform in accordance with everything that they will instruct you" (Deut. 17:10). The Torah goes on to state: "The man who shall perform with intent, to not heed the priest...or the judge, that man shall die" (Deut. 17:12). This means that the Sages received overarching authority from God, so to speak, regarding anything they say and decree, and that it is a mitzva for us to listen to them. If so, one who rebels against the words of the Sages thereby violates not only a specific commandment of the Torah but the entire system, in principle. What is more, he slights the honor of God Himself, as He appointed the Sage to be His representative in this regard. For this, one is liable for death.

On a deeper level, God desires and takes delight, as it were, especially in what is defined and formulated by the Sages, who represent Israel down below. His innermost will is hidden in these very matters, to the extent that it cannot be defined explicitly through the words of the Torah, but only, at best, by means of allusion. The following example has been suggested in this regard: When a person wants to convey to someone else what he wants from him, provided that his request is simple and practical, he can formulate what he seeks in words. However, when his desire is internal, when it is difficult to define merely by stating "do this and that," when a certain sensitivity in required for comprehension, then his wishes can be expressed only through hints, and sometimes not even that, but only if the other person understands his mindset. That individual will answer and perform an action in response, and then it will become apparent that this was his desire. Naturally, such an outlook is available only to those who are accustomed to such matters, who study and act accordingly, who have thereby attained a grasp of the particulars of God's will on the one hand, and remain active in the world below on the other. These are the wise men of every generation.

will raise anything he does beyond his own limited reach. Therefore, in this situation one should not withdraw from the public to learn alone, but rather he should study together with the community.

וְאֵין צָרִיךְ לוֹמַר שֶׁלֹּא יֵצֵא הַחוּצָה אִם לֹא יִהְיוּ עֲשָׂרָה מִבַּלְעָדוֹ, וְעָלָיו אֲנִי קוֹרֵא הַפָּסוּק: "וְעוֹזְבֵי ה' יִכְלוּ כּוּ'" (ישעיה א, כח).

Needless to say, he may not go outside, if there will not be ten left **without him, and to him I apply the verse, "And those who forsake the Lord will perish…"** (Is. 1:28).

If one leaves a group of exactly ten people, he has disbanded the "quorum," the *minyan,* and thus he has not only lost out himself, but he has caused others to miss out as well, since there will no longer be the same lofty revelation above the *minyan*. A person who forsakes it, who fails to maintain and thereby spoils the *minyan*, is compared to one who forsakes the Lord.[48] As stated at the beginning of the letter, "ten who are sitting and engaged with the Torah, the Divine Presence rests amongst them." The Divine Presence is there, and thus one who leaves has in a literal sense, abandoned God.

כְּמוֹ שֶׁאָמְרוּ רַבּוֹתֵינוּ ז"ל (ברכות כא,ב) עַל כָּל דָּבָר שֶׁבִּקְדוּשָּׁה, כִּי אֵין קְדוּשָּׁה כִּקְדוּשַּׁת הַתּוֹרָה, דְּאוֹרַיְיתָא וְקוּדְשָׁא בְּרִיךְ הוּא כּוּלָּא חַד.

As our Rabbis said, "for any expression of sanctity may not be [said in a quorum of] fewer than ten (*Berakhot* 21b)," **as there is no sanctity like the sanctity of the Torah,** since **the Torah and the Holy One, blessed be He, are entirely one.**

The simple intention of this statement refers to, according to *halakha,*[49] those sections of prayer that can be recited only in a quorum of ten Jews. These are called "expressions of sanctity," such as Kaddish, *Kedusha,* and *Borkhu*. However, beyond the compulsory meaning of the *halakha,* one can extend this concept to include all matters

48. See *Berakhot* 8a: "They who forsake the Lord will perish" – this is referring to one who abandons a Torah Scroll and leaves.

49. Rambam, *Sefer HaAhava, Hilkhot Tefilla* 8:6; *Shulḥan Arukh, Oraḥ Ḥayyim* 55:1.

of holiness, including the study of the Torah, that they are also an "expression of sanctity."

The holy, truly separate One, is God alone; there is nothing else in Judaism that is holy. Any other sanctity to which one might refer, such as the holiness of the Jewish People and the holiness of the Land of Israel, are sacred only due to their connection to God Himself. In this regard, there is nothing that is more connected to, unified with, and representative of God, than the Torah itself, as formulated in the saying quoted here: "The Torah and the Holy One, blessed be He, are entirely one." It is of course permitted, and even a mitzva, to learn Torah when one is not in a group of ten, but there is no doubt that the Torah study of ten has special value, in that it fully expresses the concept of holiness. ☞

וְכָל הַפּוֹרֵשׁ מִן הַצִּיבּוּר כו׳ וְ״שׁוֹמֵעַ לִי יִשְׁכּוֹן בֶּטַח״ (משלי א,לג), וּבְיָמָיו וּבְיָמֵינוּ ״תִּוָּשַׁע יְהוּדָה וִירוּשָׁלַיִם תִּשְׁכּוֹן לָבֶטַח״ (ירמיה לג,טז), אָמֵן כֵּן יְהִי רָצוֹן.

And whoever separates from the community will not see the consolation of the community" (see *Ta'anit* 11a), **"but one who heeds me will reside securely"** (Prov. 1:33), **and in his days and ours, "Judah will be saved and Jerusalem will dwell in security"** (Jer. 33:16; see also 23:6), **amen, so may it be** God's **will.**

SERVING GOD IN A COMMUNITY

☞ In general, there is an essential connection between holiness and the congregation. Holiness is what is separate, what lies beyond, and the community of Israel, whose minimum definition is a *minyan*, is basically the only receptacle in reality that can contain the transcendence of holiness. It might seem that by definition there is no vessel that can hold the holy, which is that which lies beyond. Only the public, the totality of Jews, can serve as a receptacle for this purpose, since the community expresses and reveals what goes beyond the individual. Together, they unify and bind the transcendent realms of all the individuals into a palpable reality. This existence, even if it is all-encompassing with regard to the individual, is internal with respect to the whole, as it contains, like a receptacle, the reality of sanctity.

The assertions made here, with regard to public Torah study etc., are not halakhically defined, unlike, say, *Kedusha*, *Borkhu*, and the Reading of the Torah. They are too subtle and abstract to be unambiguously defined before their spiritual light shines.

One who does not pray and study with the community will not be alongside them to receive the influence from above either, as only the community can receive it.[50] The converse is also the case – one who does pray and study together with the community, who "heeds me," he "and Jerusalem will dwell in security." This mention of the future redemption in the context of one who does not separate himself from the community is a kind of continuation of the statement from *Ta'anit*, as the Talmud there proceeds to add: "Anyone who is distressed together with the community will merit seeing the consolation of the community."[51]

The connection between this letter and the future redemption can be explained in light of its earlier statement on the difference between the allocation of a reward and the manifestation of the Divine Presence. It was explained that the reward is the limited illumination that a person receives, mainly in the Garden of Eden but also in this world, whose content is the revelation that can be granted to someone from the Torah he has learned and the mitzvot he has performed. This is why the reward is always limited, as it accords with that individual's spiritual capabilities, what he can currently receive, understand, and feel. By contrast, the manifestation of the Divine Presence is the illumination of the Divine Presence itself – not what a particular person can feel, but as is: an immense illumination that is not enclothed within the vessel of the soul, but which resides over it in an encompassing manner. This distinction resembles the difference between the reward that a person receives now (in the Garden of Eden) and the reward that he will receive in the future, at the time of the ultimate redemption. The revelation will be complete at the future redemption; it will not be merely the limited illumination of the Torah one has studied, but the

In the daily reality of life down here, they can take varying forms. However, within a particular framework of life, such as between a Rebbe and his hasidim, who are connected to him and can express his inner feeling, such a requirement can also be issued in an unequivocal and binding form.

50. See also e.g., *Evel Rabbati*, chap. 3; Rambam, *Sefer HaMadda, Hilkhot Teshuva* 2:8; *Shulḥan Arukh, Oraḥ Ḥayyim* 574:5.

51. As noted by the Lubavitcher Rebbe.

full revelation of the Torah and mitzvot as they are, the true realization that "the Torah and the Holy One, blessed be He, are entirely one." These two aspects refer to the two levels of Torah study that were clarified in this letter: The study of Torah even by an individual, for which God allocates reward, and communal Torah study, when the Divine Presence rests one each person, together with the community.

This short letter can be divided, as stated, into two parts. Its first section focused on the rabbinical saying: "Ten who are sitting and engaged with the Torah, the Divine Presence rests amongst them." It explained how this differs from learning that is conducted without a group of ten, regarding which it is stated, that even if one person sits and engages in the Torah, God allocates him reward. This led to a clarification of the nature of this resting of the Divine Presence and why it occurs specifically in a company of ten. The second part of the letter set out the practical conclusions from what had been stated, namely a demand that the hasidim should not speak during prayer, and that every day between the afternoon prayer and the evening prayer they should study in public an *aggada* from the book *Ein Yaakov* and a ruling of *halakha* that they require for the fulfillment of the mitzvot.

This combination of these two sections in a single letter creates an unusual tension, as the loftiest heights of exposure to the holy descends to the simplest actions that are within reach of the ordinary folk who comprise each *minyan*.

In light of this, we can understand the comment of the sixth Lubavitcher Rebbe, Rabbi Yosef Yitzḥak Schneerson, that this letter is "a very difficult section of the *Tanya*" (*Sefer HaSiḥot*, 5704 [1944], p. 28). The expression "very difficult" is not typically used in reference to the *Tanya*. After all, the *Tanya* is the "Book of *Beinonim*," geared towards the wisdom, understanding, and knowledge of the *beinoni*, rather than the loftier tzaddik. The statement that a section of the *Tanya* is difficult therefore requires explanation. It seems that this is referring not to the standard difficulty of comprehension, but rather the difficulty in absorbing its message into our human state, into the ordinary life of our *minyan*. As the sixth Lubavitcher Rebbe, Rabbi Yosef Yitzḥak Schneerson noted in that talk, this letter does not describe the ascent that comes after a descent – when the descent is for the sake of the subsequent ascent – but rather the ascent that lies within the descent itself, when "His power's presence" descends and is currently residing in our synagogue, amid the ten simple Jews who are there studying *Ein Yaakov* and a little *halakha* between the afternoon and evening prayers.

Bringing these ideas down to reality, like their performance in practice, means to transform them from a potential to an actual state, and in a certain sense transporting them from the abstract future to the concrete present. This explains the conclusion of the letter: "But one who heeds me," to all the words of this letter, "will reside securely, and in his days and ours, Judah will be saved." For one who heeds me and acts accordingly, by studying Torah in a company of ten… is already right now ("in his days and ours") activating the future redemption, or, in the words of the sixth Lubavitcher Rebbe, Rabbi Yosef Yitzḥak Schneerson, the ascent that is present within the descent itself.

Epistle 24

CONTINUING WITH THE THEME ADDRESSED IN THE previous epistles, this letter discusses various aspects of prayer: the essence of prayer which is standing before the King, the place of prayer – in the synagogue, and the set times at which prayer is recited. This epistle, like the one before it, is divided into two parts. The first describes the spiritual stature of a person who is praying in the synagogue: he should contemplate that he is standing before God, connected to Him and nullified to Him. The second discusses the practical ramifications of this contemplation: how it affects the way that a person should act in that holy place and at that holy time.

This epistle was written soon after the previous one, apparently during the early years that the author of the *Tanya* was living in Liozna, in about the year 5545 (1785).[1]

Perhaps due to the urgency of the topic, the epistle begins with a direct appeal to the reader that he not engage in conversation during prayers. Further on, the epistle will go on to discuss the deeper meaning of this topic - in particular, inferring the positive from the negative: the power of clinging to God with love and fear, literally like standing before the King.

אֲהוּבַי אַחַי, **My beloved ones, my brethren,**

24 Tishrei

23 Tishrei (leap year)

1. See *Iggerot HaKodesh Admor HaZaken* (ibid., where this letter is identified as epistle 6).

This epistle begins with a salutation frequently employed in *Iggeret HaKodesh*, which is directed principally to the Rebbe's close Hasidim: those who are not only "beloved" and influenced by him but who are also his "brethren," in that they help, by being influential leaders along with him. As was the case in earlier epistles, this salutation precedes a demand that goes beyond minimum requirements: a demand that the hasid strive to attain a profound level in serving God that will be noticeable by others and, therefore, influence them.

אַל נָא תָּרֵעוּ, רֵיעִים, הָאֲהוּבִים לְיוֹצְרָם וּשְׂנוּאִים לְיִצְרָם.

please do not do evil, friends, beloved by their Creator [*Yotzram*] **and who are hated by their** evil **inclination** [*yitzram*].

This wordplay (which appears in *Berakhot* 61a) adds that the Rebbe's "beloved friends" are those who are beloved to God and hated by their evil inclination. The opening phrase, "do not do evil," means that even if at present a person does not palpably love God with strong feeling, he should at any rate serve God so that his situation will not worsen, but he will remain on the level of a *beinoni* who does not become evil.[2]

Beloved to their Creator, hated by their evil inclination.

Loving God and hating evil is a special level that cannot be demanded of every person (see *Likkutei Amarim*, chap. 10). Yet as the author of the Tanya explains here and elsewhere, "Beloved to their Creator" are people who wish to be on that level and so they serve Him with that intent. Those who are "hated by their inclination" are those who, even if they do not hate evil completely, do not want to grow distant from God, and so they remove themselves from evil in all ways. However, even these people, that want to love God, do not always succeed in actuality. That is because their love for their Maker and their hatred for their evil inclination do not always penetrate all of the layers of their soul, but remain theoretical. As a result, they do not feel entirely obligated to act accordingly. This letter comes for that purpose: to strengthen their love of God on the one hand, and their hatred for their evil inclination on the other.

---

2. See *Likkutei Amarim*, chap. 1, "Do not be wicked," and as explained ibid. in chaps. 13–14.

The two qualities of being a beloved friend of the Creator and being hated by one's evil inclination express the approach, that appears in several places in the *Tanya*, that the contrast between them is significant. Those beloved by their Creator are those who are hated by their evil inclination, and vice versa. A person who truly loves God hates evil. If a person does not hate evil, that indicates that his love for God is incomplete. There is no neutral realm. There is no valid time or psychological state in which a person would not love God and hate evil and instead just exist. A person must always serve God: whether he is "racing forward" or "returning," whether he is in a state of expanded consciousness or restricted consciousness. If at any moment he is not loving God, he must at least hate evil, in all of its forms, as much as he can, with fear and trepidation.

וְאַל יַעֲשֶׂה אָדָם עַצְמוֹ רָשָׁע שָׁעָה אַחַת לִפְנֵי הַמָּקוֹם

A person should not make himself wicked before the Omnipresent for even **one hour,**

The simple meaning of this Talmudic statement (*Nidda* 13a)[3] is that there is no period of time in which a person may allow himself to be wicked. The reference is not to someone who is truly wicked, someone who literally commits a sin, but to a person who allows himself a period of time in which he does not serve God: whether in actuality, in preparation, or even in waiting to do so. Here the author of the *Tanya* employs an additional meaning of the word *sha'a*, "a brief period of time." It also means "to turn to"[4] – in particular, in the sense of prayer (as that usage is employed by the Sages).[5] Therefore, this quotation is speaking especially of the time of prayer, when a person turns to God.

אֲשֶׁר בָּחַר בָּהּ מִכָּל הַיּוֹם לְהִקָּהֵל וְלַעֲמוֹד לְפָנָיו בְּשָׁעָה זוֹ,

which is chosen from the entire day for people **to assemble and stand before Him at that hour,**

3. Also *Eduyyot* 5:6. And see *Likkutei Amarim*, chap. 14.
4. As in the verse, "God turned to Abel and his offering" (Gen. 4:4).
5. As in the phrase, *ḥayei sha'a*, "transient life." And see *Likkutei Torah, Derushim LeRosh HaShana* 63d.

Prayer has set daily times. The very fact that these times have been chosen, makes them deeply and intrinsically propitious for prayer. Furthermore, since all Jews gather to pray together during these particular, set times, these times are imbued with additional auspiciousness.[6]

שֶׁהִיא עֵת רָצוֹן לְפָנָיו, **which is a time of favor before Him,**

The time of prayer is "a time of favor before Him." The set time for prayer is not only an arbitrary establishment of an agreed-upon time for all Jews to gather, but it is intrinsically propitious. It is "a time of favor" from the point of view of God Himself. Prayer is a meeting of two parties coming together. We come to that meeting when we gather in the synagogue, prepare ourselves and stand in prayer. And God, as it were, comes to meet us by revealing the depth of His will to us. ☞

לְהִתְגַּלּוֹת לָבוֹא אֶל הַמִּקְדָּשׁ מְעַט, when He **comes to the miniature sanctuary to reveal Himself,**

God reveals Himself at this time of favor by coming to the "miniature sanctuary," which is the synagogue.[7] Since prayer substitutes for the sacrificial offerings, the synagogue is a "sanctuary," analogous to the Temple. Just as the Divine Presence was revealed in the Temple during the services, there is a revelation of the Divine Presence at the time of

A TIME OF FAVOR

☞ By way of analogy, a person's soul is truly present not in what he feels obligated to do, but rather, where he deeply wants to be, where he genuinely feels is the center of his life. So too the time of prayer is "a time of favor" before God. The word for "favor," *ratzon,* literally means "desire." This is the time that God deeply desires in His inner being. Therefore, He comes there, and we stand before Him face-to-face. We turn to Him and He adjusts His presence to align with our feelings, needs and words - just as a person listening to his friend aligns himself to hear his voice and the expression of his needs. Thus, the time of prayer is "a time of favor before Him," before His inner will, when He readily listens to us.

6. See Esther 8:11 ("to assemble and stand") and see II Chronicles 29:11, "and stand before Him," in keeping with the language in Deuteronomy 10:8 ("stand before God to serve Him").

7. See. Ezekiel 11:16 and *Megilla* 29a.

the service of the heart, which is prayer. In the Temple in Jerusalem, the revelation of the Divine Presence, the source of the souls of the people of Israel, was total. However, the synagogue is only a "miniature" sanctuary because, during this time of the exile, when the people of Israel are scattered across the world and distracted in mind, the revelation of the Divine Presence in every "miniature sanctuary" is not complete but only a revelation of part of the Divine Presence that relates to and rests upon that particular congregation and each of its members.[8]

לִפְקוֹד לִשְׁכִינַת כְּבוֹדוֹ "הַשּׁוֹכֵן אִתָּם בְּתוֹךְ טוּמְאוֹתָם" (ויקרא טז,טז),

to visit the Divine Presence of His glory, "which dwells with them in the midst of their impurity" (Lev. 16:16),

God's coming to the "miniature sanctuary" is the unification of God with His Divine Presence. In Temple times, God was united with His Divine Presence. However, in the time of exile, and overall, in the external aspect of the world's existence, God is not a revealed partner with the world, meaning, He is not united with His Divine Presence. Within this world, the Divine Presence is sunken in impurity. It is in exile. It gives life to the husk that exists as though it is independent, with no apparent connection to God. But during the time of prayer, when Jews pray "in the midst of their impurity" and cling to God to unite with Him, then He comes to visit them, as it were. His Divine Presence rests upon and is revealed in that congregation in the miniature sanctuary.

וּלְהִמָּצֵא לְדוֹרְשָׁיו וּמְבַקְשָׁיו וּמְיַיחֲלָיו.

and He **makes Himself available to those who seek Him, request Him, and hope for Him.**

That is the meaning of the time of favor: God is revealed to a person who seeks Him and yearns for Him in prayer. Furthermore, God Himself comes - not with other names and forms, not via messengers. That is the time of His deepest desire, when He Himself is revealed and unites with those who seek Him.

---

8. See *Ma'amarei Admor HaZaken* 5566, part 1, p. 207.

וְהַמְסַפֵּר בִּצְרָכָיו מַרְאֶה בְּעַצְמוֹ שֶׁאֵינוֹ חָפֵץ לְהִתְבּוֹנֵן וְלִרְאוֹת בְּגִילּוּי כְּבוֹד מַלְכוּתוֹ,

A person who speaks of his own **needs** when he prays **shows that he does not desire to contemplate and see the revelation of** God's **glorious kingdom,**

A person who speaks of his worldly needs at the set time for congregational prayer is not a wicked, sinning person. He is requesting that God should grant him permitted worldly things that, at other times, are necessary. However, at this time dedicated to prayer, when God, as it were, makes Himself available to those who seek Him, when a person is focused on his own needs, he shows that he does not desire to contemplate the revelation of the glory of God's sovereignty. Not only is he not praying, but he is by definition someone who does not want to pray. This indicates that deep within he does not desire the revelation of the Divine and closeness to the Divine. If a person does something wrong, while internally, he is going against his inner desire, we say that he is under compulsion or mistaken. We take the state of his inner being as the more significant factor at that time, and we minimize the seriousness of the act. On the other hand, if a person does something permitted, but his inner will in doing so is not to grow close to God, that is something that warrants even more serious concern.[9]

וְנַעֲשָׂה מֶרְכָּבָה טְמֵאָה

and that person **becomes an impure chariot**

The concept of "chariot" refers to something that is entirely an instrument for another, greater entity acting through it. In general, this term is used to characterize the realm of the holy. Thus, the patriarchs were a chariot for holiness, as is a Jew when he performs a mitzvah.[10] However, the concept can apply to impurity as well, when the entity to which a person nullifies himself and that acts through him is the husk and the evil inclination. Just as in the realm of holiness, being a chariot is on a higher level than performing a good deed, conversely in the realm of impurity being a chariot is a more complete connection to impurity than is committing a

9. The Hebrew word used here for "desire" indicates an inner will (see *Likkutei Torah, Bemidbar* 38c; *Siddur im Divrei Elokim Ḥayyim* 293b; *Derekh Mitzvotekha, Korban Pesaḥ*) that shows the soul's inclination to a specific direction.

10. See *Likkutei Amarim*, chap. 46.

sin. When a person is a chariot for impurity, not only is his deed subjected to the husk, but so are his feelings and his deepest desires.

לַ'כְּסִיל הָעֶלְיוֹן', שֶׁנֶּאֱמַר עָלָיו: "לֹא יַחְפּוֹץ כְּסִיל בִּתְבוּנָה כו'" (משלי יח,ב), כְּמוֹ שֶׁכָּתְבוּ הַזֹּהַר וְהָאֲרִיזַ"ל.

for the "supernal fool," regarding whom it is stated, "A fool does not desire sagacity…" (Prov. 18:2), **as written in the** ***Zohar*** (1:179a) **and by the Arizal.**

The "supernal fool" refers to the evil inclination.[11] A fool is the opposite of a wise person. A wise person nullifies himself to holiness, to that which is beyond his own existence, and consequently he receives from that holiness. On the other hand, the fool is not nullified. He is filled with his own ego, which constitutes a screen beyond which he cannot see. He is not stupid (he can be very clever) but neither is he wise. The fool represents the husk, confinement, and coarseness, and all of the evil that results from that.[12] ☞

THE SUPERNAL FOOL

☞ The evil inclination is not stupid, and woe to the person who thinks otherwise. It is no less intelligent and clever than the person fighting it, but all of its wisdom is merely a reflection of that person's intelligence. That is to say, a person's evil inclination acts like a mirror to all of the forces that he enlists. If he is wise, it acts to block and uproot his wisdom and transform it to foolishness. Just as a fisherman is called a fisherman because he deals with fish, so too the evil inclination is called a fool because it deals with foolishness. Foolishness is the commodity that it buys and sells.

In a few places, the *Tanya*[13] quotes the statement of the Sages, "A person does not sin unless a spirit of foolishness enters into him" (*Sota* 3a). The assumption behind this statement, which the *Tanya* establishes on the basis of its profound description of the nature of the soul, is that a Jew never does evil of his own accord. Evil means disconnection from God. Jewish history is replete with examples of the fact that every Jew will sacrifice his life before allowing himself to be disconnected from God. If a Jew does commit a sin that disconnects him from God, that is because he thinks that he it will not disconnect him. This thought is the "spirit of foolishness." He knows that the deed is not approved of, that it is problematic,

---

11. Ecclesiastes 4:13 and *Kohelet Rabba*, ibid.

12. Perhaps the reference to the Arizal is to the commentary of the Ramaz (Rabbi Moshe ben Mordekhai Zacuto) on the *Zohar* ibid. and see *Emek HaMelekh, Sha'ar* 16, chap. 11. Perhaps the reference is to *Etz Ḥayyim, Sha'ar* 32b.

13. See *Likkutei Amarim*, chaps. 17, 24, 25, and elsewhere.

דְּהַיְינוּ שֶׁאֵינוֹ חָפֵץ לְהִתְבּוֹנֵן וְלִרְאוֹת בִּיקַר תִּפְאֶרֶת גְּדוּלָּתוֹ שֶׁל מֶלֶךְ מַלְכֵי הַמְּלָכִים הַקָּדוֹשׁ בָּרוּךְ הוּא, הַנִּגְלוֹת לְמַעְלָה בְּשָׁעָה זוֹ,

This means that he does not desire to contemplate and see the glorious splendor of the greatness of the King of kings, the Holy One, blessed be He, which are revealed above during this time,

This person becomes a chariot for the "supernal fool," which is active within him at the time of prayer.

Ideally, prayer is a time of Divine revelation. That is not to say that God's inner being is revealed at that time, but rather "the glorious splendor of the greatness of the King of kings" – how He appears to this world that He created, the finite garment via which He makes and enlivens the world of which we are a part. *Sha'ar HaYiḥud VeHa'emuna* explains that this refers to God's sovereignty, *Malkhut*, which is not only His rulership over Creation but His attribute that brings Creation into being. *Malkhut* manifests itself in various forms: in fear, splendor and greatness. At the time of prayer, the principal revelation of *Malkhut* is that of the splendor of His greatness, which inspires and invites a person to come closer to God with love and fear, and to unite with Him in the words of prayer.

וְגַם לְמַטָּה אֶל הַחֲפֵצִים לְהַבִּיט אֶל כְּבוֹדוֹ וְגָדְלוֹ,

including below, to those who wish to gaze upon His glory and greatness,

This revelation exists not only above in supernal, spiritual existence that openly expresses the Divine splendor and greatness, but also below in the physical world of deed that in general hides the Divine. At the time of prayer, those who desire to gaze upon God's glory and greatness – those who come to pray, who wish to gaze upon His glory and greatness - experience that revelation.

but he thinks that it is not so terrible, that he is still connected to the Divine, that he is still essentially a good Jew. The evil inclination sells this foolishness to him together with a long list of justifications and excuses, with a complete web of foolishness that can give even a person who does everything low and disgusting the feeling that he remains a good Jew.

הַמִּתְעַטֵּף וּמִתְלַבֵּשׁ בְּתוֹךְ תֵּיבוֹת הַתְּפִלָּה הַסְּדוּרָה בְּפִי כֹל,

the revelation that happens when **He is enveloped and clothed within the words of the prayer that is fluent in every person's mouth,**

All people pray – not only righteous and holy people abstracted of physicality who have insights into the supernal worlds. That which can clothe God's glory and greatness to the lowest places, in each individual's awareness and feeling, is the simple text of the prayer written in the *siddur* that every person can recite.

The text of prayer that we have, which was instituted by the Men of the Great Assembly for all Jews at all times, was not instituted for people on some particular level of attainment. Unlike the way in which a particular human intellectual message descends to be enclothed in speech, the Men of the Great Assembly took their universal comprehension that was imbued with divine inspiration, that came from being the central representatives of the totality of the congregation of Israel, and created this template that resonates with the intrinsic character of the congregation of Israel: that is to say, to every Jew in every era. This template is not based on the faculties and intellectual abilities of the particular person who is praying. Therefore, this template of the *siddur* can be fluent in the mouth of every Jew, because it contains this revelation in itself and descends with it to the "physical" plane of words and letters. ☞ ☞

THE PRAYER TEXT RECITED BY ALL JEWS

☞ Beyond a standard recitation of the familiar words in the siddur, every person must personalize them according to his awareness and abilities. He is able to do so because the world of the holy text is not one of inanimate, arbitrary words in which it is almost impossible to find the Divine, but rather a lofty, precisely ordered and rectified world, consisting of letters and words (of the Torah and prayer) that communicate the revelation of the Divine. This is not the place to expound upon these concepts that are explained at length elsewhere according to hasidic and mystical teachings. Yet, simply understood, one can see how the order of prayer elevates a person from one world to the next: from the poetic praise of Creation in this world, to a description of and identification with the angels and seraphim as absolute expressions of love and fear, to expiration of the soul and acceptance of the yoke of the kingdom of heaven, to a description of the Divine oneness that contains all of Creation, and then, the highest of all, to meeting the Divine face-to-face.[14]

---

14. These are the parts of prayer: *Pesukei DeZimra,* the blessings of the *Shema,* the *Shema,* and the *Amida.*

וּמִתְגַּלֶּה לְכָל אֶחָד לְפִי שִׂכְלוֹ וְשׁוֹרֶשׁ נִשְׁמָתוֹ.

a revelation **that is revealed to each** person **in accordance with his intellect and the root of his soul.**

God's revelation of Himself to an individual at the time of prayer is in accordance with the individual's intellect and soul root. Every revelation requires a vessel in which it is contained and through which it is revealed. If a person lacks the words and concepts to encompass what he sees, then even if he is aware that something is happening – a change in the atmosphere, new abilities that arise in him – it is not yet revealed to him. A person's intellect – comprised of his thinking, concepts, and knowledge – is the vessel in which the divine illumination is contained and via which it is revealed. The revelation is in keeping with the vessel. The more expansive a person's concepts, the more refined and abstract his discernment, the more developed his ability to interpret and arrange the revelation, then the higher, more expansive and more tangible will the revelation to him be.

These matters have boundless depth, beyond anything that a person can comprehend. At the very least, the order of prayers, in contrast to our confused world, enables a person who recites them humbly and attentively, to see something of God's glory and greatness.

Moreover, these are the letters and words of the Divine speech with which God creates the world and through which He is revealed. When a person recites these words, he rises from the level of the created world and connects himself with the act of Creation, the power of Creation and even the aspect of the Divine itself that is even higher than the Creator aspect of God. That is because, unlike inanimate objects, the letters of the Creation are alive and active, they are connected as words to their speaker, to God. When a person recites the words with absolutely no preconceived notions of life and of himself, with attention and connection, he need only recite them and they themselves, say what his soul says, what the heavens and earth say, and what God says.: That which is clothed in the words of the siddur, therefore, is not a text written only so that even simple people will be able to comprehend it. It is beyond any human comprehension, beyond any comprehension at all. That makes it possible for the power of these words to be spoken by all Jews.

FLUENT BY ALL

☞ The very fact that there is a text of prayer shared by all Jews is itself a great advantage. As explained in the previous epistle, when people pray or learn Torah in a congregation, that increases the value of their prayer or learning, so that it is incomparably greater than when performed by an individual. Similarly, in addition to all of the wisdom and divine, holy inspiration in the prayer text, the fact that it is designed for all Jews to recite together makes it especially valuable, because at that time, as it were, the entire Divine Presence recites the text along with them, with

In a deeper sense, the root of a person's soul determines the manner of the revelation. A person's intellect, which fumbles its way forward, feeling and reaching conclusions, is the outermost tool of his soul. As his soul and the root of his soul receive these signs and signals, they respond in their individual way. Two people who have grown up in the same environment and learned the same topics from the same teachers should apparently have similar comprehension. However, they see things completely differently because the root of their soul is different. ☞

כְּדִכְתִיב: "לְפִי שִׂכְלוֹ יְהֻלַּל אִישׁ" (משלי יב,ח) "יְהַלֵּל" כְּתִיב.

As the verse states, "According to his intellect, a man will be praised (*yehulal*)" (Prov. 12:8). "*Yehulal* (will be praised)" **is written** in a way that it can be read as ***yehalel*** ("will praise").

an all-encompassing scope that extends beyond all details, divisions and concealments, and unites completely with the supernal revelation.

THE ROOT OF A PERSON'S SOUL

☞ Although there is one root to all Jewish souls (see *Likkutei Amarim,* chap. 32), nevertheless, each individual has a soul root unique to him. There is a long path from the supernal point where all souls are identical to the reality in which every individual is unique. There is a locus on the path where a defined individual soul begins, where one can point it out and identify it and its root. From that point onward, the soul is different from other souls in terms of its task, its character, its ability, and so forth. That is the place of the light of the soul's individual root. By analogy, a person's limbs all share a single "I." They are all united in that root. Nevertheless, each limb has a separate task, character and ability. The power of a particular limb is separate from the power of the soul itself. The level on which that occurs is different for each limb. For instance, the head has a higher root on the level of the soul's awareness, whereas the foot has a lower root on the level of action in the soul.

The soul's root determines its most basic character and ability: what it is sensitive to, what is meaningful to it. That is particularly the case in the realm of holiness, because sensitivity to holiness is the deepest part of the soul. Generally, that means that "high" souls have especial sensitivity to holiness, to the Divine. Such a soul will be inspired quickly in prayer. It requires only one or two psalms, imagery, and thought on a spiritual topic to break out of its boundaries with love and yearning. On the other hand, a "lower" soul barely feels anything even when it is provided with psalms and hasidic teachings, spiritual imagery and metaphors. And there is also a lateral distinction between one soul and another. Every person has a particular passage in the siddur that speaks to him and moves him: a description, an image, a song that touches his soul so that he feels the Divine. In that passage, the divine revelation in the words of prayer reaches him: the high finds the low.

Whenever a word in Tanakh is not read the same way that it is written, that means that it has two meanings: revealed and hidden.[15] Here, the revealed meaning is that a man will be praised in accordance with his intellect, that others will recognize him and praise him. But the hidden meaning is that a person praises God in accordance with his understanding of God's greatness.

This second meaning is considered hidden because it is something that others do not see. A person's praise of God is initially internal, something between him and God. Also, his praise of God is an expression of the essence of his soul. At that moment, the soul does not relate to the world, and the world does not relate to it. The soul is alone with God. Its entire being is its experience of the revelation of God, and its praise is the light that it reflects back to Him. On the other hand, the pronounced form of the word, *yehulal,* is that which is revealed: the way in which the soul is revealed to others and to itself.

וּמַלְכוּתָא דִּרְקִיעַ כְּעֵין מַלְכוּתָא דְּאַרְעָא, **The kingdom of heaven reflects the kingdom of earth,**

This Talmudic statement has far-reaching meaning. It implies that the sovereignty of heaven, meaning, the sovereignty of God, resembles the orders of sovereignty of a flesh-and-blood king in this world, and that which we know of sovereignty below applies above as well. The topic of this epistle is a person's connection with God, with heaven, with prayer. Therefore, the author of the Tanya reverses the Talmudic statement. He teaches that not only does that which happens above mirrors that which happens below. The converse is also true and a person can shape heaven in accordance with what he does here below.

שֶׁדֶּרֶךְ הַמֶּלֶךְ לִהְיוֹת חֶבְיוֹן עוּזּוֹ בְּחַדְרֵי חֲדָרִים, **as it is the way of a king for the hidden shelter of his might to be in the innermost chamber,**

This refers to a human king. He is not revealed to everyone. The glory that characterizes his sovereignty inheres in the fact that he is hidden,

---

15. See above, epistle 19; *Torah Or, Megillat Esther* 99a; *Likkutei Torah, Devarim* 92c.

that there is distance and difference between him and the people, chamber after chamber.[16]

וְכַמָּה שׁוֹמְרִים עַל הַפְּתָחִים, **with several guards before the entrances,**

Between every chamber, between every level, there is an opening, since the essence of sovereignty is not absolutely differentiated and disconnected from the people, but rather a classified connection. Not everyone may enter and even those who are granted permission may do so only at certain times. The guards only allow the elite to enter or merely glance inside, and that, only after they prepare themselves.

In terms of the heavenly kingdom, these "guards" are not angels of destruction standing with a sword in their hands or anything else external. Rather, they are a person's internal obstacles. God reveals Himself to everyone. That being the case, the only factor that prevents the revelation is the person himself: his intellect, the root of his soul and, principally, his will and his striving, and at the very least the fact that at the time of prayer he turns his attention to other things.

(עַד) אֲשֶׁר כַּמָּה וְכַמָּה מְצַפִּים יָמִים וְשָׁנִים לִרְאוֹת עוּזּוֹ וּכְבוֹדוֹ. **(until) numerous** people **wait days and years to see his might and glory.**

People who want to see a human king must wait and prepare themselves for years for the chance to do so.

וּכְשֶׁעָלָה רְצוֹנוֹ לְהִתְגַּלּוֹת לַכֹּל, **And when it has arisen in his will to reveal himself to all,**

And when this wondrous moment happens, that the king desires to reveal himself - not in response to the will of those who wished to see him, but for his own intrinsic reason. The author of the *Tanya* uses precise language here, "to reveal himself to all;" the king decides to reveal himself to all people equally. They are all invited to come before him. In terms of the kingdom of heaven, this refers to all Jews – as a

16. See *Likkutei Amarim*, chap. 27, which states that "the hidden shelter of his might" is related to the level of the "hidden world," which cannot be presently revealed in the parameters of our world.

whole and as individuals – who are invited to come to the synagogue to pray.

וְהֶעֱבִיר קוֹל בְּכָל מַלְכוּתוֹ לְהִקָּהֵל וְלַעֲמוֹד לְפָנָיו לְהַרְאוֹתָם כְּבוֹד מַלְכוּתוֹ וִיקַר תִּפְאֶרֶת גְּדוּלָּתוֹ,

and he circulates a proclamation throughout his kingdom that the people should **assemble and stand before him** so **that** he may **show them his glorious kingdom and the honor of the greatness of his majesty,**

The will of the King does not remain hidden, but rather, "circulates," is the significant bridge between the inner and external dimensions. He draws down a "proclamation throughout His kingdom," which implies, throughout all the worlds.[17]

Although this revelation arose in the King's will in a one- sided way, in actuality it cannot occur only one-sided. There are some things that can be done unidirectionally, such as creating infinite worlds. But revelation cannot be unidirectional. As stated earlier, revelation is in accordance with the recipient's intellect, with his soul. This applies to all domains. Even if a person is shown sights and visions, that does not mean that he comprehends them. He must want, seek, understand and process what he sees within his soul. Only then is something revealed to him.

Here too, in order for Hashem to be revealed to all, people must gather together, to congregate in one place and open themselves to each other – they must have a single will with a united intent and a single way of thought, in order to be together in that experience. They must stand, because standing always indicates self-nullification (like standing in prayer and like the standing in place of the seraphim). That nullification is a vital condition for revelation: every revelation of something new requires the nullification of a person's previous knowledge, and in a certain sense even of the recipient's personhood and being. All the more so, regarding a public community: it is impossible for there to be a public if the individuals do not nullify themselves in some way to each

17. See *Torah Or* 68c and *Likkutei Torah, Devarim* 20:1.

other; and how much more before Him. By way of analogy, relating to another person superficially does not require self-nullification: one takes from him what one needs, and that is all. But every instance of relating to the inner essence of another requires self-nullification: what is relevant is not what I want and think, but what the other being wants and thinks, and so forth. In order to receive, a person must first nullify (in that context) his own will and understanding. All of this, as stated earlier, is a preparation that people must make so that the King will show them the glory of His sovereignty. ☞

מִי שֶׁעוֹמֵד לְפָנָיו then, if a person **who stands before him**

People who stand before the king are no longer at the starting point: the king has issued his proclamation, and the people have come and they are standing before him. After all of the effort and striving, from the highest to the lowest level, the tension reaches its pinnacle. Even before any revelation, the king is already present. From the aspect of the anticipation and intention of the king and the people, this is the peak moment, even more than the subsequent moment of revelation.

וְאֵינוֹ חוֹשֵׁשׁ לִרְאוֹתוֹ, וּמִתְעַסֵּק בִּצְרָכָיו, **does not care to see him but is preoccupied with his** own **needs,**

TO ASSEMBLE AND STAND

☞ This expression is taken from the book of Esther. There it has the meaning of assembling and standing in order to engage in battle. And the *Zohar* states that "the time of prayer is a time of battle" (see *Zohar* 3:243a; *Likkutei Torah*, Deut. 34c, Num. 72a, 6–26b). When a person stands up to pray from the material world, he is working to distill the good, to elevate it from reality, from his bodily connections and his animal soul. He engages in the work of refining and elevating aspects within a reality that wants otherwise, that is subjugated to battle and struggle. That struggle is not simply an inevitable byproduct of life, but rather is crucial so that a person may fulfill the task of his soul and the task of prayer: to bring about a reality in which that the revelation of the divine will come not only to his holy soul but also to his natural-animal soul and indeed to the entire world, so that they will rise and be united in a state of holiness.

If, at that moment, a person has no interest in seeing the king, if he is not entirely concerned with standing before him, but he instead attends to his own needs – he answers the phone, he counts his money – then even if he does not leave (and he does nothing forbidden) his behavior is unimaginable. What can possibly be said about such a person?

כַּמָּה גָּרוּעַ וְסָכָל וּפֶתִי הוּא! וְנִמְשַׁל כַּבְּהֵמוֹת נִדְמָה בְּעֵינֵי כָּל הַבְּרִיּוֹת.

how inferior, foolish, and witless that person **is! All people view him as comparable to the beasts that perish.**

One cannot say that this person is wicked, because he has no tangible benefit from his behavior. He is simply an utter idiot!

Whoever sees a person acting this way cannot understand how it is possible for someone to fail to appreciate the situation he is in. The only way to explain this is by saying that he is like an animal that lacks the intelligence to understand and distinguish between one situation and another (e.g., between the Temple and a barn), and to act accordingly.

וְגַם הוּא בִּזְיוֹן הַמֶּלֶךְ, בְּהַרְאוֹתוֹ לְפָנָיו שֶׁאֵינוֹ סָפוּן בְּעֵינָיו לְקַבֵּל נַחַת וְשַׁעֲשׁוּעִים מֵהַבִּיט אֶל כְּבוֹדוֹ וְיָפְיוֹ יוֹתֵר מֵעֵסֶק צְרָכָיו.

In addition, this person **has insulted the king, because he shows** the king **that to have gratification and pleasure from gazing at** the king's **honor and beauty is not** more **important** to him **than dealing with his** own **needs.**

Besides the fact that the person's behavior is idiotic and disgraceful, it constitutes an insult to the king. The fact that in his idiocy the person loses this rare chance that was given to him is his own problem. But when he insults the king, that is altogether a different problem. ☞

וְגַם הוּא מִתְחַיֵּיב בְּנַפְשׁוֹ לַמֶּלֶךְ, עַל הַרְאוֹת קְלוֹנוֹ וּבִזְיוֹנוֹ אֶת הַמֶּלֶךְ לְעֵין כָּל רוֹאֶה.

He also incurs death before the king because he displays his disrespect and contempt for the king for all to see.

If a person insults the king in private, the king can respond in whatever way he desires. He can even overlook the slight. But when a person insults the king in public, in the sight of everyone, that constitutes rebellion against the sovereignty, the punishment for which is death. Even the king cannot forgive him, as it were.[18]

וְעַל זֶה נֶאֱמַר: "וּכְסִילִים מֵרִים קָלוֹן" (משלי ג,לה). כְּלוֹמַר, אַף שֶׁהוּא כְּסִיל לֹא יְהְיֶה מֵרִים קָלוֹן, שֶׁיִּהְיֶה נִרְאֶה הַקָּלוֹן לְעֵין כֹּל.

Regarding this, the verse states, "And fools raise shame" (Prov. 3:35). **That is to say, even if** a person **is a fool, he should not lift up** the king's **shame, making** his **shame visible to all.**

Even if a person is a fool, an idiot and a sinner, he should not act that way before others so that they may see and participate. This is an allusion to public prayer in the synagogue. A person who acts in such a disgraceful way ruins not only his own standing before God, but that of the entire congregation. And from the perspective of God the King, a public insult is an insult to the higher and much more perfected level that is manifested especially in the congregation, in particularly a group of ten Jews.

24 Tishrei (leap year)

וְעַל כֵּן קָבְעוּ חֲכָמֵינוּ ז"ל (ברכות לג,א) בַּתְּפִלָּה כְּאִלּוּ עוֹמֵד לִפְנֵי הַמֶּלֶךְ.

Therefore, our Sages instituted the principle (*Berakhot* 33a) **that in prayer** a person should feel **as though he is standing before the king.**

INSULT TO THE KING

☞ When, as a person stands before the king and attends to his own needs, he shows that he considers his needs, whatever they may be, equal to the importance of the king! He relates to the king not even as to another person but as one of his needs. A person is honored when people relate to his feelings, his needs, his perspective. And he is insulted when people relate to him as a mere object, as the supply for others' needs. This is true when it comes to any person, however, when it comes to the king, whose whole essence is his honor, which is higher than and separate from the nation, the disgrace is a denial of the king's existence.

18. See *Kiddushin* 32b, *Sanhedrin* 19b, and in Rambam, *Hilkhot Melakhim* 2:3–5.

This is the image that our sages depicted for every person to imagine in his mind's eye. God reveals Himself in many ways: as a father, as a rabbi, as a hasid or as a warrior; every one of his names and *sefirot* is essentially another form in which he expresses Himself. Yet, when a person prays, he must imagine that he is standing before the King. ☞

עַל כָּל פָּנִים יִהְיֶה מַרְאֶה בְּעַצְמוֹ כְּאִלּוּ עוֹמֵד כו׳ **At the very least, he should present himself as though he is standing...,**

It is proper and desirable that a person feel that he is standing before the King of kings, because that is in fact the case. However, even if he cannot, he should at any rate, act as though he is standing before the King.

לְעֵין כָּל רוֹאֶה בְּעֵינֵי בָּשָׂר אֶל מַעֲשָׂיו וְדִיבּוּרָיו, **in the view of all who see his conduct and speech with** their **physical eyes,**

He should at least act appropriately in physical and exterior matters - in his actions and speech - that other people can see. No one else knows what a person experiences, but others can hear and see what he says and does. ☞

AS THOUGH HE IS STANDING BEFORE THE KING

☞ Since prayer is one's ascension from this world and his own existence, to cling to the Divine, the starting point of all prayer is the ability to relate to the other that stands before him: to emerge beyond the question of how he sees and what he needs, and to relate to the one who stands before him. The essential idea of God as an absolute other who stands before a person is captured by the hasidic concept of the king. The king is elevated beyond, separated from and distinctive from the people. Nevertheless, He is not disconnected from them. He is the ruler, the sovereign. He takes and He gives. Without Him, nothing in the kingdom is accomplished. His governance is not at all dependent on the people. He can do whatever He wants and He need not ask permission of anyone. When a person about to pray bears this concept in mind, his prayer will proceed in the proper fashion. By analogy, when a person is in a deep and dark pit and he wants to extricate himself, he must grasp a rope tied above to the outside. Only then can he climb out. His grasp of the rope parallels a person praying who grasps the King who stands before him. There are many ledges and steps that can help a person climb. But without his constantly holding onto the rope that is tied above, nothing will help him.

אַף שֶׁאֵין לוֹ מַחֲשָׁבָה לַכְּסִיל. **even though a fool has no thought.**

In *Likkutei Amarim,* the author of the *Tanya* discusses three categories of people: the tzaddik, the *beinoni,* and the wicked person. He states that the *beinoni* exercises control over the three garments of his soul: thought, speech, and deed.[19] Here, he discusses the fool, who is not presently a *beinoni,* yet is still part of the congregation, one of the ten that the Divine Presence rests upon. He is neither a *beinoni,* nor is actually wicked. In relation to the service of the congregation, the author of the *Tanya* speaks of this additional distinction between garments of the soul, that he does not discuss in *Likkutei Amarim.* Although he does not control his thought, he does control the two external garments of his soul: his speech and deeds, and that suffices for him to be a part of the congregation. As for the internal garment, that of thought, even if he has no thought, even if he cannot think and imagine that he is standing before the King, he can still be part of the congregation, as long as he can speak and act like a person standing before the King.[20]

וְעַל זֶה הָעִנְיָן נִתְקַן כָּל הַתְּפִלּוֹת, לַמִּתְבּוֹנֵן בָּהֶם הֵיטֵב. **All of the prayers were established after this** pattern, as may be seen by anyone **who reflects deeply on them.**

IN THE VIEW OF ALL WHO VIEW HIM WITH THEIR PHYSICAL EYES

☞ This advice is first and foremost for the person himself. A person is required to act in a way that appears right to others, because when he does so, even if that is not aligned with his understanding and feelings, his prayer is proper. And, as he prays, he will come to feel what he had not originally felt. Another layer of this advice relates to the congregation. What the people in a congregation think and feel is first of all based on what they simply see with their physical eyes. The all-encompassing power of the congregation transcends the abilities of all its constituents. Yet, for this to actually happen, for them to be privy of the power of the group, they must feel that they are a connected group, moving with each other, and assisting one other, not each man for himself. When each person looks at the others in the congregation, and does not view them as separate from him, but rather as standing together before the king, this is what holds the congregation's prayer.

---

19. *Likkutei Amarim,* chaps. 4, 12.

20. See Mishna *Taharot* 8:6 and more, which state that "a deaf person, fool and minor…have deed, but they do not have thought."

The structure of the prayer service and all of its laws and customs were established to support the pattern of a person standing before the King. The King invites each of us to a private and personal meeting, for which we prepare ourselves. First, we dress appropriately, in *tallit* and *tefillin*. We prepare our mind by reflecting on the King's greatness and on His lovingkindness in having agreed to receive us. Then we enter the palace and pass from room to room. We go from the outer chamber (*Pesukei deZimra*) to the chamber where the great servants stand (the blessings on the *Shema*) and from there to the inner chamber where the important ministers stand. At last, as we recite the *Amida*, we stand before the King in awe, fear and love, and we bow before Him. We do not immediately state what we want, but first address Him with words of praise. After that, we make our requests, following which we again bow and thank Him. And then we take our leave, not turning away but stepping backwards. We retrace our steps from room to room, as we leave the palace. As the kabbalistic books state, the order of prayer after the *Amida* parallels in reverse order the prayer leading to the *Amida*.

וּמִי שֶׁאֵינוֹ מַרְאֶה כֵּן מִתְחַיֵּיב בְּנַפְשׁוֹ, A person **who does not present himself in this manner incurs the death penalty,**

This is no game: it is really the case. Even if a person does not feel that he is standing before the King, that does not change the fact that he in fact is. When we come to pray, regardless of what we feel, we are standing before Him, and we are not free to act otherwise. ☞

INCURS THE DEATH PENALTY

☞ Clearly there is no place for a person to artfully claim that if he does not think that he is standing before the King, he is not. This is in keeping with the well-known statement of the Ba'al Shem Tov: "In a place where a person thinks, there he is found" (see *Keter Shem Tov* 56, and addenda 48). This psychological subjectivity does not apply here. When a person comes to the synagogue and people see him; he can no longer say that the reality depends solely on his thought. His personal obligation depends on the degree to which he has resolved to live this truth. A person who thinks about standing before the King, in addition to speaking words and acting in a way that attests to this, may incur the death penalty even by simply thinking about something else, even if he does not perform any heretical act. Here, however, a person who only acts inappropriately, incurs the death penalty only when he does not act appropriately.

וְעָלָיו אָמְרוּ בַּזֹּהַר הַקָּדוֹשׁ (חלק ב קלא,ב): דְּאַנְהִיג קְלָנָא בְּתִקּוּנָא עִילָּאָה וְאַחֲזֵי פְּרוּדָא, וְלֵית לֵיהּ חוּלְקָא בֶּאֱלָהָא דְּיִשְׂרָאֵל, רַחֲמָנָא לִיצְּלַן.

and the holy *Zohar* says of such a person (2:131b) **that "he brings the shame to the supernal rectification and shows** that he is **separate, and** thus **he has no share in the God of Israel," God save us.**

The "supernal rectification" is the unification and perfection of the supernal faculties. Intrinsically, these faculties are already rectified. Damage, destruction, confusion, and concealment exist only in the worlds below. However, since what is below descends from and is linked to what is above, any damage below affects that which is above. As long as that which is below remains unrectified, the rectification above is no longer whole and genuine. And only a person who is himself in the world below can rectify it. When he rectifies himself and the worlds via his Torah, service of God and deeds of lovingkindness, he draws the oneness, God's unity with His Divine Presence, up to the highest heights, higher and higher. However, if a person does not bring about any rectification below – for instance, if, during prayer, which is the time of unification and bonding of all the worlds, he acts as though he is not standing before the King, and he separates himself from the King – then, because he does not attend to the supernal rectification, he disgraces it. With that, he demonstrates separation from the rectification and from the supernal oneness. Consequently, "he has no portion" – bond and relationship - "with the God of Israel," who is one.

Saying that a Jew has no portion in the God of Israel is extremely grave, perhaps the gravest statement that one can make, one that is even frightening. Therefore, the author of the *Tanya* adds, "God save him."

עַל כֵּן שְׁלִיחוּתַיְיהוּ דְּרַבּוֹתֵינוּ ז"ל קָא עָבֵידְנָא לִגְזוֹר גְּזֵירָה שָׁוָה לְכָל נֶפֶשׁ

Consequently, I am coming as an agent of our Rabbis to impose a decree applying equally to everyone:

The author of the *Tanya* is not initiating anything new. He comes as an agent of our Sages, who established the text and order of the prayer, and stated that a person should view himself as standing before the King. The decree of excommunication that the author of the *Tanya* institutes is based on the authority of the early Sages, to whose words all Jews are obligated.

Just as the order of prayer applies equally to all and is not unique to a spiritual elite – to Torah sages or tzaddikim – so too this decree applies to and obligates every individual: a simple Jew and a pious scholar alike. ☞

שֶׁלֹּא לָשׂוּחַ שִׂיחָה בְטֵלָה, מִשֶּׁיַּתְחִיל הַשְּׁלִיחַ צִיבּוּר לְהִתְפַּלֵּל הַתְּפִלָּה עַד גְּמַר קַדִּישׁ בַּתְרָא, שַׁחֲרִית עַרְבִית וּמִנְחָה וכו׳.

That a person should **not engage in idle conversation from when the Prayer Leader starts the prayers until the end of the last** ***Kaddish*****:** In **the morning prayer, the evening prayer, and the afternoon prayer…**

This decree does not add to the halakha, which states[21] that a person may not engage in any trivial conversation in the synagogue, and certainly not when the Prayer Leader starts the prayers.[22] Apparently, this is a "decree" in that it imposes excommunication upon a person who transgresses this rule.[23]

A DECREE THAT APPLIES EQUALLY TO EVERYONE

☞ Every person tends to have an excuse why a rule does not apply to him. A simple, unlearned Jew might think that this decree about prayer applies only to spiritually elevated people who understand the content of the prayer and feel connected to the Divine, whereas if he only feels like an onlooker, then he is not included in this obligation. While an intellectual hasid and a person dedicated to serving God, might think that these matters relate to regular people who pray in a congregation and at best think about the simple meaning of the words, whereas he is beyond all that, because his understanding and contemplation transcend the time and space of the congregational prayer.

---

21. See Rambam, *Hilkhot Tefilla* 11:6; *Tur VeShulḥan Arukh, Oraḥ Ḥayyim* 151:1.
22. It is possible that the ellipses here come to include the *Musaf* prayers, or perhaps every recitation of praise and beseeching in the public services in the synagogue. Alternatively, it might be referring to the continuation of the epistle from this point onward, which is not included in the first edition.
23. The three elements in the phrase, "the morning prayer, the evening prayer

וְהָעוֹבֵר עַל זֶה בְּזָדוֹן יֵשֵׁב עַל הָאָרֶץ, וִיבַקֵּשׁ מִ־ג׳ אֲנָשִׁים שֶׁיַּתִּירוּ לוֹ נִידּוּי שֶׁלְּמַעְלָה.

A person **who purposely violates this** decree **must sit on the ground and ask three people to nullify the supernal excommunication** that has been imposed upon **him.**

If a person is aware that such conversation at the time of prayer is forbidden yet he engaged in it, this decree of excommunication applies to him.

To rectify that, he must sit on the ground like a mourner (an excommunicated person must engage in a number of mourning customs).

Excommunication may be removed only by three Jewish men, who constitute a Jewish court of law. Even if a person was excommunicated by a single sage or via a decree (as the one here) or even if he accepted excommunication upon himself, he requires a Jewish court of law to release him. That is because excommunication is not a punishment imposed solely by human beings, but punishment in which human beings participate with God, as it were. Therefore, releasing a decree of excommunication also requires the participation of human beings with God. This is accomplished by a Jewish court of law, since God's Presence rests[24] on every such court and so is considered God's own court of law.

"וְשָׁב וְרָפָא לוֹ" (ישעיה ו,י) וְלֹא חָל עָלָיו שׁוּם נִידּוּי לְמַפְרֵעַ כָּל עִיקָּר.

"And he will repent and be healed" (Isa. 6:10). **Retroactively, no excommunication** will have **applied to him at all.**

---

and the afternoon prayer," are out of order. The Lubavitcher Rebbe writes (in *Shiurim BeSefer HaTanya*),

> It appears to me that a possible way to explain the order [is to read this as] "the morning prayer, the evening prayer and *even* the afternoon prayer." That is to say, even in the afternoon prayer, which comes [as a] continuation of the morning prayer (as seen [by the fact] that there is no need to recite the *Shema* again), there is a strict [prohibition against] interrupting the prayer with speech (although he interrupts, in the simple sense, between the *Shema* of the morning prayer that relates also to the afternoon prayer – to the afternoon prayer)."

See also *Likkutei Levi Yitzḥak LaTanya*, p. 48, for in a different explanation.

24. *Avot* 3:6, *Berakhot* 6a, and elsewhere.

After having made grave statements about this sin and its punishment, the author of the *Tanya* concludes with words of appeasement and consolation.

Excommunication is like illness. Therefore, being released from it is the equivalent of healing. However, this healing is not like that in the case of a physical disease, in which a person was ill and is now cured. With this healing, it is as though the person had never been "ill," as though he had never been excommunicated.

כִּי מִתְּחִלָּתוֹ לֹא חָל כִּי אִם עַל הַמּוֹרְדִים וְהַפּוֹשְׁעִים שֶׁאֵינָם חוֹשְׁשִׁים כְּלָל לְבַקֵּשׁ כַּפָּרָה מִן הַשָּׁמַיִם וּמִן הַבְּרִיּוֹת עַל הֶעָוֹן פְּלִילִי הַזֶּה.

That is **because from the outset** this excommunication **applied only to rebels and transgressors, who have no intent whatsoever to request forgiveness of Heaven and of people for this criminal offense.**

Although this person acted willfully, there is a great difference between being willful and being rebellious and sinful. Even as a willful person sins, he knows that he is committing a sin, and he also knows the severity of the sin. Nevertheless, he is not rebelling against God. He sins because his evil inclination has overcome him, because a thought of foolishness has entered into him. But in essence, he is still sound. However, a rebellious person turns his back on God's sovereignty. Therefore, he does not request forgiveness for this sin. But when a person understands that he deserves excommunication and so he sits on the ground and asks three people to release him, he demonstrates that that he was not acting as a rebel. Therefore, from the outset the excommunication had never applied to him.

וְגַם דַּוְקָא כְּשֶׁמְּדַבְּרִים בְּזָדוֹן בִּשְׁאָט נֶפֶשׁ, וְלֹא עַל הַשּׁוֹכֵחַ אוֹ שֶׁנִּזְרְקוּ מִפִּיו כַּמָּה תֵּיבוֹת בְּלֹא מִתְכַּוֵּין, שֶׁאֵין צָרִיךְ הַתָּרָה כְּלָל.

Also, this applies **specifically when** people **speak willfully, with contempt, not when** a person **forgets** to refrain from speaking **or when a few words have slipped unwittingly from his mouth. That does not require annulment at all.**

He is not even like a person who did something wrong thinking that it is permitted. Rather, he had acted without thinking. Such a person does not require to be released from excommunication, because he had never really incurred excommunication. Even when it does not occur to him to seek atonement, and so allegedly he does not repent, that is not necessarily a sign that he is being rebellious, because it is possible that he is completely oblivious to what he has been doing.

"וּבוֹחֵן לִבּוֹת וּכְלָיוֹת אֱלֹקִים צַדִּיק" (תהלים ז,י). **"The God of righteousness probes men's minds and hearts"** (Ps. 7:10).

Only God can see such differentiations in a person's intent, even when the person himself does not really know the nature of his impetus when he acted as he did. A person may rely on the "God of righteousness" to see and judge him truly and fairly.

"הֵטִיבָה ה' לַטּוֹבִים וְלִישָׁרִים בְּלִבּוֹתָם" (תהלים קכה,ד). **"Be good, Lord, to those who are good, and to the upright of heart"** (Ps. 125:4).

The author of the *Tanya* concludes with the language of prayer and blessing: May God, who probes the heart, be good to a person who is good and upright in his heart, even if he does not always appear to be. May God treat him well and not judge him as guilty.

Principally, this short epistle has expressed a single idea: that a person should not converse or engage in his own needs at the time of prayer. It is true that this is self-evident. This is a halakha that is stated explicitly in the *Shulḥan Arukh* and it also constitutes simple good manners. Nevertheless, as we see today in every synagogue, people do not conduct themselves this way. The principal reason for this is that most people do not see God's kingdom openly revealed in the world. Because the world seems to revolve on its own, people do not sense the King's boundless rulership over everything and every occurrence. As a result, it is hard for them to relate to the King and, when they pray, to feel that they are standing before Him. The first part of the epistle comes to help a person praying to understand and picture that when he stands in prayer, in particular with the congregation in the synagogue, he is standing before the King.

The problem is not quite as severe regarding a person's individual prayer and personal service of God because when he desires to approach the King, he does so because his mind and heart are opened and inspired: he experiences the preparation, the emotion, and the stepping forward all as one thing. However, public prayer is different: when people come to a synagogue at a designated time, and recite the same text in unison, they do not necessarily feel the import of their action. Therefore, this epistle comes to bolster a person's awareness that he is standing before the King. When a person realizes this, it is impossible, or at least uncomfortable, not to act as though he is standing before the King. And in case this does not suffice to affect the reader, the author of the *Tanya* imposes excommunication on a person who engages in trivial speech and the like. Excommunication is a serious step. Since it is not the way of the author of the *Tanya* to speak in such terms, he emphasizes that he views this matter as gravely as rebellion against the King. It is true that there are excuses, that people are insensitive to this and so they converse although they do not intend any sort of rebelliousness. But still, how is it possible to engage in conversation at the time of prayer?

Epistle 25

THIS EPISTLE, ONE OF THE LONGER ONES OF *IGGEROT HaKodesh,* deals entirely with the explanation of a short statement of the Ba'al Shem Tov. The epistle seems to have been written around the years 1795–1796, against the backdrop of increasing resistance of the opposition to Hasidism. It may have been written as a response to the well-known event of the burning of the book *Tzava'at Rivash,*[1] mentioned in this epistle (as stated in the introduction to this epistle in the *Iggerot HaKodesh* of the author of the *Tanya,* where it is epistle 45).

This epistle is different from the other epistles in a few respects. Firstly, in its context: In contrast to the other epistles, it is not directed to hasidim, but rather toward the *mitnagdim.* Even if it was not written directly to them, it is a response to their claims nonetheless.[2] The author of the *Tanya*'s general approach was not to enter into arguments and confrontations with the *mitnagdim.*[3] Therefore, this epistle is not written in the style of polemics.[4] Even so, there

1. As stated in the introduction to this epistle in the *Iggerot HaKodesh* of the author of the *Tanya* (there it is epistle 45).
2. Accordingly, the following appears as a title to this epistle in a hand-written manuscript: "*Iggeret HaKodesh* written by the author of the *Tanya* to the congregation of Vilna."
3. See epistle 2 above.
4. The author of the *Tanya*'s aversion to relating to the conflict over the Ba'al Shem Tov has been explained differently, more internally, in that his connection to the Ba'al Shem Tov was so close that the author of the *Tanya* was unable to utter even a small, quoted contradiction or rejection of the words of the Ba'al Shem

is a deep and expansive explanation of the words of the Ba'al Shem Tov, with hints of the opinions of the *mitnagdim* that are in the background, with the assumption the disagreement is known and that there is no reason to review it explicitly.

The other unique aspect of this epistle is its direct, even explicit, relating of the Torah of the author of the *Tanya*, the Torah of Chabad, to that of the Ba'al Shem Tov. Although it is known that the author of the *Tanya* had a profound soul-connection with the Ba'al Shem Tov, and thus, that there is a tight linking of the Torah of the author of the *Tanya* with that of the Ba'al Shem Tov (as all leaders of Chabad emphasize),[5] this connection is not usually visible to the eye. This illustrates the importance of this epistle, in which the author of the *Tanya* relates directly to the Torah of the Ba'al Shem Tov and explains it in his own way. Moreover, as is stated at the end of the epistle, this is not only an explanation of a specific piece of the teachings of the Ba'al Shem Tov, but rather it is an example and archetype for how to understand and elucidate the many Torah ideas and statements of the Ba'al Shem Tov.

25 Tishrei

25 Tishrei (leap year)

לְהָבִין אִמְרֵי בִינָה **To comprehend statements of discernment,**

This is the same epistle called in many places in the writings of Chabad, "to comprehend statements of discernment."

"Statements of discernment" is an expression in the book of

Tov, not even the appearance of a rejection or a quote in someone else's name. Just speaking such words appeared to him as separating himself from the Ba'al Shem Tov, and the author of the *Tanya* was not willing to separate himself like that even for an instant (see *HaTamim*, booklet 2, p. 56, and also *Lessons in Tanya*).

5. As is told, when the author of the *Tanya* was in prison, his teachers, the Maggid of Mezeritch and the *Ba'al Shem Tov* came to visit him. They gave their support of his Torah as theirs, and directed him to continue teaching (see *Beit Rebbe* part 1, chap. 16, in the comments, and see *Likkutei Siḥot* vol. 30, p. 170). See *Iggeret HaKodesh* of the fifth Lubavitcher Rebbe, Rabbi Sholom Dovber Schneerson, part 1, p. 259: "The Torah of Chabad Hasidism is identical to the Torah of the Ba'al Shem Tov."

Proverbs,[6] and the author of the *Tanya* here relates it to words of Torah that relate to understanding, the level of *Bina*. This is also the way he relates to the statement here of the Ba'al Shem Tov, in a way that allows it to be understood and explained to others. ☞

מַה שֶּׁכָּתוּב בַּסֵּפֶר הַנִּקְרָא 'צַוָּואַת רִיבָ"שׁ' **which are written in the book called *Tzava'at Rivash*,**

The Ba'al Shem Tov himself did not write any books or record his teachings in writing. The teachings that we have are collections from the writings of his students and teachings that spread by word of mouth. Many of these teachings are collected into the book, *Tzava'at Rivash*, which literally means, the Testament of Rabbi Yisrael Ba'al Shem Tov. It is one of the first books of Hasidism, and the first of the collected works[7] that attempted to clarify the words of the Ba'al Shem Tov and organize them. It is not clear why the book was named this way, but perhaps a hint to this can be found in the responsa of the author of the *Tanya* from his period of imprisonment,[8] in which he relates to this question. He writes that the book "was composed by a person who

STATEMENTS OF DISCERNMENT – THE *TANYA* AND THE BA'AL SHEM TOV

☞ It can also be said that these words somewhat define the nature of this epistle as an expression of the relationship between the author of the *Tanya* and the Ba'al Shem Tov. Among the hasidim of Chabad, it is accepted to describe this relationship as that of *Hokhma* and *Bina*, and thus, as the author of the *Tanya* approaches the Torah of the Ba'al Shem Tov, he relates to it as the relationship of *Bina* to *Hokhma* (see the lecture of the sixth Lubavitcher Rebbe, Rabbi Yosef Yitzḥak Schneerson, *Parashat Ki Tisa*, 5688 (*Sefer HaSihot* 5688–5691, p. 19 and onward), and *Likkutei Siḥot* vol. 19 p. 255; see also *Keter Shem Tov, Hosafot*, Section 420, in the seven teachings of the *Ba'al Shem Tov*, and the explanations of the Rebbe). He does so in the manner of a modest person who has not come to say anything new, but rather to reveal and detail what is already there.

6. Based on Prov. 1:2.
7. In the words of *Amud HaSha'ar*: "As was found in the pouch of a hasid, and explained by the man of God, our teacher Rabbi Yeshaya, the head judge and leader of the holy congregation of Yanov." First printed in Zalkwa, 5553 (1793).
8. Translated and published by Rabbi Yehoshua Mondshein, in *Kerem Chabad* vol. 4, and printed in *Iggeret HaKodesh* of the author of the *Tanya*, epistle 74.

was present at the passing of the Ba'al Shem Tov." It was this book that particularly aroused the ire of the *mitnagdim* and was even burned at the direction of the Vilna Gaon. It is therefore no surprise that the author of the *Tanya* chose to specifically explicate this book in his epistle to the congregation of Vilna.

Before beginning to explain the book itself, he prefaces with some general points about the book.

הֲגַם שֶׁבֶּאֱמֶת אֵינָהּ צַוָּאָתוֹ כְּלָל **although in truth it is not his testament at all**

The author of the *Tanya* first relates to the title of the book. Although it is called "the testament," it is not actually the testament of the Ba'al Shem Tov. Any person who actually reads the book will observe immediately that it is not a testament, not even a spiritual one. Meaning, this is not a thoughtful summation left behind by a person after his death, in which he is concerned about clarifying his thoughts such that no one should be confused after his death at which time he would be unable to correct them. That is what the author of the *Tanya* is explaining here, that this is not a testament. Therefore, one should relate to the ideas of the book as if they were spoken by a living person to other living people who shared a spiritual connection and atmosphere. Such things, when approached by later generations in a different spiritual environment, are often difficult to understand. In order to grasp them, they must first be broadly introduced and contextualized, in order to create an atmosphere similar to that of the original context, in an organized way. That is the purpose of the author of the *Tanya* in this epistle.

וְלֹא צִוָּה כְּלָל לִפְנֵי פְּטִירָתוֹ. **and he did not issue any command before his passing.**

By adding the phrase "he did not issue any command before his passing," perhaps the author of the *Tanya*'s purpose is to mention that this was not the way of the Ba'al Shem Tov at all. It is not a coincidence that the Ba'al Shem Tov did not write, for he was a vibrantly living person, and everything he said and did was within the vibrancy of life, the ways of living people and situations. This was his greatness, and such a quality cannot be captured in any text, or crystalized for later generations.[9]

רַק הֵם לִקּוּטֵי אִמְרוֹתָיו הַטְּהוֹרוֹת **Rather, they are a collection of his pure sayings,**

The statements of the Ba'al Shem Tov – he doesn't even call them by the more official word *ma'amar,* discourse, but by the more casual term "his sayings" – are themselves pure. Meaning, they are something which emerged from the inner dimension and entered into the inner dimension, from one divine soul to another (regarding which we say, "the soul you gave me is pure") without the garments or covers that exist for things that traverse the outer world.

שֶׁלִּקְּטוּ לִקּוּטֵי בָּתַר לִקּוּטֵי **which they collected, collection after collection.**

However, the writing of these statements led to them no longer being in their initial, "pure" form, since "they collected, collection after collection." This expression, taken from the Talmud,[10] references the commandment of *leket,* one of the agricultural gifts to poor people, the collection of fallen harvested crops. The Talmud says that after the poor would make their first round of collection gleanings, and the poorest of them would make a second gleaning (collection after collection), there was nothing of value remaining in the field, and anything left was permitted to any person. Here as well, the sayings of the Ba'al Shem Tov which were collected in this book were before any "collection," meaning they were not spoken by him directly, but rather they were collected by his students, things he said in different places and contexts. They were then compiled in an order that was not always coherent. Additionally, they are actually a "collection after collection," for they are not only a collection of the clearly central and important statements, but also contain secondary elements mixed in that are less

9. One can assess at this point what the author of the *Tanya* is taking upon himself, both specifically in this epistle, "to understand statements of discernment," and in the broader sense of the Torah of Chabad.

10. *Ta'anit* 6b, *Bava Metzia* 21b.

important and less clear. These are things that are attributed to the Ba'al Shem Tov, but brought by one student in the name of another student, second- or third-hand.

וְלֹא יָדְעוּ לְכַוֵּין הַלָּשׁוֹן עַל מַתְכּוּנְתּוֹ **And they did not know how to formulate the language properly,**

A collection of sayings that are taken out of their context often requires a reformulation of the statements and their presentation in order to make the collection coherent. Additionally, as the author of the *Tanya* observes, the Ba'al Shem Tov spoke in Yiddish, while the book (like all hasidic writings from that time) was written in Hebrew. This meant that the composers of the collected writings had to translate them. Thus, the combination of the required editing of the collection for the sake of coherence, with a translation process that necessarily grappled with the loss of nuance from the original language, meant that it was impossible to avoid errors in the intent of the sayings, both for the composers as well as the readers.

אַךְ הַמְכוּוָּן הוּא אֱמֶת לַאֲמִיתּוֹ. **nevertheless, the intended meaning is absolutely true.**

THE INTENDED MEANING IS ABSOLUTELY TRUE

☞ Seemingly, there is no purpose to this statement. It is intrinsically obvious that the intent of the Ba'al Shem Tov was truth. Perhaps this can be explained based by what is written elsewhere, that the phrase "absolutely true" indicates that something is "the fullest truth," something that is revealed to a person both from above as well as below (see *Likkutei Amarim,* chap. 44; *Torah Or,* 47:4; *Likkutei Torah,* Lev. 40:1; see also *Noam Elimelekh, Beḥukotai*; this is also somewhat implied by the statement of the Sages (e.g., *Shabbat* 10a) that "any judge who judges a case according to truth...the Torah views him as if he acted as a partner with God in the act of creation"). It is revealed from above through service below, in which the revelation from above is simply a confirmation of a truth that is already known and spoken of below. If this is the explanation, the author of the *Tanya* is hinting here that the true intentions of the Ba'al Shem Tov within the words are actually the understanding the reader reaches specifically through his efforts and divine service. There is no perfect formulation, served on a spoon, and the words of the Ba'al Shem Tov require toil to be understood. Errors in formulation need not discourage a reader, for they do not conceal the truth. The fullest truth may be difficult to reveal, but it is also impossible to conceal. One way or another, it will emerge, as will be shown in this epistle.

Despite the errors, the book has tremendous value, as the underlying intent is true. The intent of the Ba'al Shem Tov, and the intent of his students who collected his sayings, are found in the book. The only limitation is that sometimes it is necessary to clarify and explain the language utilized, so that the true meaning can be extracted. ☞

Here begins the explanation of that passage from *Tzava'at Rivash* that caused so much controversy. Although the author of the *Tanya* does not quote the passage here, we thought it appropriate to print it as it is printed in our version of *Tzava'at Rivash*.[11]

"And similarly, if a person engaged in prayer hears someone speaking, he should say, why did God bring that person to speak during my prayer? This is certainly divine providence. The speech is the Divine Presence that manifested (enclothing itself) as it were, in this person's mouth in order that I should strengthen myself (a different version reads: motivate myself) to service. There is so much for me to do to strengthen myself in service, meaning in prayer. This is even more so if the person speaking is not Jewish, or a child as it means that it is as if the Divine Presence has (constricted itself and) manifested in such a person, and how much more appropriate that the person should pray with alacrity."

It seems that the controversy emanating from this passage is that it sounds like the Divine Presence can rest upon a non-Jewish person, and even upon an evil gentile who is disturbing a Jewish person from prayer. Ostensibly, this does seem very problematic. How can such a thing be said?!

In order to understand this, the author of the *Tanya* presents a lengthy introductory explanation, built with a number of layers based upon the words of the Sages and the Arizal. This allows even those who are not hasidim to understand the words of the Ba'al Shem Tov.

וְהוּא בְּהַקְדִּים מַאֲמַר רַבּוֹתֵינוּ ז״ל: כָּל הַכּוֹעֵס כְּאִילּוּ עוֹבֵד עֲבוֹדַת כּוֹכָבִים וּמַזָּלוֹת וכו׳.

I will **preface** my explanation with a **statement of our Rabbis: Whoever gets angry, it is as though he is worshipping the stars and constellations...**

11. *Tzava'at Rivash* 120, and in the edition of *Karenei Hod Torah (Kehat)*. The parentheses are additions to this edition, and relate, among other things, to what is written in this epistle.

The author of the *Tanya* prefaces his explanation of the words of the *Tzava'at Rivash* with a statement from the Rabbis. The intent of this passage[12] is not that anger literally is idol worship. It is part of a broad perspective found among our Sages, especially in works of Kabbala and Hasidism, that sins (and performed commandments) have broad spiritual scopes beyond the action delineated by *halakha*. This affect includes, not only the action, but also one's thoughts and even emotional states, all of which can fall under the parameter of a particular sin. This does not mean that such an emotional state or thought is literally considered that sin, with all of its practical ramifications, however, it shares a certain intersection with it, in which such thoughts or deeds are to some degree, a manifestation of that actual sin as it is defined in the Torah. ☞

וְהַטַּעַם מוּבָן לְיוֹדְעֵי בִינָה **The reason is understood by those who know discernment,**

Since "anger abides in the bosom of fools" (Eccles. 7:9), and "those who know discernment" are the opposite of fools.[13]

"Those who know discernment" are not special people with a unique ability to understand this. Any person (a *beinoni*, which is the measure of "any person") who uses his ability to discern can internalize his

AS IF HE HAD WORSHIPPED IDOLS

☞ An expression of this perspective can be found in the text of the recitation of *Shema* prior to going to sleep (based on the version of the Arizal, in the prayerbook of the author of the *Tanya*). "That if I have sinned...and damaged the letter *yod* of Your great name, by not reciting *Shema*...I have become liable for the death penalty through stoning, ..." Meaning, a person accepts the four forms of death of the lower courts, not because he has truly committed a sin worthy of such a penalty, but rather for the failure of not reciting *Shema,* or donning *tzitzit*,... Something similar is being conveyed here regarding anger and idol worship. Further along, the author of the *Tanya* will explain the inner connection between these two things, how anger is similar to idol worship.

12. *Shabbat* 105b. See *Zohar* part 1, 27b, and 182b; part 3 179a, and 234b. See also *Rambam, Hilkhot De'ot*, 2:3.

13. See in *Likkutei Levi Yitzhak LaTanya*, p. 49, an explanation for the usage of this phrase here, based on the approach of the Kabbala.

understanding and link it to the inner knowledge and attributes of his soul, every person according to his ability. This will make him "one who knows discernment," meaning that his understanding becomes the reality of his tangible lived experience.

"Those who know discernment" are able to actually detach themselves from anger and relate to its underlying root. They can understand the mechanism that gives rise to it and that the way to prevent and heal it lies above, in the root that precedes *da'at*, which is *emuna* (faith).

since when one is angry, faith departs from him.	לְפִי שֶׁבִּשְׁעַת כַּעֲסוֹ נִסְתַּלְּקָה מִמֶּנּוּ הָאֱמוּנָה.

This is faith in the oneness of God and His Providence over every detail in creation at all times and in all events that transpire in a person's life.

The author of the *Tanya* is not speaking here of understanding or internalized knowledge that have been lost, but rather to faith. Anger is not something intellectual, and even if a person understood, that would not cause his anger to dissipate. Therefore, the author of the *Tanya* speaks of faith, for faith is the inner layer, more essential than the intellect, and, when facing off against anger, faith is deeper than intellect. ☞

FAITH

☞ Faith is the one of the highest powers of the soul in one sense, yet one of the lowest in another. On the one hand, it is a higher power, as it lies above the soul's powers of awareness, relating to lofty levels of divine being that are beyond the faculty of the intellect to comprehend, and must be believed with faith. Simultaneously, it is one of the most basic, simple ways of perceiving that which happens to the soul. The faith discussed here seems to be the simple kind of faith, in which a person perceives events happening to him, even things he does not like or understand, as coming from God. The inner dimension of this faith, while simple, draws from the higher form of faith that relates to the loftiest and broadest reaches of existence. It is the faith that God is one and unified, and there is nothing other than Him. This form of faith is its other, higher aspect, for if there is nothing other than God, that indicates that He presides over and directs every detail of the things happening in the world. This connection between the one who transcends all, with the Divine which lies within every detail of existence (or in other words: between "the one who surrounds all worlds" and "the one who fills all worlds") is the depth of the concept of faith.

כִּי אִילּוּ הָיָה מַאֲמִין שֶׁמֵּאֵת ה׳ הָיְתָה זֹאת לוֹ לֹא הָיָה בְּכַעַס כְּלָל.

For if he believed that this happened to him from God, he would not grow angry at all.

When a person lives with the belief that everything comes from God, he does not become angry. This kind of faith, in which a person has no need to ponder whether God exists, or whether everything comes from Him, since these truths are simply known, has the power to prevent a person from becoming angry.

Why is it that when a person believes that everything that happens to him come from God, he does not become angry?[14] Anger is comprised of multiple layers. The first layer is when there is something that a person experiences as bad, something uncomfortable and a violation of the person's expectations. The last layer is when there is someone or something to blame for this, someone upon whom to heap one's frustration in the form of anger. There is a combination of arrogance and frustration that accumulates and operates within a life that is empty of faith. In contrast, a person who has a simple belief that everything is from Hashem will not even initially think that something happening to him is bad, for "nothing bad descends from above."[15] God certainly only does that which is good, even if the person does not feel it at that moment.

It is easier to relate to anger as a lack of faith in simpler situations, like one in which the blame falls on oneself, happenstance, or higher forces. Examples such as when a person bumps into something and gets injured, or just misses the last bus are such situations. It is much more difficult to see things this way when another person is mixed into the situation and it is clear that this other person is doing problematic things and is to blame. What does such a situation have to do with faith in God?

---

14. As appears to be the case in other contexts, this is not only referring to anger, but also to broader negative emotional reactions like sadness, despair, jealousy and like.

15. See *Bereshit Rabba*, 51:3, and see previously, epistle 11, and many places in Hasidism.

וְאַף שֶׁבֶּן אָדָם שֶׁהוּא בַּעַל בְּחִירָה מְקַלְּלוֹ אוֹ מַכֵּהוּ אוֹ מַזִּיק מָמוֹנוֹ, וּמִתְחַיֵּיב בְּדִינֵי אָדָם וּבְדִינֵי שָׁמַיִם עַל רוֹעַ בְּחִירָתוֹ אַף עַל פִּי כֵן, עַל הַנִּיזָּק כְּבָר נִגְזַר מִן הַשָּׁמַיִם וְהַרְבֵּה שְׁלוּחִים לַמָּקוֹם.

And although a person with free will has cursed him, or struck him, or damaged his property – and the assailant **is held liable by human laws and the laws of Heaven for his bad choice – even so,** this was **already decreed upon the injured party from Heaven, and the Omnipresent has many messengers.**

One would think that in such a situation it is appropriate to be angry at the person, since he chose to do this damage and is responsible.

This is not relevant to the victim, as this "was already decreed upon the injured party from Heaven" even before the assailant chose to cause damage, and irrespective of the assailant's bad choice. The perspective here is to differentiate between the assailant and the victim. Each person has a tally with God directly, and people are not supposed to make tallies with one another (and become angry with each other), because the tally is only between us and God.

God does not operate directly in the world, but rather enclothes Himself in the vessels of the world, in "messengers." These include things like the forces of nature, animals, as well as people. The expression "many messengers"[16] says that God is not obligated to use any particular messenger or method. This allows God the freedom for His providence to act according to His wishes in the world, with independence. It also allows man the freedom to choose and to take responsibility for his actions. ☞

THE OMNIPRESENT HAS MANY MESSENGERS

☞ Unlike other messengers (objects, animals, angels), when a person is used as a messenger, he has choice and responsibility for his actions before God. Even so, God has the power to "sew" all the different people together, each one with his merits, obligations, needs and qualities. The fact that a person is a messenger for God is no justification for anything, for no one forced him to be the messenger for this

16. See, for example, *Ta'anit* 18b.

וְלֹא עוֹד, אֶלָּא אֲפִילוּ בְּשָׁעָה זוֹ מַמָּשׁ שֶׁמַּכֵּהוּ אוֹ מְקַלְּלוֹ - מִתְלַבֵּשׁ בּוֹ כֹּחַ ה׳ וְרוּחַ פִּיו יִתְבָּרֵךְ הַמְחַיֵּיהוּ וּמְקַיְּימוֹ.

Moreover, even at that actual moment when he is striking him or cursing him, he is enclothed with the strength of God and the breath of His mouth, which gives him life and sustains him.

Even if we view this person as a messenger, it is not like a messenger of another person, that after he is sent, he acts as an independent agent, and there is reason to hold him responsible and even be angry with him. When God sends a messenger, He does not leave him. The calculations and responsibility of the sender are with the messenger on the front line of his mission, at every moment and with every move. ☞

particular damage and if he commits the destructive act, that is his decision and responsibility. Even if the outcome was required by God, there are "many messengers" at the disposal of the "Omnipresent," and if this person decided to volunteer and become the vehicle for this damage, he deserves the resulting consequence. In the book of Kings, there is a story told about Ahav, the king of Israel. Before going out to war in Ramot Gilad, he asked the council of the prophets. The prophet Mikhayhu, son of Yimla, said he saw a vision of God sitting on His throne with all the hosts of the heavens to either side, and He asked them: "Who will go seduce Ahav so that he will go up to Ramot Gilad and fall there?" One spirit stood up and said: "I will go, and I will be a false spirit for his prophets." God said, "go and do so." In the Talmud (*Sanhedrin* 102b), it is written regarding this that God said to that spirit, "leave My domain." God asked for a volunteer, but regarding one who volunteers to lie it is written, "No...liar will stand firm before me" (Ps. 101: 7). Ahav was meant to die, and deserved death. But the one who took that action upon himself would be punished, for he chose to do evil. (Despite that which is written there, that the spirit was actually that of Navot who had been killed by Ahav, and who presumably had a justification to cause his death.)

EVEN AT THAT ACTUAL MOMENT

☞ As will be explained further, when God created the world, it is as if He left Himself a role within the world. This "role," while much larger than our role, still is within our terms, within our dimensions. God is revealed in the world, speaks like a person who speaks, rules like a king of flesh and blood, goes to war, judges.... Yet still, and more so, God manifests and animates all of existence from nothing. By way of analogy, the entire creation is like a story that God is telling. The characters live, the plot unfolds, as long as the storyteller continues the story. The moment he stops, there is nothing. It can also be the case that the storyteller talks about himself as part of the story, to such an extent that he is similar to the other characters in the story, though perhaps a little bigger. Similarly, a person can think that he can choose to listen or not listen to God, to choose whether to relate to God as existing or not. Similarly, he can relate

However – and this is a confusing point – God animates him even when he does not agree with him and speaks through him even when it seems that he is not fulfilling God's wishes (and even in times in which he is actually not fulfilling His wishes). A person is punished for these violations. Yet even so, in the bigger picture, these violations are the will and speech of God, and this person fulfills those things when speaking.

וּכְמוֹ שֶׁכָּתוּב: "כִּי ה' אָמַר לוֹ קַלֵּל" (שמואל ב טז,י) וְהֵיכָן אָמַר לְשִׁמְעִי?

For it is written: "Because the Lord said to him: Curse" (II Sam. 16:10). **Now, when did He say** this **to Shimi?**

The author of the *Tanya* brings a textual example about when David and his men were fleeing from Avshalom, and Shimi was standing in their path, throwing stones at them and cursing David. Avishai ben Tzruya protests and wants to execute judgment upon him – "please let me cross, and I will remove his head" – but David refuses and tells him, "He curses because the Lord said to him: Curse David.... Leave him alone and let him curse, because the Lord said to him."

The fact that David accepted this judgment is understandable, but the statement that "the Lord told him to curse" appears extreme. It is not written explicitly in the text, and it also did not appear that God wanted this.

אֶלָּא שֶׁמַּחֲשָׁבָה זוֹ, שֶׁנָּפְלָה לְשִׁמְעִי בְּלִבּוֹ וּמוֹחוֹ, יָרְדָה מֵאֵת ה', וְרוּחַ פִּיו הַמְחַיֶּה כָּל צְבָאָם הֶחֱיָה רוּחוֹ שֶׁל שִׁמְעִי בְּשָׁעָה שֶׁדִּיבֵּר דְּבָרִים אֵלּוּ לְדָוִד. כִּי אִילּוּ נִסְתַּלֵּק רוּחַ פִּיו יִתְבָּרֵךְ

Rather, this thought, which fell into Shimi's heart and mind, descended from God, and the breath of His mouth, which gives life to all their hosts, gave life to Shimi's spirit when he spoke these words to David. For

to God's messengers in the same way. He can also be unaware (if he is evil, for a righteous person who constantly unifies God and the Divine Presence is certainly aware of this) that God is the storyteller and that the messenger has no independent existence. God creates and manifests this messenger at every moment and wants his existence, speaking through him. Without God's power, he would be nothing. There would be no speech nor speaker, nor perpetrator nor action.

רֶגַע אֶחָד מֵרוּחוֹ שֶׁל שִׁמְעִי, לֹא יָכוֹל לְדַבֵּר מְאוּמָה

had the breath of His mouth departed even for **a single moment from Shimi's spirit, he would not have been able to say anything**

"God told him to curse" is not referring to a prophetic incident in which God tells a prophet to speak certain words. Rather, it is a borrowed phrasing to express the idea discussed here: everything which happens in the world and which transpires in a person's life, is from the power and actions of God Himself, and should be accepted as such. Any existing aspect of reality must be from God and sustained by God with His speech (which creates and sustains all being). Accordingly, any part of reality, even one such as this, is the word of God. For David, who understands and accepts this, even Shimi, standing and cursing, is as if God is speaking to him.

The text does not say that God told Shimi to curse David, because in fact, He never did so, and Shimi was not obligated to curse. David said this because from his perspective, one of seeing God within all events in his life, it is God who told Shimi to curse him. David expresses this in such an extreme way because this is what he wants to emphasize right now[17] – that currently, in his situation, he accepts whatever befalls him with complete humility and love, as if it was the word of God Himself speaking to him.

Additionally, David did not say that God cursed him, but rather that God told Shimi to do so. The difference here is that when God speaks to a prophet, and the prophet is nullified before the holiness of God, he expresses God's inner word and will into the world without any internal barrier between himself and God.[18] This is not the case regarding Shimi's curse of David. It is certain that this curse was not the inner will of God. God's will here was David's act of humility and his response. Shimi's curse was simply a means, the "back-end" of the inner divine intent. David's extreme response to this incident was an act

17. As we see at another time, in his deathbed instructions to Shlomo, David relates to this event with a different emphasis, that Shimi was a rebel against the throne and is liable for the death penalty.

18. See *Sha'ar HaYiḥud VeHa'emuna*, 2.

of repentance, moving to the opposite extreme. Sin is the substitution of the inner divine intent with the outer, the "back-end." Repentance is the reversal of this, the bringing of the inner intent to its outer context. This is what David achieved here. The curse of Shimi was a form of the back side of the divine intent, and David turns it toward the inner divine intent when he says, "God told him to curse."

(וְזֶהוּ כִּי ה' אָמַר לוֹ בָּעֵת הַהִיא מַמָּשׁ קַלֵּל אֶת דָּוִד. וּמִי יֹאמַר לוֹ וגו'

[**This is** the meaning of the phrase, **"because the Lord said to him" – at that very moment – "curse David." And who would say to him...** 26 Tishrei (leap year)

When God animates Shimi during that moment and gives him the desire[19] and ability to curse David, it is as if "He literally told him to do it at that moment." If God told him to curse, who can tell him that he should not, and who could attack him the way that Avishai ben Tzruya wanted?[20]

At this point, the author of the *Tanya* brings an entire section which appears in *Sha'ar HaYiḥud VeHa'emuna*, with some changes in wording and order (the sentences of the introduction and the summary are from chapter 1, and the remainder are from chapter 2).

וְכַנּוֹדַע מַה שֶּׁאָמַר הבעש"ט ז"ל עַל פָּסוּק: "לְעוֹלָם ה' דְּבָרְךָ נִצָּב בַּשָּׁמָיִם" (תהלים קיט,פט).

as is known from **what the Ba'al Shem Tov said on the verse "Forever, Lord, Your word stands in the heavens"** (Ps. 119:89). 26 Tishrei

19. In a simplistic sense, the words "And who can say to him" relate to the words of David, "because the Lord said to him: Curse David. Who can say, 'why did you do so?'" If so, the word "him" is extraneous here. This observation is made by the Lubavitcher Rebbe, Rabbi Menaḥem Mendel Schneerson, in *He'arot VeTikkunim BeDerekh Efshar*, printed at the end of the *Tanya*. There is also a hand-written manuscript in which this word is missing. However, it should also be pointed out that a verse with a similar syntax to this does appear in Ecclesiastes (Ecc. 8:4): "Since governance is by the king's word, and who will say to him: What are you doing?" See the commentary for the *Tanya*.

20. In the first edition and manuscripts, this parenthetical section does not appear.

These words allude to the divine words that create the heavens and which remain there sustaining them constantly.[21] ☞

WHAT THE BA'AL SHEM TOV SAID

☞ The third Lubavitcher Rebbe, Rabbi Menaḥem Mendel Schneerson observed (in *Hagahot* on *Likkutei Torah, Vayikra* 25:3; see there 29: 3; he is also quoted in *Or HaTorah, Parashat Aḥarei Mot*, p. 255 and elsewhere)that similar ideas can be found in the *Midrash Tehillim* on this verse. This is the wording of the Midrash quoted by the Tzemaḥ Tzedek: "What is something that is standing in the heavens? Rather, God said: upon what do the heavens stand? On that which I said, 'let there be a firmament within the waters,..., and with that same thing with which they were created, they continue to stand forever. Therefore, it is written, 'Forever, Lord, Your word stands in the heavens.'" The language of the *Midrash Tehillim* there: "...Regarding that same thing about which I said, 'let there be a firmament within the waters,..., and it was so,' and it is written, 'For He spoke, and it was done' – that which He said, He did. Therefore, it is written, 'He commanded and it took form,' and 'by the word of the Lord, the heavens were made.' Through that same thing with which they were created, they remain standing today. Therefore, it is written that 'Forever, Lord, Your word stands in the heavens.'" It was asked (see *HaYom Yom*, 26 *Tishrei; Likkutei Siḥot*, vol. 8, p. 64, and elsewhere) why did the author of the *Tanya* bring this in the name of the Ba'al Shem Tov, and not in the name of the Midrash, especially since it was not usually the author of the *Tanya*'s way to cite teachings in the name of his teachers?[22] The obvious answer is that the meaning of something cannot only be viewed in isolation, but also in its contextual relationship with other ideas, and with the person who said it, his perspective and personality. The Midrash can be understood in different ways and on different levels, but the relating of the concepts it raises to the words of the Ba'al Shem Tov ties them to him and his Torah. This includes the ideas of divine oneness, that there is nothing other than God, the implication that He controls every detail of existence, and that there is no event in the world that is not under the direct power and control of God. It is true that these principles are accepted by most of Israel, but for the Ba'al Shem Tov, these concepts are absorbed to their core, able to be perceived in the physical world and to act according to them within one's life. This is especially so in this epistle, in which the author of the *Tanya* only wants to teach one point: The Ba'al Shem Tov did not invent anything that was not known, but rather, he simply related seriously to these ideas and their implications, ideas that are known and accepted by all of Israel.

---

21. This explanation of the Ba'al Shem Tov appears in other works of early Hasidism. See *Ba'al Shem Tov al HaTorah, Parashat Bereshit*, 48 and onward, and in *Mekor Mayim Ḥayyim* there.

22. As the author mentions at the beginning of the book, and through the name of the book, all his words are just a collection of the words of his teachers. Therefore,

שֶׁצֵּירוּף אוֹתִיּוֹת שֶׁנִּבְרְאוּ בָּהֶן הַשָּׁמַיִם **That the combination of letters with which the heavens were created,**

God created the world with speech. Divine speech is not only a bestowal of something to created reality. It is itself the creation, and the divine speech is a combining of letters. This perspective, which forms the basis of many of the ideas of the Ba'al Shem Tov (and extensively explained throughout *Sha'ar HaYiḥud VeHa'emuna*) is that the twenty-two epistles of the Hebrew alphabet are the root forces of creation from which all things stem, like foundational stones that are organized to build a house. Just as a lone stone is not a house in any way, so each letter, in isolation, lacks meaning and is not yet speech. Speech begins by combining the letters. This gives them meaning and transforms them from potential creation into actual creation. This is why the author of the *Tanya* speaks here of the combinations of letters that created the heavens.

שֶׁהוּא מַאֲמַר ״יְהִי רָקִיעַ כו׳״ (בראשית א,ו) **which is the utterance "let there be a firmament..."** (Gen. 1:6),

This is one of the ten utterances that God used to create the world, recorded in the first chapter of Genesis. This chapter describes that act of creation through the speech of God. God spoke ten sentences, "let there be a firmament," "let the land," "let there be plants and animals,"... This is unlike the speech of man which we generally perceive as a transference of information. God's speech actually creates and manifests those things when He speaks.

In the *Tanya* it is explained that the speech of God is like the speech of man in the sense that it reveals that which was hidden, from thought and the hidden recesses of one's soul, from an undifferentiated state to one in which they are manifest, standing on their own, allowing the person speaking, as well as others, to relate to them. Similarly, and even more so, the speech of God constitutes the emer-

---

when he explicitly quotes someone, there must be a unique explanation for the deviation in style. Here, the statement is meant to tie these ideas to other words of the Ba'al Shem Tov, and to his unique perspective regarding this topic.

gence of God's hidden essential being into revelation. This is divine creation. ☞

הֵן נִצָּבוֹת וְעוֹמְדוֹת מְלוּבָּשׁוֹת בַּשָּׁמַיִם לְעוֹלָם לְהַחֲיוֹתָם וּלְקַיְּימָם.

they stand firm, enclothed in the heavens, to give them life and sustain them.

As explained, these letters that God speaks, which combine to form the words "let there be a firmament," are enclothed in the heavens that we see (and those we do not see) and animate and sustain them. We do not hear these letters and words like the speech that we use, but rather we experience them as the perpetuation of the heavens,... An analogy for this is when a king issues instructions, "do such-and-such," only those in his inner circle actually hear him speak. The rest of the populace only witness the results of the speech, the actions taken as a result of the orders of the king. Here as well, the "inner circle" is that which is written in the Torah: the letters combine to form the words "let there be a firmament." The "outer circle" is reality, and that is where one sees the heavens and the earth. However, unlike the analogy, the words of the omnipresent God are not separate from the results. There

THE SAYING "LET THERE BE A FIRMAMENT"

☞ Of all the ten utterances, why did the author of the *Tanya* choose this one regarding the "firmament"? The simple explanation is that these points are mentioned in the context of the Midrash regarding the verse in Psalms, "Forever, Lord, Your word stands in the heavens," which relates to this statement. Despite this explanation, the third Lubavitcher Rebbe, Rabbi Menaḥem Mendel Schneerson, (see *Or HaTorah al Ma'amarei Raboteinu z"l VeInyanim,* p. 52.) observes that the same point could have been made with the first of the ten sayings, "In the beginning..." (considered one of the ten utterances). This is because once the Sages learned from the verse in Psalms, that "Forever, Lord, Your word stands in the heavens," they could have explicated from this first saying that it is He who stands in the heavens. Additionally, it seems that this first saying is more appropriate, for it is the first one and includes all the subsequent sayings within it. He explains that the saying of "let there be a firmament" was used because it is the first saying that relates to the divine light that "fills all worlds," the light that is enclothed in the details of the heavens, in contrast to the earth. The first saying, by comparison, relates to the entirety of creation, to the light that "encompasses all worlds" and is not enclothed in created beings, but rather encompasses them from above.

is no person who hears the words and then commits the actions. Rather, it is the speech itself that manifests the person hearing it, that which he hears, and the action that he does. It is all just divine speech.

This is the point that the author of the *Tanya* comes to emphasize here: The entire creation, while appearing to be an independent reality, seeming to be even more tangible than the Creator Himself, is only the speech of the Creator. Just as speech has no tangibility and existence separate from the one speaking – when he is silent, there is nothing – so it is with the entirety of creation. The heavens, the earth, and all they contain, have no existence of their own without God speaking them into being.

וְלֹא כְּהַפִּלוֹסוֹפִים שֶׁכּוֹפְרִים בְּהַשְׁגָּחָה פְּרָטִית

This is not as claimed by **the philosophers who deny** God's **divine providence**

The quote from chapter 1 of *Sha'ar HaYiḥud VeHa'emuna* ends here, and now the author of the *Tanya* quotes from chapter 2:

This reference to "philosophers,"[23] does not imply people who totally deny the existence of God (it is unclear if there are actually people like this, but either way, it is not a position the author of the *Tanya* wishes to assess). Rather, he is referring to those who deny God's divine providence.[24] The question of divine providence stands at the foundation of faith: In what kind of God do we believe? What is the relationship between Him and the created beings? Does His state of being, or lack thereof, matter relative to us?

The perspective of the philosophers mentioned here is that there is a God, and that He created the world, but that there is no direct connection between Him and the world He created. This world is merely an emanation of the Creator, a result of His cause and effect, in which each entity and each thing that happens has a cause that drives it. This array of causes is rooted in the first cause, the cause of all causes, which is found in God. Within this perspective, in which

23. The wording in *Sha'ar HaYiḥud VeHa'emuna,* instead of "philosophers" is "heretics."

24. The wording in *Sha'ar HaYiḥud VeHa'emuna,* instead of personal providence, is "in the signs and proofs of the Torah."

the narrow cause-effect dynamics of the physical world are applied to all of existence, God is not present. He is present only as "beyond" (the power of all powers, the God of all gods[25]), but not as an involved party that relates directly to us and to whom we must relate directly in return. The author of the *Tanya* refers to those who espouse such a view as "those who deny personal providence," which is a denial of the direct relationship between God and the world, that every detail of every living thing lives and exists in each moment because God personally animates it exactly as it is. This conception also operates in reverse: Every detail relates to God directly, with no barriers, and draws its life-force and existence only from God.

וּמְדַמִּין בְּדִמְיוֹנָם הַכּוֹזֵב **and who compare, with their deceptive imagination,**

This perspective of the philosophers stems from the way people think they understand the small slice of reality which they observe and then apply that way of thinking to far broader aspects of reality about which they have no conception. Many of these flawed understandings evolved from exactly such false comparisons and equations between different parts of existence. The fact that things operate in a certain way and rhythm in one context does not mean that things work the same way in another context, in different times or under different conditions. There is a strong, seductive pull to extend what we know to that which we do not know, to apply things that are familiar and easier to contemplate to that which is less comfortable and requires more. The Hebrew word for false that the author of the *Tanya* uses here is "*akhzav*" which can be compared to the river called Akhzav: In one area, it is full of water, and we want to think it has always been so. But the next day, or in a different location, it can be completely dry.[26]

---

25. Based on *Menaḥot* 110a and brought in many places in hasidic writings. See *Likkutei Amarim*, chap. 22 and 24, as well as *Likkutei Torah, Shir HaShirim*, 36:2, and elsewhere.

26. See similar ideas in a number of the author of the *Tanya*'s epistles regarding the age of the world. For example, that which appears in *Iggeret HaKodesh*, vol. 18, epistles 876 and 898.

אֶת מַעֲשֵׂה ה׳ עוֹשֵׂה שָׁמַיִם וָאָרֶץ לְמַעֲשֵׂה אֱנוֹשׁ וְתַחְבּוּלוֹתָיו.

the work of God, who created heaven and earth, to man's creative **work and his schemes.**

We understand, with certain limits, how to do certain things, even sophisticated things: we build houses, construct tools and vessels, create and prepare things.... We imagine, implicatively, that this understanding extends to a completely different area, to the actions of God who created the heavens and the earth. Certainly, this comparison is not entirely false, for man was created in the image of God, and our entire ability to interact with the Divine is predicated on this connection and comparison, as is written in many works of Hasidism, "from my flesh, I will view God" (Job 19:26). However, in order to correctly employ this comparison, a person must be aware of the immense differences between man, a created, limited being, and God, the one Creator of which there is nothing outside Him. One of the differences is:

כִּי כַּאֲשֶׁר יֵצֵא לַצּוֹרֵף כְּלִי שׁוּב אֵין הַכְּלִי צָרִיךְ לִידֵי הַצּוֹרֵף, שֶׁאַף שֶׁיָּדָיו מְסוּלָּקוֹת הֵימֶנּוּ הוּא קַיָּים מֵעַצְמוֹ.

For when a smith completes a vessel, the vessel has no further need of the smith's hands, since even when his hands leave it, it exists on its own.

When a person acts in the physical world, he operates in an environment that is external to him, one with independent existence relative to him, just as he independently exists. When he creates something in the world, he is only combining elements that previously existed, and even the combination itself is not something new from nothing, but a possibility embedded within the details of existence. Therefore, when a person creates a tool, when he combines different materials, these materials continue to exist in this new state, it is for this end that they were initially created, and not as a result of his actions and intent. Additionally, even man, as part of the creation, receives his life force and ability to be and create from beyond himself, from that which is above him, just like the tool he creates.

וְטָח מֵרְאוֹת עֵינֵיהֶם הַהֶבְדֵּל הַגָּדוֹל שֶׁבֵּין מַעֲשֵׂה אֱנוֹשׁ וְתַחְבּוּלוֹתָיו

Their eyes are besmeared and they see not the major distinction

שֶׁהוּא יֵשׁ מִיֵּשׁ, רַק שֶׁמְּשַׁנֶּה הַצּוּרָה וְהַתְּמוּנָה, לְמַעֲשֵׂה שָׁמַיִם וָאָרֶץ שֶׁהוּא יֵשׁ מֵאַיִן.

between man's creative **work and his schemes, which consist of making one thing out of another, of merely modifying the form and shape, and the creation of heaven and earth, which is** the creation of **existence from nothingness.**

The difference between "one thing from another" and "existence out of nothingness" is the essential difference between man's actions and the actions of the Divine. All things done by man, physical or spiritual, are only "one thing from another." We are able to alter the relationship between things (primarily the relationship between us and the things around us), but we cannot change the essence of something such that it can be something which it was not before. The difference is, as was stated, that we are part of creation, on the same plane as the things we create, and we are only able to modify our relationships with the other entities within creation, but not the essence of their existence. God, in contrast, stands outside of the creation. As the Creator, only He has the capacity to create something new in the full meaning of the word, a creation of something from nothing, something that has no precedent at all. ☞

EXISTENCE FROM NOTHINGNESS

☞ When one delves into this concept, it is clear that the true meaning of "something from nothing" cannot be something which already existed in the past. It cannot be something which, long ago, was created from nothing, and now it exists. There is no such thing as this, for after it was created, from what was it perpetuated? Is it not currently still "something from nothing?" It must be that "something from nothing" inherently means that it is renewed every moment, like the language of the prayer, "in His goodness He constantly renews the act of creation." "Something from nothing" defines the relationship between the Creator and the created, and its constant perpetuation. As long as creation continues, it means that the Creator is creating it currently "something from nothing."

It is not only the denying philosophers who struggle to grasp the concept of "something from nothing," but we as well. The reason it is difficult is because such a concept does not exist in the human experience. (See at length in epistle 20 that "something from nothing" is a capacity that is solely divine.) Even so, beyond the basic, incomprehensible distinction between "acts of man" and "acts of God," there are points of comparison (as

וְהוּא פֶּלֶא גָּדוֹל יוֹתֵר מִקְּרִיעַת יַם סוּף עַל דֶּרֶךְ מָשָׁל, אֲשֶׁר הוֹלִיךְ ה׳ בְּרוּחַ קָדִים עַזָּה כָּל הַלַּיְלָה וַיִּבָּקְעוּ הַמָּיִם. וְאִילוּ פָּסַק הָרוּחַ כְּרֶגַע הָיוּ הַמַּיִם חוֹזְרִים וְנִיגָּרִים בְּמוֹרָד כְּדַרְכָּם וְטִבְעָם, וְלֹא קָמוּ כְּחוֹמָה.

This is a greater marvel than the splitting of the Red Sea, for instance, where God caused the sea to recede with a strong east wind all night long, and the waters were split. If the wind had ceased even **for an instant, the waters would have reverted and flowed downward in their natural way. They would not have stood like a wall,**

As is written, "and the water was a wall for them, on their right and on their left" (Ex. 14:22). The miracle of the splitting of the sea was that "He turned the sea into dry land" (Ps. 66:6), that the sea behaved like dry land.

אַף שֶׁטֶּבַע זֶה בַּמַּיִם הוּא גַּם כֵּן נִבְרָא וּמְחוּדָּשׁ יֵשׁ מֵאַיִן, שֶׁהֲרֵי חוֹמַת אֲבָנִים נִצֶּבֶת מֵעַצְמָהּ בְּלִי רוּחַ, רַק שֶׁטֶּבַע הַמַּיִם אֵינוֹ כֵּן.

even though this natural tendency of water to flow downward **is also a novel** phenomenon **created from nothingness. For a stone wall stands upright by itself without** the support of the **wind, but that is not the nature of water.**

this is the meaning of "*adam,*" man, from the language of "*adameh le'elyon,*" ("I can compare to the supernal"[27]). Obviously, this does not imply a complete comparison, for "who can compare to You?" But nevertheless, the comparison is sufficient to allow a meaningful connection with divine comprehension. Even this concept of "something from nothing" can be related to by man, at least in the conceptual and spiritual sense, an imagining of creating something from nothing. A person can imagine thoughts in which he weaves an entire world, and even thoughts of new things, imaginary constructs that do not exist in our world at all. These kinds of thoughts are a kind of "something from nothing," and thus, when the person ceases to think those thoughts, those things cease to exist, leaving no remnant. However, this is still not true creation of something from nothing, as those thoughts derive from some prior spiritual reality. But to a certain degree, this is enough to allow a basic grasp of the concept.

---

27. Based on Isa. 14:14. The implication in Kabbala literature is that the "lower man" is analogous to the "supernal man," meaning to the model of divine bestowal upon the worlds of reality. This can stem from the aspect of *Zeir Anpin,* the world of *Atzilut* or even higher, but from our perspective, that is divine, the Creator.

The miracle of the splitting of the Red Sea was also a creation of something from nothing. However, it was not the creation of an entity, but rather a creation of a natural tendency that did not exist previously. ☞

וְכָל שֶׁכֵּן וְקַל וָחוֹמֶר בִּבְרִיאַת יֵשׁ מֵאַיִן **Certainly, and all the more so, with regard to the creation of existence from nothingness,**

Like the creation of the heavens and the earth, which are not only nature and its patterns, but rather their entire existence is something from nothing.

"Certainly, and all the more so" is a double language, reflecting the two ways that the creation of the heavens is a bigger miracle than the splitting of the Red Sea. Firstly, in the splitting of the Red Sea, the "something from nothing" is only the change in behavior of the water to stand as a stone wall. This was different from the natural behavior of water, but contrast that with the creation of water itself, in which its entire existence is something from nothing. Secondly, while this standing of water like a wall is a new concept for water, it is not a new

THE WONDER OF THE SPLITTING OF THE SEA

☞ What they witnessed at the splitting of the Red Sea, which we don't see in the creation of heaven and earth, is, firstly, the miracle aspect. Heaven and earth are creations to which we are acclimated, and their perpetuation is something we take as a given. We perceive the "something" and not the "nothing" from whence it came, and as a result, we are not awed by the very existence of these things. In comparison, the splitting of the Red Sea was a novel phenomenon, a miraculous change in the normal patterns of nature. We saw the water standing like a wall of stone while being fully aware that this is not the nature of water. Therefore, this deviation appeared to us as a miracle, and we felt the "east wind" that was constantly holding the water in place. As was explained, the significant element for us in the concept of "something from nothing" is the awareness that it is a constant perpetuation of something from nothing. There is nothing that stands on its own, nothing is given, each thing is created currently through the will and speech of God from absolute nothingness. In creation, however, this is not seen or felt, but in the splitting of the Red Sea, this truth was before our eyes. We saw the water standing like a wall, and as we knew the nature of water, we waited for the water to fall and flow toward us, yet we saw the east wind holding the water. In other words, everything we are told about the creation of the world from nothing, that it is a perpetual phenomenon taking place every instant, was actually visible to us in the splitting of the Red Sea.

idea intrinsically, as we have stones shaped as walls within nature. Meaning, the miracle in the splitting of the Red Sea is only in relation to the water, but the miracle of complete "something from nothing" is absolute, as there is nothing like it anywhere in reality, that there is nothing at all before the "something" is created.

שֶׁהִיא לְמַעְלָה מֵהַטֶּבַע **which transcends the** laws of **nature**

Nature (*teva*) is the built-in nature of something in the essence of its creation, as opposed to external attributes (like a coin, *matbe'a,* the same root as *teva,* that has a fixed imprint and shape, not as something added to the coin, but as the defining characteristic of that coin). In this sense, the term "above nature" relates to behavior that changes the essential qualities of something, adding a new element that was not present in its essential creation. It follows that when an entity's entire being is new, then it is called "above nature."

The term sounds absurd, like saying that the nature of something is beyond nature. This is because this term is merely borrowed to describe a phenomenon that inherently lacks nature. It is a term that points to God Himself, as it were, connecting the idea of "nature" to God, which signifies that as the Creator of the world, He must be "above nature."

וְהַפְּלֵא וָפֶלֶא יוֹתֵר מִקְּרִיעַת יַם סוּף **and is an even more astonishing wonder than the splitting of the Red Sea,**

Which is known as a miracle that is above nature. As was explained, the creation of the heavens and the earth is a bigger miracle. ☞

AN EVEN MORE ASTONISHING WONDER

☞ The problem of recognizing the miraculous nature of the creation is that, in contrast to the splitting of the Red Sea, which is a miracle we can see, the creation of existence is invisible to us. The reason is that our perceptions are always relative. We perceive contrasts, transitions, allowing us to relate the "before" with the "after." It is known that processes that are very slow are likely to be unnoticed by us, and all the more so, processes that are beyond our comprehension, such as when the "before" is utter nothingness. In a given moment, the "something" is that which exists before us, and we have no grasp of what lies beyond it. Therefore, we see no miracle in its existence, despite the fact that its existence is utterly miraculous.

עַל אַחַת כַּמָּה וְכַמָּה שֶׁבְּהִסְתַּלְּקוּת חַס וְשָׁלוֹם כֹּחַ הַבּוֹרֵא יֵשׁ מֵאַיִן מִן הַנִּבְרָא יָשׁוּב הַנִּבְרָא לְאַיִן וְאֶפֶס מַמָּשׁ.

how much more so that upon the withdrawal, God forbid, of the Creator's power of creating **existence from nothingness from the creation, the creation would literally revert to absolute nothingness.**

At the splitting of the Red Sea, the east wind held the waters as firm as a wall, and it is clear that had the wind ceased, the wall of water would have stopped standing as well. This certainly applies to the creation – like the east wind holding the waters, there is something that maintains creation at all times, which breathes and acts upon it, and if that ceased to exist, God forbid, creation would return to its "natural" state of "nothingness."

אֶלָּא צָרִיךְ לִהְיוֹת כֹּחַ הַפּוֹעֵל בַּנִּפְעָל תָּמִיד לְהַחֲיוֹתוֹ וּלְקַיְּימוֹ.

Rather, the force of the Creator must constantly be within the creation to grant it life and sustain it.

The force of God must be like the east wind, in the terms of the metaphor. As soon as we perceive "existence" not as a reality itself, as a "natural" and permanent state, but as an action, it follows that there must be someone who is constantly performing the action, and if not, we are left with nothing.

וּבְחִינָה זוֹ הוּא דְּבַר ה׳ וְרוּחַ פִּיו שֶׁבַּעֲשָׂרָה מַאֲמָרוֹת שֶׁבָּהֶן נִבְרָא הָעוֹלָם.

This force is none other than **the word of God and the breath of His mouth that are in the ten utterances through which the world was created.**

When the entire world is viewed like the wonder of the splitting of the Red Sea, then the force of the Creator within the creation, the divine speech of the ten utterances that articulates the existence of reality, becomes obvious, like the presence of the world itself. ☞ ☞

"THE TEN UTTERANCES" AND THE WORLD

☞ The entire world comes from divine speech, but there is still a fine distinction between "the ten utterances through which the world was created" and the world itself, between the utterances that are written in the Torah and the meaning

וַאֲפִילוּ אֶרֶץ הַלֵּזוּ הַגַּשְׁמִית וּבְחִינַת דּוֹמֵם שֶׁבָּהּ חַיּוּתָן וְקִיּוּמָן הוּא דְּבַר ה' מֵעֲשָׂרָה מַאֲמָרוֹת, הַמְלוּבָּשׁ בָּהֶן וּמְקַיְּימָן לִהְיוֹת דּוֹמֵם וְיֵשׁ מֵאַיִן, וְלֹא יַחְזְרוּ לְאַיִן וְאֶפֶס מַמָּשׁ כְּשֶׁהָיוּ.

Even the life and sustenance of this physical world and its inanimate components is the word of God from the ten utterances, which is enclothed in them and sustains them, to be inanimate and in a state of **existence from nothingness, and** so that **they do not revert to their previous** state of **absolute nothingness.**

and outcome of that speech. This can be seen on the mundane level of human speech. When people speak there is a difference between what one says and what others hear. That which someone says is a summary of his mental concepts and thoughts, clothed in letters and words and sent out of the mind in that form. By contrast, the speech that is heard is what is absorbed within the reality of another soul – what he hears in practice becomes absorbed within the character of the listener and his particular situation. At that stage the speech is not merely letters and words, but also their meaning and implications. In this sense, the ten utterances are the speech as God spoke them, when they are still solely His own speech, purely the letters of speech that bear His inner will and thought. That is why they are written in the Torah, because this is the essence of the Torah: the revelation of His inner wisdom and will. The world, by contrast, is that same speech, but as it is heard from the outside: What is actually stated, what it means, what forms it takes in its countless combinations, and so on and so forth.

SPEECH AND THE POWER OF SPEECH

☞ There is a more profound distinction between speech that has an effect upon the world and its internal force, which is the reason why it activates. As is the case for people, speech is not a permanent, "natural" state: A person speaks if there is a reason for doing so, when someone is listening, when he has something to say and the will to say it, and so on. If these conditions are not met, he will return to his state of silence. The same applies to the creation – the "natural" state of God, as it were, of all existence before the world, is "He and His great name alone" (as stated in *Pirkei deRabbi Eliezer* 3). Thus, His entire engagement with the world and its creation – executed with wisdom, greatness, and might – is an immeasurably large degradation and constriction of His inner self. As the Sages state: "Wherever you find God's might, there you find His humility" (*Megilla* 31a). As long as there is a good reason, a will for it, God speaks the world into existence; but if there is no such desire, God forbid, then He will not speak, and there will be no world. For us, the significance of this truth is that, as explained elsewhere, we must awaken the force of the Creator within the creation, the will to speak – which is the will for kingship and the royal crown – by listening to His speech and carrying out His will as formulated by the Torah and the mitzvot. When someone is listening, responding to the speech, the desire to speak will be awakened.

Not only is the word of God the sustenance of the animal and vegetable kingdoms, whose vitality is evident, but it also sustains inanimate objects, which do not appear to contain life. In addition to imparting life, "the word of God from the ten utterances" also constitutes their very existence from absolute nothingness. In this regard, there is no difference between an inanimate object and a living plant: Everything in the world, apart from the vital movement of animals and the power of growth within plants, also contains an "inanimate" part, which is the very existence of matter. The basic existence of any substance from nothingness is equal at all levels. ☞

וְזֶה שֶׁכָּתַב הָאֲרִיזַ"ל שֶׁגַּם בְּדוֹמֵם כַּאֲבָנִים וְעָפָר וּמַיִם יֵשׁ בָּהֶם בְּחִינַת נֶפֶשׁ וְחַיּוּת רוּחָנִיּוֹת.

This is the meaning of **that which the Arizal wrote, that even inanimate objects, such as stones, soil, and water, have a soul and spiritual life force.**

Here the "quotation" returns to the author of the *Tanya*'s comments in chapter 1 of *Sha'ar HaYiḥud VeHa'emuna*. The Arizal states[28] that all of those entities have a "soul and spiritual life force" because their very existence as specific objects, as entities that endure, is the "spirit of life" within them. This concludes the citation.

THE SPEECH OF GOD

☞ This is one of the differences between human speech, with which we are familiar, and divine speech: A person speaks to someone else and thereby conveys his thoughts, feelings, and so on. He changes reality, animates it, but does not create it from scratch. By contrast, divine speech fashions a new world from a state of "nothingness" into "existence," which lasts as long as the speech continues to be spoken. The key difference is, as will be explained, that in relation to God there is no "other." Just as it is stated with regard to knowledge, that He is the knower and He is the known...(*Rambam Sefer HaMadda, Hilkhot Yesodei HaTorah* 2:10. See *Likkutei Amarim,* chaps. 4, 42, 48; *Sha'ar HaYiḥud VeHa'emuna*, chap. 9), the same applies to all of His attributes, including His speech. God's speech includes the speaker, the speech, and who and what is addressed by the speech. He is not merely conveying information; rather, He is creating the entire situation.

28. *Etz Ḥayyim, Sha'ar Tal,* beginning of chap. 3.

וְהִנֵּה נוֹדַע לְיוֹדְעֵי חֵן **Now, it is known to those initiated in the esoteric wisdom** of Kabbala

27 Tishrei

27 Tishrei (leap year)

Since the author of the *Tanya* is about to use kabbalistic language and terminology, whose proper understanding depends on prior knowledge of these concepts, he therefore notes that they are "known to those initiated in the esoteric wisdom." ☞

כִּי דְּבַר ה׳ נִקְרָא בְּשֵׁם ׳שְׁכִינָה׳ בִּלְשׁוֹן רַבּוֹתֵינוּ ז״ל **that the word of God is called the "Divine Presence," in the terminology of our Rabbis,**

That which the *Tanakh* calls "the word of God," or "utterances," or "the breath of the mouth" of God is termed the "Divine Presence" by the Rabbis in the Talmud and midrashim.

The "Divine Presence" refers to the divine life force, and in a certain sense the existence of the Divine that is present within all things. This life force, which is constricted and delineated, vitalizes and constitutes all things, within their specific boundaries. The "Divine Presence" is also divine speech, because just as a person takes himself, his thoughts and feelings, and so on, and makes them present in his speech when

"KNOWN TO THOSE INITIATED IN THE ESOTERIC WISDOM"

☞ Admittedly, all that the author of the *Tanya* has written in the epistle up to this point is also part of the inner, esoteric wisdom of the Torah, that is, the more abstract level of meaning of the Torah, which is not clothed in the garments of this physical world but only in spiritual souls and worlds. Nevertheless, he adds the phrase "known to those initiated in the esoteric wisdom" specifically in reference to what he is about to state below. This reflects the general approach of Hasidism that the inner teachings of the Torah are not just Kabbala: The esoteric level of the Torah, or "Hasidism" in its broadest sense, can be found everywhere. There is no need for prior knowledge of language and concepts; however, spiritual preparation is required. It is thus the person himself who may eclipse the secrets of Hasidism from himself. This is why the author of the *Tanya* does not state that the hasidic teachings that he has explored up until this point are "known to those initiated in the esoteric wisdom." With that said, Kabbala and its terminology undoubtedly form the basis for most hasidic teachings, and therefore – especially when dealing with other people (the *mitnagdim*) and other areas of Torah – the author of the *Tanya* returns to using kabbalistic concepts, which are "known to those initiated."

he talks to another person, so too God makes Himself present, as it were, in the divine speech that is within created reality.

וְ'אִימָא תַּתָּאָה' וּ'מַטְרוֹנִיתָא' בִּלְשׁוֹן הַזֹּהַר, וּבִפְרָט בְּרֵישׁ פָּרָשַׁת וָאֵרָא (חלק ב כב,ב)

and "the lower mother" and *matronita* [the queen] **in the terminology of the *Zohar*, especially at the beginning of *Parashat Va'era*** (2:22b),

The language of the *Zohar* is not like the language of the Rabbis in the Talmud and midrashim, even though it resembles to the extent that it too is Aramaic and depictive. Instead, the *Zohar* uses the ancient language of Kabbala, about which we do not know much, although it forms the basis for later kabbalistic terminology and thought.

"The lower mother" contrasts with "the upper mother," which is *Bina*, the feminine, receptive counterpart of *Ḥokhma*, and the mother of the attributes in *Atzilut* (the six *sefirot*, "*Zeir Anpin*"). The lower mother is *Malkhut*, the feminine, receptive aspect of *Zeir Anpin* (the "small face" of the world of *Atzilut*, which relate to the worlds) that receives on behalf of the worlds, and she is the mother of the worlds. "The queen" is the title given to a married woman who receives the influence from her husband, with which she gives life to the reality over which she reigns, bringing it into existence and "speaking" it.

לְפִי שֶׁשּׁוֹכֵן וּמִתְלַבֵּשׁ בַּנִּבְרָאִים לְהַחֲיוֹתָם. וּבִלְשׁוֹן הַמְקוּבָּלִים נִקְרָא בְּשֵׁם 'מַלְכוּת'

because it resides in and is enclothed in the created beings, to give them life. In the terminology of the kabbalists, the word of God **is called *Malkhut*** ("Kingship"),

All of these concepts express, each in a different way, the concept of divine speech that speaks and gives life to the entire creation, in general and in particular, as explained above. The term "kabbalists" here refers mainly to the Arizal. *Malkhut* is the tenth and last of the *sefirot*. Now, one can readily understand why speech is related to the last *sefira*. As in the human soul, once all the internal processes in the soul, its achievements, understanding and emotion, have been completed, everything is brought to a conclusion in the speech that the soul produces. However, it is more difficult to understand why it is called *Malkhut*. What is the connection between speech and *Malkhut*, kingship?

עַל שֵׁם: "דְּבַר מֶלֶךְ שִׁלְטוֹן" (קהלת ח,ד), כִּי הַמֶּלֶךְ מַנְהִיג מַלְכוּתוֹ בְּדִיבּוּרוֹ

after the verse **"governance is by the king's word"** (Eccles. 8:4), **as the king rules his kingdom with his word.**

The king does not take actions himself but rather he tells others what to do. Furthermore, he does not expect them to do it because they have understood the logic and reason behind it, nor out of love for him, but rather because he is issuing a command to them, an order. In other words, he imposes his authority through speech alone, which contains nothing other than what he says. This is the meaning of "governance is by the king's word" – speech itself expresses and sustains his rule, and this is the connection between the king and kingship, *Malkhut*.

וְעוֹד טְעָמִים אֲחֵרִים יְדוּעִים לְיוֹדְעֵי חֵן.

There are also other reasons that are known to those initiated in the esoteric wisdom of Kabbala.

That is, there are other reasons known to them as to why divine speech and the "Divine Presence" are called *Malkhut*.[29] ☞

"THERE ARE ALSO OTHER REASONS"

☞ This is possibly referring to the other characteristic of the attribute of *Malkhut*, the crown of kingship, which is the status of the King as exalted and separate from his Kingdom, with only His speech descending to command and give life to the worlds. That feature of the King Himself, as the "exalted" one, does not concern this epistle, which is dealing specifically with the enclothing of the Divine Presence below. The author of the *Tanya* therefore simply notes that there are other reasons known to the initiated, which are not necessary in order to understand the point he is making here.

---

29. See *Likkutei Amarim*, chaps. 51–52; *Iggeret HaTeshuva*, chap. 11, and epistle 5, above (The sixth Lubavitcher Rebbe, Rabbi Yosef Yitzḥak Schneerson, from the edition of the *Tanya* with collected commentaries).

וּמוּדַעַת זֹאת, כִּי יֵשׁ בְּחִינַת וּמַדְרֵיגַת מַלְכוּת דַּאֲצִילוּת וּבְחִינַת מַלְכוּת דִּבְרִיאָה וכו׳

And it is known that there is an aspect and level of *Malkhut* of the world of ***Atzilut*, and an aspect of *Malkhut*** of the world of ***Beria*...**

For each of the four worlds – *Atzilut, Beria, Yetzira,* and *Asiya* – there are ten *sefirot,* which are the totality of the divine illumination which bestows influence and is revealed in that world. Thus, for example, the *sefira* of *Ḥokhma* is the source of all the wisdom [*Ḥokhma*] that belongs to that world, while *Ḥesed* (Kindness) is the source of all bestowal and giving, and so on. The summation of all sefirot is the *Malkhut* of every world, what is received from all of them, from *Ḥokhma, Bina, Ḥesed, Gevura,* and so forth. It is like speech, which receives from all the inner levels in order to constitute the external reality that expresses them. The author of the *Tanya* will proceed to explain what the *Malkhut* of each world – *Atzilut, Beria, Yetzira,* and *Asiya* – constitutes and brings to life: which world, which creatures it contains, and so on.

וּפֵירוּשׁ מַלְכוּת דַּאֲצִילוּת הוּא דְּבַר ה׳ הַמְחַיֶּה וּמְהַוֶּה נְשָׁמוֹת הַגְּדוֹלוֹת שֶׁהֵן מִבְּחִינַת אֲצִילוּת

"*Malkhut* of *Atzilut*" means the word of God that gives life and being to the great souls which belong **to** the world of ***Atzilut*,**

With respect to *Atzilut* he mentions only souls, not actual angels and worlds, because the pure, lofty souls are the main entities that are emanated in *Atzilut,* and the influence upon them is the central influence of *Atzilut.* Accordingly, when the author of the *Tanya* discusses the world of *Beria* he will speak about souls and angels, and with regard to *Asiya,* which is this world in general, he will refer to the foundation of the physical earth. ☞

What does a soul of *Atzilut* look like? How does it conduct itself in our world? In order to convey this idea, the author of the *Tanya* presents some examples of souls of *Atzilut*:

כְּמוֹ נִשְׁמַת אָדָם הָרִאשׁוֹן

such as the soul of Adam,

The soul of Adam, the first man, who was the handiwork of the God – and was thus certainly created with all the perfection that a person should have – was a soul of *Atzilut*. In other words, his soul had a direct link to the Divine, without any concealment or mediation, as though it was one with God.

"THE GREAT SOULS WHICH BELONG TO *ATZILUT*"

☞ Not all souls belong to *Atzilut*. On the contrary, most souls are not of *Atzilut* – only a minority of the souls of the greatest righteous individuals are described as souls of *Atzilut*. It is true that all souls have a lofty source, which is even higher than *Atzilut*. (They are a "portion of God on high" (Job 31: 2); see *Likkutei Amarim*, chap. 2.) Nevertheless, what is significant for the individual soul is not its original root (as all souls are united in God), nor even the place to where it descends (for all souls are enclothed in a body in the physical world). Rather, the distinction is from what level the special character of this soul began to emerge, from what level and world it is already defined as a particular individual soul. It is from there that it will draw its unique powers, to there that it belongs, whether that to the world of *Atzilut* or the world of *Beria*, and so on. (For more on this, see epistle 24 above.) In this context, it is further stated (see *Torah Or* 74d) that all the differences between souls, whether they are from a lofty or lowly source, stem from what is revealed and concealed in them. This means that all souls of Israel, even if they are souls of *Asiya*, have a connection and affiliation to the lofty concerns of *Atzilut* and even higher than that. Consequently, even if some quality might be hidden in a certain soul or at a certain time, this does not reflect a lack of belonging, but only a deficiency in terms of revelation, in the soul's sensitivity and experience. Nevertheless, every soul is truly linked to and responsible for the entire spiritual spectrum of souls.

What distinguishes a soul of *Atzilut*? Elsewhere (*Torah Or*, beginning of *Parashat Mishpatim*, 74) the author of the *Tanya* explains that all the souls of Israel can be divided into two categories: "The seed of man" and "the seed of animals" (based on Jeremiah 31: 26). "The seed of man" are the souls of *Atzilut*, while "the seed of animals" are the souls of *Beria*, *Yetzira*, and *Asiya*. The differences between them do not concern the totality of a person's abilities and talents. Rather, they are at a more internal level, the level of recognition of the Divine. The souls of *Atzilut* are those which have a direct recognition of God; as explained there, they have knowledge of the Divine, that is, the kind of knowledge to which a person is fully connected, in which he lives, as though he can actually see it. In the case of the other souls, by contrast, it is as though their recognition comes from hearing, like someone who hears an idea from another person. It is a type of recognition that one can think about or decide not to, a reality that is not lived but merely thought about. The soul of *Atzilut* – only, of course, when that person lives below in a way that expresses his higher soul – lives in a state where God is the reality that is present within it. When reality speaks, it speaks to Him or it utters His words, and when it thinks, it thinks His thought with Him. Every movement of such an individual, in his body or soul, is in accordance with a movement above – of *Ḥesed*, *Gevura*, *Tiferet*, and so on. His whole existence is not as a separate entity, but only the existence of above, and this is the world of Atzilut.

שֶׁנֶּאֱמַר בּוֹ: "וַיִּפַּח בְּאַפָּיו נִשְׁמַת חַיִּים כו'" (בראשית ב,ז)

regarding which it is stated: "And He breathed into his nostrils the breath of life..." (Gen. 2:7),

As explained in *Likkutei Amarim* (chap. 2),[30] this breathing into the soul of Adam expresses the direct bond of his soul with the Divine, not through a screen and not even by means of boundaries and the mediation of letters. This essence, which emerges from within God's internality is itself the soul that is enclothed in the human body.

וּכְמוֹ נִשְׁמוֹת הָאָבוֹת וְהַנְּבִיאִים

and such as the souls of the Patriarchs and the prophets

The author of the *Tanya* compares the souls of the Patriarchs to the souls of the prophets, despite the fact that the Patriarchs certainly possessed more all-encompassing souls. The reason is that for the purposes of defining "a soul of *Atzilut*," it does not matter how all-encompassing the soul is, whether or not that person was a leader and father of all Israel. Rather, what counts is the private relationship of this soul with the Divine, whether it was a direct relationship and entailed the complete nullification of one's own person. In this regard, the souls of the prophets are equal to those of the Patriarchs. ☞

"THE SOULS OF THE PATRIARCHS AND THE PROPHETS"

☞ It can also be suggested that the souls of the Patriarchs are actually in *Atzilut*, as stated in the sources, that they served as a "vehicle" of *Atzilut*, whereas in the case of the prophets, although they too were a vehicle and entirely negated themselves (*Atzilut*), this occurred in *Beria*, *Yetzira*, and *Asiya* (See *Likkutei Torah*, Song. 11: 3; *Ma'amarei Admor HaZaken* [5564], p. 23.)

---

30. It is true that in *Likkutei Amarim*, this verse is applied to all divine souls, not specifically Adam or souls of *Atzilut*. It can be explained that on the one hand, Adam is the general essence, the head and root of all people, and thus his soul is the root of all souls, while on the other hand, he was also a particular individual who lived and died in a specific era. Accordingly, in *Likkutei Amarim* the author of the *Tanya* is referring to the first aspect, of Adam's status as the root of all souls, whereas here he is speaking about Adam the individual, that is, this verse was stated particularly with regard to his soul. The soul that is described in this verse must be a soul of *Atzilut*.

וְכַיּוֹצֵא בָּהֶן and others similar to them

This is referring to the souls of the righteous in each generation, since although prophecy came to an end, the prophetic inspiration did not cease, and in their prophetic inspiration, the greatest righteous individuals also attain the self-abnegation of a soul of *Atzilut*. Admittedly, the prophetic inspiration is not at the level of prophecy, but it appears that the difference between them lies in the message, its higher source and its penetration of reality down to the actual material existence. However, when it comes to the personality of the recipient of the prophecy or the prophetic inspiration, they are both in a state of complete negation with respect to what is passing through them. It does not matter what exactly is occurring or at what level; as far as the person himself is concerned, at that point he is in the world of *Atzilut*.

(שֶׁהָיוּ מֶרְכָּבָה לַה׳ מַמָּשׁ, וּבְטֵלִים מַמָּשׁ בִּמְצִיאוּת אֵלָיו (who were a literal vehicle for God, and who were actually negated in existence relative to Him,

The souls of *Atzilut* are considered a vehicle, which means to have attained the deepest level of nullification of existence, *bitul bimetziut*. Hasidic thought differentiates between two types of negation: "Negation of the self," *bitul hayesh*, and "negation of existence," *bitul bimetziut*. "Negation of the self" is the level of nullification of the souls in the worlds of *Beria*, *Yetzira*, and *Asiya*. It is also a level of a "vehicle," but as explained elsewhere it is that level which every Jew attains when he performs a mitzva. He is then considered as a vehicle for that act,[31] and yet he is not a vehicle himself in terms of his personality and life in general, since he still feels himself, his will and his opinion as "an entity" in and of itself, and he can never negate this. He is a vehicle only for specific acts (or statements or thoughts), when he performs the mitzva and nullifies his own will in order to fulfill God's will. This is the "negation of the self." By contrast, "negation of existence" is a level of souls of *Atzilut*, those who are an actual vehicle in all of their physical limbs, souls, and all of the events of their lives, like the Patriarchs and the prophets. Such a person does not need to negate his self and his

31. See *Likkutei Amarim*, chap. 37; *Torah Or* 71b.

will, as he has no self or sense of existence that he has to negate; he has no other desire or opinion that he must subdue. Rather, all the movements of his soul, and even his body, are not his own, but belong solely to the one above.

כְּמַאֲמַר רַבּוֹתֵינוּ ז"ל: שְׁכִינָה מְדַבֶּרֶת מִתּוֹךְ גְּרוֹנוֹ שֶׁל מֹשֶׁה. וְכֵן כָּל הַנְּבִיאִים וּבַעֲלֵי רוּחַ הַקּוֹדֶשׁ הָיָה קוֹל וְדִבּוּר הָעֶלְיוֹן מִתְלַבֵּשׁ בְּקוֹלָם וְדִבּוּרָם מַמָּשׁ כְּמוֹ שֶׁכָּתַב הָאֲרִ"י זַ"ל).

in accordance with the Rabbis' statement: "The Divine Presence would speak from Moses's throat." Likewise, with regard to **all the prophets and those who had prophetic inspiration, the supreme voice and speech** of God **would be enclothed in their actual voice and speech, as the Arizal wrote).**

Moses was more than a messenger for a particular mission that he received from God. Instead, the Divine Presence itself would speak from his throat.[32] In other words, one who listened to Moses was hearing the actual Divine Presence. With regard to the prophets as well, they were, as explained, in a state of absolute negation of themselves and their speech. What they said was not a translation, a transmission, or a rehearsal of the divine speech they heard, but rather the divine speech itself speaking through their mouths.[33]

Malkhut of *Atzilut* is the word of God, the Divine Presence, which gives life to the emanated beings that belong to the world of *Atzilut*. Just as the world of *Atzilut* in general is not a world but the Divine, so too the souls of *Atzilut* should not be considered as the existence of separate "selves" at all, but solely divine revelations. The difference between the *sefirot* of *Atzilut* and those souls is only that the former bestow influence while the latter receive it. Furthermore, the souls are recipients only with

---

32. *Zohar* 3:234a; see *Shabbat* 87a.

33. Perhaps he is here referring to an idea expressed at the beginning of *Sha'ar Ruaḥ HaKodesh*. Although he distinguishes there between the various levels of prophecy and the levels of the prophetic intuition, the rule with regard to all of them – notwithstanding their different levels and natures – is that the voice and speech from above enclothed itself in their voice and speech. In other words, they would not speak with their own voice, and with their understanding what they had heard from above; rather, as stated here, the lofty speech itself would be enclothed in their speech at that time.

respect to the *sefirot,* whereas in relation to the world they are givers. These are the very wholly righteous individuals of all generations.

וּמַלְכוּת דִּבְרִיאָה הוּא דְּבַר ה׳ הַמְחַיֶּה וּמְהַוֶּה הַנְּשָׁמוֹת וְהַמַּלְאָכִים שֶׁבְּעוֹלָם הַבְּרִיאָה, שֶׁאֵין מַעֲלָתָם כְּמַעֲלַת הָאֲצִילוּת וכו׳

And the *Malkhut* of *Beria* is the word of God that gives life and being to the souls and angels in the world of *Beria,* whose level is not like the level of *Atzilut*...

Malkhut of *Beria* is the speech of the *sefirot* from the world of *Beria,* meaning, the summation and revelation of *sefirot* of *Beria.* The world of *Beria,* as its name implies, is the creation [*beria*] of the world *ex nihilo,* unlike *Atzilut,* which is divinity. The world of *Beria* is not a corporeal world either, and it is not a world that hides its divine vitality. However, in contrast to the world of *Atzilut* it is already a "world," an "entity" in its own right. It not only recognizes the Divine, it is entirely a recognition of the Divine, divine understanding and knowledge. However, this is the case only from the other side; it is not divine recognition itself, from the inside, but rather the recognition of the Divine as attained by another.

Therefore, *Malkhut* of *Beria* sustains not only souls but also angels. In addition, as mentioned above the souls in the world of *Beria* are not at the level of "the seed of man," but rather "the seed of animals." The difference between them is analogous, metaphorically speaking, to the difference between sight and hearing: The souls (and angels) of *Beria* can be considered to hear, but not see, the Divine.[34] "Seeing" is direct, without a barrier or mediation, and thus they themselves are a revelation of the Divine, whereas "hearing" is like hearing from somebody else what they have seen, like via a screen, which, thin as it may be, is still a barrier of the most significant kind – between "something" and "nothing" creation. ☞

"THE SOULS AND THE ANGELS"

☞ With respect to *Beria,* we also speak about created angels. At its root, the soul is above *Beria.* Thus, when the sources state that "Israel arose in thought" (*Bereshit Rabba* 1: 4, cited in many places in hasidic texts), this is referring to the thought that

34. And as is known, "sight" is *Ḥokhma* and *Atzilut,* whereas "hearing" is *Bina* and *Beria.*

The author of the *Tanya* now moves on to discuss *Malkhut* of *Asiya*, without mentioning *Malkhut* of *Yetzira*. Perhaps the difference between *Beria* and *Yetzira* is not relevant to the subject matter of this epistle. *Atzilut* is unity, *Asiya* is separation (which can lead to a lack of a relationship), while in the middle there are worlds that relate to them both. It is true that there is a difference between the two types of relationships, between *Beria* and *Yetzira*, just as there is a difference between intellect and emotion, but that is not the topic currently under discussion.

וּמַלְכוּת דַּעֲשִׂיָּה הוּא דְּבַר ה׳ הַמְחַיֶּה וּמְהַוֶּה אֶת עוֹלָם הַזֶּה בִּכְלָלוֹ

And the *Malkhut* of *Asiya* is the word of God that gives life and being to this world in general,

Malkhut of *Asiya* is the speech of the *sefirot* of the world of *Asiya* (the ten utterances), which constitutes and gives life to the world in which we live in general, in both the spiritual and the material sense. The world of *Asiya*, in relation to God, is like an action in relation to the person who performed it: It is the level furthest away from himself and his individuality, further removed than his feelings, thought, and speech, to such an extent that it can even be seen as entirely unrelated to him (similar to the way in which one cannot see in a deed the one who did it, as opposed to speech and thought). In the same manner, this physical world can be viewed as an entity in and of itself, which is detached from the divinity that sustains and brings it into being from nothingness. ☞

עַד יְסוֹד הֶעָפָר וְהַמַּיִם אֲשֶׁר מִתַּחַת לָאָרֶץ

right down to the element of earth and the water that is under the ground

came before the speech with which the world was created. Although the souls descended even lower than the angels, to be enclothed in the body that is in the material world of *Asiya*, there is nevertheless a revelation of souls above *Beria* as well, in the world of *Atzilut*. In contrast, the angels are always part of *Beria*; they are spiritual, separate intellects, messengers of God, but entirely in relation and connection to *Beria*. Even though they are in essence messengers that express the will of God alone, it is always a will that refers to *Beria*, as opposed to the lofty souls in *Atzilut*, which can relate to God Himself.

Even this world – including its material qualities – is divided into four elements: Fire; wind; water; and earth, with earth as the lowest element. The elements of earth and water are described as "under the ground," in the sense that the ground conceals the divine life force from them, in contrast to the elements of wind and fire which are "above the earth," meaning, they are not completely hidden, and they at least have the aspiration to reach higher, to the existence of holiness that they can recognize there. As mentioned in the ancient books on nature,[35] it is in

"WORLDS AND *NEFASHOT*"

☞ In contrast to *Malkhut* of *Atzilut* and *Malkhut* of *Beria,* which give life to souls and angels, *Malkhut* of *Asiya* sustains "this world in general…" The difference is that souls and angels have the status of *"nefesh,"* entities that have awareness, whereas this world is, in general terms, an entity that lacks self-awareness. (According to *Sefer Yetzira,* the names for the three dimensions of the worlds are place ["world"], time ["year"], and the *nefesh* within them. In this regard, the *nefesh* is always the part that is aware and active within the dimensions of time and place.) By "awareness" we mean an awareness of holiness, of the separate divine vitality that gives life to and constitutes the *nefashot* and the angels and their world, in every world to the greatest possible extent and totality. Therefore, in this world, where even a *nefesh* does not have a natural awareness of God, the *nefesh* is entirely like a dimension of the world, the basic inanimate "matter" that is the world, and the *nefashot* within the world have no advantage over it. The *nefashot* and angels in the world of action are in this sense like the world itself, an existing reality that possesses no clear awareness of divine life and being.

However, even in the world of *Asiya* there is a difference between the *nefashot* it contains and "this world in general." The relationship between the nefesh and the body is mirrored by the relationship between the *nefashot* and the world: They are the essence of the life force, of the light and soul within the body, and in terms of the body and the world in general they are always on the side of the divine speech rather than the subject to which it refers, of the (albeit concealed) Divine as opposed to the world and action. (See *Torah Or* 3c, for a discussion of this distinction.) Therefore, secretly, sometimes even without knowing it, the *nefesh* bears the revelation of holiness from high above. (See *Likkutei Amarim,* chap. 18.) In fact, it is precisely the *neshama* in *Asiya* that thereby discovers the meaning which exists not only in the divine revelation but also in the divine concealment, and thus it is the overall key to understanding and rectifying the whole of the progression, and reality in general, from above to below and from below to above.

---

35. With regard to the physical plane of existence, see Rambam, *Sefer HaMadda, Hilkhot Yesodei HaTorah* 4:2.

the nature of the elements of water and earth to descend, while wind and fire rise upward.

28 Tishrei

28 Tishrei (leap year)

(אֶלָּא שֶׁבְּחוּץ לָאָרֶץ הַחַיּוּת הוּא עַל יְדֵי הִתְלַבְּשׁוּת שָׂרִים הַחִיצוֹנִים הַמְּמוּנִּים עַל ע׳ אוּמּוֹת

(**however, outside the Land** of Israel, **the life force is** created **by means of the enclothing of "external** spiritual **angels" charged over the seventy nations.**

That is, outside the land of Israel the life force from the word of God, *Malkhut* of *Asiya,* does not reach the physical earth directly. Every nation and culture has a spiritual essence, "minister," from which it receives its vitality and its special character. These ministers are "external," in the sense that they convey the external aspect of the life force rather than its internal essence, the effects of the life force upon the physical earth, not its inner, divine meaning. This external effect is the existence of the *kelippa* (literally, "husk," the forces of impurity) which receives all of its life force from the sacred, but which hides this and even acts as a diametrically opposing force in the worlds. ☞

"EXTERNAL ANGELS"

☞ Each of the seventy nations has its own human trait, unique to itself. (The source for the fact that there are seventy principal nations is the list the Torah provides of the descendants of Noah, in Genesis, chapter 10. The Rabbis cite this number on many occasions.) This uniqueness, in both talents and deficiencies, distinct from all other nationalities, creates enormous strength. The essence of this power and uniqueness, of the totality of the particular occurrences and individuals, is called the "ministering angel" of that nation, meaning, the spiritual essence that characterizes the nation, from which its particulars acquire their special nature: Its unique people; land; customs; dress; and so on. However, this distinctiveness leads to the genuine flaw of an inability to connect to other nations. Each nation views itself alone and has difficulty minimizing itself and accepting the other. This in turn leads to an inability to truly accept God's unity and the yoke of His kingdom. (See *Likkutei Amarim*, end of chap. 1. As for the fact that there are, and have always been, in all generations, gentiles who are "the pious of the nations," see *Iggeret HaKodesh*, vol. 1, epistle 95 also published in the edition of the *Tanya* with references and collected commentaries, chap. 1.) In opposition to all the seventy nations there stands Israel, which contains some feature from all the seventy but nothing by itself in all of its power and strength, as is the case for the other nations. (This is why Israel can appear to be "like all the nations," as we have seen. However, since they are mere-

How is this possible? The answer is comprised of several stages. One is that the divine life force is drawn forth through its enclothing in the seventy external ministering angels, who in themselves are not evil, but rather they are messengers of God sent to constitute a reality in which the presence of God is not evident. Only this reality, which receives from them, can be evil and part of the *kelippa*. Second, as will be explained below, even this life force, through which God sustains these ministers, is not an internal, direct influence, but rather it comes by way of an illumination, in an encompassing manner.

דְּהַיְינוּ, שֶׁיּוֹרֵד נִיצוֹץ מִדְּבַר ה׳ הַנִּקְרָא בְּשֵׁם ׳מַלְכוּת דַּעֲשִׂיָּה׳

That is, a spark descends from the word of God that is called "*Malkhut* of *Asiya*,"

It is not the word of God itself, *Malkhut* of *Asiya*, that descends to the *kelippa*, but only a spark from it. A spark is merely an illumination, a glimmer of the thing itself.

In other words, God does not give life to the *kelippot* directly, with His speech, but through the illumination of sparks from His speech. A spark connotes distance, which indicates that this is not like a deliberate act of giving from a bestower to a recipient, but like a light that shines and sparkles from the illumination, so that everyone outside can enjoy it as well. On a mundane level, this can be compared to a person's daily schedule. There are things that one wants and intends to do, while

ly mimicking them, they can also be more than all the nations, in that they take on their traits in exaggerated form. Sometimes this imitation is successful, at other times it is ridiculous, while occasionally it is terrible.) Therefore, Israel is labelled "the least of all nations," which means, according to the hasidic interpretation, that they diminish themselves by accepting God's unity and reign.

A characteristic expression of these "ministers" is attributed by the prophet to the Pharaoh, king of Egypt, in acclaim that is in effect the words of the ministering angel of Egypt: "My river is mine, and I made myself" (Ezek. 29: 3). The lands of the nations, as represented by the perception and awareness of the gentiles, are the embodiment of the existential claim that we control and create our own reality, both the present reality and the reality that will come to pass. Such an outlook leaves no room for the Creator and leader of the world, and therefore not only does it not refer to Him, but it also stands in opposition to any possibility that He might appear and enter the world.

there are events that happen on their own, even when he actually does not have any interest in them. These are like a background – perhaps even taking the form of a contrast – without which his inner desire cannot be sustained. In this sense, every undertaking is surrounded by a kind of "illumination" – numerous procedures that come into being and are activated (or not) by the same deed. The same applies to the higher realm, with respect to God: These ministering angels, and the *kelippa* and evil that stem from them, certainly do not represent His inner will, and they do not receive directly from His speech. They are not the meaning and letters of the speech, but merely a spark from it, like a kind of speech within a speech.

וּמֵאִיר עַל הַשָּׂרִים שֶׁל מַעְלָה בִּבְחִינַת מַקִּיף מִלְמַעְלָה, אַךְ אֵינוֹ מִתְלַבֵּשׁ בָּהֶם מַמָּשׁ, אֶלָּא נִמְשָׁךְ לָהֶם חַיּוּת מֵהֶאָרָה זוֹ שֶׁמֵּאִיר עֲלֵיהֶם מִלְמַעְלָה בִּבְחִינַת מַקִּיף.

which shines upon the supernal ministers in the form of encompassment from above, yet is not actually enclothed in them; rather, the life force is drawn to them from this illumination that shines upon them from above, in the form of encompassment.

Even with respect to one who receives its illumination, this spark is not received as an inner light and life force, but as an encompassment from above.

As explained in *Likkutei Amarim* (chap. 48), this is not like a physical illumination, which cannot be internal if it is an encompassment. Rather, it is the illumination of a spiritual life force that is not limited in place, neither physical nor spiritual. An "encompassing illumination" means that it is not enclothed in the vessels of that reality, as the affairs and conduct of the ministering angels and the lands of the nations. However, it sustains the great ensemble of which it forms part. Even in terms of the physical world, in order for something to exist within its limits, its boundary must differ from it and even be the opposite of it. This perimeter that surrounds everything in existence has no end, since every finite entity requires an encompassment, and an encompassment for its encompassment, ad infinitum. On the spiritual plane, this does not mean that the encompassment is found only within the perimeter, as stated, because the life force of the entity – its inner essence and that which is inside its internality, its character and all the particulars of its properties – are actually received at all times from the power of this encompassment. Therefore, when it is stated regarding the supernal ministers that the divine life force shines upon them in the form of encompassment, they themselves can be described as that form of encompassment. That is, with regard to the inner desire that is revealed, for example, through the enclothing of *Malkhut* of *Asiya* in a certain person who performs a mitzva, there is an encompassing illumination for him that incorporates the gentiles and all their masses, who can also stand in opposition to and against that person, his thoughts and his deeds, in that very same movement of holiness.

It can be further understood from this observation that the inner light enclothed in the vessels is the revealed light, in contrast to the encompassing light, which is hidden. Consequently, one who acts with holiness and sustains spirituality in his life – regarding whom it is stated that the divine life force is enclothed within him – is also one who perceives the divine life force, who feels with love and awe the divine reality that constitutes and gives him life. However, one who belongs to the *kelippa*, who receives his life force from those ministering angels in the form of encompassment, is unable to see.[36]

וּמֵהַשָּׂרִים נִשְׁפָּע חַיּוּת לָאוּמּוֹת **And from the ministers, a life force flows to the nations,**

A lowlier influence descends from the ministering angels to the created beings who receive from them. While there is continuity here, the summation is erroneous. Above, with the ministers, there can be a subtle understanding of how there is nevertheless something above them, and that there is a power above all powers in existence, all the

36. The vessels are also an important factor here. One whose vessels are not ready or fine enough, will not see either. However, the very existence of the light of holiness within his vessels, even if he is unaware of it, continues to direct him toward holiness, in his actions, words, and everything that happens to him. Furthermore, the light cleans the vessel more and more thoroughly, eventually equipping him to perceive with his own consciousness.

way up to God Himself. However, the nations below no longer have such a capability; they attribute the status of a god to what they perceive as the source of their power, by worshiping and serving it, and this is idolatry. ☞

וְלִבְהֵמוֹת חַיּוֹת וְעוֹפוֹת שֶׁבְּאַרְצוֹתֵיהֶם, וְלָאָרֶץ הַגַּשְׁמִית וְלַשָּׁמַיִם הַגַּשְׁמִיִּים שֶׁהֵם הַגַּלְגַּלִּים

and to the animals, beasts, and fowl that are in their lands, and to the physical earth and heaven that are the celestial **bodies**

The life force that flows from the ministers also goes to the entire natural physical infrastructure of that land which belongs to them: The animal, vegetable, and mineral kingdoms, the earth and the sky. Each of these expresses in its own way the essence of the "minister" to which it belongs. Like all of those who receive from the ministers, these too are a form of a *kelippa* that hides the divinity which constitutes and gives life to them.

The additional phrase "that are the [celestial] bodies" refers to the boundary realm between the spiritual and the material.[37] These

FROM THE MINISTERS, A LIFE FORCE FLOWS

☞ It is significant that here he talks about the life force "flowing" from the ministers to the angels, whereas earlier he referred to the "illumination" upon the ministers from *Malkhut*. (See for example the essay *Venaḥa Alav, 5714; Sefer HaMa'amarim Melukat,* vol. 3, p. 174; *Torat Shmuel,* 5627, p. 458) As explained elsewhere, a flowing influence differs from an illumination. A flow is an actual act of giving, intentional and through engagement, while taking into account the recipient and his manner of acceptance. One can understand why the ministering angels receive illumination from above rather than a flow, and why it is in the form of encompassment and is not internal, as will be explained below. However, it remains to be understood why the ministers themselves bestow a life force to the *kelippot*. The answer must be that in order for an entity to have a genuine existence in life it must have a real inner life force, not merely an existence from the encompassment. While the ministering angels are themselves a kind of reservoir of possibilities, these nations that live here in their lands, and their deeds, are indeed real existences. What is impossible to occur is the flowing of influence from the holiness to the ministers, and therefore it is an encompassing illumination. However, the ministers themselves are entirely possibilities, and the flow from them is indeed the actualization of that possibility. (For more on these terms, see *HaLekaḥ VeHalibuv*.)

37. See Rambam, *Sefer HaMadda, Hilkhot Yesodei HaTorah,* chap. 3.

bodies [*galgalim*] include what we would call today the laws of nature, the ways in which the materials of nature develop [*mitgalgelim*] from one form to another, from one state to the next; the laws of causality; particular laws; general laws; and rules of conduct, which encompass and incorporate ever more entities and worlds. This addition serves to teach that these laws are also under the influence of the spiritual "ministers" that belong to that part of the world.

(אֶלָּא שֶׁשָּׁמַיִם וָאָרֶץ וּבְהֵמוֹת וְחַיּוֹת וְעוֹפוֹת טְהוֹרִים נִשְׁפָּעִים מִקְּלִיפַּת נוֹגַהּ, וְהַטְּמֵאִים וְנַפְשׁוֹת הָאוּמוֹת מִשְּׁאָר קְלִיפּוֹת)

(only that the heaven and earth, and the pure animals, beasts, and fowl, receive their flow from the *kelippa,* the husk, called ***noga,* whereas the impure ones and the souls of the nations** receive their flow **from the other *kelippot*)**

"The other *kelippot*" means the three impure *kelippot,* from which the souls of the nations and the impure beasts and fowl receive their flow. This parenthetical observation refers to the division between the two general levels of the *kelippa,*[38] which differ in the degree of the concealment of the divine life force within them. One level is *kelippat noga,* meaning, the *kelippa* that contains *noga,* light, such that the concealment within it is not entirely sealed up, and thus holiness can be revealed within it itself. The second level is the impure *kelippot,* which are completely sealed. There is no revelation of holiness in them themselves, and all of their flow comes by way of encompassment, as will be explained. The example he brings for *kelippat noga* is the entire existence of the physical world that is used for the performance of mitzvot, which includes all material entities – heaven and earth, the pure animals,... His example for the impure *kelippot* is the beasts that may not be eaten and the souls of the nations, as explained at the beginning of the *Tanya.* ☞

THE *KELIPPAT NOGA* AND THE IMPURE *KELIPPOT*

☞ The difference between these two is that the *kelippat noga* can itself occasionally be transparent to a certain degree, thereby revealing the light itself rather than

38. For more on the *kelippat noga* and the three impure *kelippot,* see, e.g., *Likkutei Amarim,* chaps. 1, 6, 7, 37.

וְהִנֵּה שָׁמַיִם וָאָרֶץ וְכֹל אֲשֶׁר בָּהֶם בְּחוּץ לָאָרֶץ

Now, heaven and earth and all that is in them, outside the Land of Israel,

Here the author of the *Tanya* distinguishes between the heaven and earth that are outside the Land of Israel, and the heaven and earth within Israel. The heaven and earth outside the Land of Israel are part of the lands of the nations, which receive their flow from the seventy aforementioned ministering angels. It is this heaven and earth that he is speaking of here, since the heaven and earth in the Land of Israel do not receive from the ministers but directly from the holiness, and therefore they themselves can be holy and not *kelippa* at all.

כּוּלָּם כְּלֹא מַמָּשׁ חֲשִׁיבֵי לְגַבֵּי הַשָּׂרִים שֶׁהֵם חִיּוּתָם וְקִיּוּמָם, וְהַשָּׂרִים כְּלֹא מַמָּשׁ חֲשִׁיבֵי לְגַבֵּי הַחַיּוּת הַנִּמְשָׁךְ לָהֶם מֵהַנִּיצוֹץ

are all considered insubstantial in relation to the ministers that are their life force and existence, while the ministers are considered insubstantial in relation to the life force

concealing it. This can be compared to a physical garment, which usually covers and hides its wearer but can also reveal him. When it adheres fully to its wearer, to the shape of his body, and even his mood, will, and understanding, it exposes him. The same applies to material reality in general – it can refer to, accommodate, and even negate itself in favor of its wearer, meaning we can perform mitzvot with it. This is true of the (inanimate) heaven and earth, the pure animals and beasts from which a sacrifice can be brought or which can be eaten in a state of holiness, and so on, and it is also true of the animal body and soul of Israel. By contrast, there are levels of impure *kelippot* that hide the light entirely, which do not reveal the holy light they contain. Examples of this include the impure animals, whose consumption (even if done for the sake of Heaven) does not elevate the sparks of holiness within them. Likewise with regard to the souls of the nations (meaning, when they live as gentiles. For even a gentile, if he conducts himself with integrity, performs acts of kindness, and observes the mitzvot that apply to him (the seven Noahide mitzvot), can be considered one of the "pious of the nations," who have a vital soul from the *kelippat noga*) – they themselves are unable to make the transition from focusing on their own essence (the *kelippa*) to the holy, for the sake of Heaven. (See *Likkutei Amarim*, end of chap. 1.) These *kelippot*, which reveal only their own existence, completely hide and are even "opposed" to the revelation of holiness through them and in general. (This refers to when they live as gentiles. For even a gentile, if he conducts himself with integrity, performs acts of kindness, and observes the mitzvot that apply to him [the seven Noahide mitzvot], can be considered one of the "pious of the nations," who have a vital soul from the *kelippat noga*.)

מְדַבַּר ה׳ הַמֵּאִיר עֲלֵיהֶם מִלְמַעְלָה.

that is drawn to them from the spark of the word of God that shines upon them from above.

The rule for all levels of progression is that the lower level is nullified in relation to a higher level and is not considered a separate existence at all. This rule applies to the levels of the *kelippa* as well. Since the lowest level is merely a particular that contains nothing new with respect to the general and the source, it is not considered a distinct entity, and therefore the higher level returns and essentially fills the whole space.

וְאַף עַל פִּי כֵן, הַחַיּוּת הַנִּמְשָׁךְ לְתוֹכָם מֵהֶאָרָה זוֹ הוּא בִּבְחִינַת גָּלוּת בְּתוֹכָם

Nevertheless, the life force that is drawn into them from this illumination is considered to be in exile within them.

That is, the life force drawn into all the levels of the *kelippa* from this illumination of the word of God, from the holiness, is considered to be in exile within them. Everything that we stated with regard to the negation of a lower level in favor of a higher one applies from above to below, and in the case of holiness, from below to above as well, since the lower level is aware of the upper level that constitutes and sustains it. In the progression of the *kelippot*, however, when the higher level is not revealed to the lower one, the lower one is not nullified and does not diminish itself. On the contrary, it takes everything for itself, and the more it receives the greater it appears in its own eyes. This absurd situation – in which entire beings and worlds can deny the sacred, and even fight against it, at the very moment that they receive their entire existence from it – is called "the exile of the Divine Presence." It is comparable to the state of people in exile: They are subjugated to others in a place that does not belong to them and that does not suit them, where they are unable to discover their strengths and selves and in which they suffer humiliation and what is special about them remains hidden. What is more, not only is a person in exile unable to use his strengths to express himself, but he is even compelled (and sometimes tempted) to relinquish his powers and talents in order to raise and strengthen the very one who has captured him. Similarly, the

Divine Presence, which is in the exile of the nations and all that belong to them, does not reveal itself and is even "compelled" to sustain these worlds, with all the falsehood and heresy they contain.

שֶׁלָּכֵן נִקְרָאִים בְּשֵׁם "אֱלֹקִים אֲחֵרִים"

This is why they are called "*elohim aḥerim*" (foreign gods),

Since the life force that the gentiles receive from the ministering angels is in exile, where they are unable to see the divine power in their vicinity, they attribute this power to the ministers and to themselves (either actually to themselves or to the reflection of their desires and needs in the symbols they create, such as natural forces). This is why the ministering angels are called "foreign gods." ☞

וְקָרוּ לֵיהּ "אֱלָהָא דֶאֱלָהַיָּא" שֶׁגַּם הֵם, הֵן בְּחִינַת אֱלֹקוּת.

and they, those people and nations, **call Him "the God of gods," as** they maintain that **those too,** the "*elohim aḥerim,*" **are divine.**

Those people and nations, who worship the ministering angels and the forces of the world, call the Holy One, blessed be He, "the Gods

"FOREIGN GODS"

☞ In *Likkutei Amarim* (chap. 22) it is explained why the *kelippot* and the *sitra aḥara* (the "other side") are called "foreign gods," sharing the same etymological root, "*aḥer.*" One reason is because they receive from the back side (*aḥor*) of holiness rather than from the front. In the terms of his own metaphor there, it is like "a person who begrudgingly gives something to his enemy, tossing it to him over his shoulder while turning his face away from him in hatred." If so, the *kelippa* of idolatry, which receives from the "back side" of holiness, is itself considered "back side," and when it is worshipped and treated like a god, it is called "foreign gods." Later in the same chapter another reason is given, which is a logical consequence of the first one: Since this life force that is in the form of back side is in a state of exile, the *kelippot* turn into "foreign gods" in the sense that they are foreign to and oppose holiness. There is a transition here from the stage when an entity is merely not negated in favor of holiness, meaning, it also claims existence for itself, to the extent that it is everything and holiness does not exist at all, as it were. It "raises itself like a soaring eagle, saying, 'It is I, and there is none like me' (Isa. 47: 8), and as in the statement 'My river is mine, and I made myself' (Ezek. 29: 3)" (*Likkutei Amarim,* end of chap. 22).

of gods,"[39] in accordance with their erroneous assumption that the "*elohim aḥerim*" are also divine, only that God is above them. ☞

וְלָכֵן הַגּוֹיִם הַנִּשְׁפָּעִים מֵהֶם הֵם עוֹבְדֵי עֲבוֹדָה זָרָה מַמָּשׁ,

Therefore, the nations that receive their flow from them, those supernal angels, **are actual idol worshippers,**

The ministering angels themselves are not actual idols, but in the next stage,[40] for the people who receive from them in this physical world, this can turn into proper idolatry. That is, not merely a crack in the divine unity, but an entire belief system of idolatry, which maintains that the idol itself can provide benefit and do harm, that it can give and take away. That which cannot happen above, in the spiritual realm that is never entirely sealed, can indeed occur in this world, where the divine concealment can be absolute.

עַד עֵת קֵץ שֶׁיְּבוּלַּע הַמָּוֶת וְהַסִּטְרָא אָחֳרָא

until the time of the end, when death and the *sitra aḥara* are swallowed,

There is no complete solution to this problem at this time. This is part of the essence of this world, that it has a backside, where evil, idolatry, and death exist. It will only be at "the time of the end" (Daniel 11:35, and elsewhere), in the future and complete redemption, when death

THE ROOT OF IDOLATRY

☞ As the Rambam explains (in the first chapter of *Hilkhot Avoda Zara*), the root of idolatry lies in the denial not of the existence of God, but of His unity. By "His unity" we mean that He is one and that there is no other beside Him, both down below and in the realms above. The whole conception of idolatry begins from the assumption that the idol also exists, and that it too has a mind and the power to change things down below. In hasidic thought, this approach is called "the Gods of gods," as that spiritual essence, which appears to be an idol from down below, itself cannot deny the existence of God. Even it has to admit that there is a higher power above it from which it receives, only that this supernal power is merely "the Gods of gods," of the great and encompassing entities above, while each of our fates below are determined by our idol of choice.

39. *Menaḥot* 110a.
40. See Rambam, *Hilkhot Avoda Zara*, chap. 1.

and the *sitra aḥara* (the back side) are swallowed[41] out of existence, that this state of affairs will no longer be maintained. Ever since the sin of the Tree of Knowledge, the *sitra aḥara* rules over the world, and even if it is sometimes weakened – in a particular generation, for a specific person, or at a certain time in the lives of all people – it persistently reawakens once again. It is only at the future redemption that the *sitra aḥara* will disappear from existence forever. ☞

וְ"אָז אֶהְפּוֹךְ אֶל עַמִּים כו' לִקְרוֹא כּוּלָּם בְּשֵׁם ה'" (צפניה ג,ט),

and "then I will convert all the peoples to a pure language, **for all of them to call in the name of the Lord"** (Zeph. 3:9).

Then, at the time of the redemption, there will no longer be any concealment. For the concealment stems from the back side, as explained above, whereas then God will turn His face toward all the nations, and the speech that constitutes and sustains them will be "a pure language," meaning that it will be clear to everyone that it is the divine speech. All of them will "call in the name of the Lord," that is, their sight and hearing, their speech and all their modes of expression, will be in "in the name of the Lord." At present, when the garments of the *kelippot* conceal things, it is possible for a person or a world to express something else, whether themselves, idolatry, or anything else. In the

DEATH AND THE *SITRA AḤARA*

☞ There is a difference between "death" and the *"sitra aḥara."* Death, from which there is no return, represents the three impure *kelippot* that cannot be rectified, whereas the *sitra aḥara* represents the *kelippat noga. "Sitra aḥara"* is a general term: "The other side," which is the opposite of holiness. Anything that is not part of holiness is the "other side." "Side" refers to a relationship, and a relationship can be changed. This is the *kelippat noga.* However, this is the case only "until the time of the end," since at the time of the future and final redemption, after which there will be no exile, the essence of the world as we know it will be transformed into a different essence. In that world, even death, the impure *kelippot,* and the "forbidden" will be rectified and ascend, and only then will their essence as forces of evil be nullified.

41. This expression is from Isaiah 25:8: "He will swallow death forever..."

future, however, every garment will reveal only the divine force that is enclothed in it.

The author of the *Tanya* now presents a different explanation of the concept "the exile of the Divine Presence."

וְנִקְרָא גַּם כֵּן בְּשֵׁם 'גָּלוּת הַשְּׁכִינָה' מֵאַחַר שֶׁחַיּוּת זֶה אֲשֶׁר בִּבְחִינַת גָּלוּת בְּתוֹכָם הוּא מֵהֶאָרָה הַנִּמְשֶׁכֶת לָהֶם מֵהַנִּיצוֹץ מִדְּבַר ה' הַנִּקְרָא בְּשֵׁם שְׁכִינָה

This state **is also called by the name "the exile of the Divine Presence," since this life force which is considered** to be **in exile among them is from the illumination that is drawn to them from the spark of the word of God which is called by the name Divine Presence**

This is referring to the state of the concealment of the divine life force by the ministering angels and the *kelippot*. After discussing the meaning of the term "exile," the emphasis here is on the expression "Divine Presence." The author of the *Tanya* is saying that the divine life force which is in exile is called the "Divine Presence."

(וְגָלוּת זֶה נִמְשָׁךְ מֵחֵטְא עֵץ הַדַּעַת וְאֵילָךְ,

(and this exile comes from the sin of the Tree of Knowledge and onward,

The concept of "the exile of the Divine Presence" starts from the sin of the Tree of Knowledge. It is true that even before this sin the world existed, and it was even a "broken" world, in the sense that it was in need of rectification – and hence Adam received the command "to cultivate it and to keep it" (Gen. 2:15). However, this was not yet termed "exile." Exile is a kind of concealment and affront that cannot be created from above but only from below, by man. Only man, who can choose to act against the divine will, can fashion a genuine exile, such that the Divine Presence is not only unrevealed, but also the world is operating openly against the divine will.

וְהוּא בְּחִינַת אֲחוֹרַיִים לְבַד דִּקְדוּשָּׁה

and it is only an aspect of the "back side" [*aḥorayim*] of sanctity.

This is referring to the exile that extends from the sin of the Tree of Knowledge. There are many degrees of back and front, both with respect to the revelation of the Divine Presence and the exile of the Divine Presence: How internal this divine revelation is, or the opposite, how internal this exile and concealment of the Divine Presence is. On a human level, this can be compared to a person who is compelled to do something he would rather not do. It makes a difference whether it is only an action, in which he merely does what is required while his heart and soul are not in it, or if it is a creation of his inner spirit, in which case he must invest his heart and his creative power, what is truly precious and internal to him, albeit for people or a cause in which he has no interest. In both cases it is a form of an "exile" for him, but what a fundamental difference there is between the two. Similarly, this exile in which the divine speech sustains the ministers and the lands of the gentiles, which extends from the sin of the Tree of Knowledge, is "only an aspect of the back side of sanctity," in which, as it were, the holiness provides merely from its back side and externality, so that they can exist. This is nothing more than the external framework of life.

However, when Israel was exiled among the nations – and Israel's attachment and root is considered the supernal countenance –

אַךְ כְּשֶׁגָּלוּ יִשְׂרָאֵל לְבֵין הָאוּמּוֹת וַאֲחִיזַת יִשְׂרָאֵל וְשָׁרְשָׁם הוּא בִּבְחִינַת פָּנִים הָעֶלְיוֹנִים

This is the more internal and deeper exile. The author of the *Tanya* uses here the phrase "supernal countenance" which literally means "supernal face" which is the opposite of the back side. Here the exile of the Divine Presence is not merely at the level of the Divine Presence that sustains the worlds of the ten utterances, but its inner desire, which is represented by the people and souls of Israel.

All entities, from the souls of Israel and the angels to the smallest grains of dust in the ground, receive their existence and life from the Divine Presence, the divine power that is enclothed in them and sustains them in their current state. The difference between them depends on where that power is attached and rooted, the form of the Divine Presence, the specific divine image above. The world of *Asiya*, and in a broader sense the existence of all the created worlds, are attached and rooted solely in the force of the divine action or speech, which are considered like the back side in relation to the internality of the divine will. By contrast, the attachment of Israel and their root is at the "supernal countenance," "the supernal face". This depiction of the souls of Israel, as a soul within a body down below in this world, engaged in Torah and mitzvot, is engraved in the point of the inner essence of the divine will, the inner essence of recognition, the inner essence of the attributes, and the inner dimension of the divine speech and action.

הִנֵּה זוֹ הִיא גָּלוּת שְׁלֵימָה וְעַל זֶה אָמְרוּ רַבּוֹתֵינוּ ז״ל: גָּלוּ לֶאֱדוֹם שְׁכִינָה עִמָּהֶם)).

this is a complete exile. And with regard to this, our Rabbis stated: When they were exiled to Edom, the Divine Presence was exiled with them)].

When Israel is in exile, this means that not only is the back side, the active force of the Divine Presence, in exile, but the entire level of the Divine Presence, in its complete state, has also been exiled. This exile to Edom of which the Rabbis spoke,[42] is not the exile that began with the sin of the Tree of Knowledge, but a more profound and complete state of exile. With regard to this level, they said that "the Divine Presence was exiled with them," meaning, the Divine Presence itself, the essence of the Divine Presence,[43] is in the exile of Israel in Edom.

A person can perform a marginal, superficial act, without being present himself. It can be a hassle and waste of time for him, and even a kind of "exile," while he is still thinking about, desiring, and longing for other things that resonate with him. This is not the case when he is dealing with something that truly concerns him, such as something upon which his life depends or that of his only child. In such a situation, he is entirely present. This is true of Israel's exile among the nations, and therefore "the Divine Presence is with them."

---

42. *Mekhilta deRabbi Yishmael, DePasḥa,* 14; *Sifrei,* Num. 84, 161; *Bemidbar Rabba* 7:10; see *Megilla* 29a.

43. For a lengthy discussion of the concept of "the essence of the Divine Presence," see *Ma'amar Bati LeGani* (1950).

29 Tishrei

29 Tishrei (leap year)

וְהִנֵּה אַף כִּי "ה' אֶחָד וּשְׁמוֹ אֶחָד" (זכריה יד,ט) דְּהַיְינוּ דִּבּוּרוֹ וְרוּחַ פִּיו הַמְכוּנֶּה בַּזּוֹהַר הַקָּדוֹשׁ בְּשֵׁם 'שְׁמוֹ' (תיקוני זהר תיקון כב [סו,ב])

Now, although "the Lord is one and His name is one" (Zech. 14:9), **that is, His speech and the breath of His mouth, which are termed "His name" in the holy *Zohar*** (*Tikkunei Zohar* 22 [66b]),

The divine speech, which is the Divine Presence, as explained above, is also called God's "name." It is explained in several places that just as a person's speech is not intended for him but for others, to disclose to them what he is thinking, so too a person's name is not necessary for him but for others, so that they can call upon him and refer to him. With regard to God's name and His speech, the verse states that "the Lord is one and His name is one." This does not mean that He and His name are the same, but rather that this disclosure of His name serves to reveal God Himself – not one of His deeds, nor even one of His powers, but God Himself. Consequently, when we call Him by His name, we are referring to God Himself. Likewise, the divine speech is His name, the Divine Presence, which is, as explained, the internal expression of God that is in all entities.

הוּא יָחִיד וּמְיוּחָד **is singular and unique,**

In its essence, God's name is singular and unique. Since it refers to God Himself, it follows that in every situation and place it is God's complete, unique and singular expression. The multitude of God's names, like the multitude of His acts of speech, do not express plurality but rather unity. The multiplicity stems from the multifaceted reality, from our limited ability to see further than the boundaries of our personalities, beyond one narrow angle at a time, while all the names and all the speech point to a single source: The one who is called by these names and who issues the speech. The speech acts themselves, like the names, regardless of how numerous they are, cannot exist without the one who utters them.

Not only is His name "one," it is "singular and unique." There are lengthy discussions elsewhere[44] on the difference between *eḥad,*

44. See *Torah Or* 90c; *Likkutei Torah,* Num. 70, and in many other places. See

one, and *yaḥid*, unique. One idea is that *eḥad* expresses the unity in multiplicity, in the worlds, whereas *yaḥid* refers to God's personal unity. Here too, it can be suggested that "the Lord is one [*eḥad*] and His name is one [*eḥad*]" articulates the unity of the name and the Divine Presence in all the revelations of the worlds, while His description as "singular and unique [*yaḥid*]" denotes His unity in Himself, in the one so named, that He is completely one.

אַף עַל פִּי כֵן, הַהֶאָרָה וְהַמְשָׁכַת הַחַיּוּת הַנִּמְשֶׁכֶת מֵרוּחַ פִּיו יִתְבָּרֵךְ מִתְחַלֶּקֶת לד׳ מַדְרֵגוֹת שׁוֹנוֹת.

even so, the illumination and the drawing of the life force from the breath of His mouth divides into four different levels.

God, the source of the speech, is one, and even that which He reveals is essentially one, which is the Divine Presence – the existence of God in the world, which is also one. And yet the illumination is drawn forth to the worlds from the Divine Presence itself, in a manner that can be compared to a ray of the sun, in the sense that it is not an entity in and of itself but merely progressing levels and forms of the revelation of the one sun. In general terms, there are four such levels:

שֶׁהֵן ד׳ עוֹלָמוֹת אבי״ע וְהַשִּׁינּוּי הוּא מֵחֲמַת צִמְצוּמִים וּמָסַכִּים (רַבִּים), לְצַמְצֵם הָאוֹר וְהַחַיּוּת וּלְהַסְתִּירוֹ, שֶׁלֹּא יְהֵא מֵאִיר כָּל כָּךְ בְּעוֹלָם הַבְּרִיאָה כְּמוֹ בְּעוֹלָם הָאֲצִילוּת, וּבְעוֹלָם הַיְצִירָה הוּא עַל יְדֵי צִמְצוּמִים וּמָסַכִּים יוֹתֵר וכו׳

These are the four worlds of *Atzilut, Beria, Yetzira,* and ***Asiya,* and the change is due to the (many) constrictions and veils, which constrict and hide the light and the life force, so that it does not illuminate as much in the world of *Beria* as in the world of *Atzilut,* and in the world of *Yetzira* it** arrives **via more constrictions and veils...**

These four worlds are four levels that progress from one another. Not four parallel worlds but four worlds that are arranged in descending order.

---

also *Ma'amar Tziyyon BeMisphat Tipadeh* (1975); *Sefer HaMa'amarim Melukat*, vol. 4, p. 135; and see *Kuntres HaHitpa'alut, Likkutei Biurim LaTanya*, p. 75, second edition, below.

The ellipsis [...] at the end of the sentence here refers to the world of *Asiya,* which constricts the illumination in the world of *Yetzira* to an even greater extent, down to the reality of the physical *Asiya,* in which there is a complete concealment and even a *kelippa* that resists the light. The author of the *Tanya* merely alludes to this through the ellipsis because he does not want to say it explicitly here. As stated, a single source is revealed in all these levels and worlds, only that each descent to a lower world involves the addition of increasingly more veils and constrictions. Thus, the differences between the levels lies not in what they contain but only in the particular level of revelation and concealment. ☞

THE FOUR WORLDS: *ATZILUT, BERIA, YETZIRA,* AND *ASIYA*

☞ The four worlds – *Atzilut, Beria, Yetzira, and Asiya* – are the four most comprehensive levels, which encapsulate all the constrictions and veils from the *Ein Sof* down to this material world. Although the kabbalistic and hasidic texts refer to even higher worlds, which go beyond *Atzilut,* those lofty worlds are, by their very nature, hidden and disconnected from the reality of our lives (see *Likkutei Amarim,* chap. 2, in the note and commentary there), and they are not ordinarily spoken of or taken into account in relation to our reality. Furthermore, the kabbalistic and hasidic sources use the concept of the four comprehensive levels, the comprehensive *Beria,* the comprehensive *Yetzira,* and so on – in relation to which the created worlds, to which we generally refer, are specific, particular worlds (see *Likkutei Torah,* Lev. 8d; 43d, et al). In other words, the division into these four worlds of *Atzilut, Beria, Yetzira,* and *Asiya* does indeed incorporate everything, from the light of *Ein Sof* before the constriction until *Asiya,* but within it there is a further subdivision which has the same structure, and it is this subdivision, which is more relevant to us, that we typically discuss.

If we take the human soul as an example in this regard, we can say that from the stage of the revelation of the soul itself in *Ḥokhma,* which is like a kind of flash of its infinity into consciousness, until an actual deed in practice, there are countless degrees and steps. However, all of these can be divided into four broad stages: The first is in *Ḥokhma,* and it parallels the level of the world of *Atzilut.* In other worlds, the light already relates to the concept of vessels, but the other cannot attain his vessels, because everything is still "with Him," entirely unified in the *Ein Sof* Himself. The second stage involves the entrance into the vessels of the comprehensible intellect, into a world of recognition and understanding. This stage is comparable to the constriction from *Atzilut* to *Beria.* The third stage is the transition into the realm of emotion, where the expansive spiritual attainments transition into what one feels toward it, into the immeasurably constricted area of the personal emotional attitude toward those things. This stage corresponds to the level of the world of *Yetzira.* Finally, the fourth stage is what we do in practice within the world of material action. This is an immense constriction in relation to the world of emotional reference, like a kind of partial, external summation of the internal feeling. This stage can be compared to the world of *Asiya.*

אֲבָל אֵין שׁוּם שִׁינּוּי חַס וְשָׁלוֹם בְּעַצְמוּת הַשְּׁכִינָה שֶׁהִיא דְּבַר ה׳ וְרוּחַ פִּיו.

However, there is no change, God forbid, in the essence of the Divine Presence, which is the word of God and the breath of His mouth.

This essence is one, just as God is one, on every level and in every world. The only difference is, as stated, the degree of revelation with respect to the world.

The harsh expression "God forbid" indicates that this a sensitive point, particularly here when the author of the *Tanya* is addressing *mitnagdim* as well. What is the meaning of the constriction of the Divine? One might understand[45] that He actually constricts himself and even removes Himself from a certain place. In response to such a suggestion, he cries "God forbid!" He stresses that there is no change at all, not only in God Himself, but also in the revelation itself, which is the Divine Presence. All the levels of the worlds and what they contain are nothing but degrees and modes of the revelation of the Divine Presence. The only change is from the perspective of the lower beings who receive the illumination of the Divine Presence, whether it is revealed or hidden, and the like.

וְגַם בִּבְחִינַת הַהֶאָרָה וְהַמְשָׁכַת הַחַיּוּת, הִנֵּה הַהֶאָרָה שֶׁבַּאֲצִילוּת בּוֹקַעַת הַמָּסָךְ וּמִתְלַבֶּשֶׁת בִּבְרִיאָה, וְכֵן מִבְּרִיאָה לִיצִירָה וּמִיצִירָה לַעֲשִׂיָּה. וְלָכֵן אוֹר אֵין סוֹף בָּרוּךְ הוּא שֶׁבָּאֲצִילוּת הוּא גַּם כֵּן בַּעֲשִׂיָּה וּבָעוֹלָם הַזֶּה הַחוּמְרִי

Furthermore, with respect to the illumination and the drawing of the life force, the illumination in *Atzilut* breaks through the partition and is enclothed in *Beria*, and similarly from *Beria* to *Yetzira* and from *Yetzira* to *Asiya*. Therefore, the light of *Ein Sof*, blessed be He, which is in *Atzilut* is also in *Asiya* and in this material world

45. Some did indeed understand it in this manner, as reflected in the well-known dispute over whether or not the term "constriction" is meant literally. See the commentary below, and in *Sha'ar HaYiḥud VeHa'emuna*, chap. 7. See also the *Likkutei Siḥot* of the Lubavitcher Rebbe, Rabbi Menaḥem Mendel Schneerson, *Parashat Naso* [1983], 23; *Torat Menaḥem Hitva'aduyot* [1983], vol. p. 1599 and onward.

It is not only in its source that the Divine Presence is one, but also "with respect to the illumination and the drawing of the life force," the light that passes through and seems to change in its transitions from one degree to the next. The illumination that breaks through the partition between *Atzilut* and *Beria,* and is then enclothed in *Beria,* is not a different illumination but the very same light. One might have thought that the relationship between the worlds is a causal one between different forces, that there is no actual penetration from one world to another but only an indirect effect, like the result and reaction to the supreme illumination. If so, each world would receive at most from the world that is above it. The author of the *Tanya* therefore emphasizes that this is not the case; rather, the supreme illumination itself penetrates through all the partitions and the differences between the worlds, and it itself illuminates every reality and world, only with different garments and coverings each time. This can be compared, on a mundane level, to human communication. If one person tells another about something he has seen, and what he thought and felt about it, the other will receive an indirect message, only via the person who is relating it to him. However, if the first person succeeds in conveying – whether through his speech or in some other manner – something of the actual experience he had, the sight he saw, he will be able to transfer to the second individual an element of the very same content he received. Accordingly, the other person will receive not only the speech of the person who is talking to him, but also something of what the teller himself has experienced. The same applies all the way upward.

עַל יְדֵי הִתְלַבְּשׁוּתוֹ בְּמַלְכוּת דבי״ע **by means of its enclothing in the *Malkhut* of *Beria, Yetzira,* and *Asiya,***

How does this illumination, the light of *Ein Sof* in *Atzilut,* pass all the way down to this corporeal world? This answer is by means of its enclothing in the *sefira* of *Malkhut* in each world. The *sefira* of *Malkhut* is like speech in relation to the soul. Just as the soul reveals itself, its wisdom and feelings, by means of speech, so too the divine illumination in each world reveals itself to the world below it through its enclothing in the *sefira* of *Malkhut.*

The secret of speech lies in its ability to transfer content from one realm to another, from one world to the next. This appears to be difficult to understand: If two worlds are truly separate, with no sharing and overlap between them in terms of matter, intellect, or emotions, any connection between them would seem to be impossible. However, as is the case between people, even if they are from different worlds, when they converse, they create a relationship with each other and transmit contents, emotions and the light itself from one to another. This wondrous connection happens through the letters of speech, in those primary forces whose essence no one can define in precise terms, which pass between one world and another – from high above, before any world existed, before *Ḥokhma* came into being, all the way down to this material world. Everywhere they bear the innermost content and reveal it in the terms of that place. Just like speech, it is *Malkhut* that passes from one world to the next, and when it passes, it transfers not only that world which is currently speaking, but also what is spoken to that world, and so on and so forth, all the way up. This can be compared to a rabbi teaching his student: He conveys through his speech not only what he himself is thinking or feeling, but also what he received from his own rabbi, and that rabbi from his rabbi; the very same words and letters themselves that enclothe the inner light within them.

כַּמְבוֹאָר הַכֹּל בְּכִתְבֵי הָאֲרִ"י זַ"ל. **all as explained in the writings of the Arizal.**

The above explanation refers to the descent of the divine illumination, the light of the Divine Presence, to the worlds and even the existence of the *kelippat noga*. The Rabbis call this descent "the exile of the Divine Presence." This is all explained in great detail in the writings of the Arizal,[46] in many places and from various perspectives. Here, however, he does not get into a discussion of all that, as his comments are not meant only for those initiated in the esoteric wisdom of Kabbala. Nevertheless, since he is also addressing those who rely on the writings of the Arizal, he notes in passing that the ideas are mentioned and clarified there.

The author of the *Tanya* now turns his attention to the soul of man,

46. e.g., *Etz Ḥayyim* 42:4.

as that same descent also occurs in the soul and being of man – in his experience, speech, and behavior – and this is the focus of the statement of the Ba'al Shem Tov that is under discussion. In general, this is a characteristic transition from kabbala to Hasidism – that which concerns the worlds is "all as explained in the writings of the Arizal," before he continues: "Now, the soul of man..."

30 Tishrei

30 Tishrei (leap year)

וְהִנֵּה נֶפֶשׁ הָאָדָם, יָדוּעַ לַכֹּל שֶׁהִיא כְּלוּלָה מֵעֶשֶׂר סְפִירוֹת חָכְמָה בִּינָה דַּעַת וכו'

Now, the soul of man, as known to all, is comprised of the ten *sefirot* of *Ḥokhma, Bina, Da'at...*,

This "man" means specifically a Jewish man, for he is speaking about the divine soul, which is found in the Jewish people. Man was created "in the image of God" (Gen. 1:27), and that which exists in the Divine is also present in man. Of course, there is a massive, immeasurable difference between created man and the divine *Ein Sof*. Accordingly, when this comparison[47] is made, we necessarily speak in terms of the degrees through which the structure can be defined, that is, those degrees by which the soul manifests itself and operates in relation to the ten *sefirot* through which God reveals Himself and acts. He therefore states here: "Comprised of the ten *sefirot*..."[48]

To further clarify this, the similarity between the structure of the soul and the ten *sefirot* applies only to the internal relationships between the components of the structure. For example, when talking about the kindness [*ḥesed*] of a person and the kindness of God – which, in the figurative language of the *Zohar*,[49] are called the right hand of a person and the right hand of God – there is no comparison between them. However, if one thinks about the relationship between the right and left hands, the comparison does have meaning, since something of the relationship between left and right is maintained at all levels. In this sense, there is a complete structure that preserves the

47. *Adam*, "man," is related to "I will be comparable [*adameh*] to the Most High" (Isa. 14:14). See *Shelah, Toledot Adam*, introduction, 23, and elsewhere; *Asara Ma'amarot* by Rabbi Menaḥem Azaria of Fano, *Eim Kol Ḥai* 2:33.

48. As explained in *Likkutei Amarim*, chap. 3.

49. For example in "*Pataḥ Eliyahu*," from the introduction to the *Tikkunei Zohar* (17:1): "*Ḥesed* is the right arm,..."

entirety and the core of the essential relationships – between left and right, above and below, *Ḥokhma* and *Bina,* intellect and moral attributes, and so on. This is man, who is called a "small world" and was created in the image of God. ☞

וְאַף שֶׁכּוּלָּן מֵרוּחַ פִּיו יִתְבָּרֵךְ, כְּדִכְתִיב: "וַיִּפַּח בְּאַפָּיו כו'" (בראשית ב,ז).

even though they are all from the breath of His mouth, as it is written: "And He breathed into his nostrils..." (Gen. 2:7).

All of the ten *sefirot,* and the powers that the soul is comprised of, come from the breath of God's mouth, as it states with regard to the soul of man: "And He breathed into his nostrils the breath of life." This means that the soul of man is drawn from the inner essence of God, the same interiority that precedes any constriction, splitting and demarcation of the lights into vessels of *sefirot* and letters. As explained in *Likkutei Amarim,*[50] on the verse "And He breathed into his nostrils" – "one who blows from within himself he blows." For one might have thought

THE SOUL OF MAN AND THE SEFIROT – THEIR SIGNIFICANCE FOR THE SERVICE OF GOD

☞ The depth of this insight lends supreme meaning to human actions, and lays the foundational assumption for the entire hasidic service of God. To put it another way: The similarity between man and God is not merely theoretical, but rather it is based on a real, living connection between the two. The comparison that one can observe in terms of structure mandates a closeness and unity in essence as well. For example, divine kindness and human kindness are connected in their essence and core. Indeed, if a person performs the proper service with the appropriate intention, he can also attain a unity of essence and expression. (An extreme example of this is the statement that the Patriarchs were a vehicle for the Divine Presence [*Bereshit Rabba* 47: 6, 82: 6; see *Likkutei Amarim,* chaps. 23 and 39; as well as chap. 37, in reference to all people.]) Thus, for example, the service of prayer is not merely like addressing another person, a great minister, to whom one issues a request issued which he will either grant or not. Rather, it is a service that reveals a bond of unity, enabling the power in the soul to operate in the world because the divine power is enclothed and active within it. One ramification of this concept appears below.

50. Chapter 2. See also *Iggeret HaTeshuva,* 5, citing the *Zohar.*

that the soul is nothing but a extension modelled on the lofty *sefirot*: The wisdom [*ḥokhma*] of man is drawn from the wisdom [*Ḥokhma*] above, his kindness [*ḥesed*] is drawn from *Ḥesed*, and this is the whole of man. However, here it is stated that the concept of "in the image of God" goes deeper than that, and just as there is a single, infinite divine essence within all the *sefirot*, so too within all the powers and manifestations of the soul there is one soul that was drawn from the one inner, infinite essence above. And although the similarity can be seen only in their powers and actions, the connection is actually internal and obscured – where the Divine Presence is itself one, there the soul itself is also one.

מִכָּל מָקוֹם דֶּרֶךְ פְּרָט, חָכְמָה בִּינָה דַּעַת שֶׁבְּנַפְשׁוֹ הֵן דוּגְמָא לְחָכְמָה בִּינָה דַּעַת שֶׁבְּעֶשֶׂר סְפִירוֹת

In any case, the *Ḥokhma, Bina, Da'at* that are in his soul, specifically, are a miniature **version of the *Ḥokhma, Bina, Da'at* that are in the ten *sefirot*,**

"Specifically" means in the specific details of the forces of the souls, those which we can observe. Here too there is a connection and resemblance to the forces above. The phrase "miniature version" implies that they are not merely similar, but rather that they are the very same thing, only constricted and on a smaller scale, like a particular instance and not merely comparable. The *sefira* of *Ḥokhma* is the very same as the wisdom [*ḥokhma*] in one's soul, the *sefira* of *Bina* is the understanding [*bina*] in one's soul, and so on and so forth.

הַמְכוּנוֹת בְּשֵׁם 'אַבָּא וְאִמָּא'

which are called by the name "father and mother."

The *sefirot* of *Ḥokhma* and *Bina* are called "father and mother." The kabbala of the Arizal discusses not only *sefirot* but also "*partzufim*" (divine countenances), which entails an entire structural analogue that is comprised of particulars (*sefirot*) that complement one another and together create a single essence, like the countenance of a person's face, just as the human body has a head, a right leg and a left leg, and so on. The *partzufim* of *Atzilut* are as follows: "Father" and "mother," which parallel the *sefirot* of *Ḥokhma* and *Bina*; "*Zeir Anpin*, incorporating the six *sefirot* that correspond to the emotive attributes, and the *Nukva* (*nekeva,* the feminine aspect) of the *sefira* of *Malkhut* (there are two additional *partzufim* in *Keter*: *Atik Yomin* and *Arikh Anpin*). While the *partzuf* of the father is comprised of only a single *sefira, Ḥokhma,* all the other *sefirot* are composed of it; *Ḥesed* of the father; *Yesod* of the father, and so on. In other words, not only the *sefira* of *Ḥokhma* but also the *Ḥokhma* that bestows, the *Ḥokhma* that limits, the *Ḥokhma* that connects, and so on and so forth. The difference between the *sefira* of *Ḥokhma* and the *partzuf* of the father can be summed up in the following terms: The *sefira* of *Ḥokhma* is the abstract power of *Ḥokhma,* whereas the *partzuf* of the father is like a wise person [*ḥakham*]. The same applies to the *partzuf* of the mother.... The definition of a *sefira* as a *partzuf* thus applies both to its internal complexity and its relationships with the other *sefirot* and *partzufim*.

וּמִדּוֹת אַהֲבָה וְיִרְאָה וכו' שֶׁבְּנַפְשׁוֹ - הֵן דּוּגְמָא לְמִדּוֹת שֶׁבְּעֶשֶׂר סְפִירוֹת הַנִּקְרָאוֹת בְּשֵׁם 'זְעֵיר אַנְפִּין'

And the attributes of love and fear… that are in his soul are a miniature **version of the attributes in the ten** ***sefirot*** **that are called by the name "*Zeir Anpin.*"**

These "attributes of love and fear" are the six *sefirot* that correspond to the emotive attributes: Love [*Ḥesed*]; fear [*Gevura*]; *Tiferet*; *Netzaḥ*; *Hod*; and *Yesod*. The six attributes, from *Ḥesed* to *Yesod,* when they relate and operate as a single organic unit, form a separate *partzuf* that is called "*Zeir Anpin*" ("the small countenance"). ☞

ARIKH ANPIN AND *ZEIR ANPIN*

☞ *Zeir Anpin* is called by this name, "the small countenance," because it is the opposite of the partzuf in *Keter,* which is known as *Arikh Anpin* ("the long, great countenance"). Since it is in *Keter, Arikh Anpin* incorporates all of the *sefirot* within itself, and it is therefore the large countenance of reality. It can also be said that it is the countenance of the Emanator [*Ma'atzil*] Himself, in relation to the world of *Atzilut.* By contrast, *Zeir Anpin* is the small countenance, of the attributes alone, and it can be described as the countenance of *Atzilut* that is turned toward the worlds (which are incorporated in *Malkhut*). In other words, it is not the countenance of the Emanator Himself, in His greatness, but in His "smallness," when He is attending to and bestowing upon the worlds, which are small in relation to Him. As opposed to

וְכֹחַ הַדִּבּוּר שֶׁבְּנַפְשׁוֹ דּוּגְמָא לַדִּבּוּר הָעֶלְיוֹן הַנִּקְרָא בְּשֵׁם מַלְכוּת וּשְׁכִינָה.

And the power of speech in his soul is a miniature **version of the supernal speech that is called by the name *Malkhut* and the Divine Presence.**

It was already explained earlier that the word of God is called *Malkhut* and the Divine Presence. Here the author of the *Tanya* adds that human speech is an example of this. In other words, just as the divine speech not only reveals itself to the other but also creates the other in which it is revealed, residing within it and sustaining it, so too, one should understand the power of speech in the human soul as a kind of specimen of this activity. That is, the speech that a person utters likewise provides not only a disclosure of information, but in a certain way it also creates reality – the very same reality for which this information is significant.

וְלָכֵן כְּשֶׁמְּדַבֵּר דִּבְרֵי תוֹרָה מְעוֹרֵר דִּבּוּר הָעֶלְיוֹן לְיַחֵד הַשְּׁכִינָה

Therefore, when one speaks words of Torah, he arouses the supernal speech to unify the Divine Presence.

When a person "speaks words of Torah" he is articulating God's words, not his own speech.[51] It is true that even when a person speaks his

Arikh Anpin, which is encompassing and lies the background, beyond our understanding and our ability to truly relate to it, *Zeir Anpin* is situated here, since in relation to reality (*Malkhut;* the worlds), it is the bestower who incorporates and represents all that is far above us.: Since *Zeir Anpin* is situated opposite *Arikh Anpin*, on the middle line, it expresses *Keter* and divinity itself even more than the *partzufim* of the father and mother. Similarly with regard to the soul, *Zeir Anpin*, as the totality of the attributes, is the most real and significant. A person's sense of "self" is (generally) found in the attributes. The intellect is what a person understands and knows (of what ought to be the case), while the *Malkhut* is what he does, says, and even thinks. However, the attributes, the emotions, are what he actually is, and how he is currently relating to reality.

51. This is as explained in many places in the hasidic sources (e.g., *Torah Or* 67b) on the verse: "My words that I have placed in your mouth" (Isaiah 59:21), that

own words, he likewise discloses, evokes, and to a certain extent creates the reality he speaks. However, when he speaks words of the Torah, he reveals and awakens the Torah in his world, which is the supreme speech of God, which exists beyond the reality of the world, beyond even His revelation as the Creator of the world. That is to say, speaking words of Torah is itself the revelation of God who is separate from the world, and when a member of Israel, who is an expression of the Divine Presence, speaks words of Torah, this constitutes a connection and unification of God's speech with the speech of the Divine Presence. ☞

וּמִשּׁוּם הָכֵי קַיְימָא לָן בִּקְרִיאַת שְׁמַע וּבִרְכַּת הַמָּזוֹן וְדִבְרֵי תוֹרָה, לֹא יָצָא בְּהִרְהוּר בְּלֹא דִבּוּר.

For this reason, we maintain as *halakha* **with regard to the recitation of** ***Shema*****, Grace after Meals and words of Torah,** that **one has not fulfilled his duty through** mere **contemplating without** actual **speech.**

These Torah obligations specified by the author of the *Tanya* cannot be fulfilled if one merely thinks of the words but fails to articulate them orally.[52]

"THE AROUSAL OF SUPERNAL SPEECH TO UNIFY THE DIVINE PRESENCE"

☞ As is the case for human speech, there are likewise two levels of divine speech: One level is how it is said by Him, while the other level is how it is heard and received by the other. The speech as it is heard is merely the result of the speech, what happens to the speech at the end of the entire process. In the case of divine speech, this is the world that is currently before us. Consequently, when a person down here speaks words of Torah, the words of God, from within this world, he thereby unifies the spoken speech with the heard speech, uniting the outcome of the speech and creation with the original will and intention, the Divine Presence with God, who is beyond the world.

---

when a person speaks words of Torah, God Himself speaks through his mouth, and he is like one reciting something after it has been read out to him (see e.g., *Sukka* 3:10, and the Talmud segment on that Mishna).

52. See *Likkutei Amarim*, chaps. 37–38. See also *Shulḥan Arukh HaRav*, 62:3, and his *Hilkhot Talmud Torah* 2:12.

Since the unification is created through speech, it must likewise be performed below specifically by means of speech. God created the world through speech and He also reveals Himself in the Torah through speech. Therefore, the only way to unify the two is by means of speech, rather than through the emotions of love or fear and the like, in the form of mere contemplation or thought. In all such instances we are referring only to a certain level of revelation – we are thinking about the ideas and we feel something about what we are thinking. It is only through speech that we truly unite in the thing itself. For it is there, in the letters, that God has placed Himself, as it were, and it is only when all emotions and thoughts are put into speech that the unification can occur.

Fulfilling one's duty means that unification has occurred. In order for unification to occur in its ultimate extent, the unification of God and the Divine Presence, it must transpire within the person himself. "Unification" means that two things unite, and in the case of a person this generally means between thought and speech, between his internal aspect – the intellect and emotions as they are revealed in one's thought – and between speech, which refers to the outer reality and the other, all the way down to the materiality and physicality of the world. Accordingly, no unification can happen if contemplation is not accompanied by speech. It is only together with speech that it can unite with the world and express it. When one unites it with the thought that is in his speech, he thereby unifies the Divine Presence.

1 Ḥeshvan

1 Ḥeshvan (leap year)

וְהִנֵּה זֶה לְעוּמַּת זֶה **Now, in the corresponding counterpart** to holiness,

This expression,[53] which appears frequently in the hasidic sources, is shorthand for the idea that every manifestation of holiness has its impure foil. For the existence of impurity (the *kelippa*) is not independent, it has no source of existence, no essence and structure of its own. Rather, it is merely a certain twisted reflection of holiness.

יֵשׁ עֲשָׂרָה כִּתְרֵי דִמְסָאֲבוּתָא **there are ten crowns of impurity,**

53. Derived from Ecclesiastes 7:14: "God made this corresponding to that." See, e.g., *Likkutei Amarim*, chap. 6; *Torah Or* 26c.

Corresponding to the ten holy *sefirot*, which are the divine source of all reality – and on the inner level, the source of the souls of Israel – there are "crowns of impurity," which are a source of life and power fashioned in imitation of the structure of the ten *sefirot*. The world of the *kelippa* receives from these crowns. This is the world that is not nullified with respect to the Divine, which considers itself in some way as a separate "being" of its own. Therefore, it strives to separate and prevent the unification and connection of the world with God, for if unification does occur and its "self" is negated, its whole existence will cease. This world is the exact opposite of holiness, since for every power and aspect of holiness, which seeks to unify with the Divine, there is a contrasting power of impurity and being that endeavors to block that unification. ☞

וּמֵהֶן נִמְשָׁכוֹת נַפְשׁוֹת הָאוּמּוֹת, גַּם כֵּן כְּלוּלוֹת מֵעֶשֶׂר בְּחִינוֹת אֵלּוּ מַמָּשׁ.

and the souls of the nations are drawn from them, and they are **also comprised of these very same ten aspects.**

In contrast to the souls of Israel, which are incorporated and receive from the ten holy *sefirot*, the souls of the nations are incorporated and receive from the ten "crowns of impurity." That is, corresponding to

"THE CROWNS OF IMPURITY"

☞ The crowns of impurity transfer the life force from holiness to impurity by hiding the source of the power, the one who grants this life force. This transfer is performed in a manner of "encompassment," how one receives the life force without knowing its source (this is not the case for the inner level, where the effect knows its cause). Furthermore, the crowns are not evil themselves and they do not impose evil, but merely enable it. This can be compared to human emotions: It is possible for a person to receive strength and feelings from the atmosphere of a place or a certain situation, such as a bad company or environment. One who is subject to the influence of such forces can be led to act even against his own wishes and everything that is important to him, and actually do what he himself knows is bad for him, to such an extent that he can even destroy himself completely. Since they are encompassing forces, they are called "crowns" rather than *sefirot*, similar to a crown that encompasses a person around his head. For on more on this, see *Torah Or* 20c. See also at length in *Sefer HaMa'amarim* 5602 [by Rabbi Yosef Yitzḥak Schneerson] "*Pataḥ Eliyahu*," and in several other places.

the forces of holiness, for example, the desire for closeness to God and His delight, to become wise through His wisdom, and to love and fear Him, which motivate and sustain the holy soul of Israel, the souls of the nations have a life force that comes from the side of impurity. In contrast to the power of delight in holiness, such as in attaining divinity and the delight of Shabbat, there are the forces of carnal pleasures. In opposition to the wisdom of holiness, which is the power of nullification, there is a coarse wisdom that takes the form of self-aggrandizement, when a person prides himself on his cleverness. Similarly, against the kindness and love of holiness and generosity there are evil loves and lusts. In the case of *Gevura* (Restraint), there is anger and the like;[54] for *Tiferet* (Beauty) there is idolatry, and so on and so forth.

וּמוּדַעַת זֹאת בָּאָרֶץ מַה שֶּׁכָּתוּב בְּסֵפֶר הַגִּלְגּוּלִים עַל פָּסוּק: "אֲשֶׁר שָׁלַט הָאָדָם בְּאָדָם לְרַע לוֹ" (קהלת ח,ט), שֶׁהוּא סוֹד גָּלוּת הַשְּׁכִינָה בְּתוֹךְ הַקְּלִיפּוֹת לְהַחֲיוֹתָם וּלְהַשְׁלִיטָם עַתָּה בִּזְמַן הַגָּלוּת

It is commonly known what it written in *Sefer HaGilgulim* on the verse: "Whenever man controlled man, it was to his detriment" (Eccles. 8:9)**, that this is the secret of the exile of the Divine Presence among the *kelippot*, to give them life and enable them to rule now, in the time of exile,**

This verse is interpreted in the writings of the Arizal[55] as follows: "Whenever man" – this is a wicked man, a man of the *kelippa*; "controlled man" – a man of holiness. Thus, "whenever man controlled man" is basically the secret of the existence and power of the world of the *kelippa*. For as we explained, the *kelippa* is not a separate entity of its own; it does not have its own source or purpose for its life and existence. If it does exist and is active, this is because "a man had control over man," because it takes from holiness, against its will, all of its vitality – its wisdom, powers, and capabilities. It envelops holiness and

54. See *Sefer HaMa'amarim* 5602.

55. See chapter 2 there, and in several other places in the writings of the Arizal.

sucks the life forces from it as though they were its own, as though it is not receiving from the holy, as if the holy does not exist, to such an extent that it works against the holy. ☞

אֲבָל הוּא ״לְרַע לוֹ וכו׳״ although it is "it was to his detriment..."

This is the secret of the exile of the Divine Presence. The rule of evil during the exile of the Divine Presence actually works to the detriment of evil. It only appears to be the victory and success of evil, but the secret and the truth is that it is to his disadvantage, as this rule consumes the sources of his life and existence until at the end of the process he will be completely destroyed. ☞

"WHENEVER MAN CONTROLLED MAN"

☞ Here the term "man" is an abstract concept denoting the entire spiritual structure, which resembles the form of man: The structure of the ten *sefirot* or forces of the soul (and limbs of the body). In this sense the ten *sefirot,* both in general and in relation to every world in particular, are the form of the holy life force that constitutes and gives life to all existence. Corresponding to it, as explained above, there is a parallel structure involving the bestowal of life force from the *kelippa.*

THE SECRET OF THE EXILE OF THE DIVINE PRESENCE

☞ The secret of the exile of the Divine Presence is first of all that there is a secret, that there is a meaning to all of this. Everything that seems to be an injustice, as a victory of evil, of the conquering and exploitation of the holy, actually has a purpose and justification. Not only in the final analysis, but in each and every movement of subjugation and concealment of sanctity, there is a meaning that is the opposite of what it appears, and it is to the detriment of the *kelippa.*

The nature and essence of the *kelippot* is that they constantly strive to grow bigger, to get more pleasure, conquer more, be more of an "entity" (as explained earlier, regarding the statement of the *kelippa* formulated by the prophet: "My river is mine, and I made myself," Ezek. 29:3), and to that end they capture more and more of the holy, conceal it and increase at its expense. But here lies the catch: After all, if the *kelippa* receives its life from the holy, then as the sacredness weakens and disappears, the *kelippa* will likewise weaken and vanish until its complete abolition, when it will be clearly recognized that there is nothing there but deception.

Furthermore, the innermost secret of the exile of the Divine Presence is that holiness gains from all of this. It is explained in the kabbalistic sources that from the beginning of the existence of the world, since the "breaking of the vessels," there have been sparks of holiness that are "captives" inside the *kelippot.* In the kabbalistic

וְלָכֵן הָאוּמּוֹת שׁוֹלְטִין עַתָּה עַל יִשְׂרָאֵל, לִהְיוֹת נַפְשׁוֹת הָאוּמּוֹת מֵהַקְּלִיפּוֹת אֲשֶׁר הַשְּׁכִינָה מִתְלַבֶּשֶׁת בִּבְחִינַת גָּלוּת בְּתוֹכָם.

Therefore, the nations currently rule over Israel, as the souls of the nations are from the *kelippot* in which the Divine Presence is enclothed in the form of exile.

worldview, these sparks are the secret and foundation for the existence of all worlds – both for the *kelippot,* since, as stated, they are the source of their life, and therefore they are able to keep what they have and strive to swallow more and more, and also for holiness, as they are what it lacks in order to be complete. This is thus the purpose of the descent into this world: To raise up the sparks and redeem them from the *kelippot* into which they fell.

In the hasidic texts, all of this is portrayed as occurring within the soul of man: The holiness is the divine soul in man, which descends and is swallowed up in the secret of the exile of Divine Presence within the animal soul and the body, and within all the affairs of this world. And yet, despite all the difficulty and pain involved, when the holiness descends into exile and captivity, it finds there what it lacked, and receives powers that it never had before. From that point on, the inner development works in the reverse direction: Precisely in captivity and exile, when it does not feel itself and is unable to act in its own interests, it becomes increasingly stronger, it "grows," while the *kelippa* unsuspectingly loses all the selfhood it thought it has, until the big secret is ultimately revealed, that the *kelippa* no longer exists, and everything is holy.

What is it that holiness "gains"? It would seem that if it is holy, what could it lack? Here is a metaphor – or an actual example – of what we mean: When we speak of a tzaddik, a righteous individual, we assume that he is perfect with respect to himself. However, as long as there is something lacking in a detail or one place in the entire world, he is also deficient, so to speak. It is precisely the completion of this shortcoming, which is outside of him, that leads him to a perfection that is beyond his own perfection, beyond his rectified and whole state, beyond his being everything that he is. Indeed, we do not have the words to describe this process; we can only say that it unites with the purpose of the Divine, which is within and also beyond all worlds and souls.

Why is this a "secret"? Apart from the fact that "secret" is a common term in book of the *Zohar* and the writings of the Arizal, it can be suggested that it is a secret because the *kelippa* is unaware of it. As we explained earlier, a real secret is not a secret because someone is hiding it, but because it is the intrinsic aspect of something that cannot be seen. Here too, the secret of the exile of the Divine Presence is the great secret that the *kelippa* and all of its forms are unable to see. The *kelippa* is a *kelippa* for the very reason that it is unable to perceive that all of its vitality and existence comes only from the Divine, and that it does not have any other being or source of existence. It is true that it knows it is receiving life from holiness, which is why it strives to conquer more and more of it, but it fails to make all of the connections. Indeed, it is unable to do so,

The Divine Presence is expressed and represented by the souls of Israel. The idea that was previously explained in spiritual and in abstract terms is formulated here in a more concrete manner: This state of affairs finds expression in the concepts and setting of this world in the form of the people of Israel among the nations.

וְהִנֵּה אַף שֶׁזֶּה צָרִיךְ בֵּיאוּר רָחָב אֵיךְ וּמַה מִּכָּל מָקוֹם הָאֱמֶת כֵּן הוּא

Now, although this requires detailed explanation, how and what, it is nevertheless the truth.

The enclothing of the Divine Presence in exile, the exile of Israel among the nations, and the significance of this for the *kelippa* – all of these are not simple matters, and there is not and cannot be a brief and unambiguous explanation for them. Just as the life force itself does not come directly and simply from God to the *kelippa*, so too the explanation of these concepts is necessarily extensive, through the expansion of the mind and painted on a broad canvas. For this process, of the life of the *kelippa* and the exile of the Divine Presence, can be understood only by looking at the larger picture. Nevertheless, the secret of the exile of the Divine Presence, as explained in the writings of the Arizal, is the internal truth of what can clearly be seen of the spiritual, and even material, reality of the exile of the Divine Presence and the exile of Israel.

as it cannot relinquish its being. This secret, precisely because it is a secret and is not known to everyone, sustains the exile of the Divine Presence. The meaning of a secret, and the very fact that it is called by this name, indicates that it will be revealed. The same applies to the secret of the exile of the Divine Presence: It is gradually being revealed over the course of the exile, and when it is completely revealed the exile will cease to exist.

As will be explained in the continuation of this epistle, by means of the statement of the Ba'al Shem Tov, the author of the *Tanya* will disclose a specific feature of this secret, which applies to all people and all times. That wicked nation (which is also in everyone's soul) who stands up and interferes with one's prayer, takes control in the external realm. Internally, however, a person can awaken from this very place, from such a deep point within, from the depths of his heart, and pray with an inner intention – not only despite of the exile, but because of the exile. This itself is the nullification of the exile and the revelation of the secret of the exile of the Divine Presence.

Although the author of the *Tanya* does not get into the broader explanation here, one point does require clarification:

אֶלָּא שֶׁאַף עַל פִּי כֵן, אֵין הַקְּלִיפּוֹת וְהָאוּמּוֹת יוֹנְקִים וּמְקַבְּלִים חַיּוּת אֶלָּא מֵהֶאָרָה הַנִּמְשֶׁכֶת לָהֶם מִבְּחִינַת אֲחוֹרַיִים דִּקְדוּשָּׁה

Yet even so, the *kelippot* and the nations suckle and receive their **life force only from the illumination that is drawn to them from an aspect of the "back side"** [*aḥorayim*] **of sanctity,**

Despite the fact that in the secret of the exile of the Divine Presence, the Divine Presence descends and is enclothed in the spiritual *kelippot* and among the nations, in order to sustain them, they do not receive their life force from the internality of the Divine Presence, which is the revelation of the inner divinity. Were they to receive their life force from the internality of the Divine Presence that is held captive within them, they themselves would be holy rather than *kelippa*. What makes them *kelippa*, and turns the existence of the Divine Presence within them into an exile, is their reception of the life force from the externality and back side of holiness. In other words, they do not bond with the source of their life force, but only take advantage of it in order to take the life force for themselves.

כְּמַאן דְּשָׁדֵי בָּתַר כַּתְפֵּיהּ

like one throwing to someone **behind his shoulder,**

When someone is giving what he wishes to the person to whom he desires to give it, he turns his face toward him. However, in our world, every act of giving necessarily entails that the gift is received by others as well, to whom the giver has no desire to give. He is not turning his face to them at that time, but rather – in the terms of the vivid metaphor used here – he throws to them behind his shoulder.[56]

The distinction between front and back applies to everything in reality, physical and spiritual alike. This is a necessary corollary of the

56. A similar phrase appears in the *Zohar* 3 (Lev.) 23b. We have not yet found an exact source for the expression, but it appears in this form often in the hasidic texts. See *Likkutei Amarim*, chap. 22, as explained in *Kuntres "Uma'ayan"* 2:2. See also in the *Siddur Admor HaZaken*, "*Avadim Hayinu*."

complex reality of the world, that everything in it has a front and back. Some are more front side while others are more back side, but there can be nothing in reality that does not have something of both. For the sake of illustration only (as this can be observed in all things and places, as stated) everything in the world that a person might desire has a price, and it comes with consequences that are sometimes negative. They would rather not pay the price, and they are willing to relinquish those side effects, but they realize that there is no choice, as one is impossible without the other. This limitation applies not only to us created beings, as God Himself is subject to this constraint, as it were, when He intervenes in the world. This is the image of the Divine to which the world relates – the internality and externality, so to speak, of God's relationship with His world.

In order for there to be a world (*olam*, similar to *he'elem*, unknown), and specifically this lower world, it has to perceive its existence, to a certain extent, as an entity unto itself, and such a perception of reality can be formed only when it (also) accepts the "back side." Relating to the front means, in essence, identification. The more interiority there is in the relationship, the fewer relational definitions – love, fear, self-awareness – and more of a single identification, up to the level of a face-to-face relationship, which means a complete unity that leaves no room for anything else. In the terms of the above metaphor, when a person pays for what he receives – whether through work, sorrow, money, or emotional investment – he will feel, to some degree, that he deserves something, that he himself took the trouble and got it done. The back side, which is what he pays, hides the interior, the one who gives, and creates this appearance which, as stated, enables the world to exist: That there is someone, something, who deserves this, who decides it, who exists. In contrast, when a person receives internally, he feels that he is receiving a free gift, and then he senses the reality of the Giver rather than his own, his negation with respect to the one above, not his own reality down here below.

Indeed, with regard to God Himself (who is also beyond the world) there is a level above all this, where everything is internal, for it is He who wishes that there should be a front and back. The revelation of this internal level is the Torah (as will be explained at length in the next epistle), which itself is all internality, it is entirely God's wisdom and will, and yet at the same time it defines what is front and back in the worlds. If so, those who are connected to the Torah and its mitzvot are also linked to that highest level where everything is internal, everything subsumed into unity.

וְאַף גַּם זֹאת עַל יְדֵי צִמְצוּמִים וּמָסַכִּים רַבִּים וַעֲצוּמִים **and even that** comes **via numerous and immense constrictions and veils,**

The illumination of the life force that is drawn to the nations and the *kelippot* is not only "back side," but also constricted and hidden, which is not the same thing. Although in general the interior is concealed in the back side, the initial power remains intact. For the back side of something that relates directly to the primary inner purpose and essence of that thing, is simply the back side of the inner essence, not constricting, concealing it or distorting it in any way. In other words, the back side of the entity is the way that it is compatible with the world, not by expressing its inner purpose, but rather, through delineating the means by which its existence is made possible. This can be as relating to the supreme spiritual reality of our world – its principles, models, and overarching design. It is only afterward, by means of constrictions and veils, that the back side descends to particular situations within reality, where the divine inner essence becomes entirely constricted and hidden, to the extent that what is above, the thing's ultimate spiritual purpose, may look totally different and even be nullified entirely to the back side, its secondary aspect.[57] The back side then is able to descend into a deluded sense of independent self and spout heresy and other falsities. ☞

"CONSTRICTIONS AND VEILS"

☞ The "back side" is a mode of relating from the perspective of the Creator. From His perspective, there is a front and a back, whereas for the created beings there are "constrictions and veils," all of which are entirely transparent to God. Accordingly, when discussing the nations and the kelippot of this world, in order to answer the question of where they get their life force from, one must make two claims: One, that for God they are "back side," and this is what enables their existence, despite the fact that they are not the purpose of creation; second, that they create with their imaginations the reality in which they exist in practice, as a result of numerous and immense constrictions and veils.

57. As, for example, in the parable of the prostitute that appears in the *Zohar* (2:163a; see e.g., *Likkutei Amarim*, chap. 9).

עַד שֶׁנִּתְלַבְּשָׁה הֶאָרָה זוֹ בְּחוֹמְרִיּוּת עוֹלָם הַזֶּה, וּמַשְׁפַּעַת לְאוּמּוֹת עוֹשֶׁר וְכָבוֹד וְכָל תַּעֲנוּגִים גַּשְׁמִיִּים.

until that illumination is enclothed in the materiality of this world and bestows upon the nations wealth and honor and all physical pleasures.

The materiality of this world is the lowest level of progression. Materiality in and of itself is not evil; it does not deny God nor rebel. It is simply sealed up and does not transmit any part of the inner illumination. This is why it appears as though it is the sole reality, outside of which there is nothing. "Wealth and honor and all physical pleasures"[58] are the totality of life that is bestowed by this material world. This is the life force that the physical world grants, and that is what the nations feel and live on.

מַה שֶּׁאֵין כֵּן יִשְׂרָאֵל יוֹנְקִים מִבְּחִינַת פָּנִים הָעֶלְיוֹנִים

This is not the case for Israel, who **suckle from the aspect of the supernal countenance,**

The Jewish people are inner essence with respect to the nations. In comparison to those nations which belong to the *kelippa,* who suckle from the externality of the worlds, Israel suckles from the interiority. What is more, they draw their power from "the supernal countenance," that is, from the holiness, from the relationship to the Divine in the worlds. In addition, from the perspective God Himself there is, as we explained, a "supernal countenance" that transcends even the reality of the worlds of front and back, where there is no back side at all. This is where the Jewish people receive their essential vitality. ☞

FROM WHERE DO CREATED BEINGS RECEIVE THEIR LIFE FORCE?

☞ Every creature receives its life force, its physical and spiritual nourishment, from the place where it belongs and is connected, from what it thinks about it and feels within that point. This is what interests and excites it, this is what it asks and what it receives and what gives it life. The nations, who are essentially connected to the exterior, receive their life force from there – from wealth, honor, and all physical pleasures. Israel, however, who in their essence are connected to the divine inner essence,

58. A similar idea appears in Mishna *Avot* 4:21: "Envy, lust, and honor remove a man from the world."

כְּמוֹ שֶׁכָּתוּב: "יָאֵר ה' פָּנָיו אֵלֶיךָ" (במדבר ו,כה). כָּל אֶחָד וְאֶחָד לְפִי שֹׁרֶשׁ נִשְׁמָתוֹ עַד רוּם הַמַּעֲלוֹת.

as it is written: "May the Lord shine His countenance upon you" (Num. 6:25), **each and every one in accordance with the root of his soul, until the most elevated heights.**

receive an interior divine influence that is not primarily wealth, honor, or physical pleasures. This does not mean that they do not receive those things, or that they do not need them, because even the righteous of Israel live in this material world. Rather, it means that the Jewish people use them solely for their practical usage, whereas their inner world requires other things. Without the inner essence there is no point having great external abundance. If there is no drawing forth of a holy inner light into one's wealth, honor and all physical pleasures, then for Israel, such gifts are truly repulsive. This is not the case for the nations that receive from the back side: Since this is everything for them, and they dedicate their lives to this, they are absolutely determined to receive it.

However, in practice every person has free choice, which means that he can decide from where he will receive his life. Therefore, even a member of Israel can choose to receive his life force from the back side, and even from the *kelippot,* in which case he will indeed receive it from there. Moreover, one is even tempted to take it from the back side, because that is what the body sees and what the animal soul feels. Even though he has been taught that inner essence is deep wisdom and wonderful delight, on a superficial level he sees them as the opposite: Sorrow and torment,... While he is informed that the entire back side is vanity, he sees the reverse: Wealth and honor, and so on. This can clearly be seen in the case of one whose work on his animal soul has been so successful that this interiority has become his revealed and perceived nature.

The story is told among Chabad hasidim of two brothers, one of whom became a devout hasid, while the other left the inner circle and became successful and wealthy. After a while, the hasid sought to marry off his daughters, and he felt compelled to ask his brother for a loan. The rich man was happy to see his brother, and before anything else gave him a tour of his whole house to show him his many splendidly decorated rooms. The hasid followed him into one room after another, until finally, when he couldn't take it anymore, he turned to him and said: "You know what you remind me of? There is a certain animal, which is not kosher, that sits in mud up to its neck, and eats garbage, and enjoys it."

With all that said, as the soul of every member of Israel is rooted in interiority, when that individual receives from the back side, he will feel like someone who is taking stolen waters. He will make excuses for his conduct: "It doesn't really belong to me; it's only for the time being, it's only because it is pleasant, necessary,..." By contrast, when he receives from the interiority he can sense – if he just dares to listen to the voice of his inner soul – that he is entering that realm like a fish into water, and that in one movement he can reach the most elevated heights.

This verse is from the Priestly Blessing, in which the priests, as the messengers of God,[59] bless Israel. Each and every member of Israel receives illumination from the divine inner essence above, from the most elevated heights, which is above everything. However, the revelation of the illumination for each individual person is "in accordance with the root of his soul." ☞

2 Ḥeshvan

2 Ḥeshvan (leap year)

וְאַחַר הַדְּבָרִים וְהָאֱמֶת הָאֵלֶּה, הַגְּלוּיִם וִידוּעִים לַכֹּל נַחֲזוֹר לְעִנְיָן רִאשׁוֹן בְּעִנְיַן הַכַּעַס, שֶׁהוּא כְּעוֹבֵד עֲבוֹדָה זָרָה. וְהַיְינוּ בְּמִילֵּי דְעָלְמָא

After these matters and words of **truth, which are revealed and known to all, we will return to the first topic, the issue of anger, that it is like worshipping idols. This applies to worldly affairs,**

This lengthy introduction served to explain what the entire Jewish people believes: That everything is from God, and everything that happens and exists is God's thought and speech, and there is nothing else besides Him. However, this speech of God, which is called the Divine Presence, is in exile, and therefore it is possible that the illumination of the Divine Presence, which is in everything, is not clearly evident. These explanations, which are derived on the one hand from

"IN ACCORDANCE WITH THE ROOT OF HIS SOUL"

☞ When the author of the *Tanya* says that "Israel suckles from the aspect of the supernal countenance," this means that the people of Israel below, in this world, receive their life force from the lofty root in the supernal countenance, as the act of suckling means taking from the root and the source, and the root of the souls of Israel in general indeed lies above everything. Nevertheless, each individual person, as he is in this world, a soul in a body, has a personal root of his soul, meaning, a lofty root that relates to that person with respect to the form of his specific soul and personality in his current state. This personal, exalted place can be in the world of *Asiya* (for the lower souls), in the world of *Yetzira,* the world of *Beria,* or even the world of *Atzilut* (for extremely lofty souls). Wherever one's precise root, its source lies in the supernal countenance, in God's inner will that is in every world. As stated, these personal roots reflect a person as he is below, and yet they all combine and ascend in one channel of holiness that rises to the most elevated heights, (see *Likkutei Amarim,* chap. 18) in the root of the souls of Israel that transcends everything.

59. See *Nedarim* 35a: "The priests are the messengers of the Merciful One."

the Kabbala of the Arizal – which the *mitnagdim* also accept – and from the doctrine of the Ba'al Shem Tov on the other, which Rabbi Shneur Zalman seeks to interpret and reconcile with the Kabbala of the Arizal, form the basis of his argument. He can now return to the topic from which he began.

When is it appropriate to say that anger is like worshipping idols, and that all we explained in this regard applies? This comparison is accurate with respect to worldly affairs, when one gets angry about something that has gone awry, when it is not in accordance with his wishes, involving the conduct of this world.

כִּי הַכֹּל בִּידֵי שָׁמַיִם חוּץ מִיִּרְאַת שָׁמַיִם (ברכות לג,ב).

as everything is in the hands of Heaven except for fear of Heaven (*Berakhot* 33b).

"Everything" here includes all the affairs of the world. If one grows angry, he is thereby showing that he does not believe that everything is in the hands of Heaven. On the emotional level at least, he feels that there is a force or someone else who is doing this to him, to which he directs his anger. After all, one cannot be angry with God, and if one becomes enraged, his fury is not toward God.

וְלָכֵן בְּמִילֵּי דִשְׁמַיָּא לְאַפְרוּשֵׁי מֵאִיסּוּרָא לֹא שַׁיָּיךְ הַאי טַעְמָא דַּאֲמַרַן

And therefore, in matters of Heaven, where one can **separate** himself or others **from a prohibition** (*Shabbat* 40b)**, the reason that we stated does not apply,**

Sometimes, in order to prevent someone else, or himself, from violating a prohibition, it is necessary to get angry with him, and it is not enough to speak gently. Since in matters involving fear of Heaven, and spiritual issues between man and God, one has a choice and not everything is in the hands of heaven, anger here is not a sign of heresy and lack of faith in God. Quite the contrary – the anger that is designed to stop a person from violating a prohibition is not directed toward God, but toward the *kelippa* that conceals God. If so, the comparison to an idol worshipper is especially inaccurate here, as he is actively fighting against the worship of idols. ☞

וּכְמוֹ שֶׁכָּתוּב "וַיִּקְצוֹף מֹשֶׁה" (במדבר לא,יד) וְהַיְינוּ מִשּׁוּם כִּי ה' הִקְרָה לְפָנָיו מִצְוָה זוֹ לְאַפְרוּשֵׁי מֵאִיסּוּרָא כְּדֵי לְזַכּוֹתוֹ.

as it is written: "And Moses became enraged" (Num. 31:14). **This was because God gave him the opportunity** to fulfill **this mitzva, to separate** people **from a prohibition, for his merit.**

The Torah relates that Moses became angry with the soldiers upon their return from the war against Midian for taking the women as captives rather than killing them. He saw this as a capitulation on the part of the commanders to their evil inclination, as it was on account of the people's sin with the daughters of Midian that they had gone to war in the first place. This anger of Moses was thus directed against the *kelippa* and the evil inclination, and it is an example of a permitted anger, because it helped prevent people from committing a transgression. ☞

SEPARATING FROM A PROHIBITION

☞ This example of anger involving matters of Heaven, when it is designed to "separate from a prohibition," teaches that not all anger is permitted in matters of Heaven either, and that in order for the anger to be permitted, it must serve a useful purpose. Anger is essentially a negative movement of the soul, a movement of destruction, the opposite of kindness and giving. The only benefit it provides is when, in certain situations, it is able to stop the forces of evil and devastation from damaging the structure of holiness. Even in those cases, when there is an apparent justification for the anger, it will still have a negative effect on the soul. (Accordingly, the Rabbis comment on the verse cited below: "And Moses became enraged," that "because he grew angry, he forgot the halakha" [*Vayikra Rabba* 13:1; see also Rashi on Numbers 31:21], despite the fact that the anger served to separate people from a prohibition.)

ANGER THAT SEPARATES PEOPLE FROM A PROHIBITION

☞ It can be inferred from the author of the *Tanya*'s statement that "this was because God gave him the opportunity [to fulfill] this mitzva," that Moses's conduct in this situation was not optional, meaning, that he had permission to grow angry, but rather it should be viewed like any other mitzva, as a precious, important act which one is required to perform. However, since this mitzva differs from most others, in that it is not founded on a love of the good but on the hatred of evil – and as explained elsewhere (*Likkutei Amarim,* chap. 10), true hatred of evil is the purview of the righteous alone – when fulfilling this mitzva of anger, even in order to separate people from committing prohibitions, one must proceed with great caution, in case he is unworthy of following this path.

אַךְ זֶהוּ כְּשֶׁיֵּשׁ בְּיָדוֹ לִמְחוֹת בְּקִצְפּוֹ וְכַעֲסוֹ עַל חֲבֵירוֹ. אֲבָל כְּשֶׁאֵין בְּיָדוֹ לִמְחוֹת, כְּגוֹן נָכְרִי הַמְדַבֵּר וּמְבַלְבְּלוֹ בִּתְפִלָּתוֹ

However, this is the case specifically **when one has the power to object to another through his rage and anger, but if he does not have the power to object, such as** when a **gentile is speaking and confusing him when he is praying,**

The author of the *Tanya* again emphasizes that the anger must provide the actual benefit of preventing someone from sinning, not if the object of one's anger, such as a gentile, will take no notice of his anger at all.

In a situation where "he does not have the power to object," it is as though he has encountered a force of nature. Accordingly, it is no longer a question of whether the gentile is right or not, what he deserves and what is best for him. The only issue is – as with a natural event that we have to deal with – how best to react. In this particular case, anger directed at the gentile, or at trees and stones, or even at God Himself – is irrelevant. Since the act of the gentile cannot be viewed as an opportunity one has been given to perform a mitzva, but rather as a kind of force of nature, the following question arises:

אִם כֵּן מַה זֹּאת עָשָׂה ה׳ לוֹ?

then "what is this that God has done to him?"

This question is founded on a worldview that is emphasized in hasidic thought: Everything that happens to a person, all that one hears, sees, or comes to his mind, is directed at him in particular. Not like normal daily events to which a person must respond, but as a divine statement and guidance. What he is experiencing is indeed an interruption in his service to God, which he must overcome, but he must also see beyond that: It is the path of the service of God that he is now required to follow. This is the divine speech addressed to him, instructing him: "You will ascend from here."

When this gentile plainly disturbs him in his service of God, confusing him in his prayer, and he cannot do anything to change it – he cannot ask, protest, or grow angry – what is the divine statement here? How is it possible to worship God in this situation, to transcend this obstacle?

אֵין זֹאת כִּי אִם כְּדֵי שֶׁיִּתְגַּבֵּר וְיִתְאַמֵּץ יוֹתֵר בִּתְפִלָּתוֹ בְּעוֹמֶק הַלֵּב וּבְכַוָּונָה גְּדוֹלָה כׇּל כָּךְ עַד שֶׁלֹּא יִשְׁמַע דִּבּוּרֵי הַנׇּכְרִי

It is for no other reason than that he should overcome it and make more effort in his prayer, from the depths of his heart and with such great intention that he does not hear the gentile's talk,

When there is nothing that can be done, it must be that God does not want him to engage with the gentile.[60] With that said, it is also impossible for him not to pray at all, or to pray without intention, since God certainly does not desire him to refrain from his service. It is here that the aforementioned worldview has extreme ramifications. Although he cannot alter what is happening right in front of him and ascend toward God, he still asks: "What is this that God has done to me?" He is not content with doing nothing, in cutting off contact with the Divine and turning to some other issue of concern. Rather, he descends to confront the issue: He stands in the same place, continues the same prayer, while focusing his intention more and more, until this disturbance ceases to exist, meaning, it becomes meaningless to him. The fact that something is bothering him means that his intention is incomplete, that he is not fully immersed in the prayer. The part of him that remains outside, which belongs to external matters, can go on hearing the chatter of the gentile. The gentile who is disturbing him should be read as nothing other than a sign that his intention is not complete. There are things that a person cannot know on his own, and this is God's way of telling him: "Your intention is imperfect, and you can do more."

60. As explained in several places, there are two types of obstructions to the service of God. One comes from the *kelippat noga*. Here, the act can be carried out, and therefore it must be performed properly and even in a state of holiness, and one thereby rectifies and exalts the *kelippa* while ascending along with it. The second obstacle comes from the impure *kelippot*, which cannot be dealt with in a fitting and holy state. One must therefore not engage, think, or act. Even here, if it was a hasidic Jew who was interfering with his prayer, one can prevent him from committing this bad deed and lead him to repent. But since it is an evil, unapproachable gentile, one should not attempt to talk to him at all.

אַף שֶׁלְּמַדְרֵגָה זוֹ צָרִיךְ הִתְעוֹרְרוּת רַבָּה וַעֲצוּמָה **even though one requires a great and mighty arousal** to attain **this level.**

In every prayer one has to overcome distractions, concentrate on the task at hand and disconnect from the surrounding world. This is far from easy. Typically, we construct for ourselves a supportive external environment by freeing up time, entering a quiet place that is set aside for this purpose, together with others who wish to pray. This helps turn one's attention from his affairs and concentrate on prayer alone. It is true that the mind must still dismiss internal disturbances, such as thoughts and feelings that continue to run through it, but with hard work and patience this too can be achieved. Here, by contrast, when the external disturbance is ongoing, and continues to feed one's negative thoughts and feelings incessantly, it is not enough to work quietly and patiently, to silence one's thoughts and so on. Instead, one must go on the offensive, with "a great and mighty arousal."

וְעֵצָה הַיְעוּצָה **The recommended counsel**

A counsel is not an instruction, and is therefore not binding in the same way. When a counsel is given, this effectively means: "Here is a path forward, a solution to the problem, although there might be other possibilities as well." With regard to the level of internality, the counsel is very much internal as well, on a level that a person cannot as yet be compelled to follow.[61] It is only when one chooses, and indeed marches along this path, that matters will become clear to him. ☞

לְהִתְעוֹרְרוּת זוֹ הִיא מֵעִנְיָן זֶה עַצְמוֹ: **for this arousal is from this matter itself:**

The hasidic method of awakening within a person the great power that is required for this war, is to use the same power that is interfering with him. Instead of building another opposing force, to break it, the counsel is to use that very same force itself. When one thinks about it, this idea is so obvious that it cannot be otherwise. The only force that

---

61. See *Likkutei Torah*, Deut. 80c.

can fully match the disturbance is the force of that distraction itself. One just needs to know how to do it, how to direct the forces, as will be explained below. ☞

THE COUNSEL OF A REBBE

☞ The difference between a counsel and an instruction is like the difference between the category of "an attribute of piety [*hasidut*]" and that of a mitzva. The concept of "an attribute of piety" does not originate with Hasidism, but rather, is found as a general instruction that appears in the Talmud as well (see for example *Bava Metzia* 52b; Jerusalem Talmud, end of Tractate *Shevi'it* [10:4]). It refers to matters that one is permitted to accept upon himself, and which are even recommended, but which are not obligatory. In this sense, the hasidic movement in general – especially from the outside – was perceived as involving the attribute of piety, the optional realm, that whoever wishes to do so may accept such-and-such requirements upon himself. In contrast, among hasidim themselves the perception is usually rather different: Once the path of Hasidism has been revealed in the world, this approach is no longer discretionary but obligatory. It is still classified as an "attribute of piety," a "recommended counsel," but not because the hasid has the option of whether or not to follow it. Rather, as explained here, it is because its root is too lofty and subtle to be defined as a comprehensive and unequivocal obligation. The same applies in this context: For a hasid who is connected to the Rebbe, who attunes himself with the Rebbe – as one soul to another – the Rebbe's counsel is an absolutely binding personal obligation.

FOREIGN THOUGHTS AND DISTURBANCES IN THE TEACHINGS OF THE BA'AL SHEM TOV

☞ The hasidic view (and that of faith in general) is that any rectification is always similar to the corruption. Since God and His providence exist, it follows that every corruption, every disease and every disorder comes into the world together with its rectification. Just as there is no question from above without an answer, so too there is no corruption merely for the sake of spoiling, no disease simply for the sake of getting sick, and no disorder just to cause a disturbance: The essence of any corruption is the awakening of the path of rectification; the disease – how to heal it; and the disorder – how to reach a deeper state of attentiveness.

In the teachings of the Ba'al Shem Tov,[62] this counsel is virtually a comprehensive solution of how to treat disturbances, whether they come from the outside or the inside ("foreign thoughts"). Instead of resisting the disturbance, by exerting external pressure to make it disappear, he suggests actively moving toward it, taking it and using it in a different direction. In this case too, instead of distancing himself and disconnecting from that gentile, the Ba'al Shem Tov would advise almost the oppo-

62. See the *Ba'al Shem Tov al HaTorah, Noaḥ,* 117 and on.

כְּשֶׁיָּשִׂים אֶל לִבּוֹ וְיִתְבּוֹנֵן עִנְיַן יְרִידַת הַשְּׁכִינָה כִּבְיָכוֹל "וַתֵּרֶד פְּלָאִים" (איכה א,ט) לְהִתְלַבֵּשׁ נִיצוֹץ מֵהֶאָרָתָהּ, אֲשֶׁר הִיא בִּבְחִינַת גָּלוּת, בְּתוֹךְ הַקְּלִיפּוֹת דֶּרֶךְ כְּלָל לְהַחֲיוֹתָם.

When one contemplates and reflects on the matter of the descent of the Divine Presence, as it were – "it has descended in an extraordinary fashion" (Lam. 1:9) **for a spark from its illumination to be enclothed, such that it is in a form of exile among the *kelippot* in general, to give them life.**

The reflection must be accompanied by contemplation. Not merely a general, theoretical reflection on the matter, but a personal, private contemplation that penetrates the heart – one must sense and feel what he has understood in his mind. In the mind we only think about reality, whereas in the heart we actually feel it and are within it. He adds the phrase "as it were" because, as will eventually become clear, this is not a real descent but only an apparent one, for the needs of the present.

"It has descended in an extraordinary fashion [*pela'im*]." *Pele* refers to something that is distant and detached from our understanding. The verse is thus speaking of a descent that goes so far down that one cannot see the place from where it began, and one does not understand why it dropped so far. This "form of exile among the *kelippot* in general" has been discussed at length in this epistle. There are two stages here. The first stage is a general reflection – to understand the mechanism, the principle, of the secret of the exile of the Divine Presence. This is followed by the particular reflection, with regard to the specific gentile who is before us, and his speech.

וְעַתָּה הַפַּעַם, נִיצוֹץ הֶאָרָתָהּ מִתְלַבֵּשׁ בִּבְחִינַת גָּלוּת דֶּרֶךְ פְּרָט בְּדִבּוּר נָכְרִי זֶה הַמְדַבֵּר דְּבָרִים הַמְבַלְבְּלִים עֲבוֹדַת ה׳, הִיא כַּוָּונַת הַתְּפִלָּה

Now, on this occasion, the spark of its illumination is enclothed in a form of exile specifically through the speech of this gentile, who is saying things that can confuse someone involved in **the service of God, which is the intention of prayer,**

site: To attend to the disturbance, not its externality, which is the interference with prayer, but its internality, which is the divine intention within it. God's will is undoubtedly that one should strengthen his intent in prayer, as will be explained.

The process that was explained in general terms with respect to the exile of the Divine Presence is happening here to this particular person: A spark of the Divine Presence, which is the life force within the gentile's speech, is disturbing him in his efforts to serve God and reveal the Divine Presence in the world.

The difference is that when one think and talks on the level of theory, the ideas have to be organized in the mind – they must be structured properly, without internal contradictions, and so on. However, when one meets an actual example, it must fit in with one's living, breathing, harsh reality. When a person contemplates the exile of the Divine Presence, he is not experiencing it at that moment. However, in the situation itself, when this gentile is standing and interfering with one's prayer – the act is real, and the entire logical structure that we have built around the secret of the exile of the Divine Presence has no effect on him at all. He continues in his own way – he talks, taunts, and confuses, and it is disturbing, annoying, and discouraging. And yet, as the author of the *Tanya* will proceed to point out, this particular case, for the very reason that it is very much real and unbearable, has the power to bring the exile of the Divine Presence to its breaking point and reversal. ☞

as explained above, that there is a corresponding counterpart to holiness.	**וּכְמוֹ שֶׁנִּתְבָּאֵר לְעֵיל, כִּי "זֶה לְעוּמַּת זֶה וכו'".**

THE POWER OF PRAYER FOR PERSONAL DISTRESS

☞ Every prayer is, in essence, a prayer over the exile of the Divine Presence. All private requests amount to a single request: Act for the sake of Your Divine Presence in all areas, with regard to the exile and hardship, health and livelihood, and so on. However, whenever one is personally affected, when the distress is private and real, the power of the prayer is on a completely different level. A person might recite the prayer "Heal us" for the Divine Presence that is sick in exile, or for the ailing of Israel in general, and that is fine. But if he has an invalid in his own home, or, alternately, if he has attained a higher level of identification with the Divine Presence, it becomes something else entirely. Here too, when one can actually perceive the exile of the Divine Presence, when what is happening is truly confusing him and preventing him from praying – this is exactly what he should cry out and pray for: For the prayer that he cannot deliver. After all, he will be using the very same power that is preventing him from praying in order to pray in such a way it will no longer interfere with him.

What is the internal mechanism that one should reflect upon in order to transform the power of interference into the power of prayer? As explained above, the principle of "God made this corresponding to that" (Eccles. 7:14) refers to the structure of the *kelippot* that corresponds to the structure of holiness. This means that this *kelippa* which is so disturbing and frightening has no reality of its own. There is nothing within a *kelippa* that is not in holiness, in terms of its power, structure, and method; it contains nothing original, as it takes and receives everything from holiness like a shadow merely duplicating the source – only in reverse, in its outer contours. If so, the entire reality of that *kelippa* and disorder is subjective; it is completely dependent on what the praying person thinks and feels. If he lets it bother him and distract him, then it exists, but if he pays no attention to it and continues to pray with intent, it will be nullified.

וְדִבּוּר הָעֶלְיוֹן מִתְלַבֵּשׁ בְּדִבּוּר הַתַּחְתּוֹן וכו׳

The upper speech is thus **enclothed in the lower speech…,**

The "upper speech" is the Divine Presence, the word of God enclothed in the "lower speech," which is spoken by man below. Since there is "a corresponding counterpart," the lower speech can also be the speech of this gentile who is disturbing. Therefore, when the individual who is praying pays no attention to what the gentile is saying, but continues to recite the sacred lower speech, he thereby transforms the power of speech that was enclothed in that gentile into the holy speech of prayer. As stated, the existence of the gentile's speech is from the shadows, where no direct clear light of holiness shines; he draws out the power of holiness from there and turns it into a destructive force. However, when one prays and the higher speech is directly enclothed in his speech shedding light at that moment, the shadow will disappear.

וְזֶהוּ מַמָּשׁ ״אֲשֶׁר שָׁלַט הָאָדָם בְּאָדָם לְרַע לוֹ״. דְּהַיְינוּ, שֶׁעַל יְדֵי זֶה מִתְעוֹרֵר הָאָדָם לְהִתְפַּלֵּל יוֹתֵר בְּכַוָּונָה, מֵעוּמְקָא דְּלִבָּא, עַד שֶׁלֹּא יִשְׁמַע דִּיבּוּרָיו.

and this is a real example of **"whenever man controlled man, it was to his detriment." In other words, through this** disturbance, **the person is aroused to pray with greater intention, from the depths of the heart, until he does not** even **hear his speech.**

This is a practical example of the lesson we previously learned in general terms. When the Divine Presence is enclothed in this gentile, who is talking and interfering with one's prayer, this would appear to be a case of "whenever man controlled man." It is as though the *kelippa* rules over the power of holiness "it was to his detriment." However, it is actually "to do him harm" – to the *kelippa,* as this disturbance itself awakens one to pray with greater intent, until the *kelippa* has no existence at all. Beforehand, it had a meager existence, since although the man was focused on his prayer, he lacked full intention, and the proof of this is that the gentile bothered him when he talked. There was holiness, but there was some room in both the soul and the world, for the *kelippa* as well. However, after the state of "when a man controlled a man," when the speech of the gentile enclothed the speech of holiness in order to disturb it, the intention of the one praying was awakened to an even greater extent, "from the depths of the heart." Here there is no longer any place for the *kelippa,* not even a little. The depths of the heart, as explained elsewhere, is the point of the revelation of the soul itself – when the soul is aroused from this spot, there is no longer any place for anything else. The principle of "a corresponding counterpart" applies to the revelations of one's soul and its illuminations, but when it comes to the soul itself, within the heart of man, there is no opposing force at all.

The downfall of the *kelippa* occurs after the stage of "whenever a man had controlled a man." It is only then, when one becomes aware of and senses the ruling power of the *kelippa,* when he feels like an animal in a trap, he is awakened, through this power, to fight for his life. As the author of the *Tanya* says elsewhere,[63] when a person finds himself in a position in which his life is hanging in the balance, this affects him all the way down to the bones, to the innermost point of his heart, and he discovers within himself powers of which he was previously unaware. At that juncture, he will focus on nothing else, nothing will distract him, not anything similar to this nor a counterpart to it. ☞

THE OBSTACLE AWAKENS ONE'S INTENTION

☞ This aspect of prayer applies to all types of obstacles, even the most common of them (at least in our time), when the words and content of the prayer simply

63. Epistle 4, above.

The author of the *Tanya* now returns to his starting point. Thus far he has explained the statement in *Tzava'at Rivash* – which so upset the *mitnagdim* – that the Divine Presence "rested" upon that evil gentile who was standing and disturbing a person trying to pray. Even according to the explanation offered here by the author of the *Tanya,* the term "rested" has misleading implications, and he therefore notes:

וּמַה שֶּׁכָּתַב הַמְלַקֵּט "שָׁרְתָה" לֹא יָדַע לְכַוֵּין הַלָּשׁוֹן בְּדִקְדּוּק, כִּי הבעש"ט ז"ל הָיָה אוֹמֵר דִּבְרֵי תוֹרָה בִּלְשׁוֹן אַשְׁכְּנַז וְלֹא בִּלְשׁוֹן הַקּוֹדֶשׁ

As for what the compiler wrote, that the Divine Presence **"rested"** upon that gentile, **he did not know how to render the language in a precise manner, as the Ba'al Shem Tov would say words of Torah in Yiddish rather than in the Hebrew.**

do not feel relevant us – when we do not feel any connection to the words. Then prayer feels like a mere arrangement of sentences, someone else's words, whose content belongs to a different world that does not apply to me and does not express my feelings. Here too, the "recommended counsel" is to pray for this very quality itself – for the ability to pray, to find the meaning, the cultivation of a personal touch. However, this should not come from another direction and place, but from this very state of concealment in which he finds himself. The person praying should come to understand that it is in this concealment, in the experience of the lack of meaning that he is currently feeling, that the speech of God is enclothed and directed to him. If so, the meaning he will find in those words will leave nothing behind from the concealment and lack of meaning that were there before.

There is a type of prayer called the "prayer of a poor man," (see Ps. 102: 1, *Zohar* 319a, *Torat Menaḥem,* vol. 16 [5716] pp. 73) meaning, the prayer of one who lacks something, and more significantly, of one who feels that he himself is lacking and damaged. It is stated in the name of the Ba'al Shem Tov (*Ba'al Shem Tov al HaTorah, Noaḥ, Amud HaTefilla,* 102) that on the inner level, a "prayer of a poor man" is a prayer for the ability to pray. Every prayer of a poor person is a request to be someone who "pours out his woes before the Lord." He cites the parable of a commoner who always wished to talk to the king, but when he manages to approach the king to submit his request, he becomes afraid that if the king will grant his wish, he will no longer have any reason to talk to him. As a result, he asks only for the right to "pour out his woes before the Lord," that the king will permit him to come before him at any time and petition him. In this sense, the "prayer of a poor man" includes the idea formulated here: When there is a preventive factor, a hindrance to prayer, the "recommended counsel" is to turn and pray to God concerning this obstacle, to feel it as deeply as possible, to see the larger picture from this predicament, as the exile of

It was not only the Ba'al Shem Tov, but rather, all the hasidic Rebbes would speak Torah in the vernacular, in Yiddish. As explained at the start of the commentary on this epistle, the Torah of Hasidism was and is essentially an Oral Torah, which lives and breathes life, and like every oral law it is spoken in the vernacular. Nevertheless, when the hasidic Torah was written down it was typically translated into the holy language, Hebrew. Even in the case of Chabad Hasidism, almost all the articles on Hasidism, in their hundreds and thousands, were originally taught in Yiddish. However, in the particular case of Chabad Hasidism, which held the actual written words of the Torah in very high regard, the Rebbes were careful to translate the articles into Hebrew, and they would proofread them and make sure that they were accurate. Many of them were even written in Hebrew from the outset. The same cannot be said for statements cited in the name of the Ba'al Shem Tov, as these were certainly not compiled with the same strictness. Furthermore, since Hebrew was not a spoken, living language like Yiddish, even if those translators had the precise version of the words of the Ba'al Shem Tov before them, they would not have been able to translate them faithfully, by finding the exact words required while conveying the spirit of the ideas. Indeed, it is not only in *Tzava'at Rivash*, but rather, in many writings that are attributed to the Ba'al Shem Tov, that one can find corruptions and inaccuracies. One who is familiar with the language and the spirit of the times can often decipher from the words how the idea was originally formulated in Yiddish and the way that it was translated, not always successfully, into Hebrew.

וְרָצָה לוֹמַר "נִתְלַבְּשָׁה", **He meant to say "became enclothed,"**

In other words, an exact translation is "became enclothed." There is a fundamental difference between the terms "resting" and "enclothing" – in fact, they are almost antonyms. The resting of the Divine Presence upon a person or place means the revelation of the Divine Presence

the Divine Presence encapsulated in the pain, frustration, and reality of the personal case and which is intensified along with them. The "prayer of a poor man" will then emerge from the bottom of the heart, over the exile of the Divine Presence, which is currently expressed in one's personal and palpable poverty and exile.

through him, whether he is a prophet through whose mouth the Divine Presence speaks, or whether it has the more general and less explicit meaning of a person whose deeds and entire manner of conduct express the divine revelation in his own way. It is true that every revelation, including that of the Divine Presence, occurs through the enclothing of the vessels, but in the case of the revelation and resting of the Divine Presence the vessel forfeits its own existence (it is nullified in existence) and in its totality it solely expresses the bond between the Divine Presence that is revealed in it and the world to which it is connected. This vessel – whether it is a person, an angel or a place – maintains only a superficial connection to the world. It looks like any other person, any regular object, but inside it is one thing alone: The revelation of the Divine Presence. The concept of "the enclothing of the Divine Presence," by contrast, signifies an enclothing that is not the resting of the Divine Presence, that is, the clothing reveals itself rather than what is enclothed in it. For in truth, everything exists by virtue of the Divine Presence that is enclothed in it; there is no other source of life and existence. However, there is a difference between clothing that is nullified (in its own awareness or the awareness of the one looking at it) in favor of the Divine Presence that is revealed within it – and is therefore a reality of holiness and the resting of the Divine Presence – and between a clothing that is not nullified in this manner, and which displays its existence, from its perspective, while hiding the Divine Presence that is within it. This type of clothing, when it conceals in an extreme manner, is the *kelippa* itself. Accordingly, with regard to the statement attributed to the Ba'al Shem Tov, that "the Divine presence rested in that person's mouth," referring to the mouth of the gentile who is standing and interfering with one's prayer, the author of the *Tanya* maintains that it should have said "became enclothed."

וְהַיְינוּ בִּבְחִינַת גָּלוּת, וְזֶהוּ, "וּבִפְרָט אִם הוּא נָכְרִי כו'" שֶׁאָז הִיא בְּחִינַת גָּלוּת בְּיוֹתֵר

which refers to exile, and the proof of **this is** the ensuing statement: **"And especially if he is a gentile...," in which case this is a state of absolute exile.**

The enclothing of the Divine Presence is itself the exile of the Divine Presence. The proof that this is referring to the enclothing and exile of the Divine Presence, rather than its resting upon the gentile, is the statement later in *Tzava'at Rivash* that when one reflects on how the Divine Presence is enclothed in that person's mouth, he should declare: "How I must strengthen myself in the service, which is prayer, and especially if he is a gentile or a minor..." In other words, the fact that he is a gentile only emphasizes the above, that an enclothing of the Divine Presence is happening here, rather than a resting. An adult Jew is a fitting vessel for the resting of the Divine Presence; in its essence, his soul is a reflection of the Divine, while his body is a vessel designed for engaging in holiness and performing mitzvot. This is not the case for a gentile, as he and his body are a *kelippa* that conceals the Divine. Thus, when the Divine Presence is enclothed in this gentile, it is in a state of complete exile. Not only is it not revealed as the resting of the Divine Presence, but it is even giving life to the person who is concealing it!

וְאֵין לִתְמוֹהַּ אִם נִיצוֹץ מִן הֶאָרַת שְׁכִינָה נִקְרָא בְּשֵׁם שְׁכִינָה

One should not be surprised that a spark from the illumination of the Divine Presence is itself **called the Divine Presence,**

As stated by the Ba'al Shem Tov, "the Divine Presence was enclothed in this man's mouth...," as only a spark of the Divine Presence is in exile. A spark is merely an illumination of something, not the thing itself. This illumination can appear as though it is detached from its source, as if it exists separately from the source, until it might seem to be an entity of its own. This is why it is specifically in connection to the exile of the Divine Presence (such as the breaking of the vessels) that we speak of sparks – the descent of sparks and the refinement and ascent of the sparks.... In contrast, whenever we speak of the Divine Presence itself, we refer not to the exile but to the resting and revelation of the Divine Presence. Nevertheless, this perception of a spark, which is merely a part, as the whole, should come as no surprise:

דְּהָא אַשְׁכְּחַן שֶׁאֲפִילּוּ מַלְאָךְ נִבְרָא נִקְרָא בְּשֵׁם ה׳, בְּפָרָשַׁת וַיֵּרָא (בראשית יח,ג) לְפֵירוּשׁ הָרַמְבַּ״ן. וּכְמוֹ שֶׁכָּתוּב (בראשית טז,יב):

as we find that even a created angel is called by the name of God, in ***Parashat Vayera*** (Gen. 18:3)**, according to the commentary of the Ramban. And it is likewise written: "She**

"וַתִּקְרָא שֵׁם ה' הַדּוֹבֵר אֵלֶיהָ וכו'", וּכְהַאי גַּוְונָא טוּבָא.

called the name of the Lord who spoke to her..." (Gen. 16:13), **and there are many other similar instances.**

When Abraham saw the angel, he declared: "My Lord...please do not depart from upon your servant" (Gen. 18:3), and the Ramban explains[64] that although he was merely a created angel, Abraham called him by the name of God, "Lord."

The second example comes from Hagar, who "called the name of the Lord who spoke to her: You are the God of my vision" (Gen. 16:13), even though it was an angel who spoke to her, as explicitly stated in the verses. We find many other instances that an angel, or any other divine revelation, even if only partial, is called by the name of God.

It must be admitted that these examples cited by the author of the *Tanya* are not the same as the case described by the Ba'al Shem Tov. The angels that are called by the name of God are not a spark of the Divine Presence hidden in exile, but messengers of God who reveal Him and speak in His name. Nevertheless, once it has been explained that even an evil gentile can enclothe a spark of the Divine Presence, it no longer matters whether this spark is in a state of concealment and exile or revelation and holy light. The principle is the same either way: Even a mere spark and the barest illumination of the Divine Presence is the Divine Presence and it is called thus.

The truth is that the Divine Presence is one (just as "God is one," so too "His name is one"; see Zech. 14:9), and there is no such thing as a spark that is separate from Him. It just appears that this is the case, and that is the exile of the Divine Presence. When it is observed that the spark is not separate, that it is unified with the Divine Presence, this is the ascent of the spark and the redemption of the Divine Presence. Then it will be seen that the spark is the Divine Presence itself.

Up to this point, the author of the *Tanya* has elucidated the statement of the Ba'al Shem Tov. His interpretation is both profound and true, both for hasidim and for all those who take the words of the

64. The Ramban clarifies this opinion at length in his commentary to the first verse of the chapter, and on verse 3 he expressly states that Abraham "called [the angels] by the name of their Master."

Ba'al Shem Tov seriously. From here until the end of the epistle, he will mainly address the *mitnagdim*, those who oppose the path of the Ba'al Shem Tov and are unable to see its inner depth (even though their entire original question probably focused on a different point). For them he takes a step back to add a level of clarification, in their language and mode of thought.

3 Ḥeshvan

3 Ḥeshvan (leap year)

וְכִמְדוּמֶּה לִי שֶׁתְּפִיסָתָם אֵינָהּ מִצַּד דִּקְדּוּק הַלָּשׁוֹן, אֶלָּא מֵעִיקַּר עִנְיַן הִתְלַבְּשׁוּת הַשְּׁכִינָה בַּקְּלִיפּוֹת.

It seems to me that their approach, of those who object to the statement of the Ba'al Shem Tov, **is not based on a linguistic analysis, but due to the basic idea of the enclothing of the Divine Presence in the *kelippot*.**

Their issue is not the difference between "resting" and "enclothing," between two modes of divine expression. Rather, they have a fundamental problem here, as they object to the Ba'al Shem Tov's basic assumptions, which is what led to such extreme reactions, as even actually burning the book *Tzava'at Rivash*.

The author of the *Tanya* does not get into the details of the whole issue, which was one of the (few) real topics of dispute between the hasidim and *mitnagdim*. The problem, as presented here, is in the perception of God's reality in everything and everywhere. If that is the case, then it must be that He is not only in the upper heavens or in the synagogue, but also in places that are undignified, and even where evil and the *kelippa* reign. Such a statement is undoubtedly problematic: Can this be true? What does it mean? How should one react to these claims, if at all? These questions, whether they were posed directly or indirectly, occurred to everyone. Many preferred not to deal with them but to leave them in a state of unresolved ambiguity, and the author of the *Tanya* will address such individuals later on. By contrast, the original hasidic view, which seemed at the time to have been a novel approach that contradicted the accepted viewpoint, is that, indeed, this is the truth: There is an enclothing of the Divine Presence in all things, even the *kelippot*. Accordingly, nothing should be entirely rejected and negated, even if it is *kelippa*. Rather, one should search for the holy spark within it, and, if possible, elevate and rectify it. This is the message from *Tzava'at Rivash* here, as the author of the *Tanya* explains in this epistle, and as stated frequently in the works of the early hasidim, the disciples of the Ba'al Shem Tov. ☞

שֶׁאֵין לָהֶם אֱמוּנָה בְּמַה שֶּׁאָמַר הָאֲרִ"י ז"ל בְּסֵפֶר הַגִּלְגּוּלִים. **As they do not believe in what the Arizal said in *Sefer HaGilgulim*.**

The Arizal explains in *Sefer HaGilgulim*[65] the secret of the exile of the Divine Presence, that it follows the verse: "Whenever a man controlled a man it was to his detriment" (Eccles. 8:9). The meaning of "whenever a man controlled..." is as stated here – the enclothing of the Divine Presence in a *kelippa*. That is, a spark of the Divine Presence, which is the Divine Presence itself, when it is enclothed in a *kelippa*, is the life force of that *kelippa*.

As stated, this touches upon those issues that were considered fundamental disputes between the hasidim and *mitnagdim*. It seems

THE ENCLOTHING OF THE DIVINE PRESENCE IN THE *KELIPPOT* – A NON-LITERAL CONSTRICTION

☞ This question is related to a more well-known dispute, regarding constriction: How should one understand the claim that appears in the writings of the Arizal, that God constricted Himself and that an empty space was formed, as it were, in which the worlds were created (of course, the term "constriction" is far broader than that, as it also applies to dimensions of the soul and time, as well as the service of God.) The dispute is whether there actually is, objectively speaking, an empty space where God is not, or if that is the case only subjectively, from the perspective and understanding of the created beings, for whom there is a sense of "an empty space." The basic hasidic approach is that the empty space is subjective, and that the idea of a constriction should not be taken literally. Elsewhere, the author of the *Tanya* explains this by means of a parable: Constriction is like silence. When a person in the middle of talking goes silent, the space has been emptied of speech, but it has not been emptied of thought and certainly not of that person's essence. The space was emptied with respect to the one who was listening to the speech, but it was not truly vacated; not for those who can sense the thought, and certainly not for that person who was speaking and thinking. The same is true, to a certain extent, of the issue we are dealing with here, the enclothing of the Divine Presence in the *kelippot*.

65. In chapter 20 and elsewhere, on the verse: "Whenever a man controlled a man it was for his detriment," as explained above.

that the author of the *Tanya*'s opinion on those points was that there is no actual fundamental disagreement here, but mostly differences of formulation and divergent attitudes toward the same concepts, only that in the heat of battle there is a tendency to exaggerate and emphasize the contrasts. The point that Hasidism makes is that these claims which appear everywhere – in the Bible, statements of the Rabbis, and the teachings of the Arizal – should be treated with all seriousness, and fully absorbed into one's heart, and one's actual life in practice. Naturally, this leap from theory to reality can startle and shock people, provoking resistance. The author of the *Tanya* was aware of this potential opposition. Therefore, he attempts, both here and elsewhere, to break down the concepts into their constitutive elements and explain them rationally and logically; to show that they all share a common fundamental outlook, that what the hasidim say and do is actually the same as what the *mitnagdim* believe, only that the hasidim seek to extend those fundamental truths, using the very same logic, to arrive at more far-reaching conclusions.

The author of the *Tanya* proceeds to examine one-by-one those points that emerge from the words of the Arizal, which are accepted by everyone, and show that it is impossible to separate them from the conclusions he reached based on the statements of the Ba'al Shem Tov.

שֶׁאִם יִרְצוּ לְחַלֵּק בֵּין קְלִיפּוֹת הָרוּחָנִיִּים לְעוֹבְדֵי גִילּוּלִים הַגַּשְׁמִיִּים אֵין לְךָ גַּשְׁמִי כַּעֲפַר הָאָרֶץ, וְאַף עַל פִּי כֵן מִתְלַבֶּשֶׁת בּוֹ מַלְכוּת דְּמַלְכוּת דַּעֲשִׂיָּה וּבְתוֹכָהּ מַלְכוּת דִּיצִירָה כו׳ וכנ״ל.

For if they wish to differentiate between the spiritual *kelippot* and the physical worshippers of molten images, that is impossible, **as you have nothing more physical than the dust of the earth, and even so the *Malkhut* of *Malkhut* of *Asiya* is enclothed in it, and within it there is the *Malkhut* of *Yetzira*..., as stated above.**

The Arizal discussed the enclothing of the Divine Presence in the spirituality of the *kelippot*. The author of the *Tanya* states that one cannot differentiate between spirituality and materiality in this context, and claim that the enclothing of the Divine Presence can occur on the spiritual levels, but not with regard to actual materiality. The reason is that that "you have nothing more physical than the dust of the earth," and yet it is explained in the writings of the Arizal[66] that "the *Malkhut* of *Malkhut* of *Asiya* is enclothed in it, and within it there is the *Malkhut* of *Yetzira*...," meaning, the *Malkhut* of *Asiya* and the *Malkhut* of *Atzilut*, that is, the Divine Presence. This shows that the Divine Presence is enclothed even in material substances, such as the dust of the earth, and in this respect, there is no difference between spirituality and materiality.

וְאִם מִשּׁוּם טוּמְאַת נַפְשׁוֹת הַנָּכְרִים, הֲרֵי נַפְשׁוֹתֵיהֶם מִזִּיווּג זו"ן דִּקְלִיפּוֹת הָרוּחָנִיִּים כְּמוֹ שֶׁמְּבוֹאָר בְּכִתְבֵי הָאֲרִיזַ"ל.

And if they were to claim that the difference is **due to the impurity of the souls of the gentiles,** that is also incorrect, **as their souls are from the coupling of *Zeir* and *Nukva*** (male and female) **of the spiritual *kelippot*, as explained in the writings of the Arizal.**

One might claim that the relevant divide is not between spirituality and materiality, but impurity and purity. The idea is that although the physical is indeed very lowly, it is at least neutral, which is not the case for the gentile, who has an element of impurity in his spiritual root, in his very essence, and it is therefore possible that the Divine Presence does not enclothe itself in him. However, that claim is also incorrect, as the source of the souls of the gentiles is "from the coupling of *Zeir* and *Nukva* of the spiritual *kelippot*, as explained in the writings of the Arizal."[67] A soul, including that of a gentile, is the offspring of a lofty, spiritual coupling, which in the case of holiness is the source of the

---

66. A similar idea appears in several places in other writings of the author of the *Tanya*, such as *Likkutei Amarim*, chap. 51, and *Likkutei Torah, Derushim LeShabbat Shuva*, where he cites the book *Etz Ḥayyim*. The Lubavitcher Rebbe, Rabbi Menaḥem Mendel Schneerson, notes that the source is from 50:1, and 43:1, in a variant form; he also adds the reference *Mishnat Ḥasidim, Masekhet Asiya Gufanit*, 1:2.

67. *Etz Ḥayyim*, 50:7 (*Kitzur ABiYA*).

flowing of the Divine Presence to the world, although here it went to the side of the *kelippa* and impurity.

Zeir and *Nukva* are kabbalistic terms that refer to the general male and female, from whose coupling all entities in the world came into being. Every creature and individual soul is the result of a particular pairing and combination of *Zeir* and *Nukva*. In the realm of holiness, *Zeir* and *Nukva* are the attributes of divinity and *Malkhut*, that is, the revelation of God, the Divine that lies just beyond the world (which is *Zeir Anpin*), and the divine reality that is within all entities in the world, which is the Divine Presence. Their coupling causes the entire existence of holiness in the world to come into being. In the case of the *kelippa*, these are their "corresponding counterpart," meaning, the coming into being of a reality that is not holy, the attributes and powers that operate in the world, and the world itself (of *Ḥesed* and *Gevura*..., which do not appear to relate to God), as well as existing reality, the "matter" of the world as it exists and stands by itself. The coupling, or pairing, of these two, forms the creatures and souls of *kelippa*, such as the soul of this gentile that is actively working against holiness.

נִמְצָא שֶׁהָרוּחָנִיִּים מְקוֹר טוּמְאָתָם.

It follows, that the spiritual forces **are the source of their impurity.**

Even the abstract spiritual *kelippot*, which have not yet formed into a specific, real evil and impurity – and thus the Divine Presence is clearly enclothed in them – are the source of impurity for the souls of those gentiles, of that tangible impurity below. We must therefore say that the Divine Presence is also enclothed in that actual impurity which is in this physical gentile below.

אַךְ בֶּאֱמֶת צָרִיךְ בֵּיאוּר רָחָב אֵיךְ הוּא הִתְלַבְּשׁוּת זוֹ

However, in truth a broad explanation is required as to **how this enclothing** occurs,

It is indeed possible to understand and justify those who find this claim hard to accept, because it is truly difficult to grasp and emotionally accept this idea. It is obvious and easy to comprehend that the Divine Presence is enclothed in holiness, that God gives life and brings into being that which is good in His eyes, which upholds and extends His wisdom and will, and so on. However, how can we understand that He is enclothed in something that goes against His will? We are comfortable with a simplistic world view: God is good, and everything He does and sustains is good, whereas that which is evil and opposes holiness is not God. However, to say that the Divine Presence is enclothed in evil as well – not only on the theoretical level but in reference to actual entities and people who are causing us harm – this is difficult to accept in one's heart. Yet the author of the *Tanya* does not shy away from this point: He agrees that these claims require a comprehensive explanation. However, this epistle is not the right forum for such an analysis. As stated, this was not an internally distributed epistle to the author of the *Tanya*'s colleagues and students, but rather it was intended for a wide range of people, including those who were categorically opposed to the path of Hasidism. For such individuals a few wise sentences are not enough; rather, they are in need of a broader exposition, including introductions that are not merely rational explanations. Understanding this issue also involves a mental readiness to accept the ideas, and this cannot be conveyed in writing, but is formed through years of study and labor. Consequently, this is not the appropriate place for a detailed discussion.

yet their complaints do not apply to us, but to the writings of the Arizal. אֲבָל לֹא עָלֵינוּ תְלוּנֹתָם כִּי אִם עַל כִּתְבֵי הָאֲרִ״י ז״ל.

After all, based on his citations here, it is clear that his main points are taken from the teachings of the Arizal. With this observation, the author of the *Tanya* diverts the conversation from the essence of the idea themselves (which, as stated, he is unable to analyze fully in this context) to a discussion of the Arizal's writings.

The writings of the Arizal form the basis of the author of the *Tanya*'s discussion here, not only because they are accepted by everyone and that they were at the time (and still are) an indisputable source of authority, but also because the Kabbala of the Arizal is in a certain sense the last accepted formulation of the Jewish religious worldview and thought. As is the case for any field of knowledge, the discussion must be grounded not only on general acceptance, but on updated consensus as well. This is true in every arena: One must refer to the most recent and most detailed source of the current ways of thinking and existing concepts. There is no point in taking several steps backward.

וְאַל יַחְשְׁדֵנִי שׁוֹמֵעַ שֶׁאֲנִי בְּעֵינַי שֶׁהֵבַנְתִּי דִּבְרֵי הָאֲרִ"י ז"ל לְהַפְשִׁיטָן מִגַּשְׁמִיּוּתָן

Nor should the listener suspect me of thinking that I have understood the words of the Arizal, by abstracting them from their physical garb.

These are not expressions of modesty; rather, after he has diverted the arguments of the *mitnagdim* from the words of the Ba'al Shem Tov to the writings of the Arizal, he wishes to emphasize that his understanding of the words of Arizal does not differ from their own. For if it were to emerge from his comments that he comprehends them differently, in a deeper and more abstract manner, any common basis for the discussion would thereby be lost, and there would be no point in him formulating his own arguments either.

Of course, on the personal level as well, he does not want them to think of him as arrogant, someone who considers himself above them: Both because if they think that way, they won't listen to him and will only hate him all the more, and also because he really does not think that he is above them.[68] This attitude of the author of the *Tanya* toward the *mitnagdim,* to truly not be condescending or patronizing toward them, remained consistent throughout the years, and this is what he demanded of his hasidim as well.[69] ☞

"TO ABSTRACT THEM FROM THEIR PHYSICAL GARB"

☞ There seems to be two ways of understanding the author of the *Tanya*'s statement here about the abstraction of kabbalistic ideas from their physical form. One is that the author of the *Tanya* is telling the truth, that he is unable to understand the real meaning of the Arizal's statements, completely stripped of their

68. For a hasid, and especially a Rebbe of hasidim, this is obviously the case. If a Jew thinks that he is above and separated from another Jew, this forms a barrier not only between himself and that Jew, but also between him and the Torah, between him and God. Furthermore, as soon as he entertains a thought of this kind, even if he previously did have an understanding and abstraction of the words of the Arizal, that would no longer hold true.

69. See the end of epistle 2, above.

material words, concepts, and metaphors. It seems that no person can fully understand them on an entirely abstract, intellectual level. This is why the Arizal and all the kabbalistic Sages enclothed them in this physical garb. In a sense, the same can be said of the prophets as well, and perhaps even of God when He handed down these ideas to us. The other way, is that it is absolutely forbidden to understand this physical garb literally: the spiritual terms are merely enclothed metaphorically, infinitely removed from the actual reality, and anyone who takes them to be actually physical is bordering on the heretical, as he errs and misleads others. (Furthermore, as in the case for all severe warnings in the *Idra Zuta,* he is virtually considered an actual idol worshipper.) It was this aspect that was most emphasized in Hasidism, both through ways of experiencing the inner essence of the ideas directly, in prayer and devotion, which would at least detach them from the physical forms, and well as by the method, which the author of the *Tanya* perfects here, of finding words and subtle, spiritual and increasingly more extensive metaphors, which will enable even someone of a simple intellect to at least discern the reality of an abstract understanding and experience of the concepts of Kabbala. The result is that even if the concepts are not completely abstracted, one can attain a larger range of concepts and ways of thinking that disconnect their inner essence from any particular form, allowing one to grasp the reality of an essence that goes beyond any physical form.

The effort "to abstract from the physical garb" applies, in the broader sense, to all realms of the Torah. Everything that is stated, whether written or oral, is formulated with words and other techniques, such as concepts, images and metaphors, that are taken mainly from the physical world. In each case, the listener has to strip away the "physicality" of the garb in order to get at the true inner meaning. After all, every language, especially Hebrew, has countless forms of expressions, symbols, and metaphors that cannot and should not be taken literally. This is immeasurably important for the study of Kabbala, and the Kabbala of the Arizal in particular. For on the one hand, Kabbala deals with issues that are entirely spiritual and abstract, on high levels and very far from the arena of physical human life, but on the other hand, since Kabbala is not merely a description of vague personal experiences but a large and detailed construction of the divine worlds and powers, it uses a complex and sophisticated system of symbols that are taken from the physical world. The result is that in the case of Kabbala, the contrast between the clothing and the content is at its most extreme. The gap between the two is so significant that it must not be taken for granted, as those who are unaware, and have not been educated in this regard, are liable to make mistakes and mislead others. An error here is especially serious and dangerous, to the extent that there is a danger of apostasy and actual idolatry. In the words of the third Lubavitcher Rebbe, Rabbi Menaḥem Mendel Schneerson, also known as the Tzemaḥ Tzedek, "The Ba'al Shem Tov commanded us not to study the books of Kabbala, since one who does not know how to abstract the concepts from their physical garb will become very earthly through this study, as he will develop an image of His blessed divinity, that fits the paucity of his mind, in accordance with his personal capacity" (cited in the book *Derekh Mitz-*

votekha, Shoresh Mitzvat HaTefilla, end of chap. 2 (115b); see *Likkutei Torah*, Addenda, 51c).

This problem has led to different approaches to the study of Kabbala. Some are content with knowing that there is an abstract spirituality within the images and garbs, but since we are unable to strip them down to their truth, we should not even try to do so, but deal only with the clothing. In Hasidism, by contrast, there is an unremitting effort, through various methods, to remove the physicality. This trend is not necessarily exhibited or proclaimed publicly, but it does occur in practice.

The real problem is that in order to abstract the ideas from their materiality, the person seeking to do so has to be, to some extent, abstracted from materiality himself. One whose own soul is immersed in physicality cannot see or sense any realm beyond the physical. Hasidim, even if they were not that abstracted personally, nevertheless discussed this idea, thought about it, and were connected to individuals who were abstracted (the Rebbes). Thus, this focus on abstraction was all around them. And when a person in is such an atmosphere, he will the courage to try himself, and will also succeed to a certain extent. In addition, the hasidic attitude toward these ideas was more than a method of study and analysis; the new spirit in Hasidism manifested itself, among other things, in the application of the ideas in practice and in one's emotional life: In the service of prayer, the performance of mitzvot, and knowing God "in all your ways." As a consequence of this practical and experiential approach, the concepts and formulations of Kabbala took on additional forms, sometimes for private individuals, in the field of action, while other occasions as personal experiences, as well as new combinations. All these, even if they are not always more abstract, do approach a state of abstraction over the course of time, due to their multifaceted nature. In any case, they are removed from a fixed, literal meaning, and are no longer identified with a single garb.

An essential feature of Hasidism, from its earliest stages, has been the translation and rendering of the physical terms and structures of Kabbala and the Midrash into spiritual and mental images. Indeed, if one can integrate all these ideas into his soul, he will no longer be in great need of all those physical images and garments. One's soul, if he allows it to experience the ideas and if he knows that this is their essence ("From my flesh I see the Divine"; Job 19:26), can inform him directly: "This is what is written in the holy books, by means of all their words and images; and here they are, abstracted from their physical garb." The "innovation" of Hasidism was not only the use of the soul as a metaphor, but also, and mainly, the inner perception that a person's soul and body, and he himself, are themselves a projection and image of the Supreme Being. Consequently, through his own experiences a person can grasp something abstracted from physicality as well, something that is essential and separate, with which he can "live." It seems that the author of the *Tanya*, notwithstanding his own claim below that he is merely interpreting the words of the Ba'al Shem Tov, actually went even further. Those ideas that other hasidic leaders felt and formulated in terse sayings which can be understood only by those in the know, he expressed in an intelligible, expansive form, more detached from personal experiences. This epistle is an example of his approach.

כִּי לֹא בָאתִי רַק לְפָרֵשׁ דִּבְרֵי הבעש״ט ז״ל וְתַלְמִידָיו עַל פִּי קַבָּלַת הָאֲרִ״י ז״ל. בְּשֶׁגַּם שֶׁעִנְיָן זֶה אֵינוֹ מֵחָכְמַת הַקַּבָּלָה וּמֵהַנִּסְתָּרוֹת לַה׳ אֱלוֹקֵינוּ כִּי אִם מֵהַנִּגְלוֹת לָנוּ וּלְבָנֵינוּ לְהַאֲמִין אֱמוּנָה שְׁלֵימָה, בְּמִקְרָא מָלֵא שֶׁדִּבֵּר הַכָּתוּב: ״הֲלֹא אֶת הַשָּׁמַיִם וְאֶת הָאָרֶץ אֲנִי מָלֵא נְאֻם ה׳״ (ירמיה כג,כד) שֶׁאֵין מִקְרָא יוֹצֵא מִידֵי פְּשׁוּטוֹ.

For my purpose is only to explain the words of the Ba'al Shem Tov, of blessed memory, and his disciples in accordance with the Kabbala of the Arizal, especially as this topic is not from the wisdom of the Kabbala and from the hidden matters **that belong to the Lord our God, but rather from those** matters **that are revealed to us and our children, to believe with a complete faith in an explicit verse that appears in the *Tanakh:* "Do I not fill the heavens and the earth, the utterance of the Lord"** (Jer. 23:24), **as a verse does not depart from its literal meaning.**

The author of the *Tanya* asserts that "my purpose is only to explain the words of the Ba'al Shem Tov," meaning, he does not aim to expand upon and clarify the concept of the enclothing of the Divine Presence abstracted from its physical garb, but only to translate the words of the Ba'al Shem Tov into the common terms of the writings of the Arizal and the statements of the Rabbis.

The expression "to us and our children" comes from Deuteronomy 29:28. If the ideas are divested of their kabbalistic terminology, the fact that God is everywhere is a basic assumption of the Jewish worldview, in every area and at every level.

"To believe with a complete faith." Even if this idea is not grasped with all the complexity and problematic aspects of the various worldviews, as explained in the books of Kabbala, in any case every Jew believes with a simple faith "in an explicit verse that appears in the Bible: 'Do I not fill the heavens and the earth, the utterance of the Lord." There are profound hasidic interpretations of this verse,[70] which is part

70. See for example, *Likkutei Torah,* Num. 53c, Deut. 9, 33. It is explained there that that this verse is referring to the divine quality of "encompasses all worlds," that in relation to Him the heavens and earth are considered a single entity, and that just as He exists in the spiritual realm above, the same applies to the physical sphere below. This and other such interpretations resolve some of the difficulties

of the reason why he quotes it here, but it can also be understood in accordance with its plain meaning. Even for those who are unfamiliar with all the deeper levels of interpretation, there is a simple meaning to this Biblical verse that everyone can understand, in accordance with his capability, even without any preliminary knowledge from other fields: God is everywhere, in heaven and on earth, the upper and lower worlds, the spiritual and the physical realms, and so on.

וְגַם הִיא אֱמוּנָה פְּשׁוּטָה בִּסְתָם כְּלָלוּת יִשְׂרָאֵל וּמְסוּרָה בְּיָדָם מֵאֲבוֹתֵיהֶם הַקְּדוֹשִׁים שֶׁהָלְכוּ בִּתְמִימוּת עִם ה׳, בְּלִי לַחֲקוֹר בְּשֵׂכֶל אֱנוֹשִׁי עִנְיַן הָאֱלֹקוּת, אֲשֶׁר הוּא לְמַעְלָה מֵהַשֵּׂכֶל עַד אֵין קֵץ

It is also a simple belief among the unlearned, general population of **Israel, handed down to them from their holy ancestors, who walked in wholeness with God, without investigating with human intellect the matter of the Divine, which infinitely transcends the intellect,**

This is "a simple belief" not because it is written in the verse, but because it is the most fundamental axiom of Jewish faith, even before anything has been said or written down: The belief in one God, with all that this entails. The phrase "the unlearned, general [population of] Israel" indicates that this belief is not limited to any particular community, movement, or individual with special intelligence. Rather, it belongs to all Israel, at whatever level or place a Jew might be. This belief was transmitted not through intellectual explanation, or anything similar, but "handed down to them from their holy ancestors" in plain terms, since it is, as stated, the basic faith that every Jew receives from his forefathers, just as he accepts from them his status as a Jew.

The content of faith is above reason. This is the definition of faith – the faculty of the soul that grasps what cannot be understood and known, what transcends reason. The intellect can attain anything that can be contained within its limits, the concepts and values that fit the dimensions with which it thinks. Anything that is not compatible with human intellect will not enter it and is termed "above the intellect." There are concepts that transcend one particular intellect but can enter

---

of how it can be said that God, the Divine Presence, is enclothed in everything, even the *kelippot*.

into a higher intellect. This is not the case when it comes to anything divine, which inherently transcends the intellect to an infinite degree; it is grasped by the faculty of simple, pure faith.

לֵידַע אֵיךְ הוּא "מְלֹא כָל הָאָרֶץ" רַק שֶׁ"חֲדָשִׁים מִקָּרוֹב בָּאוּ" לַחֲקוֹר בַּחֲקִירָה זוֹ.

to know how He "fills the whole world." It is **merely that "new ones have come recently" to delve into this investigation.**

These questions concern the "how." There is no dispute regarding the basic point that God "fills the heavens and the earth" – and if there is a question it is illegitimate, and there is no answer to it – because this is an article of faith that exists for every Jew, which is inexplicable while also incontestable. The types of questions are: How can this be; it doesn't seem to make sense; it doesn't suit a certain person's experience, and so on and so forth. These questions do not contradict the faith, but they weaken and conceal it.

As stated, those who have perfect faith do not raise such questions, but only those "new ones [who] have come recently."[71] These are "new" people, who have come from a mindset and a cultural atmosphere where this simple belief has no place, and they inquire and expect answers. Just as in the verse, they are called "new" not as a term of praise, but by way of disapproval. Their ancestors lived in a world of faith, of basic assumptions that stand by themselves rather on intellectual comprehension, and these newcomers have arrived "to delve into this investigation," to try to understand these ideas with their powers of thought. ☞

AN "INVESTIGATION"

☞ Despite the tone of disdain in his words, the author of the *Tanya* does not take the value of such an investigation lightly, or the effort to obtain answers and definitions by means of reason and understanding. On the contrary, this is exactly what the entire epistle does. When the questions are sincere, and are referring not to the basic point of faith itself but to those marginal issues where reason has a place,

71. This phrase is from Deuteronomy 32:17: "New ones that came recently, which your fathers did not consider."

וְאִי אֶפְשָׁר לְקָרֵב לָהֶם אֶל הַשֵּׂכֶל אֶלָּא דַוְקָא עַל פִּי הַקְדָּמוֹת לְקוּחוֹת מִכִּתְבֵי הָאֲרִ"י ז"ל מוּפְשָׁטוֹת מִגַּשְׁמִיּוּתָן וּכְפִי שֶׁשָּׁמַעְתִּי מֵרַבּוֹתַי נ"ע.

It is only possible to draw them close to understanding on the basis of propositions taken from the writings of the Arizal, abstracted from their physical garb, as I heard from my rabbis, whose souls are in the Garden of Eden.

Here he is not talking about real understanding by means of the intellect, as he has already stated that it is impossible to grasp these matters, but rather the effort to "draw them close to understanding" – that is, to explain them where possible, in such a manner that the issue is at least not rendered problematic, so that the learner will feel: "Although I do not understand, comprehension is possible and I am close to attaining it. The ideas do not contradict my intellectual understanding but simply extend it a little further."

He refers to "propositions taken from the writings of the Arizal," because the initial question stemmed from their supposed understanding of the writings of the Arizal, and therefore any explanation that might put their minds at ease must also be in accordance with the Arizal's teachings. The other significance of the writings of the Arizal here is that the Kabbala of the Arizal, from when it was discovered, had spread throughout the Jewish Diaspora and been accepted as the official "theology" of Judaism, as the binding foundation of any later development of a philosophy and path in the service of God. Just as

there, intellectual answers can also apply. These answers do not prove one's faith, but, when necessary, they can strengthen and uncover it.

With that said, Hasidism is not a science; it is a religious movement that focuses mainly on, and teaches one how to refer to that which cannot be attained intellectually: God; the holy; what is beyond man and the worlds. While one must believe in these with a complete and strong faith, without investigation, his faith is built and strengthened through his understanding and by knowing what can be comprehended. When one contemplates truth, in an attempt to understand, rather than in order not to understand, one realizes that there are things one cannot grasp, and yet they are true. This is perfect faith. This is not the case when one investigates in order to dismantle an idea, with the aim of not understanding it. If this is the approach, one will not achieve faith, and he may even reach a state of heresy.

the *mitnagdim* based their opposition to Hasidism on the acceptance of Kabbala of the Arizal, so too the author of the *Tanya*, when he seeks to defend Hasidism and clarify it, does so "on the basis of propositions taken from the writings of the Arizal."

Furthermore, since the difficulty was caused by a superficial ("physical") understanding of the writings of the Arizal, the explanation should take the form of an abstraction of these ideas from their physical state, as was briefly explained above. These "rabbis, whose souls are in the Garden of Eden," and who understood and taught how to abstract the words of the Arizal from their physical garb, are the Ba'al Shem Tov and the Maggid of Mezeritch.[72] Even if the author of the *Tanya* did not hear this directly from the Ba'al Shem Tov, he heard his opinion by way of his disciples, mainly from the Maggid.[73] It is important for him to note this here,[74] in order to stress that this method of abstracting the words of the Arizal from their physicality is not merely a rational idea, but a kabbalistic approach upon which the hasidic movement was founded. And particularly, this whole epistle deals with the system attributed to the Ba'al Shem Tov.

אַךְ אִי אֶפְשָׁר לְבָאֵר זֶה הֵיטֵב בְּמִכְתָּב כִּי אִם מִפֶּה לְאֹזֶן שׁוֹמַעַת

Yet this cannot be thoroughly explained in writing, but only from mouth to attending ear,

---

72. The sixth Lubavitcher Rebbe, Rabbi Yosef Yitzḥak Schneerson, relates that when his father, the fifth Lubavitcher Rebbe, Rabbi Sholom Dovber Schneerson, taught him the *Iggeret HaKodesh*, he informed him that the phrase "I heard from my teacher" (for example, in *Likkutei Amarim*, chap. 35, in the note) refers to the Maggid of Mezeritch, whereas "I heard from my rabbis" means both the Ba'al Shem Tov and the Maggid of Mezeritch.

73. As is known, the author of the *Tanya* referred to himself as the (spiritual) grandson of the Ba'al Shem Tov (like a grandson who receives from the grandfather via his father), as he himself said to the righteous Rabbi Barukh of Medzibozh, the Ba'al Shem Tov's grandson: "You are the physical grandchild, while I am the spiritual grandson." See the epistle of the sixth Lubavitcher Rebbe, Rabbi Yosef Yitzḥak Schneerson, in *HaTamim* 2, p. 58 on the connection between the author of the *Tanya* – and Chabad tradition – and the Ba'al Shem Tov. See also *Likkutei Siḥot*, vol. 4, p. 1136.

74. A similar comment appears in epistle 23, above.

This abstraction from physicality cannot be achieved in writing. Unlike speech, writing is merely letters and words, without any live and direct contact between the one bestowing the ideas and their recipient. That which is transferred through the written word is only the outer garments, which receive their meaning in accordance with the mind of the receiver; if his mind was coarse before, written paragraphs will do nothing to change that.[75]

The phrase "from mouth to attending ear"[76] refers to the verbal content of what someone says to a person standing in front of him, who can see him and relate to him specifically. Only in this manner is it possible to transfer the contents inside the garments from one person to another. An "attending ear" is thus a person who wishes to hear, who really desires to understand what was said to him, not merely in order to formulate a response. ☞

לִיחִידֵי סְגוּלָּה וְלַשְּׂרִידִים אֲשֶׁר ה׳ קוֹרֵא

and then only **to unique individuals and to the remnant whom the Lord shall call,**

These "unique individuals" have the ability, due to their talent, hard work, and inner connection, to listen and receive the interiority of ideas, on a fundamental level. The phrase "the remnant whom the Lord shall call" is derived from Joel 3:5. He again uses a Biblical expression

FROM MOUTH TO ATTENDING EAR

☞ The verse continues: "An attending ear to life's rebuke" (Prov. 15: 31). An ear that can hear the abstraction from the physicality of the words is an ear that can hear "life's rebuke." Hearing a rebuke is one of the hardest things to do, and only those who truly nullify themselves with respect to what they hear are capable of it. In this case as well, only one who hears in such a way that he negates his own understanding, his opinion, his feelings, and indeed his whole being, such that he can approach the ideas without the mediation of his former instruments and frameworks, only he can – under additional conditions – receive the ideas abstracted from their physicality.

75. See the "Compiler's Introduction" at the beginning of the *Tanya*, and the commentary there.

76. Derived from Proverbs 15:31 and 25:12.

to describe those special individuals: They are survivors of all the vicissitudes of time, as they do not depend on and are not immersed in the affairs of the world, but rather they are ready for the Lord to call upon them.

כְּדִכְתִיב: "וּמְבַקְשֵׁי הֲוָיָ"ה יָבִינוּ כֹל" (משלי כח,ה) וּמִכְּלַל הֵן אַתָּה שׁוֹמֵעַ כו'.

as it is written: "but seekers of the Lord will understand all" (Prov. 28:5), **and from the affirmative you can understand...**

Only those who, for their part, call upon God and seek Him will be able to hear the inner essence; only such a person can succeed in abstracting the words from their physicality. As a rule, these ideas cannot be transmitted by means of any object or skill on the part of the giver alone. If the recipient is unwilling and refuses to seek them, if he does not ask the questions himself, and fails to devote himself to the point of abstracting himself of his physicality, he won't hear the message. The full quote is "and from the affirmative you can understand the negative."[77] If all these conditions are not met, the abstract idea cannot be transferred from its physical state. ☞

הִנֵּה אַתֶּם רְאִיתֶם פֵּירוּשׁ מַאֲמָר אֶחָד מִסְּפָרִים הַיְדוּעִים, לְדוּגְמָא וּלְאוֹת כִּי גַּם כָּל הַמַּאֲמָרִים הַתְּמוּהִים יֵשׁ לָהֶם פֵּירוּשׁ וּבֵיאוּר הֵיטֵב לְיוֹדְעֵי חֵן.

You have thus seen the clarification of a single section from the well-known books, as an example and illustration that all the puzzling passages likewise have an explanation and a clear elucidation to those initiated in the esoteric wisdom of Kabbala.

This statement is addressed to those who expressed reservations over the statement of the Ba'al Shem Tov. He does not intend, nor does he think it necessary, to explain all the sayings of the Ba'al Shem Tov and his students in this manner. He has provided an example, which can

---

77. The cited verse itself, Proverbs 28:5, states both the affirmative and negative sides of the proposition. See also Daniel 12:10: "All of the wicked will not understand, but the wise will understand."

serve as a model, as it demonstrates that there is a valid interpretation and explanation for all the rest as well. When a person gets involved with material, he no longer needs to go back each time and clarify the basics in accordance with the introductions to the writings of the Arizal, and so on. Instead, he can skip all that and deal directly with the inner meaning of the ideas.

אַךְ לֹא יְקַוּוּ מַעֲלָתָם אֵלַי לְבָאֵר לָהֶם הַכֹּל בְּמִכְתָּב, כִּי הִיא מְלָאכָה כְּבֵידָה וּמְרוּבָּה וְאִי אֶפְשָׁר בְּשׁוּם אוֹפֶן. רַק אִם תִּרְצוּ שִׁלְחוּ מִכֶּם אֶחָד וּמְיוּחָד שֶׁבָּעֵדָה, וּפֶה אֶל פֶּה אֲדַבֶּר בּוֹ אִם יִרְצֶה ה׳, וה׳ יִהְיֶה עִם פִּי בְּהַטִּיפִי. וְיִהְיוּ לְרָצוֹן אִמְרֵי פִי.

However, your honors should not expect that I will clarify everything for them in writing, for that is a heavy and extensive labor, and it is not possible in any form. But if you want, send one special person from your assembly, and I will speak with him one-on-one, God willing. May the Lord be with my mouth when I express myself, and may the words of my mouth find favor.

The author of the *Tanya* is here granting them permission to send someone to him for clarification of some particular matter that they are having difficulty understanding. He concludes with a petition to the God, as he too requires God's will and assistance to formulate the ideas. When concepts have been abstracted from their physicality, it is not as though they have been placed in a box where some individual,

FROM THE AFFIRMATIVE YOU CAN UNDERSTAND THE NEGATIVE

☞ This principle, that all these conditions must apply in order for one to understand, does not apply to all cases, but wherever it is stated, the idea is that the relationship between content and the way the message is formulated is essential, and that it could not be said in any other way. This applies to words of the Torah (see, for example, Rashi on Ex. 20:11), which have been handed down to us from above. Its words and the manner in which they are stated are no less holy than their content, and if one fails to understand them, the inadequacy is not in what is said but in the one who was listening. (See Deut. 32: 47, and Rashi and the *Sifrei* on that verse, and many other places.) Here too, the author of the *Tanya* is emphasizing that if one fails to understand the comments of the Ba'al Shem Tov (and the Arizal), the fault lies not with their statements but with the recipient of their message.

whoever he might be, has ready access to them. Just as there must be, as stated, a high level of devotion and preparation on the part of the hearer so that he can receive the ideas, the same applies – to an even greater extent – to the speaker. If that is the case, he will be able, God willing, to convey his message successfully.

This epistle, which was written for the purpose of explaining to the *mitnagdim* a difficult statement of the Ba'al Shem Tov, ended up dealing with topics that are central to the faith, while straddling the line of disagreement between the hasidim and *mitnagdim*. The author of the *Tanya* was "dragged" into this not only because the Ba'al Shem Tov's statement is indeed bold and problematic – for it is possible to resolve the main difficulty simply by correcting one word, as the author of the *Tanya* himself does toward the end of the epistle – but also because he sought the opportunity, it would seem, to clarify these ideas, both to hasidim and *mitnagdim*, and this was the best forum that he found for that purpose.

The difficulty in the words of the Ba'al Shem Tov, to which the author of the *Tanya* refers, is his statement that the Divine Presence is enclothed even in a gentile who is disturbing a Jew from praying. In order to explain this, he first clarifies the saying of the Rabbis that whoever gets angry is considered as though he is worshipping idolatry. He states that anger results from a lack of faith that God is found in all things and brings everything into being. For whoever truly believes in this will be at peace with everything that happens, and will not get angry. To elucidate this idea further, he cites a section, which is also quoted in *Sha'ar HaYiḥud VeHa'emuna*, to the effect that the essence of created reality is nothing but the speech of God. Just as speech has no reality in and of itself without the one uttering it, so too creation and everything that occurs in it has no reality of its own without the Creator, who intends it and speaks it. He adds that the divine speech which speaks creation into being is called "the Divine Presence [*Shekhina*]," because it rests [*shokhen*] and descends and enclothes all creatures into being and sustains them. However, this descent and constriction of the revelation of the Divine Presence can, in certain circumstances, reach such an extent that the Divine Presence is no longer revealed, but only influences events covertly, and sometimes even in a way that is the opposite of and contrary to the revelation and purpose of the Divine Presence. These degrees of the enclothing of the Divine Presence in *kelippot* are called "the exile of the Divine Presence." He next explained – based on the writings of the Arizal – that the secret of the exile of the Divine Presence is in accordance with the verse "whenever man had control over man it was to his detriment." This teaches that the whole process is ultimately to the detriment of the *kelippot*, in order to nullify them and reveal the Divine Presence even more powerfully, from a place and in a manner that was not previously attained. The saying of the Ba'al Shem Tov is an example of this principle: When the one who is praying focuses on these ideas, that the Divine Presence is enclothed in exile, through the mouth of this gentile, that it is not a chance occurrence that this evil gentile is here, and so on, but rather that this is the Divine Presence's way of encouraging him to grow stronger in prayer, then the "*kelippa*" will be nullified and the Divine Presence will be revealed through his prayer in a higher form, which had not been present before.

Addressing the *mitnagdim*, the author of the *Tanya* stresses that these are not the Ba'al Shem Tov's own, novel ideas. Rather, they are well-established themes that were already articulated by the Arizal in his own style, and which are based on a simple faith that was once the portion – and basically still is – of every Jew. And yet he also delivers, over the head of the *mitnagdim*, virtually the opposite statement to the hasidim (and to the "pious" [*hasid*] among the *mitnagdim*), that this is in fact a novel approach. Just as the words of the Arizal are not merely another way of saying various ideas, but rather a new worldview and the opening of a path to the service of God, the same applies to the words of the Ba'al Shem Tov with respect to the teachings of the Arizal. It is true that there is no new theory with novel concepts here (as the Arizal introduced during his time), because the revolution and innovation are of a different kind, which does not require new terms. He uses what is already there, in order to say in the most direct and simple manner, that which has already been stated in complex terms and in reference to unique cases: That these concepts, which appear in the writings of the Arizal (and other works of Kabbala), which the Sages studied and understood, are not found only there and in the manner they are written there. Rather, they are here, within us, and in the lives of each one of us. The writings of the Arizal provide explanations of the *sefirot*, the worlds, the enclothing of the Divine Presence, and the exile of the Divine Presence, and along comes the Ba'al Shem Tov and declares: "When a gentile is actually standing in front of you and disrupting your prayer, this is the enclothing (and exile) of the Divine Presence." When one becomes aware of this and reflects upon it, and also extracts from the experience a new aspect of the service of God, this itself is the redemption of the Divine Presence.

However, the biggest novelty of the Ba'al Shem Tov and Hasidism that is communicated in this epistle is not on the level of theory, but rather the service of God that it teaches. Until the time of the Ba'al Shem Tov, the attitude toward the interruption of prayer – and the service of God in general – whether it came from external or internal factors, was as a negative occurrence that must be avoided by any means possible. The Ba'al Shem Tov's perspective is almost the reverse: The foreign thought, even when it comes from the outside and against one's will, is not an undesirable element interfering with the service of God, but rather it is the very object of that service. Its purpose is not to cause the person to stumble, but to bring out the best in him, above and beyond what he thought possible. Therefore, that person is not expected to remove it from his path, but the opposite: To venture toward it, to search for the holiness within it, to separate it from the *kelippa* and raise it up through his service – of prayer, Torah and mitzvot. This was the well-known method of the Ba'al Shem Tov, of raising up foreign thoughts through "submission, separation, and mitigation." See the lengthy discussion on this in *Ba'al Shem Tov al HaTorah, Noaḥ, Amud HaTefilla*, 106. Nevertheless, the author of the *Tanya*'s approach in the *Tanya* is more cautious. As he states explicitly in *Likkutei Amarim*, chap. 28: "Also, one should not be so foolish as to engage in elevating the attributes of the foreign thought, as is known." Not all are equally capable of implementing this method, and one who is not blessed with the requisite skills should not engage in the practice at all. This is perhaps due to the large number of hasidim who listened to his message in general, and in particular the *Tanya*, the "Written Torah," which can be read by anyone at any time. He does not talk about elevating foreign thoughts in general and express terms, but only concerning a case like the one in this epistle, when it is not in one's power to protest, when he is unable to rid himself of the disturbance in any other way. With that said, the principle remains in force, and in the larger scale of the events of one's life it is effectively present at all times. When the author of the *Tanya* says about this epistle that it presents "the clarification of a single section…as an example and illustration that all the puzzling passages have an explanation," this should be interpreted broadly, as referring not only to other sections and sayings but also to other events: The Divine Presence is enclothed in every incident that occurs to a person during his lifetime; no matter what each person is saying or doing, at that very moment he can be raising up and elevating the Divine Presence as well.

Epistle 26

Epistle 26 is one of the letters that were written specifically for the purpose of explaining Hasidism. These letters were actually not originally written as letters but rather as part of the author of the *Tanya*'s written teachings.

The entirety of the discourse contained in this letter revolves around a certain statement in the *Zohar*. Notwithstanding this focus, this letter belongs within the framework of *Iggeret HaKodesh* because it is not simply an in-depth commentary on the *Zohar*'s statement, but it also contains significant and fundamental observations about the issues that were current at the time of the writing of the *Tanya*. These include the conflict between hasidim and their opponents, the *mitnagdim*, which revolved around the study of Kabbala as well as the role that such study plays in Jewish life. At the time when the letter was written, both hasidim and *mitnagdim* studied the hidden wisdom of Kabbala.[1] The difference between the two factions was that Kabbala wisdom was part of the hasidim's oral discourse, a component of their social milieu. Hasidic groups emphasized a relationship with the hidden higher spheres of reality. They applied the kabbalistic concepts in reality, such concepts being embedded in their thoughts and approach to life, and attempted to implant this hidden wisdom in every aspect of their lives. Within such an atmosphere lay the risk of encouraging a greater

1. Both groups studied Kabbala, but there was not yet a systematic framework for the teaching of Hasidism. Hasidic teachings were primarily transmitted orally, while the written literature mainly comrised works of Kabbala.

focus on studying Kabbala at the expense of the revealed Torah, which raised the likelihood of an erosion of stability in the spiritual state of Jewish society. This, in turn, aroused others' hostility and even total opposition to the study of the hidden wisdom of Kabbala. The author of the *Tanya*, in his explanation of the statement in the *Zohar*, sheds light on this issue, utilizing both the hidden and revealed Torah, and addresses the need for both spheres of study, with respect to both groups, the hasidim and their opponents.

Regarding the placement of the letter,[2] it is a continuation of the previous letter, which dealt with the enclothing of the Divine Presence in exile, and in the *kelippot* that disrupt and obstruct divine service through prayer. In it, the author of the *Tanya* explained how a person can utilize these very obstacles to reach greater heights, both personally and in his service of the Divine. In this letter, epistle 26, he addresses the same subject, but in the context of Torah study. He states that the Torah is enclothed in the lower worlds and in the *kelippot* and that Torah study and upholding its teaching leads to an extraction [*birur*] of evil from good, which operates not only in a specific circumstance but generally and collectively, at all times and in all worlds, until the time of the final redemption.

The letter begins with a lengthy statement quoted from the *Zohar*:

4 Ḥeshvan

4 Ḥeshvan (leap year)

בְּרַעְיָא מְהֵימְנָא' פָּרָשַׁת נָשֹׂא **In *Raya Meheimna, Parashat Naso*:**

In *Raya Meheimna* ("The Loyal Shepherd" or "The Shepherd of Faith"),[3] *Parashat Naso*. The quoted section appears in the *Zohar, Parashat Naso* [*Zohar* 3:124b]. ☞

2. As was explained, the order of *Iggeret HaKodesh* is topical and not chronological. See the comment of the Lubavitcher Rebbe on this (printed in Lessons in *Tanya*).

3. In hasidic texts, the name is usually rendered as "The Shepherd of Faith"; see *Likkutei Amarim*, chap. 42, and *Torah Or* 75b. See also *Sefer HaMa'amarim Melukat*, vol. 3, p. 35.

The passage quoted here is part of a very lengthy section that describes the exile, and the struggles that will take place during its final phase. The purpose of these struggles will be to differentiate between the righteous, who will be redeemed, and the evildoers, etc. (analogous to the test and challenge of the *sota*, an allegedly adulterous woman, to assess whether or not she had, in fact, committed adultery). However – and this is the point of the quoted section – there will be some who will not need to undergo such a test at all. These are the people who immerse themselves in the *Zohar*, meaning, in the innermost aspect of the Torah.

"וְהַמַּשְׂכִּלִים יַזְהִירוּ כְּזֹהַר הָרָקִיעַ" (דניאל יב,ג)

"The wise will shine like the radiance of the firmament" (Dan. 12:3),

This verse is the biblical source for the name of the book of the *Zohar*. The verse also serves as the opening for several passages in the *Zohar*. It states that those who study the words of the *Zohar* that appear in the particular section, and the Torah secrets that are mentioned within it, will shine and illuminate "like the radiance of the firmament" as a result. This refers to the illumination of the higher spheres, as opposed to the illumination of this world, which emanates from the revealed Torah.

בְּהַאי חִבּוּרָא דִּילָךְ דְּאִיהוּ סֵפֶר הַזֹּהַר מִן זֹהֲרָא דְּאִימָּא עִילָּאָה

with that composition of yours, of Rabbi Shimon bar Yoḥai, **which is the book of the *Zohar* from the splendor** [*zohar*] **of the supernal mother,**

THE LOYAL SHEPHERD

☞ This term is a name applied to Moses in the *Zohar*. It is also the title of a section in the *Zohar*, so named because the contents of that section are attributed to Moses. In effect, this section of the *Zohar* is a book in its own right, structured according to the order of the 613 commandments. In our editions of the *Zohar*, "The Loyal Shepherd" does not appear as a separate section (like *Tikkunei Zohar*), but rather it is scattered in small passages throughout the *Zohar*, which is organized primarily according to the weekly Torah portions. Wherever they appear, these pieces are listed under the heading of "The Loyal Shepherd."

The light and intellectual perspective that are revealed in the *Zohar* come from the light that is the level of the supernal "mother," referring to *Bina* that is found in the world of *Atzilut.* ☞

תְּשׁוּבָה repentance.

For *Bina* is referred to as repentance. As is explained elsewhere,[4] repentance is the returning and elevation of elements of holiness that had descended into the lower worlds and *kelippot* back to their roots in *Atzilut.* It is explained there (based on the statement in the *Zohar*) that the word *teshuva* (repentance) is comprised of "*tashuv*" (return) and the letter *heh,* representing the four-letter name of *Havaya.* Just as the letter *heh* appears twice the four-letter name, so are there two levels of repentance: lower repentance and higher repentance. Lower repentance is the returning (*teshuva*) to the latter *heh* in the name of *Havaya,* which is the *Malkhut* of the world of *Atzilut.* Higher repentance is the upper, first *heh,* which is the *Bina* of *Atzilut.*

The service of higher repentance is, therefore, through *Bina.* In this repentance, not only the person's actions and speech, but also his spiritual attributes, ascend to the place in his soul which, according to his understanding, is worthy and perfected. *Bina,* in this sense, is the place in his soul within which aspects of himself are increasingly perfected. It is not simply a static state of being a righteous person, with holy and perfected traits. Rather, it is an ongoing process of contemplation, service, and improvement upon prior states. This is the *Bina* that is referred to as "higher repentance."

THE SPLENDOR OF THE SUPERNAL MOTHER

☞ It is explained in the commentary on the *Zohar* of *Kisei Melekh*: "This refers to the fact that *Bina* is freedom; through it, Israel left Egypt, and it is called the "Tree of Life." Those who study the *Zohar,* which is also the "Tree of Life," so named because of the radiance of *Bina* through which they were able to attain freedom (the radiance of *Bina* through which the slaves became free), will also leave exile and become free.

---

4. *Iggeret HaTeshuva,* chap. 9. See also *Zohar* part 1, 79b, and part 3, 216a, and elsewhere.

בְּאִילֵין לָא צְרִיךְ נִסָּיוֹן וּבְגִין דַּעֲתִידִין יִשְׂרָאֵל לְמִטְעַם מֵאִילָנָא דְחַיֵּי דְּאִיהוּ הַאי סֵפֶר הַזֹּהַר יִפְּקוּן בֵּיהּ מִן גָּלוּתָא בְּרַחֲמִים

No test is required for these. And since in the future Israel will taste from the tree of life, which is this book of the *Zohar*, they will emerge through it from the exile with mercy,

Those who study the *Zohar*, and immerse themselves in the inner aspect of Torah, will not need any tests or purification for the future redemption. Engaging in the inner aspect of Torah reveals the "Tree of Life." Although the entire Torah is a tree of life, as will be elucidated below, it is through the inner aspect of Torah that this facet, the facet of life and light, is revealed, isolated from and unconnected with evil and the *kelippa*. This revelation and experience themselves represent one's personal emergence from exile, within his awareness and sensibility. It prepares him so that his general emergence from exile is experienced without hardship, but rather mercifully.

וְיִתְקַיַּים בְּהוֹן: "ה' בָּדָד יַנְחֶנּוּ וְאֵין עִמּוֹ אֵל נֵכָר" (דברים לב,יב).

and the verse **will be fulfilled in them: "The Lord alone would lead him, and there was no foreign god with Him"** (Deut. 32:12).

This means that God Himself will take them out of exile. "Foreign god" refers to the perspectives of the other nations and their angelic ministers, through which God executes judgment against the people of Israel when they are culpable. "The Lord alone would lead him" refers to when God will redeem them, and that the redemption will not be effected through judgments and reckonings, but with simple mercy.

וְאִילָנָא דְטוֹב וָרָע דְּאִיהוּ אִיסּוּר וְהֶיתֵּר טוּמְאָה וְטָהֳרָה לֹא יִשְׁלְטוּ עַל יִשְׂרָאֵל יַתִּיר

And the tree of knowledge of **good and evil, which is** related to the topics of **prohibited and permitted** matters and **impurity and purity, will no longer rule over Israel.**

This is the part of Torah (the revealed Torah) that relates to this world, which is the reality of the *kelippat noga*. In this world, there is good and evil, which the Torah categorizes as prohibited and permitted, pure and impure. They will no longer rule over Israel. For Israel will receive their life force directly from a level that is both higher and deeper, and not through the tree of knowledge of good and evil.

דְּהָא פַּרְנָסָה דִּלְהוֹן לָא לֶהֱוֵי אֶלָּא מִסִּטְרָא דְּאִילָנָא דְּחַיֵּי, דְּלֵית תַּמָּן לָא קַשְׁיָא מִסִּטְרָא דְּרַע וְלָא מַחֲלוֹקֶת מֵרוּחַ הַטּוּמְאָה, דִּכְתִיב: "וְאֶת רוּחַ הַטּוּמְאָה אַעֲבִיר מִן הָאָרֶץ" (זכריה יג,ב)

For their sustenance will come only from the side of the tree of life, where there are neither difficulties raised **by the evil side nor disputes** emerging **from the spirit of impurity, as it is written: "I will remove the spirit of impurity from the land"** (Zech. 13:2),

דְּלָא יִתְפַּרְנְסוּן תַּלְמִידֵי חֲכָמִים מֵ'עַמֵּי הָאָרֶץ', אֶלָּא מִסִּטְרָא דְּטוֹב דְּאָכְלִין טָהֳרָה כָּשֵׁר הֶיתֵּר, וְלָא מֵ'עֵרֶב רַב' דְּאָכְלִין טוּמְאָה פָּסוּל אָסוּר וכו'

The result will be **that Torah scholars will not receive their sustenance from "the ignorant," but from the good side, as they will eat in purity kosher, permitted** food, **nor from the "mixed multitude** [*eirev rav*]," **who eat impure, disqualified, prohibited** food....[5]

וּבִזְמְנָא דְּאִילָנָא דְּטוֹב וָרַע שָׁלְטָא כו', אִינּוּן חֲכָמִים דְּדָמְיָין לְשַׁבָּתוֹת וְיָמִים טוֹבִים לֵית לְהוֹן אֶלָּא מַה דְּיָהֲבִין לְהוֹן אִינּוּן חוֹלִין כְּגַוְונָא דְּיוֹם הַשַּׁבָּת דְּלֵית לֵיהּ אֶלָּא מַה דְּמִתַּקְנִין לֵיהּ בְּיוֹמָא דְּחוֹל

But during the time when the tree of knowledge of **good and evil rules..., those scholars, who resemble Shabbatot and festivals, have only what is given to them by these weekdays, like the day of Shabbat, which has only that which is prepared for it on the weekdays.**

5. Here the author omits the sentence "For they are unclean, sullying themselves with [sexual relations with] menstruating women, maids, non-Jewish women, and prostitutes. For they are the children of *Lilith*, for she is these women, and [by doing so] they return to their roots. Regarding them it is said, "From the root of the snake will emerge a viper" (Isa. 14:29).

This can be paraphrased as follows: But during the time when the tree of knowledge of good and evil rules etc.,[6] meaning, this time period of the exile of the Divine Presence in *kelippat noga*, those scholars, who resemble Shabbatot and festivals, have only what is given to them by the weekdays, which refers to the ignorant who are compared to the days of the week. Like the day of Shabbat, which has only that which is prepared for it on the weekdays. The *Zohar* expresses a harsh contrast between two types of people, scholars and the ignorant. These two types are parallel to two phases of time, the days of the week, contrasted with the Shabbatot and festivals. During the exile, one prepares for Shabbat during the weekdays, so that he cannot eat anything on Shabbat except that which was prepared during the week. Similarly, during the exile, scholars receive their sustenance from the ignorant. ☞

וּבִזְמְנָא דְשַׁלְטָא אִילָנָא דְחַיֵּי אִתְכַּפְיָיא אִילָנָא דְטוֹב וָרָע וְלָא יְהֵא לְעַמֵּי הָאָרֶץ אֶלָּא מַה דְּיָהֲבִין לְהוֹן תַּלְמִידֵי חֲכָמִים וְאִתְכַּפְיָין תְּחוֹתַיְיהוּ, כְּאִלּוּ לָא הָווּ בְּעָלְמָא

And during the time when the tree of life rules, the tree of knowledge of **good and evil is subjugated, and the ignorant will have only that which the Torah scholars will give them, and they will be subjugated to them, as though they did not exist in the world.**

DURING THE TIME OF EXILE, THE SCHOLARS RECEIVE FROM THE IGNORANT

☞ This receiving by the scholars from the ignorant (who have the status of "days of the week") refers to the scholars taking on the perspectives and ways of thinking of the ignorant. The ignorant are those who are bound to materialism, to the ways of thinking and the behavior that are associated with the physical world. In times of exile, scholars must also think and behave according to these norms, in order to survive in this world. Nevertheless, there is a difference. For the ignorant, this is real life. They truly believe that everything is subject to the rules of this world, and the effort they invest in abiding by those rules. In contrast, the scholars know that in truth, nothing is dependent on these things, but only on divine providence. But they also know that, at least outwardly, they must function within the confines of the system of this world and of the ignorant.

6. Here in the letter the author omits the words "For they are weekdays of purity and weekdays of impurity."

At the time of redemption, the situation will reverse. The ignorant will receive from the scholars both their physical needs as well as their spiritual perspectives. They will see the direct flow of the path of holiness, so that all boundaries and distortions of the *kelippot* of this world will not be an obstacle, and it will be as if they do not exist.

וְהָכֵי אִיסּוּר הֶיתֵּר טוּמְאָה וְטָהֳרָה לָא אִתְעֲבַר מֵעַמֵּי הָאָרֶץ דְּמִסִּטְרַיְיהוּ לֵית בֵּין גָּלוּתָא לִימוֹת הַמָּשִׁיחַ אֶלָּא שִׁעְבּוּד מַלְכֻיּוֹת בִּלְבַד

And thus, the topics of **prohibited and permitted** matters and **impurity and purity will not be removed from the ignorant, as from their perspective there is no difference between the exile and the days of the Messiah, other than the subordination to the** gentile **kingdoms alone.**

Here, the statement relates to two opinions found in the Talmud (*Berakhot* 35b, and elsewhere) regarding the nature of the messianic era. One opinion is that there will be a completely different reality at that time. The other opinion (which is the opinion of Shmuel in the Talmud, and the Rambam rules that the *halakha* is in accordance with Shmuel)[7] is that there will be no difference between this time period and the messianic era except for subordination to the rule of other nations. This means that, other than Israel no longer being subjugated to the other nations, which will allow them to fulfill the Torah and commandments without interference, the world will continue as it was before. Here, the *Zohar* allows space for both opinions and distinguishes instead between types of people. It posits that a complete change in the nature of reality will take place, but only for the scholars, while the ignorant will continue to experience this world as unchanged, except for the subjugation to other nations. The perspective here is that the nature of the change will depend on those experiencing it. Whoever is not prepared for it, and lacks the tools and words to think about it, will not sense and experience the qualitative, internal change of the redemption. For such a person, apart from the fact that there is no longer any subjugation, including

7. *Sefer HaMadda, Hilkhot Teshuva* 9:2 and *Sefer Shofetim, Hilkhot Melakhim* 12:2.

subjugation to the evil inclination, this world will continue to exist as it is now, even during the messianic era.

דְּאִינּוּן לָא טַעֲמֵי מֵאִילָנָא דְּחַיֵּי וּצְרִיךְ לוֹן מַתְנִיתִין בְּאִיסּוּר וְהֶיתֵּר טוּמְאָה וְטָהֳרָה.

For they did not taste from the tree of life, and they require the teachings of prohibited and permitted matters and **impurity and purity.**

Since their world will remain, in some way, as it is now, including prohibited and permitted matters, and purity and impurity, they will need to continue learning *halakha* as it is today, in order to live with these things.

עַד כָּאן בְּרַעְיָא מְהֵימְנָא.

Here ends the citation from the ***Raya Meheimna.***

This is the conclusion of the quote from the *Zohar*. The author of the *Tanya* only cites an excerpt from that passage in the *Zohar* because it is not his intention to explain the entire text. Rather, he only intends to address certain ideas mentioned in the excerpt.

It appears that the *Zohar* depicts a situation of two worlds as being at opposite extremes from each other: The world of the hidden Torah, which is entirely good and pure, in opposition to the world of revealed Torah, which is its opposite. In the following sections, by negating this perspective and clarifying the meaning and intent of the *Zohar,* the author of the *Tanya* will reconstruct the relationship between revealed and hidden Torah, according to both the revealed and hidden traditions.

First, he will state what one should not understand from the words of the *Zohar*. He will also prove that this approach and its conclusions are incorrect.

וְהִנֵּה הַמּוּבָן מֵהַשְׁקָפָה רִאשׁוֹנָה לִכְאוֹרָה מִלְּשׁוֹן זֶה הַמַּאֲמָר לַחֲסֵירֵי מַדָּע

Now, on first reflection, the meaning of this passage to those who lack understanding 5 Ḥeshvan (leap year)

There are two negations here. This understanding is only that of a "first reflection," and anyone who delves further will understand differently.

Additionally, this understanding is that of those who lack understanding. ☞ ☞

The phrase "those who lack understanding" refers not only to those lacking knowledge, but also to those who lack understanding, *"da'at,"* in the deep sense of the word. *Da'at,* as is well known, is located on

THOSE WHO LACK UNDERSTANDING

☞ From the context here, it appears that the author's intent when mentioning "those who lack understanding" refers not only to those who do not understand the *Zohar*, but also those who do not accept other parts of the Torah (the Oral Law, the *Shulḥan Arukh*, etc.). As will be explained, the incorrect interpretation of this statement in the *Zohar* leads to a rejection of the revealed Torah and the practice of *halakha*. "Those who lack understanding" is not merely an abstract term. It refers to specific people and groups (such as the Sabbateans and the Frankists, who lived close to the author's time) who brought extensive spiritual destruction to the Jewish world. This destruction undoubtedly serves as some of the backdrop for the resistance to Hasidism. These groups made claims, with some variations, that match the "first reflection" in understanding this section of the *Zohar*. The perspective was one of opposition between the revealed and hidden aspects of Torah, of a time period when the kabbalistic wisdom would override the revealed Torah. According to the extreme implication of this perspective, there would be no need to learn or observe the laws of the revealed Torah, of the prohibited and permitted, pure and impure. In his words in this letter, both those relating to the plain meaning of the revealed Torah as well as the deeper explanations of the hidden aspect, the author portrays the extent of the danger posed by these distorted perspectives. Primarily, he explains the correct places for the hidden and revealed aspects of Torah, and thus clarifies for the *mitnagdim* the degree to which Hasidism is far removed from these distorted perspectives.

THOSE WHO LACK UNDERSTANDING IN THE *ZOHAR*

☞ In addition to that which has been said, there is a real problem with understanding the *Zohar,* which is not only a work focused on the hidden aspect of Torah but also a book that is unique in its style and themes. As a result, not everyone is able to understand the intent of the words of the *Zohar*. The book is written in a language that is not organized linearly, but it is rather written in a very graphic language of other-worldly analogies and images that flow from world to world. One who is not versed in this language will find it difficult to understand what these ideas refer to and how to relate them to other matters. Additionally, like many books that deal with the hidden aspect of Torah, in places where these ideas intersect with the revealed, practical world, ideological positions are taken, both positive and negative ones. One who is unable to follow the various inner concepts, and to understand their intent, can reach incorrect conclusions, even conclusions that are contrary to what was intended.

the middle line, and the middle line always includes the two extremes and is constituted from this inclusion. This is true in the intellect, in emotions, and in the practical behaviors of a person. Only a person who can accommodate the revealed and the hidden aspects of Torah, love and fear, the nuanced details of practice together with the abstract depth of the inner side of Torah, can correctly understand the meaning of this statement of the *Zohar*, and other similar statements. Such a person will thus avoid being in the category of "those who lack understanding."

שֶׁלִּימּוּד אִיסּוּר וְהֶיתֵּר וְסֵדֶר טָהֳרוֹת הוּא מֵאִילָנָא דְּטוֹב וָרָע.

is **that the study of prohibited and permitted** matters **and the order of purities is from the tree of** knowledge of **good and evil.**

This is the incorrect understanding. It is referring to the tree of knowledge of good and evil that is mentioned in *Parashat Bereshit* (Gen. 2:9), and which has symbolized evil and the *kelippa* ever since Adam sinned through it. The tree of knowledge is not intrinsically evil (for the tree was not evil; the actions of man in eating of its prohibited fruit were), but it carries the possibility of evil.[8] As a result, it is the doorway and beginning for the existence of evil and the *kelippa* in this world within which we live. The connection that those who lack understanding make is this: Since the Torah of prohibited and permitted touches the low level of existence in which there is good and evil, and relates to it, it must therefore be a part of that reality, which began through the consumption of the fruit of the tree of knowledge of good and evil.

מִלְּבַד שֶׁהוּא פֶּלֶא גָּדוֹל מֵחֲמַת עַצְמוֹ וְסוֹתֵר פְּשָׁטֵי הַכְּתוּבִים וּמִדְרְשֵׁי רַבּוֹתֵינוּ ז״ל, שֶׁכָּל הַתּוֹרָה הַנִּגְלֵית לָנוּ וּלְבָנֵינוּ - נִקְרָא: ״עֵץ חַיִּים לַמַּחֲזִיקִים בָּהּ״, וְלֹא סֵפֶר הַזֹּהַר לְבַד.

First of all, such an idea **is astonishing in and of itself and it contradicts the plain meaning of sayings and expositions of our Sages, that the entire Torah that was revealed to us and our children is called "a tree of life for those who hold on to it," not only the book of the *Zohar*.**

8. See *Torah Or* 5c and onward, and further in this letter.

The contradiction is internal: The Torah is holy, and it is the essence of the definition and instruction of that which is good. How can one say that some aspect of the Torah is from the tree of knowledge of good and evil," which represents the reality of the profane, and the *kelippat noga*?!

It also contradicts the plain meaning of sayings and expositions of our Sages,[9] that the entire Torah, including that which was revealed to us and our children, is called in the language of the Torah "a tree of life for those who hold on to it" (based on Prov. 10:8), not only the book of the Zohar, as one might have misconstrued from this statement of the *Zohar*. In any case, it is clear that the intent of the phrase "tree of life" is referring not only to the *Zohar*, but to the Torah in its entirety. ☞

וּבִפְרַט שֶׁהָיָה גָּנוּז בִּימֵיהֶם, וְגַם כָּל חָכְמַת הַקַּבָּלָה הָיְתָה נִסְתָּרָה בִּימֵיהֶם וְנֶעֱלָמָה מִכָּל תַּלְמִידֵי חֲכָמִים כִּי אִם לִיחִידֵי סְגוּלָּה, וְאַף גַּם זֹאת בְּהַצְנֵעַ לֶכֶת וְלֹא בָּרַבִּים, כִּדְאִיתָא בַּגְּמָרָא (חגיגה יא,ב. יג,א).

This is **especially** the case **as it,** the *Zohar*, **was secreted in their days, and** indeed, **all the wisdom of Kabbala was concealed in their days and hidden from all Torah scholars, apart from singular individuals, and even then,** only **in private settings, not in public, as stated in the Gemara** (*Ḥagiga* 11b, 13a).

THE WHOLE TORAH IS CALLED A TREE OF LIFE

☞ In a very general sense, it can be said that the tree of knowledge represents this world, while the tree of life represents the Torah. Therefore, when discussing the tree of life, both here in the *Zohar* and elsewhere, the intent is to refer to the idea of the Torah in general. It refers to pure, unsullied divine revelation, of the divine will, wisdom, and truth that illuminate and descend in the form of inner divine light into all the worlds. The Torah is called the "Tree of Life" because it is the life force of all things, in the form of the inner will and divine pleasure within all things. In this sense, there is no distinction between the revealed Torah and the hidden Torah. The divine line, in its essence, is one, the inner truth of all, with no back side and no

9. Mishna *Avot* 5:7; *Berakhot* 32b, *Ta'anit* 7a, *Arakhin* 15b, and many other places.

The Talmud discusses the study of the hidden side of Torah, the Act of Creation and the Act of the Chariot. It is thus possible to see the role and standing of this type of Torah study in Jewish society. The approach was that since these concepts are not enclothed in our world, in our shared environment, but only within the eye of man's inner spirit, it is difficult, and nearly impossible, to pass this knowledge from one person to another. As a result, in the Gemara there, it is taught that one does not teach the Act of Creation to two people, and the Act of the Chariot to one person, etc. That is to say that these ideas are not taught except to individuals, and only if those individuals are wise and learned, able to understand these matters on their own. Only the introductory ideas are taught to those people, in a general direction, and the individual conceptual constructs should be developed personally by each person. Regardless, it appears that during those times, just like in later generations, it was not thought that every person should study the hidden aspect of Torah. Practically speaking, only select individuals studied it, and they did not do so openly. Most of the Torah scholars studied the revealed Torah, and how is it possible to say regarding their Torah, from which we all live, that it is not a "tree of life"?

וּכְמוֹ שֶׁכָּתַב הָאֲרִיזַ"ל דְּדַוְקָא בְּדוֹרוֹת אֵלּוּ הָאַחֲרוֹנִים מוּתָּר וּמִצְוָה לְגַלּוֹת זֹאת הַחָכְמָה, וְלֹא בַּדּוֹרוֹת הָרִאשׁוֹנִים וְגַם רַבִּי שִׁמְעוֹן בַּר יוֹחַאי אָמַר בַּזּוֹהַר הַקָּדוֹשׁ, שֶׁלֹּא נִיתַּן רְשׁוּת לְגַלּוֹת רַק לוֹ וְלַחֲבֵירָיו לְבַדָּם.

As the Arizal wrote, it is specifically in these later generations that it is **permitted – and** in fact **a mitzva – to reveal this wisdom, but not in the earlier generations. And Rabbi Shimon bar Yoḥai also said in the holy *Zohar* that permission was granted solely to him and his colleagues to reveal it.**

"other." Even when the Torah is enclothed in the lower worlds, it never ceases to be the pure, direct inner divine will. But in this state, there is a distinction between the revealed and the hidden Torah. Those who misunderstand this also err in their grasp of this statement of the *Zohar*. The hidden Torah does not truly become enclothed in this world (hence, it is "hidden"), and the revealed Torah is enclothed, in the good and evil and all that is in the world. As a result, it is referred to as the "Tree of Knowledge of Good and Evil."

The Arizal emphasizes[10] that specifically in these final generations it is permitted and is a commandment to study and reveal the wisdom of the Kabbala. But in the "first generations," there was no commandment to study it like the revealed Torah, and so only a select few studied it, and in a private way.[11] ☞

SPECIFICALLY IN THESE LATER GENERATIONS THAT IT IS PERMITTED AND COMMANDED TO REVEAL

☞ The perception that the hidden Torah is increasingly being revealed specifically in these final generations requires explanation. In what way were the merits and qualifications of these generations superior to those of the preceding generations? This question is compounded when a contrast is made with the general conception of the "decline of the generations" (see *Shabbat* 112b, and many other places citing the sayings of the early and later Sages), according to which the earlier generations were holier, and their grasp of Torah was deeper and broader than that of the later generations, and that darkness and divine concealment increases over the course of the progression of the generations.

Generally, there are two explanations for this (see the general ideas in *Kuntres* "On the Essence of Hasidism," by the Lubavitcher Rebbe, and similarly in *Siḥat Leil Simhat Torah* 5711, in *Torat Menaḥem*, vol. 2, p. 41): The first is that of necessity. Since in the final generations, especially during the period directly preceding the messianic era, there is an increase in darkness, that darkness cannot be nullified except through the powerful illumination of the inner aspect of Torah. An approach along these lines can be found in relation to the revelation of the Torah of Hasidism, such as in the well-known analogy shared by the author regarding the sick prince and his father, the king, who was willing to remove the most precious stone from his crown in order to grind it into a medicine that could perhaps heal his son ("*HaTamim*," booklet 2, p. 49; *Iggerot Kodesh* of Rabbi Yosef Yitzḥak Schneerson, vol. 3, p. 326 and onward, as well as elsewhere), as well as the analogy of the treasury of the king that was hidden away for the purpose of winning the war (*Torat Ḥayyim, Parashat Shemot*, p. 227 and onward; *Ma'amar Bati LeGani*, chap. 11) and elsewhere. The second is that the final generations that are nearing the messianic era are already receiving some of the revelation that will take place in the messianic era itself, which is the revelation of the inner aspect of Torah. This means that from either

---

10. This language is not found in the writings of the Arizal, and it is unclear which part of the Arizal's work is being referred to here by the author of the *Tanya*. A similar idea appears in the introduction of Rav Ḥayyim Vital to the *Sha'ar HaHakdamot* and *Etz Ḥayyim*, in the *Sha'ar Gilgulim* at the end of Introduction 15, and elsewhere. See *Kuntres Etz Ḥayyim* by the fifth Lubavitcher Rebbe, Rabbi Sholom Dovber Schneerson, chap. 13 and onward, and in the addendums.

11. A note by the Lubavitcher Rebbe: "See *Idra Rabba* at the beginning (*Zohar*

perspective, both in terms of the darkness preceding the messianic era, as well as the light during it, the further the generations progress, the greater the need as well as the capacity to study the hidden side of Torah. This idea can also be found in the words of the Messiah to the Ba'al Shem Tov in the well-known letter, in response to the question "When will my master arrive?" He answered, "This is how you will know, at the time that your learning is publicized, and is revealed in the world, and the wellsprings of what I have taught you will be spread outward, and also those others will be able to achieve unifications and ascensions, etc." (from the letter of the Ba'al Shem Tov to his brother-in-law in Israel. Printed at the beginning of the book *Keter Shem Tov*, and in other places).

This kind of process has a simple explanation. In order to grasp something that is more novel and abstract than already accepted ideas, both by individuals and by the people of Israel on a societal level, time is required to acclimate and to absorb the concepts within our awareness and social discourse. For the first generations, Kabbala was something that was otherworldly, and in order to study it, one had to actually ascend to higher worlds. In the later generations, as the hidden aspect of Torah descended, there was less need to ascend. Even someone who is here, in this world, can relate to these matters, because they are now here. It is not that previously they had not descended, and now they have, but rather, we have changed, so that before we could not see these things, and now we can.

In a certain way, it is actually the "decline of the generations" that allows for the revelation of the hidden. It is not a true "decline," but rather a decline in one sense that yields ascents when viewed differently. As is observable even in the physical world, when a person becomes weaker in one area, he gains strength in another. If one's eyesight is weakened, his other senses become more sensitive. This is also true for the powers of the soul. Although, over the progression of the generations, there was a weakening of clarity in perceiving the holy (which is what occurred during the times of the Temple and of the prophets), this led to a strengthening of other powers that had not previously existed. There is an amplification of the powers of awareness, abstraction, understanding, and contemplation of the things that we see. We now require mechanisms and structures to relate to things that were obvious in the past. This very process of seeking and constructing these mechanism leads to a revelation of what is more deeply hidden, the supernal essence within the vessels of the lower world.

There is a stage at which things are not spoken of, because they are simple and clear – "That's just the way it is." During this stage, speaking of such things is immodest; it is like a desecration of something holy. At a different stage, when there are many things that are not implicitly understood, people speak in an eloquent, complex language about things that clearly exist but can be properly comprehended by only a few. As this process progresses, the tools of understanding are increasingly improved, becoming simpler and more aligned with the person and the divine light within him. He can then perceive with simplicity and clarity what is being articulated through all these complex words.

Part 3, 127b and onward) and also other passages in the *Zohar* that take the same line as the words of Rabbi Shimon Bar Yohai."

וְאַף גַּם זֹאת פְּלִיאָה נִשְׂגָּבָה, דִּלְפִי זֶה לֹא הָיָה לִימּוּד אִיסּוּר וְהֶיתֵּר, וְכָל שֶׁכֵּן דִּינֵי מָמוֹנוֹת דּוֹחִין מִצְוַת תְּפִלָּה

Moreover, it is a great marvel, since according to this claim, that only the *Zohar* is called the "Tree of Life," **the study of** what is **prohibited and permitted, and all the more so monetary law, would not override the mitzva of prayer,**

According to this claim, that only the *Zohar* is called the "Tree of Life," and the study of *halakha* derives from the tree of knowledge of good and evil, the study of what is prohibited and permitted, which focuses on defining permitted and prohibited items, mainly foods, and all the more so monetary law, the main laws governing transactions between individuals, involving matters of this world, including cheating, lying, etc., would not override the mitzva of prayer. With regard to the laws of the prohibited and permitted (that is, legal, rather than ritual laws), there is still an observable connection between the laws and God, who commands them. In monetary law, even this connection is not visible, and all that apparently remains are the procedures that regulate commercial relationships between people, that they should not cheat or harm each other. As he says, if these matters were derived from the tree of knowledge of good and evil, they would not, in some cases, override the commandment of prayer.

Not all Torah study overrides the commandment of prayer, since prayer is like all positive commandments that cannot be fulfilled through the actions of another person. This is why prayer generally overrides Torah study. However, since there is a case (such as a person who studies Torah as his primary daily activity) in which Torah study does override prayer, this illustrates that if we compare these two areas, there is no clear preference toward prayer over Torah study.

שֶׁנִּתְקְנָה עַל פִּי סוֹדוֹת הַזֹּהַר וְיִחוּדִים עֶלְיוֹנִים לַיּוֹדְעִים, כְּרַבִּי שִׁמְעוֹן בַּר יוֹחַאי וַחֲבֵירָיו.

which was enacted on the basis of the secrets of the *Zohar* and lofty unifications, to those who know them, such as Rabbi Shimon bar Yoḥai and his colleagues.

The text of prayer that we use, even in terms of its level of basic intent, was assembled in accordance with the concepts of the hidden aspect of Torah. Prayer is fundamentally an elevation of the soul from this world to a unification with the divine,[12] and this is the purview of the hidden Torah. ☞

IN ACCORDANCE WITH THE SECRETS OF THE *ZOHAR* AND THE SUPERNAL UNIFICATIONS

☞ Prayer itself is not Torah study, neither of the hidden nor the revealed Torah. It is a separate area[13] of divine service of the soul, elevating a person and uniting him with the divine. In this sense, it is impossible to compare prayer with Torah study, as is being done here. However, the prayers that we say, in the language established by the Sages of the Great Assembly[14] (and even more so today, when the mystical side, based on the intentions shared by the Arizal, are more revealed), are prayers that are structured worded according to the secrets of the *Zohar* and supernal unifications.

The phrase "secrets and supernal unifications" refers to the secrets that are unifications and unifications that are secrets. The meaning of "unification" is "oneness," primarily between above and below. When a person performs actions or thinks thoughts through which he aligns himself with a supernal structure, he unites himself with that supernal existence, and more broadly, he unites the realities of above and below. Since the definitions and structures of above are secrets, in the sense that they relate to the higher realities and not to these lower ones, all these unifications are secrets. The great secret of lower existence is that it aligns with higher existence, and the details of this secret are included in the individual unifications of individual spoken prayers. Thus, the unifications that are known to those who study the hidden aspect of Torah are, to one degree or another, part of the realm of prayer, and one who

---

12. As is explained, the word *tefilla* (prayer) comes from the language of connective interaction, like "I engaged in a great struggle" (Gen. 30:8), and in the language of the Mishna, "One who lines a vessel" (*Keilim* 3:5. Also see *Tikkunei Zohar* 84b, "There is *tafal* with a *tet* and there is *tafal* with a *tav*"; and see the observation of the Lubavitcher Rebbe in the *Sefer HaMa'amarim*, 5709, p. 79). Similarly, prayer is described as the connection and cleaving of the soul with its source (*Torah Or* 79d), and the explanation of *tefilla* is that it connects the form to its creator (see *Ba'al Shem Tov al HaTorah, Parashat Noaḥ, Amud HaTefilla* 79).

13. Perhaps also previously, when there was no set text for prayer, and each person would simply pray using his own words and expressing his own personal feelings (see Rambam, *Sefer Ahava, Hilkhot Tefilla*, chap. 1), it could be said that prayer was not entirely separate from Torah study, even if this is true in a way that we would have difficulty recognizing. In such a situation, all the thought patterns and concepts utilized in prayer would be taken from Torah anyway, even if the language itself would differ from today's recognizable liturgy.

14. Following the language of the Mishna in *Pirkei Avot* (1:2): "The world stands

וְזֶה אֵינוֹ, כִּדְאִיתָא בַּגְּמָרָא (שבת יא,א) דְּרַבִּי שִׁמְעוֹן בֶּן יוֹחַאי וַחֲבֵירָיו, וְכָל מִי שֶׁתּוֹרָתוֹ אוּמָּנוּתוֹ, אֵין מַפְסִיקִין לִתְפִלָּה.

And yet **that is not** the case, **as it is stated in the Gemara** (*Shabbat* 11a) **that Rabbi Shimon bar Yoḥai and his colleagues, and anyone whose Torah is their vocation, do not stop for prayer.**

"One whose Torah is his vocation" implies that this is how he spends his time.[15] His whole life, including his physical life, are spent learning Torah. Therefore, just as he does not cease from learning in order to do other things, he also does not stop for prayer. It is interesting that these things were said specifically regarding Rabbi Shimon and his colleagues, who

delves into prayer is automatically involving himself in the secrets of the Torah.

For example: In the blessing of *Barukh She'amar* (which is said to have been established by the Sages of the Great Assembly based on a note that fell from the heavens),[16] there are eighty-seven (*paz*) words that, according to the hidden Torah, parallel the verse "His head is the finest gold [*paz*]." This blessing is meant to be recited while standing, parallel to the supernal form expressed by the verse "Seraphim were standing above Him," with the inner intent that there are ten praises in the blessing, parallel to the ten sayings of creation and the ten *sefirot* (*Turei Zahav* on the *Shulḥan Arukh, Oraḥ Ḥayyim* 51:1). This is also the case with more general intentions, such as when a person who is praying comes to any part of prayer and reflects on the meaning of the words he is saying. Another example is when he recites *Kedusha* and then thinks about what he knows and has learned about the concept of holiness, about the three sayings of "*Kadosh*" and the recitation of the angels who similarly say "*Kadosh*." When a person stands while reciting *Shmoneh Esrei* and contemplates the world of *Atzilut* within which he stands, and everything he knows about the world of *Atzilut*, he tries to instill these ideas into his sense of reality. Thus, when a person considers these concepts during prayer, not only is he engaging in prayer, he is also immersing himself in the realm of the secrets and inner workings of Torah.

---

upon three things: upon Torah, service, and acts of lovingkindness." Torah refers to the study of Torah, service in our times is prayer, and acts of lovingkindness are the commandments. Thus, prayer independently serves as the pillar that is divine service and is not a part of the other two categories of Torah study or performance of commandments.

15. The Lubavitcher Rebbe observes (in relation to a question someone asked him: If people did not pray every day, how could all the unifications that are required each day be fulfilled?), "See *Torah Or* 38d, 69a, and other places."

16. *Turei Zahav* commenting on the *Shulḥan Arukh, Oraḥ Ḥayyim* 51:1.

certainly knew the secrets of prayer and immersed themselves in those secrets during their prayers.

וַאֲפִילוּ כְּשֶׁעוֹסֵק בְּדִינֵי מָמוֹנוֹת, כְּרַב יְהוּדָה דְּכוּלְּהוּ תְּנוּיֵי בִּנְזִיקִין הֲוֵי וַאֲפִילוּ הָכֵי לָא הֲוֵי מְצַלֵּי אֶלָּא מִתְּלָתִין יוֹמִין לִתְלָתִין יוֹמִין, כַּד מַהְדַר תַּלְמוּדָא כִּדְאִיתָא בַּגְּמָרָא.

And this applies **even when dealing with monetary law,** as related about **Rav Yehuda, that his entire study was** focused **on** the Order of *Nezikin* [Damages], **and even so, he would pray only once every thirty days, when he reviewed his studies, as stated in the Gemara.**

This means that he would not stop his study of *Nezikin* in order to pray. Rather, he would pray once a month, after he had finished reviewing his studies, and before beginning to review them again.[17]

וּבִירוּשַׁלְמִי פֶּרֶק קַמָּא דִּבְרָכוֹת סְבִירָא לֵיהּ לְרַבִּי שִׁמְעוֹן בַּר יוֹחַאי דַּאֲפִילוּ לִקְרִיאַת שְׁמַע אֵין מַפְסִיקִין כִּי אִם מִמִּקְרָא, וְלֹא מִמִּשְׁנָה, דַּעֲדִיפֵי מִמִּקְרָא לְרַבִּי שִׁמְעוֹן בַּר יוֹחַאי.

And in the Jerusalem Talmud, the first chapter of *Berakhot*, Rabbi Shimon bar Yoḥai maintains that even for the recitation of *Shema* one stops only from the study **of the Bible, not of the Mishna, which is more important than the Bible, according to Rabbi Shimon bar Yoḥai.**

The Sages there disagree regarding the question of whether it is only for prayer that one should not stop learning (since the liturgy and times of prayer are only ordained by the Sages, not the Torah), or whether this is also true regarding the recitation of *Shema*, which is a commandment from the Torah. The opinion of Rabbi Shimon there is that one should stop learning the Written Torah in order to recite the *Shema*, but the study of Mishna (Oral Torah) should not be paused to

---

17. *Berakhot* 20a, that all his study was of the laws of damages in *Nezikin*. Also, in *Rosh HaShana* 35a, that he would pray once every thirty days, and Rashi's commentary there that he would do so because he was reviewing his Torah learning then.

recite the *Shema*. His reason is that the study of the Oral Torah, such as Mishna, is more important than the study of the Written Torah. He says this despite the fact that presumably the Written Torah is holier. The Oral Torah is more stringent with regard to the precedence of Torah study, because it has a relationship with and descent into this world and real life. Therefore, one should not stop studying the Oral Torah even for recitation of the *Shema,* despite *Shema* being a commandment from the Torah.

וְלֹא חִילֵּק בֵּין סֵדֶר זְרָעִים וּמוֹעֵד וְקָדָשִׁים טָהֳרוֹת לִנְזִיקִין

And he did not differentiate between the Orders of *Zera'im, Mo'ed, Kodashim,* and ***Taharot*** as opposed **to *Nezikin***

The Orders of *Zera'im, Mo'ed, Kodashim,* and *Taharot* are the orders that mainly focus on the commandments between a person and God. In contrast, the Order of *Nezikin* (and *Nashim*)[18] is focused primarily on commandments between one person and another, and on the framework of relationships between human beings. In other words, a large part of the Order of *Nezikin* is not at all concerned with the relationship with God, but only with the relationships between people. It includes issues like how to deal with people who cheat, steal, or harm each other. Despite this, there is no difference between the orders in terms of their importance, or the holiness of studying their Torah, which takes precedence even over the supernal unification of the recitation of *Shema*.

(וְסוֹתֵר דַּעַת עַצְמוֹ בְּרַעְיָא מְהֵימְנָא בְּכַמָּה מְקוֹמוֹת דְּמִשְׁנָה אִיהִי שִׁפְחָה כו׳ וְהַמִּקְרָא, שֶׁהוּא תּוֹרַת מֹשֶׁה, וַדַּאי עֲדִיפָא מִקַּבָּלָה, דְּאִיהִי מַטְרוֹנִיתָא, בְּרַעְיָא מְהֵימְנָא שָׁם, וְתוֹרָה שֶׁבִּכְתָב הוּא מַלְכָּא

(**and** in this regard Rabbi Shimon bar Yoḥai **contradicts his own opinion in several places in *Raya Meheimna,* that the Mishna is a handmaid…, and the Bible, which is the Torah of Moses, is certainly more important than Kabbala, as it is the queen** – as stated **in *Raya Meheimna*** there **– whereas the Written Law is the king**

18. A comment by the Lubavitcher Rebbe: "(For the reason why) he left out the order of *Nashim* here, see *Likkutei Levi Yitzḥak He'arot LeSefer HaTanya*."

The Written Torah is the king, the Kabbala is the queen, and the Mishna is the handmaid. This indicates that Kabbala, and the study of Kabbala, is more important than, and elevated above, the study of the Mishna.[19]

[דְּהַיְינוּ יְסוֹד אַבָּא הַמְלוּבָּשׁ בִּזְעֵיר אַנְפִּין, כְּמוֹ שֶׁכּוֹתֵב הָאֲרִ"י ז"ל]).

[that is, the foundation [*yesod*] of the father that is enclothed in *Zeir Anpin*, as the Arizal writes]).

The author comments here parenthetically on the words of the *Zohar*, that the Written Torah is the "king."[20] The focal point of the Written Torah is "the foundation [*yesod*] of the father that is enclothed in *Zeir Anpin*." The "foundation [*yesod*] of the father" is the bestowal of wisdom, for the father is the *sefira* of *Ḥokhma*, and *yesod* is the attribute of connection and bestowal. When it states that he is enclothed in *Zeir Anpin*, meaning in the *yesod* of *Zeir Anpin*, it signifies that the *sefira* of *Ḥokhma* is bestowing, through *yesod* of the mother, and *yesod* of *Zeir Anpin*, to the *sefira* of *Malkhut*, and the one who bestows to *Malkhut* is the king. In other words, the king that bestows to *Malkhut* is not only *Zeir Anpin*, but rather, *Zeir Anpin* is a garment to the bestower, which is *Ḥokhma*. The direct connection between *Ḥokhma* and *Malkhut* is along the lines of the verse (Prov. 3:19) "The Lord founded the earth with wisdom," as well as the language of the *Zohar* (part 3, 248b, and elsewhere): "The father founded [*yasad*] the daughter." This expresses the direct connection between *Ḥokhma* and *Malkhut*, of the bestowal of wisdom that reaches so low.[21]

וְגַם פִּלְפּוּל הַקּוּשְׁיוֹת וְתֵירוּצִים, דְּמִסִּטְרָא דְּרַע וְרוּחַ הַטּוּמְאָה

Also, regarding **the analysis of the difficulties and resolutions, which are from the side of evil and the spirit of impurity,**

19. A comment by the Lubavitcher Rebbe: "This requires study and research. See *Zohar* part 1, 27b (the introduction to *Tikkunei Zohar* 14, end of p. 1, and onward). See the explanations of the *Zohar* there (also in *Tzemaḥ Tzedek*, part 2)."

20. See *Ta'amei HaMitzvot*, at the beginning of *Parashat Va'etḥanan*, and in various other places.

21. And as will be explained later, that the Written Torah is enclothed in *Asiya*.

The difficulties and resolutions are not evil, but they still derive from the existence of evil, and of the concealment. When the inner substance of things is unclear, when the one speaking of them is not clear in his understanding of them, there are questions. Those studying them must then engage in the process of questioning and answering in order to uncover the truths concealed within. On the contrary, it is specifically the difficulties and resolutions that clarify and reveal the holy truth. This is the way that truth is uncovered from the place of concealment, evil, and impurity.[22] Nevertheless, this entire process relates to the side of concealment, to evil and impurity, and the very fact of this struggle with them testifies to their existence. ☞

אַשְׁכְּחַן בְּרַבִּי שִׁמְעוֹן בַּר יוֹחַי דְּעָסַק בֵּיהּ טוּבָא גַּם בִּהְיוֹתוֹ בַּמְּעָרָה.

we find that Rabbi Shimon bar Yoḥai dealt with them a great deal, even when he was in the cave.

Rabbi Shimon bar Yoḥai is known not only from the *Zohar*. He is one of the most respected *tanna'im*, involved in all the various issues of the revealed Torah. Even when he presumably had no reason to involve himself in the revealed Torah, since his lifestyle in that setting did

DIFFICULTIES AND RESOLUTIONS IN THE REVEALED AND THE HIDDEN

☞ In general, difficulties, disagreements, and resolutions are more common in the study of the revealed Torah than of the hidden. In the hidden Torah (obviously, on the assumption that the study is being conducted correctly, as those who are experienced with this kind of study are aware), the holiness inherent in the contents is revealed to a greater degree, and the "Giver of Torah" is more extensively present. Regarding the studied material, the learning is generally "from above to below": A statement that presents some initial form of revelation is then developed and elucidated. The questions that arise in this study are methodological questions, as a way of expressing and explaining the ideas. This is not the case with the revealed Torah: When the study is "from below," the question can be an actual starting point, a real problem from within the darkness and concealment.

22. See *Torah Or* 49a, based on the *Zohar*, part 3, 153a: "They embittered their lives with hard work, with mortar and with bricks…, 'hard work' refers to difficulties and questions; 'mortar' refers to extrapolations of leniencies and stringencies…'and bricks' refers to the clarification of *halakha*, etc."

not raise any questions of *halakha*, and no people came to ask him questions or to judge cases involving damage, his main area of study remained the revealed Torah. The cave was a type of self-contained world, within which Torah study was not engaged in according to the needs of the moment or of the outside world, but only for its own worth. The fact that Rabbi Shimon engaged there in the study of the revealed Torah illustrates that this study has intrinsic holiness and value, which is not clearly understood from the words of the *Zohar*, as will be explained further.

וְאַדְּרַבָּה, בִּזְכוּת צַעַר הַמְּעָרָה זָכָה לָזֶה, כִּדְאִיתָא בַּגְּמָרָא (שבת לג,ב) דְּאָמַר לְר׳ פִּנְחָס בֶּן יָאִיר אַכָּל קוּשְׁיָה כ״ד פֵּירוּקֵי, וְאָמַר לוֹ: אִילוּ לֹא רְאִיתַנִּי בְּכָךְ כו׳

On the contrary, he merited this by virtue of his **suffering in the cave, as it is stated in the Gemara** (*Shabbat* 32b) **that he responded with twenty-four answers to each difficulty of Rabbi Pineḥas ben Ya'ir, and he said to him: Had you not seen me in this state....**

The Talmud relates the story of how Rabbi Shimon and his son hid from the Romans, who had decreed death upon them. Over the course of thirteen years, they sat in one cave, eating the fruit of a carob tree and drinking water from a stream, both of which had been created for them. During the day, they would remove their clothing (so that they would not become worn out) and cover themselves with sand. Then, they would study Torah, and only get dressed in order to engage in prayer. When the decree against them was annulled, they emerged from the cave. Rabbi Pineḥas ben Ya'ir (who was the father-in-law[23] of Rabbi Shimon) took them to a bathhouse. When he saw Rabbi Shimon's skin that was cracked from the sand and heat, he said, "Woe is me that I have seen you in this state!" Rabbi Shimon answered, "You are blessed that you have seen me in this state, for if you had not seen me thus (enduring these types of suffering), you would not have found me thus (with this greatness in Torah)." As is further told there, before the cave, when Rabbi Shimon would ask a question, Rabbi Pineḥas

23. According to the Talmud, Rabbi Pineḥas ben Ya'ir was the son-in-law of Rabbi Shimon, and according to the *Zohar*, he was his father-in-law. There have been several resolutions to this contradiction.

ben Ya'ir would answer with him twelve answers. After their time in the cave, Rabbi Pineḥas ben Ya'ir would ask the questions, and Rabbi Shimon would answer with twenty-four answers.

Regardless, it is clear that in the cave, they immersed themselves in the difficulties and resolutions of the revealed Torah.

(וְגַם בֶּאֱמֶת עַל כָּרְחָךְ עִיקַּר עִסְקֵיהֶם בַּמְּעָרָה הָיָה תּוֹרַת הַמִּשְׁנָיוֹת ת״ר סִדְרֵי שֶׁהָיָה בִּימֵיהֶם עַד רַבֵּינוּ הַקָּדוֹשׁ

(and in truth, it is necessarily the case that **their main preoccupation in the cave was the law of the *mishnayot*, the six hundred orders that were extant in their days, until our holy Rabbi,** Rabbi Yehuda HaNasi.

Rabbi Yehuda HaNasi's great achievement when he organized the Mishna was to clarify one approach out of the numerous approaches that had accumulated over many generations.[24] But before Rabbi Shimon, in the generation prior to that of Rabbi Yehuda HaNasi, all of this multitude of approaches and opinions served as material for study.

דְּאִילּוּ סֵפֶר הַזֹּהַר וְהַתִּיקּוּנִים הָיָה יָכוֹל לִגְמוֹר בב׳ וג׳ חֳדָשִׁים, כִּי בְּוַדַּאי לֹא אָמַר דָּבָר אֶחָד ב׳ פְּעָמִים).

For he could have completed the book of the *Zohar* and the *Tikkunei Zohar* in two or three months, as he certainly did not recite anything twice).

The book of the *Zohar*, which comprises in concentrated form the hidden Torah studied by Rabbi Shimon bar Yoḥai, is not a large work, in terms of its size. Over the course of later generations, sages would sit and recite one passage of the *Zohar* over a period of months or years, in order to grasp the secrets within. But Rabbi Shimon bar Yoḥai certainly did not say these things more than once. When a person expresses to himself those things that he knows and thinks internally, in a way that it is simply a description of the basic reality of his life, he has no need to review those expressions. Just as a person does not forget the basic truths of his life, and has no uncertainty regarding them, so it is with

24. See *Ḥagiga* 14a.

someone like Rabbi Shimon, who had no uncertainty and no need to review these things a second time in order to clarify and memorize what is written in the *Zohar*. This is different from a person who comes from the outside, who reads these things and attempts to understand them, especially given that these are the secrets of the Torah. He will need to review them repeatedly, in order to fully understand them, if at all. ☞ ☞

גַּם אָמְרוּ רַבּוֹתֵינוּ ז"ל (ברכות ח,ב): מִיּוֹם שֶׁחָרַב בֵּית הַמִּקְדָּשׁ אֵין לוֹ להקב"ה אֶלָּא ד' אַמּוֹת שֶׁל הֲלָכָה בִּלְבַד.

Our Sages also stated (*Berakhot* 8b): **Since the day the Temple was destroyed, the Holy One, Blessed be He, has only the four cubits of *halakha* alone.**

TO COMPLETE IT IN TWO OR THREE MONTHS

☞ What are these two or three months? Perhaps they are analogous to the two and three months between the exodus from Egypt and the receiving of the Torah. It took two months to finish the preparations of "the forcing" and "the subdual," and in the third month, the Torah was received in a state of nullification. If this is the case, then receiving the Torah is a process that if not reviewed, takes two or three months (see the discourse given on the night of Shavuot, 1953, printed in *Torat Menaḥem*, vol. 8, p. 184).

WHILE STUDYING THE HIDDEN TORAH, HE DID NOT REPEAT ANYTHING

☞ Why is not the same thing said regarding the revealed Torah? (see the observation here in Lessons in *Tanya*, in which a question is asked and answered by the Lubavitcher Rebbe). We can answer this based on what was explained previously, that questions in the revealed Torah arise not because of a shortcoming in the person studying, but rather because of a concept's inaccessibility. This is unlike the hidden Torah, in that there is no option for a person to ascend to a higher level where everything becomes clarified for him. The wisdom that deals with the higher realities in their revealed form requires only that a person be on that level in order to see. This is not the case with the revealed Torah. Since the Torah is enclothed and revealed specifically in the lower realities, and the lower reality is wholly typified by concealment and distortion, then even when a person is within that context, he cannot see. As will be explained, in order to learn the revealed Torah, one must be below, and one who is below is by definition in a context of concealment. Lack of clarity, difficulties, and resolutions are an intrinsic aspect of the revealed Torah and cannot be omitted. In order to reveal this Torah, any person must struggle. This requires much time, and even after such efforts, many sections will still remain difficult and require resolution.

As a result, it is specifically in the study of *halakha* that the Divine Presence dwells. And that which is said, that "since the day the Temple was destroyed," will be explained shortly, as these points are primarily referring to the time of exile.

"The four cubits of *halakha*" is a definition that connects the Torah to a place. The four cubits of *halakha* are not merely a place where one learns Torah, but rather the place in which Torah is enclothed, and that is repaired by the Torah. This Torah that is enclothed in a particular place, in the material existence of this world, and which impacts and changes this place, is the conclusive *halakha*. As long as the intentions and reasons for different approaches are under discussion, the Torah is still on the levels of the spirit and the soul. Only after the *halakha* is decided, to do or not to do a particular action, does the Torah penetrate into the physical space.

5 Ḥeshvan
6 Ḥeshvan (leap year)

וְעוֹד יֵשׁ לְהַפְלִיא הַפְלֵא וָפֶלֶא: אֵיךְ אֶפְשָׁר שֶׁלִּימוֹת הַמָּשִׁיחַ לֹא יִצְטָרְכוּ לֵידַע הִלְכוֹת אִיסּוּר וְהֶיתֵּר וְטוּמְאָה וְטָהֳרָה?

Furthermore, there is an even greater cause for astonishment: How is it possible that in the days of the Messiah they will not have to know the laws of prohibited and permitted matters **and impurity and purity?**

According to this incorrect understanding of the *Zohar*, in the messianic era they will no longer study the laws of prohibited and permitted matters. This cannot be, for they will still need to have knowledge of these issues.

כִּי אֵיךְ יִשְׁחֲטוּ הַקָּרְבָּנוֹת, וְגַם חוּלִּין, אִם לֹא יֵדְעוּ הִלְכוֹת דְּרָסָה וַחֲלָדָה וְשֶׁהִיָּה הַפּוֹסְלִים הַשְּׁחִיטָה וּפְגִימַת הַסַּכִּין?

For how will they slaughter the sacrifices, or even non-consecrated animals, **if they do not know the laws of pressing** the knife, **concealing** the knife under the windpipe or the gullet, **and interrupting** the act of slaughter, **which invalidate a slaughter, or** the laws governing **the notches on a knife?**

These laws form the main body of the laws of slaughtering, and it is impossible to slaughter without knowing them.[25]

וְכִי יִוָּלֵד אִישׁ בְּטִבְעוֹ שֶׁיְּהֵא שׁוֹחֵט בְּלִי שְׁהִיָּה וּדְרָסָה? וְגַם הַסַּכִּין תִּהְיֶה בְּרִיאָה וְעוֹמֶדֶת בְּלִי פְּגִימָה לְעוֹלָם? וְעוֹד הַרְבֵּה הֲלָכוֹת, חֵלֶב וָדָם וּשְׁאָר אִיסּוּרִין

Is anybody born with the natural ability to slaughter without interrupting or pressing? And also the knife, how will they ensure that **it will remain forever in the proper state, without a notch? There are also many** similar **laws,** such as **prohibited fat, and blood, and the other prohibitions,**

Is anybody born with the natural ability to slaughter without interrupting or pressing? In the messianic era, people will be no different than they are now, and they will not have a new nature. When they will fulfill one of the commandments at that time, it will still be the result of a learning process, not an instinctive physical response. The laws of nature will not change, and a knife naturally becomes notched through use over time. One must know these matters in order to avoid them, whether they apply to consecrated or unconsecrated animals.

וְגַם טוּמְאַת הַמֵּת יִהְיוּ צְרִיכִין לֵידַע, כְּדִכְתִיב: "הַנַּעַר בֶּן מֵאָה שָׁנָה יָמוּת" (ישעיה סה,כ).

as well as the impurity of the dead, which they will have to know, as it is written: "The youth will die when he is one hundred years old" (Isa. 65:20).

This illustrates that fundamentally the world will not change. People will live for longer, in a healthy and youthful state, but there will still be death, and the impurity of death. Thus, in order to fulfill the laws of the Torah in general, and the service of the Temple specifically, they will need to know the laws of the impurity of the dead.

---

25. An observation by the Lubavitcher Rebbe: "He did not mention the laws of slaughtering within the prescribed space of the neck (*hagrama*) and avoiding tearing the esophagus and windpipe (*ikur*)." See *Rambam, Sefer Kedusha, Hilkhot Sheḥita* 1:1.

וְגַם טוּמְאַת יוֹלֶדֶת צָרִיךְ לֵידַע, כִּדְכְתִיב: "הָרָה וְיוֹלֶדֶת יַחְדָּיו" (ירמיה לא,ז) אִם תֵּלֵד אִשָּׁה בְּכָל יוֹם מִבִּיאָה אַחַת

Knowledge of the impurity of a woman after childbirth is also necessary, as it is written: "Women with child and women in childbirth together" (Jer. 31:7). Even **if a woman will give birth every day from a single act of intercourse,**

In the messianic era, a woman will give birth naturally, and according to the Torah, she will be impure following childbirth. Even if a woman will give birth every day (see *Shabbat* 30b), as this is the explanation of "women with child and women in childbirth together," that on the same day she becomes pregnant, she will give birth,[26] from a single act of intercourse,[27] that is, she will give birth every day from one previous act of intercourse.

אַף עַל פִּי כֵן, דִּין אִיסּוּר טוּמְאָתָהּ לֹא יִשְׁתַּנֶּה.

even so, the law of the prohibition of her impurity will not change.

Relationships will change, durations will change, as there will no longer be a need for nine months of pregnancy,[28] and a woman will be able to give birth multiple times from one act of intercourse. Still, the law of the prohibition of her impurity will not change. Since there will be births, impurity of birth will still exist, and the laws of purity and impurity of a woman who gives birth will still need to be known. ☞

וְאֵין לְהַאֲרִיךְ בְּדָבָר הַפָּשׁוּט, וּמְפוּרְסָם הֶפְכּוֹ בְּכָל הַשַּׁ"ס וּמִדְרָשִׁים, דְּפָרֵיךְ 'הִלְכְתָא

There is no need to elaborate on such **a simple matter, as the opposite** of the claim **is evident from the entire Talmud and the midrashim,** such **as** when

26. According to the Arizal's commentary in *Likkutei Has,* as well as Rashi and other commentaries; and see *Shiurim BeSefer HaTanya,* in the name of the Lubavitcher Rebbe, which deals with these issues at length.

27. The Lubavitcher Rebbe explains that the author of the *Tanya* is adding this. For if the laws of purity and impurity are unchanged, it is impossible that there would be a new act of intercourse each day, as the woman would still be in a state of impurity from the birth of the previous day.

28. See *Likkutei HaShas,* there.

לִמְשִׁיחָא?' they ask: "Does one issue a ***halakha*** for **the messianic** era?"

In the future the laws of the Torah will not be nullified, and there will be a need to assess each situation according to the laws and principles of the Oral Law in the form in which we currently possess it.[29]

This is like what the Sages are saying when they ask: "Does one issue a halakha for the messianic era?"[30] This means: "Do we issue a halakhic ruling regarding that which will only be true in the messianic era?"

THERE IS NO DIFFERENCE BETWEEN THIS WORLD AND THE DAYS OF THE MESSIAH

☞ The basic perspective here, as was mentioned in the *Zohar* previously, is that there is no difference between nowadays and the messianic era except for subordination to the gentile kingdoms. This means that the nature of the world as we know it currently will not change during the messianic era. Despite this, the author here is referring to biblical verses and statements of our Sages (relating to the messianic era) that apparently depict a deviation from the natural order with which we are familiar. The answer to this is that while the natural order in these statements "extends" beyond what is familiar to us, these new outcomes are not entirely outside the boundaries of the natural order. It is specifically in our times that our understanding of this is greater than it was in previous generations, as things that previously would have been regarded as impossible miracles are now commonplace. Accordingly, it appears that what transpires today is merely a minor preparation for what will take place in the messianic era, which will differ more significantly. The laws of nature are exactly as described here: things to which the laws of the Torah still apply. The author is intentionally emphasizing these points because he is trying to explain that the revealed Torah is not just part of a particular state of good and evil. Rather, it is part of the eternal holy Torah, on the level of the tree of life that is beyond today's temporary chaotic mix of good and evil. Therefore, it is important to emphasize that even in the messianic era, even beyond the natural world that we know, and even in a reality of supernal holiness, when evil will become a purely theoretical entity, as merely an accessory and underpinning of holiness, all this will still be encompassed within the realm of the revealed Torah, the same Torah in which we are engaged today.

---

29. A similar perspective can be found in the words of our Sages regarding the patriarchs who lived before the giving of the Torah at Mount Sinai, and even with regard to the angelic hosts and God Himself, that it is as if they are all bound by the laws and principles of the Oral Law with which we are familiar.

30. *Sanhedrin* 51b, *Zevaḥim* 45a, and *Tosafot* there.

This illustrates that even according to those who think that nowadays we should not issue rulings relating to the messianic era (for there are some halakhic authorities who did issue such rulings, like the Rambam and other Torah leaders who followed in his path), nevertheless, in the messianic era, they will certainly need to issue rulings and know the *halakha*.

וְ'אֵלִיָּהוּ בָּא לִפְשׁוֹט כָּל הַסְּפֵיקוֹת', וּ'פָּרָשָׁה זוֹ עָתִיד אֵלִיָּהוּ לְדוֹרְשָׁהּ כו'"

and "Elijah is coming to resolve all uncertainties," and "Elijah will interpret this passage...."

These expressions are from the Talmud: "Elijah is coming to resolve all uncertainties,"[31] and "Elijah will interpret this passage."[32] Elijah will arrive in the messianic era and resolve uncertainties in *halakha*. From this we can understand that we will continue to engage in *halakha*, both to study it, as will be explained, and also in order to know how to act in practice.

וְעוֹד אֵינוֹ מוּבָן מַה שֶּׁנֶּאֱמַר דְּלָא יִתְפַּרְנְסוּן תַּלְמִידֵי חֲכָמִים מֵעַמֵּי הָאָרֶץ כו' וְלָא מֵעֵרֶב רַב דְּאָכְלִין פָּסוּל טָמֵא וְאָסוּר חַס וְשָׁלוֹם.

In addition, the meaning of **the statement** cited above from the *Zohar*, **that Torah scholars will not receive their sustenance from the ignorant..., nor from the mixed multitude, who eat disqualified, impure, and prohibited** food, **God forbid, is unclear.**

The implication is that apparently, in the future, the Torah scholars will not receive their sustenance from the ignorant, but rather they will sustain themselves from the side of holiness alone.

"God forbid" is an addition by the author of the *Tanya* that relates to

31. See *Tosfot Yom Tov*, end of *Eduyyot*; Shelah, *Torah She'Be'al Peh*, and elsewhere, that every time the Talmud says "*teku*" (regarding disagreements and uncertainties that have no resolution), it is an acronym for "*Tishbi* will resolve these difficulties and questions."

32. See *Menaḥot* 45a and *Bava Metzia* 114a–b.

the "first impression" presented here, as if impure and prohibited things are actually eaten, which is certainly a reprehensible thing to say.

שֶׁהֲרֵי תַּלְמִידֵי חֲכָמִים שֶׁבִּזְמַן בֵּית שֵׁנִי לֹא הָיוּ מִתְפַּרְנְסִין מֵעַמֵּי הָאָרֶץ דְּאָכְלִין פָּסוּל אָסוּר חַס וְשָׁלוֹם. שֶׁהָיָה לָהֶם שָׂדוֹת וּכְרָמִים כְּעַמֵּי הָאֲרָצוֹת

For Torah scholars in the times of the Second Temple did not receive their sustenance from the ignorant, who would eat disqualified and **pro-hibited** food, **God forbid, as they owned fields and vineyards like the ignorant** did,

It appears that at that time there was no separation between Torah scholars and the ignorant in the sense that the ignorant would provide the sustenance while Torah scholars only studied. Rather, even the scholars would support themselves through their own efforts like the ignorant.

וַאֲפִילוּ הָכֵי הָיוּ עוֹסְקִין בְּלִימּוּד אִיסּוּר וְהֶיתֵּר וְטוּמְאָה וְטָהֳרָה כָּל הַזּוּגוֹת שֶׁהָיוּ בִּימֵי בַּיִת שֵׁנִי, וְהֶעֱמִידוּ תַּלְמִידִים לַאֲלָפִים וּרְבָבוֹת

and even so, all the Pairs from the times of the Second Temple were engaged in the study of prohibited and permitted matters **and impurity and purity, and they established thousands and myriads of disciples,**

Even though the scholars did not depend on the ignorant for their physical needs, all the Pairs, the scholars listed at the beginning of Mishna *Avot*, from the times of the Second Temple were engaged in the study of prohibited and permitted matters and impurity and purity, and they established thousands and myriads of disciples in the study of the revealed Torah. This illustrates that study of this kind was not only appropriate for the ignorant, but was equally relevant to the scholars themselves.

וְלִימּוּד הַנִּסְתָּר בְּהֶסְתֵּר כוּ'.

and yet **the study of esoteric mat-ters was** conducted **in secret....**

It was in the days of the Second Temple and onward, which were the times of the *tanna'im* and *amora'im*, that the Oral Torah in the format with which we are familiar was formed. As is explained here, the main focus of Torah study at that time was the revealed Torah – prohibited and permitted matters, impurity and purity, etc. Study of the hidden Torah was conducted in secret, and this activity was not discussed, nor perpetuated for future generations.

Until this point, the author of the *Tanya* has been illustrating in a simple manner, without delving into any deeper meaning, that there is no basis whatsoever to the notion that the study of the hidden aspect of Torah opposes that of the revealed Torah, as the tree of life opposes the tree of knowledge. Such an idea is inconsistent with historical reality, as well as the most fundamental perspectives regarding Torah and its study.

After the author of the *Tanya* explained at length what is *not* claimed in the *Raya Meheimna*, he discusses what *is* stated there. For these ideas, the author will provide an inner explanation of the nature of these things: the nature of the revealed Torah, the hidden Torah, and Torah study. He will begin his explanation with an implication gleaned from the language of the *Raya Meheimna*.

6 Ḥeshvan
7 Ḥeshvan (leap year)

אַךְ בֶּאֱמֶת כְּשֶׁתְּדַקְדֵּק בִּלְשׁוֹן רַעְיָא מְהֵימְנָא דִּלְעֵיל, וְאִילָנָא דְּטוֹב וָרַע דְּאִיהוּ אִיסּוּר וְהֶיתֵּר כו׳, וְלֹא אָמַר ׳תּוֹרַת אִיסּוּר וְהֶיתֵּר׳ אוֹ ׳הִלְכוֹת אִיסּוּר וְהֶיתֵּר׳, אֶלָּא רוֹצֶה לוֹמַר דְּגוּף דָּבָר הָאָסוּר וְדָבָר הַמּוּתָּר הוּא מֵאִילָנָא דְּטוֹב וָרַע

However, in truth, when you examine closely the language of the above citation from ***Raya Meheimna***: **"And the tree of** knowledge of **good and evil, which is** the topics of **prohibited and permitted** matters…," you will see that **it does not state "the Torah of prohibited and permitted" or "the laws of prohibited and permitted." Rather, it means that the prohibited item itself – and the permitted item – is from the tree of** knowledge of **good and evil,**

When the *Zohar* states that prohibited and permitted things belong to the tree of knowledge of good and evil, it is not relating to the Torah that analyzes such prohibited and permitted things. Rather, it relates to the real existence of things that are prohibited or permitted. Certainly, the Torah instructs us as to what is prohibited and permitted, but the Torah itself is not part of the realm of the prohibited and permitted. The Torah relates to one thing only: to the will and wisdom of God. Just as these are holy, so is the Torah holy, no matter what subject the Torah is discussing. The Torah which says "permitted" is holy, and the Torah which says "prohibited" is holy, just like the Torah that says "God is one" is holy. Given this, the Torah is not from the tree of knowledge of good and evil, because a holy reality is separated from evil. In contrast, the tree of knowledge of good and evil is, in its very definition, a reality that is not separated from evil.

If this is so, then what is that reality in which evil exists, if not always in actuality, at least in potential? What is this reality of the tree of knowledge of good and evil? Does it have another side?

The answer to this question, based on the writings of the Arizal, is the key to the continuation of this letter.

שֶׁהוּא 'קְלִיפַּת נוֹגַהּ' כְּמוֹ שֶׁכָּתוּב בְּעֵץ חַיִּים.	**which is *kelippat noga,* as is written in *Etz Ḥayyim.***

Etz Ḥayyim[33] speaks of the *kelippat noga* as the reality that exists between holiness and the *kelippot.* It is explained there that there is such a *kelippa* in all the worlds. But in *Atzilut,* it is a reality that is wholly good, while the other worlds contain a mix of good and evil, which is the tree of knowledge of good and evil. ☞

THE TREE OF KNOWLEDGE OF GOOD AND EVIL – WHICH IS THE *KELIPPAT NOGA*

☞ The reality that consists of good and evil, prohibited and permitted, impure and pure, is a unique reality in the spiritual worlds. This reality exists only on the edge of total concealment, in the "no-man's-land" that belongs neither to the *kelippa,* nor to the realm of holiness. This area is called "*kelippat noga*" by the kabbalists. In the language of the talmudic Sages, there is a concept that parallels this area, the area of "*ḥullin*" (profane entities).[34] *Ḥullin* are not evil, but they are also not holy. They are that thin region in between, in a unique state, in the line of tension that runs between holiness and the *kelippa.* This realm of *ḥullin* characterizes the reality of the world within which we live: the body and soul, the heavens and the

33. *Etz Ḥayyim, Sha'ar* 49 (*Sha'ar Kelippat Noga*), chaps. 1–2.
34. See *Torah Or* 12b and onward.

After an explanation has been given that this realm of the tree of knowledge is the realm of the *kelippat noga* and about the struggle to separate out good from evil, the meaning of what was said, that it is "prohibited and permitted," is clear, for this is the reality of this world, that it contains that which is prohibited and that which is permitted.

וְזֶהוּ לְשׁוֹן 'אָסוּר', שֶׁהַקְּלִיפָּה שׁוֹרָה עָלָיו וְאֵינוֹ יָכוֹל לַעֲלוֹת לְמַעְלָה כַּדָּבָר הַמּוּתָּר, דְּהַיְינוּ שֶׁאֵינוֹ קָשׁוּר וְאָסוּר בַּקְּלִיפָּה

And this is the meaning of **the term** ***asur***, "prohibited," **that the** ***kelippa*** **resides over it, and it cannot ascend upward like the permitted item, namely that which is not tied and bound** [***asur***] **to the** ***kelippa,***

"Prohibited" and "permitted" are meant here in their semantic sense. "*Asur*" (bound) means to be tied[35] to the *kelippa* with no way to separate from it. "*Mutar*" (released) refers to that which is not tied, or that the shackles imprisoning the being were opened so that it could ascend. ☞

earth, the material and the spiritual, the plants, animals, and inanimate objects. All of these are part of the world of *ḥullin*. Holiness is on one side, impurity on the other, and these are the options that stand before us in our world.

"PROHIBITED," THAT THE *KELIPPA* RESIDES OVER IT

☞ A *kelippa* is not something separate, external, like an independent entity of evil in contrast to holiness. A *kelippa* is a state in which something exists, such that in that state, the entity either conceals or reveals. When that entity is in opposition to the will of God, against the divine wisdom, against love, its own existence is what conceals, not anything else. In this state, the entity is imprisoned (*asur*), unable to ascend and connect to holiness. It can only wait for a different state and world to arrive, in which it will be unbound (*mutar*). Something which is unbound is that which is in a state of synchrony with the will of God. In this state, there is a path through which the various vessels and screens can be raised up, not concealing the Divine, but revealing the inner divine will. Any entity on this path, whether things or people, is raised up through this to spiritual heights.

35. Like "the place where Joseph was incarcerated" (Gen. 40:3) and "If they bind me with new ropes" (Judg. 16:11).

וְיוּכַל לַעֲלוֹת עַל יְדֵי הָאָדָם **but can ascend by means of the person**

As explained previously, forbidden (*asur*) and permitted (*mutar*) are not adjectives to describe something, but definitions attributed to a person. They describe whether a person is able to elevate something to holiness in a particular situation or not.

The distinction between prohibited and permitted is the distinction between *kelippat noga* and the impure *kelippot*. Prohibited things are part of the impure *kelippa* because they are confined (*asur*) in their concealment, and a person is unable to repair them. Permitted things are the *kelippat noga*, not holy, but a person can elevate them to holiness. Despite this, here the definitions of *asur* and *mutar* are actually both of *kelippat noga*. They both express the concept of optionality, and the option to be prohibited or permitted is the meaning of *kelippat noga*. It is specifically within this reality of *kelippat noga*, since it is not an objective reality but is subjectively related to a person, that a person can accomplish something. The prohibited is the option to descend into the *kelippa* of impurity, and the permitted is the option to ascend to holiness.

הָאוֹכְלוֹ בְּכַוָּונָה לַה' **who eats it with the intention of** serving **God,**

The example of prohibited and permitted presented here is that of eating.[36] There are foods that are prohibited to eat and those that are permitted to eat. The prohibited ones cannot be elevated, and therefore they are not to be consumed. But even with regard to the permitted ones, it is not sufficient to just casually consume them. The rule is that in order to elevate something spiritually, the one raising (the person differentiating the holiness from the mundane) must be higher than the entity being raised (differentiated). When a person eats in order to eat, without any deeper intent or connection to higher spiritual

36. This is the accepted and typical example in kabbalistic and hasidic writings. It is also found in *Likkutei Amarim*, chap. 7; and see *Torah Or, Parashat Ḥayei Sara*; *Likkutei Torah*, Lev. 7:2 and 13:2; Num. 26:3 and 81:2; Deut. 14:1. *Derekh Mitzvotekha*, p. 90a; and elsewhere.

realities, then he is like the very food which he eats, and he will not elevate anything to higher states. Spiritual ascent begins when a person places himself in a higher place with his intentions, thoughts, and actions. There are two main levels to this. The first, the more ideal, is one who "eats it with the intention of serving God." This means that the person has no personal intent or desire in the eating, only that the existence of the food should be elevated and connected to God, each food item according to its place and level in the spiritual worlds. ☞

וְגַם בִּסְתָם כָּל אָדָם הָעוֹבֵד ה' **or through any person who is simply serving God,**

This refers to the second level, at which a person is not spiritually capable of attaining the first level. This level applies to any person at any time, even when he is not able to think about God directly and about connecting to God, like when he is tired or hungry, or distracted by the issues and events of the world. In such situations, his mental space is constricted, and unable to relate to the Divine. But even such a person, if generally in his life he is a "servant of God," seeing himself as a servant, and striving to live accordingly, has another path.

שֶׁבְּכֹחַ הָאֲכִילָה הַהִיא לוֹמֵד וּמִתְפַּלֵּל לַה' **as through the strength of that consumption he studies and prays to God.**

Although currently he is not able to directly focus his intentions toward serving God, as this requires mental clarity that is not always available, nevertheless he can still say to himself: I am weak, and I am eating now

HE EATS IT WITH INTENTION OF SERVING GOD

☞ When a person has this superior intent, his concentration is focused on the action he is performing, not as a preparation for any other action (or commandment), but only on this entity that he is elevating, and through which he is ascending to holiness. There is nothing higher than this level in service of God, and a person who lives his life in this way is on the level of "chariot." It is the level of the great and righteous people, people who made every movement, in body and soul, only for God. Even if a person cannot do this perfectly throughout his whole life, or even not for one day or in performing one action, a person can accomplish this for at least part of an action, or with a partial intention, in order to occasionally ascend this way.

in order that I will have strength afterward to study Torah and pray to God. The conception is that the studying and praying are holy. When he links his eating to them, even if he is not directly eating to serve God, he is still elevating his eating and the food to holiness.

Additionally, even when he eats with no intention at all, even if he forgot that he ate, but if he later studies Torah and prays, and he does so as a result of the strength he derived from that eating, it retroactively indicates that the eating was linked to the side of holiness, and when his Torah and prayers ascend, so will the eating and the food.

וְנִמְצָא שֶׁנַּעֲשָׂה אוֹתִיּוֹת הַתּוֹרָה וְהַתְּפִלָּה הָעוֹלָה לַה׳ מִכֹּחַ הַנִּבְרָר מֵהַמַּאֲכָל הַהוּא.

It thus **turns out that the letters of the Torah and prayer, which ascend to God, are formed from the strength that is extracted from that food.**

Torah and prayer are enclothed in letters. We learn Torah and pray using letters, and in general, we think and speak in that same way as well. These letters serve to connect prayer and Torah not only to the soul, which feels and thinks using the letters, but also to the body, which speaks and thinks using the letters.[37] Additionally, there is the aspect of the world that the body employs in order to express the letters, like the food which it eats in order to gain strength to articulate the letters. Since the letters are letters of Torah and prayer, they relate to that which is above, and ascend upward, with the person and the food he consumes. ☞

THE LETTERS OF TORAH AND PRAYER THAT ASCEND TO GOD

☞ On the more internal plane, a person comprehends and feels the limits of what he is, and therefore what he does (and eats) does not ascend, diverging from its hierarchical place (it does slightly, when he himself ascends, but that is not the point being discussed here). That which generally does ascend, and ascends to *Ein Sof*, are the letters alone. The letters that a person recites (without the actual content of what he is thinking), when he is studying Torah or praying, are the same letters of the divine speech that carry the divine wisdom, will, and love that we can never

37. As the author of the *Tanya* quotes in many places, in the name of the Sages of the Talmud, that the "movement of his lips is considered an action" (*Sanhedrin* 65a; and see *Bava Metzia* 90b, and later in epistle 29, and other places).

וְזֶהוּ בַּחוֹל **That is** the case **on weekdays.**

Weekdays are the time of labor,[38] in contrast to the Sabbath, which is the time for rest. On the wider scope, weekdays represent the time of this world, which is the phase of "to do them,"[39] the actions of extracting the sparks from the world of *tohu*, as opposed to the future time which will be to "receive their reward." Therefore, the eating referenced until now, of service and refinement, is the eating of the weekdays.

אֲבָל בְּשַׁבָּת, שֶׁיֵּשׁ עֲלִיָּה לִקְלִיפַּת נוֹגַהּ בְּעַצְמָהּ עִם הַחִיצוֹנִיּוֹת שֶׁבְּכָל הָעוֹלָמוֹת **However, on Shabbat, the *kelippat noga* itself ascends, together with the externality which is in all the worlds.**

On Shabbat, when *borer* (separating and differentiating mixed objects) is prohibited, there is no spiritual differentiating either. *Borer* is one of the primary forms of labor prohibited on the Sabbath, even in the spiritual form, and the Sabbath is a time of rest in which one may not engage in forms of creative labor. The inner, spiritual reason for the prohibition of *borer* on the Sabbath, is that these things are not necessary. The days of the week, the days of this world, the mundane days, are the reality of the *kelippat noga*. During these days, the permitted entity, when left alone, resides down below, in this world, in the *kelippat noga*. In order to connect it to holiness, it must be differentiated, and then elevated from the *kelippa*. But on the Sabbath, the kelippat noga itself ascends, together with the externality which is in all the worlds. This means that the whole level of *kelippat noga* ascends to holiness

comprehend. We can detect a hint of this, a hint of a hint, in the experience through which we send the letters upward. As it famously states in *Tikkunei Zohar* 25b: "Torah without fear and love does not ascend upward." See also *Likkutei Amarim*, chap. 16; *Reshimot Devarim*, vol. 1, p. 55.

---

38. For a general treatment of this topic, of eating during the week and on the Sabbath, see *Torah Or, Parashat Ḥayei Sara*, 15c.

39. Based on the verse "...today to do them" (Deut. 7:11), and the Sages derive from this: "Today (in this world) to do them, and tomorrow (in the World to Come) to receive their reward" (*Eiruvin* 22a).

through the holiness of the Sabbath, and therefore, there is no need for the labor of differentiation and elevation of things from within the *kelippat noga.* ☞

לָכֵן מִצְוָה לֶאֱכוֹל כָּל תַּעֲנוּגִים בְּשַׁבָּת וּלְהַרְבּוֹת בְּבָשָׂר וְיַיִן אַף שֶׁבַּחוֹל נִקְרָא זוֹלֵל וְסוֹבֵא.

It is therefore a mitzva to eat all delights on Shabbat, and to increase one's consumption **of meat and wine, even though** one who did this **on a weekday would be called a glutton and a drunkard.**

Things that are only "permitted" during the week are "commandments" on the Sabbath. The difference is that during the week, the permitted can be elevated to higher levels, through our efforts of thoughts and intent at the time of consumption. If someone fails to have this intent, the eating remains in the realm of the *kelippa* (called "a glutton and a drunkard"). On the Sabbath, the eating is itself a commandment, and not of *kelippat noga*. The commandment is intrinsically holy, and there is no need to differentiate it from the *kelippa*. All that is required is that we do the action, and in this example, that just means to eat.

Despite this distinction, in a commandment there is still room for

BUT ON THE SABBATH, THERE IS AN ASCENDING

☞ As is known, the inner reality of the Sabbath is that it is a time in which the various spiritual worlds ascend. An analogy that is cited in a number of places (e.g., *Torah Or* 9b, and elsewhere; see also *Torah Or* 16c): When a person is involved in his labors, he lowers his intellect and attention to that physical entity with which he is involved. When he rests from that labor, these attributes return and ascend to his soul, to become thoughts, feelings, and understandings within himself. Additionally, within his soul, he ascends from his external relationships with the world around him to the internal relationship he has with himself, until he is fully immersed in the essence of his soul. This is true regarding the spiritual worlds as well. On the Sabbath, when God rests from the labors of creating the worlds, all the worlds ascend from the profane reality and *kelippat noga* to holiness. They transition from their external existence to the deeper, internal existence, ascending upward from below. Given this, that which was only "permitted" during the week, profane things and the *kelippat noga*, ascend on the Sabbath to become holy and commanded. This ascent is not one of labor and differentiation through human effort, as it is during the week. Rather, it takes place on its own. The arrival of the Sabbath, and the resting of God, lead to this mass ascent.

intent, to have the intent toward heaven, not in order to differentiate the eating from the *kelippa,* but for the ascent. As is explained elsewhere, a commandment, and even the Torah, without love and fear [*deḥilu ureḥimu*], which are the essence of intent, does not ascend upward. The higher the intent, and the underlying thoughts and connections to the soul, the higher the commandment ascends. ☞

After the explanation of the idea of that which is permitted, and how to differentiate it and raise it from the *kelippa,* the concept of the prohibited will now be explained.

מַה שֶּׁאֵין כֵּן בִּדְבַר אִיסּוּר, שֶׁאֵינוֹ יָכוֹל לַעֲלוֹת לֹא בְּשַׁבָּת וְלֹא בַּחוֹל גַּם כְּשֶׁמִּתְפַּלֵּל וְלוֹמֵד בְּכֹחַ הַהוּא

This is not the case with regard to a prohibited item, which cannot ascend either on Shabbat or on a weekday, even if one prays and studies through that strength,

The prohibited entity, in contrast to the permitted, is not part of the *kelippat noga,* so that it can ascend. Rather, it is part of the impure *kelippa,* so that the holiness within it is bound up, and cannot be released to ascend at all.

Even if one prays and studies through that strength. In contrast to

A COMMANDMENT TO EAT PLEASURABLE FOODS

☞ It is a commandment not only to eat on the Sabbath, but to enjoy the eating. Therefore, the commandment is to partake of many things that enhance pleasure, like meat and wine, or desserts. The inner reason for this is the highest and most essential expression is pleasure, in the Divine, the worlds, and the soul. In this sense, the pleasure one experiences from food expresses the divine spark within all things, the point of light and its connection with *Ein Sof.* It is true that when the worlds descend, in the breaking of the vessels, etc., pleasure falls as well, and gives life to the lower worlds of the *kelippa.* Here, however, we are discussing pleasure in commandments, in the "joy of commandments," in which the pleasure is in its proper, supernal place, like the pleasure in the Divine specifically. When a person derives pleasure from food on the Sabbath (and more broadly, from any commandment, which is referred to as the "joy of the commandment"; see *Torah Or* 46c; *Likkutei Torah, Vayikra* 20:3, as well as *Devarim* 43: 1, and elsewhere), through his own pleasure he connects the divine point within himself to the pleasure of the Divine, beyond all things. It can be said that the "service" of the soul on the Sabbath (and in a certain way, in every commandment), is the pleasure that a person has from eating, and the joy through which he fulfills the commandment.

that which is permitted, whose consignment to good or evil is dependent on the person's relationship with it, the prohibited is the essence of *kelippa*, which cannot be changed irrespective of the relationship and intentions of a person toward it. Even if a person intends, in consuming something prohibited, that it should be for the sake of Heaven, even if a person then studies Torah through the strength gained from the prohibited sustenance – the prohibited entity remains prohibited and embedded in the *kelippa*.

As was explained, the elevation of a permitted action is through the power of the soul. When a soul is attached at a very high point, both in intent and feeling, this soul then raises up the actions of the person to this level as well. This is not the case regarding a prohibited action, on which the soul's relationship to a person has no impact. This is comparable to trying to convince and emotionally move stones. In fact, it is even worse than this, for the prohibited thing will not only remain prohibited, but it will also ultimately impact and taint the intent of the person engaging with it, as well as the "benefits" of the Torah study and prayer that are powered by it. ☞

אִם לֹא שֶׁאָכַל לְפִיקּוּחַ נֶפֶשׁ שֶׁהִתִּירוּ רַבּוֹתֵינוּ ז״ל וְנַעֲשָׂה הֶיתֵּר [גָּמוּר].

unless he ate it **due to a life-threatening circumstance that was permitted by our Rabbis and** thus **turned into a [completely] permitted** food.

A PROHIBITED THING THAT CANNOT ASCEND

☞ The points raised here more clearly delineate the boundaries between holiness and impurity, intent and action. When these boundaries are unclear, questions arise, usually in the context of impurity: Can there be such a thing as a sin for the sake of Heaven? There is not only a temptation to seek permission for a sin; it is deeper and more serious than this. As is explained in many places, specifically below, in the place of the *kelippot* there are very powerful and primitive forces (these are the sparks of the world of *tohu* that fell during the shattering of the vessels). It occurs to someone occasionally that if he could free these forces, he could achieve a shortcut to holiness. This shortcut could benefit himself, as well as the process of rectification of all the worlds. This kind of question also arises less sharply: Until what point, if any, does the end justify the means? The goal of rectifying the worlds is certainly holiness. The question is whether it is possible to cut small corners for the sake of this tremendous goal. The answer to all these questions in Torah is clear: The

What does this observation add to our discussion? Firstly, it teaches that the idea of something being prohibited is not some kind of rigid divine decree regarding some entity, so that it can never be raised to holiness. As was explained, prohibited and permitted are, to some extent, a function of the specific situation. In many situations, the prohibited cannot be elevated, but situations can change.[40] We do not always know how or when, and these kinds of changes may not always be under our control. However, times do arise in which such things happen. ☞

אֲבָל הַלִּימּוּד בַּתּוֹרָה, אַף הִלְכוֹת אִיסּוּר וְהֶיתֵּר טוּמְאָה וְטָהֳרָה, שֶׁהֵם הַמִּשְׁנָיוֹת וּבָרַיְיתוֹת שֶׁבַּגְּמָרָא וּפוֹסְקִים הַמְבָאֲרִים וּמְבָרְרִים דִּבְרֵיהֶם לַהֲלָכָה לְמַעֲשֶׂה

However, the study of Torah, including the laws of prohibited and permitted matters and **impurity and purity, which are the *mishnayot* and *baraitot* that** are discussed **in the Gemara, and the authorities who explain and clarify their statements for** the purpose of **practical rulings,**

However, the study of Torah, not only of the book of the *Zohar* and other kabbalistic works, is not included in the category of the "Tree of Knowledge of Good and Evil."

When studying *halakha* in order to practice it, the Torah penetrates

status of something as prohibited does not change as a result of good intentions, and not as a result of good outcomes either. Prohibited stays prohibited, and cannot ascend, neither itself, nor anything that is connected to or derives from it.

COMPLETELY

☞ Regarding the word "completely," which is in square brackets, the Lubavitcher Rebbe points out that there are printings of the *Tanya* in which this word does not appear. He explains that while the prohibited is permitted in such contexts, the ill effects of the prohibited food upon the soul remain (see Ramban, Lev. 11:13). As a result, there is reason to remove the word "completely" (see *Likkutei Siḥot*, vol. 3, p. 984, which appears as an appendix in Lessons in *Tanya* to this letter).

40. Such as in *Yoma* 82a, and in the halakhic decision of the *Shulḥan Arukh, Oraḥ Ḥayyim* 617.

in the world of physical, practical application, touching things that are prohibited and permitted. Therefore, the author emphasizes here that when studying the laws that deal with the prohibited and permitted, there is no mixing together of good and evil.

הֵן הֵן, גּוּפֵי תוֹרָה שֶׁבְּעַל פֶּה **these are themselves the essence of the Oral Law,**

Moreover, these *halakhot* are not merely an addendum to the Torah, implied outgrowths of its concepts in the world of action, but rather, it is specifically these that are themselves the essence of the Oral Law. It is specifically these laws, which are the main parts of the Oral Torah, that touch the physical world. The essence of the Oral Law is the idea of bringing the Torah into the world: How does it appear there? What is the image, the physical, tangible form taken by the divine will and wisdom? The practical *halakha* is the primary method of constructing this, taking form in the lowest parts of existence, the thoughts and actions of this physical world. It is only from here, from the edge, that a projection of this finite reality can be transmitted to all the worlds, of the ideal relationship with Torah and holiness. Therefore, it is specifically the practical *halakha* that is the essential part of the Oral Law.

The Oral Torah is divine essence that is unified with the Divine, yet is able to descend to any place. It reaches the material realm, and even the prohibited and impure. Despite this, it always remains divine, holy. In order to understand this, the author will relate to another principle, one which comes from a different aspect of the Oral Law.

שֶׁהִיא סְפִירַת מַלְכוּת דַּאֲצִילוּת כִּדְאִיתָא בַּזּוֹהַר הַקָּדוֹשׁ בִּמְקוֹמוֹת אֵין מִסְפָּר, וּבְרֵישׁ תִּיקּוּנִים מַלְכוּת פֶּה, תּוֹרָה שֶׁבְּעַל פֶּה קָרֵינָן לָהּ.

which is the *sefira* of *Malkhut* of *Atzilut*, as stated in innumerable places in the holy *Zohar*, and at the beginning of *Tikkunei* Zohar: The *Malkhut* that is mouth [*peh*; speech], **we call it the Oral Law** [*Torah shebe'al peh*].

Generally, the Torah is, in a certain way, like the *sefirot* of the world of *Atzilut*: It is a force and revelation of pure and whole divinity, completely transparent and subservient to the Divine. Of all the *sefirot*, *Malkhut* is unique in that it not only transmits the divine abundance flowing through, it also expresses that which is received from this divine abundance. This is similar to the difference between the Written and Oral Torah.[41] The Written Torah expresses the will and wisdom of God, what He thinks, and what He wants to say to us. The Oral Torah, like the *sefira* of *Malkhut*, expresses that which we and the world hear and understand, at any particular time or place: what so-and-so manages to understand, what moves him, drives him. The novelty of the Oral Torah and, in a certain way, of all of Judaism, is that the Oral Torah is also holy Torah!

In order to understand this connection between the Oral Torah and the *sefira* of *Malkhut*, the author will further explain the nature of the *sefira* of *Malkhut* of *Atzilut* and its connection with the *sefirot* above it.

And in *Atzilut*, He and His attributes are one in them. That is, that the light of *Ein Sof*, blessed be He, is unified in *Atzilut*, in the ultimate union,

וּבַאֲצִילוּת אִיהוּ וְגַרְמוֹהִי חַד בְּהוֹן דְּהַיְינוּ שֶׁאוֹר אֵין סוֹף בָּרוּךְ הוּא מִתְיַיחֵד בַּאֲצִילוּת בְּתַכְלִית הַיִּחוּד

The meaning of the statement, "in *Atzilut*, He and His attributes are one in them,"[42] is that the light of *Ein Sof*, blessed be He, is unified in *Atzilut*, in the ultimate union. The world of *Atzilut* is not like the other worlds. It is not really a world in the normal sense, because God, *Ein Sof*, is not concealed there. Additionally, there is a certain amount of revelation of the Divine (in the ten *sefirot*). How is this possible? It is because the vessels (the *sefirot*) of the world of *Atzilut* are unified completely with the Divine that is revealed through them. They have no independent existence, no other revelation, neither in light nor in vessel, other than the revelation of the divine Self.

41. The quote in the text is from Introduction to *Tikkunei Zohar* 17:1 (the section entitled "Elijah Began").

42. Introduction to the *Tikkunei Zohar* 3:2. See previously at the beginning of epistle 20, the explanation of this statement in its entirety.

שֶׁהוּא וּרְצוֹנוֹ וְחָכְמָתוֹ הַמְלוּבָּשִׁים בְּדִבּוּרוֹ שֶׁנִּקְרָא מַלְכוּת - הַכֹּל אֶחָד.

such that He and His will and His wisdom are enclothed in His speech that is called *Malkhut* – all is one.

The ultimate unification of *Atzilut* takes place in *Malkhut*, the *sefira* that receives all the divine lights. This is because it is only when the receiver is as one with the sources of bestowal that there is the complete unification in which there is nothing other than Him.

Here, three things are mentioned: "He, His will, His wisdom." "He" refers to Himself. His illumination into the worlds splits into two: the encompassing light and the inner light. "His will," which is the *sefira* of *Keter*, is the encompassing light and "His wisdom" is the *sefira* of *Ḥokhma*, the initial inner light. The goal of the unification is that both God's Self, and His illumination in the encompassing and inner forms, are unified in *Malkhut*.

The *sefira* of *Malkhut* is, seemingly, of a different nature than the lights that bestow, since *Malkhut* is the one receiving, limiting, and concealing the light. However, in the world of *Atzilut*, and in the *Malkhut* of *Atzilut*, *Malkhut* does not express something different, but rather it expresses the other side of the thing itself, which, according to the divine wisdom and will, it is. Just as it is in the *sefirot*, so it is in the Torah. "He, His will, and His wisdom" are the Written Torah, which reveals the will and wisdom of God that descends and is enclothed in "His speech," the vessels (reality) of this world, without losing its holiness. Not only does this divine flow of God remain a clean and unified expression of God, enclothed in this world of separation without being fragmented, it even repairs and unifies this world through the Divine. The concepts of God's will and wisdom are enclothed in our limited understanding and are actualized in the world through our limited capability. Yet, our limited understanding and capability do not limit or distort the supernal will; they only serve to draw it in and complete it, as this outcome is exactly the goal of the divine will and wisdom. As a result, it is not only that the Oral Torah does not conceal and limit the divine will and wisdom; it is actually the method through which they reach their completion.

וּמַה שֶּׁאוֹמֵר הָאֲרִ"י ז"ל שֶׁהַמִּשְׁנָיוֹת הֵן בְּמַלְכוּת דִּיצִירָה

And as for **what the Arizal says, that the *mishnayot* are in *Malkhut* of *Yetzira*,**

7 Ḥeshvan

8 Ḥeshvan (leap year)

It is explained in the teachings of Hasidism that the Mishna belongs to the world of *Yetzira*,[43] the world of attributes, all generally included within the two attributes of love and fear.[44] The Mishna presents the halakhic rulings: what is permitted, what is prohibited, what is pure, what is impure. These rulings are expressions of love and fear, that which we love and do, and that which fear and refrain from doing; what draws us closer, and distances us.[45] Presumably, that perspective of the Mishna is different from what is said here, that the Mishna is in *Malkhut* of *Atzilut*.

רְצוֹנוֹ לוֹמַר לְבוּשׁ מַלְכוּת דִּיצִירָה שֶׁנִּתְלַבְּשָׁה בָּהּ מַלְכוּת דַּאֲצִילוּת

the Arizal **means the clothing of *Malkhut* of *Yetzira*, in which *Malkhut* of *Atzilut* is enclothed,**

In truth, there is no contradiction between these two opinions. There is a process through which the *Malkhut* of *Atzilut* descends into the lower worlds. Every descent (in spiritual matters) is an enclothing of the upper reality within the lower realm. *Atzilut* represents being subsumed in the Divine. *Malkhut* of *Atzilut*, upon descending into the lower worlds, is that subsummation now enclothed in each lower world according to its nature. In the world of *Yetzira*, which is the world of attributes that determine the relationships between different entities, both negative and positive, that subsummation in the Divine is enclothed in physical expression (*Malkhut*) of the attributes of *Yetzira*: Do this, and do not do that.

וּמַלְכוּת דִּיצִירָה נִקְרָא 'שִׁפְחָה' לְגַבֵּי מַלְכוּת דַּאֲצִילוּת

and *Malkhut* of *Yetzira* is called a "maidservant" in relation to *Malkhut* of *Atzilut*,

---

43. See *Pri Etz Ḥayyim, Sha'ar Hanhagat HaLimud*, chap. 1; *Sha'ar HaMitzvot, Parashat Va'etḥanan*, and elsewhere.

44. As is cited in various places, fear is the root of "distance yourself from evil," which refers to the negative commandments, and love is the root of "Do good," which refers to the positive commandments (see *Likkutei Amarim*, beginning of chap. 41, the introduction to *Sha'ar HaYiḥud VeHa'emuna*, and many other places).

45. Similarly, it is said that the six orders of the Mishna are analogous to the six attributes. *Zera'im* is *Ḥesed*, *Moed* is *Gevura*, etc. (See *Kuntres Aḥaron* 158b, *Likkutei Torah, Pekudei* 4:2, and elsewhere.)

The relationship between the clothing and the entity being enclothed is like the relationship between a maid and her mistress. The directing entity, which determines how everything below it should be conducted, is the *Malkhut* of *Atzilut*. Its clothing serves as its accompaniment, transporting and revealing this *Malkhut* to the external reality (the lower worlds). This clothing is the *Malkhut* of *Yetzira*.

וּמַלְכוּת דִּבְרִיאָה נִקְרָא 'אָמָה'. **while *Malkhut* of *Beria* is called** "Jewish **maidservant."**

Between the worlds of *Yetzira* and *Atzilut* lies the world of *Beria*. Accordingly, the order is that *Malkhut* of *Yetzira* enclothes the *Malkhut* of *Beria*, which in turn enclothes the *Malkhut* of *Atzilut*. This means that the more inner garment of *Malkhut* of *Atzilut* is the *Malkhut* of *Beria*, which is called "maidservant" in relation to the *Malkhut* of *Atzilut*.

In the halakhic perspective, the difference between an *ama* (Jewish maidservant) and a *shifḥa* (maidservant) is that the latter is of Canaanite descent (like a male Canaanite servant). Such a person is not fully non-Jewish, but is also not yet fully Jewish. An *ama*, in contrast, is a Jewish maidservant, and is fully Jewish in every way. This illustrates clearly that a Jewish maidservant is more fully a member of the inner circle of closeness and service to her mistress, while the Canaanite maidservant remains at a greater distance. In other contexts,[46] an analogy is presented as possibly providing a deeper explanation of these relationships: The Jewish maidservant and the Canaanite maidservant are akin to the relationship between a servant who works in the house and a servant who works out in the fields. A servant of the house serves the master himself, caring for his personal life and needs. A servant of the field looks after the master's property and fields. The servant who works in the home knows his master, his thoughts and feelings, and even begins to identify with them, thinking and feeling like his master (within the servant's own capacity). In contrast, the servant in the field does not see the master and does not know him. His connection to the master is expressed only through his actions, serving merely as an external expression of love or fear. In this sense, the Canaanite maid, the *Malkhut* of *Yetzira*, is

46. See *Derekh Mitzvotekha* 83b. See also the discourse of the Lubavitcher Rebbe, beginning with "*Ve'eleh hamishpatim*," *Parashat Mishpatim*, 5714.

like the Mishna, which is the practical *halakha,* expressing how things are meant to be performed practically. The Jewish maidservant, like the Talmud, expresses the more internal layer of the will of the King, and the underlying reasoning as to how the divine will reached its conclusions.

וְתֵדַע מִמַּה שֶּׁאוֹמֵר הָאֲרִ"י ז"ל דְּמִקְרָא, דְּהַיְינוּ תּוֹרָה שֶׁבִּכְתָב, הוּא בַּעֲשִׂיָּה

Know that this is so **from the Arizal's statement that the Bible, that is, the Written Law, is in** ***Asiya,***

This is extrapolated from the Arizal's[47] statement that the Bible is in *Asiya*. The perspective that the Written Law is in *Asiya* means that the Written Torah is revealed in the clothing of the world of *Asiya*. This refers to the form of the words as they are written physically, as well as the act of reading them. This is in contrast to their underlying meaning and reasoning, which relate to the feelings and thoughts of the soul, yet are not revealed.

וַהֲרֵי מְפוֹרָשׁ בַּזֹּהַר וּבְכִתְבֵי הָאֲרִ"י ז"ל מְקוֹמוֹת אֵין מִסְפָּר שֶׁהִיא תִּפְאֶרֶת שֶׁהוּא זְעֵיר אַנְפִּין דַּאֲצִילוּת?

and yet is it not explicitly stated in innumerable places in the ***Zohar*** **and the writings of the Arizal that it is** ***Tiferet*****, which is** ***Zeir Anpin*** **of** ***Atzilut*****?**

Given this, the question must be asked: Yet is it not explicitly stated in innumerable places in the Zohar and the writings of the Arizal[48] that the Written Torah is Tiferet, which is the *partzuf* of *Zeir Anpin* of *Atzilut*? (The *sefira* of *Tiferet* is the main one representing the *partzuf* of *Zeir Anpin*, which includes all six *sefirot,* and it is sometimes referred to by the name *Atzilut*.)

As was explained, *Malkhut* is the Oral Torah, and *Zeir Anpin* is the Written Torah, the male aspect and the bestower with respect to *Malkhut*. All things are found in the Written Torah, all the concepts and *halakhot,* but only in the form of seeds. It is the Oral Torah in which their details are developed within the context of reality. This illustrates that the Written Torah is above the Oral Torah of *Atzilut*. If this is so,

47. *Pri Etz Ḥayyim,* and *Sha'ar HaMitzvot* there.

48. Such as *Tikkunei Zohar* 40a; *Etz Ḥayyim, Sha'ar* 37, chap. 1; and elsewhere.

then how can we understand that which is said here, that the Written Torah is within the world of *Asiya*?

אֶלָּא שֶׁמִּתְלַבֶּשֶׁת בַּעֲשִׂיָּה וְכֵן הוּא בְּהֶדְיָא בְּסֵפֶר הַכַּוָּונוֹת, שֶׁמִּקְרָא וּמִשְׁנָה וְתַלְמוּד וְקַבָּלָה כּוּלָּם בַּאֲצִילוּת, אֶלָּא שֶׁמִּקְרָא מִתְלַבֵּשׁ עַד עֲשִׂיָּה וּמִשְׁנָה עַד הַיְצִירָה וְתַלְמוּד בִּבְרִיאָה.

Rather, it means **that** the Written Law **is enclothed in *Asiya*, and it is similarly** stated **expressly in *Sefer HaKavanot* that the Bible, Mishna, Talmud, and Kabbala are all in *Atzilut*, only that the Bible is enclothed until *Asiya*, and the Mishna until *Yetzira*, and the Talmud in *Beria*.**

"The Written Torah is in *Asiya*" means that the Written Torah is enclothed in *Asiya*, that it illuminates and is revealed within *Asiya*, even though its origin in *Atzilut* is even above the Oral Torah of *Atzilut*.

And it is similarly stated expressly in Sefer HaKavanot,[49] where all four parts of the Torah are mentioned: the Bible, Mishna, Talmud, and Kabbala are all in Atzilut, only that the Bible is enclothed until Asiya, and the Mishna until Yetzira, and the Talmud in Beria. It appears that in the writings of the Arizal that are in our possession, these things are written slightly differently. (It says there that all parts of the Torah are found in *Atzilut*, while in *Beria*, Kabbala is missing, in *Yetzira*, Talmud is missing, and in *Asiya*, Mishna is missing.) The language of the author of the *Tanya* here provides further elucidation: Kabbala is in *Atzilut* – this means solely in *Atzilut*, for Kabbala is not enclothed at all in the lower worlds of the created beings. Talmud is in *Beria*, because it is enclothed until *Beria*, but is not enclosed within *Yetzira*, etc. ☞

THE BIBLE IS ONLY ENCLOTHED UNTIL *ASIYA*

☞ The implication of the idea that the entire Torah, in all of its parts, is in *Atzilut*, is that all the parts are independent divine will and wisdom in a state of subsummation in the Divine Himself. The difference between the parts of the Torah relates to which parts are enclothed in which levels of the unfolding layers of the spiritual worlds (and their respective impacts within those worlds). In the process of the unfolding of these layered worlds, entities descend and become enclothed in in-

49. See *Pri Etz Ḥayyim, Sha'ar Hanhagat HaLimud*, chap. 1.

creasingly dense and thick spiritual garments. Each garment both conceals and reveals: It reveals and expresses the aspect of the entity that is connected to the garment, while concealing those aspects that are not related to the garment of that particular world. The question asked here is at what level the garment does not yet fully conceal and distort, but rather still reveals the quality that exists above in *Atzilut*. Regarding this issue, there are distinctions between the different parts of the Torah. The biblical text is enclothed all the way until *Asiya*, meaning that the ideas of the Written Torah can be revealed even in the lowest level of full *Asiya*, without any internal connection. The reason for this is that since the root of the Written Torah is so lofty, it cannot be thought about or felt emotionally except through the practical world of *Asiya*, by speaking the words or writing the letters. In contrast, Mishna is enclothed only until *Yetzira*. This is because the Mishna, the rulings of what is prohibited or permitted, pure or impure, can also be enclothed in terms of an emotional relationship, like "for and against, attraction and repulsion." But the Mishna cannot be enclothed below this, in *Asiya*, because *Asiya* is the actualized result of the complex, confusing process of revealing the divine will itself below as it is above. Talmud is only enclothed until *Beria*, because the Talmud, which is the reasoning and understanding of the Torah and its *halakhot*, cannot be understood in *Yetzira*, and certainly not in *Asiya*. The vessels of those lower layers are not precise and fine enough. The intellect of *Asiya* is sufficient for inserting a nail into a piece of wood, and even for building a computer, but not sufficient for the spirituality of the Torah. The intellect of *Yetzira* can differentiate between different feelings, but cannot conceive of things beyond existing sensations, or realities beyond the current one. This kind of intellect only exists in the world of *Beria*, which is the world of pure intellect, and therefore, that is where the Talmud is enclothed. Regarding the final piece, Kabbala, it is not mentioned here, but elsewhere (*Pri Etz Ḥayyim* there, and see *Likkutei Torah*, Lev. 4:1, 5–6:1) it is explained that Kabbala is in *Atzilut*. This means that Kabbala is not enclothed in any created level of reality from *Beria* and below. This is because Kabbala, the inner aspect of the Torah, is, in a certain way, the Torah as it is in isolation, with no relationship to anything external, including the worlds. This includes the physical realities, as well as the more conceptual and emotional aspects of existence that relate to the other worlds. The garments, within which Kabbala is depicted in various writings, are just the external garments and nothing more (similar to the garments of *Asiya* for the Mishna, which are just written words on a page). Therefore, the true understanding of the Kabbala (when it is stripped of its garments and its physical analogies) can only be achieved through what one person conveys to another, a communication between intellects, not by means of some kind of external vessel. Only a person who knows and understands these things, can serve as a true garment for the Kabbala.

It is clear from what has been said that all Torah study, as well as the *halakhot*, are in *Atzilut*. The Torah is always the "Tree of Life." Even when it is enclothed in the lower worlds of created beings, in the worlds of *Asiya* and the *kelippat noga*, prohibited and permitted, it still remains *Atzilut*, unified with God. The places the Torah reaches do not change the Torah, not even in its appearance. In fact, the Torah changes the places it touches, repairing and elevating them through its contact with them.

8 Ḥeshvan

וְהִנֵּה כְּשֶׁהַמַּלְכוּת מִתְלַבֶּשֶׁת בִּקְלִיפַּת נוֹגַהּ כְּדֵי לְבָרֵר הַנִּיצוֹצוֹת שֶׁנָּפְלוּ בְּחֵטְא אָדָם הָרִאשׁוֹן, וְגַם הָרְפָּ"ח נִיצוֹצִין שֶׁנָּפְלוּ בִּשְׁבִירַת הַכֵּלִים

Now, when the *Malkhut* is enclothed in *kelippat noga,* in order to extract the sparks that fell with the sin of Adam, and also the two hundred and eighty-eight sparks that fell with the breaking of the vessels,

Now, after this introduction regarding the Torah and its enclothing in the worlds, the author returns to the main topic of this letter, in explaining the statement of the *Zohar*. The *Malkhut* of *Atzilut,* which is the Oral Torah, is enclothed, as was explained, in the *kelippat noga,* in the *halakhot* and definitions of prohibited and permitted, pure and impure.

It is enclothed in *kelippat noga* in order to extract the sparks that fell with the sin of Adam, and also to extract the two hundred and eighty-eight sparks that fell with the breaking of the vessels. In our world, the world of *kelippat noga,* there are hidden sparks of holiness. These sparks did not descend into the layer of existence of the *kelippot* in an organized, directed way (a process like the unfolding of the layers of worlds, which always leaves a connection between higher and lower worlds); rather, the way they fell there was as if it was not by divine design, not intellectually or emotionally planned (a way that left no connection with the divine root, which is the meaning of the concealment and the existence of the *kelippa* that is below). This kind of fall took place because of the sin of Adam, and even before the creation of the world, in the cosmic "breaking of the vessels" mentioned in the Kabbala.

The *kelippot* conceal these sparks, blocking their existence, despite the fact that the whole existence of the *kelippa* only derives from those very sparks. The *kelippa* does not have life force or sustenance of its own (to remain a *kelippa*). It does not recognize holiness and its Divine Presence as the root of all life and therefore is not subsumed within that holiness. As a result, the *kelippa* receives nothing from holiness. All its life sustenance derives from the sparks of holiness that are concealed within it. It continues to exist because of those sparks, and for their sake, in order conceal them for a time, and then to ultimately reveal them at the proper time, as will be explained. For now, they remain hidden within the *kelippa* (which is the reason for the *kelippa*). This is the intent behind the descent and enclothing of *Malkhut,* which is the Oral Torah, into the *kelippa*: It is to seek and extract these sparks, to reveal and elevate them, and ultimately, to nullify the existence of the *kelippa* and concealment in the worlds. ☞

אֲזַי גַּם הַמַּלְכוּת דַּאֲצִילוּת נִקְרָא בְּשֵׁם 'עֵץ הַדַּעַת טוֹב וָרָע' לְגַבֵּי ז"א דַּאֲצִילוּת, שֶׁאֵינוֹ יוֹרֵד שָׁם וְנִקְרָא 'עֵץ חַיִּים'.

then the *Malkhut* of *Atzilut* is also called by the name "the Tree of Knowledge of **Good and Evil," in relation to *Zeir Anpin* of *Atzilut,* which does not descend there and is called the "Tree of Life."**

ADAM'S SIN AND THE BREAKING OF THE VESSELS

☞ These sparks can be divided into two groups: those that fell through the sin of Adam and those that fell during the breaking of the vessels. This is because Adam, the first man, and in some sense, all people at all times, can act against the will of God. When a person acts against the divine will that is manifested in all being, he generates spiritual cracks in that will which cause aspects of the supernal light and divine holiness to disappear, concealed behind the existence of a *kelippa*. These are the sparks that fell during the sin of Adam. In addition, there are earlier, more fundamental sparks, called the "two hundred and eighty-eight sparks" that fell during the breaking of the vessels. The kabbalistic approach views our world as having been built out of the fragments of an ancient, former world (in terms of both time and spiritual loftiness) that was broken. Its pieces lost their place in relation to each other, as well as in relation to the source of holiness. The soul of man can illustrate this point by way of analogy: This is similar to a very old memory that was lost and forgotten, but there are sparks of this memory in all corners of his life, in the people he encounters, in the things he sees or smells, in all things. When he senses these sparks along the path of his life, he tries to extract them and connect them in order to reconstruct the picture and meaning of his life. In a simpler analogy, which appears in the writings of the author of the *Tanya*, it is like a group of sentences and words that have become fragmented and scattered, and a person tries to clarify and reorganize them in order to uncover their meaning. Similarly, this is the service of man throughout the ages: to organize and reveal the ancient broken fragments referred to as the "two hundred and eighty-eight sparks."

In referring to these two kinds of sparks, the author of the *Tanya* is reversing the order, mentioning the sparks that fell during the sin of Adam before those that fell during the breaking of the vessels. This is because, in this context, he is not speaking about the descent of these sparks, but rather about their rectification and elevation, and it is the person who makes the repairs. When one begins this process of rectification, he starts with his own sins, and through them, he can then elevate the sparks that fell during the breaking of the vessels.

The *Malkhut* of *Atzilut* descended only in order to extract these sparks. But in the meantime, since it is enclothed in this lower reality of *kelippat noga*, the Malkhut of Atzilut is also called by the name the "Tree of Knowledge of Good and Evil," in relation to Zeir Anpin of Atzilut, which does not descend there and is called the "Tree of Life." The *Malkhut* of *Atzilut* is the Oral Torah, referred to by the *Zohar* as the "Tree of Knowledge of Good and Evil." This is not because the Oral Torah is actually this tree, but because it descends to the place of this tree, to the dense, material worlds, and the *kelippot*, that contain good and evil within them. This is in contrast to *Zeir Anpin* of *Atzilut*, and the parts of the Torah that do not descend to become enclothed in the lower worlds, which are accordingly called the "Tree of Life."

In the following sections, the author will explain the implications and purpose of this descent and enclothing:

וְהִנֵּה הִתְלַבְּשׁוּת הַמַּלְכוּת בִּקְלִיפַּת נוֹגַהּ הוּא סוֹד גָּלוּת הַשְּׁכִינָה, "אֲשֶׁר שָׁלַט הָאָדָם בְּאָדָם כו'" (קהלת י,ט)

Now, the enclothing of the *Malkhut* in *kelippat noga* is the secret of the exile of the Divine Presence; "whenever man controlled man, it was to his detriment" (Eccles. 8:9).

The secret of the exile of the Divine Presence is explained extensively in other contexts in kabbalistic writings.[50] In short, it is a situation in which the Divine Presence (the *Malkhut*) and the sparks of the Divine Presence sustain the reality of the *kelippat noga*, even though that reality conceals holiness and even denies its existence. The "secret of the exile of the Divine Presence" is the statement that there is a secret here, that there is a hidden explanation for this that is not currently evident. That which we see, comprising concealment, confusion, and evil, is only a piece of a larger process, described in this verse: "Whenever man controlled," referring to the man of the *kelippa*, "man," referring to the man of holiness, and the purpose of this power was "to his detriment," of the man of the *kelippa*. This is because the dominion over and exploitation of the Divine Presence by the *kelippa*, the depletion of all its powers, will ultimately be used primarily against the *kelippa*. The

50. See above, letter 25, which refers to *Sefer HaGilgulim*, and see the lengthy explanation there.

kelippa lacks any life force of its own and when it drains the power of the Divine Presence and the holiness deriving from it, it is the *kelippa* that will first be damaged. The Divine Presence is itself the source of life, and therefore it is always alive, existing, and sustaining. The *kelippa,* in contrast, only relates to a certain "back" part of holiness from which it draws its sustenance, and therefore the *kelippa* will no longer exist once it drains this. To explain in greater depth: "to his detriment," to the man of the *kelippa,* meaning, to the benefit of the man of holiness. The good which brings out the holiness from this exile is the "very good" that comprises the advantage of the light over the darkness. This is like the true understanding of an answer that can be reached only after a question has been elucidated, or like an act of joining things together, which can be done only if they had previously been separate.

Nevertheless, during the time of the exile of the Divine Presence, the apparent situation is of the power and domination of the *kelippat noga* and of the tree of knowledge of good and evil over holiness. Here, the author returns to the statement of the *Zohar* (from the *Raya Meheimna*) that was cited initially, in order to explain what was stated there.

וְזֶה שֶׁאָמַר בְּרַעְיָא מְהֵימְנָא: וּבְזִמְנָא דְּאִילָנָא דְּטוֹב וָרַע שָׁלְטָא כו׳ אִינּוּן כו׳

And this is the meaning **of the statement in *Raya Meheimna*: But during the time when the tree of** knowledge of **good and evil rules…, those…**

The Torah scholars, who are comparable to the Sabbath and holidays, are sustained only through that which is given to them by the ignorant, who are comparable to the weekdays.

דְּהַיְינוּ בִּזְמַן גָּלוּת הַשְּׁכִינָה, שֶׁמַּשְׁפַּעַת לַחִיצוֹנִים

That is, during the time of the exile of the Divine Presence, which bestows life **to the external** forces of impurity

During the period of the exile of the Divine Presence, which is the *Malkhut* of *Atzilut,* the Divine Presence bestows life to the external forces of impurity, and not the internal divine intent, only its external aspect. This external aspect is not even cognizant of the internal aspect.

The bestowal of life from the Divine Presence during the period of exile is not upon something completely foreign to the inner essence of the Presence. Rather, it is bestowed upon the external aspect of itself. All things in existence, both physical and spiritual, possess an internal and external aspect. The only differences lie in the variable distance between internal and external aspects. When the distance is so great that the two aspects are completely alienated, the external aspect transforms into a *kelippa*. These external aspects are the means by which to reach a particular end. It is impossible to achieve that end without these aspects, but when they become an end in themselves, they turn into *kelippot*.

שֶׁהֵם בִּקְלִיפַּת נוֹגַהּ, שֶׁהָ'עֵרֶב רַב' יוֹנְקִים מִשָּׁם

that are in *kelippat noga*, from where the "mixed multitude [*eirev rav*]**" suckles,**

Those external forces of impurity are in *kelippat noga,* which is the intermediate *kelippa* in which there can be an elevation from the *kelippa* to holiness, as well as a descent of holiness into the *kelippa*. The transfer of life force to the *kelippa* is through the external forces of impurity of the holiness that reach the *kelippa*.

From where the "mixed multitude [*eirev rav*]" suckles. The term "mixed multitude" relates to what is said further in the "*Raya Meheimna,*" that Torah scholars should not support themselves from the ignorant and from "the mixed multitude that eats impure, invalidated, or prohibited things, etc." This means that the "mixed multitude" suckles and receives its life force from the external aspects of holiness that reach the *kelippa*, not the internal aspects. Therefore, they "eat impure, invalid, etc." ☞

"MIXED MULTITUDE"

☞ "Mixed multitude" is a term that originally applied to the converts from other nations who joined the people of Israel when they were leaving Egypt, as it is written, "And a mixed multitude came up with them, etc." (Ex. 12:38). In the tradition of the Sages of the Talmud, and specifically in kabbalistic writings, this term applies to anyone who is like a *kelippa* for Israel, connecting to the external aspect of Israel but

וּמִתַּמְצִיתָן נִיזּוֹנִין תַּלְמִידֵי חֲכָמִים בַּגָּלוּת

and from whose inner essence the Torah scholars are sustained in exile,

During the time of exile, the flow of *Malkhut* of *Atzilut* is upon the *kelippat noga,* sustaining the external aspects of existence which contain both good and evil, as well as much futility. The nations of the world and the mixed multitude, who themselves are composed of these external aspects, connect well with this world, and succeed, materially as well as spiritually to a certain degree. Even so, as was explained, each external aspect has an internal essence of good and holiness, such that even if that internal side is not visible, it sustains all the futility of the outer layer. Even when that external aspect eventually vanishes, the internal side remains, and it is from there that Torah scholars are sustained. These righteous scholars live in holiness even in the world of exile and *kelippat noga.* They do not live in a separate time or world, nor is the sustenance they receive any different. They live here, in exile, with the rest of the people of this world, subject to the laws of nature, economics, and politics of this world. Through their efforts to only partake of the inner essence of good and holiness in this world, they are able to extract and elevate this world of *kelippat noga* to holiness.

וְאָז עִיקַּר עֲבוֹדַת הָאָדָם וְעִיקַּר עֵסֶק הַתּוֹרָה וְהַמִּצְוֹת הוּא לְבָרֵר הַנִּיצוֹצוֹת כַּנּוֹדָע מֵהָאֲרִ"י ז"ל.

the main service of man and the main engagement in Torah and mitzvot is then to extract the sparks, as is known from the teachings of **the Arizal.**

not to the inner faith and unity that forms their internal aspect, ultimately expressed as giving up one's life for God. See *Torah Or* 74c (end of *Parashat Yitro*), where it is explained that such people had no comprehension of or wonder at the greatness of God Himself, but only in relation to the revelation of God through the measurable and finite worlds and spheres. As a result, they later asked for "a God that will go before us," one that they could see with their physical eyes. Therefore, whenever the Torah relates a story of the sins of Israel (the primary example being the story of the golden calf), it is said that it was the "mixed multitude" who sinned. Similarly, here, when discussing those who suckle from the external flow of the Divine Presence, they are referred to as the "mixed multitude."

The Divine service during the time of exile is to extract sparks.[51] There is divine service that does not consist of extracting sparks, and that kind of service belongs to other times, that are not the time of the exile of the Divine Presence. There is divine service within a reality in which there is no evil or impurities to extract, which is the service of elevation and unifications, expanding good and elevating holiness to ever-greater heights (as will be explained further in the letter). But during the time of the exile of the Divine Presence, of *kelippat noga* and the mixing of good and evil, when it is almost impossible to differentiate that there is holiness here, the main divine service is to perform this differentiation. This means to extract the holy sparks from within the evil and futility that abound in life, and to elevate and gather those sparks into a holy edifice. This service of extraction from the *kelippa* is mainly from within the world of action, through the performance of commandments and Torah study that relates to that performance.

לָכֵן עִיקַּר עִנְיַן הַלִּימּוּד הוּא בְּעִיּוּן וּפִלְפּוּל הֲלָכָה, בְּאִיסּוּר וְהֶיתֵּר טוּמְאָה וְטָהֳרָה, כְּדֵי לְבָרֵר הַמּוּתָּר וְהַטָּהוֹר מֵהָאָסוּר וְהַטָּמֵא עַל יְדֵי עִיּוּן וּפִלְפּוּל הֲלָכָה בְּחָכְמָה בִּינָה וָדַעַת

Therefore, the main focus of learning is through inquiry and analysis of *halakha*, on the topics of **prohibited and permitted** matters and **impurity and purity, in order to distinguish the permitted and the pure from the prohibited and the impure, by means of inquiry and analysis of *halakha* with wisdom, understanding, and knowledge,**

This refers to the practical application of Torah study: to clarify exactly what is prohibited and what is permitted, what to do and how to do it, as well as what not to do, etc. This study is the main purpose of the Oral Torah, the Torah that many contemplate, scrutinize, and analyze, using human intellect, an intellect that operates within this world. These matters are not inscribed, and indeed cannot be inscribed, in the Written Torah, since they relate to the complex and ever-changing reality of the *kelippa* and the concealment. Therefore,

51. See *Etz Ḥayyim, Sha'ar HaKlalim*, chap. 1. See also *Torah Or* 49a and onward, and in other places as well.

it would be insufficient to simply transmit traditions of what do from one generation to another. The only way is to try to attain this understanding through inquiry and analysis, using the three powers of the mind, which are wisdom, understanding and knowledge, which are also part of this world.[52]

כַּנּוֹדָע דְּאוֹרַיְיתָא מֵחָכְמָה נָפְקַת וּבְחָכְמָה דַּיְיקָא אִתְבְּרִירוּ.

as is known, that **the Torah emerges from** ***Ḥokhma*** (wisdom), **and** the sparks **are extracted specifically in** ***Ḥokhma.***

Although the Torah at its source is above the level of *Ḥokhma,* nevertheless, in the lofty *Keter,* the way that it emerges and is revealed in the world is through *Ḥokhma.*[53]

Elsewhere it is said: And the sparks are extracted specifically in Ḥokhma,[54] and the good is separated from the bad. The power of Torah to clarify the world stems from its origin in the level of *Ḥokhma,* and it is the level of *Ḥokhma* specifically that clarifies and allows for extraction. The level of *Ḥokhma,* in this world as well, differentiates between good and evil, between false and true. Accordingly, it is through *Ḥokhma* specifically that there can be extracting of holiness from the *kelippot,* etc. This is especially true when a person immerses himself in Torah with *Ḥokhma* (wisdom), understanding, and knowledge, as was mentioned, enclothing his own *Ḥokhma* in the supernal *Ḥokhma* (and the supernal *Ḥokhma* in his own, as is explained in *Likkutei Amarim,* chap. 3). This allows him to draw the supernal *Ḥokhma,* the revelation of the light of *Ein Sof* Himself, into this world. By way of analogy, when a world of vague shapes and shadows is suddenly flooded with powerful light, everything becomes clarified, each entity and situation understood. ☞

52. In contrast to Kabbala and the inner world of Torah, which is not meant to be analyzed and debated using reasoning of this world, but rather, only through tradition and intellectual pathways of the Torah itself.

53. *Zohar,* vol. 2, 85a, and elsewhere. See *Torah Or* 19d, and in many hasidic writings.

54. *Zohar,* vol. 2, 254b.

EXTRACTED THROUGH *ḤOKHMA*

☞ Why does this occur specifically through *Ḥokhma*? One reason is that extraction cannot be performed from within. One who finds himself within a jumbled reality, and is a part of that reality, cannot differentiate between the good and evil within it. Only an outsider, who is above the various parts of that reality, can distinguish between these aspects and begin the process of extraction. Just as this is true regarding a person, it is the case in the spiritual worlds more generally. *Ḥokhma* is that which is beyond, illuminating the soul with the brilliance of a new light that the soul has not yet encountered. Our attributes are mixed together with the events encompassing us, even forming those events to some degree. Even the *Bina* component of our intellect is biased, connecting to our lower attributes and unable to free itself in order to receive the clarification of the extraction. Only the illumination of *Ḥokhma*, which is above all that we see and feel, can make this leap and decisively declare: This is truth, that is falsehood, this is good, that is evil, etc.

On a deeper level, it can be seen that extraction and rectification can only be achieved by someone who has himself undergone extraction and rectification. In a general context, this refers to the world of *Atzilut* relative to the other worlds, etc. More specifically, this refers to *Ḥokhma*, the *Atzilut* of *Atzilut*. Understandably, there is no corruption in the world of *Atzilut*. *Atzilut* is the perfected reality that is completely holy. But *Atzilut*, serving as the soul and life for the other, lower worlds, is enclothed and relates through its lower aspects to the aspects of the other worlds: the attributes in *Atzilut* relate to the world of *Yetzira* (in the language of Kabbala: "*Zeir Anpin* dwells in *Yetzira*"). *Malkhut* of *Atzilut* to *Asiya*. *Bina* to *Beria* ("*Imma* dwells in *Beria*"). Only the level of *Ḥokhma* relates purely to *Atzilut* ("*Abba* of *Atzilut*"). Accordingly, these levels that are within the enclothing, while they are themselves rectified, they appear in garments relating to a reality that is not rectified, except for the level of *Ḥokhma* of *Atzilut*, which is the *Atzilut* level of *Atzilut*. This level is not enclothed and has no connection with mortality or breakage, and it is the level from which all rectification and life begin.

This enclothing is not just a concealment of something in a foreign covering that has no relationship to that which is within (like a house inhabited by people who do not belong there). Rather, it is like a body that is within a garment, where there is a connection between the two, a point of contact and closeness between the wearer and the garment. This is like the animal soul within man that is enclothed in the body because it relates, subtly, to that body. Similarly, the attributes of *Atzilut* are enclothed in the lower worlds and sustain them, because those attributes contain the trace beginnings of the breaking of the vessels. Therefore, in the most slight and subtle of ways, the attributes of *Atzilut* must undergo extraction. This is not because they themselves are corrupted, but because they serve as the pathway for the rectification all the way to the depths of existence, to extract from there the most basic essence of the chaos of reality. This pathway provides the channel for the unbridled power that shattered the primordial vessels, giving the alternative of the vessels of rectification. The key to this is *Ḥokhma*, for the illumination of *Ḥokhma*, which nullifies the attributes and allows them to receive and contain each other, converts

וְהַיְינוּ חָכְמָה עִילָּאָה דַּאֲצִילוּת הַמְלוּבֶּשֶׁת בְּמַלְכוּת דַּאֲצִילוּת. **That is, the supernal *Ḥokhma* of *Atzilut*, which is enclothed in *Malkhut* of *Atzilut*.**

For even with the descent of this *Ḥokhma* to the lower levels of *Ḥokhma* (including that of a person studying Torah), it remains supernal *Ḥokhma*. This is the essence of Torah, which descends below and appears in lower and smaller forms at lower levels, yet remains supernal *Ḥokhma*, retaining the true relationships between the levels, just as it does at higher levels. It is this that allows supernal *Ḥokhma* to descend into the worlds in order to perform extractions.

This descent does not follow the unfolding succession of the worlds, for if it did, the supernal *Ḥokhma* would not retain its higher level, but instead become a product of the world to which it was connected. Further on, the author will explain the process of supernal *Ḥokhma* descending in the Torah.

Which is enclothed in Malkhut of Atzilut. Although there is a full structure of *sefirot* for *Atzilut*, from the intellectual ones through those of the attributes in between *Ḥokhma* and *Malkhut*, in the Torah there is a skipping of *Ḥokhma* over the order of the middle *sefirot* and directly enclothing in the *Malkhut* (which becomes enclothed in the worlds).

סוֹד תּוֹרָה שֶׁבְּעַל פֶּה This is **the secret of the Oral Law**

When the supernal *Ḥokhma* itself is enclothed in the level of *Ḥokhma* in each world, even the lowest one, the realm of *kelippa* and falsehood, this is the "secret of the Oral Law." The meaning of this enclothing is that a person, who dwells below and functions through an intellect and understanding that is a product of the reality in which he lives, can

these vessels from attributes of chaos to ones of rectification.

It is further explained that *Ḥokhma* (formed of the letters that spell out "force of what") is the level of nullification, and true rectification can only begin when it passes through the point of nullification. True rectification means a new beginning, which can only happen after a reset of the previous existence. This does not mean, God forbid, a reset of God Himself, but rather a reset of His manifestation as existence. According to Hasidism, this appears to be the essence of extraction: the distinguishing between the essence of Him, which is goodness and rightness, and between His manifestation of this existence, which can sometimes be twisted to evil and corruption.

still understand the supernal *Ḥokhma* that is enclothed in that level. Moreover, it is specifically through the understanding that belongs to that lower world, according to the ability of the person's *Ḥokhma* and understanding, that he can attain a comprehension of the higher, supernal *Ḥokhma*. ☞

(בְּסוֹד 'אַבָּא יָסַד בְּרַתָּא') **(in the secret of** "the **father that founded the daughter**")

"Father" is the term for the *sefira* of *Ḥokhma,* and the "daughter" refers to *Malkhut*.[55] These terms have multiple layers of meaning. The main one is that a father and daughter, like *Ḥokhma* and *Malkhut,* share a unique relationship. On the internal plane, there is more than just a direct flow from one to the other. As was mentioned above, there is a connection of imagination, and even of an essential identity, between a father and daughter. *Malkhut* perhaps reveals *Ḥokhma* more than the other *sefirot,* because it is truly linked with *Ḥokhma* in its essence more than with any other *sefira*. ☞

THE SECRET OF THE ORAL TORAH

☞ What is the meaning of this term? Why "secret?" The answer appears to be that "secret" relates to a phenomenon that is inexplicable. Anything which descends through the layers of the unfolding succession from above, cause and effect, has an explanation. Every event has a reason, and even if a person does not perceive or understand something, or even many things, that results from his own limitations, not because the event is truly a secret, truly inexplicable. A true secret is where the entity, in its essence, is beyond explanation or understanding in its given context, because there was a skipping of steps that our awareness cannot comprehend. Here as well, the enclothing of the supernal *Ḥokhma* in *Malkhut* (and all the levels of the worlds) skips over the levels of the unfolding succession and manifests in the low level of reality: From one angle, it is like *Ḥokhma* and intellect that can be understood, but from another angle, and this is crux of the secret, it is in fact the supernal *Ḥokhma* itself.

"THE FATHER THAT FOUNDED THE DAUGHTER" – THE CONNECTION OF *ḤOKHMA* AND *MALKHUT*

☞ Something of this connection can be perceived in the experiences of our souls. *Ḥokhma* in isolation, in its nature and essence as *Ḥokhma*, is principally revealed in

55. *Zohar,* vol. 3, 248a, 256b, 258a. And see also previously, epistle 5. Similar language was used in Proverbs: "The Lord founded the earth with wisdom" (Prov. 3:19).

הַמְלוּבֶּשֶׁת בְּמַלְכוּת דִּיצִירָה **that is enclothed in *Malkhut* of *Yetzira*,**

The *Malkhut* of *Atzilut* is not the end of the road. In order to extract the sparks that are in the lower worlds, that *Malkhut* must enclothe itself in the lower worlds, which are, for these purposes, *Yetzira* and *Asiya*.

The author of the *Tanya* mentions specifically *Yetzira* here because that is where the extraction begins. It was already explained that in the world of *Atzilut*, the breaking of the vessels primarily touches the attributes, and not the *sefirot* of the intellect. The attributes are drawn in and enclothed in the world of *Yetzira*. The world of *Yetzira*, which is the "world of attributes," is, therefore, the world in which the extracting begins. Different terminology is used in other places:[56] The world of *Atzilut* is entirely good and holy. The world of *Beria* is mostly good, with small amounts of evil. The world of *Yetzira* is half good and half evil. The world of *Asiya* is mostly evil, etc. Given this, the world of *Atzilut* clearly does not need extracting. Neither does the world of *Beria*, as its default state is to continue the process of rectification. Only from the world of *Yetzira* and below must effort be employed to divert the reality to extraction and rectification.

(וְסוֹד) [סוֹד] הַמִּשְׁנָיוֹת וּבָרַיְיתוֹת **(and)** *Malkhut* of *Yetzira* in **the secret of the *mishnayot* and *baraitot***

This enclothing is the secret, the hidden meaning, that is within the *mishnayot* and *baraitot*.[57] Externally, *mishnayot* only reveal relation-

the study of the Oral Torah, specifically in those matters that are part of the tangible reality of our lives (which are the *Malkhut* relative to us). Above this, we know of things, we understand, but we do not generate new perspectives or ideas. Expressions and illuminations of the wellspring of *Ḥokhma* are mainly found in the space called *Malkhut*.

56. See *Etz Ḥayyim, Sha'ar* 43 (*Sha'ar Ziur Olamot*), introduction to the explication. See also there, *Sha'ar* 47 (*Sha'ar Seder Abiya*), chap. 4, and *Sha'ar* 48 (*Sha'ar HaKelippot*), chap. 3. See *Likkutei Amarim*, chap. 7; *Likkutei Torah, Bemidbar* 58:3; *Ma'amarei Admor HaZaken* 5672, p. 79; and elsewhere.

57. The correction notes state: "It should say: (the *baraitot* that are in *noga*)."

ships: This is permitted, this is prohibited, this is what you should do, this is what you shouldn't do, etc. They do not reveal the underlying reasoning, neither human reasoning (as appears in the Talmud) and certainly nothing above human reasoning. But it is specifically this fact that contains a big secret, a momentous secret, that it is the divine supernal *Ḥokhma* itself that is embedded in these distinctions: this is prohibited and that is permitted, etc. There are no natural reasons, like those that descend and appear through the unfolding succession of the worlds. Rather it is the inner divine *Ḥokhma,* in its pristine form, that cannot be revealed in the intellect of any world, yet is revealed in those practical outcomes in the worlds of *Yetzira* and *Asiya.*

הַמְלוּבָּשׁוֹת בִּקְלִיפַּת נוֹגַהּ שֶׁכְּנֶגֶד עוֹלָם הַיְצִירָה, שֶׁשָּׁם מַתְחִיל בְּחִינַת הַדַּעַת [נוּסָּח אַחֵר: הָרַע] שֶׁבְּנוֹגַהּ

that are enclothed in the *kelippat noga* that corresponds to the world of *Yetzira,* as the knowledge [alternative version: the evil] that is in *noga* begins there

The meaning of these words, which is captured by both versions to some degree, is that the world of *Yetzira* enters into the realm of the tree of knowledge of good and evil. As was explained, this is the mixing of good and evil that allows for the existence of the *kelippat noga* in the world of *Asiya.* The knowledge of good and evil exists in higher worlds as well. There, the knowledge exists in the theoretical, intellectual form, that there are evil things with which we have no connection. But in the world of *Yetzira,* the world of attributes, which has no independent intellectual reality, all that exists is one's awareness is part of me and I am part of it. If one knows evil, that means one knows it through direct personal experience, with the same feelings that a person feels himself. This feeling, when it descends lower, into the world of *Asiya,* where it can no longer see its supernal source, forms into a *kelippa.* These *halakhot,* that this is prohibited or permitted, are exactly what

---

Baraitot are extraneous *mishnayot,* meaning older halakhic rulings, from the same time and with the same authority as the *mishnayot,* but which were not included in the Mishna. They are therefore called "*baraitot,*" which means "outsiders." According to Hasidism, the main extracting process is specifically in the *baraitot,* etc.; see *Torah Or* 17a and 49c.

the worlds of *Yetzira* (and *Asiya*) need for their rectification: clear definitions that differentiate and separate out the mixture, delineating that which is good and that which is evil.

[נוּסָח אַחֵר: וְהַבָּרַיְיתוֹת הַמְלוּבָּשׁוֹת בִּקְלִיפַּת נוֹגַהּ שֶׁכְּנֶגֶד עוֹלָם הָעֲשִׂיָּה שֶׁשָּׁם מַתְחִיל בְּחִינַת הָרַע שֶׁבְּנוֹגַהּ] כַּנּוֹדַע מֵהָאֲרִ"י ז"ל.

[alternative version: and the *baraitot* that are enclothed in the *kelippat noga* that corresponds to the world of *Asiya*, as the evil that is in *noga* begins there] as is known from the teachings of **the Arizal.**

The difference between the versions[58] is whether the *mishnayot* and *baraitot* are enclothed in the *kelippat noga* that is parallel to the world of *Yetzira* or to the world of *Asiya*. It appears that they are both correct, for the Torah is certainly enclothed in parallel to all the levels. The difference is one of emphasis: whether we are discussing the knowledge and feeling of evil, which begins in *Yetzira*, or the evil that is actualized practically, which begins in *Asiya*. In both of these, there is the essence of *kelippat noga*, a *kelippa* that has light and is not a purely evil *kelippa*. In *Yetzira*, it is potentially further away from the actualization of evil, and in *Asiya*, it is closer. In *Yetzira*, there are multiple steps required for the materialization of evil (in feeling and thought), but in *Asiya*, all that remains is the last step, of the practical commission of the evil (and in this sense, complete evil and darkness do not exist independently in our reality, but only as a possibility and threat).

An essential aspect of *kelippat noga*, whether in *Yetzira* or *Asiya*, is that it has light (which is more revealed in *Yetzira*). The revelation of the light within the *kelippa*, and in its world, is through the enclothing of the Torah within it. The Torah enclothed in the worlds generates a structure that is parallel to the worlds. Because this structure is rectified and extracted independently, it contains all the answers and clarifications for all the confusions, uncertainties, and threats that arise from the worlds. While it is true that we may not see a direct answer to every person and for every situation, but through delving into and

58. The alternative version is not found in the first edition.

analyzing the relationship of words to other words, of written to oral texts, of the Torah to people, and among people, it is possible to extract the truth, revealing the divine holy sparks and elevating them.

Until this point, the discussion focused on the Torah as a means for us to extract sparks, and how to do so. In the next sections, the discussion turns to the inner side of the Torah, illustrating how Torah study is intrinsically a value.

וְהַמַּשְׂכִּיל יָבִין עִנְיָן פֶּלֶא גָּדוֹל מִזֶּה מְאֹד מַה נַּעֲשָׂה בַּשָּׁמַיִם מִמַּעַל

An intelligent person will understand the meaning of a far more wondrous concept – of **what occurs in the heavens above** 9 Ḥeshvan

Until this point, we also understood a wondrous matter, called a "secret": what takes place in the world when the supernal *Ḥokhma* descends into it. Now we will understand a greater wonder: of what occurs in the heavens above through the study of Torah in the earthy, lower intellect of man. This second wonder is truly greater than the first, as is explained in several places regarding the virtues of light that ascends from below compared to light which descends from above.[59] It is more understandable that it is within the power of *Ein Sof* to animate and inhabit all things. It is more incredible that the lower, limited reality is able to ascend upward, to influence the higher spheres. This is what will be explained here: What is the study below that has an impact and rejuvenating influence above?

עַל יְדֵי עִיּוּן וּבֵירוּר הֲלָכָה פְּסוּקָה מִן הַגְּמָרָא וּפוֹסְקִים רִאשׁוֹנִים וְאַחֲרוֹנִים, מַה שֶּׁהָיָה בְּהֶעְלֵם דָּבָר קוֹדֶם הָעִיּוּן הַלָּז

through the in-depth study **and the clarification of halakhic rulings from the Gemara and the early and later halakhic authorities, which were hidden matters before that in-depth** study.

Here, he discusses the study of only revealed Torah, for even in this study he can reveal things which were hidden matters even in the Torah before that in-depth study. There are things that are written in the Written Torah, and there are things that are explained and detailed

59. See *Torah Or* 53b and elsewhere.

in the tradition of the Oral Torah, which are revealed even before a person examines them. But there are also things in the Torah that seemingly were not in it. They were hidden until people, through their study, revealed these new ideas that were never mentioned, neither in the Written Torah, nor in the Mishna, nor in the *baraita*, things that were never known before.

This idea is wondrous in every sense, from the practical, halakhic sense, that *halakhot* are revealed and established for new situations, to the sense of extracting abstract principles of *halakha* and its reasoning, both revealed and hidden, on the earth and in the heavens above. This wonder occurs when Torah study is directed not only at knowing what actions to take, but also at knowing the divine *Ḥokhma* that is enclothed in the Torah at all levels of reality.

There is a basic perspective here regarding the essence of Torah, and Oral Torah. As we see, the Written Torah, and to a certain extent, the Oral Torah that has been written down (the Mishna, etc.), mainly present details, scenarios, conceptual connections, and sometimes principles. But they cannot, due to their essential limitations, present understandings and ideas in abstract form. It is understood, however, that Torah is absolute truth that has descended from above, and it cannot descend into the world except in the form of a story (or like a photograph) relating to the things and situations that are within it. The picture beyond those details, the connections, principles, and implications, can only be generated through our understanding and acceptance of the written ideas, understandings that change and adjust themselves, that relate to us differently every time and according to our own individual capabilities, efforts, and opportunities. In other words, this is the Oral Torah, in which people learn, examine, and clarify within their souls that which they have received.

For he thereby elevates this *halakha* from the *kelippot* that were hiding and covering it, so that it was not known at all or so that it was not thoroughly understood in accordance with its reason, as the reason is the secret of the *sefira* of the supernal *Ḥokhma*

כִּי עַל יְדֵי זֶה מַעֲלֶה הֲלָכָה זוֹ מֵהַקְּלִיפּוֹת שֶׁהָיוּ מַעְלִימִים וּמְכַסִּים אוֹתָהּ, שֶׁלֹּא הָיְתָה יְדוּעָה כְּלָל אוֹ שֶׁלֹּא הָיְתָה מוּבֶנֶת הֵיטֵב בְּטַעְמָהּ שֶׁהַטַּעַם הוּא סוֹד הַסְּפִירָה חָכְמָה עִילָּאָה

Halakha is the revelation of *Ḥokhma* within the practical world. As always, the *kelippot* of the physical world conceal and distort the light of supernal *Ḥokhma,* and that which reaches below is either not seen or is not clear. Yet, through the study and clarification of *halakha,* a person can open the channel of *Ḥokhma* from above to below and reveal the existence of *halakha* that was not known, and even clarify its definitions and reasons.

As the reason is the secret of the sefira of the supernal Ḥokhma. "Reason" (*ta'am*) here is meant both in the sense of an internal, causal reason (not an external influencing reason), as well as in the sense of the pleasure of a taste (*ta'am*), like that experienced by a person in food. This reason is the beginning of the reality of each thing, that at its inner core is the pleasure of the one who created it, and in its external dimension, it is the way that it emerges from its inner essence into an external reality. This is the definition of *Ḥokhma*: the reason and beginning of each thing.

The reason is the secret of the sefira of the supernal Ḥokhma: It is explained in kabbalistic writings that there are four levels of the written letters of the Torah which are expressed in the acronym *TNT"A.* This stands for *ta'amim* (the melody of a word), *nekudot* (the vowelizing of the word), *tagim* (the written crowns attached to certain letters), and *otiyot* (the bodies of the letters themselves). These four levels are parallel to the four worlds and four *partzufim* of *Atzilut.* The level of the *ta'amim,* according to this, is that of the secret of the supernal *Ḥokhma.*

שֶׁנָּפְלוּ מִמֶּנָּה נִיצוֹצִים בַּקְּלִיפּוֹת בִּשְׁבִירַת הַכֵּלִים. **from which sparks fell into the *kelippot* at the breaking of the vessels.**

The falling of the sparks of supernal *Ḥokhma* to the *kelippot* is linked to that which is described in the language of Kabbala as "the breaking of the vessels." The breaking of the vessels is a fundamental concept in the worldview of the Kabbala (mentioned in many places, and this is not the context for explaining it). For our purposes, it suffices to say that the breaking of the vessels was a catastrophic event (as its name suggests), an event in which the manifested results lost their (visible) connection with the underlying causes. Therefore, when discussing the breaking of the vessels, we speak of the sparks having "fallen," not "descended." Descent implies the idea of the light descending through the unfolding succession, in which there is incrementally less light, but not necessarily distortion, and certainly not a total darkening of the divine light. Falling is different: When something occurs that was presumably not planned, the connection with the root is lost. This is what is written here regarding the sparks of supernal *Hohkma* which fell to the *kelippot*.

וְהֵם שָׁם בִּבְחִינַת גָּלוּת, שֶׁהַקְּלִיפּוֹת שׁוֹלְטִים עֲלֵיהֶם וּמַעֲלִימִים חָכְמַת הַתּוֹרָה מֵעֶלְיוֹנִים וְתַחְתּוֹנִים.

They are there in exile, as the *kelippot* rule over them and conceal the wisdom of the Torah from higher and lower beings.

The sparks that fell to the *kelippot* are there in a state of "exile." This means that those sparks of divine revelation and life force are dominated and covered over by the *kelippot*, so that what is seen is the *kelippot* – the natural and material aspect of the worlds – while the *Ḥokhma* of the Torah, which is the divine revelation of life force and meaning everywhere, is not visible.

From higher and lower beings. The new idea here is that this concealment also derives from the higher realities, the angels and souls that are above (and there are few people who live through their souls and not their bodies). Concealment deriving from the lower beings makes sense, since that is where the sparks are, concealed within the *kelippot* in this world, in the body and animal soul. But the concealment is also from the higher beings, for this concealment of the *kelippot* is a concealing of the *Ḥokhma* of the Torah itself, not just from those who receive it. There are things we cannot grasp because of our own limitations, because we haven't studied, or we lack the intellectual capacity. In those situations, the more we free ourselves from the *kelippot*, the more we are able to understand. But then there are things that we cannot grasp because they are themselves locked away in a box, and one who lacks the key to this box cannot reveal what lies within.

Additionally, as will explained, there is even a certain advantage for the lower realities in the elevation of the sparks. Since the sparks themselves are found below, and the elevated stages of reality only have a faint remnant of them, it is specifically the lower realities that possess this advantage since they interact directly with the sparks. This advantage is both in terms of that which is elevated, which is endlessly more valuable than that which is above, as well as in the power they can receive from the spark itself below for the purposes of their service, which is more powerful than what the elevated stages receive.

וְזֶה שֶׁכָּתוּב בְּרַעְיָא מְהֵימְנָא שֶׁהַקּוּשְׁיָה הִיא מִסִּטְרָא דְּרַע.

This is the meaning **of the statement in** *Raya Meheimna,* cited at the beginning of this letter, **that a difficulty is** raised **by the evil side.**

It is written there that in the inner, hidden side of the Torah, which will be studied in the future and which derives from the side of the tree of life, there will be no difficulties from the side of evil, and no disputes from the side of the impure spirit. Even though it was explained there that it was not implying that the revealed Torah derives from the tree of knowledge of good and evil, nevertheless it does indicate that difficulties and disputes arise from the side of evil.

But according to that which is explained here, this difficulty is not part of the Torah, but rather part of the concealment of the *kelippa* upon the *Ḥokhma* of the Torah. The Torah is holy, but a context in which there is a difficulty means a situation where information is missing, where there is a concealment, which comes from the side of evil and *kelippa*. If the side of evil did not exist, there would be no difficulties, as everything would be clear and revealed. However, there is a difficulty that is a part of the clarification of truth and construction of holiness, but it also begins from the fact that we lack information, from a place of difficulty and lack of clarity, in which we do not see the *halakha* or its reasoning. Through examination and clarification of the *halakha,* specifically here, down below, in the place where there is difficulty, we reveal the *Ḥokhma* of Torah to the lower beings as well as the higher ones.

וְהִנֵּה הָעֶלְיוֹנִים אֵין בָּהֶם כֹּחַ לְבָרֵר וּלְהַעֲלוֹת מֵהַשְּׁבִירָה שֶׁבִּקְלִיפַּת נוֹגַהּ אֶלָּא הַתַּחְתּוֹנִים לְבַד

Now, the higher beings **have the power to extract and elevate, from the breaking in the** ***kelippat noga,*** **only the lower** beings,

10 Ḥeshvan
9 Ḥeshvan (leap year)

These sparks of *Ḥokhma* are locked inside of the *kelippa,* in exile. The *kelippa* enclothes them, and they can only be revealed through the garments and ways of the *kelippa.* Therefore, the higher holy angels, who lack anything like a *kelippa,* like difficulty, concealment, lies, and willful sin in their world, are unable to relate to such a reality. Since they don't have this, they cannot arrive at such contexts in order to elevate the holy sparks from there. ☞

לְפִי שֶׁהֵם מְלוּבָּשִׁים בְּגוּף חוּמְרִי 'מַשְׁכָּא דְחִוְיָא' מִקְּלִיפַּת נוֹגַהּ

because they, the people of the lower world, **are enclothed in material bodies, "the skin of a serpent" from the *kelippat noga.***

The "skin of the serpent"[60] is the external *kelippa* of the primordial snake, symbolizing evil and the impure *kelippot.* Its outer *kelippa* is

THE HIGHER ONES LACK POWER

☞ Many have asked, not always seriously: It is known that something impure which touches something pure makes it impure. Why should this not work in the opposite way as well, that when something pure touches something impure, it purifies it? There was someone who answered, entirely seriously: Something impure would touch something pure, but something pure would never touch anything impure. A pure entity would never touch an impure one, because it is pure, and therefore it lacks any point of connection or contact with the impure item. Similarly, the higher angels only understand the holy tongue and do not speak any other language or understand this world of good and evil. They live in an abstract and perfect reality of complete good and anything beyond this is outside their sphere. It can be said that only God Himself, since He is above all definitions, is able to relate to the world of impurity, or man, who is himself within this mixture of good and evil. At the moment when a person performs this extraction of good from evil within himself, he is also able to sift the good from the evil in the part of reality within which he belongs.: "They lack the power" (and not just that "they are unable") hints, perhaps, to an additional nuance here. The *kelippot* and fragments of the world of *tohu* which exist below contain hidden things concealed within them, the primal forces of the world of *tohu* that are beyond anything that exists in the realm of the higher "perfected" beings. In this sense, only someone who resides below, as part of that lower existence, has any capacity for relationship with these imprisoned sparks, as well as with these forces that are with them. It is incumbent upon such a person to use those forces that exist in the *kelippa* in order to break it open, for there is no other way to penetrate the *kelippot.*

60. *Tikkunei Zohar* 48b. See *Likkutei Amarim,* chap. 31.

the *kelippat noga* that is above the three *kelippot* of impurity,[61] and it stands between the impure *kelippot* and the world of holiness. ☞

וְהֵם מַתִּישִׁים כֹּחָהּ בִּשְׁבִירַת הַתַּאֲווֹת וְאִתְכַּפְיָא סִטְרָא אָחֳרָא וְ"יִתְפָּרְדוּ כָּל פּוֹעֲלֵי אָוֶן" (תהלים צב,י).

They sap its strength through breaking lusts and subduing the *sitra aḥara*, and "all evil-doers are scattered" (Ps. 92:10).

They close off and conceal the *Ḥokhma* of the Torah, and thereby cause evil acts to appear in the world. Through the breaking of lusts, etc., the *kelippot* will be separated, and the *Ḥokhma* of Torah will be revealed in the world.[63]

In order to win a war, there must be soldiers on the battlefield, willing to struggle, to endanger themselves. An enemy cannot be

SKIN OF THE SERPENT

☞ As is related in Genesis (2:25), initially man did not have clothing (or, at least, not separate clothing that concealed, only garments that perfectly revealed his holy soul). After the sin, that was due to the snake, the Torah says that God fashioned "garments of skin, and He dressed" (Gen. 3: 21) the man and his wife. What was this garment, and of what skin was it fashioned? As is explained here, these were the physical body and animal soul as we know them today. The reference is to the garment of *kelippat noga*,[66] which allowed man to leave the Garden of Eden and enter this physical world of *kelippat noga*, to live and labor in it. The "skin" is a euphemism for *kelippat noga* because it is like the skin of the physical body, the outer *kelippa* of the body. It is called the "skin of the serpent" after the snake which caused it. On a deeper level, the spiritual essence of this garment of *kelippat noga* is the mixing together of good and evil, in which life cannot be distinguished from death, nor the good inclination from the bad. This is the cause of the sin, and it itself is the serpent.

---

61. *Likkutei Amarim*, chap. 6. See also *Sefer HaḤakira* by the Tzemaḥ Tzedek, pp. 68a–b.

62. *Likkutei Amarim*, chap. 1.

63. When the Tanya was published with the *Likkutei Peirushim*, it listed a footnote here from *Or Torah* of the Tzemaḥ Tzedek: Despite all these things, the angels requested the Torah! (This is difficult to understand, given that which is explained here, and the answer is) that it is through the inner side of Torah, which is the drawing in of supernal lights without requiring any extraction of sparks from the *sitra aḥara*, but only through the performance of commandments with lofty intentions toward those lights (and this will be explained more in this discourse, regarding the inner Torah that will be revealed in the future times).

vanquished without touching him, making contact with him. This is true of the soul as well. There is a *kelippa* in the world, and the only place where one can damage it, exhausting, breaking, and ultimately removing it, is in the one place where a person meets it, in the personal *kelippa* within his soul. This path always begins with a small detail, but from there it grows immeasurably. ☞ ☞

וְלָכֵן בָּאִים הָעֶלְיוֹנִים לִשְׁמוֹעַ חִידּוּשֵׁי תוֹרָה מֵהַתַּחְתּוֹנִים מַה שֶּׁמְּחַדְּשִׁים וּמְגַלִּים תַּעֲלוּמוֹת הַחָכְמָה שֶׁהָיוּ כְּבוּשִׁים בַּגּוֹלָה עַד עַתָּה.

Therefore, the higher beings **come to hear novel Torah ideas from the lower** beings, **when they formulate new ideas and discover the mysteries of wisdom that until then were suppressed in exile.**

As was explained, these new ideas of Torah were not only concealed from the lower beings,[64] who are found within the *kelippot* and con-

SUBDUING

☞ The author of the *Tanya* speaks of "breaking" and "subduing," but not of the "reversing." Subduing and reversing are two levels and two phases of the challenges of the soul. In the first phase, one subdues the evil inclination, while in the second phase, one no longer needs to force the evil inclination, since it has reversed itself to goodness. From the moment a person achieves such a reversal, he is no longer the same person. He is no longer the person down below with the *kelippot*; he is of the higher realms and not the lower. He no longer belongs to that lower service of breaking the *kelippa* and extracting the sparks.

WHY DID THE TORAH DESCEND SO LOW?

☞ Initially, one could have asked: Why is the Torah there, among the *kelippot*? Why is it not given in simplicity, without concealments, without questions? This is one of those eternal questions to which no complete answer can be given by man, only descriptive statements. One possible statement is that it descended together with us. This means that it is not only we who are with it, but that it is here with us, as if it is following after us. This is because, in the end, it is only with us that the Torah has meaning and purpose. The deeper point is that this Torah is divine, and the divine expression is truly beyond *Ein Sof*. If *Ein Sof* is beyond any end, that means that end and boundary are beyond *Ein Sof*. Only within the friction between *Ein Sof* and boundar-

64. As was said by our Sages in *Shir HaShirim Rabba* 8:13, on the verse

cealment and therefore cannot see, but also from the higher beings. Here, the intent is that only the lower beings can reveal these things, because the keys to do so are with them, down below, and therefore, the higher beings come to listen to the lower ones. ☞

וְכָל אִישׁ יִשְׂרָאֵל יוּכַל לְגַלּוֹת תַּעֲלוּמוֹת חָכְמָה, (לְגַלּוֹת) וּלְחַדֵּשׁ שֵׂכֶל חָדָשׁ

And every Jew can discover the mysteries of wisdom, (to reveal) and to innovate new insights, in the Torah,

Every Jew, whether he is a great scholar, or has little scholarship, or is someone who is not a scholar at all, can uncover new insights in the Torah. This appears to be a difficult concept. It is accepted thinking that innovative ideas of Torah are only the purview of great scholars, for only they can penetrate beneath all that has been said before and reconstruct the ideas in a novel way.[65] However, this is not precisely true (and this applies to other fields as well): The capability to generate new ideas belongs to anyone who is able to perceive the subject in a

ies – blockages and breaks, questions and answers, lust and its subdual – can there be a precious contact between the infinite and finite. It is there alone that the divine essence which is above both finite and infinite can be revealed.

THE HIGHER BEINGS COME TO LISTEN TO THE LOWER ONES

☞ How are we meant to understand this, that the higher beings descend to listen? They cannot descend without clothing themselves in a body, etc., and they will become lower beings, no longer higher ones. Rather, the meaning is that in this context, they are receiving from the lower beings. In general, the process is that the lower beings receive from the higher ones, and those higher ones from those higher than them, etc. This statement shows that there is a way in which the higher beings receive specifically from those below them. In other words, in this sense, the lower beings are actually "higher." This accords with the more general truth about the world of God, that there is no absolute state of "higher" and "lower," but rather it is relative, depending on the situation.

This perspective has broad implications,

"Companions listen to your voice." See also *Devarim Rabba* 2:14; *Zohar,* Part 3, 173a; Jerusalem Talmud, *Rosh HaShana,* 1:3.

65. See *Hilkhot Talmud Torah* by the author of the *Tanya,* chap. 2, *halakha* 2.

different way, and sometimes this capacity exists specifically in a person who lacks knowledge. ☞

הֵן בַּהֲלָכוֹת הֵן בְּאַגָּדוֹת הֵן בְּנִגְלֶה הֵן בְּנִסְתָּר, כְּפִי בְּחִינַת שֹׁרֶשׁ נִשְׁמָתוֹ

involving *halakhot, aggadot,* the revealed Torah, **or the esoteric** teachings of the Torah, **in accordance with the root of his soul.**

The root of the soul of each person belongs to a certain spark and part of the Torah. In general, the Torah can be divided into categories of *halakha* and *aggada* which is, to a certain degree, the division between revealed and hidden aspects of Torah. Just as the Torah can be divided into these two categories of revealed and hidden, so too the souls can be divided. There are those that, like the revealed Torah, are enclothed in the world of *Asiya* and in the revealed Torah that descends into it, and it is there that such souls experience vibrancy and life. Then there

including for our lives here, for each person. It impacts how we each see ourselves and how we perceive each other, who is higher and who is lower.

EVERY JEW CAN DISCOVER

☞ It is true that the more a person knows, and as his soul assumes a more general disposition, the more broadly and deeply he perceives reality, even on behalf of others. But in this context, we are not discussing what is considered innovative in the eyes of the world, but an idea that is novel personally, not relatively. Just as every soul has a root and point of truth of its own, so every spark of *Ḥokhma* that is concealed within the *kelippot* has a root of truth unique to it. As is known, souls are linked to sparks. For it is stated in kabbalistic writings that there are 600,000 letters in the Torah, correlating to the 600,000 souls (see "*HaYom Yom,*" 13 Adar Bet) and the hint to this is in the acronym formed by the letters of "Yisrael," spelling out in Hebrew: "There are 600,000 letters in the Torah" (*Megaleh Amukot, Ofan* 186). Every spark of a Jewish soul descends to this world in order to reveal and elevate the spark of Torah unique to itself, and every spark of *Ḥokhma* waits through time for that one soul that can redeem it. It can thus be said that the novel idea of that person which awaits him derives from the root of his soul, and when that insight is revealed, the inner depths of his soul are revealed. The revealer and the revealed operate so closely that it is truly all one revelation. The innovation of this one specific soul needs to be revealed in the world as part of the overall rectification of existence, and the world cannot function without both this insight and the soul to which it belongs.

are those that, like the hidden Torah, are tied to the higher worlds. These souls are also present within a body in this world, eating and drinking, walking the earth. But their root, their drive, is found above, in the underlying hidden reasons of reality and the lofty meanings and connections. While every soul is a complete structure, and interacts with every aspect of the Torah, nevertheless, the innovative insight that is unique to a particular soul is only manifested in specific circumstances.[66]

וּמְחוּיָּיב בַּדָּבָר לְהַשְׁלִים נִשְׁמָתוֹ בְּהַעֲלָאַת כָּל הַנִּיצוֹצוֹת שֶׁנָּפְלוּ לְחֶלְקָהּ וּלְגוֹרָלָהּ, כַּנּוֹדָע

This is imperative, in order **to complete his soul through the elevation of all the sparks that fell into its portion and lot, as is known**

A person – every person – not only can innovate in Torah, he is obligated to do so. It is more than a role that is assigned to him.[67] It is an internal, personal necessity that the soul requires in order to bring itself to wholeness. It is just as the author of the *Tanya* writes in his *Hilkhot Talmud Torah*[68] in the name of the scholars of the Kabbala: If a soul does not succeed in perfecting itself by revealing its unique insights, it must return as a further reincarnation, etc. Since this is an internal personal responsibility, it is impossible to be satisfied with only partial success. This role cannot be given over to another

66. See similar ideas in epistle 7, that every person is obligated in all the commandments, yet each person also has a specific commandment with which he is "more careful," and a unique "share" in Torah and in God. See also in epistle 13, that every person contains all attributes, and that the differences between people are based on that which is revealed and concealed and that each person's revelation is utterly unique.

67. See, at length, regarding the concepts of "portion" and "lot" previously in epistle 7, and the commentary there.

68. See *Hilkhot Talmud Torah* by the author of the *Tanya,* chap. 1, *halakha* 4, where he quotes from the scholars of the Kabbala that one who has not achieved what he was meant to achieve in the four levels of Torah must return to life as a reincarnation, etc. See citations for other locations in kabbalistic writings in *Likkutei Siḥot,* vol. 19, p. 231, footnote 31.

to complete, for it is the portion and lot of this soul, and only this soul can achieve it. ☞ ☞

(all words of Torah, and especially a matter of *halakha*, is a spark from the Divine Presence, which is the very word of God, as stated in the Gemara: "The word of God, this is *halakha*" (Shabbat 138b),

(וְכָל דִּבְרֵי תוֹרָה וּבִפְרָט דְּבַר הֲלָכָה הִיא נִיצוֹץ מֵהַשְּׁכִינָה, שֶׁהִיא הִיא דְּבַר ה׳ כִּדְאִיתָא בַּגְּמָרָא: דְּבַר ה׳ זוֹ הֲלָכָה

These points have already been made, but here the author reviews them for the purposes of summary and emphasis (and this is, perhaps, why they are in parentheses).[69] Sparks of holiness that fell from above into this world are elevated through the *halakhot* (more than any other aspect of Torah) that descend into the physical context, including even into the *kelippot*. The spark of the Divine Presence is the word of God, for just as speech emerges from the soul, so does the spark of the Divine Presence emerge in order to dwell and live in the separated worlds. Such is the case for the commanded *halakhot* below that emerge from the inner divine reality. This emergence creates a situation in which the inner reasoning of the *halakhot* is not visible, and they appear only as the commands of the King: Do this and do not do that.

ITS PORTION AND LOT

☞ The concept of "lot" relates to the essence of the soul, prior to any of its manifestations, just as the lot is not set based on intellect or emotions, but only on "This is how it is, and this is what must be done." It is to this portion and lot of the soul that the sparks of Torah are linked, and it is only through them that these sparks can be elevated, when a person uncovers these things in his mind. This is his unique Torah insight, one that no other person could see or imagine.

TORAH INSIGHTS COME SPECIFICALLY FROM BELOW

☞ These insights are truly innovations, even from the perspective of God. That which descends from above is not an insight. God speaks it and the layers of worlds simply reflect what He says. Innovation comes from below, and "below" is where the individual soul exists in its body, in a particular time and with a particular *kelippa*. That which ascends from there is an innovation in all the worlds!

69. In the first edition there were no parentheses.

סוֹד מַלְכוּת דַּאֲצִילוּת הַמְּלֻבֶּשֶׁת לְחָכְמָה דַּאֲצִילוּת **the secret of *Malkhut* of *Atzilut* that enclothes the *Ḥokhma* of *Atzilut***

In the language of Kabbala, this descent is the secret of Malkhut of Atzilut that enclothes the Ḥokhma of Atzilut. As was explained, *Malkhut* is expressed through the commands of *halakha*. But these commands and the distinctions between permitted and prohibited are garments for the supernal *Ḥokhma*, points of divine revelation in the world. This indicates that it is as if God Himself is clothed and revealed within the *halakhot*.

וּמְלוּבָּשִׁים בְּמַלְכוּת דִּיצִירָה, וְיָרְדוּ בִּקְלִיפַּת נוֹגַהּ בִּשְׁבִירַת הַכֵּלִים). **and which are enclothed in *Malkhut* of *Yetzira* and descended into *kelippat noga* at the breaking of the vessels).**

In the breaking of the vessels, holy sparks descended and were enclothed in the *halakhot* into the *kelippa* itself.

In these short phrases, there is an emphasis and even a small addition to what was said previously. Before, the discussion was about sparks that fell and the extraction that is performed through the study of *halakha*. Here, the author adds that these sparks, seemingly aspects of divinity in exile, are themselves the "word of God is *halakha*." If this is the case, the in-depth study of *halakha* and the insights and innovations that are revealed through study, are not merely vessels that allow for the extraction of the sparks, but rather they are the sparks themselves. The *halakha* that is clarified and innovated in its details and reasonings is itself the spark that is being unlocked from within the *kelippa*. This is a perspective of Torah study as not just a preparatory tool to attain practical extraction of the sparks, but rather it is the essence of the redemption of the sparks themselves.

וְזֶה שֶׁנֶּאֱמַר בַּגְּמָרָא: כָּל הָעוֹסֵק בַּתּוֹרָה אָמַר הקב"ה מַעֲלֶה אֲנִי עָלָיו כְּאִלּוּ פְּדָאַנִי וְאֶת בָּנַי מִבֵּין הָאוּמּוֹת הָעוֹלָם. **This is** the meaning **of the statement in the Gemara: Whoever engages in the Torah, the Holy One, blessed be He, says** about him, **"I ascribe** credit **to him as though he redeemed Me and My children from among the nations of the world."**

As was explained, engagement in Torah, especially in the innovative revelation of the details and reasons for *halakhot* that were not known previously, is the redemption of the Divine Presence from exile.[70] When a person breaks the *kelippa* and forces it (similar to the breaking of desires for things of this world), and involves himself in the exploration of Torah, he extracts and frees the Divine Presence from the *kelippa* that he broke. The Divine Presence then ascends and unites with God and through this unification, it is as if the person has redeemed God Himself from among the nations of the world (the *kelippot*). "My children" refers to the souls of Israel that ascend, together with the novel Torah concepts they revealed. This is because the innovated concept of Torah a person reveals is a spark of his own soul. This spark ascends with the spark of the Divine Presence, for when it redeems the Divine Presence, it also redeems itself from exile.

Until this point, the author explained the essence and virtue of studying the revealed Torah, based on the passage he initially cited from the *Zohar*, which is nearly the opposite of the superficial meaning of the phrase "those who lack knowledge." It does not refer to Torah study that is flawed in its holiness, embedded in the *kelippa*. Rather, it is study that is so lofty in its holiness that it is capable of descending to incredibly low levels in order to raise up holiness from the *kelippot*. Given this, it is this kind of Torah study that applies especially to the time of exile, during which good and evil are mixed together and must be separated. In this phase, holiness is not visible and gives its strength to the sustaining of a world of lies and evil. It is only Torah study that can relate to these different areas that is capable of elevating them.

From this point onward in this letter, the author will explain the main point of the *Zohar*, in relation to the study of the hidden Torah. If study of the revealed Torah, the Mishna, etc., belongs primarily to the time of exile, as was explained, then the study of the hidden Torah belongs primarily to the time of redemption.

---

70. *Berakhot* 8a. For more on this topic, see *Keter Shem Tov* 127:2.

11 Ḥeshvan

10 Ḥeshvan (leap year)

אֲבָל בְּצֵאת הַשְּׁכִינָה מִקְּלִיפַּת נוֹגַהּ [נוּסָּח אַחֵר: מֵהַקְּלִיפּוֹת], אַחַר שֶׁיּוּשְׁלַם בֵּירוּר הַנִּיצוֹצוֹת וְיוּפְרַד הָרַע מֵהַטּוֹב, וְיִתְפָּרְדוּ כָּל פּוֹעֲלֵי אָוֶן, וְלָא שַׁלְטָא אִילָנָא דְּטוֹב וָרַע.

However, when the Divine Presence will emerge from the *kelippat noga* [alternative version: from the *kelippot*], after the extraction of the sparks has been completed and the evil has been separated from the good, and all evildoers will be scattered, and the tree of knowledge of **good and evil will not rule.**

The time of exile is the time when the Divine Presence is here, ruled over by the *kelippat noga* and the tree of knowledge of good and evil. This means that the dominant perspective in this reality is that of the tree of knowledge of good and evil, a perspective of hidden divine light and lack of clarity as to what is good and what is evil, what is a commandment and what is a sin. In this reality, as was explained, the service of man is to clarify and extract sparks of holiness, to clarify good and evil. This service has an endpoint, when all the sparks are extracted and evil is separated from good, etc. It is explained in Kabbala writings that there are a finite number of sparks that fell during the breaking of the vessels, and a time will come when this extraction process is complete.

בְּצֵאת הַטּוֹב מִמֶּנָּה, אֲזַי לֹא יִהְיֶה עֵסֶק הַתּוֹרָה וְהַמִּצְוֹת לְבָרֵר בֵּירוּרִין

Then, **when the good is extracted from it, the engagement in Torah and the mitzvot will not be for** the purpose of **performing the extractions,**

When this service has concluded, when the good is extracted from it, the engagement in Torah and the mitzvot will not be for the purpose of performing the extractions. After the extraction of good from evil is complete, there will be a different purpose for the study of Torah and performance of commandments. ☞

THE EXISTENCE OF EVIL AFTER THE CONCLUSION OF THE EXTRACTION

☞ Presumably, upon the completion of the extraction when all good has emerged from the *kelippa*, evil would cease to exist. The life force of evil was derived from

כִּי אִם לְיַחֵד יִחוּדִים עֶלְיוֹנִים יוֹתֵר, לְהַמְשִׁיךְ אוֹרוֹת עֶלְיוֹנִים יוֹתֵר מֵהָאֲצִילוּת, כְּמוֹ שֶׁכָּתַב הָאֲרִ"י ז"ל.

but for uniting loftier unifications, to draw down loftier lights than *Atzilut*, as the Arizal wrote.

But for uniting loftier unifications, to draw down loftier lights than *Atzilut*,[71] as the Arizal wrote,[72] the change of state in the future will not be, as some might think, that there will no longer be divine service (and all divine service is, in one form or another, through Torah and

good, from its relationship with and distortion of good. It is like a person who is constantly thinking about its connection with good, "What is it doing, what is it thinking, how can I deceive and plunder it?" Ultimately, what is evil in isolation? It is nothing! It is like a smile, or anger, or a relationship with someone who does not exist. It seems right to say that evil as a reality that we experience, and are occasionally dominated by, will cease to exist. There will no longer be the life we know today, in which evil is as present as good, and sometimes in more substantial form. Currently, evil is part of the experience of life, sometimes overpowering good, sometimes conceding to good, with no clear victor. After the conclusion of the extraction, the *kelippa* will remain, but like a distant memory, something experienced by someone else. It will be almost the opposite of the current state, in which the physical world is tangible, and spirituality and holiness are things we read about in a book, like the experiences of other people. This kind of distinction appears in other places: Before the divine constriction, the Divine was the simple default and reality was the novel innovation (and so it still is, in the level of *Atzilut*, as well as prior to the first sin, and in the lives of the greatest tzaddikim. It will be again, in the future). But now, the Divine is the novel innovation, and reality is the simple default (see *Hemshekh Ayin Beit* 2: 934 and onward, and the writings of the Lubavitcher Rebbe in many other places). Something similar to this is told as a story about Rabbi Levi Yitzḥak of Berditchev, who used to claim: "Master of the universe, you did not design this world in an orderly way, for this world is here, and we read about Gehenna in the book *Reishit Ḥokhma*! I promise you that if it would have been the other way around, no Jewish person would ever sin." The implication of these ideas is that the world will not change into a totally different world. What exists today will also exist then, in the world and within our souls. Only our relationship with these things will change (to a state similar to those experienced by rare exceptional people who are already on this level, and to some degree, to the state all people reach in moments of elevation). As will be explained in the continuation here, in the future there will also be a place and need for the continuation of life with Torah and commandments, the same Torah and the same commandments, just in a different way.

---

71. In the edits the phrase could be "above *Atzilut*."

72. See the introduction to *Sha'ar HaYiḥudim* and other places, regarding the lofty unifications that draw higher lights that are above *Atzilut*. It appears from these ideas that this will primarily take place in the future.

commandments). Rather, it will take a different form. If currently the form is the necessity of extracting good from the *kelippa* and repairing the world, in the next phase it will be service directly with good and the divine light. The Torah and its commandments are the divine will of God. There is an external aspect to them that relates to the world and its problems. When these problems are solved, the inner aspect will come to expression. This is the aspect of His wisdom itself, its true inner nature.

As an analogy, like a project in any other field, there is an initial phase of differentiation. From the mixture of this world, of opinions, desires, needs, and falsehoods, one must clarify what kind of work is going to be done. The materials to be used in this work must be selected, as well as the methods that will be employed. When these choices are being made, while the different possibilities may all seem equivalent, they are not. There are good and bad options, possible and impossible routes to take. This important first phase is the establishment of basic infrastructure. More advanced phases follow in which the structure is built upward toward its purpose. In these more advanced phases, there is also clarification and choice, but it is not a choice and differentiation between "yes and no," or "good and evil." Rather, it is the service and choice between "good and better," that which is cleaner and more elevated, forever upward.

The author of the *Tanya* speaks here, using the language of the Arizal, of "unifications." A unification means the union between the spark and its source, between the Divine Presence and God. This is the service we perform at all times. Currently, when the Divine Presence and the spark are hidden within the *kelippa,* the action of unification is to separate it from the *kelippa,* after which it automatically unites with the Divine, like a small light with a large one. This unification relates to the world of *Atzilut* because that is the world of unity regarding the lower worlds of *Beria, Yetzira,* and *Asiya,* which are the worlds of separation. During this time, in relation to the worlds and the *kelippot, Atzilut* is the aspect of divinity, in the sense that the lights above *Atzilut* are not really relevant to us. However, after the phase of extraction from the evil is complete, the meaning of unifications will no longer be that of separating the spark from the *kelippa.* Rather, it will be the elevation of that spark to a higher level of unification. Light, even holy light, is considered a part of reality that must be unified with, and subsumed to, higher states of unity that do not yet exist. Divine service at these levels of unification is what the author here refers to as "uniting loftier unifications, to draw down loftier lights than *Atzilut*." *Atzilut* is the oneness contrasting with the separation, the divine relative to the broken, separated lower worlds. But once the relationship is with the divine oneness itself, the service will be to unify unifications at higher levels, drawing down lights that are above *Atzilut*.

וְהַכֹּל עַל יְדֵי פְּנִימִיּוּת הַתּוֹרָה, לְקַיֵּים הַמִּצְוֹת בְּכַוָּונוֹת עֶלְיוֹנוֹת, שֶׁמְּכַוְּונוֹת לְאוֹרוֹת עֶלְיוֹנִים כו'

All this will be achieved **by means of the inner dimension of the Torah, by fulfilling the mitzvot through lofty intentions, with the intent toward the supernal lights...**

These lofty intentions are part of the inner dimension of Torah. This illustrates that Jewish life, Torah study, action, and experience are all within the purview of the inner dimension of Torah; not what to do and not to do, or how to do, but rather, the inner meaning of all these things. This means from the soul and inward, upward, to the spiritual worlds that are the inner aspect of this physical world. ☞

TO FULFILL THE COMMANDMENTS WITH LOFTY INTENTIONS

☞ Most of the Torah, written and oral, *halakha* and *aggada*, relates to this world, the people who live in it and the physical things and events it contains. However, each of these things, on a broad scale as well as in every individual detail, has a spiritual root that is above, abstract and more inclusive. One can get glimpses of this in some of the texts that discuss Torah study in the Garden of Eden (the "study hall of the heavens"; see *Likkutei Torah*, Lev. 22: 2 and onward): There, too, our Torah is studied, the same verses and Mishna, but they are studied in relation to the spiritual essence of all things, abstracted and broadened. This will not only happen in the future in the Garden of Eden, but even now, there are people who see and live this side of Torah and the world.

Since, at that time, the service will not be extracting good from evil, we will no longer need to involve ourselves in the aspect of Torah that relates to this mixture, the world of action of *kelippat noga*, neither its actions, nor the basic study and thought about these things. Since the service will be to unite higher unifications, it will be necessary to study the Torah that deals with that. As was previously mentioned, the inner dimension of Torah (Kabbala) is not enclothed in the physical world, but only in the higher supernal worlds, and

כִּי שֹׁרֶשׁ הַמִּצְוֹת הוּא לְמַעְלָה מַעְלָה בָּאֵין סוֹף בָּרוּךְ הוּא **For the root of the mitzvot is higher above, in *Ein Sof*, blessed be He**

The action of a commandment is in this world, for this is the world of action, but the root of the commandment is higher above. This is true not only for commandments. All physical things have their initial roots above. Every object and action is the outgrowth of the unfolding succession from above downward, from the abstract and general structures of the higher worlds down to the detailed diversity we see in this world. Yet, the actions and objects of the commandments are different from all other things in that they are not only the result of the supernal lights, but they are themselves, here, the supernal lights. Not as a general root, but the specific root of this commandment as it is performed below, arriving from *Ein Sof* above. Therefore, the intention of this commandment when directed downward, in all its details, both practical and not practical, ascends upward. It is not only awakening something which in turn awakens something else. Rather, it itself ascends, separate from the *kelippot* of this world, level by level, until *Ein Sof*.

sometimes not even in those. This dimension deals with lofty unifications, the relationships of the supernal concepts, lights, meaning, abstract utterances to the Divine. It is not that it denies the existence of our world, for it also relates to the underlying reasoning of the practical commandments and their meaning. Rather, its relationship is similar to the circumstances that prevailed prior to the sin of the tree of knowledge. There is physical and material reality, there is evil and *kelippa*, but they are far away, in another place and time, completely separated from our holy reality. They are like the thoughts and experiences of a different person, and we only relate to these matters through the internal aspect that is within all holy things.

Therefore, for example, the relationship to practical commandments will no longer be one of practical definitions as to what is permitted or prohibited. Instead, it will relate to the meanings of such actions above, the inner intent and spiritual service that we are fulfilling with our physical action. While action is directed and constricted downward, to the material that gives it form, intention is directed upward, to the supernal lights, the underlying meaning. This is done not through constriction but through expansion, higher and higher to infinity, as well as downward and to the sides, in terms of implications and connections to ever-increasing parts of existence.

(וּמַה שֶּׁאָמְרוּ רַזַ"ל דְּמִצְוֹת בְּטֵילוֹת לֶעָתִיד לָבוֹא, הַיְינוּ בִּתְחִיַּית הַמֵּתִים

(and as for our Sages' statement that the mitzvot will be annulled in the future, that is referring to the resurrection of the dead,

The Sages' statement that the mitzvot will be annulled in the future apparently contradicts what is written here, that in the future the Torah and commandments will be fulfilled in their inner dimension. He answers that that is referring to the resurrection of the dead. The concept of "in the future" has two meanings in the words of our Sages: One refers to the time of the Messiah. The second refers to the period after the Messiah, when the world will change fundamentally, and the dead will walk. In that time, the commandments will be annulled. ☞

אֲבָל לִימוֹת הַמָּשִׁיחַ קוֹדֶם תְּחִיַּית הַמֵּתִים אֵין בְּטֵלִים).

but in the messianic era, before the resurrection of the dead, they will not be annulled).

It is emphasized that only in the time of resurrection will the commandments be annulled. In the time preceding this, the messianic era, they will not. This means that after the period of exile, when the service of extractions has been completed, there will still be a context and time in which the commandments will not be annulled. On the contrary, during that time they will be fulfilled in their entirety. Their actions will be perfected, as all commandments will be performed, and their inner intentions will be fulfilled in all their spiritual loftiness, reaching ever higher. ☞ ☞

THE COMMANDMENTS WILL BE ANNULLED IN THE FUTURE

☞ In the Talmud (*Nidda* 61b), it is written that a garment made with prohibited diverse materials, and which is prohibited to wear, can be used as a shroud for the dead. From this it is derived that commandments will be annulled in the future. The author of the *Tanya* deduces from the words of the Sages (as do the *Tosafot* commentaries there) that the meaning of "the future" in this context is the time of resurrection, when the dead will rise in garments of prohibited materials. However, the Rashba interprets this to be referring to the individual future of each person after he dies, since a dead person is exempt from commandments. This is also implied somewhat by the later part of the passage in the Talmud there. See also the observation of the Lubavitcher Rebbe there, printed in Lessons in *Tanya*.

וְלָכֵן יִהְיֶה גַּם עִיקַּר עֵסֶק הַתּוֹרָה, גַּם כֵּן בִּפְנִימִיּוּת הַמִּצְוֹת וְטַעֲמֵיהֶם הַנִּסְתָּרִים.

Therefore, the main engagement in Torah and mitzvot will also focus **on the inner dimension of the mitzvot and their hidden reasons.**

THE MESSIANIC ERA AND THE RESURRECTION OF THE DEAD

☞ Regarding the different periods of the future, the messianic era and the resurrection of the dead, there are different opinions among the Sages of Israel, and these issues are not completely clear. The kabbalists and hasidim think that the period of resurrection is one of a completely altered reality in which the nature of the physical world and the relationship between body and soul will change. Therefore, they rarely discuss this period, except to indicate that it will be different from what we know now, and that this is the meaning of the statement that the commandments will be annulled during that time. (See further on in greater detail.) In contrast, the messianic era is a period they do discuss, described as a time that represents the continuation of our world with all its features. But instead of the distorted place it is now, the world will become aligned, the distortions corrected, the proportions balanced, with each thing in its proper place. Then, too, material will remain material, spiritual will remain spiritual, Jews and non-Jews will retain their distinctiveness, but with a rectification and balancing of the relationships between them. Therefore, the messianic era is not one in which the commandments will be annulled. On the contrary, they will be revealed in all their glory and greatness, from their lowest point up to their root above *Atzilut*. They will be like pillars upon which the whole world rests, a subject on which the whole world focuses (see Rambam, *Sefer Shofetim, Hilkhot Melakhim* 12: 5).

IN THE FUTURE, THE COMMANDMENTS WILL BE ANNULLED

☞ The Lubavitcher Rebbeexplains that the intent here is with regard to the idea of being commanded. Commandments will no longer be "commanded," like an order of a king to his servants (cited in the explanation of the Lubavitcher Rebbe on *Pirkei Avot*, chap. 5, in the section "*Halakhot* of the Oral Torah that are never annulled," *Sefer HaSiḥot* 5752, p. 31). But the existence of these actions as expressions of God's will is eternal and will exist even during the time of resurrection. He explains that the idea of a command to a person only applies to a person who perceives himself as a totally independent entity, in which case there is a need to command him to behave in accordance with the will of God. After this period of man's service has concluded, when a person's existence is filled with the will of God, and he is unified with God in the sense of "Israel and God are entirely one" (as will be the case in the future), there will no longer be a category of "commands." At that time, a person will no longer be his own individual self, but rather an aspect of God's existence and will, automatically expressing himself through the natural actions of the commandments.

This is referring to the inner dimension of the mitzvot and their hidden reasons, meaning the inner dimension of Torah that relates to these aspects of the commandments, their hidden inner reasons. ☞

Studying the hidden dimension of Torah will be necessary at that future time, for it will delineate the service that is needed then, the performance of increasingly ascendant unifications. Since each level of elevation will have higher forms and meanings, concepts we do not yet know, it will be necessary to learn these things continuously.

אֲבָל הַנִּגְלוֹת יִהְיוּ גְּלוּיִם וִידוּעִים לְכָל אִישׁ יִשְׂרָאֵל בִּידִיעָה בִּתְחִלָּה בְּלִי שִׁכְחָה.

However, the revealed matters **will be revealed and known to every Jew, as innate knowledge, without forgetfulness.**

In contrast to the hidden Torah, which we will need to study, the revealed Torah, which is the clothing of the Torah in this world, will no longer need to be studied. It will instead simply be known as the reality of life, self-evident. In this world, the reality of life is the physical nature of the world, so the commandments that are enclothed in this world must be learned from a book. In the future, when this world is organized and straightened in accordance with Torah and

THE HIDDEN REASONING OF THE COMMANDMENTS

☞ There are both hidden and revealed reasons for the commandments. The revealed Torah mentions specific reasons for certain commandments. The commandments do not appear in the Torah as random orders – "Do this and don't do that" – without any logical basis to explain how and why. In many instances, it is possible to discern the connection between different commandments, as well as their broader connection to Torah and the world. This illustrates that it is possible to understand something of the reason for a commandment using the revealed intellect of this world. There are also many hidden reasons for the commandments in the inner dimension of Torah which are linked to the inner space of the soul. The physical action of a commandment that is visible in our lower world has spiritual roots that broaden and interconnect with all of reality above. In this world, those reasons are hidden, just as the inner Torah is hidden in the world and the inner soul is hidden in the body. In the future, in the messianic era (and even in this world, within special people, or at special times, and even within every person occasionally), after the period of extraction is completed and this world is no longer dominated by the distortions of the *kelippa*, these inner roots will be revealed. At that time, people will immerse themselves in the inner dimensions of the commandments.

its commandments, tangible reality will be in alignment with the commandments. This is similar to the way that any person has certain areas within his life that he intrinsically knows and has no need to study. A child knows the difference between a door and a wall and does not attempt to pass through a wall. He has no need to study this point and he will not forget it. Similarly, in the future, we will not need to study the revealed Torah.

וְאֵין צְרִיכִים לַעֲסוֹק בָּהֶם, אֶלָּא לְ׳עֵרֶב רַב׳ שֶׁלֹּא יִזְכּוּ לְמִטְעַם מֵאִילָנָא דְחַיֵּי שֶׁהוּא פְּנִימִיּוּת הַתּוֹרָה וְהַמִּצְוָה

They will not have to be occupied with them, the revealed Torah and mitzvot, **apart from the "mixed multitude** [*eirev rav*]," **who will not merit to taste from the tree of life, which is the inner dimension of the Torah and mitzvot.**

The revealed Torah is also part of the tree of life. Its taste, however, is only experienced through learning the inner dimension of Torah and the reasons for the commandments. In order for the revealed Torah to become part of a person's instinctive knowledge, he has to "be there." This means he has to experience the taste and reasoning of the Torah as if these things are real life, and that it is from these things that he draws his life force, with love and fear. When a person does not study Torah this way, and while he is learning he is actually "somewhere else," he still has not comprehended these matters through his own independent understanding, and he will have to continue studying the Torah then as we do now.

Here the author speaks explicitly about the "mixed multitude" in comparison to Israel. The reason is that here we are discussing future times, after the extractions have been completed. Just as the different sparks will have been extracted from the *kelippot,* so will all the souls of Israel be extracted, from both physical and spiritual exile. Given this, those who remain then within the *kelippa* will be those who were externally attached to Israel, and they form the "mixed multitude."

וּצְרִיכִים לַעֲסוֹק [בַּתּוֹרָה] בַּמִּשְׁנָה, לְהַתִּישׁ כֹּחַ הַסִּטְרָא אָחֳרָא הַדָּבוּק

They will need to engage [**in the Torah**] **in the Mishna, to sap the**

בָּהֶם (עַל יְדֵי עֵסֶק הַתּוֹרָה. בִּכְתַב יָד לֵיתָא) שֶׁלֹּא תִּשְׁלוֹט בָּהֶם לְהַחֲטִיאָם.

strength of the *sitra aḥara* that is attached to them (by engaging in the Torah; this does not appear in the manuscripts), **so that it does not rule over them, to cause them to sin.**

They will not be able to fully separate themselves from the *sitra aḥara*, as Israel will during that time, but they will be able to weaken its hold over them. This will transform sin into a distant possibility, like a threat uttered from far away, a wish that has no possibility of materializing, so that it does not rule over them, to cause them to sin. ☞

כְּדִכְתִיב ״וְהַחוֹטֵא בֶּן מֵאָה שָׁנָה יְקוּלָּל״ (ישעיה סה,כ) שֶׁיִּהְיוּ חוֹטְאִים מֵעֶרֶב רַב, וְגַם לְמַעֲשֶׂה יִהְיוּ צְרִיכִים לְפִרְטֵי הִלְכוֹת אִסּוּר וְטוּמְאָה יוֹתֵר מִיִּשְׂרָאֵל, שֶׁלֹּא יְאֻרַע לָהֶם פְּסוּל וְטוּמְאָה וְאִסּוּר כִּי ״לֹא יְאוּנֶּה כוּ׳״ (משלי יב,כא).

As it is written: "And the sinner will be cursed when he is one hundred years old" (Isa. 65:30), which shows **that there will be sinners from the mixed multitude. Also, in practice they will require the details of the laws of prohibited** items **and impurity more than Israelites, so that they do not suffer** cases of **disqualification, impurity, or prohibited** matters, **as "no** iniquity **will befall** the righteous" (Prov. 12:21).

Accordingly, this study will not be something the Israelites engage in, in contrast to the mixed multitude. ☞

THEY NEED TO SAP THE STRENGTH OF THE *SITRA AḤARA*

☞ There is a certain parallelism between the messianic era and the time of the exile, in the sense that everything that exists in one, exists in the other, but for different people and with different frequencies and relationships. This parallelism expresses the idea that these are not two separate worlds with different times, places, and souls. Everything is here, at all times, and the only question is "Where is the person, what does he think or feel, what is his life?" Even now, a person can sometimes reach the state of being in the Garden of Eden and existing in the messianic era. Similarly, it may be that during the actual messianic era, there will be people who, in various senses, will still be here, in this time.

וְגַם אֶפְשָׁר וְקָרוֹב הַדָּבָר שֶׁיֵּדְעוּ מִפְּנִימִיּוּת הַתּוֹרָה כָּל גּוּפֵי הַתּוֹרָה הַנִּגְלֵית כְּמוֹ אַבְרָהָם אָבִינוּ עָלָיו הַשָּׁלוֹם, וְלָכֵן אֵין צְרִיכִים לַעֲסוֹק בָּהֶם כְּלָל.

It is also possible, and indeed likely, that they will know the inner dimension of the Torah, the whole essence of the revealed Torah, like our forefather Abraham, may he rest in peace, and therefore they will not need to engage in them at all.

This is an additional element that has not been discussed previously. Before, the discussion was of natural knowledge, innate understanding, that people would know the laws. Additionally, the author discussed that "no iniquity will befall the righteous." Now, the author speaks about a different kind of knowledge.

Our forefather Abraham lived prior to the giving of the Torah. He did not receive the Torah, yet our Sages say that he fulfilled the entire Torah (*Yoma* 28b, and elsewhere). The Torah he studied was not our revealed Torah, for that was only given at Mount Sinai. It appears that the Torah that Abraham fulfilled was the inner dimension of Torah, the Torah as it exists above, not how it is enclothed below (as this lower state was conferred at Sinai, as explained in Hasidism). This leads to the question: How did Abraham know the practical details of the Torah to such an extent that the Sages said that he fulfilled the

NO INIQUITY WILL BEFALL THE RIGHTEOUS

☞ There is a perception, even nowadays, that "no iniquity will befall the righteous." For a righteous person, reality is structured in such a way that bad things do not happen to him. An ordinary person who does not rule over his soul and body, experiencing the fluctuations of the spirit and body, is subject also to the vicissitudes of his surrounding reality. Moreover, it is on this area that such a person's service is focused to integrate and clothe everything that happens to him within the laws of the Torah. Since things do happen to him, this includes matters that he must guard against. A righteous person, in contrast, no longer serves himself, as he has repaired himself. His service is with others, and with other planes, beyond his own personal sphere. For such a person, the setting adjusts itself to fit his needs and comforts, both physically and spiritually. No iniquity will befall him, for his service has no need for that and it would only distract and hinder his true service. In this sense, during the messianic era, after the service of extraction from the *kelippot* is complete, all of Israel will be as if on the level of the righteous. They will no longer need to be concerned about encountering something that is prohibited or impure in their service of God.

entire Torah, even matters like *eiruv tavshilin* (which is only a rabbinic requirement)? The answer is similar to what is said here: Based on his study of the inner dimension of Torah, he knew the practical actions that needed to be done as well.

The inner dimension of Torah does not teach the details of practical *halakha*, but it does reveal the inner meaning: the process of activation, the elements that bring about the different kinds of enclothing in the world. As an analogy, it is possible to observe a person and see what he is doing and how he is doing it. It is also possible to peer into his soul and see what he loves, how he thinks, etc. If one's understanding is deep enough and broad enough, it is possible to predict what such a person will do in a given context or situation. However, similar to the analogy, the method is not foolproof. There are many factors, and there may be multiple possible outcomes. Therefore, as described, the commandments that our forefathers fulfilled were not necessarily performed in a specific way, and not always in a form we would recognize today.[73] By contrast, following the giving of the Torah, these things were enclothed in one fixed and specific manner.

In this sense, immersion in the revealed Torah is like observing external factors and trying to depict the structure. What effect one element has on another, what the connections are between them and what can be learned from them, etc. The hidden Torah attempts to understand the internal logic. When this inner aspect is understood, the complex, detailed, and almost limitless content of the revealed Torah is rendered as very simple, almost self-evident, to the point where it is unnecessary to delve into it in isolation. By way of analogy: If one presents to an undiscerning person or child a sequence of numbers, like 3-6-9, as long as he is unable to find a logical relationship between them, he will struggle to remember them. The minute the underlying pattern is revealed, it becomes simple, and he no longer needs to learn or remember, but he simply knows intuitively.

---

73. See *Degel Maḥaneh Efrayim, Parashat Tzav*; *Ba'al Shem Tov* on the Torah, *Parashat Toledot*, epistle 4. For example, the service of Isaac was in the digging of wells. Jacob fulfilled the commandment of *tefillin* through the story of the sticks. See *Zohar*, part 1, 161b and onward; *Likkutei Torah, Bemidbar* 51:1; *Ma'amarei Admor HaZaken* 5562, p. 12; *Or HaTorah, Vayetzeh*, p. 223b, and elsewhere.

מַה שֶּׁאֵין כֵּן בִּזְמַן בַּיִת שֵׁנִי, הָיוּ צְרִיכִים לַעֲסוֹק

That was not the case in the time of the Second Temple, when **they had to engage** in them,

In the time of the Second Temple the Torah study of the scholars was mainly in the revealed Torah, and this would remain, to some degree, until the messianic era. They had to engage in them, and there was no possibility, as there will be in the future, to understand the revealed concepts from within the hidden ones. ☞

גַּם כִּי לֹא בִּשְׁבִיל הֲלָכָה לְמַעֲשֶׂה בִּלְבַד, אֶלָּא שֶׁזֶּהוּ עִיקַּר עֲבוֹדָה: לְהַתִּישׁ כֹּחַ הַסִּטְרָא אָחֳרָא וּלְהַעֲלוֹת נִיצוֹצֵי הַקְּדוּשָּׁה עַל יְדֵי הַתּוֹרָה וְהָעֲבוֹדָה כְּמוֹ שֶׁמְּבוֹאָר בְּמָקוֹם אַחֵר.

not only for the purposes of practical *halakha*, but because that was the main service: To sap the strength of the *sitra aḥara* and to elevate the sparks of holiness through the Torah and service, as is explained elsewhere.

THEY NEEDED TO STUDY THE REVEALED AND IT WAS IMPOSSIBLE TO KNOW THE INNER SIDE OF TORAH

☞ This must be said, for the idea occasionally arises that it is sufficient, even today, to study only the hidden aspect of Torah, and this idea poses a danger. While it is true that Abraham studied the hidden Torah, and this possibility will exist the future, that is not the situation currently. Initially, prior to the giving of the Torah, when things were not fixed into one form, it was possible to extract practical applications from the inner themes. The specific detail was not really understood, but rather the general principle was studied, and it could be actualized practically in some form. Following the giving of the Torah, when the final form was fixed, there was no longer an option for each person to decide the practical expression of Torah by himself. Even more so, the solution was necessarily dependent on what was decided down in the world below ("It is not in the heavens"), and one who does not possess the knowledge of the world below cannot reach it by only studying the hidden knowledge of above. Only in the future, after everything is revealed through service in the lower world, through the struggle of challenges and solutions through the days of exile, then it will be possible to know the entire revealed Torah through the hidden dimension. When these things are revealed, all one will have to do is "remember," and that will be possible even from the perspective of "above." We will live the inner dimension and see the possibilities, and we will remember the specific solution with our internal knowledge.

Until this point, it was explained that we need to study the revealed Torah to reach the practical *halakha*, as there is no other way. Now he will explain that there is another, central element to this.

This study of the revealed Torah through analysis, challenges, and solutions is the main service for exhausting the strength of the *sitra aḥara* and the elevation of holy sparks (of the Sages of the Mishna, the Talmud, and, to a certain extent, all those who study this teaching).[74] ☞

THE MAIN SERVICE TO SAP THE STRENGTH OF THE *SITRA AḤARA*

☞ One side here is that in order to battle the *sitra aḥara*, a person must make contact with the enemy, as in a physical war. This means to sense the strength and difficulty of the *sitra aḥara*, the concealment and confusion, and even the trepidation. Only when he has overcome and broken these tangible aspects, through this contact, can a person finally integrate the *sitra aḥara* into the larger existence.

This service, on a broader scale, is not only through the study of Torah. It is found in any context in which a person encounters the other side, with force and with conversion, with the fulfillment of positive and negative commandments, with performing good deeds and through prayer. Here, the discussion is focused on the study of Torah.[80] The study of Torah that deals with and is enclothed within this world is the revealed Torah, which is the study of *halakha* based on Mishna and Talmud, etc. This is true not only in terms of the topics of study, but also the method of study. Learning through asking questions and solving problems occurs where the Divine is concealed, in the battlefield of the *kelippa*, in a fog of war where it is not known who the enemy is and from where he will attack. The clarification of *halakha* is not through illumination from above, but through information found below, in the vessels of this natural world, seemingly with no involvement from above. If there is a lack of understanding or a question, that is the *kelippa*. When a solution is found, resolving matters so the problem is eliminated, that is the removal of the *kelippa* and the revelation of a holy spark, and then another, and another, until the final redemption and the completion of the extraction.

There is also another side to the extraction of sparks effected through Torah study. The study of *halakha* actually has exactly the same effect. It clarifies the divine truth that is buried within the falsehoods, fantasies, and natural boundaries of this world. The question "What is the *halakha* in this situation, or at this time?" is essentially the question "What does God want? What is His inner will regarding this aspect of the world?"

On a deeper level, when a person performs a commandment, he is like a servant fulfilling the will of the king. This is a very

74. See *Kuntres Aḥaron*, s.v. "*hineh lo tova hashmua*"; *Likkutei Torah, Bemidbar* 32:4.

75. Especially the study of Torah of the Sages of the second Temple. At that time,

וְאַחַר הַדְּבָרִים וְהָאֱמֶת, יוּבַן הֵיטֵב בְּתוֹסֶפֶת בֵּיאוּר הָ'רַעְיָא מְהֵימְנָא' דִּלְעֵיל, בְּמַה שֶּׁאָמַר 'אִילָנָא דְּטוֹב וְרַע כו'', רוֹצֶה לוֹמַר - קְלִיפַּת נוֹגַהּ שֶׁהוּא עוֹלָם הַזֶּה הָעִיקָּר

And so, **following** these **words and truth, the above** citation from **the** ***Raya Meheimna*** **will be thoroughly understood, with additional clarification,** that **when it refers to the "Tree of** Knowledge of **Good and Evil...," it means the** ***kelippat noga*****, which is mainly this world,**

The intent of the *Zohar* when it refers to the "Tree of Knowledge" is to the *kelippat noga* itself, which is the central aspect of this reality, which mixes good and evil, etc. The Torah which deals with these things, however, is itself holy, purely good, and an aspect of the "Tree of Life,"

lofty level of self-nullification to the divine will that is above everything. Yet, this self-nullification only operates on the level of *Malkhut*, the level of the practical world of the soul. By contrast, Torah study reaches levels of nullification that are deeper, relating not only to the divine will but to the wisdom and reasoning of the king. This extends so far as to say that a person who studies the *halakha* is not only like a servant fulfilling his king's wishes, but it is as if he is the king himself, who is giving the commands. One who studies Torah is nullified at all levels of his soul. It is not he who is speaking, but rather it is the king speaking, thinking, and understanding through him, and he has no role to play on all those levels. See *Torah Or* 56a, and other places, regarding the statement of our Sages: "Who are the kings? The Sages" (*Gittin* 62a, and see *Zohar,* Part 3, 253b). This can also be said regarding the extraction that takes place during Torah study. It is not only the spark that is released as a result of God's will being fulfilled. Rather, the entire structure of this world that concealed and imprisoned that spark – the concealed, the concealment, and the method of concealing – are all clarified and extracted through this study. This Torah study is not a substitute for the practical action, but it completes the action, both before and after its performance. Before – it first saps the strength of the *kelippa*. The practical action is a frontal assault and is not always possible. The Torah study disintegrates the *kelippa*, stripping it of its threats. It does not totally break the *kelippa* but it does increasingly crack it, until the spark is released almost automatically. After – Torah study elevates the *kelippa* itself alongside the ascent of the spark. Thus, both the concealed and the concealment, the concealing force itself, is elevated. This illustrates that the complete form of the service of extraction, the service of this world of exile, is only through both study and practical performance.

---

as the author states elsewhere (e.g., in *Kuntres Aḥaron*) that at that time the main service was specifically through Torah study.

like the hidden Torah and the *Zohar*. The difference is, as the author explained, that the revealed Torah which deals with the prohibited and permitted laws is enclothed in all the issues of this world, themselves part of the *kelippat noga*, while the hidden Torah is not enclothed in them.

כְּמוֹ שֶׁכָּתוּב בְּעֵץ חַיִּים וְדַי לַמֵּבִין. **as written in *Etz Ḥayyim*.** This is **sufficient** explanation **for one who understands.**

The connection between the tree of knowledge of good and evil and the *kelippat noga* is mentioned there, as well as a general explanation of the *kelippat noga* and the impure *kelippot*. This is sufficient explanation for one who understands the writings of the Arizal, and can study these things independently.[76]

As was said initially, this letter is not only a commentary on the statement from the *Zohar*, and also not of what is written in *Etz Ḥayyim*. Rather, it is a letter from a rebbe to his hasidim based on the words of the *Zohar*, with an explanation clarifying certain issues that are mentioned there, which the author deems important to clarify.

The main topic was the study of Torah and the clarification here was based on two focal points and the interaction between them. The first is the Torah, both the revealed and hidden Torah, and the second is the world, this world and the world of the future.

The first meeting point is that the place and significance of the study of revealed Torah primarily belongs to this time, the period of exile and extraction. It was explained that the main purpose and service of man during this time, in his extraction and rectification of this world, is through the study of the revealed Torah. It involves clarifying halakha, the actions one should perform, where to descend and what to do in order to extract and elevate the holy sparks. Additionally, the actions on their own are not enough, for the study of the Torah, the immersion in the underlying spiritual reality, its reasoning, and the reasons for

76. The citation from *Etz Ḥayyim* is from *Sha'ar* 49 (*Sha'ar Kelippat Noga*), mainly chap. 3.

its concealment, complete the extraction in the inner dimensions as well. Yet, even though the main aspect of the study of the revealed Torah is in this world, the author explained that it will also have a role and continuation in the future. "There is no difference between the messianic era and this world except etc.," and there will still remain an aspect of reality in the future that will require this type of Torah study. It will be necessary for the continuous elevation of the world through the service of the righteous and their study of the hidden Torah.

The second meeting point is that of the hidden Torah, which primarily belongs to the future period. At that time, when there will no longer be holy sparks to extract, divine service will consist of continuously unifying and elevating this post-extraction world, as well as the people in it. After the completion of the previous extraction service below, a person can ascend above all of reality, to his own source in the divine root. It was explained that these elevations are all through the hidden Torah, which is concealed below but revealed above, like rungs on a ladder, on which we can ascend and unify increasingly supernal layers of existence.

In parallel to what was explained regarding the revealed Torah, the hidden Torah has a place now as well, even during the time of exile and extraction service. While the primary aspect of divine service down below is that of extraction, it cannot be performed without vitalizing energy that descends from above. Additionally, if the spark below does not receive that vitality, it cannot ascend. The necessity for this dimension of the service of extraction expands over time, deepening into the darkness of the kelippa. Things that were understood in earlier phases now require explanations in order to persuade others of their truth. What was once part of the accepted and simple perspective of the social world is now known by only a few individuals, transformed through the darkness of the exile. The longer the exile extends, the more the hidden Torah is revealed, because the world needs these deeper truths and is determined to uncover them. It is specifically because the Torah is hidden, not enclothed in the vessels of this world, that it is able to extend light and vitality to the world. While this light is not fully comprehended, it is clear to all that it is light and a divine life force without any garments or coverings. This is what is deeply needed in this world, a world advancing more and more deeply into the darkness of the kelippot, becoming ever thirstier for every drop of light, for any hint of the presence and hope of the Divine.

The study of Torah, both the revealed and the hidden, is what moves the world toward its purpose and redemption. It pushes from one side and pulls from the other.

Glossary

alef First letter of the Hebrew alphabet
aliya Immigration to the Land of Israel
Amida Silent prayer recited three times daily
amora'im Sages of the Talmud who lived from approximately 200 to 500 CE
Arizal Rabbi Yitzḥak Luria of Tzefat (1534–1572), the most influential kabbalist of modern times
Ashkenazic A Jew who originated from northern and eastern Europe, primarily Germany and its environs
Asiya The world of Action, the fourth and lowest of the spiritual worlds
Atzilut The world of Emanation, the highest of the four spiritual worlds and closest to the source of creation
ayin Nothingness; the sixteenth letter of the Hebrew alphabet
Ba'al Shem Tov Rabbi Yisrael ben Eliezer (1698–1760), founder of the hasidic movement
beinonim Literally, "intermediates"; those who are on a level where he is neither wicked nor righteous
Beit Hillel Literally, "House of Hillel"; a school of thought named after the mishnaic Sage Hillel, who founded it
Beit Shammai Literally, "House of Shammai"; a school of thought named after the mishnaic Sage Shammai, who founded it
Beria The world of Creation, the second of the four spiritual worlds
bet The second letter of the Hebrew alphabet
Bina Understanding, one of the ten divine attributes known as *sefirot*
Chabad An acronym of the three cognitive attributes, *Ḥokhma, Bina,* and *Da'at*; the name attributed to Lubavitch Hasidism, founded by Rabbi Shneur Zalman of Liadi

Da'at Knowledge, one of the ten divine attributes known as *sefirot*
dalet The fourth letter of the Hebrew alphabet
Ein Sof God's infinite being
etrog Citron, one of the four species waved on the festival of Sukkot
gaon An outstanding Torah scholar
Gevura Restraint, one of the ten divine attributes known as *sefirot*
gimmel The third letter of the Hebrew alphabet
Haggada Book that tells the story of the Exodus to be related at the Seder on the first night of Passover
halakha (pl. halakhot) Jewish law
hasid (pl. hasidim) Literally, "pious individual"; a follower of Hasidism, the movement initiated by the Ba'al Shem Tov
Havaya A reference to the four-letter name of God known as the Tetragrammaton
ḥaya The second highest of the five soul levels
ḥayot Angelic creatures that appear in Ezekiel's mystical vision
heh The fifth letter of the Hebrew alphabet
Ḥesed Kindness, one of the ten divine attributes known as *sefirot*
ḥet The eighth letter of the Hebrew alphabet
Hod Splendor, one of the ten divine attributes known as *sefirot*
Ḥokhma Wisdom, one of the ten divine attributes known as *sefirot*
Ḥumash The five books of the Torah
Ibn Ezra Abraham ben Meir ibn Ezra (c. 1092–1167), a Spanish poet, grammarian, and biblical commentator
Kabbala The mystical teachings of the Torah
kaf (or khaf) The eleventh letter of the Hebrew alphabet
kelippa (pl. kelippot) Literally, "husk"; the aspect of the universe that is unholy and conceals the Divine
kelippat noga Literally, "glowing husk"; a form of *kelippa* that contains an element of goodness that can be elevated
Keter Crown, one of the ten divine attributes known as *sefirot*
Kislev The third month in the Jewish calendar, which falls out during winter
kof The nineteenth letter of the Hebrew alphabet
lamed The twelfth letter of the Hebrew alphabet
lulav Palm frond, one of the four species waved on the festival of Sukkot

Maggid of Mezeritch Rabbi Dovber (d. 1772), a disciple of the Ba'al Shem Tov and the teacher of Rabbi Shneur Zalman of Liadi, author of the *Tanya*, who strengthened the Hasidism of his master, anchoring it firmly in Jewish thought and practice

Maharal An acronym for Rabbi Yehudah Loew of Prague (1525–1609), one of the outstanding scholars and Jewish leaders of the sixteenth century

Malkhut Kingship, one of the ten divine attributes known as *sefirot*

mem The thirteenth letter of the Hebrew alphabet

menora Candelabrum with eight lights traditionally lit during the festival of Hanukkah, also known as a *ḥanukkiya*

mezuza A parchment scroll on which four portions from the Torah are inscribed and affixed to the doorpost of a Jewish home

Midrash Collection of homiletic interpretations of the Scriptures by the Sages of the Talmud

mikveh Bath used for ritual immersion

Mishna A concise summary of the teachings of the Sages on all topics of Torah, which was redacted in the beginning of the third century CE by Rabbi Yehuda HaNasi

mitzva (pl. mitzvot) A Torah commandment

moḥin Literally "brains"; the *sefirot* corresponding to the cognitive faculties

nefesh The soul; specifically, the lowest of the five levels of the soul

neshama The soul; specifically, the third of the five soul levels

Netzaḥ Dominance, one of the ten divine attributes known as *sefirot*

nun The fourteenth letter of the Hebrew alphabet

parasha (pl. parashiyot) Torah portion

partzuf (pl. partzufim) Literally, "divine countenance"; a particular arrangement of the ten *sefirot*

peh The seventeenth letter of the Hebrew alphabet

peruta Coin of a small denomination

Rabba Rabba bar Naḥmani (died c. 320 CE), a prominent third-generation talmudic Sage from Babylon

Rabbeinu Baḥya A rabbi and scholar (1255–1340), best known for his commentary on the Torah

Rambam Maimonides; Rabbi Moses ben Maimon (1138–1204), a leading halakhic authority and philosopher

Ramban Nachmanides; Rabbi Moses ben Naḥman (1194–1270), renowned for his commentary on the Torah and Talmud

Rashi Rabbi Shlomo Yitzḥaki (1040–1105), one of the foremost commentators of the Torah and Talmud

resh The twentieth letter of the Hebrew alphabet

Rosh HaShana Jewish New Year

ruaḥ Second of the five soul levels

samekh The fifteenth letter of the Hebrew alphabet

Sanhedrin A tribunal of sages consisting of seventy-one members

se'a A unit of volume measurement used in talmudic times

sefira (pl. sefirot) One of the ten divine attributes with which God creates, sustains, and directs the worlds

shamash Attendant

Shema Prayer recited three times daily in which one declares one's faith in the oneness of God

shin The twenty-first letter of the Hebrew alphabet

shofar Ram's horn sounded on the festival of Rosh HaShana

siddur Prayer book

sitra aḥara Literally, "the other side"; a general term for evil, including all aspects of the universe that counter the Divine

sukka Hut or shelter with a roof of branches and leaves used as a temporary residence during the festival of Sukkot

Sukkot The harvest festival celebrated in the fall during which Jews leave their houses to live in temporary shelters

tallit Prayer shawl

Tanakh An acronym for *Torah, Nevi'im, Ketuvim* (Torah, Prophets, Writings), comprising the twenty-four books of the Scriptures

tanna'im Sages who lived in the period spanning 332 BCE to 220 CE whose views were recorded in the Mishna

tav Twenty-second letter of the Hebrew alphabet

tefillin Leather boxes worn on the arm and forehead containing certain biblical passages that declare the unity of God and the miracles of the exodus from Egypt

tet Ninth letter of the Hebrew alphabet

Tiferet Beauty, one of the ten divine attributes known as *sefirot*

Tosafot Medieval commentators of the Talmud

tzaddik (pl. tzaddikim) Righteous individual; a person born with the extraordinary ability and brilliance to perceive God

Tzemaḥ Tzedek The third Lubavitcher Rebbe, Rabbi Menaḥem Mendel Schneerson (1789–1866), grandson of the author of the *Tanya*, Rabbi Shneur Zalman of Liadi

tzadi Eighteenth letter of the Hebrew alphabet

tzitzit Strings that are affixed to four-cornered garments

vav The sixth letter of the Hebrew alphabet

Vilna Gaon Rabbi Eliyahu of Vilna (1720–1797), a commentator and kabbalist who was known as a leader of the opponents of Hasidism

yeḥida The highest of the five soul levels

yesh Existence, substance, entity

yeshiva (pl. yeshivot) An academy dedicated to the study of Torah

Yesod Foundation, one of the ten divine attributes known as *sefirot*

Yetzira The world of Formation, the second of the four spiritual worlds

yod The tenth letter of the Hebrew alphabet

Yom Kippur The Day of Atonement, when the Jewish people engage in fasting, prayer, and repentance

zayin The seventh letter of the Hebrew alphabet

Works Cited in This Volume

Avodat HaKodesh A kabbalistic work by Rabbi Meir ibn Gabbai, a kabbalist born in Spain in 1480

Avot deRabbi Natan A commentary and exposition of the teachings of the *Pirkei Avot,* compiled during the geonic period (c. 700–900 CE)

Ba'al Shem Tov al HaTorah A compendium of teachings on the Torah and the festivals by the founder of the hasidic movement, anthologized by Shimon Menaḥem Mendel Vodnik

Beit Rebbe A biography of the author of the *Tanya,* Rabbi Shneur Zalman of Liadi (1745–1812), and his successors by Chaim Meir Heilman

Beit Yosef Written by Rabbi Yosef Karo (1488–1575), a commentary on the halakhic work *Arba'a Turim* by Rabbi Yaakov ben Asher

Bemidbar Rabba Midrash comprising a collection of homiletical interpretations of the book of Numbers

Bereshit Rabba Midrash comprising a collection of homiletical interpretations of the book of Genesis

Degel Maḥaneh Efrayim A work of hasidic teachings on the Torah by Rabbi Moshe Ḥayyim Efrayim of Sudilkov (c. 1748–1800)

Derekh Ḥayyim A work by the second Lubavitcher Rebbe, Rabbi Dovber Schneuri (1773–1827), on the subject of repentance

Derekh Mitzvotekha Hasidic discourses on the esoteric meaning of the mitzvot by the third Lubavitcher Rebbe, Rabbi Menaḥem Mendel Schneerson (1789–1866), also known as the Tzemaḥ Tzedek

Devarim Rabba Midrash comprising a collection of homiletical interpretations of the book of Deuteronomy

Eikha Rabba Midrash comprising a collection of homiletical interpretations of the book of Lamentations

Etz Ḥayyim The fundamental work of the Arizal's Kabbala, compiled by his disciple, Rabbi Ḥayyim Vital

Gevurot Hashem Commentary on the exodus from Egypt and the Passover Haggada by Rabbi Judah Loew, the Maharal of Prague (c. 1520–1609)

HaMa'asar HaRishon An account of the incarceration of the author of the *Tanya* by Rabbi Yehoshua Mondshein

HaYom Yom An anthology of hasidic aphorisms and customs arranged according to the days of the year, compiled by Rabbi Menaḥem Mendel Schneerson, the Lubavitcher Rebbe (1902–1994)

Hemshekh Samekh Vav Compilation of hasidic discourses by the fifth Lubavitcher Rebbe, Rabbi Shalom Dovber Schneerson, all of which were taught between 1905 and 1908

Hemshekh Ayin Bet Compilation of the hasidic treatises of the fifth Lubavitcher Rebbe, Rabbi Sholom Dovber Schneerson (1860–1920), from the Hebrew year 5672 to 5676 (1911–1916)

Ḥiddushei HaRim Work of hasidic teachings by Rabbi Yitzḥak Meir Rothenberg Alter (1799–1866), the first Rebbe of Gur

Hilkhot Talmud Torah Literally, "Laws of Torah Study," published anonymously by the author of the *Tanya* in 1794

Idra Rabba A section of the *Zohar* on *Parashat Naso*, in which kabbalistic mysteries that Rabbi Shimon bar Yoḥai revealed to nine of his students are transcribed

Iggeret HaTeshuva The third section of the *Tanya*

Iggerot Kodesh A comprehensive collection of correspondence written by the Rebbes of Chabad, including those of the fifth Lubavitcher Rebbe, Rabbi Shalom Dovber Schneerson (1860–1920), and seventh Lubavitcher Rebbe, Rabbi Menaḥem Mendel Schneerson (1902–1994)

Jerusalem Talmud Written in the Land of Israel, an extensive work built upon the foundation of the Mishna like its better-known counterpart, the Babylonian Talmud

Kad HaKemaḥ An encyclopedic work of ethical instruction and self-improvement written by Rabbeinu Baḥya ben Asher, the topics organized alphabetically according to the letters of the *alef-bet*

Kehillat Yaakov Kabbalistic dictionary by Rabbi Yaakov Tzvi Yalish of Dinov (1778–1825)

Kerem Chabad A journal founded and edited by Rabbi Yehoshua Mondshine, comprising articles on Chabad hasidic teachings and history, published between the years 1987 and 1992

Keter Shem Tov Collection of teachings of the Ba'al Shem Tov (c. 1698–1760), compiled from the works of his disciples, by Rabbi Aharon HaKohen

Kol Mevaser A collection of essays compiled from the works of the students of Rabbi Simḥa Bunim of Peshisḥa and published by Rabbi Yehuda Menaḥem Baum in 1991

Kol Sippurei HaBa'al Shem Tov A collection of stories and chronicles on the life of the Ba'al Shem Tov compiled and arranged according to topic by Rabbi Yisrael Yaakov Klapholtz

Kuntres Aḥaron The fifth and final section of the *Tanya*

Likkutei Amarim The first section of the *Tanya*

Likkutei Amarim Also known as *Maggid Devarav LeYaakov*, a collection of teachings of Rabbi Dov Ber, the Maggid of Mezeritch (c. 1700–1770), compiled by his disciple, Rabbi Shlomo of Lutzk)

Likkutei Biurim LaSefer HaTanya Explanations on the *Tanya* culled from other works of Chabad Hasidism, including the discourses of the seventh Lubavitcher Rebbe, Rabbi Menaḥem Mendel Schneerson (1902–1994), compiled by Rabbi Yehoshua Korf

Likkutei Dibburim A series of books containing the teachings of the sixth Lubavitcher Rebbe, Rabbi Yosef Yitzḥak Schneerson (1880–1950)

Likkutei HaShas A collection of the Arizal's writings on the Talmud

Likkutei Levi Yitzḥak A collection of marginalia from the *Tanya* of the kabbalist Rabbi Levi Yitzḥak Schneerson, the father of the Lubavitcher Rebbe, Rabbi Menaḥem Mendel Schneerson

Likkutei Siḥot The collected discourses of the seventh Lubavitcher Rebbe, Rabbi Menaḥem Mendel Schneerson (1902–1994) on the Torah and festivals

Likkutei Torah Hasidic discourses by the author of the *Tanya*, Rabbi Shneur Zalman of Liadi (1745–1812) on the last three books of the Torah and the festivals

Likkutei Torah Collection of mystical teachings of the Arizal (1534–1572) on the Torah (not to be confused with the work written by the author of the *Tanya* of the same name)

Ma'amar Bati LeGani The title of the last hasidic discourse of the sixth Lubavitcher Rebbe, Rabbi Yosef Yitzḥak Schneerson (1880–1950), and the first, as well as subsequent, discourses of his successor Rabbi Menaḥem Mendel Schneerson

Ma'or Einayim Hasidic teachings on the Torah by Rabbi Menaḥem Naḥum Twersky of Chernobyl (1730–1798)

Me'orei Or Kabbalistic reference book by Rabbi Meir Paprish (1624–1662)

Metzudat Zion A commentary on Prophets and Writings by Rabb David Altshuler that focuses on explaining difficult or unfamiliar words in the verses

Metzudot Referring to the commentaries of Metzudat Tzion and Metzudat David on Prophets and Writings by Rabbi David Altshuler, Metzudat Tzion focusing on unfamiliar and difficult words in the verses and Metzudat David delving into the meaning of the verses

Mevo She'arim An introduction to the wisdom of Kabbala from the writings of Rabbi Ḥayyim Vital

Midrash Shoḥer Tov Midrash comprising a collection of homiletic teachings expounding the Psalms; another name for *Midrash Tehillim*

Midrash Tanḥuma Midrash comprising a collection of homiletic teachings expounding the Torah

Midrash Tehillim Midrash comprising a collection of homiletic teachings expounding the Psalms

Mishneh Torah Code of Jewish law composed by Rambam (1138–1204), containing fourteen books, including *Sefer HaMadda* (the Book of Knowledge), which addresses fundamentals of Judaism

Olat Tamid A work on meditations in prayers by Rabbi Ḥayyim Vital based on the teachings of the Arizal

Or HaTorah Compilation of hasidic discourses on the *Tanakh* and festivals by the third Lubavitcher Rebbe, Rabbi Menaḥem Mendel Schneerson (1789–1866), also known as the Tzemaḥ Tzedek

Otzar HaMidrashim Collection of two hundred minor midrashim, compiled by Yehuda David Eisenstein

Pardes Rimmonim The primary exposition of the kabbalistic system of Rabbi Moshe Kordevero, famously known as the Ramak (1522–1570)

Pirkei Avot Literally, "Chapters of the Fathers"; a tractate of the Mishna dealing with ethics and piety

Pirkei deRabbi Eliezer Homiletic work on the Torah containing exegesis and retellings of biblical stories

Pri Etz Ḥayyim Mystical teachings of the Arizal on rituals and holidays as recorded by his disciple Rabbi Hayyim Vital

Raya Meheimna Subsection of the *Zohar* presenting a kabbalistic exposition of the commandments and prohibitions of the Torah

Sefer HaArakhim An encyclopedic work of hasidic concepts compiled by Rabbi Yoel Kahn and Rabbi Shalom Dovber Lipsker

Sefer HaBahir A kabbalistic work attributed to first-century talmudic Sage Rabbi Neḥunya ben HaKanah

Sefer HaIkkarim A fifteenth-century work on principles of Judaism by Rabbi Yosef Albo (1380–1444)

Sefer HaKen An anthology of articles on the life and work of the author of the *Tanya*, Rabbi Shneur Zalman of Liadi, compiled and edited by Rabbi Adin Even-Israel Steinsaltz at the behest of the Lubavitcher Rebbe, Rabbi Menaḥem Mendel Schneerson

Sefer HaMa'amarim A series of works containing the collected hasidic discourses of the Lubavitcher Rebbes, arranged by year

Sefer HaMa'amarim Melukat Selected discourses by the Lubavitcher Rebbe, Rabbi Menaḥem Mendel Schneerson, arranged according to the festivals

Sefer HaSihot A compilation of discourses delivered by the sixth Lubavitcher Rebbe, Rabbi Yosef Yitzchak Schneerson

Sefer Mitzvot Katan A halakhic work by Rabbi Yitzḥak of Corbeil (d. 1280) that is a summary of *Sefer Mitzvot Gadol* by thirteenth-century scholar Rabbi Moshe of Coucy, containing an enumeration of the 613 commandments

Sefer Yetzira Ancient mystical work attributed to the biblical Abraham

Sha'ar HaGemul Treatise on divine justice by Nachmanides

Sha'ar HaGilgulim A kabbalistic work based on the teachings of the Arizal on the topic of reincarnation and the nature of the soul

Sha'ar HaKavanot A kabbalistic work based on the teachings of the Arizal on the mystical underpinnings of daily rituals and the daily prayers

Sha'ar HaYiḥud VeHa'emuna The second section of the *Tanya*

Sha'ar Ruaḥ HaKodesh A kabbalistic work based on the teachings of the Arizal containing hundreds of meditations geared toward purifying the soul and attaining higher levels of consciousness

Sha'arei Kedushah Mystical work on piety by Rabbi Ḥayyim Vital (1542–1620)

She'eilat Ya'avetz Halakhic responsa by Rabbi Yaakov Emden (1697–1776)

Shemot Rabba Midrash comprising a collection of homiletic interpretations of the book of Exodus

Shir HaShirim Rabba Midrash comprising a collection of homiletical interpretations of the book of Song of Songs

Shivḥei HaBa'al Shem Tov Biographical stories of the Ba'al Shem Tov and his disciples

Shulḥan Arukh The most important and influential codification of Jewish law, compiled by Rabbi Yosef Karo of Tzefat (1488–1575)

Siddur Admor HaZaken Prayer book edited in accordance with the teachings of the author of the *Tanya*, Rabbi Shneur Zalman of Liadi (1745–1812)

Sifra Midrash containing halakhic exegesis on the book of Leviticus

Sifrei Midrash containing halakhic exegesis on the books of Numbers and Deuteronomy

Tanna deVei Eliyahu A compilation of midrashic teachings ascribed to the prophet Elijah

Targum Yerushalmi An Aramaic translation and commentary on the Torah

Targum Yonatan Aramaic translation and commentary on Prophets composed by Rabbi Yonatan ben Uziel

Tikkunei Zohar Also known as the *Tikkunim*, an appendix to the *Zohar* consisting of seventy commentaries on the opening word of the Torah, *bereshit*

Torah Or Hasidic discourses by the author of the *Tanya*, Rabbi Shneur Zalman of Liadi (1745–1812), on the books of Genesis and Exodus, as well as on Hanukkah and the book of Esther

Torat Ḥayyim The collected discourses of the second Lubavitcher Rebbe, Rabbi Dovber Schneuri (1773–1827), on the books of Genesis and Exodus

Torat Kohanim The halakhic Midrash to the book of Leviticus

Torat Menaḥem The comprehensive collection of discourses and speeches of the seventh Lubavitcher Rebbe, Rabbi Menaḥem Mendel Schneerson (1902–1994)

Torat Shmuel A collection of discourses by the fourth Lubavitcher Rebbe, Rabbi Shmuel Schneerson (1834–1882)

Vayikra Rabba Midrash comprising a collection of homiletical interpretations of the book of Leviticus

Ya'arot Devash Collection of the sermons of Rabbi Yehonatan Eibeshitz

Yalkut Shimoni Collection of homiletic teachings on the books of *Tanakh*, compiled between the eleventh and fourteenth centuries

Zohar One of the fundamental texts of Kabbala (Jewish mysticism) that consists of the teachings of Rabbi Shimon bar Yoḥai (second century CE), as recorded by his close disciples

אגרת הקודש

לכ״ק אדמו״ר הזקן

הרב רבי שניאור זלמן מליאדי

בעל התניא והשו״ע

אגרות יח-כו

אגרת יח

כז באלול פשוטה
כג באלול מעוברת

כתיב מה יפית ומה נעמת אהבה בתענוגים. הנה ב׳ מיני אהבות הן הא׳ אהבה בתענוגיםדהיינו שמתענג על ה׳ עונג נפלא בשמחה רבה ועצומה שמחת הנפש וכלותה בטעמה כי טוב ה׳ ונעים נעימות עריבות עד להפליא מעין עוה״ב ממש שנהנין כו׳ וע״ז כתיב שמחו צדיקים בה׳ ולא כל אדם זוכה לזה וזו היא בחינת כהנא ברעותא דלבא שבזוה״ק וע״ז נאמר עבודת מתנה וגו׳ והזר הקרב וגו׳ כי אין דרך להשיגה ע״י יגיעת בשר כמו היראה ששואלין עליה יגעת ביראה ואוי לבשר שלא נתייגע ביראה כמ״ש בר״ח וכתיב ביראה אם תבקשנה ככסף וגו׳ מלמד שצריכה יגיעה רבה ועצומה כמחפש אחר אוצרות. אבל אהבה רבה זו [אהבה בתענוגים] נופלת לאדם מאליה מלמעלה בלי שיכין ויכוון לה אך ורק אחר שנתייגע ביראת הרוממות והגיע לתכלית מה שיוכל להשיג ממנה לפי בחינת נשמתו אזי ממילא באה האהבה בתענוגים מלמעלה לשכון ולהתייחד עם היראה כי דרכו של איש לחזר כו׳ כמ״ש בלק״א.

כח באלול פשוטה
כד באלול מעוברת

והשנית היא אהבה ותאוה שהנפש מתאוה ואוהבת וחפיצה לדבקה בה׳ לצרור בצרור החיים וקרבת אלהים טוב לה מאד ובו תחפוץ ורע לה מאד להתרחק ממנו ית׳ ח״ו להיות מחיצה של ברזל מהחיצונים מפסקת ח״ו ואהבה זו היא מוסתרת בלב כלל ישראל אפילו ברשעים וממנה באה להם החרטה אך מפני שהיא מוסתרת ונעלמה בבחינת גלות בגוף הרי הקליפה יכולה לשלוט עליה וזהו רוח שטות המחטיא לאדם וע״כ עבודת האדם לקונו היא להתחזק ולהתגבר על הקליפה בכל מכל כל דהיינו מתחלה לגרשה מהגוף לגמרי ממחשבה דו״מ שבמוח ולשון ורמ״ח אברים ואח״כ יוכל ג״כ להוציא ממסגר אסיר בחוזק יד דהיינו להיות חזק ואמיץ לבו בגבורים להיות האהבה המסותרת נגלית בגילוי רב בכל כחות חלקי הנפש שבגוף דהיינו העיקר בשכל ובמחשבה שבמוח שהשכל יחשב ויתבונן תמיד כפי שכלו והשכלתו בבורא יתברך איך שהוא חיי החיים בכלל וחיי נשמתו בפרט וע״כ יכסוף ויתאוה להיות דבוק בו וקרוב אליו כוסף טבעי כבן הכוסף להיות תמיד אצל אביו וכמו אש העולה למעלה תמיד בטבעה למקורה וכל מה שיתמיד לחשוב בשכלו כוסף זה ככה יתגבר ויתפשט כוסף זה גם בפיו ובכל אבריו לעסוק בתורה ומצות לדבקה בהם בה׳ ממש דאורייתא וקוב״ה כולא חד ועל כוסף זה שבגילוי רב כתיב צמאה נפשי וגו׳ כאדם הצמא למים ואין לו תענוג עדיין כלל וגם על כוסף זה ואהבה זו המוסתרת בנו אנו מעתירים לה׳ להיות בעזרנו להוציאה ממסגר ושיהיה הלב מלא ממנה לבדה ולא תכנס צרתה בביתה שהיא תאות עוה״ז רק

שתהיה היא עקרת הבית למשול בצרתה ולגרשה החוצה ממחדו"מ עכ"פ הגם שלא יוכל לשלחה לגמרי מלבו עכ"פ תהיה היא מוסתרת בבחי' גלות ועבדות לעקרת הבית גברתה להשתמש בה לדברים הכרחים לה לבד כאכילה ושתיה כדכתיב בכל דרכיך דעהו:

אגרת יט

כט באלול פשוטה
כה באלול מעוברת

עוטה אור כשלמה וגו'. הנה בלקוטי תורה של האריז"ל פ' כי תשא ופ' ויקרא כתב כי השגת מרע"ה לא היתה בבחינת פנימיות דחכמה עילאה הנקרא אבא דאצי' וכ"ש בספירת הכתר שלמעלה ממנה הנקרא א"א כ"א בבחי' אחוריים דחכמה המתלבשים בבינה המתלבשת בז' ספירות תחתונות שנק' ז"א סוד התורה ומתפשטת עד סוף ד' ספירות התחתונות שהן נהי"מ ושם היתה השגת נבואתו בבחי' פנימיות דהיינו מבחי' פנימיות דנהי"מ. אבל למעלה מנהי"מ לא היתה לו שום השגה בפנימיות כ"א בבחי' אחוריים דחכמה המלובשים בבינה המלובשת ומתפשטת תוך פנימיות דנהי"מ בסוד נובלות חכמה שלמעלה תורה שהיא בבחי' ז"א וכדכתיב וראית את אחורי ופני לא יראו ע"ש ובשער הנבואה פ"א. ולכאורה יש להפליא הרי נאמר ולא קם נביא עוד בישראל כמשה ואיך השיג האריז"ל יותר ממנו ודרש כמה דרושים בבחי' פנימיות אפילו בספירות ומדרגות רבות שלמעלה מהחכמה וכתר דאצילות. אך הענין הוא פשוט ומובן לכל שיש הפרש גדול בין השגת חכמי האמת כרשב"י והאריז"ל שהיא השגת חכמה ודעת ובין השגת מרע"ה ושאר הנביאים בנבואה המכונה בכתוב בשם ראיה ממש וראית את אחורי וראה את ה' וירא אליו ה' ואף שזהו דרך משל ואינה ראיית עין בשר גשמי ממש. מ"מ הנמשל צ"ל דומה למשל וכתרגום וירא אליו ה' ואתגליא ליה וכו' שהוא בחי' התגלות שנגלה אליו הנעלם ב"ה בבחי' התגלות משא"כ בהשגת חכמי האמת שלא נגלה אליהם הוי' בבחי' התגלות רק שהם משיגים תעלומות חכמה הנעלם [נ"א בנעלם] ומופלא מהם ולכן אמרו חכם עדיף מנביא שיכול להשיג בחכמתו למעלה מעלה ממדרגות שיוכלו לירד למטה בבחי' התגלות לנביאים במראה נבואתם כי לא יוכלו לירד ולהתגלות אליהם רק מדרגות התחתונות שהן נהי"מ שהן הן היורדות תמיד ומתגלות מהמשפיע להמקבל בבחי' מוחין וחיות כידוע לי"ח שהנהי"מ של העליון מתלבשים בתחתון להחיותו שהן הן כלי ההשפעה והורדת החיות מהעליון לתחתון בכל העולמות והמדרגות ולכן ג"כ הן הן המתגלות לנביאים בבחי' התגלות ממש ובתוכן מלובש אור הבינה שהיא בחי' הבנת האלהות מאור [נ"א ואור] א"ס ב"ה ובתוכה מלובשים אחוריים דחכמה שהיא מדרגה שלמעלה מהשכל

א בתשרי פשוטה
כו באלול מעוברת

וההבנה באלהות ב״ה כי שם חכמה מורה על מקור השכל וההבנה ולכן אמרו בזהר דאורייתא מחכמה נפקת כי טעמי מצות לא נתגלו והם למעלה מהשכל וההבנה. וגם באיזהו מקומן שנתגלה ונתפרש איזה טעם המובן לנו לכאורה אין זה הטעם המובן לנו לבדו תכלית הטעם וגבולו אלא בתוכו מלובש פנימיות ותעלומות חכמה שלמעלה מהשכל וההבנה וכן בכל דיבור ודיבור שיצא מפי הקב״ה לנביאים הכתובים בתנ״ך הן דברי תוכחה והן סיפורי מעשיות מלובש בתוכם בחינת חכמת אלהות שלמעלה מהשכל וההבנה כנראה בחוש מענין הקרי והכתיב כי הקרי הוא לפי ההבנה הנגלית לנו והכתיב הוא למעלה מהשכל וההבנה שתיבה זו ככתיבתה אין לה לבוש בבחינת ההבנה ובקריאתה בפה יש לה לבוש וכן הענין באותיות גדולות שבתנ״ך שהן מעלמא עילאה ומאירות משם בגילוי בלי לבוש כשאר האותיות. והנה בחי׳ חכמת אלהות ב״ה המלובשת בתרי״ג ב בתשרי פשוטה
מצות התורה נק׳ בשם בחינת אחוריי׳ דחכמה כי כל אחוריים שבספירות כז באלול מעוברת
הן מדרגות החיצונות והתחתונות במעלה שבספירה זו מה שיוכלו לירד ולהתפשט למטה להתלבש בברואים להחיותם ובחי׳ הפנים היא הספירה עצמה המיוחדת במאצילה א״ס ב״ה בתכלית היחוד כגון ד״מ ספירת חכמה שהיא מיוחדת במאצילה א״ס ב״ה בתכלית היחוד כי הקב״ה וחכמתו אחד (כמ״ש לעיל) ומה שמאיר ומתפשט מחכמתו ית׳ למטה בתחתונים שהם בעלי גבול ותכלית ומתלבש בהם נק׳ אחוריים ונק׳ ג״כ בחי׳ עשיה שבאצי׳ פי׳ עד״מ כמו שבאדם התחתון שיש בנשמתו ה׳ מדרגות זו למטה מזו שהן בחי׳ השכל והמדות ומחשבה ודבור ומעשה והמעשה היא התחתונה שבכולם שהחיות המתפשט מהנשמה ומלובש בכח המעשה הוא כאין לגבי החיות המתפשט ממנה ומלובש בכח הדבור שהוא כאין לגבי החיות המתפשט ממנה ומלובש במחשבה ומדות ושכל כן עד״ז ממש היא בחי׳ כח באלול מעוברת
חכמתו ית׳ מה שיוכל להתפשט ממנה (להשפיע) [להתלבש] בתחתונים כולם הם כאין לגבי בחינת פנים המיוחד במאציל ב״ה דכולא קמיה כלא חשיב וההשפעה לכל הנבראים כולם שהם בעלי גבול ותכלית נחשבת ירידה וצמצום כביכול לגבי המאציל א״ס ב״ה עד״מ כמו שנחשבת ירידה וצמצום לשכל האדם המשכיל המצומצם באיזה עשיה גשמיות וחומרית ממש ולכן משה רבינו ע״ה שהשיג עד אחוריים דחכמה זכה שתנתן ע״י התורה שהיא נובלות חכמה שלמעלה פי׳ מה שנובל ממנה ויורד למטה ומתלבש בתורה גשמיות שלנו שעיקרה ותכליתה הוא קיום המצות ל״ת ועשה בפועל ומעשה ממש כמאמר היום לעשותם וגדול תלמוד שמביא לידי מעשה והלומד שלא לעשות נוח לו שנהפכה שלייתו וכו׳ וכל אדם מוכרח להתגלגל עד שיקיים כל התרי״ג מצות בפועל ממש כנודע מהאריז״ל:

ג בתשרי פשוטה
כט באלול מעוברת

האותיות הנגלות לנו הן במעשה דבור ומחשבה. דמעשה הן תמונת האותיות שבכתב אשורי שבס״ת. ואותיות הדבור נחקקות בהבל וקול המתחלק לכ״ב חלקים שונים זה מזה בצורתן. שהיא הברת ומבטא הכ״ב אותיות בכל לשון. כי אין הפרש בין לה״ק ובין שאר לשונות במהות הברת האותיות כ״א בצירופן. ואותיות המחשבה הן ג״כ בכל לשון שאדם מחשב תיבות ואותיות הלשון שהן כ״ב לבד. רק שבמחשבה יש בה ג׳ מיני בחי׳ אותיות. שהרי כשרואה בס״ת תמונת האותיות הן מצטיירות במחשבתו וזה נקרא בחינת עשי׳ שבמחשבה. וכן כאשר שומע אותיות הדבור הן נרשמות במחשבתו ומהרהר בהן וזה נקרא בחינת דבור שבמח׳ ובחי׳ יצירה. ואותיות המחשבה לבדה בלי הרהור אותיות הדבור נק׳ מח׳ שבמחשבה. בחי׳ בריאה. והנה אותיות הדבור ממש הן מתהוות ומקבלות חיותן מאותיות אלו עצמן שבמח׳. ואף שלפעמים מדבר אדם ומהרהר בדבר אחר. הרי אינו יכול לדבר כ״א אותן דבורים וצירופים שכבר דברם והיו במחשבתו פעמים רבות מאד ונשאר בדיבורים וצירופים אלו הרשימו מהמחשבה שנכנסה בהם פעמים רבות. וזהו בחי׳ אחוריים וחיצוניות נה״י מפרצוף העליון שנכנס בתחתון להיות לו בחי׳ מוחין וחיות כנודע:

אגרת כ

ד בתשרי פשוטה
א בתשרי מעוברת

איהו וחיוהי חד איהו וגרמוהי חד בהון. (פי׳ ע״ס דאצילות חיוהי הן האורות וגרמוהי הן הכלים שכולן אלקות משא״כ בבי״ע כו׳). וצריך להבין היטב איך הא״ס חד עם גרמוהי הן הכלים הרי הכלים הן בבחי׳ גבול ותכלית כמ״ש בע״ח. אמנם הכוונה היא לומר שהן אלקות לברוא יש מאין כמו הא״ס ולא בבחי׳ השתלשלות עילה ועלול לבד ומ״ש הרמ״ק ענין השתלשלות עילה ועלול וכ״ה בזוה״ק פ׳ בראשית היינו בהשתלשלות הספירות בספירות עצמן (בבחי׳ הכלים) שנקראות בלי מה בס״י שאינן בבחי׳ יש ומהות מושג וכמו הא״ס דלית מחשבה תפיסא ביה כלל וכמ״ש ופני לא יראו ונבואת משה רבינו ע״ה והשגתו היתה מפרק עליון דנצח דז״א ובהשתלשלות העלול הוא מוקף מהעילה ובטל במציאות אצלו כזיו השמש בשמש כמ״ש בפרדס מהרמ״ק ואף גם צמצומים רבים מאד לא יועילו להיות גשם עב כעפר מהשתלשלות הרוחניות משכלים נבדלים אפילו של המלאכים אלא להיות רוח הבהמה מפני שור כמ״ש

ה בתשרי פשוטה
ב בתשרי מעוברת

במ״א וע״ש ויש מאין נקרא בריאה בלה״ק והגם שהיש הנברא הוא ג״כ כלא חשיב קמיה דהיינו שבטל במציאות לגבי הכח והאור השופע בו מהכלים די״ס דאבי״ע שהקו אור א״ס ב״ה מאיר בהם וכזיו השמש בשמש כמ״ש בלק״א ח״ב. היינו קמיה דוקא שהיא ידיעתו ית׳ מלמעלה למטה.

אבל בידיעה שממטה למעלה היש הנברא הוא דבר נפרד לגמרי בידיעה
והשגה זו שממטה כי הכח השופע בו אינו מושג כלל וכלל וגם אין ערוך
זה לזה כלל וכלל לא מיניה ולא מקצתיה מהערך שמהעלול אל העילה
שהעלול יודע ומשיג איזה השגה בעילתו ובטל אצלו ע״י ידיעה והשגה זו
וגם במהותם ועצמותם אין הפרש גדול כ״כ רק שזה עילה וזה עלול ולא
מיניה ולא מקצתיה מההפרש שבין מהות היש הנברא למהות הכח והאור
השופע בו להוותו מאין ליש ולכן נקרא יש מאין דוקא והנה ראשית היש ו בתשרי פשוטה
הנברא ותחילתו הן הכלים די״ס דבי״ע וגם האורות נפש רוח ונבראו מבחי׳
הנשמה די״ס דבי״ע שהוא אלקות והן הלמ״ד כלים דמל׳ דאצילות וכן
באצילות מחיצוניות הכלים די״ס דאצי׳ שהן אלקות נבראו ההיכלות
דאצילות שמתלבש בהן בחי׳ העיגולים די״ס וגם גופות המלאכים דאצי׳
שהן בחי׳ יש וכמ״ש ובמלאכיו ישים תהלה. שאינן בבחי׳ ביטול לגמרי
כעלול לגבי עילתו אך נשמות המלאכים שיצאו מזיווג הנשיקין וכן נשמות ז בתשרי פשוטה
האדם שיצאו מזיווג דזו״נ דאצי׳ קודם שירדו לבי״ע אינן בכלל יש ודבר ג בתשרי מעוברת
נפרד בפ״ע אלא הן מעין בחי׳ אלקות בצמצום עצום וכעין הכלים די״ס
דאצי׳ שהן בבחי׳ גבול ע״י צמצום אור הא״ס הוא הקו המלובש בנר״נ
שלהם וכמו צמצום הראשון להיות חלל וכו׳ (ואף גם לאחר שירדו הנר״נ
דאצי׳ לעולם הזה לצדיקים הראשונים אפשר שלא נשתנה מהותן להיות
דבר נפרד מאלקות ולכן היו מסתלקות כשרצו לחטוא בטרם יחטאו וקרוב
לומר שגם האלפים ורבבות עלמין דיתבין בגולגלתא דא״א וז״א אינן עלמין
ממש כעין ההיכלות דאצי׳ ובחינת יש אלא כעין נשמות המלאכים שיצאו
מזיווג הנשיקין ונקראו עלמין לגבי בחי׳ הגולגלתא ודיקנא) אך אינן אלקות
ממש לברוא יש מאין מאחר שכבר יצאו ונפרדו מהכלים די״ס שבהן מלובש
הקו מאור א״ס שהאור הוא כעין המאור הוא מהותו ועצמותו של המאציל
ב״ה שמציאותו הוא מעצמותו ואינו עלול מאיזה עילה שקדמה לו ח״ו
ולכן הוא לבדו בכחו ויכלתו לברוא יש מאין ואפס המוחלט ממש בלי שום
עילה וסיבה אחרת קודמת ליש הזה וכדי שיהיה היש הזה הנברא בכח
הא״ס בעל גבול ומדה נתלבש אור א״ס בכלים די״ס דאצילות ומתייחד
בתוכן בתכלית היחוד עד דאיהו וגרמוהי חד לברוא בהן ועל ידן ברואים
בעלי גבול ותכלית ובפרט ע״י התלבשותן בבי״ע. אמנם מודעת זאת שעיקר ח בתשרי פשוטה
התהוות היש ודבר נפרד לגמרי הוא ממל׳ דאצילות שנעשה עתיק דבריאה ד בתשרי מעוברת
כי אין מלך בלא עם וכו׳ וגם ריבוי הנבראים והתחלקותן שנבראו בכח
הא״ס יחיד ומיוחד בתכלית הוא ע״י ריבוי האותיות היוצאין ממל׳ פי ה׳
וברוח פיו כל צבאם וה׳ מוצאות הפה הן מה״ג דנוק׳ ולזאת נקראת עלמא
דאתגליא כי בה נגלה כח אור אין סוף לברוא יש מאין שלא ע״י עילה

ועלול אבל ט׳ ספירות הראשונות נאצלו בהשתלשלות עילה ועלול ואור הא״ס הוא מלובש בחכמה לבדה. וז״ש נעוץ תחלתן בסופן כי כתר הוא ממוצע בין המאציל לנאצלים ויש בו בחי׳ האחרונה של הא״ס ולכן נקרא כתר מלכות כי אין כתר אלא למלך וגם כי בחי׳ אחרונה דא״ס היא מל׳ דאין סוף ולכן גם המל׳ דאצי׳ נקרא כתר ממטה למעלה ומה גם כי בריאת הנשמות ממנה להיות יש ודבר נפרד בפ״ע בעולם הבריאה ונקרא בשם לידה בקריעת י״ס דבעתיקא תליא וגם כל גידול הנשמות כל ז׳ חדשים מזיווג של שמיני עצרת עד שביעי של פסח הוא כמו גידול זו״נ בבטן אימא עילאה שהוא ע״י אורות עליונים מאימא עילאה ומלמעלה למעלה עד אין סוף המתלבש בה כל ט׳ או ז׳ ירחי לידה. וככה הוא בבריאת נשמות ומלאכים לעולם הבריאה וגם כל עיקר ושרש הטיפה שמקבלת ומתעברת מז״א הוא ממוחין דאו״א ובכל זיווג נמשכת לאו״א מא״א וע״י ומלמעלה למעלה עד אין סוף רק שהכל בהעלם במוחין עד לידת הנוק׳ הנשמות והמלאכים וההיכלות לעולם הבריאה. נמצא שזהו גילוי אור א״ס ממש ע״י העיבור והלידה. ובזה יובן היות המצות במל׳ ה׳ של שם הוי׳ והתורה בז״א וא״ו של שם הוי׳. הגם שלמעלה בא״א המצות הן בגולגלתא בלבנונית היא האורחא דבפלגותא דשערי דמתפלגא לתרי״ג אורחין דאורייתא שבז״א ושרש התורה דנפקא מח״ע הוא במו״ס דא״א והיינו החכמה דטעמי המצות אלא שהוא כחותם המתהפך ונעוץ תחלתן בסופן הוא כח הא״ס ב״ה לברוא יש מאין ולא ע״י עילה ועלול שיהיה העלול מוקף מעילתו ובטל במציאות רק יהיה היש דבר נפרד מאלקות בכדי שיהיה המאציל ב״ה מלך על כל הנפרדים ע״י שיקיימו מצותיו שיצוה עליהם וסוף מעשה במחשבה תחלה ולכן אמרו בירושלמי ולית ליה לר״ש שמפסיק ללולב וכו׳ וכל הלומד שלא לעשות נוח לו שנתהפכה שלייתו ע״פ וכו׳ כי השליא נוצרה תחלה מהטיפה והיא לבדה היתה עיקר הולד עד מ׳ יום שהתחילה צורת הולד. וככה המצות הן עיקר התורה ושרשה הגם שהמצוה היא גופנית והתורה היא חכמה רק שזה בחיצוניות וזה בפנימיות וכדלקמן. והנה כמו״כ מזיווג זו״ן דבי״ע נבראו מאין ליש כל הנבראים והנוצרים והנעשים ע״י אור הנשמה שבתוכן שהיא אלקות מהכלים די״ס דמל׳ דאצי׳ וגם בתוכה הארת הקו דאור א״ס המלובש באצי׳ עד הפרסא והארת הקו שהיה מאיר בכלים די״ס דמל׳ בקע הפרסא עמהם ומאיר בהם בבי״ע כמו באצילות ממש וכן גם הקו בעצמו המלובש בסיום וסוף נה״י דא״ק שהוא סוף רגלי היושר שלו המסתיימים במל׳ דעשיה הנה הארת הקו מאירה משם ומתלבשת באור הנשמה די״ס דבי״ע שהוא אלקות והארה דהארה מתלבשת בנפש רוח די״ס דבי״ע ואף גם

ט בתשרי פשוטה
ה בתשרי מעוברת

י בתשרי פשוטה
ו בתשרי מעוברת

בכל הכלים שלהם והארה דהארה הוא בכל הנבראים ונוצרים ונעשים
כמ"ש הימים וכל אשר בהם ואתה מחיה את כולם וכל זאת בבחינת
התפשטות החיות להחיותם אמנם מציאותו ומהותו של אור הא"ס אינו ז בתשרי מעוברת
בגדר מקום כלל וסובב כל עלמין בשוה ואת השמים ואת הארץ אני מלא
בהשוואה אחת ולית אתר פנוי מיניה אף בארץ הלזו הגשמית רק שהוא
בבחי' מקיף וסובב וכמ"ש הפי' בלק"א ולא התפשטות והתלבשות החיות
להחיותם ולהוותם מאין ליש כ"א ע"י הארה דהארה דהארה וכו' מהקו
כנ"ל וגם מאור א"ס הסובב ומקיף לארבע עולמות אבי"ע בשוה מאיר אל
הקו הפנימי דרך הכלים די"ס דבי"ע ובהארתו תוך הכלים נותן בהם כח
ועוז לברוא יש מאין ומאחר שהבריאה היא ע"י הכלים לזאת הם הנבראים
בבחינת ריבוי והתחלקות וגבול ותכלית ובפרט ע"י האותיות כנ"ל. ועוד יא בתשרי פשוטה
זאת יתר על כן על כל הנ"ל הארה דהארה וכל הנ"ל היא מראה ח בתשרי מעוברת
כחה ויכלתה ביסוד העפר הגשמי בגילוי עצום ביתר עז מיסודות העליונים
ממנו וגם מצבא השמים שאין בכחם ויכלתם להוציא יש מאין תמיד כיסוד
העפר המצמיח תמיד יש מאין הם עשבים ואילנות (והמזל המכה ואומר
גדל היינו לאחר שכבר צמח העשב ואינו אומר לו לצמוח מאין ליש אלא
מקוטן לגודל ולשאת פרי כל מין ומין בפרטי פרטיות. אבל בטרם יצמח
למי יאמר כל מזל ומזל לכל עשב ועשב בפרטי פרטיות) מהכח הצומח
שבו שהוא אין ורוחני והם גשמיים ואין זאת אלא משום דרגלי א"ק
מסתיימים בתחתית עשי' ותחת רגליו מאיר אור א"ס ב"ה הסובב כל עלמין
בלי הפסק רב ביניהם רק עיגולי א"ק לבדו וגם הקו מאור א"ס המסתיים
בסיום רגלי א"ק מאיר ממטה למעלה בבחי' אור חוזר כמו שהמלובש
בא"א ואו"א וזו"נ דאצי' מאיר באור חוזר ממל' דאצי' ומל' דאצי' היא
בחי' כתר ממטה למעלה ונעוץ תחלתן בסופן. וככה הוא בסיום הקו דאור
א"ס המסתיים בסיום היושר דרגלי א"ק מאיר ממטה למעלה לבחי' אור
הנשמה דמל' דמל' דעשיה שהוא אלקות ממש מחיצוניות הכלים דמל'
דאצי'. ולפמ"ש בס' הגלגולים פ"כ הובא בלק"א מתלבשת תחלה הארה ט בתשרי מעוברת
זו של הקו דאור א"ס באור האצי' שבעשיה וממנה לבריאה ויצירה
שבעשיה ומהן לבחי' אור הנשמה דמל' דמל' דעשיה ועי"ז יש כח ועוז
בסיום הכלי דמל' דמל' דעשיה שביסוד העפר והוא מאמר תדשא הארץ
וכו' להיות פועל בקרב הארץ תמיד לעולם ועד (בחי' אין סוף ולא בלבד
בששת ימי בראשית כמאמר ישרצו המים ומאמר תוצא הארץ נפש חיה
מחכמה דמל' דמל' דעשיה שבז' ימי בראשית האיר בעולם הזה הארה
מאור אין סוף בחסד חנם בלי העלאת מיין נוקבין כלל) להצמיח עשבים
ואילנות ופירות מאין ליש תמיד מדי שנה בשנה שהוא מעין בחי' א"ס

שאם יתקיים עוה"ז ריבוי רבבות שנים יצמיחו מדי שנה בשנה אלא שיש מהן ע"י העלאת מ"נ והם הזרועים והנטועים ואעפ"כ הם כמו יש מאין שהגרעין הנטוע אין לו ערך כלל לגבי הפרי וגם נגד כל האילן עם הענפים והעלין וכן במיני זרעונים וירקות וגם במיני תבואה להתהוות מאות גרעינין מגרעין א' הוא כמו יש מאין ומכ"ש הקשין והשבלים והנה הפירות שע"י העלאת מ"נ היא הזריעה והנטיעה הם משובחים מאד מאד מהעולים מאליהן מכח הצומח לבדו שבארץ ומזה נשכיל המשכות אורות עליונים באבי"ע (שהוא תכלית בריאת האדם) כמ"ש במ"א. ומזה יובן היטב בענין סדר מדרגות דצח"מ שהן בחי' עפר מים אש רוח שאף שהחי הוא למעלה מהצומח והמדבר למעלה מהחי אעפ"כ החי ניזון וחי מהצומח והמדבר מקבל חיותו משניהם וגם חכמה ודעת שאין התינוק יודע לקרות אבא ואימא עד שיטעום טעם דגן כו' ועדיין לא אכילנא בישרא דתורא כו' כי הוא בחי' אור חוזר ממטה למעלה מתחתית העשיה שמתגלית שם ביתר עז הארה דהארה כו' מאור א"ס הסובב כ"ע ומהקו אור א"ס שבסיום רגלי היושר דא"ק בבחי' אור חוזר כנ"ל. ויובן היטב בזה טוב טעם ודעת מה שמלאכים עליונים שבמרכבה פני שור ופני נשר נהנים מאד וניזונים ומסתפקים מרוח הבהמה והעוף העולה אליהם מהקרבנות שע"ג המזבח וכדקדוק לשון הזוה"ק ואתהניין מיסודא ועיקרא דילהון.

יב בתשרי פשוטה
י בתשרי מעוברת

ואחרי הדברים והאמת האלה דעת לנבון נקל להבין ע"י כל הנ"ל גודל מעלת המצות מעשיות אשר הן תכלית ירידת הנשמות לעוה"ז הגשמי כמ"ש היום לעשותם ויפה שעה א' בתשובה ומעשים טובים בעוה"ז מכל חיי עוה"ב ע"כ מצאנו מכיה"ק:

אגרת כא

יג בתשרי פשוטה
יא בתשרי מעוברת

אד"ש כמשפט לאוהבי שמו אל המתנדבים בעםלעשות צדקת ה' עם ארצו הקדושה לתת מדי שנה בשנה חוק הקצוב מעות אה"ק תוב"ב אליהם תטוף מלתי ותזל כטל אמרתי לזרז לזריזים ולחזק ידים רפות במתן דמים מעות א"י מדי שבת בשבתו ולפחות מדי חדש בחדשו מערכו הקצוב לערך שנה וכל כסף הקדשים אשר עלה על לב איש להתנדב בלי נדר לפרנסת אחינו יושבי אה"ק מדי שנה בשנה.

כי הנה מלבד הידוע לכל גודל מעלת הזריזות בכל המצות הנאמר ונשנה בדברי רז"ל לעולם יקדים אדם לדבר מצוה כו' וזריזותי' דאברהם אבינו ע"ה היא העומדת לעד לנו ולבנינו עד עולם כי העקדה עצמה אינה נחשבה כ"כ לנסיון גדול לערך מעלת א"א ע"ה בשגם כי ה' דיבר בו קח נא את

בנך כו׳ והרי כמה וכמה קדושים שמסרו נפשם על קדושת ה׳ גם כי לא דיבר ה׳ בם רק שא״א ע״ה עשה זאת בזריזות נפלאה להראות שמחתו וחפצו למלאות רצון קונו ולעשות נחת רוח ליוצרו וממנו למדו רז״ל לקיום כל המצות בכלל ובפרט מעשה הצדקה העולה על כולנה המגינה ומצלה בפירותיה בעוה״ז מכל מיני פורעניות המתרגשות כדכתיב וצדקה תציל ממות וכ״ש משאר מיני יסורים הקלים ממות כ״ש שטוב לנו גם בעוה״ז להקדימה כל מה דאפשר שהרי אדם נידון בכל יום:

יד בתשרי פשוטה | יב בתשרי מעוברת

אך גם זאת מצאנו ראינו בעבודת הצדקה מעלהפרטיות גדולה ונפלאה אין ערוך אליה להיות מעשה הצדקה נעשית בפעמים רבות וכל המרבה ה״ז משובח ולא בפעם א׳ ובבת אחת גם כי הסך הכולל אחד הוא כמ״ש הרמב״ם ז״ל בפירוש המשנה ששנו חכמים ז״ל והכל לפי רוב המעשה:

והנה מלבד כי הרמב״ם ז״ל ביאר היטב טעמו ונימוקו כדי לזכך הנפש ע״י רבוי המעשה הנה מקרא מלא דיבר הכתוב פעולת צדקה לחיים דהיינו שפעולתה וסגולתה להמשיך חיים עליונים מחיי החיים א״ס ב״ה לארץ החיים היא שכינת עוזינו שעליה נאמר ואתה מחיה את כולם והיא סוכת דוד הנופלת עד עפר וכמארז״ל גלו לאדום שכינה עמהם כו׳ כי באתערותא דלתתא להחיות רוח שפלים דלית ליה מגרמיה כלום אתערותא דלעילא ובפרט בהתנדב עם להחיות יושבי ארץ החיים ממש וד״ל. וכל משכיל על דבר גדול ונפלא כזה ימצא טוב טעם ודעת כמה גדולים דברי חכמים ז״ל שאמרו הכל לפי רוב המעשה דהיינו מעשה הצדקה הנעשה בפעמים רבות להמשיך חיים עליונים ליחד יחוד עליון פעמים רבות. והיינו נמי כעין מ״ש הרמב״ם לזכך הנפש כנודע מזוה״ק דשכינה נקראת נפש כי היא חיינו ונפשנו וכתיב כי שחה לעפר נפשנו. ולכן ארז״ל גדולה צדקה שמקרבת את הגאולה להקימה מעפר מעט מעט עד כי יבא שילה:

אגרת כב

טו בתשרי פשוטה | יג בתשרי מעוברת

אהוביי אחיי ורעיי מאהבה מסותרת תוכחת מגולה לכו נא ונוכחה זכרו ימות עולם בינו שנות דור ודור ההיתה כזאת מימות עולם ואיה איפוא מצאתם מנהג זה באחד מכל ספרי חכמי ישראל הראשונים והאחרונים להיות מנהג ותיקון לשאול בעצה גשמיות כדת מה לעשות בעניני העולם הגשמי אף לגדולי חכמי ישראל הראשונים כתנאים ואמוראים אשר כל רז לא אנס להו ונהירין להון שבילין דרקיע כ״א לנביאים ממש אשר היו לפנים בישראל כשמואל הרואה אשר הלך אליו שאול לדרוש

ה׳ על דבר האתונות שנאבדו לאביו כי באמת כל עניני אדם לבד מדברי תורה וי״ש אינם מושגים רק בנבואה ולא לחכמים לחם כמארז״ל הכל בידי שמים חוץ מיראת שמים ושבעה דברים מכוסים כו׳ אין אדם יודע במה משתכר כו׳ ומלכות בית דוד מתי תחזור כו׳ הנה הושוו זה לזה ומ״ש בישעיה יועץ וחכם חרשים וכן משארז״ל ונהנין ממנו עצה ותושיה היינו בד״ת הנקרא תושיה כמארז״ל יועץ זה שיודע לעבר שנים ולקבוע חדשים כו׳ שסוד העיבור קרוי עצה וסוד בלשון תורה כדאיתא בסנהדרין דף פ״ז ע״ש בפרש״י:

אך האמת אגיד לשומעים לי כי אהבה מקלקלת השורה והנה היא כסות עינים שלא לראות האמת מרוב אהבתם לחיי הגוף לש״ש לעבוד בו את ה׳ ברשפי אש ושלהבת גדולה מאהבת נפשם את ה׳ וע״כ היטב חרה להם בצער הגוף ח״ו ה׳ ירחם ואין יכולין לקבל כלל עד שמעבירם על דעתם לכתת רגליהם מעיר לעיר לשאול עצות מרחוק ולא שעו אל ה׳ לשוב אליו ברוח נמוכה והכנעת הגוף לקבל תוכחתו באהבה כי את אשר יאהב ה׳ וכו׳: טז בתשרי פשוטה / יד בתשרי מעוברת

וכמו אב רחמן חכם וצדיק המכה בנו שאין לבן חכם להפוך עורף לנוס למצוא לו עזרה או אפילו מליץ יושר לפני אביו הרחמן והצדיק וחסיד רק להיות ישר יחזו פנימו עם אביו פנים בפנים לסבול הכאותיו באהבה לטוב לו כל הימים. והנה למעלה בחי׳ פנים הוא הרצון והחשק אשר אבינו שבשמים משפיע לבניו כל טוב עולמים וחיי נפש וגוף באהבה ורצון חשיקה וחפיצה ע״י תורת חיים שהיא רצונו ית׳ אשר נתן לנו כמ״ש כי באור פניך נתת לנו תורת חיים כו׳ לעשות בה רצונו וע״ז נאמר באור פני מלך חיים ורצונו כו׳. משא״כ לעו״ג משפיע חיי גופם שלא ברצון וחשיקה וחפיצה לכך נק׳ אלהים אחרים שיונקים מבחי׳ אחוריים וכך הוא באדם הרצון והחשק הוא בחי׳ פנים ואם אינו מקבל באהבה ורצון כאלו הופך עורף ואחור ח״ו. ועצה היעוצה לקבל באהבה היא עצת ה׳ בפי חז״ל לפשפש במעשיו וימצא לו עונות הצריכין מירוק יסורים ויראה לעין גודל אהבתו אליו המקלקלת השורה כמשל מלך גדול ונורא הרוחץ בכבודו ובעצמו צואת בנו יחידו מרוב אהבתו כמ״ש אם רחץ ה׳ צואת בנות ציון כו׳ ברוח משפט כו׳ וכמים הפנים אל פנים תתעורר האהבה בלב כל משכיל ומבין יקר מהות אהבת ה׳ אל התחתונים אשר היא יקרה וטובה מכל חיי העולמים כולם כמ״ש מה יקר חסדך וכו׳ כי טוב חסדך מחיים כו׳ כי החסד שהוא בחי׳ אהבה הוא חיי החיים שבכל העולמות כמ״ש מכלכל חיים בחסד ואז גם ה׳ יתן הטוב ויאר פניו אליו בבחי׳ אהבה מגולה אשר היתה תחלה

טו בתשרי מעוברת (beside "וכמו")

יז בתשרי פשוטה (beside "הופך עורף ואחור ח״ו")

מלובשת ומסותרת בתוכחה מגולה ויתמתקו הגבורות בשרשן ויתבטלו הדינין נס"ו:

יח בתשרי פשוטה / טז בתשרי מעוברת

אהוביי אחיי ורעיי מגודל טרדתי אשר הקיפו עלי יחד וסבוני כמים כל היום וכל הלילה תמיד לא יחשו. לא אוכל מלט משא לאמר עם הספר כל אשר בלבבי. אך בקצרה באתי כמזכיר ומחזיר על הראשונות בכלל ובפרט אל המתנדבים בעם לעמוד על העבודה זו תפלה בקול רם להתחזק מאד בכל עוז ותעצומות נגד כל מונע מבית ומחוץ ביד חזקה כמשמעו שהוא רצון יריאיו אשר למעלה מן החכמה והתבונה אשר נתן ה' בהמה לדעת לעשות את כל אשר צוה ה' בהשכל ודעת. רק רצון פשוט ורוח נדיבה בכל איש אשר ידבנו לבו לעבוד עבודה תמה לעשות נ"ר ליוצרו. ועז"נ כי עם קשה עורף הוא וסלחת. כי הסליחה היא ג"כ למעלה מן החכ'.

יט בתשרי פשוטה

כי שאלו לחכמה כו' ומשה רבינו ע"ה ביקש מדה כנגד מדה וד"ל. ועוד זאת אדרוש ממעל' שלא להשליך דברי אחריכם אשר ערכתי שיח להיות כל איש ישר והולך בתומו כאשר עשה האלקי' את האדם ישר ולא לבקש חשבונות רבים מעלילות מצעדי גבר ומחשבות אדם ותחבולותיו. כי זו מלאכת שמים היא ולא מלאכת ב"ו. ולהאמין באמונה שלימה במצות חז"ל והוי שפל רוח בפני כל אדם בכלל כי יציבא מלתא ותקין פתגמא שכ"א מתוקן מחבירו. וכתיב כל [איש] ישראל כאיש אחד חברים. כמו שאיש א' מחובר מאברים רבים ובהפרדם נוגע בלב כי ממנו תוצאות חיים. א"כ אנחנו היות כולנו כאיש א' ממש תיכון העבודה בלב ומכלל הן כו'. וע"כ נאמר ולעבדו שכם אחד דוקא. וע"כ אהוביי ידידיי נא ונא לטרוח בכל לב ונפש לתקוע אהבת רעהו בלבו. ואיש את רעת רעהו אל תחשבו בלבבכם כתיב ולא תעלה על לב לעולם ואם תעלה יהדפנה מלבו כהנדוף עשן וכמו מחשבת ע"ז ממש. כי גדולה לה"ר כנגד ע"ז וג"ע וש"ד. ואם בדבור כך כו' וכבר נודע לכל חכם לב יתרון הכשר המח' על הדבור הן לטוב והן למוטב. וה' הטוב המברך את עמו בשלום ישים עליכם שלום וחיים עד העולם כנפש או"נ מלו"נ:

אגרת כג

כ בתשרי פשוטה / יז בתשרי מעוברת

בגזירת עירין פתגמא ומאמר קדישין חכמי המשנה ע"ה ששנו במשנתם עשרה שיושבין ועוסקין בתורה שכינה שרויה ביניהם כי זה כל האדם ואף גם זאת היתה כל ירידתו בעוה"ז לצורך עליה זו אשר אין עליה למעלה הימנה כי שכינת עוזו אשר בגבהי מרומים והשמים ושמי השמים לא יכלכלו אימתה. תשכון ותתגדל בתוך בני ישראל כמ"ש כי

אני ה׳ שוכן בתוך בנ״י ע״י עסק התורה והמצות בעשרה דוקא כמ״ש רז״ל
אתיא תוך תוך כו׳ וע״ז נאמר בקרבך קדוש ואין דבר שבקדושה בפחות
מעשרה ומשום הכי נמי אצטריך להו לרז״ל למילף מקרא מנין שאפילו
אחד שיושב ועוסק בתורה כו׳ ואף גם זאת לא מצאו לו סמך מן המקרא
אלא לקביעת שכר בלבד ליחיד לפי ערכו לפי [נ״א ולפי] ערך המרובים
יח בתשרי מעוברת אבל לענין השראת קדושת הקב״ה אין לו ערך אליהם כלל וההפרש שבין
כא בתשרי פשוטה השראה לקביעות שכר מובן למביני מדע. כי קביעת שכר הוא שמאיר ה׳
לנפש תדרשנו באור תורתו שהוא מעטה לבושו ממש ולכן נקראת התורה
אור שנאמר עוטה אור כשלמה והנפש היא בעלת גבול ותכלית בכל
כחותיה לכן גם אור ה׳ המאיר בה הוא גבולי מצומצם ומתלבש בתוכה
וע״כ יתפעל לב מבקשי ה׳ בשעת התפלה וכיוצא בה כי בו ישמח לבם
ויגיל אף גילת ורנן ותתענג נפשם בנועם ה׳ [נ״א על ה׳] ואורו בהגלותו
ממעטה לבושו שהיא התורה ויצא כברק חצו וזו היא קביעת שכר התורה
יט בתשרי מעוברת הקבועה תמיד בנפש עמלה בה. אבל ההשראה היא הארה עצומה מאור
ה׳ המאיר בה בלי גבול ותכלית ואינו יכול להתלבש בנפש גבולית כ״א
מקיף עליה מלמעלה מראשה ועד רגלה כמו שאמרו חז״ל אכל בי עשרה
שכינתא שריא כלומר עליהם מלמעלה כמ״ש ויהי נועם ה׳ עלינו ומעשה
ידינו כוננה עלינו כלומר כי נועם ה׳ אשר הופיע במעשה ידינו בעסק התורה
והמצות דאורייתא וקוב״ה כולא חד יתכונן וישרה עלינו מלמעלה להיותו
בלי גבול ותכלית ואינו מתלבש בנפשנו ושכלנו וע״כ אין אנו משיגים
בשכלנו הנעימות והעריבות מנועם ה׳ וזיו השכינה בלי גבול ותכלית
אשר מתכונן ושורה עלינו במעשה ידינו בתורה ומצות ברבים דוקא. וע״ז
ארז״ל שכר מצוה בהאי עלמא ליכא כי אי אפשר לעולם להשיגו כי אם
בהתפשטות הנפש מהגוף ואף גם זאת על דרך החסד כמ״ש ולך ה׳ חסד
כי אתה תשלם לאיש כמעשהו וכמו שארז״ל שהקב״ה נותן כח בצדיקים
כו׳. משא״כ במלאכים כמו ששמעתי מרבותי כי אילו נמצא מלאך אחד
עומד במעמד עשרה מישראל ביחד אף שאינם מדברים בדברי תורה
תפול עליו אימתה ופחד בלי גבול ותכלית משכינתא דשריא עלייהו עד
כב בתשרי פשוטה שהיה מתבטל ממציאותו לגמרי וע״כ רע בעיני המעשה אשר נעשה תחת
כ בתשרי מעוברת השמש בכלל ובפרט בין אחיי ורעיי הנגשים אל ה׳ הגשה זו תפלה ואחר
התפלה או לפניה נעשה מושב לצים ר״ל כמו שארז״ל שנים שיושבין ואין
ביניהם ד״ת כו׳ ואם נעשה מושב לצים בעשרה דשכינתא שריא עלייהו
אין לך עלבונא וקלנא דשכינתא גדול מזה רחמנא ליצלן ואם אמרו רז״ל
על העובר עבירה בסתר שדוחק רגלי השכינה ח״ו העובר עבירה ברבים
דוחק כל שיעור קומה של יוצר בראשית כביכול כמ״ש רז״ל אין אני והוא
וכו׳ אלא שמלך אסור ברהטים כו׳. אבל ווי למאן דדחקין לשכינתא כד

יוקים לה קודשא ב״ה ויימא לה התנערי מעפר קומי וגו׳ ועל תלת מילין מתעכבי ישראל בגלותא על דדחקין לשכינתא ועל דעבדין קלנא בשכינתא וכו׳ כמ״ש בזוה״ק. על כן אהוביי אחיי ורעיי אל נא תרעו הרעה הגדולה הזאת ותנו כבוד לה׳ אלהיכם בטרם יחשך דהיינו בין מנחה למעריב כל ימות החול ללמוד בעשרה פנימיות התורה שהיא אגדה שבכס׳ ע״י שרוב סודות התורה גנוזין בה ומכפרת עונותיו של אדם כמבואר בכהאריז״ל והנגלות שבה הן דרכי ה׳ שילך בהם האדם וישית עצות בנפשו במילי דשמיא ובמילי דעלמא וכידוע לכל חכמי לב וגם ללמוד מעט בשו״ע או״ח הלכות הצריכות לכל אדם וע״ז ארז״ל כל השונה הלכות בכל יום כו׳ שהן הלכות ברורות ופסוקות הלכה למעשה כמבואר בפרש״י ז״ל שם ובשבת קדש בעלות המנחה יעסקו בהל׳ שבת כי הלכתא רבתא לשבתא ובקל יכול האדם ליכשל בה ח״ו אפילו באיסור כרת וסקילה מחסרון ידיעה ושגגת תלמוד עולה זדון ח״ו ואצ״ל באיסורי דברי סופרים שרבו כמו רבו למעלה ובפרט באיסורי מוקצה דשכיחי טובא והחמורים ד״ס יותר מד״ת כמ״ש רז״ל שכל העובר על דברי חכמים אפילו באיסור קל של דבריהם כמו האוכל קודם תפלת ערבית וכה״ג חייב מיתה כעובר על חמורות שבתורה וכל יחיד אל יפרוש עצמו מן הציבור אפילו ללמוד ענין אחר כ״א בדבר שהציבור עסוקין בו ואצ״ל שלא יצא החוצה אם לא יהיו עשרה מבלעדו ועליו אני קורא הפסוק ועוזבי ה׳ יכלו כו׳ כמשארז״ל על כל דבר שבקדושה. כי אין קדושה כקדושת התורה דאורייתא וקוב״ה כולא חד. וכל הפורש מן הציבור כו׳ ושומע לי ישכון בטח ובימיו ובימינו תושע יהודה וירושלים תשכון לבטח אמן כן יהי רצון:

כג בתשרי פשוטה

כא בתשרי מעוברת

כב בתשרי מעוברת

אגרת כד

כד בתשרי פשוטה

כג בתשרי מעוברת

אהוביי אחיי אל נא תרעו ריעים האהובים ליוצרם ושנואים ליצרם ואל יעשה אדם עצמו רשע שעה אחת לפני המקום אשר בחר בה מכל היום להקהל ולעמוד לפניו בשעה זו שהיא עת רצון לפניו להתגלות לבוא אל המקדש מעט לפקוד לשכינת כבודו השוכן אתם בתוך טומאותם ולהמצא לדורשיו ומבקשיו ומייחליו והמספר בצרכיו מראה בעצמו שאינו חפץ להתבונן ולראות בגילוי כבוד מלכותו ונעשה מרכבה טמאה לכסיל העליון שנאמר עליו לא יחפוץ כסיל בתבונה כו׳ כמ״ש הזהר והאריז״ל דהיינו שאינו חפץ להתבונן ולראות ביקר תפארת גדולתו של מלך מה״מ הקב״ה הנגלות למעלה בשעה זו וגם למטה אל החפצים להביט אל כבודו וגדלו המתעטף ומתלבש בתוך תיבות התפלה הסדורה בפי כל ומתגלה לכל אחד לפי שכלו ושורש נשמתו כדכתיב לפי שכלו יהולל איש יהלל

כתיב ומלכותא דרקיע כעין מלכותא דארעא שדרך המלך להיות חביון עוזו בחדרי חדרים וכמה שומרים על הפתחים (עד) אשר כמה וכמה מצפים ימים ושנים לראות עוזו וכבודו וכשעלה רצונו להתגלות לכל והעביר קול בכל מלכותו להקהל ולעמוד לפניו להראותם כבוד מלכותו ויקר תפארת גדולתו מי שעומד לפניו ואינו חושש לראותו ומתעסק בצרכיו כמה גרוע וסכל ופתי הוא ונמשל כבהמות נדמה בעיני כל הבריות וגם הוא בזיון המלך בהראותו לפניו שאינו ספון בעיניו לקבל נחת ושעשועים מהביט אל כבודו ויפיו יותר מעסק צרכיו וגם הוא מתחייב בנפשו למלך על הראות קלונו ובזיונו את המלך לעין כל רואה וע״ז נאמר וכסילים מרים קלון כלומר אף שהוא כסיל לא יהי׳ מרים קלון שיהי׳ נראה הקלון לעין כל. וע״כ קבעו חז״ל בתפלה כאלו עומד לפני המלך עכ״פ יהי׳ מראה בעצמו כאלו עומד כו׳ לעין כל רואה בעיני בשר אל מעשיו ודיבוריו אף שאין לו מחשבה לכסיל וע״ז הענין נתקן כל התפלות למתבונן בהם היטב ומי שאינו מראה כן מתחייב בנפשו ועליו אמרו בזהר הק׳ דאנהיג קלנא בתקונא עילאה ואחזי פרודא ולית ליה חולקא באלהא דישראל ר״ל ע״כ שליחותייהו דרז״ל קא עבידנא לגזור גזירה שוה לכל נפש שלא לשוח שיחה בטלה משיתחיל הש״ץ להתפלל התפלה עד גמר קדיש בתרא שחרית ערבית ומנחה וכו׳. והעובר ע״ז בזדון ישב על הארץ ויבקש מג׳ אנשים שיתירו לו נידוי שלמעלה ושב ורפא לו ולא חל עליו שום נידוי למפרע כל עיקר כי מתחלתו לא חל כ״א על המורדים והפושעים שאינם חוששים כלל לבקש כפרה מן השמים ומן הבריות על העון פלילי הזה. וגם דוקא כשמדברים בזדון בשאט נפש ולא על השוכח או שנזרקו מפיו כמה תיבות בלא מתכוין שא״צ התרה כלל ובוחן לבות וכליות אלקים צדיק. הטיבה ה׳ לטובים ולישרים בלבותם:

כד בתשרי מעוברת

אגרת כה

כה בתשרי פשוטה

כה בתשרי מעוברת

להבין אמרי בינה מ״ש בספר הנק׳ צוואת ריב״ש הגם שבאמת אינה צוואתו כלל ולא ציוה כלל לפני פטירתו רק הם לקוטי אמרותיו הטהורות שלקטו לקוטי בתר לקוטי ולא ידעו לכוין הלשון על מתכונתו. אך המכוון הוא אמת לאמיתו. והוא בהקדים מארז״ל כל הכועס כאילו עובד עכו״ם וכו׳. והטעם מובן ליודעי בינה לפי שבעת כעסו נסתלקה ממנו האמונה כי אילו היה מאמין שמאת ה׳ היתה זאת לו לא היה בכעס כלל ואף שבן אדם שהוא בעל בחירה מקללו או מכהו או מזיק ממונו ומתחייב בדיני אדם ובדיני שמים על רוע בחירתו אעפי״כ על הניזק כבר נגזר מן השמים והרבה שלוחים למקום ולא עוד אלא אפילו בשעה זו ממש שמכהו או מקללו מתלבש בו כח ה׳ ורוח פיו ית׳ המחייהו ומקיימו וכמ״ש כי ה׳

אמר לו קלל והיכן אמר לשמעי אלא שמחשבה זו שנפלה לשמעי בלבו
ומוחו ירדה מאת ה׳ ורוח פיו המחי׳ כל צבאם החיה רוחו של שמעי בשעה
שדיבר דברים אלו לדוד כי אילו נסתלק רוח פיו ית׳ רגע אחד מרוחו של
שמעי לא יכול לדבר מאומה (וזהו כי ה׳ אמר לו בעת ההיא ממש קלל כו בתשרי מעוברת
את דוד ומי יאמר לו וגו׳ וכנודע מ״ש הבעש״ט ז״ל ע״פ לעולם ה׳ דברך כו בתשרי פשוטה
נצב בשמים שצירוף אותיות שנבראו בהן השמים שהוא מאמר יהי רקיע
כו׳ הן נצבות ועומדות מלובשות בשמים לעולם להחיותם ולקיימם ולא
כהפלוסופים שכופרים בהשגחה פרטית ומדמין בדמיונם הכוזב את מעשה
ה׳ עושה שמים וארץ למעשה אנוש ותחבולותיו כי כאשר יצא לצורף כלי
שוב אין הכלי צריך לידי הצורף שאף שידיו מסולקות הימנו הוא קיים
מעצמו וטח מראות עיניהם ההבדל הגדול שבין מעשה אנוש ותחבולותיו
שהוא יש מיש רק שמשנה הצורה והתמונה למעשה שמים וארץ שהוא
יש מאין והוא פלא גדול יותר מקריעת ים סוף עד״מ אשר הוליך ה׳ ברוח
קדים עזה כל הלילה ויבקעו המים ואילו פסק הרוח כרגע היו המים חוזרים
וניגרים במורד כדרכם וטבעם ולא קמו כחומה אף שטבע זה במים הוא ג״כ
נברא ומחודש יש מאין שהרי חומת אבנים נצבת מעצמה בלי רוח רק שטבע
המים אינו כן וכ״ש וק״ו בבריאת יש מאין שהיא למעלה מהטבע והפלא
ופלא יותר מקריעת י״ס עאכ״ו שבהסתלקות ח״ו כח הבורא יש מאין מן
הנברא ישוב הנברא לאין ואפס ממש אלא צ״ל כח הפועל בנפעל תמיד
להחיותו ולקיימו ובחי׳ זו הוא דבר ה׳ ורוח פיו שבעשרה מאמרות שבהן
נברא העולם ואפילו ארץ הלזו הגשמית ובחי׳ דומם שבה חיותן וקיומן הוא
דבר ה׳ מי׳ מאמרות המלובש בהן ומקיימן להיות דומם ויש מאין ולא יחזרו
לאין ואפס ממש כשהיו וז״ש האריז״ל שגם בדומם כאבנים ועפר ומים יש
בהם בחי׳ נפש וחיות רוחניית. והנה נודע לי״ח כי דבר ה׳ נק׳ בשם שכינה כז בתשרי פשוטה
בלשון רז״ל ואימא תתאה ומטרוניתא בלשון הזהר ובפרט בר״פ וארא לפי כז בתשרי מעוברת
ששוכן ומתלבש בנבראים להחיותם ובלשון המקובלים נק׳ בשם מלכות
ע״ש דבר מלך שלטון כי המלך מנהיג מלכותו בדיבורו ועוד טעמים אחרים
ידועים לי״ח ומודעת זאת כי יש בחי׳ ומדריגת מל׳ דאצילות ובחי׳ מל׳
דבריאה וכו׳. ופי׳ מל׳ דאצילות הוא דבר ה׳ המחי׳ ומהוה נשמות הגדולות
שהן מבחי׳ אצילות כמו נשמת אדה״ר שנא׳ בו ויפח באפיו נשמת חיים כו׳
וכמו נשמות האבות והנביאים וכיוצא בהן (שהיו מרכבה לה׳ ממש ובטלים
ממש במציאות אליו כמארז״ל שכינה מדברת מתוך גרונו של משה וכן כל
הנביאים ובעלי רוה״ק היה קול ודבור העליון מתלבש בקולם ודבורם ממש
כמ״ש האריז״ל) ומל׳ דבריאה הוא דבר ה׳ המחיה ומהוה הנשמות והמלאכי׳
שבעולם הבריאה שאין מעלתם כמעלת האצי׳ וכו׳ ומלכות דעשיה הוא דבר
ה׳ המחיה ומהוה את עוה״ז בכללו עד יסוד העפר והמים אשר מתחת לארץ.

כח בתשרי פשוטה
כח בתשרי מעוברת

(אלא שבחו"ל החיות הוא על ידי התלבשות שרים החיצוני' הממוני' על ע' אומות דהיינו שיורד ניצוץ מדבר ה' הנקרא בשם מלכות דעשיה ומאיר על השרים של מעלה בבחי' מקיף מלמעלה אך אינו מתלבש בהם ממש אלא נמשך להם חיות מהארה זו שמאיר עליהם מלמעלה בבחי' מקיף ומהשרים נשפע חיות לאומות ולבהמות חיות ועופות שבארצותיהם ולארץ הגשמית ולשמים הגשמיים שהם הגלגלים (אלא ששמים וארץ ובהמות וחיות ועופות טהורים נשפעי' מקליפת נוגה והטמאים ונפשות האומות משאר קליפות). והנה שמים וארץ וכל אשר בהם בחו"ל כולם כלא ממש חשיבי לגבי השרים שהם חיותם וקיומם. והשרים כלא ממש חשיבי לגבי החיות הנמשך להם מהניצוץ מדבר ה' המאיר עליהם מלמעלה ואעפ"כ החיות הנמשך לתוכם מהארה זו הוא בבחי' גלות בתוכם שלכן נקראי' בשם אלקי' אחרים וקרו ליה אלהא דאלהיא שגם הם הן בחי' אלקות ולכן הגוים הנשפעים מהם הם עע"ז ממש עד עת קץ שיבולע המות והסט"א ואז אהפוך אל עמים כו' לקרוא כולם בשם ה' ונקרא גם כן בשם גלות השכינה מאחר שחיות זה אשר בבחי' גלות בתוכם הוא מהארה הנמשכת להם מהניצוץ מדבר ה' הנקרא בשם שכינה (וגלות זה נמשך מחטא עה"ד ואילך והוא בחי' אחוריים לבד דקדושה אך כשגלו ישראל לבין האומות ואחיזת ישראל ושרשם הוא בבחי' פנים העליונים הנה זו היא גלות שלימה וע"ז ארז"ל גלו לאדום שכינה עמהם)):

כט בתשרי פשוטה
כט בתשרי מעוברת

והנה אף כי ה' אחד ושמו אחד דהיינו דבורו ורוח פיו המכונה בזוה"ק בשם שמו הוא יחיד ומיוחד אעפ"כ ההארה והמשכת החיות הנמשכת מרוח פיו יתברך מתחלקת לד' מדרגות שונות שהן ד' עולמות אבי"ע והשינוי הוא מחמת צמצומים ומסכים (רבים) לצמצם האור והחיות ולהסתירו שלא יהא מאיר כ"כ בעולם הבריאה כמו בעולם האצילות ובעולם היצי' הוא ע"י צמצומים ומסכים יותר וכו' אבל אין שום שינוי ח"ו בעצמות השכינה שהיא דבר ה' ורוח פיו וגם בבחי' ההארה והמשכת החיות הנה ההארה שבאצילות בוקעת המסך ומתלבשת בבריאה וכן מבריאה ליצירה ומיצירה לעשיה ולכן אור א"ס ב"ה שבאצילות הוא ג"כ בעשיה ובעוה"ז החומרי ע"י התלבשותו במלכות דבי"ע כמבואר הכל בכתבי האר"י ז"ל:

ל בתשרי פשוטה
ל בתשרי מעוברת

והנה נפש האדם ידוע לכל שהיא כלולה מי"ס חב"ד וכו' ואף שכולן מרוח פיו ית' כדכתיב ויפח באפיו כו' מ"מ דרך פרט חב"ד שבנפשו הן דוגמא לחב"ד שבי"ס המכונות בשם או"א ומדות אהבה ויראה וכו' שבנפשו הן דוגמא למדות שבי"ס הנקראות בשם ז"א וכח הדבור שבנפשו

דוגמא לדבור העליון הנקרא בשם מלכות ושכינה ולכן כשמדבר ד״ת מעורר דבור העליון ליחד השכינה ומשום הכי קיי״ל בק״ש ובהמ״ז וד״ת לא יצא בהרהור בלא דבור:

א בחשוון פשוטה
א בחשוון מעוברת

והנה זלעו״ז יש עשרה כתרי דמסאבותא ומהן נמשכות נפשות האומות ג״כ כלולות מעשר בחי׳ אלו ממש ומודעת זאת בארץ מ״ש בספר הגלגולים ע״פ אשר שלט האדם באדם לרע לו שהוא סוד גלות השכינה בתוך הקליפות להחיותם ולהשליטם עתה בזמן הגלות אבל הוא לרע לו וכו׳ ולכן האומות שולטין עתה על ישראל להיות נפשות האומות מהקליפות אשר השכינה מתלבשת בבחי׳ גלות בתוכם והנה אף שזה צריך ביאור רחב איך ומה מ״מ האמת כן הוא אלא שאעפ״כ אין הקליפות והאומות יונקים ומקבלים חיות אלא מהארה הנמשכת להם מבחי׳ אחוריים דקדושה כמאן דשדי בתר כתפי׳ ואף גם זאת ע״י צמצומים ומסכים רבים ועצומים עד שנתלבשה הארה זו בחומריות עולם הזה ומשפעת לאומות עושר וכבוד וכל תענוגים גשמיים. משא״כ ישראל יונקים מבחי׳ פנים העליונים כמ״ש יאר ה׳ פניו אליך כל אחד ואחד לפי שרש נשמתו עד רום המעלות:

ב בחשוון פשוטה
ב בחשוון מעוברת

ואחר הדברים והאמת האלה הגלוים וידועים לכל נחזור לענין ראשון בענין הכעס שהוא כעובד ע״ז והיינו במילי דעלמא כי הכל בידי שמים חוץ מי״ש ולכן במילי דשמיא לאפרושי מאיסורא לא שייך האי טעמא דאמרן וכמ״ש ויקצוף משה והיינו משום כי ה׳ הקרה לפניו מצוה זו לאפרושי מאיסורא כדי לזכותו:

אך זהו כשיש בידו למחות בקצפו וכעסו על חבירו אבל כשאין בידו למחות כגון נכרי המדבר ומבלבלו בתפלתו א״כ מה זאת עשה ה׳ לו אין זאת כ״א כדי שיתגבר ויתאמץ יותר בתפלתו בעומק הלב ובכוונה גדולה כ״כ עד שלא ישמע דבורי הנכרי אך שלמדרגה זו צריך התעוררות רבה ועצומה. ועצה היעוצה להתעוררות זו היא מענין זה עצמו כשישים אל לבו ויתבונן ענין ירידת השכינה כביכול ותרד פלאים להתלבש ניצוץ מהארתה אשר היא בבחי׳ גלות בתוך הקליפות דרך כלל להחיותם ועתה הפעם ניצוץ הארתה מתלבש בבחי׳ גלות דרך פרט בדבור נכרי זה המדבר דברים המבלבלים עבודת ה׳ היא כוונת התפלה וכמש״ל כי זה לעומת זה וכו׳ ודבור העליון מתלבש בדבור התחתון וכו׳ וזהו ממש אשר שלט האדם באדם לרע לו דהיינו שעי״ז מתעורר האדם להתפלל יותר בכוונה מעומקא דלבא עד שלא ישמע דיבוריו. ומ״ש המלקט שרתה לא ידע לכוין הלשון בדקדוק כי הבעש״ט ז״ל היה אומר ד״ת בל״א ולא בלה״ק ור״ל נתלבשה

והיינו בבחי׳ גלות וזהו ובפרט אם הוא נכרי כו׳. שאז היא בחי׳ גלות ביותר ואין לתמוה אם ניצוץ מן הארת שכינה נקרא בשם שכינה דהא אשכחן שאפילו מלאך נברא נקרא בשם ה׳ בפ׳ וירא לפי׳ הרמב״ן וכמ״ש ותקרא שם ה׳ הדובר אליה וכו׳ וכה״ג טובא וכמדומה לי שתפיסתם אינה מצד דקדוק הלשון אלא מעיקר ענין התלבשות השכינה בקליפות שאין להם אמונה במ״ש האריז״ל בס׳ הגלגולים שאם ירצו לחלק בין קליפות הרוחניים לעו״ג הגשמיים אין לך גשמי כעפר הארץ ואף על פי כן מתלבשת בו מלכות דמלכות דעשיה ובתוכה מלכות דיצירה כו׳ וכנ״ל. ואם משום טומאת נפשות הנכרים הרי נפשותיהם מזיווג זו״ן דקליפות הרוחניים כמ״ש בכהאריז״ל. נמצא שהרוחניים מקור טומאתם אך באמת צריך ביאור רחב איך הוא התלבשות זו אבל לא עלינו תלונתם כ״א על כהאריז״ל. ואל יחשדני שומע שאני בעיני שהבנתי דברי האריז״ל להפשיטן מגשמיותן כי לא באתי רק לפרש דברי הבעש״ט ז״ל ותלמידיו עפ״י קבלת האריז״ל בשגם שענין זה אינו מחכמת הקבלה ומהנסתרות לה׳ אלוקינו כי אם מהנגלות לנו ולבנינו להאמין אמונה שלימה במקרא מלא שדבר הכתוב הלא את השמים ואת הארץ אני מלא נאם ה׳ שאין מקרא יוצא מידי פשוטו וגם היא אמונה פשוטה בסתם כללות ישראל ומסורה בידם מאבותיהם הקדושים שהלכו בתמימות עם ה׳ בלי לחקור בשכל אנושי ענין האלקות אשר הוא למעלה מהשכל עד אין קץ לידע איך הוא מלא כל הארץ רק שחדשים מקרוב באו לחקור בחקירה זו וא״א לקרב להם אל השכל אלא דוקא עפ״י הקדמות לקוחות מכאריז״ל מופשטות מגשמיותן וכפי ששמעתי מרבותי נ״ע אך א״א לבאר זה היטב במכתב כי אם מפה לאזן שומעת ליחידי סגולה ולשרידים אשר ה׳ קורא כדכתיב ומבקשי הוי׳ יבינו כל ומכלל הן אתה שומע כו׳.

הנה אתם ראיתם פי׳ מאמר אחד מספרים הידועים לדוגמא ולאות כי גם כל המאמרים התמוהים יש להם פי׳ וביאור היטב לי״ח. אך לא יקוו מעלתם אלי לבאר להם הכל במכתב כי היא מלאכה כבידה ומרובה וא״א בשום אופן. רק אם תרצו שלחו מכם אחד ומיוחד שבעדה. ופא״פ אדבר בו אי״ה. וה׳ יהי׳ עם פי בהטיפי. ויהיו לרצון אמרי פי:

אגרת כו

בר״מ פ׳ נשא והמשכילים יזהירו כזהר הרקיע בהאי חבורא דילך דאיהו ספר הזהר מן זהרא דאימא עילאה תשובה באילין לא צריך נסיון ובגין דעתידין ישראל למטעם מאילנא דחיי דאיהו האי ספר הזהר יפקון ביה מן גלותא ברחמים ויתקיים בהון ה׳ בדד ינחנו ואין עמו אל נכר ואילנא דטוב ורע דאיהו איסור והיתר טומאה וטהרה לא ישלטו על ישראל יתיר

ג בחשון פשוטה

ג בחשון מעוברת

ד בחשון פשוטה

ד בחשון מעוברת

דהא פרנסה דלהון לא להוי אלא מסטרא דאילנא דחיי דלית תמן לא קשיא מסטרא דרע ולא מחלוקת מרוח הטומאה דכתיב ואת רוח הטומאה אעביר מן הארץ דלא יתפרנסון ת״ח מע״ה אלא מסטרא דטוב דאכלין טהרה כשר היתר ולא מערב רב דאכלין טומאה פסול אסור כו׳ ובזמנא דאילנא דטוב ורע שלטא כו׳ אינון חכמים דדמיין לשבתות ויו״ט לית להון אלא מה דיהבין להון אינון חולין כגוונא דיום השבת דלית ליה אלא מה דמתקנין ליה ביומא דחול ובזמנא דשלטא אילנא דחיי אתכפייא אילנא דטוב ורע ולא יהא לעמי הארץ אלא מה דיהבין להון ת״ח ואתכפיין תחותייהו כאלו לא הוו בעלמא והכי איסור היתר טומאה וטהרה לא אתעבר מע״ה דמסטרייהו לית בין גלותא לימות המשיח אלא שעבוד מלכיות בלבד דאינון לא טעמי מאילנא דחיי וצריך לון מתניתין באיסור והיתר טומאה וטהרה ע״כ בר״מ:

והנה המובן מהשקפה ראשונה לכאורה מלשון זה המאמר לחסירי מדע ה בחשוון מעוברת
שלימוד איסור והיתר וסדר טהרות הוא מאילנא דטוב ורע מלבד שהוא פלא גדול מחמת עצמו וסותר פשטי הכתובים ומדרשי רבותינו ז״ל שכל התורה הנגלית לנו ולבנינו נקרא עץ חיים למחזיקים בה ולא ספר הזהר לבד ובפרט שהיה גנוז בימיהם וגם כל חכמת הקבלה היתה נסתרה בימיהם ונעלמה מכל תלמידי חכמים כ״א ליחידי סגולה ואף גם זאת בהצנע לכת ולא ברבים כדאיתא בגמרא וכמ״ש האריז״ל דדוקא בדורות אלו האחרונים מותר ומצוה לגלות זאת החכמה ולא בדורות הראשונים וגם רשב״י אמר בזוה״ק שלא ניתן רשות לגלות רק לו ולחביריו לבדם ואף גם זאת פליאה נשגבה דלפי זה לא היה לימוד איסור והיתר וכ״ש דיני ממונות דוחין מצות תפלה שנתקנה ע״פ סודות הזהר ויחודים עליונים ליודעים כרשב״י וחביריו וזה אינו כדאיתא בגמ׳ דר״ש בן יוחאי וחביריו וכל מי שתורתו אומנתו אין מפסיקין לתפלה ואפילו כשעוסק בדיני ממונות כרב יהודה דכולהו תנויי בנזיקין הוי ואפ״ה לא הוי מצלי אלא מתלתין יומין לתלתין יומין כד מהדר תלמודא כדאי׳ בגמ׳ ובירושלמי פ״ק דברכות ס״ל לרשב״י דאפי׳ לק״ש אין מפסיקין כ״א ממקרא ולא ממשנה דעדיפי ממקרא לרשב״י ולא חילק בין סדר זרעים ומועד וקדשים טהרות לנזיקין (וסותר דעת עצמו בר״מ בכמה מקומות דמשנה איהי שפחה כו׳ והמקרא שהוא תורת משה ודאי עדיפא מקבלה דאיהי מטרוניתא בר״מ שם ותורה שבכתב הוא מלכא (דהיינו יסוד אבא המלובש בז״א כמ״ש האריז״ל)). וגם פלפול הקושיות ותירוצים דמסטרא דרע ורוח הטומאה אשכחן ברשב״י דעסק בי׳ טובא גם בהיותו במערה ואדרבה בזכות צער המערה זכה לזה כדאיתא בגמ׳ דאמר לר׳ פנחס בן יאיר אכל קושי׳ כ״ד פירוקי וא״ל אילו לא ראיתני בכך כו׳ (וגם באמת ע״כ עיקר עסקיהם במערה הי׳ תורת המשניות ת״ר סדרי שהיה

בימיהם עד רבינו הקדוש דאילו ספר הזהר והתיקונים היה יכול לגמור בב׳ וג׳ חדשים כי בודאי לא אמר דבר אחד ב׳ פעמים) גם אמרו רבותינו ז״ל מיום שחרב בהמ״ק אין לו להקב״ה אלא ד׳ אמות של הלכה בלבד. ועוד יש להפליא הפלא ופלא איך אפשר שלימות המשיח לא יצטרכו לידע הלכות איסור והיתר וטומאה וטהרה כי איך ישחטו הקרבנות וגם חולין אם לא ידעו הלכות דרסה וחלדה ושהי׳ הפוסלים השחיטה ופגימת הסכין וכי יולד איש בטבעו שיהא שוחט בלי שהי׳ ודרסה וגם הסכין תהי׳ בריאה ועומדת בלי פגימה לעולם ועוד הרבה הלכות חלב ודם ושאר איסורין וגם טומאת המת יהיו צריכין לידע כדכתיב הנער בן מאה שנה ימות וגם טומאת יולדת צריך לידע כדכתיב הרה ויולדת יחדיו אם תלד אשה בכל יום מביאה אחת אעפ״כ דין איסור טומאתה לא ישתנה ואין להאריך בדבר הפשוט ומפורסם הפכו בכל הש״ס ומדרשים דפריך הלכתא למשיחא ואליהו בא לפשוט כל הספיקות ופרשה זו עתיד אליהו לדורשה כו׳: ועוד אינו מובן מ״ש דלא יתפרנסון ת״ח מעמי הארץ כו׳ ולא מערב רב דאכלין פסול טמא ואסור ח״ו שהרי ת״ח שבזמן בית שני לא היו מתפרנסין מע״ה דאכלין פסול אסור ח״ו שהיה להם שדות וכרמים כע״ה ואפ״ה היו עוסקין בלימוד איסור והיתר וטומאה וטהרה כל הזוגות שהיו בימי בית שני והעמידו תלמידים לאלפים ורבבות ולימוד הנסתר בהסתר כו׳:

ה בחשון פשוטה

ו בחשון מעוברת

אך באמת כשתדקדק בלשון ר״מ דלעיל ואילנא דטוב ורע דאיהו איסור והיתר כו׳ ולא אמר תורת איסור והיתר או הלכות או״ה אלא ר״ל דגוף דבר האסור ודבר המותר הוא מאילנא דטוב ורע שהוא קליפת נוגה כמ״ש בע״ח. וזהו לשון אסור שהקליפה שורה עליו ואינו יכול לעלות למעלה כדבר המותר דהיינו שאינו קשור ואסור בקליפה ויוכל לעלות ע״י האדם האוכלו בכוונה לה׳ וגם בסתם כל אדם העובד ה׳ שבכח האכילה ההיא לומד ומתפלל לה׳ ונמצא שנעשה אותיות התורה והתפלה העולה לה׳ מכח הנברר מהמאכל ההוא וזהו בחול אבל בשבת שיש עליה לקליפת נוגה בעצמה עם החיצוניות שבכל העולמות לכן מצוה לאכול כל תענוגים בשבת ולהרבות בבשר ויין אף שבחול נקרא זולל וסובא. משא״כ בדבר איסור שאינו יכול לעלות לא בשבת ולא בחול גם כשמתפלל ולומד בכח ההוא אם לא שאכל לפיקוח נפש שהתירו רז״ל ונעשה היתר [גמור]. אבל הלימוד בתורה אף הלכות איסור והיתר טומאה וטהרה שהם המשניות ובריית ות שבגמרא ופוסקים המבארים ומבררים דבריהם להלכה למעשה הן הן גופי תורה שבע״פ שהיא ספי׳ מלכות דאצילות כדאי׳ בזוה״ק במקומות אין מספר ובריש תיקונים מלכות פה תורה שבע״פ קרינן לה ובאצי׳ איהו וגרמוהי חד בהון דהיינו

ו בחשון פשוטה

ז בחשון מעוברת

שאור א״ס ב״ה מתייחד באצילות בתכלית היחוד שהוא ורצונו וחכמתו המלובשים בדבורו שנקרא מלכות הכל אחד:

ומ״ש האריז״ל שהמשניות הן במלכות דיצירה ר״ל לבוש מלכות דיצירה ז בחשוון פשוטה
שנתלבשה בה מלכות דאצילות ומלכות דיצירה נקרא שפחה ח בחשוון מעוברת
לגבי מלכות דאצילות ומלכות דבריאה נקרא אמה ותדע ממ״ש האריז״ל דמקרא דהיינו תושב״כ הוא בעשי׳ והרי מפורש בזהר ובכתבי האריז״ל מקומות אין מספר שהיא תפארת שהוא ז״א דאצילות אלא שמתלבשת בעשי׳ וכן הוא בהדיא בספר הכוונות שמקרא ומשנה ותלמוד וקבלה כולם באצילות אלא שמקרא מתלבש עד עשיה ומשנה עד היצירה ותלמוד
בבריאה. והנה כשהמלכות דאצי׳ מתלבשת בקליפת נוגה כדי לברר ח בחשוון פשוטה
הניצוצות שנפלו בחטא אדה״ר וגם הרפ״ח ניצוצין שנפלו בשבירת הכלים אזי גם המלכות דאצי׳ נקרא בשם עץ הדעת טוב ורע לגבי ז״א דאצילות שאינו יורד שם ונקרא עץ חיים והנה התלבשות המלכות בקליפת נוגה הוא סוד גלות השכינה אשר שלט האדם באדם כו׳ וז״ש ברע״מ ובזמנא דאילנא דטו״ר שלטא כו׳ אינון כו׳ דהיינו בזמן גלות השכינה שמשפעת לחיצונים שהם בקליפת נוגה שהערב רב יונקים משם ומתמציתן ניזונין תלמידי חכמים בגלות ואז עיקר עבודת האדם ועיקר עסק התורה והמצות הוא לברר הניצוצות כנודע מהאריז״ל לכן עיקר ענין הלימוד הוא בעיון ופלפול הלכה באיסור והיתר טומאה וטהרה לברר המותר והטהור מהאסור והטמא ע״י עיון ופלפול הלכה בחכמה בינה ודעת כנודע דאוריי׳ מחכמה נפקת ובחכמה דייקא אתברירו והיינו חכמה עילאה דאצילות המלובשת במלכות דאצי׳ סוד תורה שבע״פ (בסוד אבא יסד ברתא) המלובשת במלכות דיצירה (וסוד) [סוד] המשניות ובריייתות המלובשות בקליפת נוגה שכנגד עולם היצירה ששם מתחיל בחי׳ הדעת [נ״א הרע] שבנוגה [נ״א והברייתות המלובשות בק״נ שכנגד עולם העשיה ששם מתחיל בחי׳
הרע שבנוגה] כנודע מהאריז״ל. והמשכיל יבין ענין פלא גדול מזה מאד ט בחשוון פשוטה
מה נעשה בשמים ממעל ע״י עיון ובירור הלכה פסוקה מן הגמרא ופוסקים ראשונים ואחרונים מה שהיה בהעלם דבר קודם העיון הלז כי ע״י זה מעלה הלכה זו מהקליפות שהיו מעלימים ומכסים אותה שלא היתה ידועה כלל או שלא היתה מובנת היטב בטעמה שהטעם הוא סוד הספי׳ חכמה עילאה שנפלו ממנה ניצוצי׳ בקליפות בשבה״כ והם שם בבחי׳ גלות שהקליפות שולטים עליהם ומעלימי׳ חכמת התורה מעליונים ותחתונים וז״ש בר״מ
שהקושי׳ היא מסטרא דרע. והנה העליונים אין בהם כח לברר ולהעלות י בחשוון פשוטה
מהשבירה שבקליפת נוגה אלא התחתונים לבד לפי שהם מלובשים בגוף ט בחשוון מעוברת
חומרי משכא דחויא מקליפת נוגה והם מתישים כחה בשבירת התאוות

ואתכפיא ס״א ויתפרדו כל פועלי און. ולכן באים העליונים לשמוע חידושי תורה מהתחתונים מה שמחדשים ומגלים תעלומות החכמה שהיו כבושים בגולה עד עתה וכל איש ישראל יוכל לגלות תעלומות חכמה (לגלות ולחדש שכל חדש הן בהלכות הן באגדות הן בנגלה הן בנסתר כפי בחי׳ שרש נשמתו ומחוייב בדבר להשלים נשמתו בהעלאת כל הניצוצות שנפלו לחלקה ולגורלה כנודע (וכל דברי תורה ובפרט דבר הלכה היא ניצוץ מהשכינה שהיא היא דבר ה׳ כדאיתא בגמרא דבר ה׳ זו הלכה סוד מלכות דאצילות המלבשת לחכמה דאצילות ומלובשים במלכות דיצירה וירדו בקליפת נוגה בשבירת הכלים). וז״ש בגמרא כל העוסק בתורה אמר הקב״ה מעלה אני עליו כאלו פדאני ואת בני מבין האומות העולם. אבל בצאת השכינה מקליפת נוגה [נ״א מהקליפות] אחר שיושלם בירור הניצוצות ויופרד הרע מהטוב ויתפרדו כל פועלי און ולא שלטא אילנא דטוב ורע בצאת הטוב ממנה אזי לא יהיה עסק התורה והמצות לברר בירורין כ״א ליחד יחודים עליונים יותר להמשיך אורות עליונים יותר מהאצילות כמ״ש האר״י ז״ל והכל ע״י פנימיות התורה לקיים המצות בכוונות עליונות שמכוונות לאורות עליונים כו׳ כי שרש המצות הוא למעלה מעלה בא״ס ב״ה (ומ״ש רז״ל דמצות בטילות לע״ל היינו בתחיית המתים אבל לימות המשיח קודם תחה״מ אין בטלים) ולכן יהי׳ גם עיקר עסק התורה גם כן בפנימיות המצות וטעמיהם הנסתרים. אבל הנגלות יהיו גלוים וידועים לכל איש ישראל בידיעה בתחלה בלי שכחה וא״צ לעסוק בהם אלא לערב רב שלא יזכו למטעם מאילנא דחיי שהוא פנימיות התורה והמצוה וצריכים לעסוק [בתורה] במשנה להתיש כח הס״א הדבוק בהם (ע״י עסק התורה. בכ״י ליתא) שלא תשלוט בהם להחטיאם כדכתיב והחוטא בן מאה שנה יקולל שיהיו חוטאים מערב רב וגם למעשה יהיו צריכים לפרטי הלכות אסור וטומאה יותר מישראל שלא יארע להם פסול וטומאה ואסור כי לא יאונה כו׳ וגם אפשר וקרוב הדבר שידעו מפנימיות התורה כל גופי התורה הנגלית כמו אברהם אבינו ע״ה ולכן א״צ לעסוק בהם כלל. מה שאין כן בזמן בית שני היו צריכים לעסוק גם כי לא בשביל הלכה למעשה בלבד אלא שזהו עיקר עבודה להתיש כח הס״א ולהעלות ניצוצי הקדושה ע״י התורה והעבודה כמ״ש במ״א. ואחר הדברים והאמת יובן היטב בתוס׳ ביאור הר״מ דלעיל במה שאמר אילנא דטוב ורע כו׳ ר״ל קליפת נוגה שהוא עולם הזה העיקר כמ״ש בע״ח וד״ל:

יא בחשון פשוטה

י בחשון מעוברת